# IN DEFENCE OF CANADA

# In Defence of Canada

PEACEMAKING
AND DETERRENCE

JAMES EAYRS

UNIVERSITY OF TORONTO PRESS
Toronto and Buffalo

Toronto and Buffalo
Reprinted in paperback 1977
Printed in Canada
ISBN 0-8020-1907-2 (cloth)
ISBN 0-8020-6328-4 (paper)
LC 66-3834

*To Betty Gordon Lofft*

STUDIES IN THE STRUCTURE OF POWER:

DECISION-MAKING IN CANADA

EDITOR: JOHN MEISEL

1 In Defence of Canada: From the Great War to the Great Depression. BY JAMES EAYRS

2 The Vertical Mosaic: An Analysis of Social Class and Power in Canada. BY JOHN PORTER

3 In Defence of Canada: Appeasement and Rearmament. BY JAMES EAYRS

4 Canadian Labour in Politics. BY GAD HOROWITZ

5 Federal-Provincial Diplomacy: The Making of Recent Policy in Canada. BY RICHARD SIMEON

6 In Defence of Canada: Peacemaking and Deterrence. BY JAMES EAYRS

7 The Canadian Public Service: A Physiology of Government 1867–1970 BY J.E. HODGETTS

STUDIES IN THE STRUCTURE OF POWER:

DECISION-MAKING IN CANADA

The series 'Studies in the Structure of Power: Decision-Making in Canada' is sponsored by the Social Science Research Council of Canada for the purpose of encouraging and assisting research concerned with the manner and setting in which important decisions are made in fields affecting the general public in Canada. The launching of the series was made possible by a grant from the Canada Council.

Unlike the books in other series supported by the Social Science Research Council, the studies of decision-making are not confined to any one of the disciplines comprising the social sciences. The series explores the ways in which social power is exercised in this country: it will encompass studies done within a number of different conceptual frameworks, utilizing both traditional methods of analysis and those prompted by the social, political, and technological changes following the Second World War.

In establishing the series, the Social Science Research Council has sought to encourage scholars already embarked on relevant studies by providing financial and editorial assistance and similarly to induce others to undertake research in areas of decision-making so far neglected in Canada.

J.M.

# Preface and Acknowledgements

My wish for this book is that it will be thought to go some way towards fulfilling an undertaking – brashly and rashly declared in July 1964 in a preface to *In Defence of Canada: From the Great War to the Great Depression* – to write a further volume 'concerned with Canadian national security policy as it unfolded to meet the ... threats of the long-range bomber and the intercontinental missile in the nuclear age...'

In the same place – land o' Goshen, in the same sentence – I promised to deal as well with the opportunities and problems created for Canada by 'para-military skirmishing along the Great Powers' spheres of influence.' That aspect of our national security policy does not seem to me to fit, physically or conceptually, into the themes of peacemaking and deterrence with which the present volume is concerned. My mood is far from that of George Sand who, writing a novel at 1 A.M., exclaimed 'Good Heavens, I've finished!' and promptly began writing another. But I have started to work on a fourth volume – through the generosity of the Canada Council, which has awarded me a Killam Senior Research Scholarship for the purpose – which will deal with Canada's experience as North Atlantic ally and global peacekeeper.

It was my hope that volume III would appear in 1966: here it is in 1972. The long delay has not been due to 'creative pause' (that euphemism for sloth), nor to the kind of hammer-blow from Fate that consigns one's manuscript to flames or city dump. It has been due to a fiat from the government of Canada.

Late in 1963, I was informed that I should present some notes I'd made from material in the custody of the Public Archives in Ottawa to the Department of External Affairs for 'vetting' for 'security.' As I have explained elsewhere,* the frail apparatus of its Historical Division proved unequal to the task of deciding which material could be declassified and which could not. Accordingly, instead of censoring my work, it confiscated it. 'I have to tell you, regretfully,' a letter prepared for the signature of Arnold Smith advised me in April 1964, 'that it has been ruled that the documents which you left with the Department ... cannot be quoted or referred to in any publication ... I have also been asked to tell you that the copies of these documents which you sent to the Department must be kept here, since under the law you are not entitled to keep copies of classified material.'

Accompanying this decision, in a gesture which may have been intended to be mollifying, was the assurance that it had been 'very carefully considered by the Under Secretary of State for External Affairs, Norman Robertson, and the Acting Under Secretary, Marcel Cadieux, on the basis *inter alia* of the advice of a well known University Professor who had previously had some years of experience in the government service.' If there were such a practice as the opposite of dedicating a book, I should wish to opposite of dedicate this book to that 'well known University Professor.'

Because the material withheld by the Department of External Affairs was indispensable to the writing of volume III, I was obliged to abandon work upon it until such time as the Department saw fit to revoke its edict of 1964. This it did in 1970. Hence the delay. Better now – I trust– than never.

My greatest indebtedness in writing this book is to the officials of the Department of External Affairs who in 1970 changed the ruling of their predecessors. To A.E. Ritchie, the present Under Secretary of State for External Affairs, and A.E. Blanchette, the present Director of the Department's Historical Division, go my thanks and appreciation not only for their help on my behalf but for bringing about a new deal for all who are interested in the history of Canadian defence and foreign policy.

I am grateful as well to Dr S.F. Wise who, in his capacity as Director, Directorate of History, Department of National Defence, made it possible for me to make use of important documents in his custody; and to Mr P.A.C. Chaplin, of the staff of the Directorate, for his cheerful and efficient assistance.

For permission to make use of the various collections of papers on

* See James Eayrs, *Diplomacy and its Discontents* (Toronto 1971), viii–ix.

which this book is mainly based, I am grateful to their custodians (who are listed in the note on the sources). I wish particularly to record my gratitude to Mrs Brooke Claxton, who offered me the hospitality of her home in which to work as well as access to the papers of her late husband. I have tried to do justice to his public service.

In addition to these written materials, I have benefitted from interviews with those who have had first-hand knowledge of the events with which my book is concerned. The late Right Honourable Vincent Massey, CH, the late General the Honourable A.G.L. McNaughton, CH, the late Air Marshal Robert Leckie, CB, and the late General Charles Foulkes, CB, all gave generously of their time to share with me their recollections and reflections. I have learned much from talks with the Honourable Mr Justice D.C. Abbott, Air Marshal W.A. Curtis, Mr G.P. deT. Glazebrook, Dr C.J. Mackenzie, Lt-General Maurice Pope, Lt-General G.G. Simonds, and Dr O.M. Solandt. The late Colonel the Honourable Colin Gibson, PC, MC, and Mr George Ignatieff kindly clarified some points by mail.

A few of my helpers are my friends as well as actors on the stage of Canadian history. To John Holmes, Douglas LePan, and John Meisel go special thanks for their encouragement and for their comments on my manuscript. I shall not say they are responsible for any merits what I've written may possess. But they are not responsible for any of its shortcomings.

My labour with the index was eased by Barbara Beach and Jonathan, Jimmy, and Susan Eayrs.

For financial aid I am grateful to the Social Science Research Council of Canada, the Canada Council, the Guggenheim Foundation, the University of Toronto, and the Canadian Institute of International Affairs.

To Rik Davidson of the University of Toronto Press and impresario of this work, and Jean Wilson, also of the Press and my esteemed editor, homage and hosannas.

JE

1 June 1972
Toronto

# Contents

# IN DEFENCE OF CANADA

# INTRODUCTION

## Personalities and Policies

Wherein the infirmities of some, and the malice of others, both in persons and things, must be boldly looked upon and mentioned...

*Edward Hyde, Earl of Clarendon*

Modern political science rejects, correctly, the notion that one man – be his name Lenin or Stalin, Mussolini or Hitler, Chamberlain or Churchill, Roosevelt or Kennedy, Nehru or Nasser – can make his country's foreign policy just as he pleases. Modern political science asserts, correctly, that behind every 'output,' or policy decision, there lurk a dozen 'inputs' – the economy, opinion, military might and morale, political structure, political culture, competing elites, and all the others – that constrain the would-be foreign policymaker on horseback. It was Mussolini himself who remarked in a moment of clarity that 'there is no such thing as originality in foreign policy.'

Grant that the most charismatic leader must obey a hard if not an iron law that limits his scope, that narrows his options, that brings down to earth and sometimes buries beneath the earth his lofty conceptions of the public good. Canada's leaders do more than grant it, they grovel before it. If one prime minister has publicly proclaimed that 'Canada is a difficult country to govern,' most have said it privately, nearly all have believed it to be true.* A precarious economy, regional rivalry, cultural diversity, a small and scattered population, the looming proximity of a great, if mostly

* Prime Minister Pierre Elliot Trudeau may be an exception: 'If Canada is a difficult country to govern, if the governing of a free society is never easy at any time, and if it's difficult in Canada now,' he told an interviewer on 21 December 1971, 'how much more difficult it must be in bigger countries like the United States, countries with much more serious problems, the Middle Eastern problems, sub-continent ones, totalitarian societies.' (Text supplied by the Prime Minister's Office.)

friendly, foreign power – all these, and more, are invoked as extenuating circumstances.

Circumstances – 'inputs' in the jargon – are what they are; to what degree extenuating is for historians to decide. (Statesmen are not to be entrusted with deciding, for they have a vested interest in over-estimating the burden of constraints.*)

Since statesmen stress determinism, historians by stressing free will may bring their assessment back in balance. That is why this study of Canada's search for security in a better world during the closing years of the Second World War and the opening years of the Cold War is introduced by a discussion not of the political culture or the Precambrian Shield – important as such factors are – but of some leading personalities and the policies they espoused.

## CABINET MINISTERS

As the Second World War came to its climax and its close, W.L. Mackenzie King approached the age of seventy. For a quarter century he had led the Liberal Party. For eighteen years he had been prime minister, ten of them – since 1935 – consecutive, and his own foreign minister as well. For six years he had been the head of a government at war.

Managing the nation's war effort had been a punishing grind for most of the members of his Ministry (the sixteenth since Confederation), but Mackenzie King stood the strain far better than his colleagues. Durability derived from his single-minded dedication to the craft of state, his long experience of political turmoil, his sturdy physical constitution, his unparalleled capacity for believing that he always did the right thing for King and country. His physical no less than his political stamina are shown during the day of 22 November 1944 – no ordinary day in the life of the Prime Minister, far from it, but the day he faced and surmounted the supreme crisis of his career. It was then he decided to introduce conscription for overseas military service. After taking the decision, persuading rebellious colleagues not to resign, securing agreement from his Cabinet, meeting with Parliament and party caucus, conducting perhaps a score of other conversations – all activities, as his biographer notes, 'of the utmost consequence to his country's future' and all making 'extraordinary demands on his power of persuasion, his gifts of leadership, his nervous energy, and his vitality' – he returned that night to Laurier House (his home in the Sandy Hill district of Ottawa, about a mile east of Parlia-

* See James Eayrs, *Diplomacy and its Discontents* (Toronto 1971), 81–155.

ment) unruffled and unwearied. 'Today has gone well,' he wrote serenely in his diary – for in its course he did not fail to dictate and write the usual quota of five or six thousand words for his record – and added: 'I believe the right decision has been reached.'[1] How could it be otherwise? Consoled and refreshed by the thought he slept the sleep of the Liberal just.

Such peak performance could hardly be sustained much longer. Nor was it. The descent at first was slow, to the outsider imperceptible. An anniversary tribute, written in 1946 by one of Mackenzie King's most persistent critics, was mocking, as might be expected – 'Now he is celebrating either the beginning or the end of his twentieth year in office as prime minister – we forget which' – but deferential, too: 'From the respectful attention which he receives when he speaks for us abroad – in London, Washington, San Francisco, Geneva, and elsewhere – the Canadian qualities which are summed up in his character do meet with considerable approval from the peoples of the world with whom we have business to transact. And we should be willing to pay cordial tribute to him for this fact.'[2] Had the truth been known that was not so much fact as fancy. Only those working most closely with him on affairs of state – his valets, as it were, of the conference room – knew the extent to which the old man's powers had begun to fail and his influence to wane.* And good valets tell no tales. Not until after his death did it emerge that the Prime Minister of wartime Canada had cut rather a forlorn figure at those post-war conferences where – Roosevelt dead, Churchill out of office, de Gaulle about to enter his retreat – he had become, with Smuts, the senior statesman of the group. But where Smuts was still in his element – 'the old Zealander,' he told the States General of Holland on 11 October 1946, 'who in 1692 left Middelburg in Walcheren to seek a home in the far south has the honour to address you today through his descendent'[3] – Mackenzie King was out. At Paris in particular, he was ill in body, ill at ease, sick at heart: 'I do not know the personages ... I realize I am not quick-witted in some things.'†

Prime ministers whose reflexes fail towards the close of their career may make life awkward for their colleagues; prime ministers who develop

* Deterioration had set in even before the conscription crisis. One of Mackenzie King's advisers at the Prime Ministers' Meeting in London in May 1944 recalls that 'he did not speak up until he was goaded, and he always sounded petty – even to one of his humble servants who had no doubt that the centralized concept should be shot down.'

† Quoted in J.W. Pickersgill and D.F. Forster, *The Mackenzie King Record,* III, *1945–1946* (Toronto 1970), 296. [Hereafter cited as *Record III.*] See below, 180–1.

quirks and aberrations along with their faltering synapses threaten parliamentary government itself.* This threat was posed for Canada during Mackenzie King's last two years of power.

From the end of 1946 to his retirement on 15 November 1948, the Prime Minister was a liability to colleagues, Party, country. Mackenzie King, writes one of his biographers, 'could work for only three hours at a stretch. After such a spell he could not work at all the next day ... His memory was failing ... Among the inner circle of King's counsellors it was realized that soon someone must tell him the truth and advise him to retire. Nobody volunteered for that duty.'[4] It was not that no one cared, it was that no one dared. Never had it been easy to serve the man whom one of his most able and senior servants has called 'as complicated a being as Canadian public life has ever produced.'[5] A quarter century earlier, when he first became Prime Minister, he had been an exacting taskmaster: † time did not improve his disposition.

One after another the records of political longevity were broken. On 7 June 1946, Mackenzie King exceeded Sir John A. Macdonald's length of service as Prime Minister. His staff presented a copy of F.S. Oliver's *The Endless Adventure* to mark the occasion and, as more months passed with retirement nowhere in sight, must have wondered whether the adventure would ever end. For to irascibility had now been joined the still more unsettling trait of unpredictability. 'Mackenzie King had by this time become incalculable on major issues of foreign policy,' one of his advisers

* For some chilling case histories, consult Hugh L'Etang, *The Pathology of Leadership* (London 1969).

† Mackenzie King's secretary and Fidus Achates during the Great War and early 1920s, recalls, with delicacy of phrase, what it was like to work for him:

> While he could be exceedingly kind at times in his personal relations with his staff, he could never quite conceal his opinion of them ... The search for the perfect secretary always ended in futility, and unfortunately the incumbents, even the best of them, were not unaware of his feeling of their inadequacy ... I can recall, more than once or twice ... a withering comment about some shortcoming, ending with ... 'The Lord knows, McGregor, I am not criticizing' ...

F.A. McGregor, *The Fall and Rise of Mackenzie King: 1911–1919* (Toronto, 1962), pp. 7–8. A diary entry (30 August 1946) suggests what his entourage of later years had to endure: '... said ... I had never felt so let down in all my life as I had been by some of those around me in the last couple of weeks. That except where there was something that they wanted for themselves, there had not been even a question as to whether there was anything they could do in furthering my interests or wishes ... I again repeated I had never felt so let down in my life nor had I suffered as much in mind and heart...' Quoted in *Record III*, 330–1. Bearing the brunt of the Prime Minister's wrath on this occasion was Arnold Heeney, then Secretary of the Cabinet and Clerk of the Privy Council. See below, 44.

has since testified. 'During the war he had urged the creation of an effective collective security system but as soon as the war was over he began to retreat to his pre-war isolationism. We, in the External Affairs Department, never knew which way he would jump.'[6] But jump he did – at his colleagues, at his counsellors, at his allies. His irascibility, his unpredictability, his xenophobia, his paranoia – the list is long, and could be longer – all but brought his Government to rebellion in the last year of his rule.*

Pride alone saved him from a fall. Four months more, and Sir Robert Walpole's record of 7619 days in power would be broken: Mackenzie King drew back – just in time – that he might break that record too. The great day came on 20 April 1948, but the Liberal Party leadership was not surrendered until August and the prime ministership was not surrendered even then. Mackenzie King clung to office as if to life itself – which for him it was. Eventually illness and infirmity made it impossible to cling longer. He ceased being Prime Minister on 15 November 1948. He ceased to live on 22 July 1950. But he did not cease, and has not ceased, to influence the country he had governed for so long – for better or for worse Canadians may never be able to decide.

Throughout these trying years, Mackenzie King maintained an almost mesmeric hold upon the members of his Ministry. None cared or dared to challenge his authority until the last months of his rule.

During the war, the Prime Minister's mastery of his ministers was awesome to behold. 'I'm called in to the War Committee occasionally,' L.B. Pearson had written in 1942, 'and it's enlightening to notice Mr King's absolute ascendency over & complete domination of his colleagues. There are, in fact, only four of them who count – Ilsley, Power, Howe & Ralston.'[7]

Here was an imposing quadrumvirate. It did not impose upon Mackenzie King. He took care that they did not act collectively. ('Always interview your creditors,' he quoted approvingly on one occasion, 'one at a time.') Individually they were no match for him.

J.L. Ilsley was perhaps the most prestigious of the four. Granitic, incorruptible and dour, he had been Minister of Finance since 8 July 1940. The strain of managing the nation's economy throughout the war had by its end brought him close to mental and physical collapse, and on 10

* The issue was whether to withdraw from the United Nations Temporary Commission for Korea, on which Canada's delegates to the UN had accepted representation without Mackenzie King's consent. See Bruce Hutchison, *The Incredible Canadian* (Toronto 1952), 432–4; and J.W. Pickersgill and D.F. Forster, *The Mackenzie King Record*, IV, *1947–1948* (Toronto 1970), 133–53. [Hereafter cited as *Record IV*.]

December 1946 he assumed the less strenuous position of Minister of Justice.

Mackenzie King respected Ilsley but for some reason did not like him. When they clashed, in December 1947, over Canada's representation on the United Nations Temporary Truce Commission for Korea, his dislike became contempt. 'Nothing could better illustrate than his attitude in today's discussion,' Mackenzie King wrote in his diary on 22 December, 'how ill suited Ilsley is for leadership. I think toward myself he has a very bitter feeling ... Running back into the years, he has been protectionist in the matter of apples.[*] I think he was annoyed at the decision in Geneva to do away with preferences; probably feels that I have had to do with that. Apart from all else in his overtaxed condition ... his judgment has become far from sound.'[8] Ilsley resigned from the Ministry of Justice on 30 June 1948 to become Chief Justice of Nova Scotia.

C.G. Power was a very different case. By reason of his wartime portfolios – Minister of National Defence for Air, and Associate Minister of National Defence – 'Chubby' Power was close to the conduct of grand strategy. By reason of his person he was close, or closer than most, to the remote figure of his chief who felt for him a kind of affection, sharply qualified by Mackenzie King's limited capacity for friendship with associates invariably valued more for their political than for their personal qualities. Such, certainly, was the Prime Minister's attitude towards Chubby Power. 'I pray ... that he will be spared,' Mackenzie King wrote in March 1942, when some occult voice whispered that his colleague might soon meet an untimely death, 'for he is very helpful and able.'[9]

Power's helpfulness and ability were at a premium during the crisis over conscription. His rare understanding of the feelings of French-speaking Canadians rendered him unable to take in stride his leader's sudden decision to send conscript soldiers overseas. On 22 November 1944 Mackenzie King met with him to try to keep him in the Government, at least to ask him to leave quietly. Every device of cajolery, Power recalled, was used:

He then made a very personal appeal saying he had always stuck by me and had been my friend, hinting there were times when he need not have done so, and he thought I should be his friend at this stage. If later on I felt like retiring and did not care to face an election I could be assured of something worth while. He said the problem for him was not so much to remain at the head of a government but to have a government in Canada. He feared it was im-

* Ilsley at least came by his protectionism honestly: Digby-Annapolis-Kings, his constituency, contained many of those orchards which are to Nova Scotia a source of pride and revenue.

possible to have any government other than a Liberal one (presumably with himself at the head). I left him without changing my attitude in any way, though he kept on reiterating that he thought I would help him.[10]

Power resigned four days later, without furor, fuss, or others in his wake.

This fall from office brought no corresponding fall in grace or favour; there was even some discussion, in November 1947, of his returning to the Cabinet.[11] His influence on affairs was exercised hereafter as a kind of loyal opposition within the Liberal Party; he entered the Senate on 28 July 1955.

Then there was C.D. Howe. Howe's enormous energy, his administrative flair, went entirely into the crucial task of ensuring that munitions and supply continued to flow from the facilities of defence production which, by the war's end, were entirely in his charge. Only a threatened interruption to that flow would drive him to distraction and, on one occasion – a strike in July 1941 at the Arvida, Quebec plant of the Aluminium Company of Canada – almost to resignation. But so long as it continued Howe remained content.

By 1944 the flow had become a torrent, Howe's stature towering. But by normal political ambitions he was not possessed. His instincts were entrepreneurial, his impulses managerial, he collected means of production (including 28 crown corporations), not cabinet portfolios. The nickname 'Minister of Everything' was his but not by choice. On 7 September the Prime Minister asked him at a meeting of the Cabinet to become Minister of Reconstruction. 'Howe objected very strongly,' Mackenzie King recorded, 'saying ... it involved nothing but the receiving of delegations from all over the country and that he was not a good receiver of delegations.'[12] It was perfectly true; nevertheless the ministry became his the next month, *faut de mieux*. He held the new portfolio concurrently with that of Munitions and Supply (his since 9 April 1940), and the two were combined into a single Ministry of Reconstruction and Supply on 1 January 1946, of which Howe was the first and only minister until its abolition on 14 November 1948.

That left 'C.D.,' as a grateful country knew him, minister merely of Trade and Commerce, which he had become on 19 January 1948. It was in this post, held uninterruptedly until the defeat of the Liberal Government in June 1957,* that he became the first 'strong man' in a Canadian cabinet, prime ministers excepted, since W.S. Fielding had taken charge of fiscal policy in the Ministry formed by Mackenzie King as a freshman prime minister more than a quarter century before. As Minister of Trade and Commerce, Howe more or less made policy towards the United

* See below, 16.

States; as Minister of Defence Production (a portfolio created on 1 April 1951 as the result of the Korean War), he more or less made policy on defence. But it was not under Mackenzie King that Howe exercised these powers. 'My own opinion is that in matters of the kind, Howe is almost an innocent abroad.'[13]

Of the quadrumvirate there remains J.L. Ralston. Alone of the four Ralston challenged Mackenzie King's authority. He did not want to become Prime Minister in his place. He wanted to force the policy of conscripting troops for overseas service upon a Government still doing all it could to avert it. If that meant the break-up of the Government, the dislodging of the Prime Minister, even a second wartime election, Ralston was ready to do his duty.

But things never came to that. On 1 November 1944, in the presence of all his ministerial colleagues, Mackenzie King asked Ralston for his resignation, and got it. He resigned not only from the Government but from political life. He parted more in anger than in sorrow, and may never have spoken to his leader again, certainly never with warmth or cordiality. Some weeks after Ralston's departure, Mackenzie King told the House of Commons: 'All of us revered our colleague the Minister of National Defence, and may I say that many of us, including myself, personally loved him.'[14] The reader should discount that declaration of love.

None of the four ministers singled out by L.B. Pearson was regarded by the Prime Minister as the most able member of his Cabinet. That accolade Mackenzie King bestowed (though as yet only in the form of an entry in his diary) upon Louis Stephen St Laurent.

St Laurent had been unwillingly recruited in the Mackenzie King Ministry, was indeed a virtual conscript. He had no very obvious preparation for cabinet office. He was devoid of political ambition. When Mackenzie King turned to him, early in December 1941, St Laurent was nearly sixty years of age, the head of a closely-knit and demanding family, with a prospering and expanding law practice that engaged his full attention.*

* From St Laurent's legal background derived his powers of concentration upon a document or brief which, according to an associate, were truly formidable:

> His eye went down the first page – very quickly. He read the second and the third pages at the same rapid speed. Then he turned back to the beginning; read the first page slowly; turned over to the second page, reading slowly. When his eyes reached the middle of the second page, I saw him pause in his reading for about two seconds. He said nothing. He continued to read the memorandum slowly till the end. Then he turned back to the second page. This time he did not start reading at the top of the page. He started in the middle of the page. He studied the paragraph in the middle of the page. Then he spoke for the first time. Politely he questioned an argument in that paragraph, doubted the

He was a modest man who sincerely doubted his capacity to make a worthwhile contribution to the government of Canada.

But Mackenzie King was not accustomed to returning empty-handed from such overtures. In fact, as he stressed to St Laurent, he was not accustomed to making such overtures. 'In my leadership of the Liberal party,' the Prime Minister had written to his prospective recruit, 'I have never before, that I am able to recall, begged of any man to become a member of any government of which I have been the head. I do not hesitate, however, to urge you just as strongly as I possibly can to come to Ottawa, and that at once.'[15]

Eventually St Laurent yielded before a combination of pressures – the blandishments of the Prime Minister, the counsel of friends, his sense of duty. On 10 December 1941 he was sworn in as Minister of Justice, and took his place in the Cabinet as Mackenzie King's French-speaking lieutenant in Quebec, replacing Ernest Lapointe who had died in office a fortnight before. 'When I took the oath of office today,' St Laurent told a press conference, 'I felt that oath to be identical in effect to the oath taken by many thousands of Canadians at this time. This is a war job.'[16]

Within a year, Mackenzie King had come to think of St Laurent as the person he would most like to have succeed him as leader of the Liberal Party. 'He would be my choice in a moment,' he wrote on 16 October 1942, 'were he not of the minority in both race and religion.'[17] The qualities which appealed to the Prime Minister in St Laurent were his modesty, his diffidence, his disdain for political intrigue and self-seeking, all joined to a tireless mastery of the tasks of his new career.

If being French Canadian and Roman Catholic was thought by the Prime Minister to rule out, for the time being, St Laurent's succession to the leadership, it need not rule out, he thought, his acquiring some of the responsibility for the conduct of foreign policy. From time to time Mackenzie King had considered making Ernest Lapointe Secretary of State for External Affairs; now he considered St Laurent. A trial run was arranged during April and May 1944, when the Prime Minister (who also held the External Affairs portfolio) attended the Prime Ministers' Conference in London. The Acting Secretary of State for External Affairs told a French-speaking audience in Hull, Quebec, on 21 May, that since his duties would lapse on the Prime Minister's return, it was 'perhaps the

validity of the conclusion derived from that argument. He was right. He had put his finger on the weak point...

Escott Reid, 'Memories of Louis St Laurent, 1946–9,' in Norman Penlington (ed.), *On Canada: Essays in Honour of Frank H. Underhill* (Toronto 1971), 71–2.

first and last occasion I will have to speak in public in this capacity.' The theme of his address – that Canada should follow a middle road between 'extreme nationalism and exaggerated internationalism' – was certainly not calculated to offend his chief. Mackenzie King (according to St Laurent's biographer) 'was so pleased on returning to Canada at the way St Laurent had handled the Department of External Affairs that he increased rather than decreased his colleague's responsibilities in that field.' He put St Laurent up to reply to the criticism by Quebec nationalists of the Government's plans for relief and rehabilitation of the newly-liberated countries of Europe; and it was St Laurent who spoke for the Government when General de Gaulle visited Ottawa in August 1944.[18]

Late in February 1946, the Prime Minister reached, under pressure from the Opposition and the press, the long-delayed decision to divest himself of the External Affairs portfolio. He asked St Laurent to accept it. The Minister of Justice demurred; he recalled their understanding that his sojourn in politics was to be only for the duration, and protested that his return to private life was already overdue. Nothing was more likely to persuade the Prime Minister that St Laurent was the man for the job than so sincere a display of reluctance to accept it. When their conversation ended, St Laurent had agreed to serve once again as Acting Secretary of State for External Affairs, during Mackenzie King's forthcoming absence at conferences in London and Paris.

The Prime Minister's first move on his return in September was to attempt to persuade his acting foreign minister to continue to serve his country, first as Secretary of State for External Affairs, ultimately as his successor in the leadership. When it became apparent that St Laurent was determined not to be drawn into a permanent arrangement, Mackenzie King quickly agreed that it might be transitional. It was on this understanding that St Laurent allowed himself to be sworn in as Secretary of State for External Affairs on 5 September 1946. But Mackenzie King had calculated correctly that this further extrication in the affairs of state would make it next to impossible for St Laurent to leave at the end of the year. 'The reaction to his appointment,' writes St Laurent's biographer,

> was even stronger than he had anticipated. He tried in vain to explain to his colleagues and other close associates that he was just making the Justice portfolio available for Ilsley, and giving the Prime Minister time to find a more permanent Minister for External Affairs; his many admirers were encouraged to increase the pressure on him to remain in Ottawa. Negotiations were about to be undertaken to bring Newfoundland into Confederation, the removal of the Department of External Affairs from the Prime Minister's cautious direction opened up the possibility of new initiatives in Canadian foreign policy, and several items of legislation that would shape the country in the years ahead

were being prepared for the new session of Parliament. The new challenges were interesting to him, and the argument that he could play a uniquely useful role again proved irresistible; he acquiesced...[19]

St Laurent's acquiescence had been secured on false premises. Seeking to retain him in his Government as the indispensable spokesman for Quebec, Mackenzie King had stressed the opportunities of the portfolio he sought to have him accept. But, contrary to the impression he may have conveyed, it had not been Mackenzie King's intention to slough off, along with the portfolio, responsibilities for the great affairs of state. Far from it. His whole idea had been that by devolving the portfolio upon someone else he himself would be relieved of the more tiresome details of departmental administration and management and thus enabled to devote more time and care to those matters of high policy with which, as he still supposed, he was uniquely equipped to deal.

As long as St Laurent busied himself with the housekeeping aspects of foreign policy – such as supervising the acquisition and outfitting of the new Canadian missions then being opened up abroad – relations between Prime Minister and foreign minister proceeded free from strain. But that was not for very long. It was not in the nature of the job, nor as it proved in the nature of the man, that St Laurent should stay content with a technician's role. The new foreign minister had a mind of his own and a temperament of his own. The mind was imaginative; the temperament, stubborn. It soon transpired that the Secretary of State for External Affairs entertained ideas about Canada's role in world affairs very different from those in the mind of Mackenzie King.

By 1947, the Prime Minister of Canada had reverted to the isolationism of his pre-war years. For this reversion he offered no convincing intellectual justification – no justification, indeed, of any kind – but sought simply to impose his will upon his colleagues (and, through them, upon the country) by the sheer force of his personality and by the authority of his office. In contrast, the Secretary of State for External Affairs had by 1947 become the foremost exponent of a new Canadian internationalist outlook. The diverging views of prime minister and foreign minister were first displayed to an astonished Cabinet in May 1947, when Mackenzie King took exception to the positive response that St Laurent wished Canada to make to the imminent independence of India and to Asian membership of the Commonwealth.* On this occasion a collision was averted only by St Laurent's refusal to make an issue of the affair – a refusal explained by his biographer as evidence of a sympathetic understanding that his leader's powers were failing. 'The incident was closed, but rumours cir-

* See below, 235–6.

culated in the corridors of Parliament Hill that relations between Mackenzie King and St Laurent had become strained.'[20]

There were limits even to St Laurent's capacity for loyal understanding and forbearance. These were reached by the end of the year. St Laurent had agreed to the appointment of a Canadian representative on the United Nations Temporary Commission on Korea. Mackenzie King wanted the representative withdrawn. This time Mackenzie King backed down, though not before each had threatened resignation and the Cabinet been convulsed by the most serious ministerial crisis since the conscription issue over three years before. 'Both men,' writes St Laurent's biographer, 'were immensely relieved to have found a way out of the impasse, and to put an end to their most serious disagreement in six years of constant collaboration.'[21]

Nevertheless, Mackenzie King regretted his decision to allow St Laurent to prevail. He resented his colleague's initiatives in foreign policy. His diary, hitherto lavish in its praise, became more and more critical of him. 'I confess that I get increasingly alarmed at the lack of judgment on the part of External Affairs in these matters,' runs a typical entry, 'and am beginning to mistrust St Laurent's judgment in them.'[22]

The Prime Minister's regard for his foreign minister's judgment was certainly lessened; but his belief in his integrity remained intact. St Laurent remained Mackenzie King's choice for the leadership. He duly became his successor, but only in stages: first, in August 1948, as leader of the Liberal Party; second, on 15 November 1948, as Prime Minister of Canada.

St Laurent's two ministries were never marred by the extreme tension which so disfigured the final months of Mackenzie King's protracted reign. He got on well with his colleagues. He contrived with them a productive division of labour. The inner harmony of the Government owed much, perhaps owed most, to the personality of its Chief Minister. St Laurent's courtly manner and consideration for others were not a disguise assumed for the purposes of public life: they were as much a part of him as his Gallic charm and his Irish temper. He was no more disposed to trespass upon the prerogatives of fellow Ministers than to trespass upon their properties. So long as they did their job to his satisfaction, he was content to leave them alone. It helped, as well, that they all saw eye to eye on most of the issues of the day. They were all committed, as Mackenzie King had never been committed, to an internationalist view of Canada's external responsibilities. Finally, St Laurent profited by his experience. He had known what it was like to serve under a jealous and intrusive chief. He was determined to spare them his own ordeal.

The principal beneficiary of St Laurent's administrative latitude was his new Secretary of State for External Affairs. If Mackenzie King and St Laurent provide a lesson in how a Prime Minister and a foreign minister ought not to work together, St Laurent and L.B. Pearson provide a lesson in how they should. 'With their offices just a few doors apart on the second floor of the East Block, St Laurent and Pearson met frequently, going over the voluminous dispatches received from other parts of the world, and working out the Canadian policy together. While the Prime Minister allowed Pearson an unusual amount of freedom of action, the Secretary of State for External Affairs never abused that confidence, keeping his superior closely informed of all developments, discussing his ideas with him, and obtaining his approval for any significant initiatives.'[23] Their relationship was as idyllic as it was rare. 'Mr St Laurent was more than a prime minister to me,' Pearson has since testified, 'he was always a very close friend. "Don't worry," he told me. "Do what is best. Do the right thing, and I'll back you." '[24] And he did. No foreign minister could wish for more.

Another beneficiary was the Minister of National Defence. In Brooke Claxton, St Laurent knew he had a loyal and diligent colleague. He was perfectly content to repose in Claxton the enormous responsibility of safeguarding Canada's interest in the esoteric matters with which a North American defence minister of the 1950s had to deal, and about which his own knowledge was less than perfect. 'I will have to be careful in what I say about military matters,' St Laurent had written to Claxton on the eve of a parliamentary debate on defence policy, 'because my background may be something like our radar screens – its coverage is not very extensive.'[25]

The third minister to profit by St Laurent's indulgence of his colleagues was the Minister of Trade and Commerce. St Laurent and C.D. Howe got on well together. 'Both had entered politics from a sense of patriotism rather than from partisan considerations or personal ambition. They shared a feeling of disdain for men who played politics with war issues; and they both preferred blunt honesty to the circumspection so often imposed on them in what they considered to be their temporary public-service careers.'[26] St Laurent had helped to persuade Howe to remain in the Government after the war, as he had been persuaded to remain. He was more than happy to allow Howe to continue into peacetime his war-time role as a kind of general manager of the Canadian economy. In the course of their collaboration, a serious clash over policy occurred between them: St Laurent favoured a cash payment to western wheat farmers, Howe opposed it. One man or the other had to give way and in the event

Howe gave way. In contrast with the outcome of St Laurent's confrontation with Mackenzie King, 'St Laurent's and Howe's mutual regard was enhanced rather than diminished as a result of the clash ...,'[27] and thereafter Howe, in St Laurent's view, could do no wrong.

Or so he may have thought. In 1956 C.D. Howe went too far for his own good, and for that of the Government. The nature of his deal to finance the Trans-Canada pipeline, and even more the way he defended his deal in the House of Commons, convinced the voters of Canada that their rulers had become too arrogant. St Laurent sat, or rather slumped, silent at his desk during the pipeline debate, his emotion betrayed only by the reddening of his neck clearly visible from the visitors' gallery, while his Minister of Trade and Commerce proceeded to hang the Government by the rope too generously allotted to him by its leader. The country was witnessing the twilight of the Grits. Night fell, as night must fall, on 10 June 1957.

Canada's first post-war Minister of National Defence was General Andrew George Latta McNaughton.* But not for long.

Mackenzie King had picked McNaughton for a special wartime purpose. Realizing that J.L. Ralston, Minister of National Defence since 5 July 1940, might resign in protest at the delay in instituting conscription for overseas service, Mackenzie King had begun to cast about for a successor who could carry the country as well as the load. His thoughts turned at once to 'Andy' McNaughton, who had been languishing in unaccustomed idleness since the end of 1943 when he had relinquished, not of his own volition, command of the First Canadian Army.

The same considerations which had led Mackenzie King to appoint McNaughton to the command of the 1st Canadian Division at the outset of war† now commended his candidacy for the Defence portfolio. He was passionately attached to the voluntary ideal for summoning a nation to arms. No barrage was too profligate if it saved the lives of troops. To these qualifications, which during the conscription crisis had become all-important, could be added 'a tremendous popular reputation which' – it is the opinion of Mackenzie King's official biographer – 'had not been greatly

* On McNaughton's personality and earlier career, see James Eayrs, *In Defence of Canada*, I, *From the Great War to the Great Depression* (Toronto 1964), 256–8. The official biography is John Swettenham, *McNaughton*, 3 vols. (Toronto 1968, 1969). For the vicissitudes of McNaughton's service in the Second World War, see C.P. Stacey, *Arms, Men and Governments: The War Policies of Canada, 1939–1945* (Ottawa 1971), 224–8, 231–47.

† 'His nomination by the Prime Minister was an act of the highest political importance, and Mackenzie King so regarded it.' James Eayrs, *The Art of the Possible: Government and Foreign Policy in Canada* (Toronto 1961), 77.

dimmed by his forced retirement in December 1943. He was still the idol of the army.'[28] Mackenzie King was gratified to discover, on 20 October 1944, that St Laurent shared his assessment of McNaughton's suitability. Even so, McNaughton was not approached until the eleventh hour, which struck on 1 November. The Prime Minister's careful interrogation of the General that day confirmed his initial belief that McNaughton was not just the ideal man, he was the only man. McNaughton agreed to take the job. The next day it was his.

McNaughton's task as Minister of National Defence was thus defined with unusual clarity. He had to secure sufficient numbers of volunteers to make unnecessary the conscripting of men for service overseas. If that failed, he was to make conscription palatable to the Government, to Parliament, and to the people of Canada. Unsuccessful in the first assignment, he succeeded with the second. Conscription was introduced without major political or military crisis. On the fighting front the German offensive was slowed and then repulsed. Within six months of McNaughton's appointment came victory in Europe.

McNaughton carried his new portfolio easily, when not tripped up by politics. 'The ministry,' writes his biographer, 'held no terrors for him; administration and organization came as second nature ... The arts of "man mastership" and persuasion had been familiar to him for more than thirty years, and he was a good and practised speaker.'[29] He was ready, even eager, to stay on the job in peacetime.

But his colleagues were not so keen on keeping the General in their midst. 'McNaughton ... has big ideas,' Mackenzie King noted disapprovingly on 19 July. 'St Laurent feels that the one question of the unwisdom of having him stay on is that we might never get the armed forces to the proportions they should be at. Howe feels this very strongly.'[30] An even graver liability was McNaughton's failure to secure a seat in the House of Commons. The results of the bitterly-fought by-election in Grey North on 5 February might be blamed on the Opposition's unscrupulous tactics;* those of the General Election of 11 June, in which McNaughton ran third in the Saskatchewan riding of Qu'Appelle, could only be blamed on himself.† He had now made constitutional history of an unenviable

* Its leader, John Bracken, had entered the riding on the eve of the election to charge that some of the newly conscripted soldiers had thrown rifles and ammunition from their troopships en route to Britain; in fact, one soldier had done so, and he was of unsound mind. But McNaughton's rebuttal did not avail against this roorback.

† Disregarding the advice of his campaign manager to forget about 'bombs and bullets' and talk about 'baby bottles and bonuses,' McNaughton told an audience at Moosomin on 12 May that Canada's Army would not be sent to the Pacific

kind – eight months in the Ministry but not a day in Parliament. By the last week of July Mackenzie King had concluded that McNaughton would have to go.

McNaughton took the news in good part. His Department, he told his Prime Minister, was in good shape for any successor, much as he would have liked to stay on until 'our men and women [had been] brought home from overseas, cared for and re-established, and our post-war organization set up for defence.' But his parting words only confirmed Mackenzie King's belief that he was not the man to trust with setting up the post-war organization for defence, in Parliament or not. 'He spoke very strongly,' King recorded, 'about keeping the good-will of the Army. Also keeping it to considerable size. He believes we might have a good deal of trouble through the demobilization period and immediately after. I find all these military men have an obsession about the fear of civil strife.'[31] McNaughton resigned as Minister of National Defence on 20 August 1945.

Douglas Charles Abbott was chosen to replace him. Abbott was born in 1899 in the Eastern Townships, only a few miles from St Laurent's birthplace. A signaller in the 7th McGill Battery, he had received a commission in the Royal Air Force at the end of the Great War. At the time he entered the House of Commons in 1940 he was well known in English-speaking Montreal where he had a flourishing law practice. Abbott was a natural politician, radiating energy and geniality. He possessed immense administrative talents, which his party quickly recognized and turned to its advantage. In 1943 he was appointed parliamentary assistant to the Minister of Finance – the first such appointment in the history of Canadian government. Early in 1945 he became parliamentary assistant to the Minister of National Defence.

As McNaughton was not in Parliament, being his parliamentary assistant imposed especial responsibility – particularly since the Opposition were determined to hound the absent Minister and whoever his *locum tenens* might be. With the General watching from the gallery, Abbott rose magnificently to the occasion. 'Instead of waiting for the Conservative charges and answering them,' a newspaperman who was present has recounted,

'to slug it out hand-to-hand with a foe perhaps better fitted than we to survive in the jungle war ... We will assist to smash the Jap forever with a maximum of machines and explosives.' McNaughton must have been thinking of the atomic bomb (about which he'd known from the beginning); his prospective constituents, who knew nothing about it, construed his remarks as a slur upon the Army and further appeasement of Quebec. See John Swettenham, *McNaughton*, III, *1944–1966* (Toronto 1969), 88–97.

Abbott tried to foresee and forestall them ... He cited every possible fact damaging to the Government before the Conservatives could say a word. Point by point he took their speeches out of their mouths.

When they attacked at last, there was little more to be said. Wherever they went, Abbott had been there first. As Abbott's speech began, King was alarmed by his candid admissions of mistakes but he soon saw the wisdom of it and was delighted. He marked Abbott for rapid promotion.[32]

Rapid promotion was soon forthcoming. On 18 April, a fortnight after the parliamentary performance which had so pleased his leader, Abbott was appointed Minister of National Defence for Naval Services. On 21 August, he succeeded McNaughton as Minister of National Defence.

McNaughton's mission had been to cope with conscription; Abbott's was to manage demobilization. It was job enough for any man, requiring a combination of political sensitivity and great firmness. Abbott handled it well. He employed to good effect the technique which had served the Government to such advantage during the debate over conscription, disarming criticism by conceding difficulties and admitting mistakes, and by not promising too much. 'The Department is cautious,' Abbott told the House of Commons on 16 October 1945, 'and I am most cautious about making predictions.' He allowed himself the prediction that 'we shall be able to get all our boys back, with the exception of those in the occupation forces and necessary staff, by late March or April, 1946.'[33] On that promise the Minister and his Department made good.

At the same time, Abbott had little interest in post-war policy. His mandate was demobilization rather than re-establishment. When pressed to go beyond it, he refused to go beyond it, or very far beyond it. He was glad to leave to his successor the honour of announcing in the House of Commons the Government's first comprehensive statement of future defence plans.

Douglas Abbott was succeeded as Minister of National Defence by Brooke Claxton. The careers of the two men are remarkably similar. Both entered Parliament in 1940 from constituencies in Montreal. Both became parliamentary assistants in 1943. They joined the Cabinet within six months of one another and left it on 30 June 1954. Both were veterans of the Great War: Claxton served as battery sergeant-major of the 10th McGill Siege Battery, and was awarded the Distinguished Conduct Medal and a commission in the artillery. They were classmates at McGill University, fellow-lawyers in Montreal, great friends.

Brooke Claxton looked like an intellectual in politics; in some respects he was. He had an owlish appearance. His manner in the House of Commons could be didactic. He read prodigiously. During the 1930s he had been an active member of the Canadian Institute of International Affairs. He contributed articles to learned and semi-learned periodicals. His admirers expected great things of him,* and he did not let them down. Mackenzie King immediately marked him out for advancement. He considered Claxton for a lesser Cabinet post in May 1941,† and in May 1943 appointed him Parliamentary Assistant to the President of the Privy Council (a portfolio then held by the Prime Minister). 'Told him to master all that related to Boards and Committees coming under President of Council,' Mackenzie King wrote in his diary after the appointment took effect, 'and to be prepared to make statements in the House on them.'[34] Brooke Claxton thus became in fact though not yet in name (for no such post existed at the time) Parliamentary Assistant to the Secretary of State for External Affairs. Mackenzie King was quick to take advantage of his aide's expertise in external affairs – such expertise was then in extraordinarily short supply – and, on occasion, allowed Claxton to reply to criticism of the Government's foreign policy. 'The Tory party are again talking Empire,' Mackenzie King noted on 9 July 1943, 'single foreign policy – an Imperial Cabinet and Imperial Council ... I asked Claxton to speak and present our point of view and he did so ... very well.'[35]

Anyone who could please the Prime Minister on that touchy topic had a great future. In October 1944, Brooke Claxton became the first Minister of the new Department of National Health and Welfare. His first weeks were spent more on national defence than on national health, for he plunged into the conscription crisis, juggling manpower statistics in an unavailing attempt to demonstrate that voluntary recruitment would provide sufficient soldiers. He demonstrated as well an aptitude for Liberal Party politics, and became 'a kind of junior Minister of Politics and head of a secret brain trust whose assignment was to plan the next general election campaign.'[36] All this commended him even more to his chief. When, in 1946, Mackenzie King went to Paris to attend the Peace Conference, he took Claxton with him as a member of the Canadian delegation; when, late in August, he returned unexpectedly to Canada, he left Claxton in charge.

It was then that the Prime Minister became resentful of his protégé. Brooke Claxton was no more prepared than St Laurent had been to give

* 'Brooke Claxton will make a very valuable member. I should imagine his entrance into the House will be well received on all sides irrespective of political opinions.' Vincent Massey to Mrs W.L. Grant, 9 April 1940, Massey Papers.

† Minister of National War Services. In relation to the competition, Mackenzie King considered Claxton to be 'the abler man as a student and more thorough' but lacking 'the personality ... for meeting people in public.' Since an ability to make a favourable impression on the public was an essential qualification for the job, Mackenzie King gave it to J.T. Thorson. (See J.W. Pickersgill, *The Mackenzie King Record*, I, *1939–1944* [Toronto 1960], 223. [Hereafter cited as *Record I*.])

less than his best so as to curry favour with Mackenzie King. Mackenzie King, as previously noted, was out of his element in Paris; Claxton, in contrast, revelled in the work. The Prime Minister found this hard to take. 'I have a feeling,' he had written on 5 August, while still at the Conference, 'that those around me would as soon have me avoid taking too active a part. Whether this is that they feel they are more competent or are considerate in a way, I cannot say. I have felt that Claxton was anxious to figure prominently in the debate. He knows the Conference personnel and general strategy.'[37] On returning to Ottawa, Mackenzie King read Claxton's despatches with a mixture of envy and disapproval. He noted 'that Claxton has given two dinners to which heads of the different delegations have been invited. That is right enough I assume but some day there will be a real outcry in Parliament.' A few days earlier he had listened to Claxton's radio broadcast of the work of the Conference. 'He has got a way of keeping himself before the public,' Mackenzie King wrote sourly, 'and at the same time giving an interesting account of foreign affairs.' Quickly he qualified even so slight a tribute: 'As I listened to him what struck me was how easy it is to make an address out of a commonplace.'[38]

Brooke Claxton's virtuoso performance at Paris paradoxically deprived him of the portfolio of Secretary of State for External Affairs, for the higher he soared in the realm of diplomacy, the more determined the Prime Minister became to bring him down to earth. By 6 November 1946, Mackenzie King had decided to make Claxton Minister of National Defence. 'If given that post,' he wrote, '[Claxton] will at least be kept at home and out of the international arena ... I think he has quite lost his head in the extravagant manner in which he has travelled about, indifferent to the pressure under which all here [in Ottawa] have been working. I thought he was a man of sounder judgment...'[39]

Mackenzie King was mistaken in suspecting his Minister of National Health and Welfare of a too highly cultivated taste for the diplomatic life, at least as this was to be lived at the Paris Peace Conference. Claxton worked hard as head of the Canadian delegation because it was his habit to work hard at any assignment. Privately, however, he deplored what he had to do. 'The three months I spent in Paris,' he wrote later,

> were among the unhappiest of my entire life ... The Conference and its setting were depressing enough but so was my own mood. Inactivity of any kind I have always found hard to bear even for a few hours ... At Paris there were endless opportunities for sitting and doing nothing else ... The work we were engaged on, if such a pointless activity could be called work, was boring enough in itself, but to have every word translated into two other languages was too much to bear...[40]

Clearly Claxton was not cut out for diplomacy, and he knew that he was not. There was thus no spectacular element of self-abnegation in his suggestion that St Laurent might be persuaded to remain in public life by being offered the Secretaryship of State for External Affairs. So far as Claxton was concerned, St Laurent was more than welcome to it. 'Over the years,' he wrote looking back upon them, 'people and press speculations have suggested that I would have preferred External Affairs to Defence. Nothing could be further from the truth.'

If the *longueurs* of the Paris Peace Conference developed Claxton's distaste for diplomacy, his experience there of Soviet negotiating techniques led him to believe that the time had come for Canada, in the company of friends and neighbours, to turn for protection to the military. That is why, as he wrote later, 'I preferred National Defence to any other Department, not only because it was the toughest and most challenging, but also because at the time I believed it to be the most important. Unless the free countries built up their defences together we would go down the drain one by one. About this I had no doubt and my experience at the Paris Conference ... had confirmed my conviction.'

On 12 December 1946, the Prime Minister summoned Brooke Claxton to his office to tell him that he wished to appoint him Minister of National Defence. Mackenzie King, possibly anticipating some objection from Claxton, turned on all his very considerable powers of persuasion. No situation in the country, he told his prospective recruit,

> [was] quite as important and critical as that which pertained to the three services. First of all, looking at the question as it related itself particularly to the public service of Canada, these Departments had been running too much on their own. The Ministers who had had control during the war had extravagant notions. Things had gone very far in the way of expenditures.[*] They had left

* It should be borne in mind that Mackenzie King's views on 'expenditures' – for defence or anything else – were affected by a parsimony so extreme that (to give one instance of it) in September 1945 he was ready to abandon a mission to discuss Soviet espionage with President Truman on learning that it would involve the re-routing of his railway car for which the Canadian Government would be charged $300. The Under-Secretary of State for External Affairs sought to convince the Prime Minister that the expenditure was justified, but Mackenzie King told him 'I did not wish my reputation to be damaged by any false step. I would go the next day if it could be arranged. Otherwise we might have to give up the trip altogether.' (Diary entry of 28 September 1945, quoted in *Record III*, 36.) In the event the Prime Minister made the trip by plane.

A member of his staff recalls that when travelling abroad 'King would usually manage to have one of us sign the bill, not so much to take advantage of us but in order that his own expense account should be kept to the minimum against the possibility of criticism in Parliament. As a result of such harmless strategems the Prime Minister's expenditures invariably appeared to be among the lowest of the Canadian delegates, on one occasion actually below those of his valet.' A.D.P. Heeney, *Memoirs* (Toronto 1972), 89.

before the elections and the Ministers that have since taken hold have done so without any feeling that the arrangements would be final ... There were so many watertight compartments, each demanding full equipment and the like that I thought on all things they had in common, great saving could be effected. Also that they should be made to reach joint agreement; that could never be done under different Ministers. Each would feel it necessary to defend his own Department...

I said that I thought the Services were continuing to go too far. The Army was planning for an overseas army. The Navy had no need at all for aircraft carriers. I had always opposed this from the start as unnecessary. We should have a purely coast defence. I said more important than all this was the shaping of policy in the light of discussions which have taken place in New York at the UNO on disarmament, etc. Relations with Russia. Nothing be done here to give excuse for competitive armament ... The greatest care should be taken over the question of bases and the like. That we should not go throwing money into the water in the North; breaking holes in the ice of the North, in the light of the atomic age...

All of this was a very large problem. A real world problem. I felt it would give him a knowledge and experience that would be more valuable than could be gained anywhere else. I then said to Claxton: You are interested in Health and Welfare, in social questions. You know as well as I do if we are to have money for these purposes, we cannot go on spending what we are on the Army, Navy and Air Force. Either one or the other will have to be cut down. I think your task should be to see that the utmost economy cognizant [*sic*] with security should be effected in the Defence Department and I look to you for that...[41]

Lord Curzon had declined an offer of the War Office with the words: 'No and a thousand times No. There is no reason why one should sacrifice the whole of the best years of one's life for work for which you get no gratitude and are, on the contrary, overwhelmed with ignorant calumny and scorn.' Brooke Claxton said 'Yes' to Mackenzie King's offer of the Department of National Defence. He knew most of what he was in for. 'It was going to be a tough nasty job,' he wrote afterwards. 'I was under no illusion as to that. But I felt that I would like it...'

The mandate of the new Minister of National Defence was just as specific as his predecessors'. McNaughton's had been to find men to fight while lending his military reputation to a government under attack for its military policies. Abbott's had been to bring the forces fairly home. Claxton's was to reorganize the peacetime military establishment and keep its costs down low. 'King put Claxton in as a hatchetman,' the armed forces official historian comments tersely, 'to cut the defence budget...'[42]

Brooke Claxton started to chop with all the energy and enthusiasm that Mackenzie King had known he would throw into his new job. Only a month after taking charge he was favourably impressing his leader. 'Claxton has done wonderful work,' Mackenzie King commented on 14 January 1947, 'in compelling the defence forces to cut down different establishments, effecting a saving of something like $100,000,000.'

As with his Secretary of State for External Affairs, so with his Minister for National Defence. Mackenzie King could tolerate the ability and ambition of his younger colleague only so long as these did not challenge his own preconceptions and authority. As soon as Claxton turned from the chores of budget trimming and organizational reform to assess the crisis of the Cold War, the Prime Minister's regard soured into jealousy and suspicion.

Brooke Claxton, like Louis St Laurent, would stand only so much of this treatment. In December 1947, Claxton joined with St Laurent and J.L. Ilsley in threatening to resign from the Government. He had, in fact, prepared his resignation statement, of which the final portion read in part as follows:

> Irrespective of the issue, was it right, was it just and was it necessary that a course of action should be taken in a way which would force two members of the Government to present their resignations? Here we have in [Ilsley and St Laurent*] two men who have served their country night and day, through war and peace, men whose characters and reputations are held in highest regard by Canadians, irrespective of politics, race or religion, men who by their service deserved well of their country. The records of [Ilsley and St Laurent] are matters of international renown as well as of national pride. That actions taken by them in the exercise of their own best judgments should now be repudiated and repudiated in a way to force their withdrawal from the Government is not right. The only effective way of showing where I stand on these issues and the only way in which I can protest against this treatment is to stand by their side, and it is an honour to be in such company...
>
> Altogether this is a poor incident. Repudiating our representatives, going back on our word, is unworthy, unnecessary and irresponsible. I was among the millions of Canadians who believed that [W.L. Mackenzie King†] was Canada's greatest man of all time. Such a record of achievement cannot be destroyed. It is imperishable, it is a golden leaf in the pages of our country's history. No one can doubt, however, that this action will leave a blemish on that leaf, a blot on that record, a scar on that memory which will last as long as memory itself...
>
> From the hands of [Mackenzie King] there has been shown nothing but kindness and friendship for myself and the members of my family ... But there is a limit at which loyalty to a person must give way to conviction on what one believes, rightly or wrongly, to be a moral question...

It turned out that Claxton did not have to resign, and the statement he had prepared in anticipation of his going was never delivered. Mackenzie

* In the original document these names are omitted.

† This name, also, is omitted in the original.

King thus never knew how sharply critical of his own behaviour a trusted colleague could become. Privately he became more and more critical of Claxton's performance. 'He is far too much given to an assertion of power,' he wrote on 22 December 1947, unaware how perfectly Claxton reciprocated the feeling, 'though he has real ability.' And, on 14 January 1948, *à propos* a speech given by Claxton at Annapolis in which he had promised Canada's co-operation with the United States in the event of war: 'Claxton has left nothing for Parliament's decision. Has given a decision in the name of the Government in advance ... All this is part of an engineered scheme to let some of these younger ambitious men play a role which their ambitions may feel it is their duty to play but which, if they were more experienced, they would hesitate to essay.'[43]

In what was to be the final act of their official relationship, Mackenzie King endeavoured to have Claxton switched from the Ministry of National Defence to the Ministry of Justice, and sent St Laurent (who had just become party leader though not yet Prime Minister) to try to persuade him to make the change. On 23 August, St Laurent reported to Mackenzie King that, as the latter recorded,

> he had talked with Claxton who did not want Justice. Thought it had come to be looked upon as a sort of secondary portfolio. That Defence was all-important in the public mind and he would wish to keep that post. I said it showed wherein Claxton's ambition was defeating his judgment. That Defence was the last portfolio in which people of the country were interested, important as it might be should war arise...[44]

When Mackenzie King had persuaded Claxton to take Defence eighteen months earlier, he had portrayed its opportunities in more glowing terms.

Brooke Claxton served two years as Minister of National Defence under Mackenzie King, five and a half years under St Laurent. He became the most durable defence minister of his time, weathering the formation of NATO, the war in Korea, the building of the Arctic warning systems. Other defence ministers in other allied nations were driven to resignation by the pressure, one was driven to suicide; Claxton was driven only by himself.

That he survived so long so well attests to his stamina and will. It also reflects ministerial support. Once St Laurent took over, he enjoyed the confidence of the Prime Minister. 'I do not believe he ever had anything to do with defence matters in his life until he entered the Cabinet in 1941,' Claxton remarked warmly of his chief to a gathering of Liberals in Ottawa in 1951 [see below, Document 5], 'but he shows the most complete and sympathetic understanding, and if he can do anything for our armed forces he does it.' Claxton and Pearson almost always saw eye to eye. 'During my time,' Claxton wrote of his career in retrospect, 'we had no rifts between External Affairs and Defence.' Of C.D. Howe, Claxton was inclined to be a little apprehensive (as who in that Ministry was not?), but the two men – Claxton at Defence, Howe at Defence Production (among much else) – made a strong team. So did Claxton and the Minister of Finance. 'In the following years,' Claxton wrote of Douglas Abbott,

> I frequently discussed programmes and personalities with him. It was usually, not always, of considerable advantage to have in the Minister of Finance someone who had a good working knowledge of the Defence Department and the Armed Forces and who did not automatically take the view held by some civilians that they were a group of arrogant, ignorant, and irresponsible swashbucklers. Sometimes, however, he knew just a bit too much.[45]

As Minister of National Defence, Brooke Claxton had both strengths and weaknesses. Among his strong points was a healthy scepticism – the ability, precious in any minister, above rubies in a defence minister, to question the plans and assumptions of his expert advisers. He was neither cowed by the great nor truculent in their presence. He held his own in Washington. But his greatest asset was his energy. The Defence portfolio, at that time more than at any time, was no portfolio for sluggards: Claxton was as far from sluggishness as any man alive. Late one Friday afternoon, at the end of a hectic week, he took advantage of an unexpected lull to write to a friend of his routine:

> My desk is clear; there are no Chiefs of Staff waiting in the next room with the daily crisis; we are not going to a cocktail party; everything is under control. This will last for about a minute and a half, I expect. I have got to the condition of a clear desk and a semi-clear conscience a few times during the last six years but the condition is entirely temporary. In a minute or two someone will arrive with another three feet of files for signature which should have been here yesterday; the telephone will ring with a story of rape in Korea, disaster in the Mediterranean or strike at Esquimalt; all four telephone lines will get occupied and we will all feel quite normal again...[46]

On his own assessment, Claxton believed his main fault as a Minister to be a tendency to work too hard. This was not quite right. Rather, it was his tendency to spend too much time 'anticipating' (as he put it) 'and preparing for events which sometimes did not happen.' Sedulously he guarded his Department against those misfortunes which might be turned by political opponents to their own advantage. Only Mackenzie King possessed more sensitive antennae: Claxton's were continuously attuned to the faintest murmurings of public opinion. 'Ministers propose: Cabinets dispose.' Claxton's method was to predispose. To the requirements of his Department he would apply his politician's rule: these thus received a double corrective – Claxton's and the Cabinet's – and sometimes suffered in the process. Brave in combat, Claxton was timid on reconnaissance. He approached a problem apprehensively, as if it were an ambuscade from which would leap some monstrous complication to overwhelm the Liberal Government and Liberal Party.* He was constantly on the alert against surprise attack,

> unforeseen and outside the personal control of the Minister. It may be a fire or theft; it may be an accident in training; someone may have made a ghastly mistake or a gaff in a speech or press release ... To help in this we had someone get up very early and do a note on all references to defence appearing the previous day in the press. By the time I arrived at my office, my staff would have looked through this and started inquiries about matters that were likely to give rise to calls for the press or questions in Parliament...[47]

'Worldly events are so governed by Fate and by God that men cannot by their prudence change them.' It is true that Machiavelli cites this view only to dispute it. But even he attributes about half of the misfortunes to which statecraft is prone to the operation of an inscrutable Fate. Try as hard as he could to defend his Department against them, Claxton was bound to fail. The bomber will always get through. It did so, to devastating effect, during his last year in office. A government inquiry revealed waste and dishonesty within the Department of National Defence. Claxton did not dispute its findings, but held that these had been grossly exaggerated by a hostile press and unscrupulous politicians. 'What was affected,' in his view, 'was a single Branch of the Engineers Service at a time of intense expansion when normal accounting procedures were less important than getting the troops to Korea and Germany.' The public would not regard the matter so slightly, and the prestige of the Department of National Defence and its Minister plummeted almost overnight. Claxton was understandably bitter:

> The record made by the Canadian forces in action in Korea, their remarkable response to all the challenges of peacetime emergency by flood and fire, the steady build-up after post-war demobilization, the outstanding success of new weapons, like the F-86 and CF-100 aircraft, the location of a variety of schools,

* Two examples may be cited. In the early 1950s, the official historian of the Canadian Army desired to publish a factual account of the work of the Canadian-American Permanent Joint Board on Defence during the Second World War. He sought authorization from the Minister, but months passed with no response. Recalling the political controversy aroused by the creation of the Board in 1940, Claxton was reluctant to countenance publication for fear of reviving the controversy. Eventually, and with misgiving, he gave his consent. The article was duly published (in the Spring 1954 issue of the *International Journal*), attracting no attention whatsoever.

The other example is Claxton's reaction to 'Operation Candor': this is discussed below. (See chapter 6, 366–8.)

research establishments and arrangements of every kind which put us in these respects on an even footing with Britain and the United States – these were the fruits of our work in Defence and a proper measure of its success. The Currie Report turned the sensation of accomplishment to ashes, brought the Canadian Army into disrepute and ended my own keen interest in public life...[48]

During this final, dispiriting year it was a great consolation to Claxton to have at his side an Associate Minister of National Defence with whom to share the burden. Ralph O. Campney, his parliamentary assistant since 24 January 1951, was appointed to this new portfolio on 12 February 1953. 'In our partition of the work,' Claxton wrote of it,

it was understood that he would pay special attention to the civil administration – construction, supplies and finance. However, we really acted as alter-egos for each other ... We were the right and left hands of a team organization. We had never differed over a thing. I don't suppose our relationship could have been improved. To step into the office he did not need to change his shoes, but it only needed for me to break ranks...[49]

When Brooke Claxton broke ranks on 30 June 1954, Ralph Campney succeeded him as Minister of National Defence.

## CIVIL SERVANTS

The Department of External Affairs had travelled far and high since its humble beginnings when a deputy minister, two clerks, and a secretary shared an annual budget of $14,950 and an office above a barber shop on Bank Street.* Forty years on, its *placement* at the federal table put it closest to the salt. To its ranks candidates for public service most eagerly sought admission; from them came the most powerful of mandarins. To speak of its relationships with other departments as one of *primus inter pares* is to do less than justice to its position: it cannot be first among its equals for the very excellent reason that it has no equals. Or so it was during the decade 1943–53.

The foreign service officer who, judged by longevity in office, seniority of posting, and eminence of person, ought to have been the most influential member of the Department of External Affairs was Vincent Massey.

Massey was not exactly *un diplomat comme les autres*. He entered the Department in 1926 by means of an Order-in-Council rather than by

* James Eayrs, 'The Origins of Canada's Department of External Affairs,' *Canadian Journal of Economics and Political Science*, XXV, May 1959, 109–28; also, slightly revised, in Hugh L. Keenleyside *et al.*, *The Growth of Canadian Policies in External Affairs* (Durham, NC 1960), 14–32.

competitive examination, having sojourned briefly in Mackenzie King's Government as Minister without Portfolio and failing to gain election to the House of Commons. To console him for this false start – he had given up a lucrative career in industry to enter public life – Mackenzie King made Massey Canada's first Minister to the United States. In 1930 it was the Prime Minister's intention to appoint him High Commissioner to the United Kingdom, and arrangements for this transfer were duly put in hand; they were, however, countermanded by R.B. Bennett who, on becoming Prime Minister, sent as his representative to London someone more personally and politically congenial to himself. Vincent Massey thereupon retired from the Diplomatic Service, only to join it once more in 1935, to take up the High Commissionership once deferred. He remained in that post until 1946.

During those years in London, Vincent Massey had position; but position conferred little power. Mackenzie King distrusted the views of his High Commissioner. He believed him to be overly influenced by what he disparagingly called 'this British crowd.' He suspected him of wishing overly to cultivate his importance in the scheme of things. He was determined not to let the slightest responsibility for the decision of high policy be removed from Ottawa (where little escaped his watchful eye) to London. All this was well understood by Mackenzie King's associates. With feelings ranging from remorse to satisfaction – the Massey personage was not invariably admired – they conspired to turn aside the High Commissioner's appeals to be let in on what was going on. 'I find myself,' Vincent Massey had written in some desperation to a friend in the Department of External Affairs, 'dealing more and more with problems of far-reaching importance in connection with Canada's position in the post-war world, and it would be of the greatest help not only to be kept in touch with the official point of view at home but also to exchange ideas informally and personally with people like yourself.' This plea, and others like them, fell on deaf ears. The Minister of National Defence, from whom Massey had urgently requested information about the Quebec Conference of August 1943, returned a typically dusty answer. 'While I can talk to you very personally and face to face about these matters,' J.L. Ralston had replied guardedly, 'don't you think the PM would feel that information regarding decisions made from time to time here had better go forward from him? ... We might all feel unhappy if attempts were made to short-circuit.'[50] Vincent Massey suffered these indignities with patrician stoicism.

The permanent head of the Canadian foreign office – its Under Secretary of State for External Affairs – was throughout most of the war Norman Alexander Robertson. Mackenzie King had chosen Robertson to succeed O.D. Skelton, who had worked himself to death in the service of his chief and country, in January 1941. No one was ever quite able to do for Mackenzie King what Skelton had done. Skelton's dedication to his work, his utter self-effacement, his capacity for fathoming and expressing the workings of the Prime Minister's mind, his Harry Hopkins-like loyalty,* were virtually unique. But in all these qualities Robertson was second only to Skelton. Mackenzie King was quick to mark and recognize the fact. 'With the exception of Skelton,' the Prime Minister wrote of his Under Secretary on 22 October 1944, 'he has the finest sense of duty of any man I have known. He will not accept the work of another, but verifies everything himself, if there is the slightest possibility of error.'[51] In the exacting service of the most demanding of employers, that was the beginning of wisdom.

The subject of this unusual tribute had entered the Department of External Affairs in 1929, after a Rhodes scholarship had taken him to Oxford and postgraduate study to Harvard and the Brookings Institution. His first posting was to the legation in Washington as third secretary. In 1930 he accompanied Sir Robert Borden to the League of Nations Assembly in Geneva, and favourably impressed that elder statesman. He no less favourably impressed the Department of Government at Harvard, which offered him a lectureship, to lead, within five years to a professorship. The Under Secretary of State for External Affairs, O.D. Skelton, prevailed upon his protégé to accept leave of absence from the Canadian public service, rather than to sever the connection entirely; and, in 1934, prevailed upon the Prime Minister, R.B. Bennett, to waive the civil service seniority system so as to enable Robertson to return to Ottawa as first secretary. Once he returned he never looked back.

By 1944, when Mackenzie King bestowed his praise upon him, Norman Robertson was forty years of age – perhaps not yet at the peak of his intellectual powers, certainly not yet at the peak of his influence. Within two years, however, that influence – which later justifiably became one of the legends of the capital – was great enough for the Prime Minister himself to cite it as reason enough why Robertson ought not to leave his post at Ottawa – 'the most influential post,' as Mackenzie King described it, 'in the service of the country ... not only in Canadian affairs and in Continental affairs but in world affairs'[52] – to become High Commissioner

* 'Should the President on a dull day suggest casually to his friend and confidant, Harry L. Hopkins, that the national welfare would be served if Mr Hopkins were to jump off the Washington Monument, the appointed hour would find Mr Hopkins poised for the plunge. Whether with or without parachute would depend on what the President seemed to have in mind.' Marquis W. Childs, 'The President's Best Friend,' *The Saturday Evening Post*, 19 April 1941, 64.

in the United Kingdom. In the event, Robertson did go to London in the autumn of 1946. His tall stooping figure, draped in its cape-like coat, and the high-domed forehead topped with a floppy black felt fedora, blended easily into the environment of English eccentricity – a statesman not at all disguised. He was more at home at Whitehall than at Foggy Bottom, and it was at Canada House that he made his reputation as 'a diplomatist of world rank' – the tribute is that of *The Times* – 'with world-wide interests.' He was the first Canada had produced.

In 1949 Norman Robertson returned to Ottawa to succeed Arnold Heeney as Clerk of the Privy Council and Secretary of the Cabinet. In June 1952 he began a second tour as High Commissoner in the United Kingdom. In May 1957 (the Suez crisis past), he was appointed ambassador to the United States. In 1958 he was back in Ottawa again as Under Secretary of State for External Affairs. His partial retirement in 1964 – he continued to serve on special missions and as a consultant to the government – completed a career in public service as influential as any that Canada will know. He died on 16 July 1968.*

Mackenzie King admired his aide more for selfless service rendered than for pointed criticism and devil's advocacy. Not until King left the scene could Robertson's intellect, which excelled at both, come fully into its own. 'N.A.R.,' initialled on papers of state, guaranteed bite and tartness. He did not write many: his minutes were few, his memoranda fewer still. He enjoyed Proust, but his style, abominating length and froth, was anything but Proustian. His reluctance to commit his views to paper became notorious among his colleagues. His method could be disconcerting. 'Often, when he studied a question and saw objections,' an associate recalls, 'he simply heaved a long, very long, incredibly long, sigh. He had said everything. We understood that there were a multitude of problems we had not foreseen in our plans. And we withdrew without further ado.' Documents and letters would remain on his desk for months on end, in the expectation that the problems they proclaimed would one day go away. Sometimes they did.

Outside the inner circle the Robertson manner was harder to appreciate. One could not be sure whether the reserve with which a visitor beyond the bureaucracy was received was due to shyness or disdain; perhaps a bit of both. A fault apparent even to insiders was in administering his team, for which he had neither taste nor talent. 'Norman is just himself,' an

* His death drew from colleagues appreciations marked no less by candour and sensitivity than by affectionate admiration. See the tributes by L.B. Pearson, John Holmes, and Marcel Cadieux, in *External Affairs* (Ottawa), October 1968; also Denis Brogan, 'A Balliol Man,' *The Spectator*, 2 August 1968.

associate wrote of him a few months after he had taken charge of the Department of External Affairs in 1941, '– brilliant, modest, lovable, working his head off – but no gift for organization.' Five years later the Prime Minister wrote that his deputy had 'very decidedly lost his grip on administrative end of departmental affairs.'[53] He used his pencil like a scalpel but he could never use a scalpel – much less a pole-axe.

Robertson was not the only contender for the top job in the Department when it fell vacant in January 1941. The Counsellor at the Canadian Legation in Washington also might think himself entitled to it.

Humphrey Hume Wrong had already spent fifteen years in diplomacy, most of them in an office at 1746 Massachusetts Avenue NW. Soon after his arrival at this, his first posting – it was to be as well his last – Hume Wrong had jotted down, half in fun, what he took to be essential attributes of the successful diplomatist – a good head for liquor, a way with the ladies, no need for sleep, more than average common sense. Then followed:

> (5) an orderly and methodical mind, so that one doesn't forget things and lose papers and so on – with this again nature has endowed me not too badly; (6) cynicism about governments and pessimism about human nature, with both of which I am amply provided; (7) a capacity for producing, orally and on paper, polite guff at a moment's notice; this I found trying at first, but it is becoming mechanical; it really ranks a lot higher than seventh on the list – first or second, I think.[54]

Son of a noted Canadian historian (and a tyro historian himself), grandson of Edward Blake, kin to Cronyns, in-lawed to Huttons, Hume Wrong would have been assured of a place among the ruling class had Canada been more of an aristocracy than she was; being merely meritocracy tempered by privilege, he had to content himself with a place among her power elite. His advancement in its ranks was delayed by his temperament. He did not possess that extraordinary capacity for self-effacement – one might almost say self-immolation – which so commended Skelton and Norman Robertson to their chief. As a junior foreign service officer he had refused to don diplomatic dress, preferring to make this minor tribulation of the profession into an issue of principle, which he referred to as the 'confounded uniform question.'[55] He had an acidulous wit. He once devised, during the tedium of some international gathering, 'a plan for the perfect representation of Canada at conferences. Our delegate would have a name, even a photograph; a distinguished record, even an actual secretary – but he would have no corporeal existence and no one would ever notice that he was not there.'[56] (It may be seen from this excursion how far from the truth was the official obituary in proclaiming cynicism to be 'a habit of mind at all times completely foreign to him.')

Hume Wrong had some reason to believe that he was being passed over when Norman Robertson became Under Secretary of State for External Affairs. He bore up as best he could under what he regarded as a slight and a mistake of the meritocracy. But his best was none too good and the dissatisfaction showed. The Minister, Leighton McCarthy, arranged with Mackenzie King to have Wrong transferred to Ottawa to serve under Robertson, his place as Counsellor being taken by L.B. Pearson. This move was doubly upsetting. Not only might it seem hard to work for Robertson when it might have been Robertson working for him, but leaving the Legation meant foregoing the post of Minister when it fell vacant, as it soon would do. 'Hume is taking the whole business very hard,' Pearson wrote in June 1942. 'You know his pride, his touchiness, & his sensitiveness. All these have been deeply affected.'[57]

But offsetting all these was the public servant's sense of duty, which in the end prevailed. Once in Ottawa, Wrong served Robertson, and Canada, no less faithfully than Robertson served Mackenzie King, and Canada. One who worked for both at the time records that he 'was never conscious of any friction at all.' Robertson put Wrong's talents to play upon the problems of post-war international organization. 'What particularly distinguished his contribution in this field,' a colleague has written, 'was its rational quality and its pragmatism. He did not suffer from apocalyptic delusions about the nature and the prospects of international government.'[58] These traits showed to advantage in his work on the future Charter of the United Nations and, four years later, the future treaty of the North Atlantic nations. In contrast to Norman Robertson, Wrong was a fine administrator. A mind orderly and disciplined produced decisions swift and shrewd. 'He worked his staff hard,' a member of it recalls, 'and imposed on them his own high standards, and they admired him for it.'[59]

There was a third contender for the Under Secretaryship in 1941. L.B. Pearson, many years later, described his not having attained it as the greatest disappointment of his career,[60] but it was a career singularly lacking in disappointments.

'Mike' Pearson – the nickname had stuck since the Great War and suited well a sunny, breezy disposition – entered the Department of External Affairs in 1928, not without reservations on the part of those who let him in.* The first seven years were based in Ottawa, with occasional

* 'My only criticism of him in connection with this possible appointment,' Vincent Massey had written to O.D. Skelton in July 1928, 'is that there is something curiously loose-jointed and sloppy about his mental make-up which, as a matter of fact, is reflected in some measure in his physical bearing. It is possible,' Massey

trips abroad with the then Prime Minister, R.B. Bennett, for whom he performed various minor tasks and, as secretary to the Royal Commission on Price Spreads, one major task. His first overseas posting was to London where, from 1935 to 1941, he worked closely with Vincent Massey and shared (or feigned) his chief's indignation at the High Commission's shabby treatment by Mackenzie King. Here, and at Geneva, Pearson got his first real taste of diplomatic life. He showed himself well suited to it. Of some international commodity conference at which, for the first time, he represented Canada, he wrote: 'Of course no one here has any idea as to what the Canadian attitude toward this conference is, or even if there is a Canadian attitude. But I was reluctant to say that, so I chatted amiably for 15 minutes...'[61]

Early in 1941, Pearson was recalled from Canada House to the Department's headquarters in the East Block at Ottawa. 'The imperative reason,' Mackenzie King explained to Vincent Massey, whom he knew would sorely miss his deputy, 'is ... to obtain best possible assistance for Robertson.' On 19 May 1941, the Prime Minister had his first talk with Pearson in nearly two years,* and was favourably impressed. 'Very modest, unassuming,' he wrote. 'He is going to be valuable to Robertson.'[62] But

conceded, 'that his other qualities offset this defect.' The Under Secretary, not wholly convinced that all entrants to External Affairs should combine the mind of a mathematician with the posture of a Grenadier Guard, placed somewhat greater emphasis upon those 'other qualities.' Pearson 'has very distinct capacity,' Skelton wrote in reply, 'and attractive personal qualifications.' (Massey Papers) Pearson, then a history don at the University of Toronto, topped the list of candidates. It was not a long list.

Applicants to the Department of External Affairs may possibly be heartened by the knowledge that a future Under Secretary, Minister, and Prime Minister was thought to be not altogether a safe bet for the position of FSO 1.

* They had last conversed in August 1939. Pearson, vacationing in Manitoba,

> had canoed across the lake to the village and saw a headline in a newspaper: 'Nazis threaten Danzig and Polish Corridor.' This was it, I felt sure. So I packed, left my family, hurried to Ottawa and told Dr Skelton I should get back to Canada House as quickly as possible, as war was now going to break out. He thought I was too alarmist and suggested I see Mr King. So I spent an ... afternoon at Kingsmere, with a kindly and gracious host, the Prime Minister, who thought my sense of duty was praiseworthy but my judgment was erratic. There would be no war, he said, but, if I wished to cut short my holiday, he had no objection. When I indicated that not only should I cut it short but I should fly back at once, he lost all confidence in my judgment ...

L.B. Pearson, 'Forty Years on: Reflections on Our Foreign Policy,' *International Journal*, XXI, 3, Summer 1967, 359–60. Notwithstanding the fact that war broke out within a week, Mackenzie King continued to think of Pearson as a bit on the impetuous side. He 'always wanted,' he told the American Minister to Ottawa on 9 January 1942, 'to go a little too fast.' (Quoted in Nancy Harvison Hooker [ed.], *The Moffat Papers, 1919–1943* [Cambridge, Mass. 1956], 373.)

Pearson had no sooner settled into wartime Ottawa than he was on the move once more, this time to Washington as Counsellor. He was none too sure that he would do well in the job. 'It will be difficult – very difficult – for me in Washington,' he wrote to Vincent Massey on 9 June 1942. 'I'm new there – do not know my way about. The Minister is ... not physically strong, the staff is not officially strong and its morale is, I hear, very bad ... However, I shall do my best.'[63]

He need not have worried. No Canadian diplomatist has made a more favourable impression in the American capital than Mike Pearson during the years 1942 to 1946, when he was successively Counsellor, Minister-Counsellor, Minister, and Ambassador. If Hume Wrong was the principal architect of Canada's policies on post-war international organization, L.B. Pearson was the principal agent in the attempt, far from wholly successful, to press those views upon the governments of the Great Powers, through the Government of the United States. 'Few serious officials,' James Reston wrote in an *envoi* in 1946, 'have been able to work incessantly on the problem of peace without losing either their perspective or their sense of humour ... Mr Pearson has managed to do that.'[64]

While in Washington, Mike Pearson became known for his ardent and compelling support of collective security as the basis for the post-war international order. 'A bomb dropped on a Chinese village echoes across the St Lawrence,' he told a possibly sceptical audience in March 1943; 'that is something we Canadians have learned.'[65] And a year later:

> That collective system which was spurned in peace has proven to be our salvation in war ... There is no other way to win the peace. If we want it badly enough, we can secure it. If we want other things more, individual and national gain, an easy and comfortable life, then we will once more lose the peace and enter again that wasteland of another post-war world, where queues are for bread and not for hockey tickets, and where peace sits uneasily on the top of a bayonet.[66]

On his recall to Ottawa in 1946, as Under Secretary of State for External Affairs (replacing Norman Roberson, who became High Commissioner in the United Kingdom), Pearson expected to be able to put these principles into practice. He was to be sorely disappointed. It was not just the international environment which proved stubborn and refractory. Much as the Prime Minister admired the zest and idealism of his younger deputy – in offering him the post as Under Secretary, Mackenzie King had pointed out to Pearson that it could lead to a political career, and had told him (in what was a supreme compliment) that he was 'cut out for politics' – he soon became alarmed at Pearson's attempted initiative. His diary makes clear the extent of his distress:

*6 December 1947*: ...They all use him in New York to be prominent in the Palestine affair, and he being young and no doubt feeling his ability in these matters, I think has lent himself perhaps too wholly to the desires of others ... I told Pearson in talking with him this afternoon that I thought he should put his emphasis now on developing his own staff at home. I am terribly afraid we have gone too far in the prominent part we have allowed our own people to play at the expense of our own affairs...

*18 December*: ...Pearson with his youth and inexperience and influenced by the persuasion of others around him, had been anxious to have Canada's External Affairs figure prominently in world affairs and has really directed affairs in New York when he should have been in Ottawa, and without any real control by Ministers of the Crown and proper consideration of these questions. All meant well but very much the inexperience of youth. I am sure if Skelton had been alive, he would not have advocated our going afield in that fashion...

*22 December*: ...So far as External Affairs is concerned, they have been allowed to be run far too much on Pearson's sole say so, and Pearson himself moved far too much by the kind of influences that are brought to bear upon him. He is young, idealistic, etc., but has not responsibility. I am thankful I held ... External Affairs as long as I did. At least, I did not get the country into trouble by keeping it out of things it had no business to interfere with.

*31 December*: ...While Pearson is very quick and able, he still lacks experience and, to some degree, distant vision, but next to Robertson and Wrong, is undoubtedly the best man in the diplomatic service.

*20 February 1948*: ...I really think Robertson's judgment is sounder than Pearson's on these international affairs, and that he would be better at the head of the Department here. Is less fond of speaking or of travelling or of participating in the United Nations, etc. Less likely to get the Government into trouble...

*25 February*: ...I feel a good deal of concern with the part Pearson takes in New York. I think he is much too active in the name of Canada. His own report shows he does not hesitate to advise both the United Kingdom and the United States as to what it is wisest for them to do. He likes the international arena but some day it will land us in an obligation from which we will find a great difficulty in being freed...[67]

Neither chief nor protégé had much longer to endure the want of peace of mind that each produced in the other. Pearson entered Mackenzie King's ministry on 10 September 1948 as Secretary of State for External Affairs; Mackenzie King's ministry became St Laurent's ministry on 15 November 1948. Thereafter the way was clear for Pearson's diplomatic talents to come into their own. These led straight to leadership in the affairs of the Atlantic Alliance, to conciliation in the Korean War, to peacemaking and peacekeeping in the Middle East, and to the Nobel Peace Prize.

Gifted in negotiation, Pearson was a poor administrator. He could no more wield a pole-axe than could Norman Robertson. 'Dad was a poor disciplinarian,' his daughter recalled of her childhood, 'when we got into mischief he was likely to melt away or disappear behind his newspaper.' Far from disagreeable in a parent, the trait is debilitating in a politician, deadly in a prime minister. 'As Secretary of State for External Affairs, Pearson got his deputy ... to look after whatever firing of personnel had to be done. He was hesitant to judge people and consequently not perceptive about their weaknesses, preferring to like everyone until he had been given plenty of reason to think otherwise.'[68] Not least among his charms was his utter self-awareness of this liability of leadership. An almost reckless air of diffidence marked his five years as prime minister which began in April 1963, and a highly developed (perhaps over-developed) gift for persiflage found its first target in himself.* Of such leniency colleagues and underlings were quick to take advantage. The pedagogue-turned-politician found himself headmaster of a school for scandal. A series of sordid escapades marred his administration. These, remarks a chronicler of his times and their distemper, 'would always remain on the charts of Lester Pearson's accomplishments, like a buoy that marks the position of a wreck.'[69]

'No government service,' it has been remarked, 'can be made up entirely of first-class men ... efficiency is finally determined not by the stars but by the average second class.'[70] The average second class of the Department of External Affairs during the decade 1943–53 worthily complemented the triumvirate of Robertson, Wrong, and Pearson. In time some of them would shine almost as brightly.

Among the home guard, the diplomat most deserving of mention in despatches is Escott Meredith Reid. Escott Reid was that *rara avis* of any foreign office, a genuine scholar and intellectual. Like Loring Christie before him,† he hated having to concoct and mouth the gibberish of state. Clarity in diplomatic discourse became a fetish. He strove ceaselessly, against insuperable odds, to make less circumlocutory the language of foreign affairs. The Charter of the United Nations, the Pact of the Atlantic

* As in his adieu to the Parliamentary Press Gallery, 30 March 1968:

> My sixty days of decision were too decisive. I failed to get three maple leaves on the flag and I lost the blue border. I failed to get Vancouver into the NHL or Gabon into the Canadian confederation. I failed to realize that unification of the armed forces should have been preceded by unification of the Cabinet. I was wrong in relying entirely on the Sermon on the Mount as the guideline for Cabinet solidarity ... So I leave you ... conscious of a job half-done...

Quoted in Lester B. Pearson, *Words and Occasions* (Toronto 1970), 286.

† See James Eayrs, *Right and Wrong in Foreign Policy* (Toronto 1966), 43–4.

Nations – neither, perhaps, models of concinnity and eloquence – were the better for his draftsmanship.* He indulged in speaking bluntly as well as plainly, though by 1942 Pearson thought he had 'mellowed since I saw him last and [is] not so provocatively Canadian.'[71] He had a reputation as a radical.† He would even kick against the pricks. 'Perhaps if I had done that more often,' he wrote after his retirement, 'I might even have been able to keep the bloody Portuguese out [of NATO]. I fought to the end against Portuguese membership, even putting the case against it into the final memorandum asking Cabinet approval for the Treaty.'[72] He felt a compulsion to keep watch upon himself and, even more erratically, to report on what he found. An *apologia pro vita sua diplomatica,* though offered when no longer in the profession, is a reckoning as unusual as it is poignant.‡ Needless to say, the combination of these traits kept him just below the Department's commanding heights.

Wartime offered little scope for oversea diplomacy. By 1939, there were only seven missions in the field – London, Washington, Paris, Tokyo, Brussels, The Hague and, for the League of Nations, Geneva. War closed down the Tokyo legation. Relations with the Allied governments-in-exile were conducted through a mission created for the purpose in London in 1943.

After the war, representation abroad expanded rapidly – so rapidly that, a decade later, missions of one kind or another existed in nearly fifty capitals. Despite intense recruitment there were not enough good men to go round. At their best, the good men were able enough: three were outstanding.

Major General Georges P. Vanier had entered diplomacy through the door of a disarmament conference, as technical expert to Canada's one-man delegation on the League of Nation's Permanent Advisory Commission for Military, Naval and Air questions. During the tedium of double-

* Of the proposed Atlantic Pact, Reid had written: 'Because the Treaty should be a human and compelling document, calculated to strike the imagination of the peoples of the Free World, it is important that every effort be made to write it in simple, everyday language understandable by the ordinary man ... Ancient forms and terms should be avoided ...' His chief was unconvinced. 'I fear you still have your phobia about lawyers' jargon,' Norman Robertson minuted. 'It is hackneyed, but it often helps precise statement. I see no point in trying to work in sub-crusades for basic English.' (King Papers)

† 'Preparedness for national defence,' Reid had written in an editorial for the *Trinity University Review* in 1927, 'has never yet brought a feeling of security to nations and it never will.'

‡ 'I cannot speak from personal experience about what a diplomat should do if called upon to perform unclean or indecent acts because I was never called upon in my career in the Canadian foreign service to perform such acts though I was, of course, called upon to perform unpleasant or embarrassing tasks and acts which I considered unwise.' 'The Conscience of the Diplomat,' *Queen's Quarterly*, LXXIV, 4, Winter 1967, 586.

talk and consecutive translation there was little to do but doodle; one of Vanier's *bloc-notes* catches perfectly the profile of a diplomat of the old school: 'What is he best fitted for – to create or to complicate, irritate and destroy? What a master saboteur he is, with his mobile and ravaged features, his eyes with their cobwebs of wrinkles, his thick and facile laugh, contrasting with his sinister smile.' He knew the terrain of diplomacy as well as the trenches he'd left behind.

After a stint at Canada House, where he and L.B. Pearson backed up Vincent Massey – Massey's genius lay in getting able helpers – Vanier received his first diplomatic command on 25 January 1939 as Minister to France. Love for his mother country blinded him to her faults. 'It must be admitted,' writes his biographer, 'that he at no time between September 1939 and May 1940 suspected the weakness of the French army, the deep fissures in French society, or the intrigues that were already undermining the Government.'[73] A person of exceptional probity and piety, it was not given to him to understand the damage that might be done to a great power by a Comtesse de Portes, by a Madame de Crussol, from their salients of *salon* and *boudoir*. The major accomplishment of his mission was to burn his documents, evacuate his legation and escape to England and safety.

For all his devotion to family, Church, regiment, Vanier was not deceived by Pétain's corporative slogans after the fall of France. 'The Vichy government was conceived in the sin of betrayal,' he wrote to Mackenzie King on 17 May 1941; 'its every act, therefore, must needs be marked with the original stigma.' He asked to be allowed to resign from duties impossible to reconcile 'with a sense of honour, of decency, or of patriotism.'[74] Ottawa, more concerned with the conventional diplomatic virtues of timing and expediency, kept his resignation in abeyance for a further year. But it is Vanier's distinction to have been the first Canadian diplomat to tender his resignation on an issue of principle; there have not been many since.

First in London, later (January 1944) as ambassador in Algiers, Vanier championed the cause of the Free French against their powerful detractors. Gaullism knew no more staunch supporter, its leader no more loyal upholder. 'Ever since I came to Algiers,' Vanier noted on 6 August 1944, 'I have been endeavouring to prove to the Department [of External Affairs] that the only reasonable course for us to follow was to acknowledge [de Gaulle's] Committee as the future and later "de facto" administrator in France after Liberation.'[75] He helped secure the decision to allow Free French forces to take part in the Normandy landings. Within a week of the surrender of the German garrison in Paris to General Leclerc (the cousin of his wife), Vanier flew to the liberated capital to resume his duties as Minister, soon (November 1944) as Ambassador, to France. He remained at this post until his retirement from diplomacy in 1953.

Just before returning to Canada, the Vaniers dined with de Gaulle at Colombey-les-Deux-Eglises, where the great man was in retreat to write his memoirs and regather his forces. This rare audience was justly due to one who, as de Gaulle had acknowledged, 'from the very first day [had been] the faithful friend of the Free French and the evident defender of their cause.' But there are limits to gratitude in foreign policy, in Gaullist foreign policy severe limits. When, twelve years later, Vanier lay stricken by the illness from which he did not recover, only de Gaulle's ambassador failed to call at Government House.

Pierre Dupuy was another outstanding Canadian diplomat. He had entered the Department of External Affairs in a very junior capacity as long ago as 1922; in January 1939 he was first secretary under Vanier in Paris. After the fall of France he undertook the first of three journeys to Vichy to assess its policies, mood, and future. Dupuy's modest account of his first mission* discreetly passes over the reluctance of his superiors in the Department of External Affairs to have him embark upon it. 'Ottawa is getting alarmed about his activities,' the High Commissioner in the United Kingdom noted on 31 December 1940, '...& is sending fussy telegrams ... As soon as any representative shows either imagination or initiative he calls down the displeasure of the powers that be in External Affairs. Their ideal diplomat belongs to Mme Tussaud's waxworks!'[76] As *chargé d'affaires* to the Dutch and Belgian governments-in-exile, as well as to the French, Dupuy, in Vanier's words, was 'watching by the bedside of three countries seriously ill.' In 1945 he was rewarded for these ministrations by being appointed Canada's first Ambassador to The Netherlands. He remained at The Hague until 1952, when he became Ambassador to Italy; in 1958 he became Ambassador to France.

The third member of this trio was Edward Dana Wilgress. Wilgress went to Kuibyshev, the Soviet Union's wartime capital, in March 1943, as the first Canadian accredited to a communist government. He brought to this post a unique experience of Russian life going back to 1916 when, as a very young man, he had sought out economic opportunities in Siberia on behalf of the Department of Trade and Commerce.† After the Second World War he stayed on in Moscow as Ambassador.

* 'Mission à Vichy: Novembre 1940,' *International Journal*, XXII, 3, Summer 1967, 395–401.

† These adventures are described in Dana Wilgress, 'From Siberia to Kuibyshev: Reflections on Russia, 1919–1943,' *International Journal*, XXII, 3, Summer 1967, 364–75; and in *Dana Wilgress Memoirs* (Toronto 1967), 30–56.

Having spent most of 1946 outside the Soviet Union at various international conferences, Dana Wilgress was astonished when, during a session of the Conference at Paris, the Soviet representative launched a personal attack upon him.

It was prompted by a proposal I had made for a modification of the five-year period during which Italy would be compelled to grant most-favoured-nation treatment to the other signatories of the treaty. Vyshinsky embarked upon a long tirade expressing surprise that anyone who knew as I did of the destruction suffered by the Soviet Union during the war should make such a proposal. I understood what he had said in Russian, then I had to sit through the interpretations into English and French, feeling that all in the room were looking at me. I replied very simply that I felt it was not just to deprive the Italians for so long of a period of freedom to manoeuvre...[77]

It had not been Wilgress's proposal that drew harsh words from Vyshinsky, rather the publication of the report of the Canadian Government's Royal Commission on Soviet wartime espionage in Canada. Its unflattering disclosures brought Soviet retaliation in the form of hostility towards Canada's ambassador. Dana Wilgress's position in Moscow became more and more uncomfortable, eventually untenable. 'During the war,' Wilgress recalled, 'I had felt myself at the very top in Soviet esteem, ranking just after the British and American ambassadors. Now, I had fallen to the very bottom.' Early in 1947 Ottawa decided that his usefulness in Moscow was at an end. To rebuke the Russians for their inhospitable attitude a successor was not appointed, and the Embassy remained in the hands of a succession of *chargés d'affaires* until March 1954.

Wilgress was too level-headed a diplomat to allow this contretemps to sway his assessment of Soviet policies. A summary of his views, prepared for his colleagues in the Department of External Affairs soon after he left Moscow, is wholly free from rancour or hysteria, and in striking contrast to much of the intelligence about the Soviet Union then circulating in Washington.*

Membership of the Department of External Affairs expanded rapidly during the Second World War. Marcel Cadieux, Jean Chapdelaine, John Deutsch, R.A.D. Ford, George Glazebrook, John Holmes, George Ignatieff, Jules Léger, R.M. Macdonnell, Leon Mayrand, A.R. Menzies, Herbert Norman, Saul Rae, A.E. Ritchie, C.S.A. Ritchie, Chester Ronning, Arnold Smith, Paul Tremblay, and Max Wershof were among the new recruits – 'articulate, worldly-wise yet earnest' (as an Australian scholar has described them), 'seeking few favours but determined to be active.'[78] Their efforts 'brilliantly built up from nothing' – the tribute is

* See below, 335.

a British ambassador's – 'one of the highest-powered Foreign Services in the modern world.'[79]

Not all who shaped external policy during the decade 1943–53 were members of the Department of External Affairs. The view from the top of the public service is one in which the bailiwicks of bureaucracy are blended into a continuous panorama. The senior civil servant is able to gaze across the entire horizon of public policy, the boundary between domestic and foreign affairs all but disappears.

So it comes about that many of the decisions discussed in following chapters are the work not of diplomats only, but of a select company of senior administrators outside the Department of External Affairs to whom ministers turned, collectively and individually, for advice on how to govern.

No better vantage point may be found from which to view the terrain of state than the Cabinet's Secretariat – unless it is the office of the Prime Minister.

In the United Kingdom these institutions functioned as two solitudes. 'It should be clearly understood,' an expert wrote for the benefit of the Prime Minister of Canada in 1927, 'that the Cabinet Office or Secretariat is entirely separate from the Prime Minister's office. Hankey and his assistants are established in Whitehall Gardens; the Prime Minister's personal staff ... are at 10 Downing Street or in the Prime Minister's room at the House of Commons ... The Cabinet Secretariat works in the background avoiding publicity. The chief object of Hankey and Tom Jones is to keep out of the lime-light. The success of their work depends upon this. It is not Hankey's duty but that of the personal staff at No. 10 to see individuals for the Prime Minister and to act as a buffer. Hankey does not go about with the Prime Minister nor is he seen with him.'[80] It may be doubted whether the recipient of this remonstration regarded it as the last word on its subject. With the niceties of organizational theory, the relationships of 'line' and 'staff,' Mackenzie King had no patience and nothing to do. 'The diffusion of responsibility among the members of his staff,' one of its most influential members has testified, 'and [his] comparative indifference to their respective roles, were nicely calculated to cause confusion and misunderstanding.'[81] So far from wishing to preserve the respective autonomies of Cabinet secretariat and Prime Minister's office, he had wanted to combine the two under the direction of a single official to be known as 'executive assistant to the Prime Minister.' Only grudgingly did he yield to the argument that such an arrangement would wreak havoc in both quarters, but no one could persuade him that service as a member of his staff was not the most fitting preparation for a tour of duty in the Cabinet secretariat. The two Secretaries to the Cabinet during the years 1940–1953 both served just such an apprenticeship.

A Cabinet secretariat came late to Canadian government. In 1923, Mackenzie King told Sir Maurice Hankey, who had served as secretary to British cabinets since 1916 and had come to personify the post, 'that he would like to have a Secretary to the Canadian Cabinet, and that he would have one "in his time," but that at present it wouldn't do. His Cabinet would not stand for it ... A Secretary would cause all kinds of trouble.'[82] 'In his time' proved to be 25 March 1940, by which date (according to the order-in-council authorizing the position), 'the great increase in the work of the Cabinet and particularly since the outbreak of war [had] rendered it necessary to make provision for the performance of additional duties of a secretarial nature relating principally to the collection and putting into shape of agenda of Cabinet meetings, the providing of information and material necessary for the deliberations of the Cabinet and the drawing up of records of the results.'[83]

The first Secretary to the Cabinet was Arnold Danford Patrick Heeney, who had grown up in Manitoba, been polished at Oxford on a Rhodes Scholarship, and for a decade after 1929 had practised law in Montreal. It was from this profitable and congenial milieu – he combined his practice with lecturing in law at McGill University – that the Prime Minister sought to lure him for his own staff in August 1938. 'Heeney seems genuinely interested and anxious to come,' Mackenzie King wrote after a day's assiduous wooing which included lunch at the Ottawa Country Club. 'I rather believe he will accept. It rests with a Higher Power – and for that guidance I pray for his sake & my own.'[84]

This might appear as somewhat extravagant language for a prime minister to employ about the hiring of a relatively unknown 36-year-old lawyer – even for one who, like Mackenzie King, was accustomed to calling for divine guidance the way others might call for a waiter. But there was much at stake. Mackenzie King had at last made up his mind that the time had come to create a cabinet secretariat in Canada. He looked to Arnold Heeney to set it up. The post as Principal Secretary to the Prime Minister was to be his apprenticeship for the Secretaryship of the Cabinet (along with the established position of Clerk of the Privy Council) when it became available about two years later.

For nine years – March 1940 to March 1949 – Arnold Heeney kept the minutes and the secrets of the government of Canada. He was good at the job, he relished the work, he basked in *darshan* (a Hindi word, unique in any language, for the peculiar glow of pleasurable excitation some feel in the presence of the powerful and famous).

There were tribulations, too. Following precedent in Britain – where prime minister's office and cabinet secretariat operated each unto itself – Arnold Heeney strove to remove party politics from his agenda. He might as well have striven to reverse Niagara Falls. To his prime minister, welfare of the Liberal Party, welfare of the nation, were one and indivisible. Mackenzie King could never understand why Heeney would not toil loyally for both.

In 1949 Heeney became Under Secretary of State for External Affairs. By then there was little he did not know of the arcane rites of Ottawa. One of the youngest of the mandarins, Heeney was also one of the most influential – and most worldly. Away from the habitat of the capital he did not convey, as did other public servants, 'the uncomfortable impression of shy woodland animals caught rashly far out from the undergrowth.'[85] There was nothing shy about A.D.P. Heeney, whether at home or abroad. He radiated energy and authority, breathed an air of command. With his patrician features, marcelled hair turned prematurely grey, a wide and faintly supercilious smile, he even looked like an ambassador. In due course he became one – the highly powered envoy of a Middle Power Kingdom, first to NATO, next to the United States.

During the early Eisenhower years all things, if not bright and beautiful, were at least benign and bland. Ike asked after our wartime generals, chuckled indulgently at memories of McNaughton: 'Andy thought he was fighting the British!' Dulles joshed about his offshore island in eastern Lake Ontario. Armistice in Korea had removed a major irritant. Vietnam was just a name. The long polar watch pumped cold cash into our economy. We were Uncle Sam's favourite nephew. Bliss was it in that dawn to be alive, but to be representing Canada in Washington was very heaven!

After two years as chairman of the Civil Service Commission, Heeney returned to the United States as ambassador in 1959. He now represented a different government of a people in a different mood. His mission as a Middle Power Kingdom's middle man between John G. Diefenbaker and John F. Kennedy, while not mission impossible, was certainly mission exacting. In the end it failed.*

* For Arnold Heeney's discreet recollections of his ambassiates, see 'Washington Under Two Presidents: 1953–57; 1959–62,' *International Journal*, XXII, 3, Summer 1967, 500–11; and, for a critique of his ideas about Canadian-American relations, James Eayrs, *Diplomacy and its Discontents* (Toronto 1971), 49–58.

Yet another Manitoban who had finished school at Oxford joined the Prime Minister's staff in the summer of 1938. John Whitney Pickersgill had languished, unpromoted, in the History Department of Wesley College, Winnipeg, before entering the Department of External Affairs in 1937; he was soon seconded by the Under Secretary who could recognize (having long provided it himself) that special blend of blind and competent devotion Mackenzie King demanded of his assistants.

The new arrival quickly gained grace and favour. 'Pickersgill has come into close confidential relationship,' Mackenzie King wrote of his protégé in August 1939, 'and I feel a good deal of confidence in his judgment as a young man, and appreciate the work he is doing.'[86] Having just acquired a secret too delicate to be shared with his Cabinet yet too delectable to be kept to himself – an invitation from Hitler to visit Germany that fall – the Prime Minister confided it to Pickersgill. 'Asked him ... to say nothing of it to anyone, but to think it over and if he cared to, talk to me about it later on. He was careful not to commit himself in any way.'[87] The faithful servant had soon acquired his master's style.

Skelton, Heeney, and Pickersgill, under the Prime Minister's direction, administered the country through its first few months at war. Just before its outbreak, Mackenzie King had spoken to the trio 'about the importance of organizing a staff for war purposes at the office, each one with their special duty: Heeney to be the liaison between Skelton and myself ... Pickersgill to keep to the political side, while Heeney devoted his time to the war side.'[88] Such a division of labour allotted the lion's share to Pickersgill, for 'the political side' meant everything. After Heeney's appointment as Secretary to the Cabinet in March 1940, and Skelton's sudden death in January 1941, Pickersgill's influence – the word 'clout' was just then coming into use* – grew apace. His own assessment of that influence, while not falsely modest, necessarily fails to do justice to his role:

J.W. Pickersgill was the no. 2 in the Prime Minister's Office after March 1940 but he had, since 1938, had direct contact in his work with the Prime Minister and only a minor share of the ordinary duties of a Private Secretary. Most of his time was spent in assisting Mackenzie King with the preparation of speeches, public statements, and official correspondence.[89]

From the beginning of the war, I had had a relatively close and frequent association with Mackenzie King personally. It is no exaggeration to say that

* 'The political use of the word is believed to have originated in Chicago in the 1940's, taken from the baseball phrase, "What a clout!" meaning "a powerful hit," or "a long hard drive." ' William Safire, *The New Language of Politics* (New York 1968), 81–2.

there were very few prepared speeches or statements made by him in Parliament or elsewhere in public in which I did not have some part. In the preparation of speeches, correspondence, and memoranda and in their subsequent revision with him, I gradually developed a familiarity with his attitude, with his modes of expression, and with what might be expected to be his reaction to various situations. From the first Conscription Crisis of 1942 onward, our association was much closer than it was before that year. I should, however, emphasize ... that I was not Mackenzie King's principal adviser at any time during the war, and that I was not the head of the Prime Minister's office until just after the election of 1945.[90]

When in 1927 Mackenzie King had persuaded Parliament to appropriate funds for an 'executive assistant to the Prime Minister,' he had promised that the executive assistant would resign with the Prime Minister.[91] But it was not to be. The head of the Prime Minister's office went with the office. So it was that in November 1948 Louis St Laurent inherited Pickersgill along with the Prime Ministership. 'It was decided,' writes St Laurent biographer, 'that J.W. Pickersgill, special assistant in the Prime Minister's office and an ardent admirer of St Laurent, would remain in Ottawa to help ensure a smooth transfer of power.'[92] By whom or how this was decided is not made clear.

Much of the power was transferred to Pickersgill himself. As Secretary of State for External Affairs, St Laurent had been insulated from the day-to-day political activities of which the Special Assistant had such long and exacting experience. He depended on him 'for direction on how to operate the prime minister's office ... For the first three months of St Laurent's term at least, the country was to an astonishing degree run by Jack Pickersgill ... During the 1949 election St Laurent made a pact that he would commit himself to no appointments or public appearances that weren't "cleared with Jack." '[93] St Laurent's biographer puts it this way: 'At his right hand he was anxious to have J.W. Pickersgill, whose wide knowledge of Canadian politics and government and seemingly boundless energy and initiative made him an invaluable assistant.' And again: 'Watching over every aspect of political and administrative activity, Jack Pickersgill proved an invaluable aide and counsellor. "Check it with Jack" became a watchword on Parliament Hill.'[94]

Clearing – or checking – with Jack was no guarantee of a statesmanlike result. The man was indefatigable, his knowledge of politics inexhaustible, but his judgment was not infallible. His approach to government, writes a perceptive and cutting critic, 'was so uniquely his own that his name found a place in Canada's political dictionary. The expression "Pickersgillian" came to signify any partisan ploy that was too clever by half. His strong personality, encyclopaedic knowledge of Ottawa and its ways, his mastery of Commons rules and intense loyalty ... allowed him to exercise a decisive and not always benign leverage on the course of federal events.'* But it was the Pearson Government, not the St Laurent, which became the embarrassed beneficiary of his major mistakes.

In 1952 Pickersgill, like Heeney before him, left the Prime Minister's office to become Secretary to the Cabinet and Clerk of the Privy Council. 'Through this shift in personnel,' writes St Laurent's biographer, the Prime Minister 'lost one of his most trusted advisers, for by transferring from the Prime Minister's Office to the Privy Council, Pickersgill disqualified himself from playing the role of political adviser in which he was so valuable.'[95] It may be doubted that any such disqualification occurred: Pickersgill could no more refrain from dispensing political advice, from the Cabinet Office or anywhere else, than a geyser can refrain from spouting. But the changed milieu made it more awkward. A General Election impended. Even a Pickersgill could hardly bound about the country on behalf of St Laurent and Liberalism while Clerk of the Privy Council. So he exchanged his job in the Cabinet Office for a job in the Cabinet. It was as though Sir Maurice Hankey had plunged into the fray of the Khaki Election. Still, as a 'new Canadian' from the United Kingdom had observed in 1927, 'no one who knows Canada would imagine that the British system could or should be introduced *in toto* into Canadian public life.'[96]

The making of external policy, though dominated by the Departments of External Affairs and National Defence, and peculiarly influenced from within the Prime Minister's and Cabinet Office, was not confined to these. Senior public servants from other departments and agencies of government also shared in the process of decision-making. Their number was small: perhaps a dozen in 1943, triple that number by 1953. Their composition varied, depending on the ascendant personalities of the moment and the status of their particular bureaucratic bailiwick in the hierarchy of power.

The Department of Trade and Commerce, by reason of its duties and even more (after C.D. Howe took charge) by reason of its Minister, regained the prominent role of which it had been deprived by war. Its rehabilitation in the scheme of things was helped along by its traditional rival. 'The Department of Trade and Commerce,' Norman Robertson wrote to the Prime Minister on 27 December 1943,

* Newman, *Distemper of Our Times*, 231. Chapter 17, 'A Footnote on "Sailor Jack",' offers a penetrating assessment of what it describes as 'not ... exactly a noble career.'

is directly concerned with the formulation of government policies on most economic questions and specifically with wheat and international commercial policies. Its normal activities fell off very largely with the outbreak of war, and the new war agencies progressively took over functions which might have been handled by an expanding and adaptable Department of Trade and Commerce. In the last few years the other Departments concerned with economic policy questions have all strengthened their personnel very considerably. One result of this is that they consult pretty freely with each other because they appreciate the value of each other's views on questions of joint and common concern, and tend only to consult Trade and Commerce when that Department clearly has a jurisdictional interest in a particular question. This weakness in the senior personnel of Trade and Commerce is a matter of some concern to people in other Departments of the Government who have to concert policy with them. It has also the unhappy result of producing a rather defensive state of mind and something approaching an inferiority complex within the Department.[97]

The decline in its fortunes, Robertson suggested, might be arrested by the appointment of a forceful deputy minister. He suggested the name of Hector McKinnon. But McKinnon's services were required elsewhere, and Trade and Commerce continued to flounder until 1948, when C.D. Howe came to its rescue.

The Department of Finance was especially influential, not least on account of its deputy minister, W.C. Clark, whom Mackenzie King praised as 'very clear and far-seeing' – 'far-seeing' being one of the Prime Minister's highest accolades – and to whom he thought 'the Government and the country owe almost more ... than to any other man for the war effort.'[98] W.A. Mackintosh, Clark's deputy, was a distinguished and potent influence during wartime and after. So were Graham Towers, Governor of the Bank of Canada; Hector McKinnon, Chairman of the Wartime Prices and Trade Board; Donald Gordon, deputy Governor of the Bank and McKinnon's successor; Arthur McNamara, deputy minister of Labour; and C.J. Mackenzie, President of the National Research Council.

The list, while incomplete, provides a fair example of what R. MacGregor Dawson has called 'the notable contribution made by Scotland to Canada.' It provides as well an illustration of what John Porter has called 'the vertical mosaic' – the product of those processes of Canadian society which seem to deny a fair place on its commanding heights to the two-thirds of its members who are not white, Anglo-Saxon, and Protestant.

After the Second World War, these veterans of the public service were infused by a fresh and no less gifted group of recruits. R.B. Bryce, A.K. Eaton, A.F.W. Plumptre, and K.W. Taylor occupied the higher echelons of the Department of Finance. Mitchell Sharp left Finance to become C.D. Howe's deputy at Trade and Commerce. David Golden helped Howe at another of his enterprises, the Department of Defence Production. Omond Solandt became the first chairman of the Defence Research Board (in which capacity, Brooke Claxton wrote later, he 'knew more British secrets than any American and knew more American secrets than anyone from the British Isles'). Solandt's appointment was matched in importance by that of C.M. Drury, whom Claxton obtained from the Department of External Affairs in 1948 to become Deputy Minister of National Defence, where he carried – it is Claxton's tribute – 'a load through the years such as few people could have borne, and he carried it magnificently.'[99]

The new group of higher civil servants was not markedly more cosmopolitan than the old, although the Scottish strain was less spectacularly in evidence. Like their predecessors they were an homogeneous band, with 'a common background in the social class and educational systems [and] ... commonly held intellectual values.'[100] It was enough to make a prairie populist cry 'Conspiracy!' But there was no conspiracy. There was only a common interest, or perhaps a common obsession: how to acquire, retain, deploy, augment, the power of the bureaucrat.

## ADMIRALS, AIR MARSHALS, GENERALS

Conspicuously absent from this company were members of the military profession.

Their absence, during wartime, is readily accounted for. The military were engaged in the business of war, which left little time for other business. There were a few exceptions. General McNaughton, following his enforced resignation, spent a brief interlude in politics. And three major-generals moved from army service to the foreign service.

The transition of Major-General Georges Vanier has already been noted. That of Major-General Victor Odlum was less successful. On 10 October 1941, the Prime Minister asked him to become Canada's first High Commissioner in Australia. 'The fact that, at the moment, you are filling the position of General Officer Commanding of the 2nd Canadian Division in the United Kingdom,' Mackenzie King had written, 'would cause our friends in Australia, as well as the Government of the United Kingdom, to feel that Canada was making a real contribution to the situation on the Pacific.' Odlum was reluctant to give up his command, doubtful of his abilities as a diplomatist, and sceptical that his presence in Canberra would prove a satisfactory substitute for the division of Canadian troops which was what the Australians were really after. However, he yielded to his Prime Minister's persuasion. He soon regretted doing so. 'Cut off from you,' Odlum wrote disconsolately to Mackenzie King soon after his arrival,

> I feel like a lost soul. I am still of the opinion that a natural soldier cannot make a good diplomat – at least in the height of a war fever. Everything here has to do with war ... And I am showing a lively interest in all the Australian defence problems. But while this interests me, it does not make me feel that I am tugging at the right trace...[101]

Chungking, to which capital Odlum was transferred in 1943, was better than Canberra, being the scene of great events unfolding. It is not known whether Canada's Ambassador to China (Odlum's mission was raised to the rank of embassy in 1944) provided his Government with any useful assessment of the direction those great events were soon to take. Victor Odlum remained in China until 1947, when he became Ambassador to Turkey.

The third major-general in diplomacy was Maurice Pope who, of all the wartime military, came closest to the arcana of bureaucratic power. At the outset of war, Pope was Secretary to the Chiefs of Staff Committee, as well as to the half-dozen interdepartmental committees on which the Department of National Defence was represented. Soon afterwards, he became Director of Operations and Intelligence at National Defence Headquarters. A descendant of two distinguished families prominent in Canadian political life, no officer was more conscious of the civilian implications of military policy, or less likely to take part in any revolt of the generals.* Mackenzie King, appreciating these qualities, in 1942 appointed their possessor Chairman of the Canadian Joint Staff Mission in Washington. Pope's mission was to scrounge what snippets of information he could from his highly placed friends in the US State and War

* Two passages in Maurice Pope's memoirs illustrate, respectively, each of these characteristics. His alacrity in discerning the political aspects of grand strategy is revealed in his recollection of his reaction on reading a signal from the Chief of the General Staff, concerning the possible use of Canadian troops in the Alaska theatre, in which

> there was a phrase which ran generally 'that he had not yet consulted the Minister in this respect.' In the light of this governing phrase, [his] 'heresy' ... struck my mind with the clarity of the click of a pebble thrown against a rock. Reading no further, I reached for the telephone...

Maurice A. Pope, *Soldiers and Politicians* (Toronto 1962), 215. His sensitivity to the proprieties of civil-military relations is disclosed in his description of how, on finding himself acting Chief of the General Staff in January 1942, he 'allowed myself to speak in a way quite improper for a public servant when addressing a minister of the Crown': his sin, as he thought it to be, consisted in telling J.L. Ralston not to concern himself with the shortage of rifles in the Reserve Army. *Ibid.*, 179–80.

Departments, and on the Combined Chiefs of Staff. It was not a job for most soldiers, but Pope enjoyed it and did well at it. In August 1944, the Prime Minister brought Pope back to Ottawa and created for him the posts of Military Staff Officer to the Prime Minister and Military Secretary to the War Committee of the Cabinet. Mackenzie King explained to him 'that I wanted someone to whom I would not have to tell what to do but who could tell me what was required, why and how it should be done ...'[102] Pope understood his Prime Minister well enough to realize that he wanted nothing of the sort; no one, a general least of all, ventured to tell Mackenzie King what was required, let alone why and how it should be done. It worked out just as Pope expected. 'I cannot recall an occasion when Mr King sent for me to discuss a military question. Such of these that interested him were invariably loaded with political overtones and under this head the Prime Minister was in no need of my advice.'[103]

External Affairs was Maurice Pope's spiritual home, and after the war it became his corporeal home as well. His diplomatic career began in October 1945, with his appointment as head of the Canadian Military Mission in Berlin.* It was at first not clear to him whether this was a military or a diplomatic assignment, and Pope sought guidance on the point from the Under Secretary. Norman Robertson 'replied that I should be the representative of the Canadian Government in Germany in precisely the same way as were our Ambassadors to The Hague, Brussels, and Paris ... I found this intelligence most gratifying.'[104]

So began Maurice Pope's delayed but distinguished career in diplomacy which led, after the postings in Berlin and (from 15 December 1949) Bonn, to ambassadorships in Brussels, Luxembourg, and Madrid. He relished the protocol and festive aspects of diplomatic life, but by no means gave himself over entirely to court ceremonials. He pursued intelligence as indefatigably as a pig after truffles. He took great care in the composition of reports from the field, admonishing his staff 'that while I well knew that the substance of our dispatches would duly fetch up in Ottawa as dead as mutton, it behoved us to see that they showed at least some sparkle of life when they went into the bag.'[105] But his most valuable asset by far was a sturdy common sense immunizing his judgment to alarmist assessments of the intentions of potential adversaries, which he resolutely refused to identify with their capabilities. General Maurice Pope kept his head when all about him – notably his Berlin colleague General Lucius Clay† – were losing theirs. It was no small achievement.

* See below, 200.

† 'Within the last few weeks,' Clay had cabled Washington on 5 March 1948, 'I have felt a subtle change in Soviet attitude which I cannot define but which now

The military profession played little part in the wartime higher public service because its members were at war. For the little part it played in the postwar higher public service, other explanations must be found. Its members were no longer at war. Most of the senior officers returned to that civilian life from which they came. Most of the professionals remained in uniform.* But whether in the Services or out of them, the commanders of Canada's fighting forces did not become the administrators of Canada's post-war policies. Why should this have been so?

In the United States it wasn't so. There, 'the movement of military personnel into high appointive federal agency posts was a deliberate post-war policy to meet the personnel shortage of an expanded bureaucracy, especially in foreign affairs and defense-related agencies.' There, also, 'civilian leadership sought to make use of prestigeful [*sic*] military officers to deal with difficult political problems.' General George C. Marshall's appointment in 1946 as President Truman's special representative in China was only the most dramatic example of a far-reaching trend.[106]

This trend had no counterpart in Canada. Not that there was no shortage of senior public servants, nor no vexing problems to be solved. Rather, because the professional military officer was regarded as an unsuitable choice either for filling high office or for solving national problems.

After the First World War, the attitude towards the officer class was bitterly critical. And with reason. The officers had let the country down in the very business in which they professed competence – the business of

gives me a feeling that [war] may come with dramatic suddenness.' (Quoted in Walter Millis [ed.], *The Forrestal Diaries* [New York 1951], 387.) Here is Pope's assessment of the same situation from the same vantage point:

> While ever since the cessation of hostilities, now over three years ago, it has been obvious that there was nothing to stop the Russian Armies from advancing to the western shores of Europe, were they of a mind to do so, no evidence has ever come my way which pointed to the conclusion that such a course of action lay within immediate Soviet policy. This is but yet one more instance of the United States habit of appreciating situations in terms of the other side's 'capabilities' rather than in terms of 'probability.' I would therefore venture to repeat that, while there is no restraining force in existence that could prevent the Soviet Army from advancing to Calais – or the Pyrenees – I am unaware of any evidence that would go to show that Moscow is planning to do so within the reasonably near future. It is for this reason that I have been extremely careful never to send you a single word bearing on the possibility of war.

Quoted in *Soldiers and Politicians: The Memoirs of Lt.-Gen. Maurice A. Pope* (Toronto 1962), 338.

* There were few professionals, Canada's wartime Services having been led largely by civilian officers. 'In the tragic and costly operations against Dieppe in the summer of 1942,' an Opposition defence critic observed on 16 October 1945, 'not more than half a dozen permanent force officers landed on the beaches.' Canada, *H.C. Debates*, 1945, 2nd Session, I, 1181.

war. The higher their rank, it often seemed, the graver their offence. 'The British generals one and all,' wrote a Canadian in 1915, 'are the most incompetent lot of bloody fools that have ever been collected together for the purpose of sacrificing armies.'[107] If British generals were so singled out, it was not because they were British but because they were generals. Few Canadians rose high enough to bear responsibility for what happened, but that did not spare them from becoming scapegoats for the slaughter in which 60,000 Canadians had perished in the mud.

After the Second World War, there was little criticism of this kind. Again with reason. Many Canadians perished in that war too, but, with the exception of the Hong Kong expedition and the possible exception of the Dieppe raid, their next of kin could not with reason think their deaths had been due to incompetence, their sacrifice in vain.* The generals, the admirals, the air marshals and air vice marshals, had not let their country down. They had served it with valour, and, on the whole, with competence. Tributes to these qualities were duly paid in Parliament during the autumn of 1945. The Parliament of 1919 had heard only anger and accusation.

Though the conquering heroes might be hailed, they would look in vain for worship. Their wartime service conferred a pension, possibly a place on a company's board, certainly (for those staying on in the Forces) an office on Cartier Square. But it did not confer the right to rule. In the public service the limit to favouritism was veterans' preference. That helped you start at the bottom: it was no help at all at the top.

What the public concluded by instinct, insiders concluded from experience. Two factors, in particular, caused them to close ranks so as to exclude the military from their midst.

The first was the feeling that the military were not to be trusted. They

* Doubts about the sacrifice arose only later – much, much later – and were even then repressed by all save the most hardened sceptic. One who built his career on hardened scepticism put the forbidden thought into the following words:

> Reading ... my umpteenth book on the war of 1939–45, I still have the feeling that there is some essential aspect which remains unexplored and unexpressed. On the one hand, all the writers ... accept the notion that the events described are historically momentous, and the men concerned giants who will be remembered for ever. On the other, the effect of their narrative is to make one feel that the struggle, far from being over mighty principles and the defence of civilisation, is just part of a universal crack-up; about nothing and solving nothing; no more than a footnote to the last page of the last chapter of the story of Christendom, with Churchill defending an Empire that was already over, Roosevelt freedoms he neither respected nor understood, and Stalin a revolution he had long ago liquidated.

Malcolm Muggeridge, 'Macmillan Goes to War,' *The Observer*, 10 September 1967. With Churchill, Roosevelt, and Stalin thus reduced in scale, whatever remains of Mackenzie King?

would too quickly exceed, or try to exceed, the limits of their status and jurisdiction.

This fear seems not at all to have troubled authorities in the United States. 'The great thing about an Army officer,' Henry L. Stimson had quoted approvingly from Theodore Roosevelt in nominating yet another military man to ambassadorial rank, 'is that he does what you tell him to do.'[108] It was this quality, among others, that caused President Truman to appoint no fewer than ten officers to serve as principal State Department heads and ambassadors during 1947–9;[109] this in addition to the Secretary of State himself (General Marshall) and the uniquely proconsular figure in Japan (General MacArthur) – who eventually had to be dismissed for not doing what he was told to do. But it gravely troubled authorities in Canada, at least that authority which mattered.

Mackenzie King (so his biographer informs us) 'was never a military man in any sense: his distrust of the army was deep-seated and life-long.' During the Second World War, he 'viewed the army from a remote eminence. He had little sympathy with it, virtually no contacts, and only a hazy understanding of its problems.' As early as December 1941, he had become 'convinced that unless it was carefully watched the ambition of the military officers was likely to lead the Cabinet into difficulties.'[110] His attitude was not improved by word reaching him in 1943 that 'the officers of the Army [were] practically all Tory,' nor did his informant's opinion that 'the Navy is Liberal' serve as sufficient compensation.[111] He came to believe that General Staff officers were withholding information from him, and exceeding their authority by planning military projects without his knowledge or consent. By 1944 he had developed grave doubts as to their efficiency. 'Really the more I see of it all,' he noted on 26 October, 'the more I am convinced that the Department of Defence has made a terrible mess of our whole war effort. The army has been far too large; the the planning has been anything but sound. The judgment, far from good.'[112] A few days later his darkest suspicions were confirmed. He became convinced, during the conscription crisis of November 1944, that the senior officers of the Dominion of Canada were plotting against its Government – his Government.

Plot or no plot – the evidence, while incomplete, suggests that there was none* – the Prime Minister there and then resolved that never again would he allow the military to intrude upon the making of national policy.

* 'There has been a good deal of talk,' R. MacGregor Dawson has written,

> about a possible military revolt in Canada at this time ... There was a lack of enthusiasm and a lack of effort in the cause of voluntary enlistment among the army officers who in many instances placed personal convictions and feelings above the legitimate demands of the Government; there was apathy

He had been reluctant to trust them in the past. He would not trust them in the future. Henceforth they would be confined in their small corner of the policy realm. In May 1946, a proposal emerged, in all innocence, from the British Government to the effect that military attachés be stationed at the respective missions of Canada and the United Kingdom in each other's capitals for purposes of liaison and the exchange of intelligence. Mackenzie King bridled instantly at the suggestion. 'I had a strong feeling,' he wrote, 'that the military, air and navy attaché business ought to be done away with altogether and Embassies should be left free to discharge what are obviously their right duties.'[113] Only reluctantly did he give his consent to the proposal, and then on the condition 'that whatever was done should be done quietly.'[114]

Aversion to military influence and military advice was one prejudice most higher civil servants shared to the full with their chief. 'Is it for the military staff to expound policies? Is it not for the civil arm of government to lay down the scheme of policy and liabilities, and then for the military to submit military plans accordingly?'[115] From this way of looking at it, expounded rhetorically by the Under Secretary of State for External Affairs ten years before, the civilian advisers of the post-war period differed not at all. Policy they held to be their own preserve. Any general, admiral, or air marshal so misguided as to try to enter it should be rebuffed. Usually they were rebuffed.

Such inhospitability stemmed from several causes. It was partly a simple matter of a struggle for power. The decline of military influence meant an augmentation of the influence of civilians. A few of those civilians who, while of fighting age and fighting trim, had sat out the war behind an East Block desk, may have been relieved to find that brass and braid and oak leaf clusters were not to be allowed to exploit their psychological advantage in committee. That generosity of spirit in which the Department of External Affairs had taken upon itself the role of mentor and protector of the policy community – even, as has been shown, exalting departments of low degree so as to restore balance and harmony to the whole – did not embrace the Department of National Defence.

But the most important cause of the military's ostracization by the rest

> and a disinclination to help in some quarters which may have approached a mild form of passive resistance; there was the conviction in the minds of many army officers that the civil power was not doing its duty and that therefore the army was free to do as little as it pleased to assist; there was a withdrawal of support by the Military Members of the Army Council for the Minister's policy; but there is no sign whatever of ardent soldiers in a spirit of misguided patriotism being prepared to march on Ottawa and take over the Government.

R. MacGregor Dawson, *The Conscription Crisis of 1944* (Toronto 1961), 90–1.

of the post-war policy community was the feeling that its senior officers lacked the type of training that was needed to deal with national security in a nuclear age. What in its collective experience – at sea, on land, or in the air – equipped its members to comprehend their new environment much less to shape it? The answer was thought to be not very much. 'Majors and colonels read *Time* and *Life*,' a foreign service officer wrote of them disparagingly, 'and form their appreciations which none can shake.'[116]

Admirals and commodores, more than majors and colonels, had difficulty adjusting. 'They had all joined about the year 1914,' was how their Minister accounted for it, 'had been trained largely with the RN, and served together through every rank and every course, had English accents and fixed ideas.' They also caused a lot of trouble.*

To steer the Navy into post-war waters the Government had looked to Vice Admiral George Clarence Jones. 'Jetty' Jones – the sobriquet had been flung at him in Parliament by that merciless critic of the Service brass Jean-François Pouliot, and unfairly attached itself to an officer with as much sea-time as most – became Chief of Naval Staff on 15 January 1944. To the intense pressure of running the Navy during the final year of war were added, during the spring of 1945, the additional problems caused by the explosion of the Navy ammunition dump near Halifax, the riots which broke out in that city on V-E Day, and the investigations which these events made necessary. The Admiral's health could not withstand the strain, and on 8 February 1946 he suffered a heart seizure at his desk and died. So it happened that the Chief of Naval Staff with whom Brooke Claxton first had to deal on becoming Minister of National Defence was an officer who in the normal course of events would not have occupied that post.

In many respects, Vice Admiral Howard Emerson Reid was typical of the senior officers of the senior Service. Born at Portage du Dort, Quebec, he entered the second term of the Royal Naval College of Canada in Halifax in January 1912, at the tender age of 14 years, seven months. As a junior officer during the Great War, he served in British as well as Canadian warships. Between the wars he commanded HMS *Sepoy* on the China Station and, in 1932, HMS *Warspite*. In 1931 he attended the Royal Naval Staff College. On the outbreak of war, he was Commanding Officer, Atlantic Coast. In 1940 he became Vice Chief of Naval Staff and the Canadian member of the Canada-United States Permanent Joint Board on Defence. It has been recorded that during a meeting at National

* See below, 124–7.

Defence Headquarters convened to consider what should be done about the Japanese-Canadians of British Columbia, Admiral Reid 'cheerfully stated that [the Navy] had no problem, for on the day of Pearl Harbor they had cleared every one of our Japanese fishermen off the sea.'[117] His subsequent record as Flag Officer, Newfoundland Force, pitted him against a more formidable foe: he gave a good account of himself during the U-boat war.

But as a peacetime Chief, 'Rastus' Reid was less successful. He gave little of his energies to his new duties. (A scabrous ditty of the wartime RCNVR, which begins with the lines 'Rastus was a lazy man / under a tree, / when 'long came a bee,' may conceivably have referred to him.) Reid resisted Claxton's efforts to integrate the armed forces but did not conspicuously improve the efficiency of his own. If he departed at all from tradition, it was only the tradition of the 'silent Service.' The Admiral became outspokenly critical of government policy which he construed – not without justification – as niggardly towards the post-war Navy. In due course, he over-stepped the mark, which was easily over-stepped. On 6 November 1946 he attacked the Government in a speech widely reported in the newspapers. 'The United States Navy,' Reid declared, 'plans a post-war personnel of 500,000 men. We have 10,000. Our population is one-twelfth that of the United States. You can figure out for yourself the arithmetic.'[118] The Prime Minister, to whose attention these observations were duly brought, was not at all interested in the Admiral's arithmetic; he was incensed by the impropriety of the Admiral's utterance. At a Cabinet meeting on 15 November, Mackenzie King instructed the Minister of National Defence for Naval Services to reprimand his Chief of Naval Staff. Douglas Abbott replied primly that the reprimand had already been administered. Admiral Reid retired in September 1947.

Reid was succeeded by Vice Admiral H.T.W. Grant, who remained Chief of Naval Staff until 1 December 1951. Harold Grant had the most illustrious battle record among Canadian maritime commanders. Like Admiral Jones, he had been born in Halifax and attended the Royal Naval College there as a youth, graduating as a midshipman at the age of 17 to serve for the remainder of the Great War in ships of the Royal Navy. He remained with the RN until 1923, returned for duty on the Canadian destroyers *Patriot* and *Patrician*, and between 1927 and 1931 served once again on Royal Navy warships. During the 1930s he shuttled among the usual shore postings, staff colleges, and sea duties. In 1942–3, while in command of HMS *Enterprise*, he engaged eleven German destroyers in the Bay of Biscay and was awarded the Distinguished Service Order for this action. Still commanding *Enterprise*, he took part in the

D-Day landing operation and was wounded during the bombardment of Cherbourg. Prior to his appointment as CNS on 1 September 1947, he had been commanding officer of HMCS *Ontario* and Chief of Naval Administration and Supply.

Under Admiral Grant as Chief, the post-war Navy underwent its major period of expansion. When he came to the job, the Navy had only 6814 officers and men, and eight ships in active commission; by the time he left, its strength was more than 12,000, with 24 ships at sea (including three destroyers on duty in Korean waters) and 39 vessels being built in shipyards across the country. It was also a period of crisis which, under Grant's leadership, it survived.* The Admiral's lively sense of humour, even more his absolutely disarming modesty – attributes not always found among his naval colleagues – stood him, and the Navy, in good stead during its time of testing. He was the first of the post-war naval Chiefs to develop and propound ideas about the role of the Navy in the conditions of sea warfare created by nuclear weapons and the attack submarine. [A sampling of his views is presented below as Document 4.]

If the post-war Navy had the hardest time adjusting to its peacetime role, the post-war Air Force had the easiest. That was not least due to the fact that, more than the other two armed forces, the Air Force had things pretty much its own way. Its role was more easily defined, its status more prestigious, its connections more powerful. Its funds, in consequence, were more plentiful and its future more assured.†

Two Chiefs of the Air Staff guided the RCAF during its metamorphosis.

Air Marshal Robert Leckie had become its senior officer in 1944. Leckie had an outstanding service career. Born in Scotland in 1890, he came to Canada as a youth, joining the Royal Naval Air Service in 1915. Among his wartime exploits, for which he was several times decorated, was shooting down two zeppelins. In 1920, Leckie was appointed a member of the Air Board of Canada, and so became one of the founders of the Royal Canadian Air Force.‡ Between the wars he commanded the Royal Navy aircraft carriers *Hermes* and *Courageous*. In 1940 he returned to Canada as Director of Training for the RCAF, and in this capacity was responsible for administering the British Commonwealth Air Training Plan. For his able performance of a crucial wartime command he was appointed Chief of Air Staff. He worked well and closely with the

* See below, 124–7.
† See below, 122–3.
‡ See James Eayrs, *In Defence of Canada*, I, *From the Great War to the Great Depression* (Toronto 1964), 196, 202–3.

Minister of National Defence for Air; Chubby Power considered Leckie 'in every respect well fitted for the position ... widely read even beyond his technical and professional knowledge, and [with] a thorough, strictly non-partisan understanding of politics and politicians.'[119]

Leckie got on no less cordially with Brooke Claxton. Claxton admired the tenacity with which Leckie defended the interests of his Service, and admired no less the loyalty with which he carried out policies he disagreed with – such as the reduction of the authorized strength of the RCAF to 12,000 officers and men announced on 16 January 1947 which (as a fellow-officer later recalled) 'made Bob Leckie boiling mad.' He was not one to sulk or resign over such a matter. He had developed useful contacts during the Second World War with some of the nabobs of American military aviation. General H.H. Arnold and General Carl Spaatz were fishing companions on expeditions to northern Quebec, and Leckie learned much from these apostles of air power which proved helpful to his Service when it came to solving problems of procurement and supply.

But Leckie was no lap-dog of the USAF. In 1940 he had undergone the harrowing experience of turning, in vain, to the Americans for aircraft engines no longer forthcoming from the United Kingdom and without which the Air Training Plan might be doomed. 'This must never happen again,' C.D. Howe had told him then.[120] Leckie, like Howe, never forgot this incident; both became ardent advocates of an all-Canadian aircraft industry capable of meeting out of its own production the post-war requirements of the RCAF. Nor did Leckie fall in meekly behind the plans of his American counterparts for an all-out joint Canada-US effort to defend the continent against Soviet bomber attack.*

On 1 September 1947, Leckie was succeeded as Chief of Air Staff by Air Marshal W.A. Curtis. Wilf Curtis had been acting Chief during most of 1947 when Leckie, on the verge of retirement, played a decreasing role in the major decisions of that year. If this period of *de facto* command is joined to the five and one-half years Curtis remained as CAS, he may be reckoned to have the longest run in office of any of the post-war Chiefs.

Under the leadership of Curtis the RCAF embarked upon an unprecedented peace-time expansion. It came to surpass the Army in over-all strength, and its budget became greater than those of the two other Services combined. Even so, Curtis retained the respect, rather than incurred the jealousy, of his fellow Chiefs of Staff. His wartime record was exceptional among their exceptional records. As a fighter pilot during the Great War he earned the Distinguished Service Cross and bar. He was one of a very few to hold commissions in all three Services. Unlike his fellow

* See below, 341–2.

Chiefs, he had not stayed in the permanent forces after 1918 but went into business, acquiring from the practice of insurance a familiarity with figures and accounting which later helped him cast a practiced eye over departmental estimates. Recalled from the Air Force Reserve (in which he had become officer commanding the RCAF 110th Toronto Squadron) at the outbreak of the Second World War, Curtis advanced through various administrative posts to become Deputy Commander-in-Chief of the RCAF overseas.

One of his first assignments was to try to have a number of Hawker Hurricanes, whose airframes had been made in Canada, allocated to the RCAF; the committee of supply ordered them to the Soviet Union instead. This experience, and others like it, converted Curtis (as Leckie had also been converted) into an ardent advocate of national self-reliance on aircraft production (including engines) in the post-war years. Backed by C.D. Howe, he argued successfully in 1947 for the design and development of what emerged, three years later, as the CF-100 fighter-interceptor with its Orenda engine, both all-Canadian projects.*

Like Leckie, Curtis had powerful connections in the world of American military aviation; General Hoyt S. Vandenberg (who had succeeded Spaatz as USAF Chief of Staff in April 1948) and 'Dutch' Kindelberger (president of North American Aviation) were among those whom he successfully approached during the scramble for parts and procurement during the early months of the Korean War. Nor had he neglected his wartime friendships in the RAF. Curtis was on good terms with the Air Ministry. Lord Tedder and Sir John Slessor he knew as comrades-in-arms; it was through a well-placed hint to Slessor from Curtis that the NATO Military Standing Group (on which Slessor was the United Kingdom representative) finally got round to asking the Canadian Government for an air contribution to the defence of Western Europe – a request answered, in due course, by the formation of the RCAF's air division in France. Wilf Curtis resigned as Chief of Air Staff on 31 January 1953 to watch, from the sidelines of an exceptionally active retirement, the decline and ultimately the disappearance of the Service whose strength he had done so much to build.

At the end of the war, the crisis over conscription lay less than a year in the past, and senior Army officers were still regarded with some suspicion by politicians in Ottawa. There was accordingly no more crucial position in Canada's post-war military establishment than that of Chief of the General Staff. The incumbent was Lt-General J.C. Murchie, who was due

* See below, 101–5.

to retire, and did retire, on 20 August 1945. To the selection of his successor the Government gave careful and anxious thought.

One of two obvious candidates was Lt-General G.G. Simonds. Guy Simonds was considered by many, including Field Marshal Montgomery, to be the most capable battle commander produced by Canada during the war. He was certainly the most dashing in appearance. Since 30 January 1944 he had led the second of two Canadian Corps in Western Europe, previously commanding the 1st Division during the Sicilian campaign. Against this brilliant wartime record were to be set certain adverse factors. Simonds had yet to serve at National Defence Headquarters, he had spent scant time in Canada since graduating from the Royal Military College in 1932, he was thought to possess insufficient understanding of the ways of Canadian life. He was not noted for an abundance of tact or discretion. Even Montgomery found his protégé 'a little headstrong.'[121] Fools he suffered less than gladly, politicians not at all. General H.D.G. Crerar, his Commander-in-Chief, told Mackenzie King in 1944 that while he would recommend Simonds as his own successor, 'he might not be the best man for post-war planning.'[122] That was McNaughton's judgment too, and of Douglas Abbott when Abbott became Minister of National Defence. All this tipped the balance against him. In August 1945 Simonds was ordered to remain in Europe as commander of Canadian forces of occupation. The job of Chief of the General Staff devolved upon the other candidate.

The other candidate was Lt-General Charles Foulkes. As a wartime commander Foulkes' record had been a shade less spectacular but was, even so, outstanding. Going overseas as a major in 1939, Foulkes rose swiftly to the top of the Army. As a major-general he took the 2nd Division to France early in 1944, fought the battle of Falaise and drove through the buzz-bomb coast to Antwerp and the Low Countries. In September 1944 he temporarily commanded the 2nd Canadian Corps in its victory in the battle of Walcheren. November found him in Italy, leading the 1st Canadian Corps to its capture of Ravenna. In February 1945 he took the Corps to Holland and there, on 5 May, received the surrender of the German armies from General Blaskovitz.

Off the battlefield, Foulkes' qualifications gave him the edge over his rival. He had served at National Defence Headquarters (having returned from overseas in 1940 to become, for a year, senior General Staff officer in the 3rd Canadian Division), and this experience gave him that knowledge of Ottawa which Simonds was thought to lack. Temperamentally he fitted better into the policy machine. He was mild-mannered and soft-spoken. He did not flaunt his braid. He was as at home in a government office as in a field caravan. He never made the wrong kind of public speech and his private speeches [see, for a choice example, Document 3, below] did not leak to the newspapers as Simonds' were wont to do. He developed a feeling for the political aspects of defence policy to the degree where he became the object of sneering criticism from Simonds who, once retired, charged that the Chiefs of Staff Committee (of which Foulkes became first Chairman) was ' "packed" to protect the government against the receipt of unpalatable advice...'[123] To Charles Foulkes, military politics was not to politics what military music is to music: they were one and the same. He remained the government's principal military adviser until his retirement in 1960.

Not much time elapsed before the Government had reason to believe that in choosing Foulkes, rather than Simonds, it had made the right choice. Towards the end of 1945 disturbing reports began reaching Ottawa concerning the bad conduct of some of the Canadian occupation forces in Europe.* It fell to Foulkes to find out what was going on. He cabled a résumé of alleged misdemeanours to Simonds, and ordered an inquiry. Simonds responded by arresting some of his officers. He may have arrested them too hastily, for a number sought legal counsel and mounted counter-charges against him for improper arrest. Simonds was instructed to return to Ottawa for consultation.

The General had not before met the Minister of National Defence. Indeed, his return to Ottawa, early in January 1946, was his first visit to Canada since the outbreak of war. He seems not to have realized that he was on the carpet, rather than in the role of returning hero. He took up residence in the Chateau Laurier, expecting that in due course the Minister would call upon him. Foulkes had to telephone to explain that this was not how it worked, and that Simonds should report to Abbott at the earliest opportunity. The opportunity arrived on a Monday morning. Simonds descended from his suite in the company of a couple of *aides de camp*: greatcoats flying, swaggersticks flailing, the splendid trio pushed its way out of the elevator, across the hotel lobby, and into a waiting staff car, which drove the party to the Minister's office at the Woods Building – a distance of some 300 yards. One of the civilians shouldered aside by the General's exit happened to be the Minister of National Defence himself, who emerged from the hotel in time to see Simonds' limousine pull away from the curb. Abbott then walked to his office, his anger rising with every step. 'Tell General Simonds I will see him now,' he roared to Foulkes over the office intercom on his arrival. 'And tell him the war is over!'[124]

So displeased was the Cabinet at Simonds for allowing indiscipline

* See below, 189.

among his men, and for his handling of their alleged misdemeanours, that it considered at this time whether he should be dismissed. Some influential persons (among them Leonard Brockington, a confidant and former speech-writer of the Prime Minister) intervened on his behalf; and it may be for this reason that Simonds was spared. The incident, however, had not improved his reputation in the capital. When, on 15 February 1946, the decision was taken to withdraw the occupation force from Germany by the end of the year, the problem of what to do with their erratic general engaged the Government once more.

In the normal course of events, Simonds would have replaced Foulkes as Chief of the General Staff. But Abbott would not hear of this appointment. Moreover, Foulkes, who was by this time only 42 years of age, was working out so well that it would have been foolish to transfer him and wasteful to retire him. On the other hand, there were not so many seasoned generals still on active service that the Government could afford to lose an officer of Simonds' calibre. Accordingly it cast about for some suitable employment for him. Discreet soundings were taken of the Chief of the Imperial General Staff, but Lord Allenbrooke, irked by the decision to withdraw Canadian forces from occupation duty, would only offer a place at the rank of brigadier – a rate of exchange unacceptable both to the Canadian general and to the Canadian Army. Eventually, after earnest consideration, a solution was found. 'I don't know whether it was General Foulkes or myself who thought of it,' Brooke Claxton has recorded,

> but one or the other hit on the idea of first appointing Simonds to succeed Jock Whiteley[*] at the National Defence College. This would give him a couple of years to acclimatize himself in Canada. At the NDC he would meet officers of all three Services and numbers of civilians both in the instructing and student groups. A number of cabinet ministers and other leading citizens in various walks of life would come to the College to lecture to the students. Ordinarily they would stay with Simonds in the Commandant's house ... There would be no better place for him to have a refresher course on his country, and it would be a first class opportunity for me and my colleagues to size him up.[125]

Brooke Claxton, with his own gallant soldier's record, appreciated Simonds' soldierly qualities, and understood with greater sympathy than had his predecessor the difficulty that Simonds and other senior officers, 'having been trained and achieved their high rank and honour in war,' would experience in adjusting to peacetime service. 'It might have been expected,' Claxton wrote, 'that they would be a bit "bloody minded" ... People looked to me to curtail this proclivity without cramping their style.'

* Major General J.F.M. Whiteley, British Army.

In August 1948, having returned from London (where he had put in a year at the Imperial Defence College waiting for the Commandant's post to fall vacant), Simonds met Claxton for the first time. Their meeting took place at the relaxing setting of Claxton's summer cottage. Simonds impressed Claxton more favourably than he had impressed Abbott two years before. 'I could see that almost certainly he would be a success at the Defence College,' Claxton wrote afterwards.

He had the experience and attributes necessary to fill this post with distinction. There was one proviso: he must not go about making speeches. I am all for silent soldiers as well as sailors. I had more doubts about his having the more generalized qualifications of good judgment, ability to get along with people, and the knack, the wisdom, the instinct – whatever it is – to keep out of trouble ... I voiced these views pretty plainly, and said his posting to the Defence College would be a time when he could acclimatize himself in Canada and win the confidence of those with whom he would continue to have to work should he become Chief of Staff. As to this I could make no promise. I would let him know what I thought as soon as I could after his appointment at Kingston. That would be in twelve or eighteen months...[126]

As the first Canadian commandant of the National Defence College, Simonds was an outstanding success. 'From my several visits there,' Claxton recorded, 'I got to know him well and like him a good deal more than I had.' The Minister of National Defence was sure that, thanks to the 'refresher course on his country,' Simonds would make a first class CGS. Others were not so sure. 'Quite a few people,' Claxton recalled, 'including some high-ranking military personalities from all three services, took it on themselves to state the contrary view. None gainsaid his qualifications as a soldier but they seemed to think he was so ruthless and self-seeking that he could not help but prove embarrassing and even disloyal to his Minister.'[127] Claxton was ready to run that risk.

General Simonds was appointed Chief of the General Staff on 1 February 1951. On the same date General Foulkes, whom Simonds succeeded, became the first Chairman of the Chiefs of Staff Committee. There was no question of Simonds being appointed to the more senior position. 'Among other qualities,' Brooke Claxton wrote afterwards, 'the Chairman must be good at paper work, a genius at conciliation and a man in whom the Government has complete confidence. He must fight for the Canadian point of view on all occasions. Simonds hardly knew what the Canadian point of view was.'[128]

In their new capacities the two generals, between whom in any case little love was lost, could have had their difficulties. Their relationship might have proven stormy had the Chairman concerned himself primarily with quelling inter-service disagreement by friendly persuasion or, that failing, by *fiat* from above. In the event his job turned out to be more international than inter-service. 'It fell to [the Chairman],' Claxton recorded, 'to represent the Chiefs in relations with NATO and in top level negotiations with other countries. In fact the Chairman of the Chiefs of Staff Committee is more a diplomat than a soldier: he deals with paper, and what quantities of it there are!'[129]

Such a division of labour, wherein Foulkes assumed charge of military negotiations with Canada's allies and Simonds administered the Canadian army, kept the two rivals out of each other's hair and enabled them to work reasonably well together under their Minister's direction. For Foulkes' grasp of military diplomacy and the astute manner in which he dealt with his American and British counterparts, Brooke Claxton had boundless admiration. 'His knowledge,' he was to write later, 'of the background and paperwork of NATO and international military co-operation was unequalled. On every occasion he had shown how he could watch out for and if necessary fight to protect Canadian interests.' He thought Foulkes possessed just that 'kind of judgment and understanding of the rules of the game that unfitted Simonds for appointment as Chairman of the Chiefs of Staff.'[130] Nevertheless Claxton believed Simonds to have made a success of his job as Chief of the General Staff. 'We did not by any manner of means see eye to eye about everything. When he saw he could not convince me of a course he would usually drop it. However, there were exceptions.'[131]

One such exception concerned conscription. For a Chief of the General Staff not to see eye to eye with his Minister on *that* issue was a matter of some consequence. General Simonds became critical of the Government's policy of relying solely on voluntary enlistment to meet the manpower requirements of the armed forces during the Korean War, when serious deficiencies in the numbers of available trained troops had developed. For the duration of that war he kept his heresy to himself; but with the signing of the Armistice on 27 July 1953, he began to share it with his fellow officers and, perhaps unwittingly, with the general public. In June 1954, Simonds delivered an address to an army gathering in Saint John, NB. The newspapers carried a report of his speech, and quoted him as having stated that 'the vast majority of Canadian officers share his view that every youth in the country should receive two years' military training.' Claxton was furious on reading the story. 'I at once sent for him,' he wrote afterwards, 'and indicated my displeasure.' Simonds explained that the speech was meant to have been off the record; that the context of his offending remark removed much of its offence; and that he would be more careful in his choice of words and audience in future. Mollified, Claxton defended his Chief in the House, as a good Minister should do.[132] But a few months later, Simonds was in similar trouble again. The press reported a speech he had given to the Canadian Club of Montreal on 17 January 1955, in which he had declared: 'I would like to see every young man in Canada given two years' military training ... A system of compulsory military training would be good for the boy, for the army, and for the country.'[133] By this time Claxton was no longer Minister of National Defence; it fell to his successor, Ralph Campney, to administer a second rebuke to his talkative general.

Soon after this episode, word got around that Simonds was to retire from the Army. It was widely rumoured that he had been fired. In fact, as Campney declared to Parliament, his resignation had been planned well before the spate of speech-making which got him into trouble, and 'was a normal and orderly retirement at the conclusion of his period as Chief of the General Staff.'[134] Soon after his resignation, which took effect on 31 August 1955, he became one of the most persistent and outspoken critics of the Government's national security policies. Guy Simonds was never cut out to be a silent soldier.*

For exploits in battle the post-war Chiefs bore ribbons and medals in profusion. Yet there wasn't a university degree among them. Their lack of formal higher education may not have mattered much to them. But it mattered much to their civilian counterparts. Many of the bureaucratic elite were former dons. Former dons, more perhaps than dons themselves, are given to donnish ways. The worth of a colleague is judged by academic attainment, suitably certified: the publication of a scholarly article, a speech to a learned society. A PHD conferred prestige, a DFC did not. By such criteria of worthiness the post-war Chiefs were handicapped.

In time the military's influence would be restored. Restoration required a government less biased against the profession of arms; a civilian bureaucracy more tolerant of the workings of the military mind; above all, senior officers demonstrably more proficient in coming to grips with the post-war world.

The first of these conditions was satisfied by Mackenzie King's retirement in 1948, and by the emergence to prominence of the new Minister of National Defence. Brooke Claxton strenuously sought to improve the image of the military, even as Mackenzie King had sought to undermine it. He may be the first peacetime defence minister to retain for this pur-

* See his 'Commentary and Observations,' in Hector J. Massey (ed.), *The Canadian Military: A Profile* (Toronto 1972), 267–90.

pose the services of a public relations firm. He is certainly the first defence minister to have written the advertising copy himself.* 'They would suggest the themes for the series,' Claxton wrote later of his PR consultants, 'I would set the feeling.'[135] He judged these efforts a success. 'The old attitude there used to be towards sailors and soldiers,' Claxton told the House of Commons in 1950, 'is a thing of the past.'[136] Others did not.†

It was harder to attain and earn the respect of the policy community. There is a natural antipathy between diplomatists and militarists ('militarists' as Shakespeare used the word), between the profession of words and the profession of arms. It arises out of the incompatibility of their respective missions traditionally conceived: the diplomatists', to keep the peace, the militarists', to win the war. That antipathy could not and did not abate overnight.

But by 1953, or thereabouts, it had abated quite a bit. Membership in NATO – a military alliance despite Canadian efforts to make it transcend the merely military – brought personnel of the Department of External Affairs into closer contact than they would otherwise have had with their colleagues in the Department of National Defence; a defence liaison division, with the specific object of improving the exchange of information and ideas, was created within the Department of External Affairs in 1952. Familiarity can breed contempt, and on occasion did;‡ but, by and large, the closer contact proved beneficial to a relationship already so bad that it was easily made better. The cautious demeanour of the High Command throughout the Korean War showed how little inclined were any senior officers to exploit Canada's involvement for the aggrandizement of the military. 'There was no Somme,' the official historian wrote in conclusion to his narrative, 'no Passchendaele, no Hundred Days, no Dieppe, no Hitler Line, no Victory. There was, however, no defeat.'[137] And, it could be added, no Canadian MacArthur.

Most important of all in the restoration of military influence within the policy community was the improved intellectual calibre of military advice and military opinion. This could not have come about in the absence of determined effort to make it come about. A merit of the post-war Chiefs

* See below, 121.
† See below, 127, 127n.
‡ As for example, at the NATO Defence College (created in 1951) where, according to one observer, 'foreign service officers found a bond in their common tendency to criticize the political naïveté of military personnel.' Laurence I. Radway, 'Military Behavior in International Organization – NATO's Defence College,' in Samuel P. Huntington (ed.), *Changing Patterns of Military Politics* (New York 1962), 115. This is not at all how it was supposed to work.

was their readiness to recognize that facilities for the improvement of the military mind in Canada were woefully behind the times. That readiness varied from Chief to Chief, but it was present in them all.

As long ago as 1922, the Royal Canadian Naval College had fallen victim to a government economy drive. That the axe fell on the College had been the wish of the naval authorities themselves: 'The first item for extinction,' an RCN committee recommended, 'is considered to be the Royal Naval College; whilst this is a most efficient educational establishment, the Navy derives comparatively little benefit from it, and it is not essential to the Navy.'[138] As between trigonometry and armour plate, software and hardware, the Navy would choose plate and hardware every time.

Twenty years later, a Royal Canadian Naval College was created at the Navy's wartime officer training base near Esquimalt, BC. Throughout the war, HMCS *Royal Roads* harboured naval cadets only. Early in 1946 it was decided to admit RCAF cadets to the College, and after a year of bickering between the two services – the Navy fearing erosion of its identity, the Air Force considering the Navy's educational programme insufficiently rigorous – *Royal Roads* opened its doors to cadets from both. By 1948 the Army too had gained admission, though not without a struggle.

The Royal Military College of Canada* had been closed in 1942 in deference to the feeling (as expressed by the Army's official historian) that 'a four year course to produce subaltern officers, though it paid large dividends for a peacetime regular army, was not an economic or practical arrangement in wartime.'[139] By 1945 there were those who had come to feel that it was not an economic or practical arrangement in peacetime. Among them was the first post-war Chief of the General Staff.

General Foulkes had not attended the Royal Military College. He was not a part of the RMC old boy net. He felt that the post-war army would be better off without the rivalry and rancour between those officers who had been at the College and those who had not. He proposed that officers should be trained at the universities which, in exchange for a suitable subsidy, could make the necessary provisions in their curricula. He produced figures to demonstrate that such a plan would result in a saving of $24,221.36 per officer. The Minister of National Defence, Douglas

* See James Eayrs, *In Defence of Canada*, I, 85–8, for a discussion of its inter-war role. The official history is Richard Arthur Preston, *Canada's RMC: A History of The Royal Military College* (Toronto 1969); what follows is based in part upon chapter 13, 'The Struggle to Re-open, 1942–48,' 305–31.

Abbott, who received these proposals on 28 February 1946, was favourably impressed.

The old boys now moved to the defence of their *alma mater*. The RMC Club swung into action. A special committee of the Club was formed to lobby on behalf of re-opening the College on its pre-war basis. Its members were formidably influential, and their constituency something of a fifth column, reaching as it did into the senior officer corps, Parliament and the Government itself. (Colin Gibson, an ex-cadet, was Minister of National Defence for Air until 11 December 1946, when he became Secretary of State.) Their powers of persuasion, persistently deployed, forced Foulkes to join them in recommending the creation of a special committee to examine and report on the problem; its chairman was Brigadier Sherwood Lett. The Lett Committee, having examined witnesses and briefs, recommended re-opening. It also proposed that Foulkes' plan for training officers at universities be given a chance.

Douglas Abbott deferred a decision. Perhaps he resented the intense pressure brought to bear upon him by the RMC Club lobbyists. When he resigned as Minister of National Defence at the end of 1946 the fate of the College had not yet been finally determined.

So Brooke Claxton inherited it. Seeing the Royal Military College as an aid to integrating the three services swung Claxton round to the side of the re-openers. He announced in April 1947 that the College would admit its first post-war class in September 1948, its members to be selected from army, air force, and naval cadets. 'I thought there was a great deal to be said,' Claxton wrote later, 'for continuing RMC, with its buildings, its associations and its traditions. However, it seemed to me we should do everything possible to avoid some of the bad practices. I thought a college of this type would only be justified if it had very high standards, at least as high as those of the best university.'[140] These were more easily proclaimed than arrived at.

During the Korean War, the Canadian Army had suffered from an acute shortage of French-speaking officers, so much so that at one stage it was found 'necessary to post 18 English speaking subalterns to Valcartier.'[141] To overcome this deficiency it was decided during the summer of 1952 to open a French-language equivalent to the Royal Military College. A site was chosen near the village of Saint-Jean, Quebec, and in September 1952 Le Collège Militaire Royal de Saint-Jean admitted its first class of 125 cadets, 78 of whom spoke French as their native tongue. The enterprise was well received, both in Quebec and in the rest of Canada, and in April 1953, Claxton decided to enlarge its facilities so as to provide for 400 cadets during the next academic year.[142]

How well did the Service Colleges perform their job? What job, indeed, were they expected to perform? According to a report issued by the Department of National Defence in 1951, they existed

> to instruct young men in the skills and qualities essential to development after graduation as officers in the active or reserve forces of the Royal Canadian Navy, the Canadian Army, or the Royal Canadian Air Force. Courses of instruction are designed to develop character, to provide a balanced and liberal education in arts and sciences, and to provide a broad basic military education.[143]

Such was the official view. An unofficial view could be more critical. 'The Canadian military establishment,' a critic wrote of it some years later, 'has never accepted the existence of a curriculum of university level study uniquely relevant to the military profession ... It has persisted in staffing the service colleges' military studies departments with service officers of the most modest academic attainments, in giving these officers university titles on the somewhat hilarious basis of their military rank, and in requiring them to teach courses of ostensibly university calibre which have an actual intellectual level nearer to that of the drill manual.'[144]

Catering to students of higher seniority is the National Defence College of Canada. This institution was conceived in 1946 in response to the need to bring officers of the three armed forces out of their respective solitudes. 'During the late war,' the Commandant of the College noted in 1950, 'the Canadian Naval, Military and Air Forces all had experience of working with other nations and with other Services, but had little opportunity for working with one another at the higher levels. Many senior officers in the Royal Canadian Navy, the Canadian Army and the Royal Canadian Air Force have never met one another, or at best have no more than a nodding acquaintance.'[145] The type of institution obviously suited to correct this condition was a Canadian version of the British Joint Services Staff College and the American Army-Navy-State College, and this was what the Chief of the General Staff envisaged and recommended to the Chiefs of Staff Committee on 16 May 1946. What was required, in General Foulkes' view, was a Canadian Joint Services Staff College, the purpose of which would be 'to preserve the techniques, mutual understanding, high spirit of joint service co-operation, interdependence of equipment design, and common doctrine which were major factors in the Allied victory.' What was not required was a Canadian counterpart of the Imperial Defence College, or of the National War College created in Washington that year; it would be ridiculous for a country having armed forces the size of

Canada's to try to compete with these elite institutions, the more so since each offered places to any Canadian officers able to profit by them.

This case was countered by the British officer sent out to advise the Canadian Government on what the senior service college should be like. Major General J.F.M. Whitely argued very forcibly that the joint services conception was inadequate and that what Canada really required was its own version of the Imperial Defence College. His support came not from the Canadian military but from the civilian sector of the public service. The Secretary to the Cabinet, A.D.P. Heeney, and the Under Secretary of State for External Affairs, L.B. Pearson, each took Whitely's side. A Canadian Joint Services Staff College, Pearson thought, stressed the military side of the College's concerns too much. What was needed was an institution in which military minds could be steeped in civilian modes of analysis. His Department, and other civilian agencies of government, could not be expected to spare their most promising people for the best part of a year unless the course of study in which they were to be immersed was sure to add to their usefulness on their return. He and Heeney prepared a paper to this effect, and submitted it to the Chiefs of Staff Committee on 4 June 1947. It argued that the provisional title of the proposed college be changed to The National Defence College of Canada, and that the purpose and syllabus of its work be appropriately redefined.

The Pearson-Heeney paper was discussed at the 395th meeting of the Chiefs of Staff Committee on 9 July 1947. Its arguments were opposed both by the Chief of the General Staff, General Foulkes, and by the Acting Chief of the Air Staff, Air Vice Marshal Curtis. But they were two out of five. The civilian members – the Chairman of the Defence Research Board, O.M. Solandt, and the Deputy Minister of National Defence, W.G. Mills – joined with the Chief of the Naval Staff, Vice Admiral Reid,* to carry the Committee's recommendation to proceed with the Pearson-Heeney proposals. The National Defence College located at Kingston, Ontario, began instruction on 5 January 1948. 'It is the first effort to organize in this country an institution for the advanced study of war and security problems,' the Minister of National Defence declared at the opening day ceremony. 'The programme will include the study of new and foreseeable developments in science, economics and international politics and their effects upon national security.'[146]

Sixteen students were enrolled in the first course – seven army officers, three from the Royal Canadian Air Force, two from the Navy, and four

* Admiral Reid, who was to retire in a few weeks, was not so much captivated by the prospect of a military-civilian national defence college as repelled by the prospect of increased inter-service co-operation; his vote is best interpreted as a parting shot in a long vendetta.

from the civilian public service. The second course, which opened on 1 November 1948, was enlarged to twenty-one members, of whom eight were civilians, one a US Army Colonel and one a captain of the Royal Navy. During succeeding courses the number of students was raised to around thirty, in which the proportion of military to civilian members was about three to two: the civilians were reinforced by representatives of the US State Department and the Foreign Office, as well as of businesses with defence responsibilities (Bell Telephone and Imperial Oil usually taking turns to fill the vacancy). Each year witnessed the progressive de-militarization of the curriculum, and on 1 March 1956 L.B. Pearson was able to write of the College that 'no one who has been closely associated with [its] development ... any longer thinks of it ... as a place to train officers and officials for participation in the planning and direction of a possible war; rather is it a place for developing those who may be expected to have some responsibility for advising the Government in dealing with the security problems which it now faces and will have to face in the foreseeable future.'[147] That same year the Commandant of the College described the syllabus as it had by then evolved:

> Commencing with a study of the constitutional government and working through problems dealing with the political, economic and defence factors pertaining to the countries of the West, [it] analyses Communism and its threat, not only to the Western countries but also to the uncommitted areas of the world, and ends up with a consideration of what Western foreign policy should be, with a subsequent study of the part Canada should play in the implementation of Western foreign policy through her own Canadian defence efforts.

This pattern of study, concluded the Commandant – a far from disinterested testimonialist – 'has proved to be most successful.' Not everyone agreed. One critic stated flatly that the College was 'an educational disaster.' But he did not say how you could tell.

More tangible contributions were made by the Defence Research Board, conceived in 1945.* Like the National Defence College, the Board had determined opponents, mainly in the Air Force, whose senior officers disliked the notion of a separate centre of defence research serving all three of the armed forces. There were three main reasons why.

During the Second World War, the status of the RCAF did not keep pace with its stature; despite the important role played by Canada in training aircrew and bombing Europe, few Air Force officers, by comparison with

* '...the basic reasoning which produced the DRB ... is contained in a remarkable paper dated 17 September 1945, and entitled *The Future of Canadian Army Research and Development – An Appreciation by Colonel W.W. Goforth* DSD(W).' A.M. Fordyce, 'How It All Started: The Goforth Paper,' *Canadian Defence Quarterly*, I, 4 (spring 1972), 15–16.

their Army and Navy counterparts, had been assigned to senior operational commands. Resentment at this exclusion lingered. The Air Staff were determined not to allow the RCAF to suffer so soon after this experience any further erosion of its identity.

Secondly, the Air Staff had already decided to press for the acquisition of a Canadian-designed and Canadian-built all-weather jet interceptor for the post-war RCAF. They felt that this project had a better chance of acceptance if recommendations came from their own research establishment than from one in which it would run the gauntlet of competing projects and rival expertise.

Finally, the Air Staff was reluctant to accept any radical change in the administration of defence research for fear that significant, though preliminary, accomplishments of its own wartime efforts – in radar, photography, cold weather flying, aviation medicine – would not be vigorously carried forward.

And so the post-war RCAF, tenaciously led by Air Marshal Leckie and his Air Member for Technical Services, dug in and fought. They fought a losing battle, for against them were arrayed the combined forces of the General Staff (the idea had come originally from an Army officer) and the Government. (The Navy remained neutral.) The Board came into being on 3 April 1947, after what its official historian describes as 'a great deal of work and some heartache.'[148]

Within the Board there quickly developed an Operations Research Group, obscurely positioned on its organization charts and even more obscurely preoccupied with what were described as 'problems which had certain psychological overtones.'[149] Over the next few years the emphasis of its investigations changed. Instead of working on practical military problems of the moment – radio propagation, personnel selection and training, 'human engineering' – the operations researchers developed a taste for 'futurology' – forecasting and planning for coming trends in weapons innovation, technological advance, and social and political change.

For this sort of work, already under way in the United States at several institutions of which The RAND Corporation (as reorganized in November 1948) was as yet without a peer, neither the traditional civilian bureaucrat nor the traditional military officer was properly equipped. The requirements might be more easily stated than discovered: a gift for speculative and highly abstract thought, fluency in mathematical language, a sense of science, the historical imagination, all fused within a willing servant of the state. Where did such a paragon abound? Not in the East Block, certainly, nor yet in Cartier Square. He did not abound anywhere in Canada, if the truth were known. But if he could be found at all, it was in the university, not in the bureaucracy.

So it was from the university that the first of the 'defence intellectuals,' as they came to be called, were recruited. In the United States, where need was intense and resources immense, the recruits quickly became an army. In Canada, where need seemed far less urgent and resources were harder to come by, the recruits might be counted on the fingers of a mutilated hand. A fearful asymmetry ensued, and was to last for many years. 'The smaller ally,' an informed commentator wrote in 1964, 'faces [a] serious problem in maintaining a meaningful dialogue with the United States on strategic policies. Americans, with a somewhat more categorical attitude towards facts and an infinitely vaster establishment for accumulating them, tend to turn bilateral discussions into briefing sessions in which Canadians are awed into sceptical silence.'[150] A decade earlier the Canadians barely possessed the faculty of scepticism. Yet a beginning had been made. Sophistication would follow scepticism, and a few Canadians talk back.

Admittedly a very few. Yet in strategic matters, as in other matters, it's not the size, it's the ferocity. The Canadian government got good value from its small community of defence analysts. Their intelligence product was by no means always inferior to that in the United States. On 3 December 1945, Vannevar Bush, principal scientific adviser to the Pentagon, dismissed rocketry in warfare as of no future importance. 'People ... have been talking about a 3000-mile high angle rocket shot from one continent to another, carrying an atom bomb and so directed as to be a precise weapon which would land exactly on a certain target ... I think we can leave that out of our thinking.'[151] A few months earlier his Canadian counterpart, C.J. Mackenzie, had offered a different and, as it turned out, more prescient opinion: 'I agree with many who feel that the introduction of the rocket raises possibilities which will change fundamentally the pattern of future warfare ... I feel very strongly that whatever we do in Canada in the way of military research in the future, work on rockets should be included...'[152] A senior member of The RAND Corporation testifies that 'it was a Canadian rather than an American who first drew attention to the vital distinction between first-strike and second-strike capabilities.'[153] The Canadian most likely to have made this contribution – to strategic analysis roughly as the law of gravity is to physics – is the late R.J. Sutherland, then beginning a brief but brilliant career in the Operations Research Division of the Defence Research Board. Sutherland, it has been said, was 'Canada's one-man answer to The RAND Corporation.' He was only one man, or one of a tiny band. But at least there was an answer. Before there had been none.

# 1

# Re-establishing the Military

Ah! who will guide me thro' the wood?
    I am so small to wander.
Maybe that gentleman so proud,
    He looks a brave defender!

*Canadian Folk Song*

## DOCTRINE AND ROLE

What sort and size of military establishment should Canada acquire to serve her in the post-war world? In what proportions ought its component forces to be mixed? What weapons placed at their disposal? Such were the questions on the agenda of Canada's defence planners at the end of the Second World War, as they had been at the end of the First World War. In 1945, as in 1919, their answers logically depended on answers returned to two more fundamental questions. In what manner of world would post-war Canada be likely to find herself? In such a world, what tasks should Canada's military be called upon to perform?

In August 1945, the features of the post-war world resembled the surface of some distant planet enveloped in a mysterious gas and glimpsed through the lens of a primitive telescope. No one knew for sure what it would be like. There were only hopes and fears. One could only guess. But some guesses proved better than others.

From the evidence at hand might be extrapolated, with equal credibility, one or other of two radically differing scenarios. There was first the scenario of a co-operative commonwealth. The United Nations would behave as their Charter meant them to behave. Great Powers would be models of prudence and restraint; lesser powers, eager to follow their example. Any miscreant community would swiftly be chastised by a grand coalition of peace-loving states. Atomic bombs, being internationally outlawed, would threaten no one; atomic energy, being supranationally controlled, would benefit everyone. A cluster of social welfare institutions, with the globe as their constituency and prosperity as their mandate, would make the world a better place, as it had become a safer.

No less plausible was the competing scenario of a world in conflict. The United Nations would betray their Charter. Great Powers would fall out among themselves; lesser powers would align in rival camps. No grand coalition would quell aggression at its source. Atomic weapons are instruments of national policy, threatening or obliterating as expediency dictates. The world becomes a fearful anarchy, its wealth consumed on arms expenditure, the lives of the peoples squalid and deprived.

To a defence planner of any country, it made much difference by which of these scenarios his government was guided: to a defence planner of Canada it made all the difference. If the world was to resemble a co-operative commonwealth, he should devise forces from which a respectable contribution might be made to that international military establishment which, under United Nations command, was to keep the peace on Canada's behalf and that of fifty other nations. If the world was to degenerate into anarchy, a more substantial force, more impressively armed, was presumably required. How much more substantial, how much more impressively armed, were questions the answers to which turned upon the identity of possible aggressors.

Here, at least, more was clear than a quarter century before. In 1919 it had been assumed that aggression could come from the South: plans were accordingly made for the defence of Canada in the event of armed attack from the United States.* In 1945 only the most dire scenario convincingly portrayed invasion from that quarter. But invasion was easily envisaged from another. Aggression could come from the North: plans were accordingly made for the defence of Canada in the event of armed attack from the Soviet Union. Central to those plans was the extent to which the military establishment of Canada should co-operate with the military establishment of the United States in the defence of the continent which was their common home.†

Supposing, then, the Soviet Union to be the enemy. What if it struck at Western Europe rather than, or in addition to, North America? Canadians had just fought, and died, for Europe's freedom: how could Europe's freedom suddenly become something for which in no circumstances would Canadians fight, and die, again? But in what circumstances? What form should their exertions take? Ought they to plan another expeditionary

* See James Eayrs, *In Defence of Canada*, I, *From the Great War to the Great Depression* (Toronto 1964), 70–8, 323–8.

† See below, 320–44.

force and ships to take it in? Or had the expeditionary force and the convoy gone the way of the Roman phalanx and the cavalry charge as grand tactics in a modern war? What sort of war was nuclear war? What was required to fight one?

Answers to such questions, even had they been known, would not in themselves entirely determine the nature of Canada's post-war military establishment. For fighting a war, against whatever enemy, with whatever weapons, is only one among the military's several tasks. Were there no enemy at all – as in the most optimistic version of the scenario of a co-operative commonwealth – the profession of arms might still do much for Canada. It could keep the country lawful and orderly. It could aid in its development. It could underpin its diplomacy. And it could provide it with insurance – insurance against the possibility that, in some future no one could foresee, for reasons no one could predict, the world of the co-operative commonwealth, where national fighting forces are redundant, might give way to a world of anarchy, where national fighting forces mean survival.

Considerations of this kind are indispensable for drawing up a reasoned justification for any military establishment. They entered little, if at all, into the planning of Canada's post-war defence forces during 1945. The military appropriations for that year emerged from a struggle between the desire of the Chiefs of Staff for as large a Service as each might possibly secure and the demands of the Government for the utmost possible economy. Every defence budget emerges from such a struggle, but usually not before requirements of the strategic situation have been ascertained. Canada's defence budget for the fiscal year 1946 emerged unattached to any principle other than that holding the future to be inscrutable. It was not the worst principle from which to start.

The three Services did not wait for peace before staking out their claims. As early as March 1943, the General Staff had prepared some 'Notes on Post-War Army Organization,' a paper based on a draft begun on 21 July 1941. That the future was inscrutable, this document conceded, could not be denied – 'it is quite impossible at the present time to foretell the state in which the world will find itself when hostilities cease' – but not so inscrutable as to admit the possibility that no post-war Army would be needed: 'If anything can be certain it is that the English-speaking world will not again hasten to put its faith in a League of Nations unbacked by force. It would, therefore, seem reasonable to suppose that in order to avoid a lapse into the inadequate position which the Armed Forces of Canada were in for many years prior to the outbreak of war that a compulsory system will be continued into and throughout the post-war period.' Nor did the inscrutability of the future deter this Army planner from proposing the size and composition of the post-war Army.

It seems unlikely that the Army of the future will be organized on a smaller scale than that which will have been found necessary during the present war. It is, therefore, assumed that on the cessation of hostilities our Army will be designed to provide for the progressive mobilization of not less than six Divisions, two Armoured Divisions, and a suitable proportion of Corps, Army and L. of C. troops.

Should it be thought that an Army of the strength assumed above might prove to be unduly large, it is to be borne in mind that it is not suggested that all these formations should be maintained in the same degree of readiness. Rather it is considered that roughly one-third or one-quarter should be Active Formations and the remainder divided into a First and Second reserve ... Not less than two Divisions and one Armoured Division should be maintained on an active basis ...

The system roughly sketched out in the foregoing would give Canada a standing Army of roughly 50,000 to 60,000 all ranks. Maintenance of $2.00 per day would come to some fifty to sixty millions per year...[1]

In August 1943, an Army memorandum put it to the Working Committee on Post-Hostilities Problems* that it was none too soon 'to consider the approximate size of the permanent Canadian Army of the future. If a minimum figure could be set,' it argued,

to be reviewed every five years, say, it would pave the way for the solution of many problems. Undoubtedly there would be sufficient numbers prepared to volunteer on the assurance that the Army could be regarded as a profession. On the other hand, should the set-up eventually prove to be unnecessarily large, normal wastage or inducement to return to civil life can bring about a reduction without serious difficulty.[2]

'A minimum figure' had by the autumn of 1943 been settled at 'approximately six divisions and four armoured brigades,' of which two divisions and one armoured brigade were to be kept on active service.[3] 'There can be no doubt,' another Army paper argued a year later, 'that, with or without world security obligations, Canada will be required to carry a much greater peace time defence commitment than ever before.'[4]

The civilian planners were unimpressed by the Army's assertion. 'Dissatisfaction was expressed with the case made out by the Army for large forces after the War,' a member of the Working Committee reported after its meeting on 25 August 1944. 'The paper really says nothing more than that there will be an unsettled condition and that although no major threats of attack can be foreseen, it is nevertheless a good idea to main-

* See below, 143–7.

tain large forces just in case. The feeling of the Committee was that an argument could be made for forces larger than those before the present war, but that the Army had not made it.'[5]

Not all of the Army planners were big-army men. 'I think the difference between us,' Maurice Pope wrote to Escott Reid,

> is that you have taken me to have a substantial military force in mind. I have not. You must remember that in 1939 our permanent army was less than 5000 in all. In the future I would like to see it doubled, or possibly 3 times that number, dependent on whether or not we have some form of compulsory military service, the possibility of which I think is at least doubtful. Nor do I think that in the future we should be prepared to mobilize a greater force than we mobilized in 1939, namely, the coastal garrisons and an army corps of between 60 and 70 thousand. I am by no means desirous of having a really big standing army. I only advocate that it should be increased sufficiently and be given enough to do to keep it healthy and efficient. Compared to most parts of the world I should think that a standing army of 10,000 out of a population of over 11 million is not very great...[6]

But a standing army of 10,000 was far short of what the General Staff eventually requested. To comprise what it described as 'a small self-contained and highly trained force for the development of training principles and tactical doctrine, and for immediate use in the event of emergency,' together with personnel for coastal defence and administration, a regular force of no fewer than 55,788 all ranks was proposed. The part-time militia was to consist of 177,396 men, recruited through 'a universal system of military training of young men for one year,' with a further period of service of three years 'in order to enable the volunteer [*sic*] to be trained in the collective operation of all arms.' The annual cost of such a post-war Army was estimated to be $162,000,000.[7]

The Air Force like the Army grew restive in the absence of plans for its post-war future. 'Canada has embarked on a vast programme for the training of aircrew,' an RCAF planner wrote in September 1943.

> This programme has been expanded gradually during the past four years to its present maximum. Yet, at some time before the end of the war, this programme will have to be curtailed, and eventually some disposition will have to be made of the training organization both in equipment and personnel now in operation throughout Canada. The disposition of this organization and the size and composition of the Air Force establishment which Canada is to maintain at the end of hostilities can be determined and planned for only in the light of possible post-war commitments in Europe or elsewhere ... Plans must be prepared in advance ... for any eventualities that may arise...[8]

A document described as a 'Brief on Post-War Planning for the Royal Canadian Air Force,' the work of Air Commodore K.M. Guthrie, was ready for the planners' consideration by December 1943. Acknowledging that 'the size and composition of the RCAF establishment in peacetime can be determined and planned for in detail only when ... policy decisions have been made by the Canadian Government,' it nonetheless advanced certain principles as guides for future planning. First, the RCAF should be capable of offensive and defensive air warfare. 'It is most important that the RCAF should not be organized for a purely defensive role.' Bombers would be needed as well as fighter-interceptors. Second, the post-war Air Force should be capable of a swift transition from a peace to war footing. 'It is submitted that the only difference in an air force between peace and war should be in the strength, pressure of work, and the dangers and discomforts which are inevitable in war; and that we should strenuously avoid any organization which provides for one method in peace and a different one in war.' Third, the post-war Air Force should have a permanent air and ground training organization capable of rapid expansion. For this purpose it would be prudent to maintain, albeit on a smaller scale, the British Commonwealth Air Training Plan. Finally, the post-war Air Force should be highly mobile. 'The RCAF may have to fight over either the North American continent or overseas and, owing to flexibility in the application of air power, its units must be capable of moving quickly, at short notice, over long distances.' An active Air Force meeting the requirements of these four principles would require 'a total of fifteen (15) squadrons ... comprising five (5) general reconnaissance, five (5) bomber (two to be very long range bomber units) and five (5) fighter squadrons.'[9]

The shopping list eventually drawn up by the RCAF planners followed this early estimate closely. They placed the post-war Air Force requirements at sixteen operational squadrons – four of day fighters, two of medium bombers, four of heavy bombers, two of general reconnaissance, two of long range transport, one of troop transport and one of photographic survey. 30,000 personnel would be needed to sustain such a force and train auxiliary and reserve sqaudrons. Its cost was estimated annually at $78,000,000 – on the assumption 'that there will be a fully equipped air force on the cessation of hostilities, and that only a negligible amount of equipment replacement or construction will be required during the first five years.' The planners considered that their proposals were in no way extravagant, and had been guided only by 'the need for maximum economy commensurate with a reasonable degree of security.' They had specified neither a large post-war Air Force nor lavish equipment for it.

Because air force equipment is expensive and quickly becomes obsolete, it is impracticable to maintain a large regular force equipped, as it should be, with the latest weapons. It is, however, essential to maintain a relatively small, full-time force to perpetuate and develop tactical doctrine in all fields of air warfare. Such a force is incapable of providing full, immediate protection and, therefore, must be backed up by a large Auxiliary and Reserve force, the personnel in which are trained to such a standard that they can be mobilized and complete their training in the time required to produce the weapons with which they fight.[10]

The Navy more than its sister Services planned for its post-war future. Unlike the Army and the RCAF, each overwhelmed by wartime weaponry with which to make a peacetime start, the RCN had not acquired in the war what its senior officers thought the permanent Navy needed. While 'the precise requirements in ships and personnel of ... a peacetime navy will vary according to the nature and direction of the hostile threat, and according to the strength of the other Canadian services and of Canada's probable allies' – so an RCN memorandum noted on 28 October 1943 – one point was paramountly clear. The Navy would need bigger ships. The cockleshell flotilla of frigates, corvettes, and trawlers, assigned to convoy patrol and minesweeping by the allied division of labour, could not possibly perform the duties of the post-war peacetime Navy, namely,

(a) To maintain command of the oceans adjacent to Canada, Newfoundland and Labrador, with the assistance of the RCAF, against all attacks except sustained battleship attacks launched by major naval powers.

(b) To contribute to the maintenance of Imperial sea communications at least to the extent of providing trade protection forces proportionate to the size of Canada's merchant marine.

(c) To contribute to the joint defence of the oceans adjacent to North America.

(d) To support national policies and interests generally.[11]

What kind of ships could perform such missions? 'Cruisers are clearly required.' 'It is ... essential that aircraft carriers be included in the fleet.' 'Cruisers and carriers by themselves ... are exceedingly vulnerable ... If Canada is to have large ships, they will need a screen of destroyers.'[12]

And how many? 'The minimum Navy which could be considered,' the Naval Staff agreed on 24 December 1943, 'would consist of 5 cruisers, 3 flotillas of destroyers each consisting of 8 private ships and one leader, 16 frigates, 12 minesweepers, a Naval Air Service with 2 light fleet aircraft carriers, and a fleet train of necessary supply and maintenance ships in order to give the whole fleet complete mobility.'[13] But not any old ships would do.

Irrespective of the size and composition of the post-war Royal Canadian Navy, it is essential that all ships be the most modern of their type. Should hostilities cease in the summer of 1945 only the following ships can be considered to fulfill this requirement – "Minotaur," "Algonquin," and "Sioux." The Tribals are a 1935 design and although modernized in respect of armament cannot be said to embody the lessons of this war in construction, propulsion, etc. "Uganda" is a 1936 design, and cannot be considered modern when compared with "Minotaur." All plans for the RCN should therefore take into consideration the desirability of acquiring men of war of the most modern type...[14]

The Navy planners estimated that a force on such a scale would require a complement of approximately 30,000 officers and men. However, recognizing that their plans 'might not be possible of realization for other than strategic reasons,' the Chief of the Naval Staff 'directed that the figure of 15,000 complement for post-war permanent force be considered as the firm recommendation of the Naval Staff for planning purposes,' with an equivalent number in reserve.[15] The annual operating cost of the post-war Navy was put at $48,745,000.[16]

One of the tactics employed by the Naval Staff to prepare the government for commitments on such a scale was that of acquiring carriers and cruisers on loan from the Royal Navy for wartime service. It would be easier to argue the case for retention than the case, in peacetime, for acquisition. 'There is a large RN building programme of light fleet carriers and destroyers,' the Director of Plans reminded the Assistant Chief of Naval Staff in August 1944, 'and it should be possible to obtain ships of these types by manning them and paying for their up-keep.'[17] By this device the cruisers *Uganda* and *Ontario* (formerly HMS *Minotaur*) were brought into Canadian service in 1944 for deployment in the Pacific theatre of war. The fleet carriers proved harder to come by.

At a meeting of the War Committee of the Cabinet on 8 September 1943, the Chief of Naval Staff pleaded powerfully but inconclusively for acquiring aircraft carriers from the British navy. In October, a combined RCN-RCAF committee reported in favour of obtaining carriers, again without effect. Then the Admiralty called for help. The Royal Navy had the ships but not the tars. The Vice Chief of Naval Staff went immediately to London, returning in December with several Admiralty proposals for Canadian assistance. One of them was that the RCN should man two escort carriers, *Nabob* and *Puncher*, then being readied for service with the Royal Navy. This proposal the Cabinet War Committee treated with great reserve, being anxious at all times to protect and preserve the national identity of Canadian fighting forces. It was moreover apprehensive about venturing, at so late a stage in the hostilities, upon a naval aviation role of which the Service had no recent experience. On 5 January 1944 the War Committee turned it down. But a forceful plea by the Minister of National Defence for Naval Services brought a reversal of its decision a week later. *Nabob* and *Puncher*, provided with British aircraft and Canadian crew, entered active service on the Atlantic later in the year.

Now that it was manning carriers the Navy had a stronger case for acquiring carriers. Negotiations were successfully completed with the Admiralty for taking over two light fleet carriers for service in the Pacific. The Prime Minister first learned of this deal at the Quebec Conference in September 1944. 'I could see that Jones [Chief of Naval Staff] was seeking to work in an extra carrier,' Mackenzie King wrote on 13 September, 'maintaining that having our own ships fight in the South Pacific would involve, in the way of expense, reconditioning which he said would be essential if in use there.' And the next day, at a meeting with Churchill in the presence of British and Canadian chiefs of staff, Mackenzie King 'noted particularly the mention of one carrier – Jones yesterday had spoken of two...'[18]

Clearly the carriers were headed for a rough passage. At a meeting of the War Committee on 5 October, Angus Macdonald, Minister of National Defence for Naval Services, put the case for acquisition so intemperately as to cause the Prime Minister to leave the meeting. 'I found myself getting a little incensed,' Mackenzie King recorded, 'and for that reason did not wish to wait and get into a bitter argument with my colleagues.' When discussion resumed on 11 October, the War Committee had before it a written statement about the carrier role and the need for Canada to play it. Mackenzie King 'pointed out where the memo had a new turn to it, for example, that it read the British requested certain ships. Also mentioned that others were indispensable and the like. I said this was a new attitude toward Canada on the part of the British Government. They had no business to request anything or to state that our ships were indispensable ... It was apparent,' he added, 'the memo had been prepared in the Department [of National Defence] which is really saturated with the Imperial Navy idea ... The Department has not been straightforward in dealing with the Cabinet in the way it has gone about securing these ships as a gift from England. The real object being to make a fleet unit for post-war purposes, rather than for the war ... It was a hard battle to fight but I won after struggling alone – after having fought over and over again.'[19]

As a result of Mackenzie King's opposition, a different policy was agreed to. The Government would not accept the carriers as an outright gift from the United Kingdom. Instead, it would take them on loan, with the understanding that they might be bought or returned after the war, and that in no case would they be used except in those theatres of war already prescribed for Canadian forces in the Pacific. That prescription had been determined by the Cabinet on 6 September 1944, when it had been agreed that Canada's armed forces 'should participate, as a matter of preference, in the war against Japan in operational theatres of direct interest to Canada as a North American nation, for example on the North or Central Pacific, rather than on more remote areas such as South-East Asia, and that government policy with respect to employment of Canadian forces should be based on this principle.'[20] The British Government did not much care for this principle. (Nor, for that matter, did the Minister of National Defence for Naval Services.*) On learning of the Canadian Government's conditions, the Admiralty reconsidered its original offer. There was talk of transferring the carriers to Australian service, in which they might be moved about as grand strategy rather than political sensibility dictated. But eventually the British agreed to accept Canada's terms. 'As the war in the Atlantic drew to its close' – the words are those of the official history of Canadian naval aviation – 'the RCN could look forward to a promising future with the prospect of commissioning and manning two modern aircraft carriers.'[21]

Such were the armed forces' aspirations. It now remained for them to move them from paper into land and air and sea.

A first step in this process was to acquaint their ministers with their plans. A meeting for this purpose was held on 25 June 1945 between the three Chiefs of Staff and the two defence ministers. The Working Committee on Post-Hostilities Problems was duly informed of what transpired.

> The Navy are thinking along the lines of a task force rather than an escort force, comprising 2 carriers, four cruisers and two destroyer flotillas with a total of about 20,000 personnel, half at sea and half ashore.
>
> The Army plan envisages a small self-contained and highly trained force of the order of a brigade group, in addition to personnel for defence installations, research and development work, training and administrative personnel. The Army plan apparently proposes that there should be universal training on a compulsory basis for boys from 18½ to 19½, followed by a period of obligatory service in the reserve. The manpower components would be made up as follows: Active: 55,788; Reserve: 177,396; Training force: 48,500.
>
> The Air Force is thinking along the lines of a regular force organized into four operational and one maintenance command, an auxiliary force organized into squadrons undergoing part-time training and capable of rapid expansion in war time, and a reserve. Manpower organization would be as follows: Regular force: 30,000; Auxiliary force: 15,000; Reserve force: 50,000.[22]

The total estimated cost of these proposals was $290,000,000.[23] Defence expenditure during the last year of peace had amounted to $35,000,000.

* '... Macdonald quite rightly pointed out this makes nonsense of naval warfare,' the Canadian High Commissioner recorded. 'He now has an embarrassing time with the Admiralty because we are taking over two aircraft carriers and if their movement is to be thus restricted the Admiralty quite rightly feels some doubt about their becoming units of the RCN.' Vincent Massey, *What's Past is Prologue* (Toronto 1963), 415.

A second step in the process of gaining political approval for their plans was to prepare a common appreciation of the need for the military preparations recommended in them. This the Chiefs of Staff had ready by 5 July 1945.

The roles of the post-war armed forces were defined in the Chiefs of Staff appreciation as defending Canadian territory against attack, protecting Canadian trade and strategic routes, supporting the world security organization, co-operating with the British Commonwealth, the United States, 'or other forces with which Canada may be associated in the event of another war,' and providing for the internal security of the State.

The Chiefs then took up the problem of the threat. 'It is not possible,' they admitted, 'at this time to definitely predict the sources from which a threat to world peace and to Canada may develop in the future.' So long as the victors in the war continued to be vigilant there would be no military resurgence of Germany and Japan and 'in her own interests Canada must be prepared to render such military assistance as may be necessary in support of their control.' No serious threat to world peace was likely so long as the United Kingdom, the United States, and the Soviet Union continued to work together. 'However, the possibility of war between the USSR and the Democracies cannot be ignored.' In any case, prudence dictated preparedness:

> Because of war weariness and the need for reconstruction, it is improbable that any nation will precipitate a general war within the next few years, but the possibility exists and must be guarded against. To neglect military preparations because no apparent threat now exists, would be to invite aggression, whereas adequate preparations should discourage it.

Adequate preparedness meant a force in being. A protracted period for mobilization and tooling up, such as had been available at the outset of the last two wars, would not be available in a third. 'While it may be assumed that some warning of war will be discernible, the period of warning is almost certain to be inadequate to accomplish the requisite degree of preparation. In any event any extraordinary preparation brought about by a short period of warning could not equal in effectiveness the degree of preparedness for war that would result from a planned programme of military training and equipment supply.'[24]

On 31 July, the Chiefs of Staff discussed their appreciation and their plans at a meeting of the Advisory Committee on Post-Hostilities Problems.* 'Two conflicting considerations were involved,' its minutes record Hume Wrong as having pointed out. 'On the one hand it was agreed that in the absence of plans for post-war permanent forces it was inevitable that good men would be lost to the Services; on the other hand,

* See below, 143–4.

there were too many unknown factors at present to enable plans, except of a very tentative nature, to be submitted to the Government at the present time.' The Committee agreed to inform the Prime Minister of its view 'that the reports prepared by the three Services on their post-war plans might appropriately, in the first instance, be considered by a Cabinet Committee on Defence.'[25]

That consideration the Cabinet Committee on Defence (formerly the War Committee) bestowed on 28 September 1945. Quickly and ruthlessly the recommendations of the Chiefs of Staff were trimmed and sometimes slashed. Their proposed over-all defence budget of $290,000,000 was reduced to $172,000,000. The Navy, which had asked for 20,000 men, was authorized to plan for 10,000. The Air Force was reduced to a regular strength of between 15,000 and 20,000, rather than 30,000. The Army, which had proposed a peacetime force of 55,788, was told to plan for between 20,000 and 25,000 men, and to forget about its dream of compulsory military service.[26]

It fell to Douglas Abbott, McNaughton's successor as Minister of National Defence and Macdonald's successor as Minister of National Defence for Naval Services, together with Colin Gibson, Minister of National Defence for Air, to explain and defend the Government's decisions to the House of Commons.

The air estimates were introduced first. 'No definite decision has yet been made as to the strength and composition of the post-war air force,' Colin Gibson informed the House on 4 October 1945, 'as until the nature and extent of any commitment that we may have under international or regional arrangements have been determined it is obviously impossible to reach any final decision.' Certain provisional arrangements, however, had been made. The post-war RCAF would consist of regular, auxiliary, and reserve forces. The regular force would 'comprise all branches of air force activities including bomber, fighter and transport squadrons ...' There were to be ten squadrons in all – four bomber, two fighter, three transport, and one photo-reconnaissance. The transport squadrons were to be re-equipped with the new American C-54s, but the rest would be formed out of aircraft already in service: 'While experiments and research are going on,' the Minister explained, 'we do not consider it advisable to commit ourselves to the purchase of large numbers of either fighters or bombers, but believe that we should continue for the present with those we have available.' There were many thousands of aircraft available, for by 1945 the RCAF had become 'the fourth largest air force of the Allied Powers, exceeded only by those of the United States, the Soviet Union and Britain.'[27] Whatever its eventual equipment and role, the Air Force would play a major part in the defence of Canada during the years to come. 'The production of the atomic bomb will ... have far reaching effects on the whole science of war, but whatever its effects may be upon the other services, I consider that it will undoubtedly increase the relative importance of air power.'[28]

On 9 October, Douglas Abbott, speaking as Minister of National Defence for Naval Services, discussed in the House of Commons the future of the Royal Canadian Navy. He could predict, he said, 'with some accuracy what our establishment will probably be ... At the outset, Canada's peacetime Navy should comprise two cruisers, probably two light fleet carriers, ten to twelve destroyers, and the necessary ancillary craft, all ... of the latest and most modern type, while in reserve and for training purposes, we will continue to hold a certain number of frigates.'[29] 'A good, workable little fleet,' was how the Minister described this paper flotilla a few days later. 'It can easily be expanded if need be.'[30]

Interim plans for the post-war Army were announced in the House of Commons by the Minister of National Defence on 16 October 1945. Again Abbott emphasized that they were subject to change: 'The final determination of just what military establishments we will need in peace cannot yet be made, and will be influenced to a large extent by the nature of any obligations which we may later assume under a world or regional security arrangement – obligations which have not yet been clarified – and by the character of the new and terrible weapons which have so recently been developed.' Meanwhile, there were 'certain steps which in the interval can properly be taken, and which we propose to take, to set up and maintain a basic military establishment, and which can be added to or developed as future circumstances require.' Accordingly, the post-war Army was planned to consist of a permanent active force and a part-time reserve force – the latter to be trained and administered by the former. The active force would consist of between 20,000 and 25,000 all ranks, 'fully equipped, ready to meet whatever commitments may arise.' It would comprise (Abbott further disclosed on 1 November) 'a brigade group augmented by two armoured regiments, one medium artillery battery, together ... with the usual administrative and training elements to assist the reserve army, including a coastal artillery battery on each coast, and a composite anti-aircraft battery.'[31] The reserve forces was to be organized in six divisions, 'with supporting armoured elements and selected corps and army troops for an army of two corps.'[32]

These plans, provisional and tentative as they were, nonetheless met with criticism. Grote Stirling, a former Conservative Minister of National Defence, was the most placable of the Opposition defence critics. 'I do not quarrel,' he remarked in the House of Commons on 22 October, 'with the attitude taken by the Government when it considers that the international situation is such that it is hardly feasible to proclaim a definite permanent policy for the navy.' But, primed perhaps by his son (Lt-Commander M.G. Stirling, RCN), he went on to attack Abbott's 'good, workable little fleet' as not good enough and probably not workable. 'It is entirely wrong for us to extol the magnificence of Canada's commerce, to boast that we are the fourth trading nation in the world and at the same time to provide inadequate naval defence for that commerce in the focal areas. We must be ready.'[33]

Another Opposition defence critic was Major-General G.R. Pearkes who, as General Officer Commander-in-Chief, Pacific Command, had played a prominent role in the conscription crisis of November 1944 by summoning a press conference to criticize government policy; he now rounded on the Government in the normal constitutional manner. 'The Minister of National Defence has declared that this is an interim period,' Pearkes observed in the House of Commons on 16 October.

> I do not wish to see a drifting back into the laissez-faire attitude or to conditions of prewar life. The time should be spent in planning and remodeling our forces ... There will be – and I see it in the remarks of the Minister – a tendency to get back to an organization based on our pre-war system ...
>
> I feel that not sufficient foresight is being used at this time in preparing our future defence forces so that they may assure reasonable and adequate defence of this country in another global war where we might be faced with an enemy equipped with the most scientific developments of this atomic age. We should think twice before we go back to the time-worn policies and time-worn formations which we had before this war...[34]

The most stringent criticism of the Government's interim defence plans came from Lt-Colonel C.C. Merritt, like Pearkes a former Canadian Army officer and holder of the Victoria Cross. Merritt refused absolutely to accept the view that it was premature to begin planning Canada's permanent post-war defence policy. 'Both Ministers for the defence services, in bringing down their estimates,' he remarked in the House of Commons on 22 October,

> have based their inability to make a statement, their desire to have an interim force, and their uncertainty about the future, upon the fact that they do not know what the obligations of the country will be under the United Nations Charter and also upon the fact that they do not know what the atomic bomb is going to do to the present types of service ...
>
> Just because we have the atomic bomb ... is no reason whatever to wait before making up our minds what our forces are to be. Ordinary forces still are

necessary ... The atomic bomb gives us no reason for waiting, no reason not to be decisive now and know what we are going to do.

Now let us turn to our duties under the security pact of the United Nations. Again there is no reason to wait. In the first place, those duties may be undecided for an indefinite period of time, five or six years or more. What then are we going to do in the meantime? In the second place, I suggest that when those duties are announced they will not affect us substantially in our calculations with respect to our armed forces ... Our first duty is to defend this country...[35]

Abbott replied to this criticism with some spirit. 'We have been more definite than any other allied country,' he declared,

in announcing the character and composition of our post-war forces. We have been more definite than Great Britain or the United States ... [All the same], I do not think the time is ripe to lay down hard and fast rules as to what our post-war forces are to be, whether Army, Navy or Air Force ... Only six weeks after the end of the Japanese war is a little too early to lay down hard and fast rules as to just what type of ships we are to have or just how many men will be in our post-war forces. I think we have to proceed a little more slowly than that.[36]

Abbott's defence of his policy not to embark upon hard and fast plans was sufficiently convincing when delivered in October 1945. It was less convincing when delivered in August 1946. By then a year, rather than six weeks, had elapsed since the end of the war against Japan. By then, also, some of the earlier uncertainties had been removed. Initial meetings of the United Nations Military Staff Committee had shown that the day of agreement upon a United Nations military force at the disposal of the Security Council was far in the future, if it would ever dawn. Initial meetings of the Council of Foreign Ministers had shown that the Soviet Union was more of an enemy against which to arm than an ally with which to co-operate. Initial meetings of the United Nations Atomic Energy Commission had shown how remote were the prospects of bringing nuclear weapons under international control. And by then Abbott himself had swung around to the view expressed by Colonel Merritt the preceding October, namely, that while atomic energy might work a revolution in science and politics, it was unlikely to work a revolution in warfare. 'It is doubtful whether the discovery of atomic energy has changed the fundamental requirements of conducting successful war,' the Minister told a reporter of the *Montreal Standard* in April 1946, 'any more than they were altered by the discovery of gunpowder, the submarine, gas, tanks or planes. The basic principles of war remain unchanged.'

Yet despite these clarifications of the international environment there were no comparable clarifications of Canada's military policies so long as

Abbott remained Minister of National Defence. He spoke on military matters very seldom outside the House of Commons, and his few speeches were confined to generalities:

With the possible advent of atomic war ... it becomes apparent that there is a need for the armed forces of a country to be immediately available. It is imperative, therefore, for Canada to maintain adequate active and reserve forces of the armed services and that these services be well-staffed, well-trained, well-equipped, and well-administered.[37]

The keynote in our defence policy at this time is preparedness ... We cannot forget the critical risks we have run by our previous lack of preparation ... It is an old maxim that the best defence is a strong offence and this is recognized by the ability to attack or the potential offence ... We in Canada must not forget the lessons of the past. We must guard against future optimism which would encourage too rapid disarmament. We should be cautious about reducing too greatly the size of our armed forces.[38]

Within Parliament, when presenting the service estimates for 1946–7, the Minister refused to make a general statement on defence policy. 'I thought,' he explained, 'that the general outline of our plans given last session and in statements since had pretty well indicated the general policy and that it would expedite the business if I were to answer specific questions asked by Hon. Members.'[39] This explanation did not satisfy at least one member of the Opposition. 'I want,' Colonel C.C. Merritt declared at length, 'to ask the Minister a very short question: Will he say for what purpose Canada's post-war defence forces are being designed?' The question drew forth the following exchange between the Minister and his critic:

*Abbott*: Yes, I can answer that very easily. Canada's post-war defence forces are designed to provide, first, a representative group of all arms of the services. We need them now as a permanent professional trained army. In addition they are to provide a force to train the citizen army ... which has been the basis of Canada's fighting force in two wars and would be the basis of our force in any war we fight in the future, assuming we fight a war with an army, which I take it we would. The purpose of this relatively small force is to provide a small but highly trained and skilled professional force which can be expanded in time of war, primarily to train the citizen soldiers who would have to fight that war. That is about as briefly as I can put it.

*Merritt*: Then, I understand, the permanent force is designed for training purposes only and not for the defence of Canada or for an overseas commitment. Is that correct?

*Abbott*: Well, if – which may God forbid – we should get into a war in the next two or three years they would be available to the extent of their numbers, but obviously a force of eight or nine thousand troops altogether with training cadres and administrative personnel would not have any perceptible effect in any war that we can contemplate ...

*Merritt*: I suggest to the committee that the Minister's answer leaves open, as I thought it would, the whole question of the defence of Canada, and that we should not consider that these forces are in any way adequate or even designed to defend Canada in case her borders were attacked...[40]

'In the two months during which I have been in the Department,' Brooke Claxton told the House of Commons on 13 February 1947, 'I must say I have not made many speeches about atom bombs or guided missiles or jet-propelled planes or other things to make people's flesh creep. I thought it was my job first to do what obviously was wanted, not only by the Government but by the people of Canada and by the members of the armed services themselves; that is, to endeavour to coordinate the three departments which had been developed separately during the war.'[41] The people and Parliament of Canada would have to wait a few more months before they would hear from their new Minister of National Defence what a disappointed Colonel Merritt described as 'that statement of policy and purpose in regard to our forces for which we have asked him and his predecessor ever since peace broke out.'[42]

Despite Claxton's reticence in the House of Commons, he was trying to think out in his own mind what sort of military establishment the national interest required during the years ahead. On 17 February he addressed himself to this task in a memorandum headed 'Observations on the Defence Needs of Canada,' the ideas and concepts of which would form the basis of the first statement of post-war security policy given to the House of Commons when Claxton defended the estimates of his Department later in the year.

There were two possible theatres, Claxton considered, in which Canadian forces could conceivably be called upon to fight. The first was Western Europe. It was 'very unlikely' that Canada's armed forces would be called upon to fight in this theatre within the next five years. 'Canada would only enter such a war if the United States did. The probability that the United States would win any such war is strong assurance against its taking place.' Should, however, the unlikely occur, Canada would again be called upon to play her part. Operations 'would be similar, although not identical, to the operations of the Canadian forces in the First and Second World Wars. The task of any Canadian force might, as then, be to defend our front in Western Europe and assist in the defeat of the enemy in his own country. The Navy would be engaged on escort work across the North Atlantic and in defensive operations in the North Atlantic, Pacific and Arctic. The Air Force would assist these and if bombing is still in vogue co-operate in bombing the enemy.' Such operations, Claxton assumed, would only be entered upon by Canadian forces after the war had gone on for some considerable time, during which military personnel could be trained and the necessary equipment manufactured. Thus it would not be necessary to maintain large forces in being in anticipation of war in Western Europe; and 'we should not involve ourselves in any considerable expense in building up mobilization reserves of materials of war which would only be useful in fighting a war outside of Canada.' On the other hand, 'we should, through research, assistance, industrial development, etc., maintain and increase our knowledge and industrial skills so that we would lose no time in getting into production of the kind of weapons and materials of war it will be our part to make.'

The other theatre in which Canadian forces might be engaged was North America. The North American continent, in Claxton's view, would be a secondary target, hit so as to cripple industrial production and cut off the line of supply to Western Europe. 'Attacks on North America of the kind envisaged would not require large forces immediately ready to meet them but require a relatively small, highly trained force.'

Claxton's analysis thus led to the conclusion that no good purpose would be served by Canada's maintaining a sizeable military force in being, or by stockpiling military equipment on a grand scale. For the armed forces, both active and reserve, the need was for training, not for numbers – training 'so that they can be the nucleus of a greatly enlarged war effort.' For munitions and supply, the need was to dispose of the enormous stockpile held over from the Second World War: 'certainly the purchasing of additional tanks, guns of existing types, motor vehicles, etc., to go into mobilization reserves, even at scrap values, would not be justified.'

It was just as well that Claxton's strategic survey pointed in the direction of economy; for economy was the Government's watchword where the Department of National Defence was concerned. During the weeks following Claxton's appointment as Minister, the Cabinet gave a good deal of attention to re-establishing the military. The Prime Minister had set the tone for these discussions by remarking at the outset that 'what we needed now was to get back to the old Liberal principles of economy, reduction of taxation, anti-militarism, etc.'[43] He was powerfully supported by Douglas Abbott, whose ideas about the needs of the military had undergone radical change as the result of moving from Defence to Finance. 'On Thursday, December 9, 1946,' Claxton recorded,

> as Minister of Defence, Doug [Abbott] had been looking at a figure of $365 million as the amount of money the three services would need for the year 1947–48 ... Now, as Minister of Finance, his point of view had changed; he wanted me to reduce the $365 million which he had had before him to some-

thing like $150 or 160 million ... I would not, I could not, agree to that. But I got the Deputies together and told them that they had to come down to $250 million ... Still Doug Abbott and Cliff Clark [Deputy Minister of Finance] were adamant. Cliff said we could not possibly spend $250 million or even $200 million. No one had had more experience than Cliff Clark in coping with the appetite of government departments. I could see his point; but he must see mine. I could not allow the defence programme for 1947–48 to be regarded as anything other than the irreducible minimum; the base on which we would start to build our post-war forces. At first Clark thought that this should be the level, but I succeeded in getting at least government acquiescence that it was to be regarded as a minimum. I must say I got little support for my fight in the Government or elsewhere for that matter.[44]

Claxton made his pitch for the irreducible minimum at a meeting of the Cabinet on 5 February 1947. 'Claxton made out a very good case,' Mackenzie King conceded afterwards in his diary.

Held to his position that he could not possibly go further in view of what had been understood originally and keep responsibility in the Department. I felt he was on the whole right ... though I told Council that I believed the CCF would come along and produce a motion to cut expenditures in half ... and they would have no better political capital throughout the country. I also in reply to Claxton's statement asked if he had not received communications expressing favour for reduction of army, etc. I said if not he had better see the communications that came to my office and if he wanted to test the Liberal feeling let us have the matter discussed at party Caucus. That was the place to get the views. Not as sent in by persons interested in Army to the Minister of War...[45]

In the event Claxton had to settle for a compromise. The Cabinet agreed to allot $200 million for the defence estimates for 1947–8. However, Claxton recorded, 'this was subject to informal understandings of great and, as it turned out, growing importance.' The first understanding was that the Minister of National Defence should do everything in his power to see 'that the Department and services practiced the utmost economy in every direction. Major developments in the programme would be submitted to the Cabinet or Treasury Board for approval.' A second understanding was that 'if it should turn out that we needed more money to maintain the approved programme, that money would be provided in supplementary estimates.' A third was

that while the total appropriation of $200 million was divided among different heads in the detailed estimates, the actual amount sought in the estimates for defence – for all services and branches – would be $200 million as a single item. With the approval of the Treasury Board, we could transfer sums allocated from one item in the details to meet expenditures on another. We could even transfer sums from service to service ... This device enabled us to get by with very much less money than would otherwise have been the case. For in this first post-war year we had nothing in previous experience to guide us in figuring out the cost of the armed forces for the next year...[46]

Only once during Claxton's eight years as Minister of National Defence was it necessary for him to resort to the device of supplementary estimates, and that was during the Korean War. Even so the concession had not been granted lightly. 'I can remember to this day,' he wrote in 1960, 'the hot intensity of my talks with my colleagues in obtaining this agreement ... In these first years I had the feeling that the only sentiment common to the Chiefs and my Cabinet was that all of them regarded me as unreasonable.'[47] That is probably as good a sign as any that a Minister of National Defence is doing his job.

The Chiefs, for their part, devised their own techniques of supplication. Early in January 1948, the Chief of the General Staff told his Headquarters officers something of how these worked:

What happens is that we make out the Army programme for the year, the programme is costed and comes up to twice as much as we have any chance of getting. We start to prune it down; then we have an argument for two or three weeks with the Treasury Officials. Finally we reach a compromise and then within that figure we have to do all we can of the Army plans for the next year. One of the difficulties in getting our estimates through the Treasury Board is that last year we ended up with 40 million surplus and it now looks as if we are going to end up the year with between 12 to 15 million surplus. The reaction of the Treasury is quite natural. They say: "You fellows can't estimate, you never spend what we give you, so we are going to start with taking off 40 million; that will give you what you had last year and you should be able to get along on that." I do want to impress upon you that it places me in a very difficult position and that if you over estimate and we don't spend the money that is used as a lever by the Treasury to pry off that much the next year...[48]

Brooke Claxton presented his first estimates to the House of Commons on 9 July 1947. He had by then been authorized by the Cabinet to ask for a total of $240 millions, rather than $200 millions; this sum represented, he told the House, 'about 12 per cent of our national budget.' He doubted whether more could be wisely spent during the current fiscal year. It would be possible to work within this figure because of the pruning and weeding at National Defence Headquarters, and because the three services had been told that they should recruit only up to 75 per cent of the force levels approved by the Cabinet Defence Committee in September 1945.

Claxton had announced the decision to cut recruiting by at least one quarter on 16 January 1947, and had defended it in the House of Commons on 13 February. 'If we at once recruited our three services up to the ceilings that were announced by my predecessor last year,' he declared, and fill up the establishments on the basis set forth by him, it would be difficult at a later time to make any change which might be desirable ... It seems to me that we are on much safer ground if, for this year, we limit the recruiting of the defence forces of Canada to seventy-five per cent, as I have announced. Then, at the end of the year, we would be able to see better what the future holds for us...[49]

Not everyone was ready to accept this explanation at face value. 'There are many of us who believe,' Colonel Merritt remarked in reply, 'as I certainly do, that this reduction of twenty-five per cent from the figure set last year is dictated only by economy and without regard whatever to military necessity.' He was dead right, but that did not make the reduction wrong.

On presenting the estimates of his Department on 9 July 1947, Brooke Claxton gave the Parliament and people of Canada the first rationale of military expenditure to come from the Government since the end of the Second World War. After reviewing the nation's war effort, Claxton began by setting forth the purposes for which Canada required a military establishment in time of peace. Three such purposes were discerned:

1 To defend Canada against aggression.

2 To assist the civil power in maintaining law and order within the country.

3 To carry out any undertakings which by our own voluntary act we may assume in co-operation with friendly nations or under any effective plan of collective action under the United Nations.[50]

He spoke of the new weapons, no longer weapons of the future – the atomic bomb, jet-propelled aircraft, rockets, higher-speed submarines, bacteriological and chemical warfare – weapons 'so much more devastating than anything previously used that of themselves they may make major changes in the nature of war, should war come again to scourge the earth.' At the same time, 'these new powerful weapons reinforce the powerful appeal of those who want to work to make war impossible.' Canada could no longer rely on geography for its defence. 'Distance and space still combine to give us great natural advantages for which we cannot be too grateful, but distance and space have been drastically reduced and are still shrinking; and the shaping of world events and the changing centres of power have put Canada in a more important strategic position than she has ever been before.'[51] Caution was needed, however, in assessing how these changes in weaponry and in the external environment affected Canada's defence requirements. 'There has been a great deal of talk,' Claxton observed, 'about push-button wars as well as about saucers flying in formation ... That does not mean that we should not keep up to date and do the utmost in research and industrial organization and have as much as we can afford of the most modern weapons. But it does seem to me that we should keep our feet on the ground...'[52] There was in any event 'still a lot of work to be done in reorganization before we can provide a proper organizational and administrative basis for any defence forces that we may have in the future.'[53]

What of the defence forces of the present? They stood, the Minister reported, at a total strength of 32,610. Of these, 6621 officers and men were on active service with the Navy; 11,804 with the Air Force; and 14,185 with the Army.

By then the 'good, workable little fleet' foreseen by Douglas Abbott had more or less come into being. On the West Coast the flotilla consisted of the cruiser *Ontario* and the destroyers *Crescent*, *Cayuga*, and *Athabaskan*, with ten ships (including the decommissioned cruiser *Uganda*) in reserve. A similarly minuscule flotilla guarded the Atlantic – the destroyers *Nootka*, *Micmac*, and *Haida*, the Algerine *New Liskeard*, nine ships in reserve, and HMCS *Warrior* as flagship.

*Warrior*, along with the sister aircraft carrier *Magnificent*, had been acquired for Canadian service from the Royal Navy during the war as part of the RCN's strategy for a post-war big ship navy,* and was commissioned into the Navy on 24 January 1946 at the Belfast shipyard where she had been built; *Magnificent* was still under construction. The Prime Minister did not share the Navy's enthusiasm at the prospect of Canada's taking delivery of these vessels. He felt that he had been outmanoeuvred by his Naval Staff, and there were good reasons for that feeling. 'The Navy had no need at all at the present time for aircraft carriers,' Mackenzie King wrote in his diary at the end of 1946. 'I had always opposed this from the start. We should have a purely coast defence.' His distaste was in no way lessened by the news, reaching him on a frigid winter day in Ottawa, that *Warrior* and her crew were then cavorting off Acapulco. 'What nonsense it is to see pictures of waste of money and our men travelling in cities like Mexico, etc. It all irritated the public after the war.'[54] It certainly irritated their prime minister.

No arrangement had as yet been made about purchasing the carriers. *Warrior* was on loan, as would be *Magnificent* when finished. What had been borrowed could be returned, and Mackenzie King's first impulse was to return *Warrior* as soon as might be done with decency and to decline to accept *Magnificent*. St Laurent, too (the Prime Minister recorded on 12 December), 'was feeling that aircraft carriers should go at once.' A month later, however, the Prime Minister had changed his mind. 'I am inclined to believe one aircraft carrier may be advisable. If war should come at any time flying from the northern regions would be an important factor.'[55]

* See above, 82–4.

*Warrior* was worthless for Arctic service, but it was not too late to refit *Magnificent* if work began at once. The job was thus to persuade the British to accept the return of *Warrior* in exchange for an 'arcticized' *Magnificent*. After some haggling, this transfer was arranged.

The deal was admirable for Canada but the Prime Minister still could not but 'shudder' (as Mackenzie King wrote on 9 April 1947),

> each time I think of this enormous aircraft carrier which we are having brought out under the title of "Magnificent." What Canada wants with the largest aircraft carrier afloat[*] under a title like that, I don't know. It is just to invite an enemy's attack. I venture to say should war come soon, it would be about the first of the large vessels to disappear.[56]

'Our ships will all be winterized,' the Minister of National Defence promised Parliament in the summer of 1947, 'and made as comfortable as possible for the fine young officers and men in the Canadian navy, of whom we are exceedingly proud.'[57] A year later, *Magnificent* and a destroyer escort ventured into Hudson Bay – the first Canadian warship to show the White Ensign in Arctic waters. Northern naval activity was further emphasized by the decision to construct a large ice-breaker for the RCN.

But Claxton's pride in the Navy preceded its fall. The official history of the armed forces of Canada finds the post-war pre-Korea RCN 'weak in ships and men,' all the weaker for dividing its meagre resources between two oceans so that 'squadron organization was hardly feasible and even effective training exercises difficult.'[58] By December 1947 only ten ships remained in commission, and while the defence budget for the following year added four more to the fleet the Navy was in the doldrums. Before emerging from them it would undergo a period of demoralization and humiliation unknown in its forty-year existence.†

The Air Force was allotted $73,000,000 of the $240,000,000 defence budget for 1947–8. At its disposal were thousands of aircraft – Spitfires, Hurricanes, Mosquitos, Lancasters – all of them out of date. 'We believe that every single one of these planes with which we ended the war is now obsolete,' the Minister of National Defence admitted in the House of Commons. 'We are waiting to receive some of the latest jet propelled planes which have been on order for a number of months, but which have been delayed in delivery.'[59]

The jets to which Brooke Claxton referred were Vampire twin-engine interceptors built by the de Haviland Company in the United Kingdom.

* By the end of 1945, *Midway*-class carriers displacing 45,000 tons were entering the US Navy; *Magnificent* displaced under 20,000 tons full load.

† See below, 124–7.

They were being made available to the RCAF as the result of the initiative of the Acting Chief of the Air Staff, Air Vice Marshal W.A. Curtis, who conceived the idea of trading Canadian Spitfires based in Britain for a number of the Vampires then on order for the RAF. Negotiations with his wartime colleague and friend Lord Tedder proved successful, the British finding that they could put the Spitfires into useful service in the Middle East. Some 200 Spitfires were exchanged for some 85 Vampires, and the Canadians considered that they for once got the better deal. But the aircraft were a long time arriving. The British insisted on equipping their own squadrons before releasing any to the RCAF, and it was not until December 1948 that Vampires entered Canadian service. Even so, their acquisition meant that the RCAF were flying jets some months before the USAF, whose F-86s did not become operational until 1949. Meanwhile, before the Vampires arrived, the air defence of Canada was carried out by units of the RCAF auxiliary, whose week-end flyers performed their simulated interceptions from P-51 Mustangs. Whether these would have been a match for the Soviet Long Range Air Force (whose first four-engine jet bombers had dumbfounded the Western air attachés at the fly-past over Moscow on 1 May 1947) was happily never put to the test.

It was just as well, also, that the Soviet Union did not try to lodge armed forces in the Canadian North. To meet such a contingency, Brooke Claxton recorded afterwards, 'we felt that we should have fully trained and ready to fight in Canada what was first called a brigade group but later was called the Mobile Striking Force of three air-borne battalions plus appropriate artillery and supporting units. These were the only front line fighting forces planned or provided for when I came in and their organization was just getting under way.'[60] When Claxton presented his estimates on 9 July 1947, Opposition defence critics were keenly interested in the state of preparedness of this force, the formation of which had been announced by D.C. Abbott as long ago as 16 October 1945. Claxton had to concede that its preparedness left much to be desired: 'It does not yet exist as a fighting unit fit to take the field at any moment.' So far it had a complement of 192 officers and 1,952 men (compared to the planned strength of around 5,000), and these, as was pointed out from across the floor of the House, were 'scattered all the way from Esquimalt to ... Halifax.' The Minister rejected the suggestion that the brigade group be recruited to full strength and kept together as an elite fighting force. 'Once one regards the armed forces of Canada,' Claxton replied,

> from what I believe is the right point of view at the present time, that is, as a training force for future staff officers and leaders, and for the reserve forces of Canada, then I should think ... keeping constantly mobilized and ready for

action anything in the nature of a brigade group in one place would be a mistake ... Given the present development of weapons ... we can take care of anything that happens in Canada in the immediate future...[61]

By 1948 it was no longer necessary to refer to 'the enemy' in hypothetical terms or in Aesopian language. On 9 February, with the ominous news from Czechoslovakia blackening the daily newspapers, Brooke Claxton spoke out, for the first time, about the threat of Soviet aggression. 'Russia is not poised on the brink of war,' he told a meeting of the McGill Liberal Club in Montreal,

no people wants war – but the record of the Soviet Union in international relations since the war unfortunately prevents our eliminating the possibility of Russian aggression. The Soviet Union's use of the veto twenty-three times when the other great powers have used it twice cannot be interpreted as evidence of her determination to make the United Nations an effective body for world co-operation. She has expanded her official borders since the end of the war so as to take in the whole or part of eight different countries having an area of 274,000 square miles and she exercises active domination over a much vaster territory. All the way round the world Russia exploits every difficulty and obstructs every constructive effort so as to prevent the establishment of conditions in which the nations can work together to build peace and prosperity on lasting foundations. By suppressing and distorting the truth behind the iron curtain, the Soviet Union has kept her teeming millions in ignorance of the infinitely better conditions prevailing in the democratic countries...

And at South Porcupine, Ontario, on 6 March 1948, the Minister of National Defence declared:

The mistakes made by other countries have been errors of judgment, failings of human personality, honest difficulties due to the magnitude and complexity of the problems confronting the world. The reasons which have led to Russia making her grand contribution to international misunderstanding have been deliberate, part of a well worked out plan. The plan, quite obviously, has been to create and exploit and magnify every difficulty, to promote chaos and disorder, to do everything possible to make democratic government unworkable.

Finally, when presenting his second set of defence estimates to the House of Commons on 24 June:

The Soviet Union has flouted ... war-won friendships, obstinately obstructed every move to arrive at understanding, and promoted chaos and disorder and the darkness of the iron curtain ... It has produced an attitude in Canada towards defence which is quite different from any that we ever had before in peacetime...

Nor was this a partisan view only. 'Those who were asleep from 1935 to 1939,' declared an Opposition spokesman in the defence debate, 'are asleep no longer. We know the issues.'[62]

It was one thing to know the issues, another thing to know what to do about them. Brooke Claxton strove hard to convince the House that, despite events in Europe during the spring of 1948, forcing 'the Western democracies together, producing Western Union and the Statements of President Truman and of our Prime Minister on March 17,' Canada was in no immediate danger. 'Theoretically it is possible for missiles to be guided by various devices to their destination hundreds if not thousands of miles away. The submarine which under water can do something like twenty-three knots is known to exist. But these new developments have not in fact yet been carried to the point where it is possible for them to change the character of war or make out of date either existing concepts or existing equipment.'[63]

Existing concepts, accordingly, remained as they had been the year before. 'In the immediate future,' Claxton declared, 'any attack on North America would be diversionary, designed to panic the people of this continent into putting a disproportionate amount of effort into passive local defence ... A potential aggressor, if it had atomic weapons at all, would use them on targets of the greatest strategical importance, and it is very unlikely that in the near future such an aggressor would use any such weapons he had on many targets in Canada.'* Canada would not be the Belgium of World War III. She would be the Canada of World War III. That is to say, her role in any conceivable global conflict of the next few years would be comparable to the role she had played during two previous world wars. 'At sea,' Claxton predicted, 'our role would largely consist of guarding the lines of communication as the Royal Canadian Navy did so well during the last war.' On land, the army, apart from dealing with a diversionary landing upon North America, was 'to provide the administrative and training staff ... to train the reserve army and with it form the

* The Chief of the General Staff meanwhile entertained a slightly different conception. 'It is very likely,' General Foulkes told his headquarters officers on 28 January 1948,

> that we will be very much like the infantry soldier in the next war. We will get the shorts, some bombs aimed at the United States will drop on Canada. I am quite sure we must expect that we will get some of the atomic bombs on this country either by accident or on purpose. There will be an air defence system across the northern part of this country and the object of this air defence system will be to bring down the airplane carrying atomic bombs before it reaches Chicago. This might mean that Canada will be on the receiving end. The one thing we can be sure about is that there will be destruction, chaos, casualties in the thousands, cities laid waste, essential services destroyed, complete and utter confusion, panic and distress in certain areas in Canada at the beginning of the war ...

See Document 3 below.

nucleus for as large a force as Canada may need' – presumably, another expeditionary force to fight in Europe. Only in the air was any major new role contemplated: 'Our main peacetime task will be to supply interceptor fighter squadrons and ground forces necessary to deal with attacks on Canadian territory.' But the Minister noted that 'these will be valuable units from which to draw the nucleus of larger forces should the situation demand it'; and he stated that the RCAF would maintain 'one permanent and two auxiliary bomber squadrons' so as to 'keep abreast of modern trends and developments in the art of bombing' – an art brought to such a pitch of perfection by Canadian airmen over German cities.[64]

At least one member of the Opposition stoutly resisted these conclusions. 'The whole tenor of the Minister's statement,' declared E.D. Fulton, 'indicates the belief in the minds of the Department that we shall again have an opportunity for leisurely preparation ... leisurely mobilization, leisurely assembling of our forces and leisurely direction of our forces to those places where we wish to send them, and that we shall be able to conduct the war as the last one was conducted in its early stages.' Such thinking, Fulton argued, was wishful, faulty, and dangerous. 'At the moment we are not preparing our defence plans to meet an immediate war in any realistic fashion; we are not bearing in mind that the character of warfare is being changed every day; and we are in fact making no effective plans to meet the next war which, whenever it comes, I am certain will be characterized by a totally new, much more rapid, and in many respects totally unexpected, form of attack.'[65]

The major beneficiary of re-equipment was the RCAF. By 1948 the Air Force was poised for take-off. It was not longer an air force without serviceable aircraft. During 1948 it took delivery of 85 Vampire jet fighters, 30 Mustangs, 23 North Star transports (a modified version of the DC 4*), 20 Firefly IVs and 27 Seafuries (to be carried by *Magnificent*), 3 Sikorsky helicopters, 3 Chipmunks, and 36 Auster trainers. As a result of these acquisitions, Brooke Claxton told the House of Commons on 24 June 1948, 'this year we shall be spending more on the air force and fleet air arm than on either the navy or the army.'[66] It would not be long before more was spent on the Air Force than on both the Navy and the Army.

Not all the Air Force's post-war aircraft were acquired from other countries. In 1946 the Government had decided to proceed with the de-

* The Chief of the Air Staff, Air Marshal W.A. Curtis, had negotiated the necessary release of patents and production processes through his contacts in American aviation circles. North Stars were the workhorses of the RCAF Transport Command and, along with aircraft chartered from Canadian Pacific Airlines, ran the airlift to Korea.

sign and development of a jet fighter built specifically for Canadian requirements. The decision had not been lightly taken, nor was it taken without opposition. Within the Chiefs of Staff Committee it had been opposed by the Chief of the General Staff: General Foulkes, recalling that Canadian industry had been unable to design a tank during the Second World War, doubted whether it would be capable of the more exacting feats of engineering and productivity required to turn out an all-Canadian fighter aircraft. No doubt he and his naval colleague reasoned, if they did not argue, that an all-Canadian aircraft would prove to be an expensive project, drawing funds away from their respective services; and that if successful it would lead to even more expensive projects in the future. But in the face of these arguments the decision to proceed prevailed.

It was based upon two main considerations. The first was the necessity of assuring the RCAF the supply of aircraft needed for it to perform its primary mission of defending Canada from enemy bomber attack. Previous experience, both in wartime and during the immediate postwar period, had shown the reluctance of both the United Kingdom and the United States to satisfy Canadian requirements, even when cash was placed on the barrel-head, until their own were fully met. If Canada was to be able to count on an adequate supply of aircraft and engines for her own Air Force, she would have to build her own.

The second consideration was the need for equipment especially designed for Canadian flying conditions. A fighter on patrol in the United Kingdom or the United States was seldom far distant from an airstrip on which to put down in an emergency: under such circumstances a single engine offered its pilot a reasonable assurance of survival. A fighter on patrol in Canada would, however, be operating far out of range of any such haven. Accordingly, two engines were indispensable. And not two engines only, but two seats in the aircraft – one for the pilot, one for the operator of the complicated electronic apparatus installed to increase the chances of successful interception in the vast areas under surveillance. No aircraft combining these specifications was then under development, let alone production, either for the RAF or the USAF. If the RCAF was to obtain the aircraft it required, the aircraft – engine as well as airframe – would have to be produced in Canada.

As between airframe and engine, the latter was the more difficult engineering feat. Fortunately there were some facilities at hand.

In 1942, the Canadian Government was informed by the British Government of work then proceeding in the United Kingdom upon a new type of aircraft engine. Experts were sent over from Canada to study its development. In 1943, as a result of their mission, a cold weather test station was opened in Canada to test the British jet power plants under severe weather conditions. The following year the Canadian Government set up, as a Crown Company, Turbo Research Limited. The first task of Turbo Research was to test engines and components for the RAF, and for this purpose it recruited and trained a number of young Canadian aeronautical engineers in the wholly new field of jet propulsion.

In January 1945, the Canadian Government awarded Turbo Research a contract to design and develop a new jet engine for the RCAF. Work was begun on a 4200 lb thrust axial flow engine known as the TR-3. In November 1945, the Company requested additional funds to carry the work through to completion. C.D. Howe, the Minister to whom the matter was referred, was not optimistic. 'I am certain,' Howe wrote to Crawford Gordon, the president of Turbo Research, on 10 November,

> that the Government will not authorize $8,000,000 to be spent over five years by Turbo Research. This is development work rather than research work and should be undertaken by private industry. The Government has certain facilities which might not be open to private industry for obtaining information but all such resources will be put at the disposal of private industry, should they be interested in carrying on...[67]

Faced by an uncertain future, the small staff at Turbo Research made little progress on their project throughout the winter and spring of 1946. In May 1946, the Government decided to liquidate Turbo Research. Development of the jet engine was transferred to A.V. Roe Canada, Limited, and basic research became the responsibility of the National Research Council. At Avro's plant at Malton, Ontario, near Toronto, two engines soon took shape. One was the 'Chinook,' designed for experimental purposes; it had its first official test running on 24 March 1948. The other engine, the 'Orenda,' begun in September 1946, was to be the power plant for the airframe being built by Avro next door.

Both the engine project, known as the TR-5, and the airframe, known as XC-100, were strongly supported by the Government. On 5 April 1948, the Chief of the Air Staff, Air Marshal Curtis, argued forcibly in a memorandum for the Minister that development on engine and airframe should be speeded up. 'The advancement of this programme,' Curtis wrote, '...should effect economy by reducing overhead which usually results from a prolonged programme of this type. But more important is, that from a defence point of view, we will be prepared to meet an emergency at least six months earlier than we are at present. This, when based on the next two years, is a saving of 25% in the time planned.'[68] C.D.

Howe, to whom Brooke Claxton had referred the Chief's recommendation for advice, was enthusiastically in favour of pushing ahead. 'I visited the plant of A.V. Roe some ten days ago,' Howe wrote to Claxton on 12 April,

> witnessed a test run of the engine and examined the progress of the Airframe. I must say I was greatly impressed by the progress being made. It seems quite possible that Canada may produce the first successful jet engine of large size...
>
> Having in mind developments in the United States towards preparedness in the Air, I believe that an additional $3,500,000, expended this year to speed up the Avro programme, is warranted. Should you decide to apply for the money required, I will be glad to support you.[69]

Brooke Claxton duly applied for, and duly received, the extra appropriation, which Avro put to good use. By January 1950, the CF-100, powered by two British-built Avon jet engines (the Orenda was not ready until the end of the year) was test-flown for the first time and underwent intensive trials during the next four months. The results were gratifying. 'Predicted performance has been realized,' Avro reported to the Government on 30 June 1950, 'and, in a number of important aspects, exceeded, under full-scale test conditions ... It is to be anticipated that appreciable improvements will take place when the fully rated engines are adopted...'

While work on the CF-100 was going forward, the RCAF required an alternative, faster than the Vampire, just in case the Avro project ran into trouble. A scrutiny of the possibilities led to the selection of the F-86 then under production by the North American Aviation Company. A senior RCAF officer flew the machine at the Company plant in Los Angeles and reported favourably on its performance. In November 1948, C.D. Howe and Air Marshal Curtis set out for Washington, DC, with an order to buy 56 F-86A jet day fighters from North American. They were authorized as well to enter into negotiation on conditions under which the F-86 might be produced in Canada under licence from the manufacturer. An aide-mémoire, carried with them on their mission, explains why the Canadian Government turned to an American rather than to a British supplier:

> By reason of the different standards, techniques and procedures employed by Canadian industry, aircraft of United Kingdom design have to be re-designed and re-engineered to such extent that the aircraft produced in Canada have to have pipeline support from this country. Aircraft of United States design can be made in Canada without such changes and both the aircraft and components can be absorbed into the normal pipeline. Since the Royal Canadian Air Force must be capable of operating with the United States Air Force in the defence of North America, the advantages of using equipment that can be supported by the industries of Canada and the United States far outweigh any other consideration.

The purchase of the F-86s was successfully arranged in Washington with officials of the US Air Force and the Defense Department. Howe and Curtis then travelled to New York to discuss with representatives of North American Aviation the terms under which F-86s might be produced in Canada under licence from the company. They talked all day Saturday at an office on Wall Street and, late in the afternoon, had reached agreement on all points save one. That concerned construction of the wing and spar components of the airframe which – so the president of the company, 'Dutch' Kindelberger, assured his Canadian visitors – lay beyond the capacity of an infant aircraft industry to produce. 'Better leave them to us,' Kindelberger urged. 'We will ship you the components from Los Angeles.' It was true that they were difficult to produce: the wing of the F-86 tapered in an aerodynamically exacting fashion in two directions, to the wing-tip and to the trailing edge. Howe was disposed to accept the proposed division of labour, but Curtis thought that Canadian technology could and should learn to master manufacture in its entirety. Curtis won the argument. Canadair – the company chosen to produce the F-86s in Canada – bought the jigs and sent their experts to California to see how it was done. All went well. Over the next nine years, Canadair produced nearly 2000 F-86 Sabres; fitted with the same engine which had been designed for the CF-100, these aircraft were used by the RCAF (which placed its first order for 300 in 1950) and the air forces of nine other nations.

By comparison with the Air Force, the Army seemed a poor relation indeed. But the Army – so Brooke Claxton insisted in the House of Commons on 24 June 1948 – was 'not short of any ... equipment.' At the end of the Second World War the Army was left with an enormous stockpile which had since been supplemented by modern weapons of various types. 'I repeat,' Claxton declared, 'I should like to know what equipment we are short of for the active or reserve forces.'[70] The Opposition parties may not have known, but the Chief of the General Staff knew very well. Five months earlier, in a speech to Army officers, General Charles Foulkes had conveyed a very different impression of the Army's combat readiness:

> We are only holding about 25% of our load carrying vehicles and that percentage goes down every day. We have no tracked vehicles except universal carriers and a deficiency of some 844 tanks. As you know we brought back no tanks from Europe. We did buy about 350 new Shermans from the USA. These are only for training purposes and we will require to make arrangements for new tanks before we go to war.[*] We hold about 50% of the medium

* Speaking in Parliament three years later, Brooke Claxton spoke as follows on the alleged deficiency in the supply of tanks for the Canadian Army:

> It would have been utterly ridiculous for us either to have contemplated the

guns. Our anti-aircraft guns, except 20mm., are woefully out of date and won't be very useful for the aircraft of the future ... We have a distinct shortage of tank spares which are in short supply and come from the US, so we may have to curtail somewhat the training of armour...[71]

The Army which had to make the best it could of what it thus received consisted of between 15,000 and 16,000 officers and men on active service, with a further 35,000 in the reserve force. The Active Force units, as they were called, were scattered in army camps across Canada. 'The two armoured regiments – the Royal Canadian Dragoons and Lord Strathcona's Horse, equipped with Sherman tanks and operating on a restricted establishment – were located at Camp Petawawa, Ontario, and Currie Barracks, Calgary, Alberta. The 1st Royal Canadian Horse Artillery was at Camp Shilo, Manitoba, armed with 25-pounder field guns. The infantry was organized in regiments of one battalion each: The Royal Canadian Regiment at Currie Barracks, and the Royal 22e Régiment at Camp Valcartier in Quebec. In addition, there were a few basic supporting units such as signals and engineers that had been kept at reduced establishments ... The rest of the Active Force was organized into schools of instruction, static service units and headquarters for five regional commands.'[72] It was fair to ask where, in this diaspora, the vaunted brigade group was to be found; and an Opposition critic did not fail to ask. 'That mobile brigade,' the Minister replied,

still forms ... the main agency by which Canada would deal with any direct attack on Canada. There has been no abandonment of it whatever. It is in training now. The armoured and infantry battalions have been grouped together at Petawawa for the first time and this summer will engage in unit training. The other branches of it are at Rivers [Manitoba], where the army-air co-operation school is located, at Chilliwack [British Columbia], where there is the engineers' school, and at Shilo [Manitoba], the artillery school; and other branches are at other places.[73]

Claxton felt it desirable to examine, in addition, the likelihood of the mobile brigade ever being called upon to repel a direct attack on Canada by forces of the Soviet Union. 'I suggest,' he remarked,

that the probability that has to be taken into account in our calculations of any such attack is so slight at the present time that it is something that hardly needs being counted in the realm of active possibility; for ... the outcome would be certain and the strategic advantages would be nil.

manufacture of tanks of an intermediate type or to have bought tanks from the United States when these tanks were still in the process of development, and were not yet in large scale production in the United States. We have now the opportunity of buying from the United States the latest tanks, and they will be coming with the equipment for the two divisions we transferred to Europe. But our tanks are by no means obsolete...

Canada, *H.C. Debates*, 1951, III, 2872.

*Mr Fulton*: Why would the strategic advantages be nil?

*Mr Claxton*: Because the forces would be destroyed within a short time.

*Mr Fulton*: By whom?

*Mr Claxton*: By our Canadians.[74]

Brooke Claxton never wavered in his view that, as the danger of direct attack upon Canadian territory was extremely remote, there was no need to maintain the brigade group or (as it was later known) the Mobile Striking Force as a powerful fighting unit. 'Some controversy came up,' he recalled afterwards, 'as to whether this relatively small mobile fighting force would be sufficient to meet an attack on Canadian territory ... The forces provided were "adequate." The territory of Canada has not been attacked...'[75] But that is not to say what would have happened had it been.

## COMMAND AND CONTROL

As demobilization and the re-establishment of the military in peacetime got under way, it quickly became apparent that the organization and administration of the armed forces needed to be changed. Three aspects of command and control were singled out for improvement. One was the political direction of the three Services. A second was the apparatus of high command. A third was the extent of duplication and overlapping within the Services themselves.

Political direction of the armed forces in wartime had been the responsibility of the War Committee of the Cabinet. It was the secretary to this Committee, A.D.P. Heeney, who suggested to the Prime Minister on 20 July 1945 that 'there is a strong case for a committee to deal with defence questions. Without such a committee,' Heeney added, 'the Service Departments tend to lose touch with the Cabinet and to proceed without adequate direction.' He recommended that he be authorized to 'prepare for a discussion with you and Robertson a proposal for a subordinate Cabinet committee on defence, international security, and mixed military-political questions generally.'[76]

On 3 August 1945, the Cabinet agreed 'that a Cabinet Defence Committee be constituted for consideration of defence questions, the said Committee to report to the full Cabinet upon major matters of policy relating to the maintenance and employment of the three Services...' It was to consist of the ministers of National Defence, Veterans Affairs, Finance, Agriculture, Justice, National Health and Welfare, and National War Services, with 'the Chiefs of Staff, the Under Secretary of State for External Affairs and the Secretary of the Cabinet, and such other officers and officials as might from time to time be required, to be in attendance upon the said Committee.' Its first assignment was to 'examine and report to the Cabinet upon the programmes of the three Services for the period of continuing hostilities against Japan and, subsequently, upon the extent and nature of post-war military establishments.'[77] It was Heeney again who suggested that 'it might be easier to obtain the essential co-operation and support of the Services if the senior Defence Minister were to be in the chair.'[78] Mackenzie King gave his approval to this proposal and, accordingly, D.C. Abbott, as Minister of National Defence, became chairman of the Cabinet Defence Committee on 21 August 1945.

In the mind of Arnold Heeney, its innovator, the Cabinet Defence Committee was to act in peace as the Cabinet War Committee had acted in war. That was very far from being Mackenzie King's conception of its proper role. On 26 September 1946, he recorded that at a meeting of the full Cabinet he had spoken 'very strongly against permitting the Committee on Defence and the Chiefs of Staff deciding any matters of importance without the Cabinet being given the fullest opportunity to approve in the first instance...'[79] A few weeks later his alarm at the tendency of his colleagues to accept without sufficient scrutiny the recommendations of their military advisers was such as to cause him to decide 'that while it would add to my responsibilities and work to take the Chairmanship of the Defence Committee, that I would have to assume this task.'[80] Mackenzie King, rather than Brooke Claxton, was chairman of the Cabinet Defence Committee when the latter became Minister of National Defence on 12 December 1946. A month later the Prime Minister recorded his satisfaction at this arrangement: 'Having a Defence Committee of the Cabinet,' Mackenzie King wrote in his diary on 14 January 1947, 'and presiding over it is all important in effecting saving of public money.'[81]

When St Laurent became Prime Minister in November 1948, he would have been perfectly willing to have Claxton assume the chairmanship of the Cabinet Defence Committee. There was really no good reason, however why he should have done so. Claxton had by then become Vice-Chairman of the Defence Committee, and he ran it pretty much as he wanted. 'Meetings of the Cabinet Defence Committee,' he recorded afterwards,

> were summoned on the Prime Minister's instruction as suggested by me whenever we had enough business to justify a meeting. The meeting was usually attended by the ... Chiefs of Staff and the Deputy Ministers of Defence, Finance, External Affairs or other senior officials of Departments. Almost invariably, matters coming before the Defence Committee had first been dealt with by the Chiefs of Staff and then by me. They would usually be introduced

in a memorandum or 'paper,' generally a page and a half in length, but forwarded by the Minister responsible, in most cases myself...

The Defence Committee ... usually met in the Cabinet room ... At these meetings the talks were very free indeed. Frequently the Ministers would exchange views (and sometimes punches) as if the Chiefs of Staff were not there. It was a valuable experience for the Chiefs of Staff to see how much interest civilians took in defence matters and how essential it was that consideration be given to the financial, economic, political, and external implications of any course of action...

Usually meetings of the Cabinet Defence Committee were held at eleven o'clock in the morning and would be over by one. On several occasions we spent parts of several days going into plans at much greater length. Some of the major operations were related to the aircraft programme, the extent of participation in Korea, the reorganization of the Reserve Army, and the organization, planning and arrangements for our forces in NATO...

Minutes of these meetings were kept by a member of the Cabinet Secretariat having to do with defence matters ... After practically every Cabinet Defence Committee meeting I would summarise the decisions and discussions to the next meeting of the Cabinet, more often than not on the same day. There would be an item on the Cabinet agenda – Report on Defence Committee Meeting. Where the Prime Minister or I considered it desirable to have formal Cabinet approval of the action taken by the Cabinet Defence Committee, that was sought. In this way we had no gap between the Armed Forces, the Department of Defence, the Cabinet Defence Committee, or the Cabinet. We worked out a complete system of interlocking memberships so that everyone responsible had had a responsible share in arriving at and approving a decision and everyone knew what was going on.[82]

By the time Brooke Claxton left the Government in 1954, two other Ministers had been added to the membership of the Cabinet Defence Committee – the Minister of National Health and Welfare (by virtue of his responsibility for civil defence), and the Minister of Justice (by virtue of his responsibility for internal security, counter-espionage, and the Royal Canadian Mounted Police).

A second reform of defence organization at the ministerial level concerned the members of the Cabinet responsible for the armed forces.

'There is on the order paper,' an Opposition defence critic noted on 19 August 1946, 'a resolution to continue the two ministers of defence ... But if we are to have any common doctrine between the three services, I think the first step should be to get those services under one minister.'[83] George Pearkes may not have known it, but he was preaching to the converted. The Prime Minister had reached the same decision a full year earlier; he would have appointed Douglas Abbott as the first post-war Minister of National Defence responsible for all three services, but political considerations, involving representation in and balance of the ministry, got the better of this project.

But by November 1946, Mackenzie King had decided that the time had come for consolidation. His decision was precipitated by what he described in his diary as 'a very great and grave concern about the manner in which the services have been pushing their end at the expense of others and the lack of any real supervision over the defence forces and their unification.'[84] On 12 November, he raised with Douglas Abbott, whom he intended to transfer from National Defence to Finance, 'the necessity of having one Minister over the Department of Defence – one head of permanent services. He was,' Mackenzie King recorded,

very strongly for that. I asked who he thought could handle Defence if he left it. He suggested either Claxton or Bridges. Did not think Bridges would be too good; Gibson not firm enough; thought Claxton would do the job well. I spoke of Claxton being very extravagant with public money. He said he certainly was, but doubted if he would be in that Department...[85]

On 15 November, the Prime Minister raised the matter with his Government colleagues. 'Cabinet was agreed,' he wrote, 'it would be desirable to have one Minister in control of the three Services.' After the meeting, Colin Gibson called upon Mackenzie King 'to say that if I wanted his resignation as Minister for Air, he of course would be ready to give it. I told him I was not thinking of resignations at all, just of what might be needed when it comes to reorganization of the Cabinet. That I would expect him and Abbott to do what they could meanwhile in the way of getting the joint reports from the services and effecting economies.'[86] But Gibson must have known then that he was being eased out. The news came a month later. 'Said to him,' Mackenzie King wrote after the interview,

I did not think I should ask him to take the three Services; that would be too heavy a load for him. Apart from that I felt it would be unwise, seeing he had become identified with one of the services, namely, Air, and that in effecting a consolidation, it would be hard to have the army and navy not feel that he was partial to the Air. This feeling would not easily be removed. I had decided therefore it would be best to bring in to the Defence Department a member of the Government who had had nothing to do with the Department up to the present. I then told him I had decided to appoint Claxton...

He was very pleasant about it. Said to me he thought consolidation was the right thing. That, as a matter of fact, I had no idea how the Departments had run of late. He had great difficulty getting all kinds of joint reports out of the staffs...[87]

In the small policy community of post-war Ottawa it was difficult to conceal disarray in one quarter of the public service from the rest. That something other than perfect co-operation subsisted among the three Chiefs of Staff was thus an open secret. On one occasion the feuding of the Chiefs aroused comment in Parliament. 'At the chief of staff level,' declared A.R. Adamson on 19 August 1946, 'you find officers who are very jealous of their prerogatives, and the co-operation is apt to be on the surface rather than genuine. A man on the chief of staff level is inclined to take the view: That is all very well, but I am running the navy. The same attitude will no doubt be found in the other services...'[88] The Minister of National Defence, then Douglas Abbott, agreed 'that there should be the closest possible liaison between the three branches of the service, and that is what we are endeavouring to achieve.'[89] But so long as Abbott remained Minister this was not achieved. The three services were as three rivals.

Just how much remained to be done to bring them closer together was borne in upon Brooke Claxton soon after he succeeded Abbott as Minister of National Defence in December 1946. He found that the meetings of the Chiefs of Staff Committee, which during the war had been held regularly every week, had

> petered out [into] infrequent, informal and *ad hoc* affairs. There was some co-operation, little coordination, and no unity ... When I came in, the three huge wartime buildings created within a few feet of each other on Cartier Square ... were each occupied by a single service and had no connecting door or tunnel. The Navy had "A" Building, fronting on Elgin Street, the Army "B" Building in the rear, and the Air Force "C" Building fronting on Lisgar Street. If any member of the staff of any one of the three services wanted to communicate with his opposite number, he could get on the telephone, he could write a letter, but he could not go by a communicating passage because until I came there, there was none.[90]

Claxton's first day on the job was spent, as many succeeding days were spent, in attempting to break down these barriers between the three services. His own office, he discovered, was located neither in 'A,' 'B,' or 'C' Building, but in the old Woods Building where, before the war, the entire Department of National Defence together with the headquarters staff of the three services had been housed. 'The office was dark and dingy, the lay-out of the rooms was inconvenient, the building was like a rabbit warren.' For these reasons alone Claxton would have moved elsewhere. But there was another reason why, as he wrote later, 'my stay in the Woods Building lasted less than half an hour:

> ...I felt it to be of importance that I should at once make some changes just to indicate there there was a change; that there was a new boss and that he was going to be the boss. I further thought that it would be highly desirable to show that I was not just another "army man." Colonel Ralston had really

been Minister for the Army only and he had been a distinguished soldier. So was Andy McNaughton. Doug Abbott had also served in the Army ... It was unfortunate that was the service I had seen in war. I felt that I must do something at once to emphasize my tri-service character ... I asked the Deputy Minister of Naval Services ... to meet me in "A" Building ... as I was thinking of establishing my office there. I then got Vice-Admiral Reid on the phone and told him the same thing ... It was arranged that I would meet them at the main door of "A" Building in five minutes. With that I left the Woods Building and I have never been back.

...Suitable space was found in the north east corner of the building on the main floor. When I suggested that this could be made entirely satisfactory by simply removing a few partitions, the naval brass [corrected me] ... : "Bulkheads, Sir, bulkheads." I was learning fast that the Navy was a different world from the Army. The three services had different uniforms, ranks and organizations: they also had different traditions, attitudes and jargon...[91]

It would be many years before the services acquired a common uniform. But Claxton lost no time in attempting to make them acquire a common attitude. His first move was to bring their headquarters under a common roof.

The more I saw of the armed forces the more I felt they needed a psychological shake-up. They simply would not accept the idea of co-operation and coordination; they were still living in the mood of the war when the sky was the limit and there was little or no civilian control. This mental attitude was duplicated in the physical arrangements of National Defence Headquarters ... Accordingly, I decided to have the Deputy Minister and his immediate staff, the Chiefs of Staff and their personal staffs, the secretariats of the principal defence committees, and the Chairman of the Defence Research Board and the headquarters of defence research, as well as joint intelligence and some other agencies of a similar character, located in one building. For this we chose "A" Building, formerly Naval Headquarters ... However, I went further ... and had all the agencies concerned with personnel located in "C" Building which had formerly been Air Force Headquarters and all those concerned with supply matters in "B" Building which had been the Army annex...

Such a shift was a major operation. From the point of view of telephones alone it had to be planned several months in advance. Close to a thousand extensions had to be changed ... There was even a traffic problem as furniture and files could only be moved one way along the narow corridors ... Altogether it was a grand upset and I think it did the Department and the services a lot of good...

While the services were being re-shuffled, we were building bridges between the three buildings. The completion of the bridge between "A" and "C" Buildings on ... March 15, 1947, was marked by an "impressive ceremony" ... A group of about forty senior officers and officials was assembled. To open the bridge I had to cut a red ribbon, in this case a long stretch of government red tape. I was given a pair of army issue wire-cutters. I assured them that we had not been able to find the red tape in National Defence but had to go to another government department for it...[92]

An early reform on the civilian side of defence administration was the abolition of deputy ministers for the three services and their replacement by a single deputy minister of national defence, together with associate deputy ministers (by law not exceeding three) whose duties were assigned functionally rather than on service lines. This step required an amendment of the Department of National Defence Act, and a resolution for this purpose was introduced by Claxton on 12 February 1947. It was designed, he told the House of Commons, 'to give further effect to the policy of the government to coordinate and consolidate the department and services,'[93] and for that reason

no service has any deputy or associate deputy particularly associated with that service. The deputy and associate deputies are appointed by the government, and their duties are given to them in accordance with their functions with regard to the Department and all three services, and not having regard to any particular service. One associate deputy will deal with finance and supply, and another will deal with personnel and pay.[94]

At the present time there is no intention of appointing a third, but in the course of developing the work of the Department we may find that there is a natural division to which effect should be given and that we should have one associate deputy minister in charge of finance and administration, a second in charge of supply, equipment, engineering, and so on ... and a third in charge of personnel and pay ... However, we believe we have divided the work in a sensible way so that we can get along with two associate deputies. They are carrying on well, and we believe they will be able to carry on.[95]

The administrative structure of the Department of National Defence was completed to Claxton's satisfaction when he acquired a deputy minister in whom he had the utmost confidence. In 1948 C.M. Drury became such an acquisition, replacing W.G. Mills, who had been deputy minister since 1942. In Drury's charge, the office of deputy minister assumed a central place in the running of the Department and in the making of defence policy. 'Without changes in the constitutional or legal position,' Claxton recorded, 'he soon established his relationship with the Chiefs of Staff on a sound working basis. He attended meetings of the Chiefs of Staff and took an active part in them. In my absence he was the Chairman of the Defence Council.'[96]

Under Brooke Claxton's guidance, the Chiefs of Staff Committee regained its former importance in the machinery of government. It now met regularly every Tuesday morning, more frequently if required. Its meetings were normally held in a conference room adjoining the office of the Chief of the General Staff in 'A' Building, sometimes in an ante-room beside the office of the Minister; occasionally, when the pressure of work mounted and there was unfinished business to take care of, the Chiefs would repair to Claxton's home on Sunday morning and work to the end of their agenda. The Chiefs of Staff Committee was serviced by a small secretariat provided by the Privy Council office, whose members prepared agenda, helped with planning, circulated papers, and steered intelligence the Chiefs' way. The Committee was strongly reinforced from the civilian sector of the public service. The chairman of the Defence Research Board attended as a full member; the Deputy Minister of National Defence attended as a regular though unofficial participant. In addition, the Under Secretary of State for External Affairs, the Deputy Minister of Finance, and the Secretary of the Cabinet would often be present at its meetings. When they were, its civilian members outnumbered its military. That was how Claxton had planned it, and that was how he liked it. 'The civilian members,' he wrote afterwards, 'brought to the meetings their own wide experience of public affairs. A direct and friendly relationship was built up between the most important civilians in the government service and the service heads, forming a basis for understanding and co-operation. We had less in-service *versus* civilian bickering and intrigue than in most countries.'[97]

On 6 November 1946, Mackenzie King recorded in his diary that he was thinking of pulling 'the three departments together into one with a single Chief of Staff and three deputies. I do not see any way more effective to bring about consolidation.'[98] That reform would only come about many years later.* Meanwhile, however, consideration was given to appointing some senior official to whom the Minister of National Defence might turn for authoritative advice in the event that the Chiefs of Staff Committee could not agree. Such an appointment formed one of the principal recommendations of an outside report on the organization of the Department in December 1948.† 'Obviously,' the authors of the report wrote with reference to the proposed appointment,

> this is a most difficult position to define and to fill. The incumbent, if he is to be successful, must have considerable tact, be impartial, and have a broad knowledge and understanding of the respective roles of the three Services. If he is to gain the confidence of each of the three Services, he should either have retired from his own Service prior to accepting the position in question or it should be understood that this position would be his last appointment. Very definitely he should not be eligible at a later date for appointment to the post of Chief of Staff of his own Service or for any other position in such Service.

* The first Chief of the Defence Staff, Air Vice-Marshal Frank Miller, was appointed in July 1964.

† The report had been commissioned by Brooke Claxton from J.D. Woods & Gordon, Ltd., a prominent Toronto firm of management consultants. 'Last night,' Claxton wrote on 23 December 1948 to Walter Gordon, the firm's senior partner and the report's principal author, 'I was able to go through the report again ... It is a very thorough and competent job.' Claxton Papers.

The report canvassed a number of possible positions which such an officer might hold within the policy community. He could be a deputy minister 'with a broad military background and experience'; he could be a senior officer who would act as secretary of the Defence Committee of the Cabinet, with *ex officio* membership of the Chiefs of Staff Committee; he could be designated 'Staff Officer,' 'Military Adviser,' or 'Military Consultant' to the Minister of National Defence; or he could be 'an independent Chairman of the Chiefs of Staff Committee ... similar to the position which Admiral Leahy holds in the United States.' The report did not venture to state a preference among these various alternatives. 'We believe,' its authors observed, 'that the exact form in which the Minister should receive independent military advice can best be worked out by him in consultation with the three Chiefs of Staff, if and when the need for such independent advice has been agreed upon by all concerned. The rank, age and experience of the men who would be acceptable to the Minister and to the three Services and who would be available for the position would also have considerable bearing upon the exact nature of the appointment.'[99]

In the event the Government, on Claxton's recommendation, opted for the post of Chairman, Chiefs of Staff Committee. Three years passed before it did; the delay was due to the difficulty of finding the right man for the job, not to doubts about the need for the job. None of the retired Chiefs of Staff was considered as a candidate. Of the three Chiefs then in harness, General Foulkes was thought to be eminently suitable: but, in the event of his elevation to the chairmanship there was no one thought suitable to take his place as Chief of the General Staff. The appointment was not made until General Simonds, then undergoing seasoning at the National Defence College, was deemed ready to take over from Foulkes as CGS. This came about on 1 February 1951.

Credible testimony to the work of a Chairman of the Chiefs of Staff Committee comes mainly from the Chiefs who serve under his chairmanship. Testimony to Foulkes's leadership is conflicting. Air Marshal W.A. Curtis, who experienced it from 1951 to 1953, told the House of Commons Special Committee on Defence that he 'always found the Chairman very fair.'[100] But Lt-General Guy Simonds, who experienced it from 1951 to 1956, told the readers of *Maclean's Magazine* that the Chairman's role had been 'to protect the government against the receipt of unpalatable advice.'[101]

Creation of the chairmanship was not intended to deny to the Chiefs of Staff the right of individual access to the Minister of National Defence. Nor did it do so. The first Chief of the Air Staff to serve under the new management testified that it was his practice to have a private consultation with the Minister 'certainly every other week. Sometimes it was weekly, and sometimes two or three times a week.' The other Chiefs sought out their Minister no less frequently. 'Our meetings would usually be of ten to fifteen minutes time in length ... except occasionally when something was important.'[102]

The Minister viewed these audiences not as a tiresome interruption of vital public business but as an essential stage in the process by which military policy was made. 'Any new development,' Brooke Claxton wrote later,

> any substantial change or any new addition to the programme on which we had settled, or a proposed major change in organization, would usually be brought about following a discussion of this between the Chief of Staff concerned and myself. After several talks he would send in a paper to me, usually a memorandum two or three pages long, with attached appendices giving tables of estimated changes of organization required, differences in expense, estimates of manpower involved, etc. At various stages the Deputy Minister would be brought in, and, after his appointment as Associate Minister, Ralph Campney. If other departments were involved we would discuss the plan with them. Frequently there would be one or more talks with the Chief at which we would agree on further modifications suggested by us. Then a revised paper might be put in on which I would simply write "concur" or "agree" and my initials. If I thought it desirable or necessary a paper would be prepared for my signature for consideration by the Cabinet Defence Committee and if the Prime Minister, the Defence Committee or I thought it desirable, the whole Cabinet. If necessary this procedure could be telescoped so that everything necessary could be got through in a day or even minutes. Unless the urgency for action demanded it, undue haste was unwise. The matters we had to deal with in the post-war period were usually new, highly complicated, of far-reaching consequence, and enormously expensive. Unless there was real need for urgency, it was a mistake for the Chiefs to try to rush me and it was still more of a mistake for me to rush the Cabinet...
>
> From time to time a Chief of Staff would send in to me a paper dealing with some knotty problem on which he wanted to put his views forward for approval or action. It was, of course, their duty to make "appreciations" but in a very few cases they would be writing "for the record" rather than for my concurrence or other action. How I reacted to this would depend on the subject and tone. If it was only fair that the Chief should put himself on record in this way and if it was done reasonably, then I would simply write on the paper "Noted" and it would go into the files. If it was similarly a proper course for the Chief to take but with which I disagreed, I would tell him so and probably write nothing on the paper. On only two occasions I found the memoranda quite improper. At once I sent for the Chief, pointed this out, which led him to withdraw it. People who were working for me could not use my office to build up for themselves a soft cushion on which to land.
>
> Usually, however, my relations with the senior officers were excellent and we had no trouble whatever ... In over nine years there were only two cases when

a Chief and I continued to differ over very senior appointments. One reason why a person should not stay too long a Minister of National Defence is that he may have been wrong about any of these cases. It is a good thing to have someone in to take a fresh look...[103]

'My job as the first post-war Minister of National Defence,' Brooke Claxton wrote in retrospect of his assignment, 'was to bring together and make into a team three mutually resistant and highly competitive services staffed by bands of aggressive young men who had little or no experience of peacetime responsibility but who had won the war.'[104] A prime prerequisite for teamwork, it appeared to him, was the elimination of that costly and cumbersome administrative apparatus by which each service sought to insulate itself from its rivals and to aggrandize rather than harmonize its place in the overall scheme.

When Claxton came on the job in December 1946, he was shocked to discover the extent to which unnecessary duplication and overlapping subsisted within the military establishment. 'My original impulse,' he confessed, 'was to go far and fast in the direction of unification.'[105] It proved easier to yield to this impulse than to gratify it. The Minister's master idea was that each service should have to carry out for itself only those functions essential and peculiar to the effective performance of its role in a theatre of war. All other functions should be performed either by civilians on behalf of all three services, or by one of the services on behalf of the other two. Where the latter procedure was employed, the service which was the largest user of personnel and equipment required for carrying out the function in question should do the job for the other two. 'This was easy to say,' Claxton conceded, 'but hard to apply.'

He first applied it close to home. Early in 1947 he discovered a perfect example of wasteful duplication in the services' motor vehicle transport system in Ottawa. Each service ran its own garage, with its own officers, mechanics, messes, telephone exchanges, equipment, spare parts, and automobiles – of which there were no fewer than fifty-one 'used for carrying officers around, frequently on purely social occasions.' Claxton 'clamped down on this and gave instructions that, as the largest user, the Army would run the only service garage in town ... We cut the number of staff cars down to sixteen, where it stayed for quite a while.' Encouraged by this success on a small scale, Claxton attempted to apply it on a larger. He ordered that the Army, as prime user of vehicular transport, should assume responsibility for major repairs of vehicles for all three services right across Canada. It sounded fine in theory. 'We tried it for a year and a half,' the Minister reported to the House of Commons in May 1951, 'and it was found that it did not work.' One of the practical problems encountered, he related, was that the Air Force blamed the Army for its failure to keep aircraft in operation throughout the winter.

The Air Force has to keep its runways open the year round. They have to contend with very heavy snowfall in many parts of the country, and they have very good heavy equipment for this purpose. When that equipment had to be maintained and supplied by the Army, the Air Force would sometimes say they were not given a sufficiently high priority...[106]

Because of this problem, and others like it, Claxton modified his earlier decision. The principle of the prime user would be applied only where experience showed it to be workable, not as a matter of headquarters doctrine. So far as motor vehicle maintenance was concerned, Claxton explained, this meant that in some cases, as at Esquimalt and Halifax, the Navy did the servicing for the other two services; in others, as Saint John, Lachine, Ottawa, Kingston, and several other centres, the Army did it; and at Calgary and Trenton the Air Force did it. The new rationale, born of unsatisfactory experience with the old, was that 'each service must have the responsibility for doing, and therefore must carry out, every part of a job which was vital to the performance and safety of its operations.' Under this dispensation, responsibility for the maintenance of snow removal equipment was returned to the RCAF.

Of all the problems of service integration considered by the Combined Services Functions Committee – which was the committee created to unify and co-ordinate different branches of the services where it seemed expedient to do so, and whose title Claxton described as 'a symptomatic mouthful' – none proved more intractable than what to do about the medical services. In 1947, when the problem was first examined, each service had its own medical corps. The Deputy Minister of National Health and Welfare, Brock Chisholm, strongly recommended that these be combined into a single medical service for all three services. In this he was supported by senior officers of the RCAF. But the Navy were strongly opposed. It carried its opposition into the Combined Services Functions Committee, and from there into the Chiefs of Staff Committee. A special committee of medical officers could not agree upon a solution. Neither could a special committee of outside experts. Reluctantly Claxton came to the conclusion that medical unification was not yet a possibility. He justified his decision to Parliament in the following terms:

Such a combination would have some desirable features, perhaps, but on the other hand there would be a loss of direct association with the traditions and work of each particular service. We would soon have a joint medical service having specialists for the Army, specialists for the Navy, and specialists for the Air Force. The advantages of unification, therefore, would not be nearly as great as might be expected. Further, there would be administrative difficulties in deciding to which officer this neutral medical service would be responsible...

'No country in the world,' Claxton concluded somewhat limply, 'has the medical services combined into one.'*

It did not always come about, either, that elimination of separate service branches brought with it the desired elimination of personnel. 'All we did in the chaplain service,' General Foulkes recalled ruefully from his experience with integration, 'was to create two new brigadiers.'[107]

## ESPRIT AND MORALE

*Esprit* and morale may be hard to measure – especially the *esprit* and morale of a volunteer military establishment just beginning to be formed. Perhaps the fairest way of measuring them is by the number and quality of the men and women who come forward to fill its ranks.

During the first few months of peace it was by no means certain that by any such test *esprit* and morale of the nascent Canadian military establishment were all they should have been. 'The great problem of this Government,' declared a member of the official Opposition during debate on the defence estimates in October 1945, 'is not to decide on the particular size of the forces. The great problem of the Government is to maintain interest in these services at a time when they are necessary and at a time when everybody is trying to get out of the services.'[108] That was no exaggeration. The Government could hardly hope to attract 55,000 qualified officers and men – the authorized strength of the three post-war services – without being able to state to prospective recruits what were the terms and conditions of service. Yet it could not state the terms and conditions of service until it had settled upon the services' post-war roles and the nature of Canada's post-war defence policies. And the Government (as has been shown) considered it altogether too soon to come to any final decisions about such roles or policies.

On 16 October 1945, the Minister of National Defence revealed that a special committee had been created to review the rates of pay and pensions, both to bring them into line with post-war civilian rates and to provide equal rates among the services. The terms and conditions of duty

* Canada, *H.C. Debates*, 1951, III, 2878. It should be noted that this is not necessarily an argument against a combined branch: it could well be an argument in its favour. See, on this point, James Eayrs, 'Canada Pioneers the Single Service,' *The Round Table*, no 234, April 1969, 156–7.

in the permanent, as distinct from the interim, forces were to be announced no later than 31 March 1946. Meanwhile the rates of remuneration would be those in force for members of the three services on active duty at the end of the Second World War. New terms and conditions would come into effect on 30 September 1947, the date when the permanent forces would also come into being. 'The pay structure,' Douglas Abbott promised, 'will provide remuneration comparable to civil employment, and the pay will be good pay. We have no intention of trying to set up a cheap permanent force.' If, on learning of the terms and conditions of permanent service, a member of the interim force did not wish to serve out the remainder of his term, he did not have to do so. Conversely, if he wished to stay on and join the permanent forces on 30 September 1947, he would be allowed to do so – 'subject of course to continued good conduct, satisfactory medical category, and military efficiency of the individual.'[109]

The Government did not anticipate any difficulty in securing recruits of the desired number and quality. The desired number became that much more easy to attain when, on 16 January 1946, its decision was announced to cut back the strength of the three services to 75 per cent of their authorized limit. A month later Brooke Claxton reported to the House of Commons that the Navy and Air Force had already recruited their new reduced quotas and that, for this reason, no further enlistment in these services would be permitted for the time being unless the candidates possessed exceptional qualifications, or were needed to meet a particular deficiency in a particular branch of the services. Enlistment in the Army had been less spectacular: still, 'recruits are coming in without any campaign, at a rate which would indicate that we are very likely to achieve the seventy five per cent during the course of the coming year.' The new rates of pay, Claxton affirmed, 'compare most favourably with rates of pay in civilian occupations,' and 'food, clothing and equipment [are] as good as we can find ... We do not aim to have anything second rate about the armed forces of Canada.' Nor, he insisted, was there anything second rate about them. 'The officers and men who are joining the armed forces are Canadians with good qualifications. They are splendid Canadians.'[110]

By the summer of 1947, as the civilian economy began to pick up steam, the armed forces were beginning to find it difficult to obtain the personnel they needed. 'We would like to see more men coming in as tradesmen,' Brooke Claxton admitted in the House of Commons on 9 July, and announced that, beginning that autumn, the Government would embark upon its first post-war recruiting campaign.[111]

Brooke Claxton was the first Minister of National Defence to take a direct and personal interest in peacetime recruitment for the armed forces.

He instructed his Chiefs of Staff to do likewise. Each service had a Director of Recruiting, and the three Directors formed the Joint Service Recruiting Committee, whose work was supplemented by a Joint Service Advertising Committee. 'I felt so keenly about the need for watching recruiting and getting results,' Claxton wrote later,

that I was in effect the head of the recruiting effort ... We used three advertising agencies and they worked closely with me. ... Every appeal must have something patriotic, something adventurous, something to build up the prestige of the services; it must have all that and then, too, it must appeal to the pocketbook ... We had surveys made to see why men joined and why they stayed and why they left. We had every kind of test made of the efficiency of various types of advertisement. We took into account the state of national and international feeling at the time of each appeal as we had found that this had a definite relationship to recruiting just as had the national and local employment situation and the season of the year ... I felt it necessary to examine and pass on every single advertisement and every bit of copy issued. This was not just a perfunctory job to make sure there were no mistakes. I took a constructive interest and frequently made substantial changes or even redrafted an entire advertisement or copy...[112]

On 24 June 1948, Claxton reported to the House of Commons on the results of his first campaign. 7029 officers and men had enlisted in the three services during the year ending 31 March. These recruits brought the Navy up to 89 per cent of its authorized strength, the Air Force to 87 per cent, and the Army to 82 per cent. These results Claxton thought very satisfactory: the intake in that one year, he pointed out, was roughly the equivalent of the total strength of the permanent armed forces of Canada, on the average, between 1930 and 1939. At the same time there was still room for improvement: 'We need numbers of good men,' he admitted, 'especially men who were too young to see service in the last war.' Not letting the opportunity pass, he made a brief recruiting speech then and there:

Every fit young Canadian should recognize his duty to serve his country. I know of no better life and I know of no better opportunity. Members, veterans and others should encourage young Canadians to serve in either the full-time active forces or the part-time reserves.[113]

One of Brooke Claxton's missions was to enhance the image of the peacetime profession of arms in the public mind. No better way existed, he thought, of elevating the mood and raising the morale of Canada's postwar military establishment. He stressed this theme in all armed forces advertising, which he

designed to build up the prestige and self-respect of the men in the armed forces ... What we had to do was to create in the minds of civilians the idea that a career in the armed forces was a good thing to have; the idea that the armed forces were not only responsible and well conducted people but that they were "citizens" as well. I coined the phrase for some of the advertisements "Citizens Plus" – that is, citizens who, in addition to their duties and responsibilities as such, were dedicated to the service and defence of their country...[114]

He stressed it too in Parliament. 'During this last year,' he told the House of Commons on 24 June 1948,

it was my privilege to visit most of the establishments of the Navy, Army and Air Force across Canada. There I met not only officers and men, but also members of the civilian community. With all of them I discussed the relationship of the forces to the community. I had one conviction. The closer the civilian comes to the armed forces, the more inclined he is to like them and to give them his approval and support ... On that account we have encouraged visits, arranged for open-house occasions, such as visits to ships and camps, and Air Force Day, and done everything possible to bring the services and civilians closer together...[115]

This policy seems to have worked. In November 1945, an Opposition defence critic had warned Claxton's predecessor that his most difficult job would be 'to build up the support of the Canadian people' for their armed forces in peacetime. 'I do not believe,' he stated, 'that our people are in the frame of mind now to support [them]. It has never been done in Canada, it is something entirely new. It will require very strong leadership if these plans are to be carried out.'[116] There was strong leadership, and they were carried out. 'Our sailors, soldiers and airmen,' remarked the Minister of National Defence on 31 August 1950, 'have attained and earned the respect of the community.'[117] But by then they were no longer members of a peacetime military establishment.

To write of esprit and morale of the post-war armed forces is misleading, for spirits varied considerably from one force to another.

Spirits were highest in the Air Force, and rose with the passing of the years. Since 1946, the RCAF, capitalizing upon (but not capitulating to) doctrines of air power sedulously propagated in the United States,* had been able consistently to attract the largest share of recruits. Since 1947, it had been able to secure the largest share of budgets. The Air Force's

* The RCAF maintained a comradely relationship with the USAF but retained throughout a separate identity of outlook. In particular its members, partly as a result of study at the National Defence College, the Air Force College and the Air Force School, rejected the simplistic SAC approach to international problems. One RCAF officer remarked of his USAF counterparts: 'They want to use a big nuke on the big problems and a little nuke on the little problems'; this was said with both distaste and incredulity, and probably typified the Air Force attitude.

share, Brooke Claxton explained in August 1950, was 'spectacular ... because aircraft cost so much money.'[118] The F-86s were working out at a comparatively modest $250,000 each. But the CF-100 was priced at $750,000, partly as a result of trouble with its Hughes electronic system causing scores of finished aircraft to fail their entrance examination. Equipping the RCAF with these two machines – 'a team,' Claxton described them, 'which we believe will not be matched in any other country in the world'[119] – meant that of the five billion dollars to be spent on defence over the next three years, the Air Force would receive as much as did the Army and Navy combined; by 1953 the RCAF was allotted about 41 per cent of the total defence appropriation, a sum amounting to $450 millions. As with money, so with men. In February 1951, Brooke Claxton predicted that the Air Force, then numbering 22,000 officers and men, would surpass the strength of the Army, then numbering 35,000; by 1955, it had reached an overall strength of 50,330, compared with the Army's strength of about 45,000.

For a force for which the sky was the environment, rather than the limit, nothing seemed impossible. In 1952 a group of experts drawn from the RCAF, the Defence Research Board, and the National Aeronautical Establishment drew up plans for a new all-Canadian fighter interceptor, designed to meet the threat posed by the expected development of a Soviet intercontinental bomber comparable to the B-52. The cancellation of this project seven years later, after the aircraft had reached the prototype stage of development and more than a billion dollars had been spent on it, dealt to the prestige and morale of the Air Force a blow from which it never fully recovered. Pride led to *hubris, hubris* to the CF-105.

The Army had its afflictions, too; but *hubris* was not among them. The ground force equivalent of the ill-fated Arrow was the Bobcat, an amphibious armoured personnel carrier of Canadian design and intended Canadian manufacture; the project had been initiated in January 1954, and was abandoned ten years later because of mechanical difficulties and soaring unit costs. $25 millions had been wasted on the Army's weapon, but that of the Air Force had wasted 40 times as much. That is a fair measure of the discrepancy between them. 'There seems to be some thought,' Brooke Claxton remarked on 31 August 1950, 'that the Army is getting the thin end of the stick with regard to equipment.' He did not deny that it was so. 'The Army,' he declared, 'is in a special position. We have in mobilization stores or on issue a large part of the equipment required, if we had to get into a war, for the first year of that war.' He promised the Army better days to come. 'We shall be adding steadily to anti-aircraft and anti-tank weapons ... We shall also be acquiring considerable quantities of ammunition and motor vehicles.'[120] But these were not there when needed. 'Many shortages of training elements are beginning to be felt,' an officer of a regiment bound for service in Korea wrote in September 1952.

There is little concertina and barbed wire, practically no ammunition for the 60 mm and 81 mm Mortars, no stripless belt for M.M.G., no ammunition for the 3.5 rocket launcher, no mines of any sort, not enough vehicles, no mobile or portable flame thrower equipment, no air photographs, no recoilless rifles, and an over-all restriction on the use of live ammunition ... Many of these shortages have existed for nearly two years...[121]

If *esprit de corps* was highest in the Air Force, it was lowest in the Navy. Discontent within the senior Service had come to light even before the end of the war, when ratings had rioted in Halifax on V-E Day. The first few months of peace brought little to alleviate the grievances of those remaining in the interim force. Some of these were mentioned in the House of Commons. They concerned the lower rates of pay relative to those of the other services; the hardships of serving at sea in the cramped quarters of frigates and corvettes; above all, the slavish conformity to the traditions of the Royal Navy and its outdated code of discipline. 'I think we have reached the time,' declared one Member of Parliament on 25 October 1945, 'when we must realize that Nelson is dead.'[122] 'I have had conversations with many young men out of the Navy,' reported another,

and with some still in it, and so far as the ratings are concerned I gained the definite impression that the service was not very popular with them, chiefly because they were subjected to a large number of petty annoyances ... One example is ... the method adopted when men go on shore leave. Whether a man is in a ship or in barracks ... when he has an evening off he has to wait for the so-called 'boat' [liberty ship] before he can go, and if he misses one mythical boat he has to wait for the next one, which may be an hour...[123]

'If a man appears with a button undone,' testified a third, 'or his shoes not shined, the captain or any of the officers can say, "You will have ten days in the brig." It is too much; it is too severe...'[124] And a fourth, the redoubtable Jean François Pouliot:

I spent a yuletide at a dockyard, and I saw the number of servants the commanding officer had at his disposal ... One was cleaning silverware; another was cleaning china; another was cleaning porcelain; one had the key to the wine cellar; another was serving wine; another was serving water; and another was serving bread and butter. They were like the sands of the sea and the stars of the sky ... Well, even if it is done that way in England, why should we follow that example here in Canada? It is time to stop those practices...

Is there anything more foolish than that they should wear a black tie to mourn the death of Lord Nelson? Not only that: they wear the most absurd trousers, with seven creases to indicate the seven seas...[125]

The Minister of National Defence for Naval Services, to whom these observations were addressed, promised to bring to the attention of the Naval Staff the fact that Nelson was dead. No doubt Douglas Abbott did as he promised. No doubt, either, that the Naval Staff paid no attention. For among the Naval Staff Nelson (or the Nelson touch) was very much alive. 'The senior officers of the Navy,' Brooke Claxton wrote of them, 'were away out of line not only with Canadian sentiment but ... with the feelings of the junior officers, petty officers and ratings of our new Navy.'[126]

Not all the brass was blind to these shortcomings. 'It is recommended that more than old-school tie thought be given to post-war relations with the RN,' a planner at Naval Headquarters urged in April 1944. 'There is little doubt that had we not blindly followed the lead of the RN our equipment and training along many lines would have been much further advanced.'[127] So would have been the life style of the lower deck. The captain of one ship, puzzled at the incidence of *accidie* among the men, asked his chaplain and his surgeon what should be done. Their recommendations, forthcoming during the summer of 1947, were homely and specific. 'There ought to be more bulk rations and more variety.' 'Food should be served cafeteria style so that it is picked up hot.' 'There should be pay increases; factories give them.' They noted that 'restlessness was not directed against officers but conditions,' and noted too that 'many lads in ships were from war homes and had never been disciplined – absent fathers and broken homes.' The captain who had requested this report found it 'exceedingly valuable.' The senior officer on the Halifax station to whose attention it was drawn 'was struck forcibly with the ... colossal ignorance of the service of both of the officers' who had prepared it.[128]

Such hide-bound traditionalism and Captain Bligh authoritarianism might have been overlooked had the new Navy performed in response to them at the highest standards of operational efficiency. But the new Navy was nowhere near such standards. From bridge to desk to syndicate stretched a sorry tale of incompetence:

Groundings – *Middlesex*, 1946; *Port Arthur*, *Magnificent*, June, 1949.

Collision between (a) *Mic Mac* and *Yarmouth County*, July 1947; (b) *Portage* and *Dundalk*, April 1949.

*X*., *Y*., and *Z*. admittedly not competent.

*A*. incapable of properly performing his duties afloat; *B*. and *C*. quite incompetent to do the work of their jobs at Washington and London.

Failure to make University Naval Training Division work.

Failure of RCN Warrant Officers in UK course.

Officers not qualified by general education for staff and planning duties.

Un-Canadian attitude illustrated ... by taking the Maple Leaf off funnels.

Attitude of non-cooperation in inter-service committees.

High accident rate in naval flying – aircraft failures, mid-air collisions.

Failure of Executive Officers at RN Staff Course.*

The general inefficiency recorded in this dispiriting document might have been corrected internally, and without public knowledge or furore. What made this course impossible were a series of events on board three of His Majesty's Canadian Ships for which no parallel could be found since Royal Navy ratings had mutinied at Invergordon eighteen years before. Seamen on board HMCS *Magnificent*, *Athabaskan*, and *Crescent* refused to obey orders.† A Royal Commission was appointed to discover the reasons why.

The commission of inquiry was composed of two civilians – Leonard W. Brockington, an adviser to and former speechwriter for the Prime Minister, and L.C. Audette, a senior public servant who had served during the war as a lieutenant with the RCNVR – and Rear Admiral Rollo Mainguy, then Vice-Chief, later (in 1951) Chief of Naval Staff, who was its chairman. Its Report almost totally exonerated the ratings; it laid the blame largely at the feet of those responsible for the formulation and execution of naval policy. Among the general causes of the breakdown of discipline in Canadian ships at sea it noted the 'absence of Canadian traditions' in the Navy. 'An opinion,' the Commissioners reported,

> is widely held amongst many ratings and some officers that the "Nelson tradition" is overdone, and that there is still too great an attempt to make the Canadian Navy a pallid imitation and reflection of the British Navy. This is in no sense a criticism of the magnificent traditions of the Royal Navy, but is a natural outcome of the growth of a healthy Canadian national consciousness.[129]

One of the recommendations of the Report was 'that the words "Canada" or "Royal Canadian Navy" be used as shoulder flashes on the uniforms of all ranks.' It was noted that, some months after the publication of the

* Claxton Papers (no date). *A.*, *B.*, *C.*, *X.*, *Y.*, and *Z.* were all in the rank of commander or above.

† The 'incidents,' as the Royal Commission referred to them, occurred within 48 hours of each other, were remarkably similar in nature, but were too widely separated geographically for anything in the nature of a conspiracy to have been suspected. In no case was insubordination accompanied by violence, nor did the incident last longer than a few hours. Full details are given in the Report of the Royal Commission. See *Report on Certain 'Incidents' which Occurred on Board H.M.C. Ships* Athabaskan, Crescent *and* Magnificent, *and on other Matters concerning the Royal Canadian Navy* (Ottawa, October 1949), 9–22.

Report, 'the Flag Officer Atlantic Coast ... had not yet mounted the ... "Canada badges" on his own uniforms. The FOAC at that point was Admiral Mainguy.'[130] It would take more than a commission of inquiry to exorcize the Nelson spirit.

Brooke Claxton, at whose instigation the Commission had been created, was satisfied with its Report. 'The whole tone,' he wrote of it afterwards, 'strengthened my hand regarding modernization of the treatment of personnel and the further Canadianization of the Navy.'[131] Yet one of its observations he could only have read with concern. 'The organization of advertised recruiting,' the Report noted reproachfully, 'had been left almost entirely to professional advertisers and specialists in commercial radio, who have known nothing of the Navy, however skilled they may be in the sale of consumers' goods to a coy and jaded public.'* Claxton, who took pride in his skill as a copywriter and (as previously shown) personally scrutinized all advertising for recruitment, must have winced at that rebuke.

Esprit and morale of one community within the post-war armed forces of Canada were worse than all the rest. The community was composed of those soldiers, sailors, and airmen whose mother tongue was French.

The situation of French-speaking Canadians in the armed forces varied considerably from one service to another. It was least complicated – and arguably least unsatisfactory – in the Royal Canadian Air Force.

The RCAF did not worry unduly about bilingualism within its ranks; it is no great exaggeration to say that it did not worry at all.

During the Great War, as many as 23,000 Canadians are known to have served with the Royal Flying Corps, the Royal Naval Air Service and, after its formation in April 1918, the Royal Air Force. No record exists of the number of French-speaking Canadians among them, but it is quite possible that it did not exceed a few hundred or even a few score. It had nothing to do with acrophobia, everything to do with the formidable obstacles in the way of French-speaking enlistment. To begin with, the prospective recruit had to make his way to Ontario for training at the Curtis flying school near Toronto (early in the war the RFC and RNAS accepted only the holders of a civil pilot's licence) or, later on, to one of the RAF training bases also in Ontario. It goes without saying that English

* *Report on Certain 'Incidents'* ..., 34–5. The official historian of the RCN chaplaincy service writes of 'ratings who had been blarneyed into enlisting by the recruiting prepared by commercial advertising firms [which] pitched their propaganda to the commercial market – comfort, security, benefits – appealing to self-interest and indulgence rather than to citizenship and manliness.' Waldo E.L. Smith, *The Navy Chaplain and his Parish* (Ottawa 1967), 211.

was the language of instruction at all these establishments. Once trained as a pilot, the fledgling airman had no national air force in which to serve, but had to enlist in an imperial force having (beyond special rates of pay) no concern for Canadian, let alone French-Canadian, interests and susceptibilities. There was, to be sure, one other option open. A French-speaking Canadian might choose to serve in the air force of his mother country under orders given in his mother tongue. Jean-Marie Landry was one who made that choice, paying his passage to the Blériot flying school in France and serving with the French air force. But he may well have been the only one.[132]

A Canadian Air Force was formed in 1920 and re-named the Royal Canadian Air Force on 1 April 1924. The permanent force on that date consisted of 66 officers and 307 airmen; two of the former and ten of the latter may be presumed (on account of their French names) to have been French-speaking. By 1930, out of 89 officers, three were French-speaking. It is not hard to account for the discrepancy. All pilot training took place at Camp Borden, Ontario; training was exclusively in the English language; no provision was made for instructing French-speaking recruits in English, let alone English-speaking recruits in French; while 'post-graduate' or specialist training was given either at the Royal Military College at Kingston, Ontario, or at the RAF Staff College at Andover, England. So things remained until the outbreak of the Second World War.

That war brought no radical change in the situation of the French-speaking Canadian airman. He might now enlist at one of three recruiting offices opened in Montreal, Three Rivers, and Quebec City. But once on active service he was still required to take all his training in English at stations for the most part located outside his native province. His chances of serving in a French-speaking operational environment were not great: of 48 RCAF squadrons overseas and 37 in Canada, only one had what could be described as a distinctively French-Canadian atmosphere. This was the 425 Alouette Squadron formed on 25 June 1942 and based in England as part of the RAF's No 4 Group. The unit was composed primarily of French-speaking Canadians; but it contained many members who were not French-speaking, its operations were conducted in English, and it is thus not comparable with the genuinely French-speaking units which were part of the wartime Canadian army. The strength of the RCAF overseas in 1944 was 11,403 officers and 32,904 airmen; of these, 471 officers and 3623 airmen were French-speaking. In 1944, for the first time, English-language training was provided for French-speaking personnel arriving overseas with what their Anglophone commanders considered to be an inadequate knowledge of the RCAF's *lingua franca*.[133]

The post-war Air Force remained the most determinedly unilingual of the three services and the most anglicized – later, as its liaison with the United States Air Force grew steadily more intimate, the most anglo-americanized. English continued to be its operational language. All personnel had to be proficient in it, even to write their professional examinations in it. Only a minuscule number of French-speaking Canadians rose in the rank structure – in 1951, ten held the rank of wing commander or higher, as against 390 English-speaking officers – and none at all rose to the top. The RCAF was run by Anglo-Canadians largely as if Canada were an Anglo-Canadian nation. It was only in 1950, on the express instructions of the Minister of National Defence, Brooke Claxton, that its communications to the Government of Quebec, French-speaking municipal authorities, and French-speaking individuals began to be written in the French language. In 1951, on orders from the Defence Council, its regulations and orders were published in both of Canada's national languages. That represented the limit to which French was formally employed.

In such a service, avowedly unilingual, frankly unicultural, the French-speaking Canadian might pursue a useful career and lead a happy life: but only by allowing himself to become completely assimilated to a life-style other than, if not alien to, his own. Most French-speaking members of the RCAF made the adjustment successfully, with neither recrimination nor regret. The Air Force became, in effect, an apparatus wherein French-speaking Canadians were reprocessed as 'anglophones.'

A plausible rationale for such a policy could be, and was, produced. The primary mission of the RCAF – deterring attack upon North America – depended upon split-second co-ordination with the USAF. Clarity in command, speed in execution, were all-important components of the strategy. To have elevated French to the status of an operational language might conceivably have led to misunderstanding and delay hideous in their consequences. Stranger things have happened in the history of war, much of which is war by accident.

Yet which of the evils is the greater? A bilingual and bicultural air force which microscopically impairs the imposing strength of the Great Deterrent? Or a unilingual and unicultural air force which weakens national unity, perhaps (in conjunction with many other grievances) to the point where a disaffected Quebec decides to secede from Canada? Only recently have such questions been raised and their implications examined. The interrogation may have come too late.*

* See *Report of the Royal Commission on Bilingualism and Biculturalism*: Book III, *The Work World* (Ottawa 1969), c. XI, 'Canadian Forces,' and the following

Like the Air Force, the Navy had always been an English-speaking service. But with less good reason for its being so. The RCAF might, and did, plead as an extenuating circumstance the need for unilingualism to ensure command and control. The Navy had no such excuse. There was no insuperable obstacle from an operational standpoint to sending to sea ships in which officers and men used French to carry out their duties. The obstacle was not efficiency, it was tradition.

To an extent far greater than in the other two services, the Royal Canadian Navy was patterned upon its sister service in the United Kingdom. It had been founded in the expectation that in times of grave imperial emergency it would take its place as a component of the grand imperial fleet. (That may not have been Laurier's expectation but it was certainly the Admiralty's.) For that purpose the Royal Navy had contributed ships, officers, personnel. With them came uniforms, ranks, regulations, and – above all – a distinctive cultural milieu. 'The professional idiom and to a lesser extent the colloquialisms,' writes the Canadian Navy's official historian, 'were the same, while the customs and etiquette of the Royal Navy as well as its incomparably rich traditions, were accepted by the younger service.'[134] In consequence, a French-speaking Canadian, be he officer or rating, might make his way in the navy of his nation only by assuming the protective coloration of an environment not just anglophone but anglophile.

Such an environment proved in the end too alien even for English-speaking Canadians; for Canadians who spoke French it was inhospitable in the extreme. 'Leave them alone,' Stephen Leacock said of the more than 400,000 Canadians of Ukrainian origin, 'and pretty soon they will think they won the Battle of Trafalgar.' French-speaking Canadians were under no such delusion. Nelson was not a French-speaking admiral; in his victories they could find little inspiration, in his touch no comfort.

The wartime Navy's concessions to bilingualism and biculturalism were few and far between. A high failure rate among French-speaking recruits led in 1943 to the establishment of HMCS *Prevost* located – with what awareness of the implication is unknown – at London, Ontario. Here those deficient in the English language were given a twelve-week course. (No facilities were provided for recruits deficient in French.) If at its close their knowledge of English was still judged inadequate, ratings were given shore duties in an English-language environment for three months; if they then failed an English-language test they were usually discharged. So that

studies prepared for the Royal Commission: Pierre Coulombe (with the collaboration of Lise Courcelles), 'Carrière militaire et dynamique culturelle'; Harold Forbell and Barry Gallant, 'Armed Forces Histories.'

their seamanship would not be lost to the Allied cause, the Navy proposed that prospective recruits who could not meet its English-language requirements be allowed to enlist in the forces of Free France.

Mackenzie King learned of this proposal at a meeting of the War Committee on 18 June 1943. He sensed at once injustice and, more to the point, political peril.

> ...in the presence of the Ministers and the Chiefs of Staff, I stated this was an indefensible procedure, and could not be for one moment, regarded or tolerated as an expression of Government policy ... [I] could not imagine any subject that would raise such a furore throughout Canada and be less defensible, should it be known that, when Parliament was appropriating millions of dollars for the three armed services, French Canadians who formed one third of the population of the country were being virtually excluded or ostracized from one of the services. I asked all present to imagine what would be said when it was placed within the power of anyone to represent that not only was this the case, but that those who were practising it were seeking two things in addition, to have the Canadian Navy so closely intertwined with the British Navy as to become virtually a part of it, and, on the other hand, were supporting a policy that many men who were precluded from enlisting in the Navy, should be conscripted for service overseas. I did not spare the expression of my indignation and said I wished to have the minutes record the fact that any practice of the kind was opposite to the policy of the Government, and should not be countenanced for a moment longer.[135]

Whatever the minutes might record the practice remained unchanged, or largely so. *Prevost* was disbanded at the end of the war, when limited instruction in French became available at the main new-entry training stations of HMCS *Cornwallis* and *Naden*. The effort was lackadaisical. French-speaking Canadians had reason to believe that the post-war Navy was not really keen to recruit among their people, however excellent their English. 'Always there are very high obstacles to cross,' Jean François Pouliot complained in the House of Commons on 19 August 1946, 'before a French Canadian is admitted, and not in the department [only] but on a ship ... It seems to me that the high officials of the department ... do not want a single French Canadian to get on board the ships...'[136]

If that had been their objective, the 'high officials' were not completely successful. Of 4865 ratings (leading seamen and above) in the Navy as of 1953, 497, or 9.8 per cent, were French-speaking: many of these, perhaps not as many as there should have been, had gone to sea. Discrimination is more evident higher up. Of 1825 officers (including cadets), 234, or 7.8 per cent, were French-speaking. No French-speaking officer had risen to the rank of commodore (of which there were in 1953 eleven in the Service), while only two were captains (compared with forty-two

English-speaking captains) and twenty-one were commanders (compared with 148 English-speaking commanders).

Given such a rank-structure, it was hardly surprising that recruiting among French-speaking Canadians lagged behind recruiting in English Canada. In 1951, reacting to the manpower shortage created by the Korean War, the Navy for the first time became anxious to remove the discrepancy. One of the twenty-one French-speaking commanders, Marcel Jetté, was instructed to report on the reasons for the lag and to recommend measures to overcome it.

The Jetté Report, based on interviews with officers and men in the Navy, retired naval officers, recruits, educators, and a few lawyers and executives, was completed in 1951. It contained few surprises. As might have been guessed, lack of enthusiasm for naval service stemmed from ancient and familiar grievances. French-speaking Canadians, Commander Jetté reaffirmed, had been brought up to believe that Canada's wars were Britain's wars, and were reluctant to take part in them. Their own imaginations and the testimony of veterans alike had led them to assume they were not wanted in an English-speaking navy. Jetté's Report made the point that a unilingual recruit from French Canada had quickly to learn not just one foreign language but two – English, and 'the Naval language, which is a language in itself.' It was too daunting a task. 'Before long [the recruit] gets discouraged and adopts a defeatist attitude – that is, if he is not discharged.' Jetté discovered that many French-speaking Canadians knew next to nothing about the Navy, which they tended to confuse with the Merchant Marine. 'This is a common fault ... Even by the top men in the Montreal Catholic School Commission it was thought that the Naval School in Rimouski, which is operated by the Provincial Government, belonged to and was operated by the RCN.'[137]

The Jetté Report considered, only to reject, the proposal that ships be sent to sea manned by French-speaking crews. Such a measure was thought to be unwise, not so much because of operational inefficiency as because it was thought likely to defeat what it was meant to win: 'It would achieve exactly the opposite of what we are trying to achieve – a united Canada. French-speaking Canadians want to be considered as Canadians, not as isolationists.' It was conceded that a French-speaking ship 'would have great *esprit de corps*' – probably too much *esprit de corps*, for 'fights would no doubt start with other ships, particularly ashore when in company.' The Report noted that where the idea was favoured, it was by civilians rather than by officers and ratings, who said they would prefer not to serve in such a ship.*

* So did some of the crew of HMCS *Ottawa* when, in September 1968, she became the first ship in the RCN to operate officially on a bilingual basis. 'The men were

The main recommendation of the Jetté Report was that an English-language school be established in Quebec City for the instruction of French-speaking ratings – regulars as well as recruits – in mathematics and seamanship, as well as in English; HMCS *D'Iberville* was duly opened for this purpose in Quebec City. A year later, in 1952, instruction in the French language was offered to naval officers at National Defence Headquarters. But, as recently as 1959, a suggestion from the commanding officer of *D'Iberville* that English-speaking ratings be given a similar opportunity was turned down; as were still more recent requests for English-speaking officers to attend French-language courses at Laval University. The first decision was defended on the grounds of a shortage of bilingual instructors, the second on the grounds of a shortage of funds. But the real shortage was of imagination – a commodity which in the Royal Canadian Navy was seldom in over-supply.

A French-speaking Canadian wishing to serve in the post-war military establishment was best advised to seek enlistment in the Canadian Army. There, more than in the other two services, he might pursue a career in his native tongue and in his own cultural milieu.

During the Second World War, it was the government's policy to maintain, so far as possible, a fixed proportion of French and English-speaking soldiers in the Army overseas; 19 per cent of the Army was French-speaking (compared to 12.6 per cent) during the Great War. To encourage French-Canadian enlistment, French-speaking soldiers were sent, all else being equal, to French-speaking units commanded by French-speaking officers. A project to form a French-speaking brigade was dropped due to a shortage of qualified French-speaking officers. As of 1 March 1944, there were in the Army some forty French-speaking formations of battalion strength, mostly artillery and infantry, with some administrative and support units. Technical personnel, especially signallers, were notably absent. English remained the operational language of the Army, and the use of French was confined to the training, administration, and tactical control of French-speaking units. There was

suspicious at first,' her commanding officer, Commander Pierre Simard, recalled. 'One said it was a form of separatism. If we got enough ships, in 25 years they could be turned over to the separatists.' 'Bilingual Ship called Experiment Important to Future of Country,' *The Globe and Mail* (Toronto), 1 October 1968. Of *Ottawa*'s crew of 215, including 17 officers, 20 per cent were English-speaking. New crews were planned to take over the ship at sixteen-month intervals. While orders on board would be in both official languages, outbound communication remained English. 'English is the language of NATO,' Commander Simard remarked, adding: 'I don't want to go through the bloody jetty.'

Among the terms devised to enable the *Ottawa* to operate bilingually are 'homme à la mer' (man overboard), 'sur farrière' (abaft), and 'top d'echo' (radar blip). See *Canadian Forces Military Dictionary* (Ottawa 1972).

no place for a unilingual French-speaking officer in the higher command. There was, however, in contrast to naval and air force practice, a place for bilingual (in practice, francophone) Army officers at all levels of seniority.

It was not, for them, a happy place. The High Commissioner in London recorded several occasions on which French-speaking officers complained to him of discrimination:

> Major ——— [an officer in a French-speaking regiment] came in to say good-bye. He feels that the relations between French and English in our Army are very unsatisfactory. In fact there are no relations except those of a purely professional nature. He said that French-Canadian soldiers in his experience were full of appreciation of their reception in Great Britain and only wished that their fellow-Canadians would treat them as well as the British public. [Diary entry, 24 September 1943]

> Colonel ——— ...called ... He is going back to Canada very bitter about the treatment of French-Canadians in the Army. He gave me instances of French-Canadian officers and other ranks being told that they were not to speak French. I am afraid there are grounds for his complaint. [Diary entry, 11 August 1944][138]

Maintaining French-language units and a fixed proportion of French- to English-speaking personnel were policies carried over to the post-war Army. The quota of French-speaking personnel in the regular Army was set at 30 per cent for the infantry and 15 per cent for other corps. English remained the operational language. Rather than relying, as in the past, upon bilingual French-Canadians, the post-war Army began to train English-speaking officers and NCOs at the Canadian Army Training School opened in 1946 originally to provide French-speaking recruits with basic instruction in the French language. In addition, the Chief of the General Staff introduced a programme of French-language instruction for Army Headquarters personnel; begun in Ottawa in November 1947, the course was later made available in other major camps and training centres across the country.

The conscription crisis of 1944, and the strains upon national unity to which it gave rise, forfeited for the post-war Army much of the trust and confidence of the people of French Canada. 'The grand total for National Defence Headquarters in Ottawa,' Boris Arsenault pointed out in the House of Commons on 30 October 1945,

> stands at three French Canadians out of a total of 72. Is that what can be termed a Canadian partnership? And the same discriminatory situation applied all the way down the list, as far down as that little Quebec farmer's son who did not speak English, and found himself lost, hundreds if not thousands of miles away from his home, where he was often requested to speak "white," or

had to hunt for a translator to try to explain his wants, if not his grievances, to the officers ... who did not understand his language...[139]

'I do not believe,' declared Wilfrid Lacroix on 2 November,

the French Canadians will ever get fair play in the Canadian Army, for, of all the parties represented in this House, the Liberal party has the most sympathy for them, and in spite of their efforts and good intentions, they have failed, during the war, to prevent discrimination being shown against them. How could they get better results in peace time when all our imperialistic brass hats will be enshrined in high army posts to form a class accountable to no one?[140]

This was a despairing view, and it was doubtless too pessimistic. The 'brass hats' were not accountable to no one: they were accountable, after December 1946, to a strong and able Minister of National Defence well aware of the grievances of French Canada and determined that these should be alleviated, not accentuated, by the armed forces in his charge. Brooke Claxton took justifiable pride in many aspects of his long administration, but few things gave him greater satisfaction than the better image the Canadian Army gradually acquired in the minds of French-speaking Canadians. Recruitment in Quebec was as good a test as any of the improvement. Of it, Claxton wrote afterwards: 'We had the best rate of recruiting in French Canada that any of the forces ever had in war or peace.'[141] Nor were the 'brass hats' themselves lacking sympathy for French-speaking members of the Army, whether officers or enlisted men. 'The study of French,' General Charles Foulkes told his fellow officers on 28 January 1948, 'should be undertaken to a greater or lesser extent by every officer in the Canadian Army ... There is no doubt that officers with bilingual qualifications have better opportunities for certain employment than those who lack similar qualifications.'[142]

Yet while the post-war Army was far less rigidly anglophonic than its sister services, it fell short of reflecting the bilingual and bicultural character of the country it existed to defend. So long as English alone remained its operational language, no soldier or officer speaking the French language only might hope to compete on equal terms with his English-speaking counterpart. He might write his examinations and receive his basic training in his own language – a privilege (or right) denied to airmen and to sailors – but once beyond that level he was distinctly disadvantaged. All senior courses and advanced technical training taught in Canada were taught in English; and English was of course the medium of instruction at staff colleges and training centres in the United Kingdom and the United States to which the more senior officers from time to time are posted. The results are evident in the Army rank-structure: the higher the rank, the lower the proportion of French-speaking to English-speaking officers, so that in 1958, 15 per cent of lieutenants were French-speaking, 12 per cent of captains and majors, 9 per cent of lieutenant-colonels, and 8 per cent of colonels and above. The post-war Army, like the post-war Navy and Air Force but to a lesser degree, remained a force in which a French-speaking Canadian might make his way in spite of what he was and not because of what he was. No grave disadvantage in this was seen, let alone injustice, until the Queen's Own Rifles were prevented by reason of their resemblance to British troops from taking up their peacekeeping assignment in the Middle East.

# 2

# Uniting the Nations

It may take a year or two, or maybe even three-o,
But some day all the world will be a happy family-o,
As we make United Nations a reality-o,
Then we will see a world where we
Are happy, safe and free-o.

*UN Department of Public Information, 1945*

## SYSTEMS OF SECURITY

On 1 November 1943, the United States, the United Kingdom, the Soviet Union, and China issued from Moscow their declaration supporting 'a general international organization, based on the principle of the sovereign equality of all peace-loving states, large and small, for the maintenance of international peace and security.' When word of its release reached Ottawa, the following statement, drafted by Norman Robertson, was given to the press by the Prime Minister's office:

I welcome this announcement most warmly. It makes clear the determination of the British, Soviet, United States and Chinese Governments that their war-time co-operation will continue, not only until victory has been achieved and the enemy has been defeated and disarmed, but indefinitely thereafter within a general international organization which will be open to membership by all peace-loving states. The declaration brings the assurance that the largest powers among the United Nations are pledged to a joint endeavour to devise in concert with other countries effective means of ending the blight of war and establishing freedom from fear throughout the world. The Canadian Government has been consulted about the terms of the Four Power Declaration and is fully in accord with its provisions.

The terms of the declaration about which the Canadian Government had been particularly concerned were the inclusion of China as one of its co-sponsors, and the suggestion of the United Kingdom, which it successfully opposed, that the declaration be issued in the name of the British Commonwealth of Nations.

The Canadian Government had by the date of the Moscow Declaration already fixed upon the three fundamental principles which would guide its policy on post-war international organization. The first of these principles was that international society required for its safety and well-being an effective system of collective security.

Collective security was by no means the only remedy recommended by those in a position to treat the world for all its ills. To the Prime Minister of the United Kingdom a different cure seemed preferable. 'I attached great importance to the regional principle,' Winston Churchill recalled in his war memoirs. 'It was only the countries whose interests were directly affected by a dispute who could be expected to apply themselves with sufficient vigour to secure a settlement.' He had therefore envisaged a series of inter-locking regional councils, 'one for Europe, one for the American hemisphere, and one for the Pacific.' There would be a World Council, to keep up appearances; but the real force for peace was the regional council. A realistic and effective system of international security had to take cognizance of areas of primary concern, indeed of spheres of influence. Otherwise the world would be no better off after the war than it had been before. 'If countries remote from a dispute were among those called upon in the first instance to achieve a settlement, the result was likely to be merely vapid and academic discussion.'[1]

These ideas, argued with powerful logic by so prestigious a figure, might easily have won the day had they not run into stern opposition from within. The British Foreign Office did not like the regional approach. In their Foreign Secretary they had an influential spokesman for their own. Early in 1943, Anthony Eden circulated his thoughts on a possible post-war system to the members of the Cabinet. They were diametrically opposed to Churchill's. 'There must not be,' Eden argued, 'a kind of "limited liability" system, whereby one power was solely responsible for keeping the peace in a given area. On the contrary, it was essential to assume that the great powers were in principle equally interested in maintaining the peace everywhere in the world, and that they would act together whenever and wherever it might be threatened.'[2]

Eden's argument, for all the tenacity with which it was pressed upon the Prime Minister, was not in itself sufficient to convert him. Help, however, arrived from an unexpected quarter. 'A very good meeting of Dominion Prime Ministers,' the Foreign Secretary wrote in his diary on 11 May 1944. 'They all took my line and not W.'s about future world set-up. This was very helpful, in particular they were nervous of regional councils and for the same reasons.'[3] They may have been nervous, but not for the same reasons.

Not, at any rate, in the case of the Prime Minister of Canada. Mackenzie King's thoughts about what had caused the war and what, therefore, would be required to preserve peace, were very different from those of Churchill or of Eden. He did not share their view that the conflict had resulted from the cowardice of Western governments and the selfishness of Western peoples. Not the lethargic pace of rearmament, not the timidity and myopia of the pre-war democracies, but the insincerity and half-heartedness of appeasement had plunged the world in war.

Only when Europe was liberated, and the death camps disclosed their ghastly secrets, would it be known that the Nazi gang were mass murderers on a scale and of a bestiality without precedent in history. But in August 1944 this was not yet known – though one might have guessed. What was known was that the Nazis were colossal liars, masters of deceit. Even so, Mackenzie King could hardly bring himself to believe that they had really been beyond the reach of reason. 'The present war,' he had written in November 1939, 'has come about through inability to hold a conference. Had Italians, Germans, etc., been mixing freely with representatives of the British Commonwealth, United States, etc. ... discussing their grievances and publicly proclaiming them to the world ... means would have been found, short of war, to bring about adjustments.'[4] Nothing during the four years of fighting that followed caused him to set aside this conviction of a lifetime.

Such a notion profoundly influenced Mackenzie King's views on post-war international organization. What was required above all was an assembly of the nations. It should not be like the League of Nations, at least not like its theory; for, as he wrote, 'If the League of Nations had not placed its reliance upon force, in other words, sought to identify collective security with coercion, sanctions, etc., I am persuaded there would have been no war in Europe.' The post-war world should not be allowed to place its trust in force, in that collective security which he would rather call collective coercion. 'Blindly to return to that sort of a remedy is simply to hasten the day for another [war].' It should place its trust in publicity – 'machinery for letting in the light to the nations concerned,' 'provision for the formation of an intelligent public opinion; above all else, means of impartial investigation of existing wrongs.'[5]

From these fundamental beliefs Mackenzie King was never dissuaded. Contrary notions might be put into his speeches by his speech-writers, but they never changed his mind. If he seemed to abandon his beliefs during the last year or two of war, he returned to them during the first year or two of peace. His conversion to collective security was grudging and temporary. On 25 October 1944, the Prime Minister told his cabinet that 'much as I did not like the use of force in any form I was nevertheless prepared to support a world organization that might have force as its ultimate means of maintaining peace.'[6] Less than a year later the Prime Minister told his party caucus that he hoped that 'they would not put their faith in any organization as to world security; that I greatly feared the new organization might in some circumstances be as much of a blind as the League of Nations.'[7] For Mackenzie King there was no harsher condemnation.

But as between collective security and the only practicable alternative, Mackenzie King was compelled to choose collective security. He chose it reluctantly, but he chose it. For the only practical alternative was regionalism. No statesman of any consequence shared Mackenzie King's personal vision of world peace sustained by conciliation, publicity, and a kind of universal International Joint Commission. And for Canada, regionalism was replete with special perils. It might be fine enough for Great Powers, each ruling its own particular regional roost. But for small powers, even for those so presumptuous as to call themselves 'Middle Powers,' it meant being ruled by the great, ignored by the great. Nor was that all. In the version being put about by Churchill, regionalism required a unitary Commonwealth in which the United Kingdom would play the leading role. Mackenzie King had spent a major part of a long political career seeking to demolish such a unitary Commonwealth. He did not take kindly to its coming to the fore.

Within the Department of External Affairs, opposition to regionalism was no less keen but based on somewhat different considerations, which Hume Wrong set out in a memorandum written as early as August 1943:

> Mr Churchill publicly referred some months ago to the possibility of establishing a Council of Europe and perhaps a Council of Asia, implying his preference for a regional organization. From the Canadian point of view there is much to be said against great emphasis being laid on regional methods, especially if the regions are taken to be the continental land masses. In such a system Canada would be in the American region but would also be intimately concerned with security in the European and Asiatic regions. Emphasis on regionalism would tend to lead the forces in the United States that are opposed to international commitments to concentrate on security in the American region as the particular responsibility of the US, and to argue for the assumption of no responsibility for European stability. We have in the last four years had a striking demonstration of the truth of the doctrine that peace is indivisible in the modern world and, therefore, that security everywhere is the concern of all countries. Furthermore, "regions" from the security point of view can no longer be identified with continents. It is more realistic to regard the North Atlantic area as a security region than the continents of North and South America. While regional

bodies should play a valuable part, it seems desirable that we should support a world system on which any regional bodies would depend.[8]

An opportunity to assert the collective principle as against the regional presented itself at the meeting of Commonwealth Prime Ministers convened in London during May 1944. On 9 May there took place what Mackenzie King described in his diary as 'a very important discussion.' In the course of it, he wrote, he 'spoke out emphatically about the danger of beginning with Regional Councils as in all probability leading – certainly in the case of America – to the continent taking a more or less isolationist position, being concerned with its own affairs. To keep the world as united as possible, the emphasis must be on a central organization.' On 11 May the Prime Ministers discussed 'the important issue of whether representation on World Organization was to be of British Empire and Commonwealth as Churchill was anxious to have it, or Britain alone.' (It was this session which proved so gratifying to Anthony Eden.) At the outset, Mackenzie King recorded, 'it looked for a while as if no one would wish to say anything. Churchill rather hesitated to begin discussion. Eden did not wish to open up particularly.' (Their hesitation was probably due to their reluctance to risk disagreeing with one another before the other Prime Ministers, or perhaps to each seeking tactical advantage in the timing of their intervention.) 'As someone had indicated I should begin the discussion,' Mackenzie King's account continues, 'I started in and read [a] statement from beginning to close.'[9] The statement had been drafted a few hours earlier by Norman Robertson and John Holmes. It dealt directly with Canada's attitude towards the regional approach to international organization:

The question of regionalism is one that must be approached with caution. This war has made it clear that countries can secure their own immediate defences only in co-operation with friendly neighbours. This principle is the basis of the Permanent Joint Defence Board, which was established in 1940 between Canada and the United States,[*] and it is, I believe, the basis of the very fruitful proposals recently made in the agreement between Australia and New Zealand...

We should not forget, however, that a major lesson of this war is the truth that the seas do not divide and that the peace and prosperity of the world are indivisible. It would not be wise to encourage the peoples of the world to return to their illusions about their ability to live in continental isolation. I am glad to

* This reference had been cunningly inserted. It served to remind Churchill that when the Canadian Government had conducted its own experiment in regional organization in August 1940, he had been disagreeably surprised. See James Eayrs, *In Defence of Canada*, II, *Appeasement and Rearmament* (Toronto 1965), 209–10.

see, therefore, the views expressed in these [Foreign Office] papers that the world organization should be established first, and that regional associations for special purposes might develop out of the particular necessities of particular areas, and should be fitted into the overall framework of world security.[10]

When Mackenzie King finished reading this statement, Churchill spoke up to say 'there were parts of it which ran counter to his views.' Eden, however, seemed 'very pleased' – so Mackenzie King noted – 'with what I had said.' The Canadian Prime Minister described his intervention as 'the hardest battle of the Conference thus far because it required very straight and direct talking to and differing from Churchill on the things he feels most deeply about.'[11]

After this exchange, perhaps because of it, Churchill abandoned his advocacy of the regional approach and of regional councils. Henceforth – much to the relief of the Foreign Office – the British Government supported a global concept of international security.

But regionalism had not been banished. It had merely been downgraded. There still remained the question of the place of regional associations within the framework of a world security system. Should the operation of the regional principle be restricted to the narrowest of sectors and the most remote of contingencies? Or ought the advantages of regionalism be widely proclaimed and generously provided for?

To this question a small number of civil servants, mostly from the Department of External Affairs, who had come together in 1943 to develop ideas about the kind of world Canada should work for after the war was won, devoted considerable attention. It is well to digress at this point in order to describe the machinery for what became known as 'post-hostilities planning.'

The realization that some systematic method of dealing with post-war problems did not exist and would be required dawned on the Department of External Affairs in June 1943, with the arrival of two telegrams from the British Government asking for a Canadian opinion on the impending armistice with Italy, the control of a defeated Germany, and Canada's participation in the proposed United Nations Commission for Europe and in a European policing system. Forced to look up from its day-to-day preoccupation with the conduct of the war, the War Committee of the Cabinet peered uncertainly at the future during its meeting on 15 July, when the two British telegrams came before it for consideration. The need for closer study and harder analysis of these and other post-war problems was obvious at once. The War Committee asked the Department of External Affairs to examine the proposals together with representatives of the Services. So it came about that on 22 July 1943, a meeting was held in Room 123 of the East Block to consider post-hostilities problems – the first of many such meetings convened during the next two years. On the Services side it was attended by the Chief of the Naval Staff, Admiral P.W. Nelles, the Chief of the Air Staff, Air Marshal L.S. Breadner, the Deputy Chief of the General Staff, Brigadier P. Earnshaw, together with their respective planning specialists – Lt-Commander G.F. Todd, Air Commodore K.M. Guthrie, and Colonel J.H. Jenkins. The representatives from the Department of External Affairs were its Under-Secretary of State, Norman Robertson, its Assistant Under-Secretary, Hume Wrong (who acted as chairman), George Glazebrook, and John Holmes (who acted as secretary). The Clerk of the Privy Council, A.D.P. Heeney, was also present at the creation of Canada's post-hostilities planning apparatus.

Committees invariably spawn sub-committees. The offspring of the meeting of 22 July was a smaller group, to be known as the Working Committee on Post-hostilities Problems, which met for the first time on 3 August in Hume Wrong's office. In addition to Wrong, who was to be the chairman of the Working Committee throughout its existence, Glazebrook, Holmes, and R.G. Robertson attended for the Department of External Affairs; representing the Services were Group Captain W.F. Hanna, Lt-Commander G.F. Todd, and Major H.C. Grant; while Lt-Commander D.K. MacTavish spoke for the Privy Council office. At its first meeting, the Working Committee decided that its functions should consist of originating proposals and offering advice on all matters relating to post-war problems. Its recommendations would be made to the group which had met on 22 July. Regular fortnightly meetings of the Working Committee were planned.

The bureaucratic need for structure and certitude in operations was not yet satisfied by these arrangements. At its fourth meeting on 12 October, the members of the Working Committee – so the minutes suggest – were assailed by a crisis of identity. 'It was pointed out that the Working Committee had been consisted to report to a body which had met only once and was very much an ad hoc affair. The scope and responsibility of the Committee was uncertain. Was it, for instance, the responsibility of the Committe to take the initiative in seeing that all post-hostilities problems were being studied by the Departments concerned? Was the Committee, on the other hand, simply a central repository of information about what government bodies were doing along these lines? Should the Committee, in fact, be re-constituted with a more certain authority?'[12] A second meeting of the parent body on 9 November dispelled some of these uncertainties. A Post-Hostilities Advisory Committee was to be created, composed of the Under Secretary of State for External Affairs, to act as chairman, the Chiefs of Staff, and the Secretary of the Cabinet. The Post-Hostilities Advisory Committe was to offer guidance and direction to the Working Committee, to refer to it matters requiring detailed study, and to submit recommendations on post-war problems and policies to the War Committee of the Cabinet. The Working Committee was specifically enjoined to keep the Advisory Committee informed on post-hostilities affairs, and to prepare special studies, either on its own initiative or at the direction of the Advisory Committee. Both these bodies were given formal status by the War Committee on 16 December, which then enlarged the membership of the Advisory Committee to include the Deputy Minister of Finance and the Vice-Chairman of the National Harbours Board; this last official was appointed not on account of the intrinsic importance of harbours in the post-war world but in order to have, in the person of J.E. St Laurent, a French-speaking representative on the Advisory Committee.

Still the machinery was not complete. The Working Committee gave birth in June 1944 to the Post-Hostilities Joint Drafting Group, known less formally as the Junior Planning Staff. This body was composed of a planning officer from each of the three Services and a representative from the Department of External Affairs – the official (first John Holmes, later – after January 1945 – George Ignatieff) who was also secretary to the Advisory and Working Committees. The Joint Drafting Group met informally as occasion required, kept no minutes, and was intended to provide a forum for frank exchanges of opinion and to study and draft papers.

The Canadian planners did not try to solve all the problems of the post-war world. 'It would be wasted effort for Canada to attempt to plan from the foundation upward,' Hume Wrong instructed his small but potent task force. 'As a secondary country we have not a great enough influence to make our views prevail. We should, however, be in a position at least to know what is not acceptable and to advocate changes or additions to fit our particular interests.' It would not be long, he predicted, before the Canadian government would 'be called upon to answer such difficult questions as: How far can authority reasonably be concentrated in the hands of the Great Powers after the war? How great commitments can be accepted to maintain peace and to further prosperity? ... Should Canada act mainly as a secondary world power or as an influential member of the Commonwealth? ... The answers to them will grow out of wartime decisions reached often in a hurry ... To pay attention now to these problems is, therefore, a necessary complement to meeting the problems of the conduct of the war.'[13]

As well as preparing position papers of their own, the Canadian planners had to digest the position papers of their allies. By far the greatest number of these arrived from the Post-Hostilities Planning Committee in the United Kingdom which (unlike its Canadian counterpart) was a sub-committee of the Chiefs of Staff. 'There has been a tremendous flow of material lately from London,' Holmes noted on 6 April 1944. Some six weeks earlier, the Canadian High Commissioner had reported that 'the Post-Hostilities Planning Sub-Committee here would be much interested to see and study papers produced by our Working Committee in Ottawa,'[14] and while the Canadian output was nothing like so voluminous as the British there was much that could have been exchanged – papers on regional vs universal security systems, post-war defence arrangements with the United States, the post-war defence of Newfoundland, the Canadian military interest in Greenland and Iceland, the Canadian position in the event of strained relations between the Soviet Union and the United States, the Canadian role in North Pacific defence, to name but a few. But it was not. A meeting of the Advisory Committee on 15 March 1945 agreed that a reciprocal exchange of post-hostilities planning papers between London and Ottawa while theoretically desirable was practically impossible. 'The London papers were essentially strategic and military studies and it was clear that we had nothing equivalent to offer to the London Committees. The papers produced by the Canadian Post-Hostilities Planning Committees contained political considerations and when approved by the War Committee were intended to serve as guidance in policy on various matters ... Few of the Canadian PHP papers were of a kind which could be shown to the United Kingdom authorities.'[15]

There was similarly little interchange on post-war planning with the United States, though the Department of External Affairs wanted to secure as much information as possible about American proposals for international organization. 'The more information that the Embassy can secure from the State Department on their plans the better,' Hume Wrong had instructed L.B. Pearson on 11 May 1944. 'I am afraid, however, that if they should prove willing to exchange papers with us on a barter basis the traffic would not be large.'[16]

It is the way with committees not only to procreate their kind but to add to their membership. By June 1944 the Working Committee had become, in the opinion of its chairman, 'too cumbrous'; Hume Wrong proposed cutting back the number of representatives from the Department of External Affairs from seven to the original three. 'I think that the best organization for us to adopt would be for the regular departmental representation to consist of myself, Holmes and Ignatieff ... The Committee is designed to be an interdepartmental study group and its membership has not been selected with a view to representing all of those concerned in its work or in other Departments.'[17] In this streamlined version the Working Committee functioned to the end of its days.

As the war approached a climax, the Working Committee was given less and less to do. Hume Wrong reported a decline in its activity to the meeting of the Advisory Committee on 15 March 1945. It was not that there were slackers, it was just that its work had been done. Further study, the Advisory Committtee agreed, 'would have to be primarily the responsibility of the Department of External Affairs.'[18] A month later, the secretary of the Advisory Committee wrote that 'in present circumstances it would seem unlikely that there will be any meetings ... for some little time and that generally the activities of the Committee will be in abeyance.'[19] On 25 July Hume Wrong prepared a memorandum on the future of the wartime post-hostilities machinery.

> It is probably desirable to wind up the existing PHP Committees (which have dealt in the main with short-range problems arising in the course of the war) and to substitute some more permanent machinery for the continuous review of policy. The Working Committee in particular seems to have lost most of its utility and has not met for some time. A senior official body should be part of the machinery with the chairman from External Affairs and with representatives of the Services and the Cabinet Secretariat. This body might establish ad hoc sub-committees to prepare studies on particular problems, the present working Committee being wound up...[20]

The Working Committee was duly wound up, but there was nothing to take its place. 'In my opinion,' R.M. Macdonnell wrote on 15 August 1946, 'all that is required for the Post-Hostilities Groups is decent burial.'[21] Hume Wrong concurred. But they did not get even that degree of consideration, much less the new lease on life that one or two had recommended. 'It does seem to me,' wrote one of the Working Committee's former secretaries at the time of its demise, 'that an organization of its kind, continually studying political-strategic matters & preparing drafts, would be most useful for those who formulate Canadian policy, & would also be the best way of supplying the trained personnel which was the most serious deficiency in our organization.'[22]

But of the possibility of a planned, as opposed to a pragmatic, foreign policy, officials of the Department of External Affairs remained deeply sceptical. 'A continuing series of ad hoc decisions,' was how one of them described the policy process to a group of academic social scientists some years later. 'It is always a case of realizing as fully as you can the implications of what you propose to do, and of doing it according to the best judgment you can make in a single circumstance at the moment of time.'[23] Such was the prevailing ethos of the next two decades.*

The Post-Hostilities planners in Ottawa approached the problems of post-war international organization with a modesty both realistic and commendable. No attempt was made to draft an all-Canadian United Nations charter. 'Canadian authorities could not try to construct a general security plan,' Hume Wrong told the Advisory Committee on 28 March 1944, 'but they should know at least what proposals would not be acceptable,' and for that purpose 'it was advisable to have some views prepared on the pros and cons.'[24] This modest note Wrong sounded again in a letter to Pearson on 11 May – 'We are refraining from any attempt to draw up Canadian schemes for the organization of world security and are confining ourselves to the study of proposals which reach us from other countries, and especially the United Kingdom. It might be advantageous for us to attempt more than this if we had the time and the people to do so'[25] – and once again, this time without the reservation, in a letter to Dana Wilgress in Moscow: 'It would be wasted effort for us to contribute any comprehensive plans of our own, for Canada, as a secondary power, would not have a great enough influence to make our views prevail. We should, however, be in a position at least to decide what is not acceptable to us, and to advocate changes to accord with our interests, through appropriate channels, in the plans of the Great Powers.'[26]

It became clear almost at once that a reversion to a regional system of security – the pet project of Winston Churchill, one which Lord Halifax's Toronto speech showed was far from dead† – was not acceptable to the Ottawa planners. 'The danger of regional security arrangements,' R.M. Macdonnell noted on 13 January 1944, 'is that they may become regional alliances against other regions. From Canada's standpoint, a most dangerous situation would arise if British-American co-operation for the preservation of peace were turned rather towards the defence of British-American interests and ideologies against the USSR and communist ideologies. It is, therefore, imperative that the USSR be a partner in any security arrangements established in these areas...'[27] 'The best opening,' Dana

* Not until 1969 did the Department of External Affairs acquire a peacetime version of the post-hostilities machinery – its Policy Analysis Group, which – according to an official statement of its origin and purpose – 'stemmed from an expression of concern by the present Government that the elements of Canadian foreign policy should be settled with an orderly coherence in a rational form, be sensitive to changing conditions and priorities and in tune with the future.'

† See below, 201–5.

Wilgress commented from Moscow, 'to render service to the cause of collective security is through behind-the-scenes prodding in Washington.'[28] John Holmes proposed behind-the-scenes prodding in London: 'The United Kingdom – no matter how small she may be – can lead the world into collective security. Her reversion to reliance on the juggling of power seems to arise out of the funk induced by the thinking of Smuts and Halifax ... Canadian intervention should be peculiarly influential because we could make it clear that, although we are not willing to commit ourselves to narrow schemes for imperial defence, the United Kingdom can count on us as the firmest of allies if they want to take the plunge into a real system of collective security.'[29]

By April 1944 the planners had assembled their various views on regionalism in one of their first major memoranda. The paper, while endorsing collective security, went through the motions of attempting to discern advantages in the regional approach. These were by no means negligible. To devolve responsibility for dealing with conflicts within defined geographic areas upon the appropriate regional council could ease the strain upon a world council likely to be over-burdened. Conflicts close to home were more likely than those remote and far away to engage the concern of governments and publics; hence, the measures recommended by a regional council were more likely to be supported. A regional system would permit smaller countries to play within their regions a more prominent part in restoring security than would be theirs on the wider stage of a global security system. It would be easier to carry out joint military operations. Finally, if Canada were a member of a region confined to North America, there would be less likelihood that Canada would be called upon to provide troops; the planners conceded that this 'danger would be somewhat increased if South America were included in the region.'

So much for the advantages of regionalism. The planners found much to say against it. First, any form of regional devolution would tend to cause governments to view their responsibilities as being confined to disputes within their region, and theirs alone; this could encourage a false sense of security. Second, the establishment of a security region confined to North America or the Western hemisphere could promote a revival of isolationist sentiment in Canada and the United States leading to an American withdrawal from world affairs. Third, any comprehensive system of regional councils would create artificial geopolitical barriers cutting across natural groupings of states. 'Regional limits,' the paper noted, 'might have to be set at such artificial boundaries as the Suez Canal, the Urals, or between Greenland and Iceland. Moreover, continental regions would be based on the false premise that the seas divide, thus ignoring one of the chief lessons of this war and the last. The creation of oceanic regions (e.g., a North Atlantic or an Indian Ocean region) would be equally arbitrary. Security regions inevitably overlap, and Canada belongs to a North American, a North Atlantic, a North Pacific, and an Arctic region.' Fourth, regions would tend to become spheres of influence for the most powerful states within each region: such spheres of influence might in the future as in the past sharpen the rivalries of the Great Powers and set back the cause of world peace. Fifth, the regional approach might run counter to and weaken the bonds of membership of the Commonwealth of Nations. Finally, complications could arise out of the possibility that some states, such as Portugal and The Netherlands, might use their colonial possessions to demand more extensive representation on the regional councils than merited by their power and status in the post-war world.

The Working Committee, having thus set out the *pros* and *cons* of the regional approach, concluded that its liabilities outweighed its assets. 'Serious dangers to general security,' its members concluded,

> while their occasions may arise within a region, are certain to involve territories and issues outside the particular region. If specific commitments to preserve the peace were confined to the elimination of dangers arising within any particular region, there would be little hope of developing a sense of responsibility for the general maintenance of security. On the other hand, regional security councils might play a limited role in finding a local solution to purely local disputes, such as border disputes between small countries.*

The Canadian government was already allowing its representatives to speak publicly along these lines. 'If the collective principle is not applied,' L.B. Pearson said in an address to the Canadian Club of Toronto on 13 March 1944,

> there will be one of three results. The states other than the "Big Four" will either try to form power groups themselves and demand a franchise in the

* 'Advantages and Disadvantages for Canada of the Regional Security Organisation and Defence,' 21 April 1944, Department of External Affairs files. General Maurice Pope, then chairman of the Canadian Joint Staff in Washington, took a keen interest in the work of the Post-Hostility planners in Ottawa, and on this matter found himself in disagreement with their conclusions. 'The note the department men produced,' his memoirs recall disapprovingly, 'seemed to evince a desire that some beginning be made towards the creation of an international police force ... It seemed to me more realistic to endeavour to ensure peace in well-defined regions comprising those nations whose oxen were likely to be gored in the particular case in question, before attempting to legislate for the entire world.' *Soldiers and Politicians: The Memoirs of Lt.-Gen. Maurice A. Pope* (Toronto 1962), 267–8.

"Major League," or they will cluster uneasily for security in the shadow of a Great Power, or they will seek security in isolation and neutrality.

None of these results will make for peace. The first simply extends the "balance of power" idea. The second merely surrounds the existing Big Four with satellites, who will share their fate and may be lost in their ambitions and their fears. Least of all is there any hope in isolation...[30]

The role of commentator on Great Power drafts for post-war security systems modestly assigned to itself by the Working Committee did not prevent the planners from developing ideas on their own. They paid particular attention to the scope and scale of an international armed force. The British planners, they felt, had too quickly brushed this project to one side as overly utopian. Hume Wrong believed it otherwise.

Might not a small beginning be made towards the creation of an International Force? It is not very far-fetched to argue that the Air Forces of the British Commonwealth are a not unhopeful indication of what might be accomplished. There are to be found in them not only nations of all parts of the British Commonwealth but also citizens of many foreign countries – Americans, Poles, Frenchmen, Czechs, Norwegians. Furthermore, the methods worked out for the training of these Forces are a promising example of international co-operation in finance and control.

Rather than summarily dismiss an international force as the British proposed, Canada should press for the creation of 'a small International Force, as part of the world security organization, which would be charged with the performance of specific duties. Such a force would not at first be a combatant force equipped to suppress or deter aggression. It might initially be used in the defence and maintenance of bases held available for the use of the combined military forces of the United Nations operating under a world security organization.'[31] Norman Robertson agreed that these views should be relayed to London. 'In putting them forward,' he commented, 'we c'd perhaps give them greater force by stressing the measure of their derivation from actual Canadian experience in this war – perhaps adding the Canada-US Special Service Force as another illustration.' Such a force, Robertson added, might contribute to post-war domestic as well as international order. 'The existence of an international police force might have something of the psychological release value in the RCMP and US Marines and French Foreign Legion, particularly for the restless and adventurous young men in small countries who might otherwise stay home and "make revolution" ... One pre-war complaint from have-not countries was their lack of a colonial service with its opportunity of a varied specialized and rather exotic employment for just these people...'[32]

The conception of an international force that eventually emerged was described by Hume Wrong for the benefit of the High Commissioner in London:

What the Working Committee had in mind ... was the desirability of setting up a small international force as part of the world security organization which would be charged with the performance of such specific duties as defending and maintaining United Nations bases. They had in mind a force with a distinctive uniform which would be responsible to an international body. This force might conceivably be directed by the Military Staff Committee ... responsible to a World Council which it would advise on military matters. The ultimate responsibility for the international force would therefore be the World Council. Its relation to the World Council would differ from that of the aggregate of the national forces of the Member States. The latter would be at the disposal of the World Council but the units thereof would continue to be subject to the ultimate authority of their own national governments. The former, however, would be responsible only to the World Council (and would presumably be made up of denationalized persons).

The Working Committee do not wish to seem Utopian. They are not proposing an over-all international police force which could by itself resist aggression by any combination of powers. They do believe, however, that some experiment in the establishment of a truly international force should be undertaken in the hope that further developments might come from the experience. They consider that successful experiments along these lines during the War should not be allowed to lapse.[33]

The role of regional arrangements within the United Nations system was discussed by the Great Powers at Dumbarton Oaks, in Washington, from 21 August to October 1944. It proved to be one of the few subjects on which the Great Powers were able to agree. Both the British and Americans looked to the Security Council as the mainspring of the machinery of peace. While the Council might 'encourage the settlement of local disputes through regional agencies' and might 'use these agencies "where appropriate" for enforcement action under [its] authority,' the agencies themselves were not to act on their own to enforce or restore peace.[34] The Soviet Union accepted this formulation.

UN CHARTER ART. 53

Canada was not represented at the Dumbarton Oaks talks. The government attempted to convey its views, and to learn what was going on, through the good offices of the British delegation. 'The Government was receiving a great deal of information on the proceedings at Dumbarton Oaks,' Hume Wrong told the Working Committee on 25 August. 'On each day on which sessions were held, the United Kingdom delegate held meetings with the representatives of Commonwealth governments in Washington and outlined what had taken place. At present there was little which could be done except to study the proceedings in Washington. The general views of the Canadian Government had already been sent to London and there was not much which could be added to them just now.'[35]

The Dumbarton Oaks discussions did not solve the problem of regionalism exactly to Canada's satisfaction. 'Section VIII(C) goes somewhat further than we should have liked,' Pearson reported from Washington in September, 'as it gives regional organizations the authority to settle local disputes whereas we should have preferred that regional organizations have no political authority.' But this was mainly a matter of emphasis. There were other features of the arrangements emerging from Dumbarton Oaks to which the Canadian Government took more strenuous objection.

It was the same at San Francisco. The Canadian delegation chose to concentrate on what was for it the more important issue of staking out a role for middle and small powers, leaving the debate over regionalism largely to the Latin American and United States representatives. The Latins were concerned lest the inter-American system be contradicted or compromised by the United Nations Charter, in which they therefore desired to emphasize as forcefully as possible the autonomy of regional organizations. The Americans, while not wanting either to weaken the inter-American system or to offend the Latins, were concerned lest the authority of the Security Council be eroded by too vigorous an assertion of regional rights. A compromise between these two positions, somewhat favouring the former, resulted in Articles 51 and 52 of the Charter. No one at San Francisco foresaw that in less than four years' time the Canadian Government would seize gratefully upon those articles as providing the legal justification for the creation of a regional security organization for the North Atlantic area. Certainly no Canadian foresaw it.

## THE GREAT POWERS AND THE MIDDLE POWER

A second fundamental principle on which the Canadian Government had settled when the Great Powers issued their declaration from Moscow on 1 November 1943 was that any future international organization ought to provide generously for the role of Member States other than the Great Powers.

As early as 1 March 1943, the Prime Minister of Canada was experiencing displeasure and misgiving at the way the smaller countries in general, and Canada in particular, were being passed by and passed over. 'We are not satisfied,' Mackenzie King had written to his Minister at Washington, 'with the place that has been accorded to Canada in some of the bodies set up for the direction of the war ... We cannot accept the idea that our destinies can be entrusted to the four larger powers.'[36] Mainly because of the special personal relationship Mackenzie King maintained with the Prime Minister of the United Kingdom and the President of the United States, Canada was better placed than any of the lesser Allies to put the case against the domination of the post-war world by the Great Powers.

Both Churchill and Roosevelt had from the outset been drawn to the notion of a Big Three, or a Big Four, concert system as the only practicable basis for a durable peace. In April 1943, the Canadian Minister at Washington reported that in conversation with the President, Roosevelt had remarked to him 'that there will be no peace conference after this war – "Winston, Stalin, and myself, and possibly the Chinese, will settle things." I jokingly said,' the Minister added, ' "Do you desire me to report this to my Government?" He said, "There is no need to do that, because I have already told Mackenzie [King] the same thing".'[37] But to Mackenzie King this was no joking matter. The prospect that the post-war world might be governed by a concert of the Great Powers was intolerable to him, as he knew it would be to most Canadians. At the Quebec Conference in August 1943, he took advantage of his role as host to Churchill and Roosevelt to tell them both straight out that, as he recorded, 'I did not believe the other United Nations would like it, and I knew the Dominions would resent it. We would not agree to a government of the world by the four most powerful powers – it was contrary to conception for which this war was being fought.' Churchill replied that he was 'all for having ... an Assembly in which all nations would be represented – they could talk all they liked.'[38] That added insult to the injury. It was not just to be able to sound off in public debate that Canada had contributed nearly a million men and women to the armed forces of the Grand Alliance.

The Canadian Government was prepared to grant that the Great Powers should have the main say in the maintenance of peace and security, for only the Great Powers would be able to maintain them. 'There should be a real relationship between power and responsibility in the new world organization,' L.B. Pearson commented from Washington in July 1944. 'It doesn't make international organization either more effective or more democratic if it is made as easy for Iran as for the USA to obstruct salutary action.'[39] But Canada would not and could not accept as a corollary the proposition that all that remained to the rest was to do what they were told. 'Unless [the smaller powers] have the voice to which they are entitled by the contributions they can make to world security and prosperity,' Mackenzie King stated at the Commonwealth Prime Ministers' Conference on 11 May 1944, 'they cannot be expected to discharge their appropriate responsibilities. They must be assured that they can bring their cases before the World Assembly or World Council, and not feel that settlements by the Great Powers will be made arbitrarily at their expense.'[40] Nor was it clear that Great Power settlements were the most effective settlements. 'The history of the League proves that not small powers but big powers cause most of the trouble and prevent most of the solutions,' Pearson wrote to Norman Robertson.

It also shows that smaller powers – when not the pawns of larger – can do good and constructive international work. Would it not, therefore, be wise to give those smaller powers as much prestige and authority in the Organization as possible, without giving them power to block moves agreed on in the Council? Otherwise, the moral and world position of the Organization will be greatly reduced and it may become a sort of Holy Alliance with a great number of indifferent or resentful states outside that alliance. Even on the lowest terms, it is surely essential to construct an impressive, dignified, universal organization within which the Big Powers can co-operate, and which will add its moral authority to the effective executive action of the smaller group of Great Powers.

The Assembly is that section of the world organization which will attract the most public attention and it will be the main outlet in the world organization for the views on international problems of the vast majority of states. It is, therefore, important, from the point of view of the prestige of the Organization as a whole, that the Assembly should be something more than a futile debating society.[41]

Upon these themes the Canadians continued to play as opportunity afforded. Opportunity did not afford much. During the summer of 1944 they did their best to press their case upon the British, through whom they hoped to influence the outcome of the negotiations at Dumbarton Oaks. 'The position proposed for secondary states in the new organization,' the British Government was informed by Ottawa on 2 August,

should receive careful and anxious attention ... The special place accorded to the Great Powers should not be extended beyond functions in which their active collaboration is indispensable. If they are given too large an authority and too extensive a right of individual veto the result may be that membership will not be sufficiently responsible to secure the participation of important secondary states whose full collaboration would be of the greatest value ... We are concerned over the very extensive powers proposed for the Council in both the United Kingdom and the United States plans...[42]

To this entreaty, and others like it – in which Canada was joined by Australia and New Zealand – the British responded with mollifying messages. The Canadians were right to remain anxious about the outcome. There was some support in the Foreign Office for the Canadian position, but that was not what ultimately counted. Churchill valued the veto as highly as did his colleagues in Washington and Moscow, which is to say very highly indeed. One of his chief preoccupations was to keep the British colonial empire out of the hands of those who, in the absence of the veto, would doubtless lay their hands upon it. Where the veto was concerned, he was not disposed to yield much, and did not yield much. When the British representative emerged from the first round of the Dumbarton Oaks meetings to tell the Dominions what had transpired, what he had to say was far from reassuring. 'From what we were told yesterday,' L.B. Pearson reported from Washington on 24 August, 'it is not much of an exaggeration to say that the points on which the Three Powers seem to find least difficulty in reaching agreement are those about which we have most doubts.'[43] 'There would be agreement between the Great Powers,' Hume Wrong duly informed the Working Committee the next day, adding that he could not be certain 'that this agreement would be palatable to the other countries. Canada had two points of view to consider. We did not want to throw a monkey-wrench into the harmony among the Great Powers but, on the other hand, we wanted to protect the Canadian position as well as that of other small countries.'[44]

On 6 September, Norman Robertson formulated the views of the Canadian Government for L.B. Pearson, whose exacting mission it had become to try to convince the Dumbarton Oaks conferees of their merit without himself taking part in the discussions.

The concurrence of important trading countries should be given in decisions involving the application of economic sanctions. In this regard, of course, Canada far outranks both the Soviet Union and China on the basis of pre-war [trade].

It is difficult to see how the Canadian Government could secure the support of Parliament and the public for the surrender to the Council of full responsibility for, in the extreme case, sending into action a substantial quota of the Canadian armed forces without themselves being a party to the decision. This would be too serious a denial of responsible government to be swallowed in the present state of international political organization. Much the same argument applies also to the imposition of economic sanctions involving a real disturbance in the Canadian economy.

If the Great Powers maintain a complete veto right for themselves (except possibly in case of disputes in which they are involved), their surrender of sovereignty scarcely exceeds what they all formally renounced in the Kellogg-Briand Pact. They commit themselves to a procedure but retain liberty to block the employment of the procedure. The propose, however, that other states should not only be bound by the procedure but should be bound to do their share in executing decisions in the framing of which they have had no part unless they happen to be elected to the Council. This might not matter much in the case of a considerable number of little countries whose collaboration in carrying out Council decisions would be unimportant. The serious difficulties concern the position of the chief secondary states, the co-operation of some at least of which would probably always be essential in the effective application of either military or economic sanctions.

The result to be aimed at is fairly clear although it is difficult to suggest an exact formula: Any Government required to participate in the execution of a decision which involves substantial action on its part should be placed in a position in which it can satisfy its legislature and people that it has had a responsible share in the taking of the decision.[45]

Reasonable as this position might have appeared, it did not make much headway. From Canada's standpoint the Dumbarton Oaks meetings went from bad to worse. 'Pearson is discouraged,' the Prime Minister was told on 10 September; that was ominous, for Pearson was not easily discouraged. The next day Hume Wrong wrote to Robertson that he had begun to feel that the fate of the world body was at stake.

I am disturbed by the serious possibility that the plan now being framed will not be accepted by a considerable number of States. Even if it were accepted, I doubt that States other than Great Powers would go on to consent to place quotas of their forces and military facilities at the disposal of the Council. This would pretty well reduce the whole organization to an alliance between great powers, with frills attached to give it the appearance of general participation. One frill would be the right of the five Permanent Council members plus one other to the active co-operation of all member states in the execution of decisions on which they might reach agreement between themselves.

The 'sovereign equality' of states becomes, in practice, the sovereign equality of Great Powers. Canada would probably be less directly affected by such a plan than any of the smaller countries in Europe or Asia. The smaller countries in those continents, or at any rate those most exposed from the point of view of security, would probably be compelled to become clients of a Great Power – in Europe either of the UK or of the USSR – thus creating new spheres of influence and a new balance of power. This would greatly complicate intra-Commonwealth relations; and its long-term effect might well be disastrous...[46]

On 14 September, Wrong predicted that 'the central Canadian difficulty over acceptance of the world security organization in the form emerging from the Washington talks will arise from the imposition of permanent and indefinite obligations which might, in the extreme case, require Canada, by order of a Council on which Canada was not represented, to impose heavy burdens on the Canadian people.'[47] Two days later, he informed the Prime Minister that Dumbarton Oaks was producing a plan which would be 'wide open to attack in Canada ... the attacks all centring around one of its central features – a Council possessing great authority to enforce settlements of disputes and to require all member states to assist in enforcement, while giving inside the Council a very special position to the Great Powers.'[48]

What was to be done? No last-minute conversion of the Dumbarton Oaks conferees, *via* the British delegate whose sympathetic and effective advocacy could not in any case be counted on, seemed likely. A suggestion by Escott Reid that the Prime Minister should make a public statement to 'demonstrate that the Government was aware of the deficiencies of the Charter'[49] was not well received. The Canadian Government decided to play for time. In this it was helped by the failure of the Big Three to reach agreement on the use of the veto. Mackenzie King urged Churchill to delay publication of the draft proposals.

> I question whether the publication of the plan in its present form, with the section on voting in the Council left blank, will help ultimate agreement. Its publication will appear to narrow the issue to the single problem of the right of great powers to vote in the Council in disputes in which they are involved, while fixing in other respects the structure and authority of the new international organs. Is it not possible that a way around the difficulty might be found even though this would involve changes of substance of other parts of the plan? Should there not be an attempt to see whether a different pattern could meet the Russian position?...
>
> It will take time to explore alternative courses, and it is important to keep the situation as fluid as possible. Hence I repeat my suggestion that the official publication of the plan should be deferred...[50]

But the British Government had no desire to explore alternative courses. It regarded the matter as settled. It wanted only to remove as quickly as possible the impasse which had developed between the Russians and Americans over the use of the veto in a way which would safeguard to the greatest possible extent the interests of the Permanent Members. 'We have received no further word from London on our suggestion that publication of the plan should be deferred,' Norman Robertson informed Pearson on 5 October, a week after Mackenzie King's message to Churchill. Meanwhile, James Reston had leaked most of its contents in the *New York Times*. The Dumbarton Oaks Proposals – minus the section on Security Council voting procedure – were published on 9 October.

The problem of the veto was held over for consideration at the summit of the Grand Alliance when its leaders would next meet. They next met at Yalta in February 1945. And what was done at Yalta was done not only without Canada's consent, it was done without Canada's knowledge. 'We had been told nothing of the proceedings at Yalta,' Mackenzie King wrote afterwards, 'had not been informed of what was going on.'[51]

The Canadian Government had been informed by Washington of the United States proposal that the veto should not apply to procedural questions in the Council. This restriction Stalin accepted at Yalta, perhaps because he knew how easily it could be circumvented. 'We cannot say that the proposed arrangement is satisfactory,' Hume Wrong remarked on learning of it, 'but we should not say that it is unsatisfactory.'[52]

By no stretch of the imagination can that be called daredevil diplomacy.

Yet, as has been said,* discretion may be the better part of valour; and a reputation for discreet statecraft was to carry Canadian diplomacy far in the post-war world. Seldom would discretion pay greater dividends than during the United Nations Conference on International Organization. There Canada, in the company of other lesser States, confronted a harsh and unyielding choice. She might accept the kind of United Nations on which the Great Powers had reached agreement; or risk the prospect of no United Nations at all.

The Canadians at San Francisco did not hesitate to choose the first. All their wartime planning had pressed for a widening of alternatives; but they had never been prepared to place the whole project in jeopardy just because Canadian interests had been insufficiently looked after. Like Voltaire, they preferred peace to Canada. They did not welcome, nor did they join, the efforts of other delegations – the Australian, the New Zealand, the Mexican – to force amendment of the Charter against the expressed desire of the Great Powers. They regarded those efforts as maladroit, jejune, dangerous. 'It seems clear to us,' a member of the delegation wrote back to Ottawa in June 1945,

> that, in this year of grace, there cannot be a world organization established, with Russia as a member, unless it provides for voting rights substantially as set forth in the Great Power memorandum ... The effective choice appears, therefore, to be between such an Organization and an organization from which the Soviet Union and those countries which feel their security must closely depend on their relations with it are excluded. Our view is that it is better to take the Organization that we can get and, having come to that decision, to refrain from further efforts to pry apart that difficult unity which the Great Powers have attained. This means foregoing the luxury of making any more perfectionist speeches...[53]

This attitude strongly commended itself to the Canadian Government. By it the conduct of its delegation was guided throughout the remainder of the Conference.

But if Canada did not wish to be a 'small power rampant'† at San Francisco, she was far from being a small power dormant. Her restraint in not attacking that which the Great Powers would not in any case surrender helped to ensure that a Charter acceptable to all finally emerged from the drafting committees. Her labours within those committees (and

* Though not, in this context, without qualm: 'I realize that I invite calumny in citing Falstaff as a patron of Canadian diplomacy.' John W. Holmes, *The Better Part of Valour: Essays on Canadian Diplomacy* (Toronto, Montreal 1970), vii.

† The expressive phrase used by Professor Wood to describe the role of New Zealand throughout the Conference. See F.L.W. Wood, *The New Zealand People at War: Political and External Affairs* (Wellington, NZ 1958), 370–84.

within the suites of the mighty at the Fairmont and Mark Hopkins Hotels) left their impress upon a number of its articles. So it was, as an exhausted member of the delegation wrote on 19 June, that the finished product appeared 'a much better document than when we started.'

The greatest improvement in the document, from a Canadian standpoint, was represented by the final form of Article 44:

When the Security Council has decided to use force it shall, before calling upon a Member not represented on it to provide armed forces in fulfillment of the obligations assumed under Article 43, invite that Member, if the Member so desires, to participate in the decisions of the Security Council concerning the employment of contingents of that Member's armed forces.

This text is a tribute to the tenacity of the Prime Minister of Canada. Mackenzie King was greatly concerned to discover that, as the Great Power delegations were disposed to view the matter, a government not represented on the Security Council might be obliged to furnish troops without any opportunity to contract out or even to express its views. Had this procedure carried, he would have had to return to Parliament with the news that, after all he had promised over the years to the contrary, it would no longer be able to decide whether or not to despatch Canadian forces for service overseas. He was determined to prevent it from carrying. On 11 May, at a meeting at General Smuts' apartment in the Fairmont Hotel, attended as well by Herbert Evatt of Australia and Peter Fraser of New Zealand, Mackenzie King sought to enlist the support of the Dominion Governments for his position. 'I did not see how it was possible,' he told the group,

to agree to a step which meant conscription of a nation's forces at the instance of four or five outside Great Powers. I doubted if such a Charter with such a provision would ever be accepted by our Parliament ... I spoke of how difficult it had been for us to come to concede the veto of the five Great Powers. We had worked ourselves into the view of granting it. Members of Parliament and certainly the country did not grasp the significance of that step, as yet. It would come to them as a shock...[54]

The Dominion leaders did not seem to share Mackenzie King's concern in this matter. Smuts, in particular, the Canadian Prime Minister recorded, 'seemed to feel in a casual sort of way to give interested countries a chance to be on the Council for consultation would be enough without sitting as temporary members with voting powers.' At a further meeting very late that night, Mackenzie King put his case to Anthony Eden and Lord Cranborne; but the British leaders were 'pretty well tired out,' and he doubted that he had made much of an impression upon them.

He had, however, impressed them sufficiently for them to raise the question with the American Secretary of State. On 14 May, Edward Stettinius called upon the Canadian Prime Minister. 'The interview,' Mackenzie King recorded,

> was a most important one. Mr Stettinius began by asking me how I thought things were going. I replied ... I did not see serious difficulties ahead except with regard to smaller powers being represented on the Security Council when matters affecting sanctions and their own interests were being considered. I stated that I thought in drafting the Dumbarton Oaks proposals and what had been done since, those working on the revisions had more in mind a plan which could be followed once the organization was formed but little in mind what was necessary to get approval of the Charter in the first instance. I thought it was very essential to get into the Charter itself something that would be reassuring to the smaller powers, when approval of the Charter was being worked out...
>
> I said ... that it seemed to me the proper procedure was for the Security Council on the basis of military advisers to determine and decide that certain forces were necessary. The next step was organization of forces. When that step was being taken, if it was proposed to take a division, say, from Canada, Canada should be asked to come and sit on the Security Council as a member and vote in the Security Council. If there were other countries that felt they were affected or were being called, they would not sit on the Security Council at the same time but could come in when their turn came. In other words, if the Council was composed of 11, there would be only an addition of one when voting took place. If the Council could not get a majority in those circumstances, there would be grounds for believing something really was wrong. I pointed out it might be helpful for the Council itself knowing of reasons whether a certain step was appropriate or not appropriate. Something they might not have thought of, for example, differences between South American Republics. The United States might not wish to use their own forces. We might prefer to have Canada's forces used rather than those from some European countries. However, if they were to be used against certain countries that were largely French, it might be a mistake to have Canadian troops sent in ... On the other hand, Canada being represented as a nation on the Security Council, provided presenting its case there. Its representatives would be able to return to their own country and explain why forces of that particular country were being requested and could state if [they] had a vote, that [they] had been overruled and that the majority rule must carry...
>
> Stettinius ... seemed much relieved at this suggestion ... Said at once it seemed to afford a way out ... I left with the distinct impression that the matter was settled ... It has really meant victory for the smaller nations in the fight that was being made for their recognition on the Security Council.[55]

It was a victory, but a victory of status rather than of substance. For not to this day has the Security Council been able to take any military action on behalf of the United Nations. Thus the question of interpreting the key provision of Article 44 secured by Mackenzie King's personal diplomacy – the right of any Member 'to participate in the decisions of the Security

Council concerning the employment of contingents of that Members' armed forces' – has never arisen over the years.

Mackenzie King's satisfaction at this job well done was tempered by his failure to receive what he considered to be adequate public recognition of his role at San Francisco. He was especially chagrined – not without reason – when, at the ceremony of the signing of the Charter, the representative of Peru singled out Evatt of Australia as the champion of the rights of the smaller powers against the Great. However, his disappointment was soon banished by his remarkable capacity for self-consolation. 'My part,' he reflected, 'has been done quietly, unobtrusively but effectively behind the scenes.' The tribute was just, even if it came better from someone other than its subject. 'A common failing with many men,' Mackenzie King added characteristically, is 'that [their] leadership consists in showing that one has power rather than in getting one's end by means that lead to agreement on the part of all.'[56]

## KEEPING UP WITH THE PATAGONIANS

In 1919, Sir Robert Borden had expended himself in Paris in an 'earnest effort' (as he himself described it) 'to hold our own with Patagonia.' Equality of status with Patagonia no longer satisfied Canadian statesmen at the end of the Second World War. It became a third fundamental principle of Canada's policy towards post-war international organization to ensure that in whatever institutions might be created to keep the peace, Member States other than Great Powers should not be indiscriminately lumped together without due regard for the important differences by which they could and ought to be distinguished.

Here was the germ of what in due course Canadian spokesmen would call 'the functional idea.' It grew out of the assumption that the world was a more complicated place than a simple division of labour between the Great Powers, on the one hand, and all the rest, on the other, might indicate. The international institutions of that world ought to reflect its complexity in the arrangements to be made for admission to membership and leadership. More specifically, as Mackenzie King once put it, 'those countries which have most to contribute to the maintenance of the peace of the world should be most frequently selected' for positions on the governing bodies of its international institutions.[57] As the war drew to a close, the Canadian Government had become firmly committed to this principle, in the exposition of which it had grown skilled by repetition.

The functional idea, thus understood, is related to, but should be distinguished from, a theory or hypothesis of international relations sometimes known as 'functionalism.' The functional theory supposes that the problems connected with the building of a peaceable and prosperous states-system are best approached by dealing, through appropriate international institutions, with economic and social shortcomings, rather than by a head-on and headlong assault upon political grievances. For political grievances, being political, are more likely to be intractable. From the functional theory derives the functional idea: those states best qualified by resources and experience to make a constructive contribution to the solution of economic and social problems ought to play a commanding role in whatever international institution is created to deal with them.

As early as 1942 the Canadian Government had asserted the functional idea in an effort to gain membership on the Executive Committee of the United Nations Relief and Rehabilitation Administration. UNRRA was the first international institution created by the Allies which was not directly related to the conduct of the war, and was widely regarded as a prototype for other international institutions which might be created later on. The Canadian Government perceived correctly that an important precedent was at stake. If Canada, by deploying the functional idea on behalf of her candidacy, successfully pressed her claim to a place on the Executive Committee, the way was opened up for her representation in other inner councils as these appeared; conversely, to be excluded from UNRRA boded ill for the status and stature of Canada in the post-war world. Exclusion, however, did not seem likely; on any fair application of the functional idea it seemed impossible. Not only had Canadian farms and factories, Canadian mines and forests, supplied the forces of the Grand Alliance with so much of what had kept them fighting: their output would be no less indispensable in the gigantic tasks of relief and rehabilitation which lay ahead, and which UNRRA had been created to organize and direct.

Confident in the justice of its case, the Canadian Government was as much startled as aggrieved to discover that the Great Powers were less than sympathetic to granting it a place on UNRRA's Executive Committee. The Russians and Americans appeared to think that by acceding to Canada's request they would be opening a Pandora's Box from which small nations by the score would emerge to demand similar treatment. The Americans, in particular, were troubled by the same spectre of 'five votes to one' which had so agitated some of their Senators during the debate in 1920 on the Treaty of Versailles. 'We should put our foot down in the very beginning,' Harry Hopkins wrote to the United States Ambassador in London, 'and insist on the main committee of four members ... [Otherwise] we would be constantly outvoted.'[58] To this was added the suspicion, which the British also shared, that Canada's zeal in claiming membership was caused less by a desire to become a philanthropist to the world than by her concern to protect her post-war markets for her produce, especially for her wheat. Fearful of creating an undesirable precedent, wary of her motives, the Great Powers refused to give in to Canada's demands.

This rebuff produced much bitterness in Ottawa. But as at San Francisco later on discretion was thought to be the better part of valour. The Canadians responded in a manner high-minded rather than high-handed, realizing that to continue the struggle would only delay the creation of UNRRA and perhaps compromise its vital work. They agreed to a compromise. Canada, while foregoing membership on the Executive Committee, would become a member of a Committee on Supplies, whose chairman should attend meetings of the Executive Committee whenever Supply was under discussion, which was expected to be practically all of the time. The Great Powers were also to be members of the Committee on Supplies. Finally, the Americans and British promised to try to secure the election of a Canadian as its chairman.

This compromise was accepted by the Canadian Government on its express understanding that it was not to be regarded as a precedent by which other international institutions would be bound or even guided. Even so, it was an unhappy outcome for the Ottawa functionalists, even for one far-flung functionalist in London. 'I confess I was disappointed,' Vincent Massey wrote to his Prime Minister in April 1943,

> that it was found necessary to give up our claim to be a full member of the post-war relief administration. We seemed to be on such sound ground in asking for full membership ... I cannot help feeling that sooner or later we shall have to be very "tough" indeed in connection with our relation to these post-war international bodies. The "Big Power" complex seems to be unfortunately far too prevalent at present and we will suffer from it, I think, until we have scored a victory in some such issue as the recent one, and have secured full acknowledgment of the right of Canada to sit on international bodies when for functional reasons it is right and proper that she should.[59]

The functional idea suffered a severe reverse in the UNRRA affair. Nevertheless, the Canadian Government, so far from abandoning functionalism as an unwanted foundling on the United Nations doorstep, determined to promote its welfare all the harder in the future. The experience taught it to be less concerned about the status of other smaller powers and more concerned about the status of Canada as a middle power. 'We are moving up in the International League,' L.B. Pearson told a Toronto audience in March 1944, 'even though we are not yet in the first division.' In a letter written around that time to Norman Robertson, Pearson reflected on the problems he was encountering as Canada sought to find her proper place among the nations:

> Canada is achieving, I think, a very considerable position as a leader, if not *the* leader, among a group of States which are important enough to be necessary to the Big Four but not important enough to be accepted as one of that quartet. As a matter of fact, the position of a "little Big Power" or "big Little Power" is a very difficult one, especially if the "little Big Power" is also a "big Dominion." The big fellows have power and responsibility, but they also have control. We "in between States" sometimes get, it seems, the worst of both worlds. We are necessary but not necessary enough. I think this is being felt by countries like The Netherlands and Belgium as well as by ourselves. That is why these countries are not only looking towards the Big Powers, but are looking toward each other for support. There is, I think, an opportunity for Canada, if we desire to take it, to become the leader of this group.[60]

The Canadian Government did what it could to develop among British ministers and officials a sympathetic understanding of what it meant to be a middle power. 'Just as we are prepared to recognize the great difference in power and responsibility between Canada and the Soviet Union,' Mackenzie King told the meeting of Commonwealth Prime Ministers on 11 May 1944, '[so] we should expect some recognition of the considerable difference between Canada and Panama.'[61] Later in the summer, during an exchange of views between the British and Canadian governments on the proposed United Nations constitution, Ottawa raised for the first time a claim for Canada's right to be represented not only on such economic and social organizations as UNRRA and FAO, but as well on the political executive charged with the maintenance of international peace and security. 'In the case of the Council,' the Canadian government's message observed, 'a major consideration [for the qualifications of membership] should be the relative military power of the member states; the actual contribution towards the defeat of Germany and Japan provides one convenient and very relevant criterion for assessing this.' By such a criterion, fairly applied, Canada would be assured a place on the Council.

In Ottawa this argument seemed logically unassailable. In London it seemed politically unacceptable. It was by no means certain, the British replied, that by making military power the basic criterion for membership on the proposed Council all British Commonwealth members would be advantaged. Nor would the criterion be to the advantage of the countries of Nazi-occupied Europe: the military contribution to victory of France, Belgium, Holland, Denmark, and Norway had been negligible, but their suffering and sacrifice far from negligible; it was not just, it was not expedient, that they should be ignored once their position among the nations had been re-established. Finally, the British argued, any arrangement which attempted a classification of secondary powers in different categories would produce not only anomalies but antagonisms among their ranks: these would be far from helpful to the United Nations organization during its formative phase.

For these reasons the British Government felt obliged to reject the Canadian position. But the Canadian Government was in no mood to have it rejected. It reaffirmed, in a message of 4 September 1944, its belief that powers other than the Great Powers should be represented on the Council, and that their selection 'should in some way be related to a dispassionate appraisal of their probable effective contribution of states to the maintenance of security. You will, I am sure,' Mackenzie King thought it well to add to this dispatch, 'appreciate how difficult it would be for Canada, after enlisting nearly one million persons in her armed forces and trebling her national debt in order to assist in restoring peace. to accept a situation of parity in this respect with the Dominican Republic or Salvador.'[63]

By sticking to their guns, the Canadians were able to extract a promise from the British Government to carry into the Great Power discussions at Dumbarton Oaks a formula on representation on the Council designed to meet their needs. The British allowed that they thought the formula might not get through intact but promised to do their best. Their best resulted in a statement issued by the Dumbarton Oaks conferees on 9 October declaring that, in electing non-permanent members to the Council, 'due regard' should be 'specially paid, in the first instance, to the contribution of Members of the United Nations to the maintenance of international peace and security and to the other purposes of the Organization.' This best was better than nothing. But the Canadian Government still felt it did not go far enough to assure Canada of an appropriate 'middle power' position in the field of international peace and security.

On 12 January 1945, Canada made a final bid for recognition. It took the form of a memorandum addressed to the four Great Powers and the Provisional Government of the French Republic. 'Canada certainly makes no claim to be regarded as a great power,' this document assured its recipients. However, it continued,

> the Canadian record in two great wars ... has revealed both readiness to join in concerted action against aggression and the possession of substantial military and industrial capacity ... The question therefore arises whether it is possible, within the framework of the general scheme, to devise means of associating more effectively with the work of the Security Council states of the order of international importance of Canada.[64]

It was very late in the day to be re-opening such a question. Having with scant success sought support from the United Kingdom, the Canadian Government now turned to the United States. To no avail. 'I was not able to make progress,' Hume Wrong admitted after discussions with State Department officials in mid-February 1945. 'The Americans produced the obvious and formidable objections to any effort to classify all the States of the world in accordance with their international significance.'[65] 'One of the most difficult things to attempt,' Wrong mused not long after this failure, 'seems to me to be to persuade a representative of a great power to see any situation from the point of view of a smaller power...'[66]

Part of Canada's difficulty in interesting the Great Powers in boosting her post-war status derived from being a group of one. Other non-Great Powers – particularly the 'band-wagon states,' mostly Latin American, which had qualified for United Nations membership by last-minute declarations of war upon the Axis – were entirely satisfied with the seating plan, and not at all disposed to favour any scheme for making post-war status depend on wartime performance. Canada had no support. There was not much more the Canadian Government could do beyond hoping that when it came to electing the first non-permanent members of the Security Council, justice would be done and right prevail.

That sometimes happens, even in international politics. But this was not one of those times. In the first election to non-permanent membership, Canada ran – and lost.

Some consolation attached, perhaps, to losing to Australia – a country which on the functional criteria had an excellent claim to a seat. But the Canadian delegation to the first General Assembly could be pardoned for believing that Canada's claim was even better. The insiders might console themselves further by reflecting that Canada's defeat came about through a technicality – in fact, a fluke – in the voting procedure.* But it was deemed inexpedient to publicize that aspect, and it did not greatly help to brood about it. 'The results,' Hume Wrong wrote from the scene of the accident, 'must have been a shock to all of you in Ottawa.'[67] They were

* Canada actually received the required two-thirds vote of 34 on the first ballot. However, the delegate of Nicaragua spoiled his ballot by signing his name, thereby making a run-off vote necessary between Canada and the next highest contender, which was Australia. Mexico having already been elected, many of the delegates, bearing in mind the injunction of Article 23 of the Charter to pay due regard to 'equitable geographical position,' voted for Australia in preference to another North American Security Council member.

More than once, Canadian diplomats had compared the countries of Central America invidiously to their own; it was, therefore, poetically just at least that the cause of the failure of Canada's candidacy and of the set-back to functionalism should be the delegate of Nicaragua.

indeed. 'Our functional principle seems to have been thrown out of the window,' Pearson commented wryly. 'In elections to the Security Council it has been subordinated to the geographical principle ... I am afraid that the election pattern which is developing in UNO, in spite of our efforts ... and all our speeches on functional representation, will not be any better than that which prevailed in Geneva in the old days.'[68]

The Canadians had reason to feel disheartened, none as yet to feel disenchanted. Pearson's natural optimism soon reasserted itself. But for Mackenzie King the episode served only to deepen his distrust of the United Nations. It seemed to him just as well that his country was not required at the outset to occupy a seat in the front parlour of what he called 'a creaking house with nothing of a solid structure about it.'[69]

# 3

# Settling Europe

And in his mind
The sifting, timeless sunlight would not find
Memories of stylish Florence or of sacked Rome,
Rather the boyhood that he left at home;
Skating at Scarborough, summers at the Island,
These are the dreams that float beyond his hand ...

*Douglas LePan*

Canada did not intend that the post-war world should be run by three Great Powers or four – not if she could help it. But her government was not averse to allowing Great Powers to work out and impose a general settlement for Europe. It was an expression of the functional approach that they should do so. Where boundaries should be drawn, peoples settled, indemnities demanded, were not first and foremost the business of Canadians. Their business lay rather in doing their best to ensure that such details of the settlement, worked out by those more familiar with the problems, should be such that the peace and prosperity of Europe would be most surely and swiftly restored. For on Europe's peace and Europe's prosperity Canada's own depended; so two world wars had shown.

For this, two requirements were essential. The Canadian government had to know what sorts of settlements were under study. The views of the Canadian government had to be taken fairly into account, should it wish to put views forward for consideration.

## THE MOODS OF KING AND COUNTRY

Mackenzie King was as diffident during the war years in venturing his views on the European settlements as he was forthright in expressing his views about post-war international organization or the future of the Commonwealth of Nations.

That diffidence was in no way due to lack of familiarity with Europe's problems. His experience might suffer if compared to that of his fellow prime minister from South Africa; but Smuts, as the only statesman to lead delegations at peace conferences following two world wars, was virtually unique. Compared to Curtin, or Evatt, or Fraser, or to any Commonwealth leader including Churchill himself (though not, perhaps, to Eden), Mackenzie King might well be considered a European area specialist. Student days in Germany, travel in France and Italy, three missions to Geneva, a score of visits to Great Britain, talks and correspondence with European luminaries and European rogues a list of whom resembles the index to Gunther's *Inside Europe*, made him familiar with the scene.

What was missing was the interest. The Prime Minister of New Zealand, admitting 'very imperfect knowledge ... of this complicated question,' did not for a moment allow so minor a liability to inhibit his sending a personal despatch to Churchill in February 1945 defending Poland's 'just claim for Lwow with or without the neighbouring oilfields.'[1] Issues such as the placing of the Polish frontier the Prime Minister of Canada was content to allow to be decided by the flow of events.

For where European problems were concerned, Mackenzie King remained an isolationist. Such had he been at the end of the First World War; such was he now at the end of a Second. On 28 August 1944, his thoughts turned towards Europe by the visit a month earlier of General de Gaulle, he confided to a member of his staff 'that some of his officials were urging him to play a role in the settlement of the political problems of Europe. He was averse to this, he said, for his feeling was that while we could properly have a voice in the solution of world economic problems, he did not judge it expedient or appropriate for us to intervene in European political affairs.'[2] A year later he told de Gaulle much the same thing. 'I pointed out,' Mackenzie King recorded, 'that we are not particularly interested in political developments, in the fixation of boundary lines, etc., in Europe, but that we were interested in the economic questions. I did not want it to be understood that we wished to get involved in all European situations. Quite the contrary.'[3] Events in Europe confirmed him in this view. 'What folly it would be,' he wrote in his diary on 14 August 1946, 'for any of our people to go poking their fingers into the European pie ... There is a mass of intrigue, grievance, etc., which none but those who are parties to them will ever be able to know or understand.'[4]

That contemptuous dismissal was by then to slight the insights of what had become the Canadian 'attentive public' – the people among a country's population who, while laying no claim to any formidable expertise, are interested in and tolerably well informed about international affairs.

At the close of the First World War such a group had been practically non-existent. The science (or art) of international politics was not even in its infancy: it was embryonic, possibly yet to be conceived. All the experts – that is to say, two or three – were in government service. A motley band of self-appointed educators – journalists, professors, presidents of banks, captains of industry – presumed to contrive a public philosophy. For what it thus received the public did not seem truly grateful. Nor had it much reason to be grateful. An historian of the period reconstructs as follows the meagre stock of ideas with which its public mind was furnished:

> There was a general but cautious endorsement of the idea of a league of nations, but no Smuts appeared in Canada to contribute towards its philosophy, and no league of nations society was formed until after the League was in being. Occasional references are found to the misrule of the Turks, and in particular a tenderness for the Armenians. On the question of freedom of the seas Canadians usually followed the British lead. Some of the newspapers took an interest in reduction of armaments and government control of the industry. One of the few questions on which Canadians showed any direct interest was reparations, in the sense that there were frequent demands that Canada should receive compensation from Germany. It was left to the imagination to estimate how large the sum received might be...[5]

The study from which the foregoing passage is quoted was commissioned in 1941 by the Canadian Institute of International Affairs in the hope that it might contribute to the formation of opinion better equipped than that of the preceding generation to ponder usefully the problems of the post-war world. The Institute had been brought into being in 1928 by a dozen public-spirited and mostly prominent Canadians, including Sir Robert Borden, Sir Arthur Currie, Sir Joseph Flavelle, N.W. Rowell, and J.W. Dafoe.* Their philosophy was frankly élitist. They sought to cultivate 'a small group of well-informed men and women in Canada who, because of their training, knowledge and position, may be of some assistance in dealing with the external affairs of our country ... We are not interested in a large membership nor in propagandist work, and aim as far as possible to keep our membership limited to those who can make some

* For a detailed description of their efforts, see Edward D. Greathed, 'Antecedents and Origins of the Canadian Institute of International Affairs,' in Harvey L. Dyck and H. Peter Krosby (eds.) *Empire and Nations: Essays in Honour of Frederic H. Soward* (Toronto 1969), 91–115, and Carter Manny, 'The Canadian Institute of International Affairs, 1928 to 1939: An Attempt to "Enlighten" Canada's Foreign Policy' (unpublished Harvard College AB thesis).

contribution to the knowledge and study of international affairs.'[6] By 1943 the number of this élite had risen to more than 1500. The Institute's membership thus included nearly all of the expertise on international affairs that Canada then could muster. It was natural that the Institute should give the lead to public discussion of the terms of the coming peace, of future international organization, and of Canada's place in the post-war world.

These efforts were at first not welcomed in high places. Mackenzie King had always thought that, so far as public opinion on foreign policy was concerned, silence was golden. 'As little discussion as possible,' he wrote to a back-bencher in April 1936, 'should be raised in our House of Commons with respect to the present European situation.'[7] And he shuddered when contemplating, as on 28 October 1937, 'the mischief that an organization like the League of Nations Society ... can work on the whole country ... allowing themselves to be used for the purpose of advocating policies which would lead to war.'[8] These were pre-war views, but wartime did not change them. 'The more [the] public ... is diverted to questions about what is going to be the attitude of this country and that country at the peace table and in the post-war period,' Mackenzie King remarked in the House of Commons in March 1943, 'the less the country will be impressed with the fact that this war itself is not yet won.'[9]

Plans for an unofficial conference to discuss post-war policies were developed by the Canadian Institute of International Affairs during the spring of 1943, notwithstanding the Prime Minister's warning that such discussion was dangerous and premature. To the planners of the conference it seemed that such discussion was if anything overdue. 'When one thinks of the immediacy of so many of the problems upon which Canada must take a stand,' E.J. Tarr, a leading member of the Institute and prime mover of the conference, wrote in September 1943, 'one shudders at the unpreparedness of public opinion.'[10] He was gratified to find that most interested Canadians felt as he did, rather than as Mackenzie King did, about the need to prepare public opinion with all possible speed. 'The interest in the little show is quite amazing,' Tarr wrote in October. 'St Laurent, Crerar, Claxton, Garson, Taggart have all accepted. We are going to have a strong CCF group.'[11] In fact every invited group – labour, management, Prairie, Maritime, academic, public service – responded enthusiastically to the invitation, with the notable exception of French Canada. 'We are going to be rather shy on French,' Tarr wrote in the final phase of the preparations, and this prediction proved correct. The few that came might just as well have stayed away. 'A sign of sickness in the

Canadian state,' noted an observer from the Department of External Affairs in a report to the Under Secretary,

> was that the French Canadian members of the Conference were silent during the discussions of general questions of post-war policy and participated in the discussions only when they touched the peculiar rights and claims of French Canada. The French Canadians behaved not as real participants in the Conference but as if they held a watching brief for the interests of French Canada.[12]

The conference convened at the Seigneury Club at Montebello, Quebec (whence derives the name 'the Montebello Conference'), between 4 and 12 December 1943. The subject of how to treat the defeated European powers occupied a prominent place on its agenda, which raised for discussion the following questions, among others: What are the implications of 'unconditional surrender,' as qualified by the Atlantic Charter and other pronouncements by Allied leaders? By what sort of government – civil or military – should the defeated countries be ruled during the period immediately following their surrender? How harshly (if at all harshly) should they be treated? Ought the peace to be imposed or negotiated? If negotiated, with what parties? What should be done with Italy's pre-war colonies? What should be done with the German *Reich*? For how long should the defeated countries be forbidden to bear arms, and how might such a proscription be enforced? How should war criminals be tried and punished? What reparations should be paid, and how distributed? What role should be given to the re-education of the defeated peoples and how could their re-education be accomplished? How much responsibility should Canada accept for any or all of these problems?

The last of these questions provoked the most spirited discussion. Some of the conferees argued that much would depend on the extent to which the Canadian Government was consulted on the European settlements. If Canada was given an opportunity to influence their form, Canadians would and should be willing to accept the various responsibilities of peacemaking, including the responsibility of providing troops for occupation duties. But if there was no such opportunity, Canadians would not nor could they be expected to interest themselves in European affairs. This statement was vigorously challenged. Suppose, it was suggested, that the worst were to happen: a peacemaking procedure which provided Canada with no chance at all to express her views. If the peace that would emerge was worth upholding – not a perfect peace, but one which offered a decent chance – should not the duty of Canadians be to play their part in promoting it, even if they had been able to play little or no part in making it? 'Could we sit back and let the world plunge again into chaos just because we weren't consulted?'[13] Some thought yes, but more thought not.

On 15 December 1943, three days after the Montebello Conference adjourned, Escott Reid, who had attended on behalf of the Department of External Affairs, reported his impressions to his chief, Norman Robertson. They were mostly favourable. 'What impressed and encouraged me most,' he wrote,

> was the very great area on which everyone present was in agremeent. In the few cases where disagreement appeared to be profound, I had the feeling that further discussion would have shown that disagreement was not of relatively great importance...
>
> I cannot recall any member of the Conference attempting to use its meetings as a sounding board for attacks on the Government. Indeed ... the only direct attack on the Government's foreign policy arose incidentally during the discussion of the general problem of the post-war treatment of the principal defeated powers when the Government was criticized for not having succeeded in obtaining a more influential role for Canada in the determination of the policies of the United Nations...
>
> The main value of the Conference, of course, was in its educational effect on the participants. We can reasonably expect that the level of discussion in Canada on the subjects dealt with at the Conference will be raised as a result of its sessions...[14]

Against these agreeable impressions may now be set, with the hindsight afforded by a quarter century, one harsher observation. Judged by the reports of the deliberations, the conferees seem somehow out of touch with their times. For all their varied store of knowledge the delegates were ignorant of what today appear as the realities of that post-war world whose future they so earnestly scrutinized. Of the holocaust in Europe they were wholly unaware. The Jewish problem was for them to secure a suitable Jew to take part in their proceedings: how different the proceedings 4000 miles to the east, where the death trains were loading with their human freight, shuttling between the ghettoes and the extermination camps. They knew nothing of the atomic bomb, they knew nothing of atomic warfare. They thus discussed the post-war world oblivious to mass extermination, on the one hand, or to massive retaliation, on the other. Yet by such diabolical forces would the post-war world be moved. Of the Montebello conferees one may write today what Auden wrote then of other well-intentioned folk:

> They attend all the lectures on Post-war Problems,
> For they do mind, they honestly want to help; yet,
> As they notice the earth in their morning papers,
> What sense do they make of its folly and horror...?[15]

## FROM POTSDAM TO PARIS

The Great Powers were no more anxious to admit the smaller members of the wartime alliance to a significant role in the making of the European settlements than they had been to admit them to positions of responsibility within the United Nations Organization. Canada's earliest dealings with the new Labour Government of the United Kingdom, which took office on 28 July 1945, were to deplore, to protest, and to resist this trend.

On 26 August, the Prime Minister of Canada received from the Prime Minister of the United Kingdom a despatch suggesting that he should arrange to visit Britain in order to be on hand for the forthcoming meeting of the Council of Foreign Ministers, about the proceedings of which the Foreign Office would be pleased to offer full information. At this procedure Mackenzie King felt highly indignant. He instructed Norman Robertson to draft

> a rather strong message ... letting the British see quite clearly I did not think it was good enough to have Canada sit on the sidelines to be called if and when it suited the UK Government to confer on something; particularly after Canada's part in the war we really deserved to be represented on the Council of Foreign Ministers, which would be making the preparations for the peace ... Also the desire of Canada not to have followed in post-war matters the pattern of a big 3, 4, or 5, to make everything themselves in advance of final settlement.[16]

Robertson's draft, slightly revised by Mackenzie King, went out to Clement Attlee on 28 August. 'I acknowledge gratefully,' it read in part, 'the steady flow of valuable information which reaches us from London, but I cannot consider that the receipt of this information gives to Canada effective participation in the great decisions that confront the world. The methods developed of arriving at private settlements between the great powers on issues of general interest are becoming a source of difficulty and even of danger.' No opportunity had been given to Canada to express her views at the time of the Potsdam Conference. The procedure agreed to at Potsdam – that the Council of Foreign Ministers, American, British, French, Russian, should draft the treaties of peace – was not acceptable to Canada. After all that the Dominion had contributed to victory, after all that her people had gone through, was she now to be offered even less scope for peacemaking than had been hers in 1919?

The new British Government was well aware of these gathering grievances. (The Australians, as well as the Canadians, were expressing them forcefully.) It was not without sympathy for the Canadian case. After all, Marshal Stalin, not Prime Minister Attlee, had expressed his contempt for the claims of the smaller powers at Potsdam. The British proposed that the Dominion should appoint representatives who might meet with their own while the sessions of the Council of Foreign Ministers were in progress; in this way they could be kept closely informed of the proceedings and might be able, as at Dumbarton Oaks, to influence their outcome by having their views transmitted to the Council by the British Foreign Secretary. This procedure was agreed to.

From the Canadian standpoint it did not work very well. The meetings with Bevin and other Foreign Office officials were dominated by Evatt of Australia, who seemed less interested in Trieste and Italy's frontiers than in protesting against his country's exclusion from the main events unfolding in Marlborough House nearby. The Australians went so far as to issue a statement objecting to the way the Council of Foreign Ministers was ignoring the views of the lesser Allies. It was due to this unquiet diplomacy (or so Evatt claimed) that the Council invited the Dominions (and the governments of Italy and Yugoslavia) to attend one of its meetings at which their views on the status of Trieste and the Yugoslav-Italian frontier might be heard.

The Canadian Government had not joined Evatt in his private grizzling to the British, nor in his public complaint about the procedure in the Council. It declined the Council's invitation to attend the special meeting, on the grounds that it was 'not in a position to put forward specific solutions of the problems of the Yugoslav-Italian frontier, or for that matter of any of the other questions affecting the future territorial boundaries of Italy.' Nevertheless, the Canadian Government continued, 'we are very much concerned with the effect which the peace settlement will have on the general relationship of a democratic Italy to the community of nations.' For that reason, it hoped that an 'adequate opportunity will be afforded to Canada and the other United Nations which have played an active part in the Italian War to consider and discuss the contents of the peace treaty as a whole at the appropriate stage in its negotiations.'[17] This response was in marked and deliberate contrast to Australia's blustering, and was (Canada House reported to Ottawa) much appreciated by the British on that account.

It also prefigured exactly Canada's approach to all of the treaties of peace. The Canadian Government was content to allow the Great Powers to work out the details of settlement, provided they would afford it adequate opportunity to comment on matters of principle. 'Questions of boundaries, of colonial administration, or regional disarmament are important,' the Prime Minister observed in the House of Commons on 27 September 1945, 'but, in the last analysis, many of them are of less consequence, even to the countries whose interests they affect most immediately, than are questions of attitudes and objectives. These are, as I see it, the big questions, the worrying questions.'[18] These were, too, the only sorts of questions that Mackenzie King thought Canada ought to concern herself with in Europe. Not the minutiae of peacemaking, which had preoccupied Sir Robert Borden in Paris in 1919 – the refinements of Article this, sub-section that of the draft treaty of such-and-such – but the grand strategy of peacemaking was the legitimate interest of Canadians in the post-world world.

By the spring of 1946 the Grand Alliance could make good use of some grand strategy of peacemaking. The meetings of the Council of Foreign Ministers (and of their deputies) had accomplished little except to demonstrate the width and depth of the rift which divided the Soviet Union, on one side, and Britain, France, and the United States, on the other. For the latter Powers, the most important question was no longer what to do with Germany: it was what to do with Russia. Had the time come already for a showdown with the Soviets? Or would a wiser policy be one of patience and restraint in the negotiations with the Russians, making every allowance for their instransigence, giving them the benefit of every doubt? Within a year of victory, the West had arrived at a fateful crossroads.

On this crucial issue Mackenzie King had views of his own. He favoured the policy of patience and restraint, as against the policy of showdown. His convictions had nothing whatsoever to do with being (in the argot of a later day) 'soft on communism.' Earlier than many Western statesmen, and with better reason than all of them, he had come to the conclusion that the Russians were not to be trusted. 'Russia,' he wrote in his diary on 3 October 1945 – a month after he had learned of the Soviet espionage ring in Ottawa – 'will not observe any pledge on paper. I am sure of that.' He approved without reservation Churchill's speech at Fulton, Missouri. 'The most courageous speech I have ever listened to' was how he described it on 5 March 1946, after the broadcast, 'in every way most opportune.' And he added: 'I confess I personally believe that as regards Russia the rest of the world is not in a very different position than other countries in Europe were when Hitler had made up his mind to aim at the conquest of Europe.'[19] Yet that bleak reflection did not lead him to want to have it out with the Russians then and there. A role remained for conciliation. Nothing should be left undone in the search for peace. If it should come to general war – and during these years Mackenzie King came more and more to believe in the imminence of general war – it should not be possible to say of the Western nations that they had insufficiently persevered in the effort to head it off.

An opportunity to present these views to others was provided by the convening, in May 1946, of the Conference of Commonwealth Prime Ministers. In London, Mackenzie King put forcefully to the British Government the case for conciliating the Soviet Union. 'I told Lord Addison [Secretary of State for Dominion Affairs],' he wrote on 20 May,

that I agreed with the view that some way would have to be found of getting the Big Four to work together. If they could not do that by themselves, putting a lot of nations around them would not make the situation any easier ... Felt we had to be very patient with the Russians. It was better to take longer and get agreement than a situation which might mean the lining up of certain nations – large number of the United Nations against Russia...

He was relieved to find that the British Ministers with whom he spoke thought this to be the proper prescription, and gratified to learn from Ernest Bevin's account of the negotiations then going on among the foreign ministers of the Big Four in Paris 'that they had made some headway. That the matter had got down pretty much to a question of the Danube and Trieste. If the Russians got their way in that particular, everything could be settled.'[20]

The following day – 21 May – it was Mackenzie King's turn to address the Prime Ministers' meeting. He told it, he wrote afterwards,

that it was [not] wise to hurry a final settlement. That the issues to be settled were very large and time was a great factor. That, of course, one did not wish the Russians to consolidate their position too much or stir up strife elsewhere but I thought, however, that the thing to do if they were in the wrong was to make that so apparent that other nations would change their views toward them. They could not go on ceasing to co-operate without different free countries getting a strong public opinion against them and equally against the spread of communism. On the other hand, if we let them get into the position before the world where they could say they were being crowded and that the other powers were ganging up against them ... we would find that within many countries there was, to our amazement, communistic sympathy in quarters we had never anticipated ... It was for this reason that I felt it undesirable to try and bring many more nations in to settle difficulties. To try and arrange to reach an agreement where the Big Four themselves had found it impossible to do so, especially as the Big Four would be a main portion of the larger number that could come together. I was afraid that would lead to a lining up in public with recriminations, positions taken, etc., which would make the last stage worse than the first...[21]

By these attitudes the Canadian delegation was guided throughout the Conference of Paris.

Word that the Big Four had agreed sufficiently upon the terms of five draft treaties of peace to invite 'all members of the United Nations which had actively waged war with substantial military forces against the European members of the Axis' to a general conference in Paris to consider their handiwork reached Mackenzie King in Ottawa on 5 July. That was less than a month after his return from the Prime Ministers' meeting in London but, even so, he decided almost immediately to return at the head of the Canadian delegation. 'The country and Parliament would expect me to,' he wrote in his diary. 'Among the public men of the world today, I was one of the few that had led his country through the war and was in the position now of the one who had held office longer than any living man. I thought Canada would expect me to go.'[22]

He selected the delegation with customary care. From the outset he opposed the view that the representation at Paris should be bipartisan, as it had been at San Francisco. The Cabinet discussed the matter on 10 July. 'St Laurent took the view that the people at large would like that attitude. I strongly opposed it myself on the score that Canada's interests in the Conference itself would not justify that and found all the other members of the Cabinet with me.' In the event, Brooke Claxton was the only politician, the Prime Minister apart, on the delegation; the remainder were drawn entirely from the Department of External Affairs: Norman Robertson, A.D.P. Heeney, Dana Wilgress (then ambassador to the Soviet Union), Georges Vanier (then ambassador to France), and Maurice Pope (then head of the Canadian Military Mission to the Allied Control Council in Germany). Considering the number and scope of the various commissions and sub-commissions of the conference, the delegation was a small one – too small, as it proved, to enter with much effect into the fray of amending and sub-amending which continued for ten weeks. But the delegation had not been assembled to try to redraw the map of Europe or to rewrite the terms of peace. Its purpose was to signify Canada's presence and to register Canada's concern. As a ceremonial delegation it was large enough.

A few hours before the formal opening of the Conference on 29 July, the delegations from the Commonwealth countries met for a preliminary exchange of views. As in London earlier that year, the meeting was monopolized by the Australians. Mackenzie King found Evatt's manner 'distinctly rude and unpleasant,' and his argument no less distasteful – 'all in the way,' he recorded, 'of objection to the Big Four having taken matters into their own hands.' When he discovered that the South African and New Zealand delegates responded favourably to Evatt's approach, Mackenzie King felt obliged to oppose it:

> I stressed the work that had already been done. Emphasized taking the long view; making this conference succeed ... At all costs keeping Russia in the conference, not allowing her to bring forward fresh difficulties each time fresh difficulties were raised by our own people ... The last thing we would wish is to have the subject-matter of this conference thrown into a United Nations as a whole. There would be no peace settlement if it ever reaches that stage.

After he had finished, Mackenzie King noted, Attlee told him privately that his intervention had been 'most helpful. I think I was.'[23]

The Conference opened at four that afternoon. 'Was somewhat disgusted,' Mackenzie King wrote after the meeting, 'at Evatt leaping into the arena at the start and making a somewhat immoderate speech in relation to procedure ... He seemed ... to want to get on record he was fighting for the small powers as against the Big Four Powers ... I personally feel it is much better to maintain a dignified silence.'[24] A dignified silence was maintained by the Canadian Prime Minister when asked, the next day, to nominate M. Spaak of Belgium as chairman of the committee on procedure. Having declined to do so – 'not knowing,' as he wrote, 'what the attitude of the delegates might be' – Mackenzie King was amazed 'when ... Evatt jumped in and proposed Spaak. Immediately after, Molotov proposed a delegate of Yugoslavia.' How wise he had been, Mackenzie King reflected, in refusing to take the initiative in nominating Spaak: he thought it 'a great pity that there had not been some arrangement in advance. It would have prevented the nomination of two candidates which gave the appearance of Russian and anti-Russian forces, thereby defeating the Conference in this way at the very beginning.' The Czechoslovakian delegation offered a compromise arrangement whereby Spaak and Molotov would occupy the chair on alternate days; and despite negative votes cast by both the United States and the United Kingdom, Mackenzie King voted in favour of it, 'glad to have a chance,' as he recorded, 'to cast a first vote which showed no antagonism toward anyone.' He confessed to feeling 'surprised at the British attitude,' and concern that 'the Big Four had not themselves taken care to see that this nomination was properly arranged without any division ... Everything that was done this morning seemed, if not to have been wrong in itself, to have been done in the wrong way and most unfortunate in serving to divide forces rather than to unite them.'[25] It had been an inauspicious start.

Three days later, on 2 August, Mackenzie King addressed the Conference in plenary session. It was his only major address while in Paris. 'Canada,' he told the delegates,

> has no specific national interest in the adoption of any particular formula for the solution of individual conflicts and differences which, in the aggregate, will

constitute the general settlement. But we have a vital and compelling interest in the kind of settlement that results from these deliberations. Our principal duty and interest lie, it seems to me, in helping the countries more directly concerned to work out agreed solutions which are fair and likely to endure. Our concern as a nation is to see that, as far as we can help to make them so, the peace treaties will be based upon broad and enduring principles of justice and equity.[26]

His audience, he noted afterwards, listened to his remarks in 'astonishing silence' – a reaction he attributed, characteristically, to its rapt attention – and it seemed to him that he was given 'a very cordial reception at the close.'*

From these lofty generalities the Conference soon descended, and within hours the delegates became embroiled in a rancorous and protracted argument over procedure. A pattern of voting appeared at once. Though Poland and Czechoslovakia had shown signs of independence at the outset, they fell in smartly behind the Soviet delegation, accepting its position on every amendment whether of consequence or not. The rest voted to show a monolithic unity of their own, with the result (as a Canadian witness reported) that 'a great number of the final votes were counted out as 15 to 6, 15 to 6, with the mechanical regularity of a cash register.'

The Prime Minister of Canada lost interest in the proceedings at an early stage. Unlike Sir Robert Borden, who in 1919 had been wholly absorbed in peacemaking at Paris – so much so that he reacted with annoyance to news from home† and only returned to his capital when his colleagues demanded it – Mackenzie King found the atmosphere disturbing and disenchanting. 'Find the whole system of amendments and sub-amendments quite wearisome,' he confided to his diary on 5 August, '...and feel that it may be just as well not to get unnecessarily involved in international entanglements.' He discovered too late that he had over-estimated his ability to make a constructive contribution. A year earlier, learning of Labour's victory in Britain, he had thought that 'my position, internationally, will be heightened as a consequence.'[27] That was wishful thinking. He did not seem to realize how much of his wartime influence

* Quoted in *Record III*, 293. It has been suggested that the enthusiasm with which Mackenzie King's audiences were wont to applaud his peroration was prompted less by their appreciation of his performance than 'by relief that the speech, like Swinburne's river, had found its way somewhere safe to sea.' Nicholas Mansergh, 'Power and Position,' *International Journal*, XIX, 1, Winter 1963–4, 63.

† 'Several dispatches from Ottawa, some of which are disturbing ... I put them aside until tomorrow morning. I want very much to reply to these dispatches "for the love of God, give me some peace".' Diary entry, 23 April 1919, Borden Papers.

derived from his powerful friends. Now, with Roosevelt dead, and Churchill deposed, and with as yet no rapport established with their successors, his influence was bound to wane, and did.

Nor was that all. The strain of wartime leadership over six hectic years had begun to take its toll. Mackenzie King was tired and ill.

The members of the Canadian delegation at Paris found the predicament of their leader poignant and affecting; they did what they could to cheer their chief in his evident distress. 'It was his habit,' one of them recalls, 'to dine every evening at a big round table in the Crillon restaurant where those of us who could made it a point to join him. One evening I ventured to observe that he seemed to be particularly fond of a favourite French course, the globe artichoke. "Yes," he replied ... sadly ... "they seem to be the only good thing about this conference".'[28] After a week of it, the Prime Minister had had enough. Though Mackenzie King stayed on in Paris, he took no further part in the work of the delegation, and on 25 August he returned to Canada, leaving Brooke Claxton in charge.

For Claxton, opportunity had knocked at last. He threw himself into the work of the Conference with all his energy and gusto. Never were such qualities more valuable. The Conference did not adjourn until 15 October; even so, some of its commissions met continuously for as long as twenty-eight hours to get through its business in time. 'Not very hopeful,' Norman Robertson reported of the atmosphere after a fortnight of discussion. 'The interminable wrangles over rules of procedure, the prolonged filibusters put up by the Soviet and satellite delegations, and the squabbles over minor points have combined to produce a somewhat cynical frame of mind among the delegates. Nor have tempers been improved by long day and night sessions in the gilded but airless salons of the Luxembourg Palace.'

Throughout the Conference, the demeanour of the Canadian delegation was in marked contrast to that of the Australian. Led or driven by the egregious Herbert Evatt,* it put forward no fewer than 70 different amendments; not one of these was adopted, and most were defeated by votes of 20 to 1 or (when the Australians were joined, probably more out

* 'His behaviour in Paris in pursuit of his ambition,' a member of the Canadian delegation recalls of the leader of the Australian,

> jarred the sensitivities of many ... Few can be more successfully abrasive than a determined Australian and Evatt was a past master in giving offence ... Maurice Pope, our representative on the committee dealing with the Bratislava bridgehead, a subject about which he confessed to know little, when questioned on the reasons for the attitude he had taken, replied quite simply, 'I wait until that bastard ... takes his position, then take the opposite.'

Brian Heeney (ed.), *The Memoirs of A.D.P. Heeney* (Toronto 1972), 87.

of mateship than conviction, by New Zealand) 19 to 2. It was a débâcle without parallel in the annals of diplomacy. Canada suffered no such humiliation, but then Canada was careful to avoid running such a risk. Her delegation offered only one amendment to the Conference – a proposal that Italy be allowed three years rather than eighteen months in which to grant reciprocal most-favoured-nation treatment to the members of the United Nations; passed by the Economic Commission (where it was introduced), the Canadian amendment was defeated at the closing plenary session. Modest as this initiative may have been, it was enough to bring down upon Dana Wilgress, the member of the delegation who had taken it, the wrath of the Russian representative, M. Vyshinsky.* The episode was brief but distinctly unpleasant; and since it had been precisely the objective of the Prime Minister at the Conference of Paris not to become embroiled with the Soviets, Mackenzie King was relieved that he had left firm instructions with the delegation to keep in the background as much as possible.

Not all its members were content to be placed under such restraint. General Pope has recorded that

> at one time I was tempted to move that a clause in the proposed treaty with Italy requiring them to tow their submarines out to sea and to sink them in 100 fathoms of water, be amended to read that they be dismantled ashore and broken up for scrap ... Italy has no iron ore and her steel industry is based entirely on scrap metal. The draft clause was, I thought, unnecessarily harsh and unjust...[29]

Maurice Pope was no Walter Riddell. He kept his convictions to himself and voted as instructed. His instructions were 'that at no time and in no circumstances should I express a view in the Commission.'[30] Mute and inglorious, the delegation did its duty.

During debate in the Canadian Parliament on the treaties drawn at Paris, a Conservative critic remarked that Canada's delegation had acted 'only as a sort of general adviser with respect to the thing without being even in the position of real advisers.' Perhaps to his surprise, the Prime Minister agreed. 'Commentator,' Mackenzie King broke in to say, 'would be a good word.'[31] The role of the commentator is not necessarily without honour, but it is often without influence. From their position of detachment the Canadians at Paris found it difficult to have much effect upon the final result. 'There is not much more we can do,' Brooke Claxton had written to Mackenzie King after the Conference entered its seventh week, 'than to watch the situation carefully, keep as close touch as we can with the various parties, and when the opportunity presents itself ... do what we

* See above, 41.

can to bring home a point of view.'[32] These tactics, Claxton later conceded to the House of Commons, 'achieved something, but not nearly as much as we would have liked.'[33]

## NAZIS AND GERMANS

As early as June 1943, the British government asked whether Canada would wish to participate in policing and occupying a defeated enemy, a task to entitle those countries whose armed forces might perform it to membership in a proposed United Nations Commission for Europe.

Hume Wrong pondered this inquiry in a memorandum of 5 July. It seemed to him to raise issues of the utmost significance for Canada.

> There is no doubt whatever that these proposals if they are adopted will have important political and economic effects. The longer the Armistice the more important will these effects be and it is by no means unlikely that the suggested United Nations Commission for Europe might become the actual machinery for framing the European peace settlement ... Only those non-European countries which were prepared to contribute to the policing of Europe would be invited to join the Commission.
>
> The question of Canadian participation may well involve a preliminary decision on our readiness to play an active part in a new world security system. Our armies are in the European theatre and so is the bulk of our operational air force. A commitment to contribute to the policing of Europe would presumably in the main involve an undertaking to participate to some degree in providing the necessary armies of occupation. The United States and Canada may be the only overseas countries with substantial military forces in the European theatre...

It was Wrong's opinion that more information should be sought from the British, and the views of the American and Soviet governments solicited, before Ottawa could give its final answer. 'It seems to me that all we can do immediately is to send an interim reply to London showing that we fully appreciate the importance of the issues and asking for further information on some points.'[34] This was duly done. 'What tentative plans,' a cable asked in turn of the Dominions Office, 'have been prepared for "the European policing system" and what would a Canadian contribution to this system be likely to involve? (b) What formula is proposed to govern the relationship of the suggested Steering Committee to the Commission as a whole? (c) What are the reactions of both the United States and the USSR to the suggested arrangements?'[35]

While awaiting answers to these questions, the Canadian planners exchanged views among themselves. The first meeting, held on 22 July 1943, of what was to become the regular machinery for post-hostilities problem-solving soon disclosed a difference of opinion.* The armed forces, particularly the Air Force, wanted to stake out at once as large a role as could be obtained in the work of occupying and policing post-war Germany, in order to ensure the survival of as much as possible of their equipment and personnel. The Chief of the Air Staff objected to what he described as a 'lukewarm' response in the draft of a telegram prepared by the Department of External Affairs for consideration by the War Committee of the Cabinet before being sent to London. 'He would like the Government to say now' – so the minutes of the meeting record Air Marshal L.S. Breadner as declaring – 'that Canada would take part in post-war policing, the extent of this participation to be decided later.'

The diplomats present at the meeting were at first inclined to be more cautious. There was something to be said against entering so soon into a commitment to post-war occupation duty. The end of hostilities in Europe might find Canadians fighting on a Far East front. Canada's contribution might take the form of supplies rather than of troops. Her soldiers would have been overseas longer than those of any other country.

Norman Robertson brought these diverging views together. Occupation duty, he pointed out, 'was the first installment in the plans for post-war world order, and ... a refusal by Canada to take part would mean a reversion to isolationism.' The meeting agreed that a note to this effect should accompany the draft cable to be considered by the War Committee. The message sent out to London on 30 July declared that 'Canada will contribute substantially to the pacification of Europe.' It added: 'The Canadian government also assumes that its participation in relief and other civil international activities proposed to come under the direction of the United Nations Commission, in addition to the military effort, would make desirable its membership on the Commission.'[36]

In this way the Canadian government agreed to make a substantial contribution to the pacification of Europe. But what dimensions did 'substantially' imply? The Department of External Affairs felt that it was much too premature to plan the scope and scale of any occupying force. The Army and RCAF felt it was not. 'The Canadian government ... is feeling its way somewhat cautiously to ascertain what commitments would be

* Attending the meeting were the Chief of Naval Staff, Admiral P.W. Nelles; the Chief of the Air Staff, Air Marshal L.S. Breadner; the Deputy Chief of the General Staff, Brigadier P. Earnshaw; the Army's Director of Military Operations and Planning, Colonel J.H. Jenkins; the RCAF's principal planning officer, Air Commodore K.M. Guthrie; the Secretary to the RCN's Plans Division, Lt-Commander G.F. Todd; the Clerk of the Privy Council, A.D.P. Heeney; and, from the Department of External Affairs, Norman Robertson, Hume Wrong, George Glazebrook, and John Holmes.

required,' an Army memorandum noted disapprovingly on 3 August 1943. It noted 'that while at the moment the development of Canadian policy seems to be directed by External Affairs, the UK Military Sub-Committee ranks equally with the Foreign Policy Sub-Committee which is studying the same problem.'[37] 'There is every reason for considering at the present time the extent to which Canada is to participate in the policing of post-war Europe,' an Air Force memorandum of 7 September argued, 'rather than postponing a decision until the pressure of events makes it imperative.' One such reason was the probable hostility of public opinion to a protracted occupation role unless such a role were early and closely defined. 'Conditions in Europe at the cessation of hostilities may be little short of chaotic; old animosities will flare up, and disputes over boundaries will undoubtedly arise. This and similar considerations, together with war weariness and a desire on the part of Canadian service men to return as quickly as possible to civilian life, may conceivably induce the Canadian government to arrive at an *ad hoc* decision based on expediency rather than on a long term policy designed to affect both national and international security.' Moreover, 'the size and composition of the Air Force establishment which Canada is to maintain at the end of hostilities can be determined and planned for only in the light of possible post-war commitments in Europe or elsewhere.'[38]

But by the end of the year the armed forces had still no clear idea of what their police and occupation duties in post-war Europe might be. It had become evident, however, that a 'substantial' contribution was not likely to be a large-scale contribution. The War Committee of the Cabinet had considered the question on 24 November. It had agreed 'that it was important to avoid commitments which would involve the use of extensive Canadian forces in Europe after the cessation of hostilities, and which would involve heavier burdens financially and otherwise than the Canadian people would be inclined to accept after the long strain of war...'[39]

Such was the sum total of policy declaration by the Canadian government available to its post-hostilities planners by early 1944. It was not much for them to go on. 'There has been no commitment or statement of policy by the Government on Canadian participation in post-hostilities activities,' Hume Wrong informed Charles Ritchie in London.

> It was the feeling of the advisory Committee at its recent meeting that, in the absence of some guidance from the War Committee, there was little that could be done in the way of offering advice on post-hostilities problems. It would be somewhat irresponsible on our part to express strong views on, for instance, the plans for the occupation of Germany if that occupation may be carried out by other countries.[40]

But by February it had been borne in upon the Canadian government that there could be really no escaping some part in the occupation of the defeated European enemy. Nearly 400,000 members of the armed forces would be in the theatre of war at the moment of surrender. It would be six months at least, more likely a whole year, before all of them could be brought back. Meanwhile it was better for some of them to undertake the tasks of policing than hang about the barracks with nothing else to do. How many might take part depended on other factors, of which first and foremost was the demand for Canada's troops in a final onslaught on Japan. But on that score the Prime Minister's mind was already firmly set. 'No place,' Mackenzie King had written on 5 January 1944, 'for sending any army over the Pacific.'[41]

Had the planners known as much, they might not have been so cautious in their earliest recommendation. This proposed an Army contribution of 5000 men to the British Commonwealth (in the event, the British) zone of occupation, an Air Force contribution of seven squadrons and the same number of personnel, with no role at all for the Navy. This commitment, the planners had to admit, 'would be less than might be assumed on a strict pro rata basis.' Nonetheless it could be justified. Canada would be called upon to supply the lion's share of supplies for the relief and rehabilitation of Europe. A much greater distance from the zone of occupation than separated Britain or France would bring far greater problems of administration, maintenance, and morale among the men. The War Committee of the Cabinet endorsed these recommendations on 1 March 1944.

In September 1944, the Prime Minister attempted to find out Churchill's views on occupation policy when they met at the second Quebec Conference. According to Mackenzie King's understanding of their talk, Churchill felt that 'all that would be expected in the light of our past contributions would be assisting in the policing of Europe for a time. He said that there would not be any attempt to have Germany controlled immediately by our forces. What would be done would be to have the Germans do the policing themselves of their own people ... They were a race that loved that sort of thing...'[42]

In the light of this assurance, the planners reconsidered their earlier recommendation. A memorandum of October 1944 incorporates their views. They began by recognizing how hard it would be to ascertain when occupation duty became the final phase of military operations against Germany and the first phase of post-war policy towards Germany. It was for the Canadian government to decide if it wished to contribute forces for the post-war policing of Germany while having no voice in the determination of post-war policy towards Germany. The principal argument against a precipitate withdrawal of all Canadian troops from Europe on the cessation of hostilities – to the extent transport allowed – was that such a speedy retreat might encourage isolationism not only in Canada but in the United States. There was some scope here for bargaining. Granted that it would be neither easy nor prudent to escape entirely from occupation duty during the months immediately following a German surrender, Canada could and should refuse to commit herself to any long-term responsibility in Europe unless arrangements for participating in the making of post-war policy were judged satisfactory. No great harm would be done by Canada's refusal to promise, say, one division for long-term service; it would simply place responsibility for policing squarely upon the Big Four. It was entirely proper that Canada's European allies, rather than Canada herself, should bear the brunt of the burden. The functional principle demanded it; common sense endorsed it.

Out of such reflections, and the Services' determination to keep their strength in being, a new set of proposals emerged – an Army force level five times that of the earlier authorization, and an Air Force contribution of eleven squadrons, rather than seven. These were endorsed by the War Committee of the Cabinet on 11 December. 'The Minister of National Defence (General McNaughton) explained that the force would be allocated to the British zone of occupation and the commitment would be specifically for Stage II, the term used for the period of adjustment and disarmament immediately following the operational occupation of Germany. Thereafter, he said, the personnel would be returned to Canada with all possible speed.'[43] This decision was communicated to the British government in January 1945. 'It would be both unwise on our part and misleading to you,' Ottawa's message to London concluded, 'were we, at this stage, definitely to undertake to furnish occupation forces for the whole period of military control in Germany.' The matter would be reviewed by the Government before the end of the next fiscal year (31 March 1946) by which date 'much that is now hypothetical should be clearer.'

The commitments thus assumed came tolerably close to what was actually contributed. In the event, the Canadian Army Occupation Force consisted of 18,000 troops, rather than the 25,000 planned. The RCAF, however, began its occupation duties with thirteen squadrons, not eleven, though two of them were disbanded in October 1945 and one more in December.

By the end of 1945 the promised review had been completed and a cabinet decision taken. The decision, as Mackenzie King informed the British Prime Minister on 8 December, was to reduce progressively the Canadian Army Occupation Force so that all its members would have left the European continent by the summer of 1946 and all remaining Army personnel overseas would be repatriated by the autumn of 1946.

This was bad news for the British. Clement Attlee earnestly beseeched the Canadian government to reconsider. Withdrawal of its troops by these dates would, he asserted, place upon the British people an added burden which in their straitened circumstances it would be hard to bear. He begged Mackenzie King at least to lengthen the time-table of withdrawal so that Canadian forces would remain in Europe until 1947, if not longer.

The Prime Minister was unmoved by this plea. Mackenzie King told the British High Commissioner, whom Attlee had instructed to reinforce his cable by personal persuasion,

> that our obligation ... was to furnish food and supplies to Britain and to the occupied territories and that he would have to tell his Government that in furnishing the United Kingdom not only with supplies on credit but giving them money with which to make purchases from other countries we were assuming an obligation that the United Kingdom was not; that we needed our men back to produce and that by remaining abroad, instead of helping us to meet the need of added supplies, they were making a demand on that. I had fully expected this appeal from Attlee, but told Malcolm [MacDonald] that I would have to remain adamant in declining.

He reflected that he had 'fought this thing all along in the Cabinet.' The Minister of National Defence had told him 'that the more he had gone into the matter of keeping our troops longer in Europe, the more he was convinced this would be a very great mistake. In these matters we have been far too lax in protecting the interests of our own people and the burdens they were bearing in the war of taxation.'[44]

The Cabinet was entirely agreed that this was the right way to look at the matter. On 14 January 1946, its decision to stick by its original decision to bring the troops back by the summer of 1946 if possible, or the autmn of 1946 at the latest, was conveyed to London. But Clement Attlee would not take no for an answer. 'The British have come back again,' Mackenzie King wrote in his diary on 23 January, 'with a request for retaining our troops longer in occupation zone, the claim being that they have so much to do in distant countries ... In these things they have an interest which we have not at all.'

If the British really believed that the Canadian Government would respond sympathetically to the argument that its troops should be left in Germany to allow deployment of their troops in Palestine, Malaya, and other imperial outposts under siege, they miscalculated. Their injection of this new factor only stiffened the Cabinet's resolve not to relent. St Laurent, in particular, was outraged at the suggestion. He had no intention, his biographer records, 'of freeing troops that would hold down other peoples in the Commonwealth,'[45] and he told Attlee as much while on a brief visit to London, pointing out (as he reported to Mackenzie King on his return) that 'our conception of the Empire was not based on an undertaking of responsibility for all parts of the Commonwealth. We had our own contribution as a nation to make.' Mackenzie King was also indignant. 'It is clear,' he reflected, 'the present Government is even worse than the last on recognition of Canada's part as a nation.'[46]

There was a further reason for the reluctance of the Government to accede to Attlee's request, beyond those of economy and autonomy. The forces overseas were becoming restive. In December 1945 a disconcerted defence headquarters in Ottawa learned that a number of Canadian officers had been implicated in looting and bootlegging activities in a number of Western European cities: on New Year's Day, the Queen of The Netherlands herself appealed in a telegram to the Canadian Prime Minister to stop the stealing of Dutch art treasures by members of the Army overseas. An investigation was begun immediately, resulting in the court-martialling of one senior officer and imprisonment for several others. Worse was still to come. ' "Sit-down" strike in the occupation zone yesterday by some of our men,' Mackenzie King wrote in his diary on 13 February. 'Foulkes [the Chief of the General Staff] had handled it tactfully but there was danger of this spreading.'[47]

That was the last straw. On learning that its soldiers were on the verge of mutiny, the Government immediately told the British authorities that its decision to withdraw the occupation force was final, that it could not and would not be reopened, and that a public announcement of the decision would be made at once. 'It would, I think, be disastrous,' Mackenzie King cabled to Attlee, 'if the announcement of decisions taken three months ago, and which has been deferred in an endeavour to find some way to meet your difficulties, should, when finally made public, appear to be the result of local pressures from within the ranks of the occupation force itself.' The announcement was made on 15 February.

By the summer of 1946 most of the troops had been repatriated on schedule. There was general satisfaction in Canada at their return. A dissenting note was sounded by the Opposition defence critic, who observed in the House of Commons on 19 August that a Gallup poll of Canadian opinion reflected the feeling that by withdrawing its troops, the Government was reneging on its responsibilities. 'Some of our allies,' George Pearkes asserted, now believed

> that perhaps this country, which had never let down any of its allies during the war, was rather letting them down during this critical stage, the early days of peace. When it was suggested that it was hard that our allies should have to bear the burden alone, the reason advanced for our withdrawal was ...

that it was for administrative reasons. If Canada hopes to hold a position and to carry out any commitments which the United Nations may call upon her to do in the future, we must learn how to overcome "administrative difficulties."[48]

Difficulties there had surely been, but they were political rather than administrative. The Government had never explained the real reasons for its decision; and when, during the course of the debate in March 1947, it was challenged to deny that Canada's exclusion from the ranks of the peacemakers might not be related to its early termination of the occupation role, its spokesmen were hard pressed to offer a reply that was both convincing and consistent.

They tried. The Minister of National Defence rejected with some heat the contention of the critics that limited participation in the settlement of Germany stemmed from limited participation in the occupation of Germany. 'There is no evidence – no proof,' Brooke Claxton insisted, 'that the presence of any force Canada might have in Europe would change our position by so much as an ounce of more power or weight. Further, I would ask my hon. friend this question: What is his idea of the size of the occupying force it would be necessary for Canada to have, in order to have some weight? Would it be five thousand or ten thousand or fifteen thousand Canadians kept from their homes?'[49] The Secretary of State for External Affairs embarked upon a different course of explanation. 'It has been suggested,' Louis St Laurent remarked in reply to the criticism of the Conservative foreign policy spokesman, Gordon Graydon, 'that we should have left troops in occupation in Germany. Well, is it suggested that they should have been part of the Russian forces? Is it suggested that they should have been part of the French forces of occupation? Is it suggested that they should have been part of the United States forces of occupation? Is it suggested they should have been part of the United Kingdom forces of occupation?' Swept up in the rush of his rhetoric, St Laurent seemed oblivious to the fact that it was as part of the British occupation forces that Canadians had remained in Germany for a full year following the German surrender, and that the Opposition's suggestion was precisely that they ought to have remained longer in that role. When Graydon reminded him of it, St Laurent denied it. Canadian troops, he insisted, had never taken any part in occupation duties properly so-called. 'Our troops were there when the surrender occurred, and we could not fly them out overnight. We immediately started to demobilize our forces and to remove them just as expeditiously as transportation conditions permitted.' Asked, finally, to explain why they had been removed so quickly, St Laurent replied: 'The occupation force in Germany was withdrawn because we were kicked out.' On reflecting upon this answer, the

Minister considered that, while its substance was correct, its language was indecorous: the Hansard record of his reply reads '...because we were left out.'[50] It might with more accuracy have been reworded to read: '...because we ducked out.'

All this testimony, replete with bluster and recrimination, did little to clarify the Government's policy and less to satisfy the Government's critics. Certainly their officials felt things had gotten out of hand. 'I am sure that you must have been somewhat perplexed over the manner in which the discussion has developed here,' the Under Secretary of State for External Affairs wrote to the High Commissioner in London. 'You know as well as I do, however, that decisions concerning tactics in debate have a way of being made informally at the last minute, and often without there being an opportunity for full consultation between members of the Government, members of Parliament and the civil servants most directly concerned.'[51]

On 10 March, the official Opposition introduced a motion in the House of Commons calling for the production of all relevant documents having to do with the decision to withdraw Canadian forces from Europe. The Prime Minister, sensing real trouble, made a bold effort to head it off. His office, under the direction of the indefatigable J.W. Pickersgill, prepared a statement which, studiously avoiding the pitfalls into which Claxton and St Laurent had strayed the week before, was designed to give the impression of candid and complete disclosure. Mackenzie King read the statement to the House; it included the full texts of the Government's despatches to London of 9 January 1945 and 8 December 1945.

To the Department of External Affairs that was telling much too much. 'We considered ... that a short answer pointing out the privileged nature of the documents and referring to explanations made when the decision was announced would have been sufficient,' L.B. Pearson reported to Norman Robertson in London.

> ...The Prime Minister's office did not consult anyone else in the Department concerning his statement, though ... Earnscliffe had been informed and Garner[*] was present in the Diplomatic Gallery. His appearance there, together with the fact that Pickersgill was seen somewhat ostentatiously handing him a copy of the text ... led the Press Gallery to conclude that Mr King was making his statement as a result of protests from the United Kingdom Government.
>
> The inclusion of extracts from two telegrams was also decided upon in the Prime Minister's office without consultation with officials of the Department, and the question of compromise of cyphers unfortunately was never considered...[52]

* J. Garner, then First Secretary, United Kingdom High Commission.

All in all, a highly unprofessional production. However, the statement itself appeared to Pearson to be 'a fair summary,' though he noted that 'it had the immediate effect of undermining Mr St Laurent's suggestion that the decision had been the result of dissatisfaction over arrangements for the control of Germany.' But the Prime Minister considered his strategy wholly successful. There was no response from the Opposition (apart from Howard Green's remark that there was 'not much indication of "kicking out" in that statement'), and the sponsor of the motion to produce the papers withdrew it. 'I felt the statement would clear the air,' Mackenzie King wrote afterwards,

> and I could see that all sides of the House were satisfied. I had stated the position very clearly. General Pearkes, in withdrawing his motion, admitted that was the case. I am sure I saved the Government a very embarrassing situation and have helped to free us from a lot of nagging for information which, subsequently, would have been extracted anyway. I think the statement went to show that it was only to our credit instead of being a source of embarrassment. It made clear that years before the war was over we were taking care to try and get our men back at the earliest date possible. I shall be surprised if the veterans will find any fault with this.[53]

Only the veterans of diplomacy found fault with it. 'I do not suppose that we have heard the last of this controversy,' Pearson summed up for Norman Robertson. 'The continuation of this discussion is particularly unfortunate from our point of view, I think, since it will divert attention from the important current question of Canadian participation in the German settlement, in which an active interest has developed both in parliament and in the country at large.'

Germany was to be occupied and policed for a period after its defeat. That much was evident to all. But what ought to be the objectives of the occupation? For what purposes ought policing to take place? What measures of punition and control might the Allies most usefully mete out? Here answers were anything but evident. Opinions gathered at one or other of two poles – a soft peace, or a hard.

Canada, as elsewhere, had its share of Carthaginians. Conspicuous within the Department of External Affairs for his advocacy of harsh punishment and radical reform was a future ambassador to Bonn. Escott Reid believed that the prime goal of the Allies ought to be creating and sustaining anti-nazi governments and anti-nazi attitudes. Such a task was by no means as difficult as some were making out. What was required was the imposition of 'certain social and economic changes of a permanent and semi-permanent character.' Such changes could be produced by redistributing the large estates among the peasantry; expropriating heavy industry, notably coal and steel; placing a capital levy which would leave no German in possession of the equivalent of more than $50,000, the proceeds to be given to victims of the war; separating church and state; and sentencing 'to varying terms of hard labour in labour camps, which would do reconstruction work in devastated areas outside Germany, about 100,000 to 200,000 of the principal officials in the Nazi administration.'[54]

Another member of the Department who approved of a Carthaginian approach was Pierre Dupuy. Dupuy was particularly concerned to make a scapegoat out of Prussia. 'It is the spirit of Prussia that has permeated and dominated the whole of Germany. For this reason I consider that Prussia should receive particularly harsh and drastic treatment. She obviously cannot be wiped off the map but she should be isolated from the rest of Germany, and a more severe military, financial, political, industrial and economic control established there.' Berlin should not be rebuilt, but left 'as a kind of Pompeii, as a lasting reminder to future generations that war does not pay.' German industry should be 'integrated into an international system of industrial production.' Germany's western frontier should be at the Rhine, and the Kiel Canal 'internationalised and guarded by an international force...'[55]

But others in the Department were sceptical that such draconian measures would eradicate what seemed to them to be primarily a cast of mind rather than the product of geopolitics. It was easy to prescribe them. Their ministration was something else again. Nor was it certain what their effect might be. 'The Allied object,' George Glazebrook pointed out in a thoughtful but inconclusive paper, 'is to create in Germany an attitude of mind that is neither desperation nor sullen determination on revenge, but a chastened spirit, a recognition of defeat, and a renewed interest in decency. What type of settlement is best calculated to produce these ends?'[56]

As the defeat of Germany drew nearer, the Canadian government veered ever closer to the advocates of a soft peace, rather than a hard. 'A rapid rebuilding of Western Europe and the United Kingdom is now more vital to the future of Europe and its security,' wrote R.B. Bryce, then a rising star in the firmament of Finance, 'than the quick destruction of the remainder of German industry. I would think that this rapid reconstruction would be helped by leaving as much as possible of German industry as can be adapted for peacetime purposes, and forcing it to be used for reparations purposes instead of destroying it.'[57] His seniors in External concurred with this assessment. 'This comment seems to me very much to the point,' Charles Ritchie minuted, to which either Hume Wrong or Norman Robertson added: 'I agree with C.R.'

To such a policy one major problem was bound to attach itself. The Soviet Union would be bound to object to it, thereby getting post-war Canadian-Soviet relations off to a rocky start. The ambassador in Moscow recognized the problem but viewed it philosophically. 'In advocating the imposition of harsh terms on Germany the more logical arguments will be at the disposal of the Soviet Union,' Dana Wilgress wrote from his post to Ottawa, 'and other countries will be suspected of seeking to maintain Germany as a force to be reckoned with in Europe if they advocate more moderate policies ... That inevitably will involve Canada in differences of views with the Soviet Union. This, however, is unavoidable if we wish to participate in the making of the peace.'[58]

The Prime Minister had given these issues only fleeting attention so long as the war was being waged. Mackenzie King's memorandum on war aims, composed within a few weeks of its outbreak, proposed but one term of peace: ' – that a plebiscite of her own people must be taken before those in authority shall have the right to invade another country or to declare war. Until a declaration is so made by whosoever may be representing the German people at the time of effecting a truce or peace, there should be no bickering [*sic*] with him.'[59] He alluded briefly to the problem of the post-war settlement with Germany in conversation with President Roosevelt in December 1942: 'If, in any peace settlement ... it could be arranged to compel representative institutions, that would be most desirable.'[60] Mackenzie King did not allow himself to dwell upon how that compulsion might be arranged.

After the war, the Prime Minister emerged as a determined opponent of a punitive peace. Mackenzie King told the Commonwealth Prime Ministers' Conference, at the meeting of 21 May 1946, that he favoured 'getting production started and taking a policy that would lead to the development of industry, getting people employed and goods produced so that they could arrange for exchange with other parts of the world and commodities. The sooner that was done, the better.' Asked by the British Prime Minister whether his remarks meant that he was 'against carving up Germany to pieces, etc.,' Mackenzie King responded:

> Certainly I was. You could not change the love of man for his own country. If the Russians were to begin to carve up the East of Germany, take away part of their territory, this would only cause people living there to be sympathetic with the Russian absorption on the East, and central Germany would be feeling that they had no better friends in the British themselves than they had in

the Russians. It would all lead to a communistic Germany and to a Germany determined to again unite as one. I said if I thought they could get industry going and definite order established, a great body of German opinion, once they felt a sense of security and had work, would be no more anxious for another war than any other of the great bodies of the people...[61]

Despite the great contribution of Canadian arms to the military defeat of Germany, the Canadian Government was given little opportunity to place these views directly before the major Allies. It was not until December 1946, after the Conference of Paris had adjourned, that the Council of Foreign Ministers turned to the German peace settlement. They turned only to appoint Deputies, who were instructed to receive the views of other governments about the terms of a peace treaty. The governments invited to express their views were those of Germany's wartime victims and of the Allies which had actively participated in Germany's defeat.

The Government of Canada was among those receiving from the Foreign Ministers' Deputies an invitation to submit its views in writing 'at its earliest convenience ... on those aspects of the German problem which are of interest to it.' If it so desired, the Government might supplement its written observations by an oral presentation to the Deputies. This curt summons reached Ottawa on 4 January 1947; the Deputies would meet on 14 January for the purpose of receiving its deposition.

All this was profoundly unsatisfactory to the Canadian Government. It objected both to the shortness of the notice and to the inadequacy of the procedure. It requested the Deputies to devise some alternative method which would enable Canada to participate more effectively in the drafting of the German peace treaty. The Government made the request public, but received no reply. Then, on 17 January, the High Commissioner for Canada in London was asked by the secretary to the Deputies if he would appear before them on 25 January to offer the views of his Government on the German settlement. 'By this action,' St Laurent (who had recently become Secretary of State for External Affairs) told the House of Commons on 30 January,

we were placed in a somewhat difficult position. We had made what we thought were reasonable and constructive representations on the question of procedure. The special deputies were not, apparently, in a position to take notice of these. We had, on the other hand, been asked again to participate in a procedure which appeared to us to provide an entirely inadequate method for associating Canada with the peace settlement.[62]

The Government felt that no useful purpose would be served by 'a Canadian representative making a formal appearance before the deputies, presenting his submission without the privilege of discussion, and then withdrawing.' It decided instead to take what advantage it could of the proposal by making public a memorandum incorporating its views on a German settlement. It still hoped that some better way would be found of allowing Canada to participate in the process of peacemaking in the manner to which she was entitled by the contribution of her armed forces to the Allied victory.

The Ottawa memorandum on Germany has been described as marking 'an important stage in the development of Canadian foreign policy.'[63] It was unquestionably more comprehensive than other comparable submissions by the smaller allies. It opposed dismembering Germany. It advocated placing German heavy industry under international control. It warned against perpetuating 'conditions of economic depression and unrest which would adversely affect the economic and political stability of Europe as a whole.' It recommended that the peace settlement take the form of an international statute rather than the form of a conventional treaty; such an instrument, it argued, would permit peace to be made with a country still lacking a recognized government and would enable the settlement to be built piece by piece, as experience might show, rather than as a prefabricated edifice thrown up while little was known of the bearing of the site, the solidity of the foundations, the character of the surrounding neighbourhood.[64]

By the quality of these representations the Big Four do not seem to have been greatly impressed. Certainly one among the Four was greatly unimpressed. Their Foreign Ministers, meeting in Moscow on 10 March 1947, soon came to a deadlock. Canada would take no part in making a peace settlement for Germany, for there would be no peace settlement for Germany. There would be rearmament instead.

By the beginning of 1944, the Big Three had agreed upon machinery for the post-war control of Germany. Over-all authority was to be exercised by a United Nations Commission for Europe. Under the United Nations Commission was to be an Allied High Commission for Germany, furnishing the commanders in their respective zones of occupation with guidance on political and economic policies and gradually assuming their powers as the need for military government diminished. Under the High Commission for Germany was to be a Control Commission, with the task of ensuring that the terms of Germany's surrender were carried out.

The Canadian Government had expressed its keen interest in membership of the United Nations Commission (though not of its Steering Committee; the 'functional principle' was felt to rule this out) as early as July 1943. A year later, however, it had become clear that, of the three organizations comprising the control machinery, the United Nations Commission for Europe would be the least influential. The High Commission and the Control Commission had become the all-important organs, and the Big Three were determined to keep them for themselves.

The looming exclusion of Canada from a role in the machinery for controlling – as distinct from policing – post-war Germany evoked a mixed response in Ottawa. Hume Wrong was disposed to believe 'that representation on a United Nations Commission for Europe would be sufficient,' noting that 'we have not pressed for a seat on the Advisory Council for Italy even though Canadian troops are engaged in that area.'[65] This opinion reflected the view of the Cabinet War Committee that 'it was important to avoid commitments which would ... involve heavier burdens financially and otherwise than the Canadian people would be inclined to accept after the long strain of war.' It was a case for the constructive acceptance of the inevitable. 'The trend seemed definitely to favour tight three-Power control,' Wrong told the Advisory Committee on Post-Hostilities Problems on 25 October 1944, 'and there was probably little that Canada could do to alter the pattern.'[66]

Others were less philosophical. W.C. Clark reminded the Advisory Committee 'that on the basis of war effort the Canadian part in the defeat of Germany was probably greater than that of France. The Canadian claim to a proper share in the direction of policy was very strong.'[67] 'Canada of her own free will declared war in September, 1939, for the purpose of helping to save Europe from German aggression,' Dana Wilgress wrote indignantly from Moscow. 'This should entitle us to membership on the United Nations Commission for Europe regardless of whether or not we participate in the policing of Europe. If we do agree to participate in the occupation of Germany we should be given responsibility for a clearly defined area of our own and not merely contribute personnel to assist the United Kingdom in policing the British Commonwealth zone.'[68] From London, Charles Ritchie commented in a way that struck Norman Robertson as 'particularly pertinent.'

> Our position differs from that of some of the other United Nations in that we have no territorial claims against Germany. But two generations of Canadians have been involved in war by Germany's aggressions. And Canada may well be asked to participate with the other United Nations in plans extending over a period of years to keep Germany disarmed. She may have to undertake long term obligations with this object in view. Moreover the problem of Germany will be one of the central problems occupying any world security organization which may be set up and in which Canada will no doubt participate. If the Canadian people are to assume these responsibilities and to continue in them for at least another generation, they must feel that Canadian policy

towards Germany has been decided in terms of Canada's interests and that full opportunity has been given for Canada's views to be heard when the policy of the United Nations towards Germany is being formulated...[69]

The most exercised foreign service officer of all was the ambassador to the United States. 'There is certainly no noticeable disposition on the part of the Big Three to confront us with the problem of making up our minds on the larger issues of what to do with Germany,' L.B. Pearson commented sarcastically from Washington.

An occasional bone of participation will be thrown to the European allies and the Dominions, but it will be done without enthusiasm and there will be little meat on it.

This attitude – I think it is probably more of an attitude than a policy – merely confirms what we found at Dumbarton Oaks. I know perfectly well that it can be defended on various grounds. It makes quick and practical decisions easier. It may possibly knit the Big Three more closely together, though I wouldn't stake very much on this. It centralizes responsibility where there is power. On the other hand, it puts the other United Nations who have contributed to the defeat of the Axis – some of which, Canada and Australia, for instance, have contributed heavily – in a position of subordination which amounts almost to disappearance; except in respect of the acceptance of new responsibilities. Here, as usual, we are to be allowed, even urged, to play a part.

My own view is that the circumstances which made it possible, even reasonable, for the Canadian Government to accept such a position during the war when we were fighting for our own existence, are radically changed when the war ceases and the menace to that existence is removed. With this change of circumstances, there will, I think, develop in Canada a change of heart and opinion about the acceptance of military responsibilities especially when they are not accompanied by any political control. Even if there were no such development, I see no reason why we should provide an army division to help the USSR and USA police Germany for a period of at least 18 months, when these governments refuse to accept any control machinery which provides, even in the most harmless way, for some recognition of the other United Nations...

I don't want to be too sensitive or too impatient about all this, or to exhibit that lack of understanding of the difficulties of the Big Three which they show about ours, but I really don't see how they can expect us to associate ourselves formally or effectively with the armistice and, later, with the peace settlement on terms like those suggested...[70]

There was not much to be rejoined to such a deposition. 'You put very forceably the difficulties,' Hume Wrong replied; and let it go at that.

Letting it go at that became, of necessity, the policy of the Canadian Government. 'Recent developments indicated that changes in the pattern of control might be anticipated,' the Under Secretary of State for External Affairs reported to the War Committee of the Cabinet on 9 November

1944, 'and more opportunity afforded for participation by European allies.' That was only wishful thinking. The inner circle was enlarged, but only to make room for France (judged at last, over Soviet objections, 'to have recovered her greatness'). Canada remained excluded from both High Commission and Control Commission.

There remained one way by which to gain admission. Canada, as a Dominion, might contribute personnel to the British Control Commission. The *pros* and *cons* of this proposal were canvassed by the Department of External Affairs. Australia, New Zealand, and South Africa each intended to take advantage of it. Of its merits for Canada there was at least something to be said. The principle was being followed so far as the policing of Germany was concerned; why not as well with the still more important function of control? 'The primary object of this control machinery is so to direct German affairs through the period of Allied occupation and control that Germany will be unlikely to make war again in the predictable future. This objective accords with the Canadian primary interest of security. Undoubtedly there are a number of Canadians with suitable qualifications who would have a contribution to make to the control of Germany to this end and who could thus serve a principal interest of Canada.' Such Canadians would be as well a means of liaison between the British Control Commission and the Canadian Government.

But these arguments were straining for effect. For Canada to play a part on a British Control Commission would be to revert to Dominion status *circa* 1919. Such a reversion was unthinkable. 'The proposal of merging Canadian personnel into the "British element" of the Control Commissions would not give the Canadian Government any direct voice in, or responsibility for, the control of Germany. They would, in fact, become part of a British staff which would be under the direction of the United Kingdom Government.'[71]

So the *cons* carried. 'It was the intention of the Government,' Norman Robertson informed a meeting of the Advisory Committee on Post-Hostilities Problems on 15 March 1945, 'to avoid having officers serving, as part of the Canadian commitment to furnish occupation forces, on the Control Commission in Berlin, for the reason that Canada had no share or responsibility in the military government of Germany. If the service of such officers was desired by the United Kingdom, individuals might be allowed to volunteer, but they would become entirely a United Kingdom responsibility and would cease to be members of the Canadian forces. It was not therefore appropriate that Canadian personnel should be included in the Control Commission.'[72] The Royal Canadian Air Force was instructed to withdraw the officers it was in the process of seconding to the British. 'We do not think it wise,' an official on duty with the delegation at San Francisco was briefed by the Department of External Affairs, 'to convey to the Canadian public the impression that Canada will be sharing in the government of Germany by the Great Powers when, in fact, this will not be the case.'[73]

For the same reason a proposal from the Chief of the General Staff that a small Canadian military liaison section be attached to the British Control Commission was vetoed. 'It ... might give the impression,' Norman Robertson explained to General J.C. Murchie, 'that Canada was sharing with the government of the United Kingdom effective responsibility for the control of the country, which would not in fact be the case...'[74]

A Canadian Military Mission to the Control Council as a whole was quite a different matter. Such a mission, Hume Wrong explained in February 1945, 'would represent the Canadian Government in Germany and would perform with respect to the Control Commission functions analogous to those performed by a diplomatic mission in normal circumstances ... As Germany will be run by Generals,' Wrong added, 'there is quite a lot to be said for having our representative an officer of a general's rank.'[75] General Maurice Pope was the obvious choice for the job, and on 26 September 1945 he got it. 'Norman Robertson told me today that the question of establishing a Military Mission in Germany ... had been pretty well decided upon, and that I should head it.'[76] Pope left Ottawa for Berlin on 17 October, conferring *en route* with Norman Robertson in London. 'I asked him point blank what he expected of me in Berlin. He replied that I should be the representative of the Canadian Government in Germany in precisely the same way as were our Ambassadors to The Hague, Brussels, and Paris.'[77]

It could not be, and was not to be, 'in precisely the same way.' General Pope was accredited not to a national government but to a committee of conquerors, envoy of a country with which the German people were not yet at peace. The normal diplomatic duty of making an agreeable impression upon the local populace was not among his mandates; nor did he behave as if it were. 'I invariably treated them with respect,' Pope wrote later of such Germans with whom he came in contact, 'but I never allowed myself any degree of familiarity, nor did I expect them to show me other than an appropriate degree of reserve.'[78] It was not yet time to fraternize – though fraternity, forced by events, would come sooner than either Germans or Canadians could then have found it possible to believe.

# 4

# Composing the Commonwealth

There once was an old sailor my grandfather knew,
Who had so many things which he wanted to do,
That, whenever he thought it was time to begin,
He couldn't, because of the state he was in.

*A.A. Milne*

## CONFRONTATION OF THE PROPHETS

Leaving a meeting of his Cabinet on 24 January 1944, the Prime Minister of Canada was told by a secretary that Lord Halifax, British ambassador to the United States, 'was making a perfectly terrible speech in Toronto.' The following morning, when Mackenzie King read press reports of what Halifax had said, he was inclined to believe that 'perfectly terrible' had been if anything too mild an appraisal of what he would later describe as a blow more severe than he had hitherto sustained. Halifax's speech, he wrote, 'simply dumbfounded' him.

It seemed such a complete bolt out of the blue, like a conspiracy on the part of Imperialists to win their own victory in the middle of the war. I could not help but feel that Halifax's work was all part of a plan which had been worked out with Churchill to take advantage of the war to try and bring about this development of centralization, of making of policies in London ... If Hitler himself wanted to divide the Empire ... he could not have chosen a more effective way.[1]

What was the fuss all about? The immediate cause of this outburst had been a few passages in Lord Halifax's speech which appeared to promote (and were so reported in Canada) a conception of the Commonwealth which Mackenzie King had spent the greater part of his long career implacably opposing. The offending paragraphs read as follows:

In the field of defence, while there must be individual responsibility, there must also be a unity of policy. I suggest that in the years of peace it was a weakness, which we should try to cure, that the weight of decision on many problems of defence was not more widely shared...

I do not mean that we should attempt to retrace our steps along the path that led from the Durham Report to the Statute of Westminster. To do so would be to run counter to the whole course of development in the Commonwealth. But what is, I believe, both desirable and necessary, is that in all the fields of interests, common to every part of the Commonwealth – in foreign policy, in defence, in economic affairs, in colonial questions and in communications – we should leave nothing undone to bring our people into closer unity of thought and action...

Today we begin to look beyond the war to the reordering of the world which must follow. We see three great powers, the United States, Russia and China, great in numbers, areas and natural resources ... If, in the future, Britain is to play her part without assuming burdens greater than she can support, she must have with her in peace the same strength that has sustained her in this war. Not Great Britain only, but the British Commonwealth and Empire must be the fourth power in that group upon which, under Providence, the peace of the world will henceforth depend.[2]

Re-read today, these sentiments do not strike one as unduly subversive. Even at the time they struck at least one senior Canadian official as 'pretty moderate and to my way of thinking pretty sound.'[3] Certainly their author had no idea of the consternation they would arouse in the mind of the Prime Minister of Canada, and he wrote to tell him so.*

That plenty of political capital might be made of the Halifax speech, Mackenzie King was well and characteristically aware. 'If it were not for the war,' he told the Governor General on 25 January, 'I would this evening be asking ... for a dissolution of Parliament to appeal to the people.'[4] If he was really that tempted, he resisted the temptation. 'Halifax has done the damage,' he reflected on second thought, 'I must seek to repair it ... Do what I can in what I say not to widen the division between different parts of the Empire which his provocative speech, made at this time, has already occasioned, but make a common statement that will make my own position clear and leave matters at that for the present.'[5] Mackenzie King no more wished at this juncture to discuss the future of the Commonwealth than, a few months previously, he had wished to discuss the future of the United Nations. But Halifax, he felt, left him no choice. A reply was essential. In that reply, some statement of his own ideas about the Commonwealth, and of Canada's place within it, would be inescapable.

Mackenzie King's response to the Halifax speech was delivered in the House of Commons on 31 January 1944. It began with a description, and

* See *Record I*, 639. In retrospect Halifax chose to attach no importance to the affair, for it is not mentioned in his memoirs, *Fulness of Days* (London 1957). His biographer, less excusably, also ignores it; see The Earl of Birkenhead, *Halifax: The Life of Lord Halifax* (London 1962).

a defence, of the system of Commonwealth co-operation and consultation developed during the war. Since September 1939 there had come into being among those governments of the Commonwealth at war what Mackenzie King described as 'a continuing conference of cabinets of the Commonwealth dealing with matters of common concern.' Such a 'continuing conference' had been made possible by the presence of High Commissioners in member capitals and, even more, by the network of cable and telegraph making the Commonwealth a communications system. There was also the advent of the aircraft, permitting 'a minister [to] cross from Canada to Britain or vice versa in less than a day.' All these links, better than an imperial conference, better by far than an imperial council meeting in London, enabled the governments of the Commonwealth to keep in close touch with each other and to co-ordinate and harmonize their respective policies.

The Prime Minister then addressed himself to the matter of Lord Halifax and his speech. He felt sure, he said, that the Ambassador had spoken for himself, not for the British Government; and had spoken, moreover, as a political philosopher, not as a policy-maker – 'allowing his mind' (so Mackenzie King alleged) 'to travel into the next hundred years as to the possible changes that might be necessary in Commonwealth organization.' Making every allowance for all of this, it was nonetheless 'unfortunate' that Halifax had spoken as he had done; for his speech had raised issues best left undisturbed for the duration of the war. Now that they had been raised, however, the Canadian Government felt obliged to place its views about them on the public record.

In dealing with the substance of the Halifax speech, Mackenzie King also took into account the views expressed in the address delivered by Field Marshal Smuts in London on 25 November 1943, in which the South African leader, like the British Ambassador, had foreshadowed the emergence of the British Commonwealth as one of the four Great Powers of the post-war world.[6] 'With what is implied in the argument employed by both these eminent men,' the Prime Minister declared, 'I am unable to agree.' It ran contrary to the spirit of the Moscow Declaration. It was peculiarly repugnant to Canada:

> Behind the conception expressed by Lord Halifax and Field Marshal Smuts, there lurks the idea of inevitable rivalry between the great powers. Could Canada, situated as she is geographically between the United States and the Soviet Union, and at the same time a member of the British Commonwealth, for one moment give support to such an idea?...
>
> What would seem now to be suggested is that the prime Canadian commitment should be to pursue in all matters of external relations – "in foreign policy, defence, economic affairs, colonial questions and communications," to cite the words of Lord Halifax – a common policy to be framed and executed by all the

governments of the Commonwealth. I maintain that apart from all questions as to how that common policy is to be reached, or enforced, such a conception runs counter to the establishment of effective world security, and therefore is opposed to the true interests of the Commonwealth itself.

We are certainly determined to see the closest collaboration continue between Canada, the United Kingdom, and other Commonwealth countries. Nothing that I am saying should be construed as supporting any other view than this. Collaboration inside the British Commonwealth has, and will continue to have, a special degree of intimacy. When, however, it comes to dealing with the great issues which determine peace or war, prosperity or depression, it must not, in aim or method, be exclusive. In meeting world issues of security, employment, and social standards we must join not only with Commonwealth countries but with all like-minded states, if our purposes and ideals are to prevail. Our commitments on these great issues must be a part of a general scheme, whether they be on a world basis or regional in nature...[7]

Contrary to his custom, Mackenzie King had delivered this statement extemporaneously, and his first reaction was one of remorse at having muffed so splendid an opportunity on so important an occasion. He was, he wrote, 'conscious of leaving out parts of what I wished to say, and really suffered a good deal of mental confusion ... I felt genuinely depressed...' However he was quickly uplifted by the response of the newspapers, whose editorials were exceptionally enthusiastic. A day later he had come to regard the speech as possibly 'one of the most significant I have made in my life. It opens up,' he asserted,

the great broad division between centralized and decentralized organization, not only of Empire activities but the larger question of power politics by a few great nations leading inevitably to war against the conception of international world co-operation of nations great and small. In other words, a future world organization. Matter of preserving peace and preventing war. The largest subject that it is possible to deal with in politics.[8]

Mackenzie King's optimistic assessment of his speech was not excessively optimistic. His own verdict proved to be the verdict of historians – 'a major pronouncement,' one of whom wrote fifteen years later, 'not only on Canadian but also on Commonwealth affairs.'

An attentive observer of these events was Halifax's Commonwealth colleague, the Canadian ambassador to Washington. 'His Lordship is, I think, somewhat surprised,' L.B. Pearson reported to Ottawa, 'at the commotion that he has caused. Those who advised him to speak as he did certainly did him no service.' The time had arrived, Pearson felt, for Canadians to think hard about their role in the British Commonwealth of Nations.

We had little to do with British foreign policy leading up to the present war, but we were as deeply involved in the results of that policy as Great Britain herself. That being the case, surely we should seek to influence British policy in some way when it appears to be going in the wrong direction. I do not mean by this that we should adopt certain ideas now being thrown out by various British Commonwealth leaders which look to the British Commonwealth as a unit in international affairs. If we act as a unit, I do not see how we can also act separately and maintain the national and international position we have gained. We can't have it both ways. Therefore, there is only one way. It is, I think, quite impossible for us, even if we so desired, to reverse the history of the last twenty years. The Prime Minister was, in my opinion, absolutely right when he deprecated this talk of a British Commonwealth unit in foreign affairs; talk based on views held, I'm afraid, in pretty high quarters, in the White House, in No. 10...[9]

Halifax's speech in Toronto was followed by one in New York. 'This Society,' he told the members of the American-Soviet Friendship League on 16 November 1944, 'speaks for two sides of the triangle. The third side is the British Commonwealth; and it is symbolic of this threefold association that the United States, Soviet Russia and the British Commonwealth are represented here tonight.' Pearson's reaction to this second intervention was almost as heated as that of Mackenzie King to the first. 'The evidence is quite clear,' he wrote to Norman Robertson,

that remarks of the kind mentioned above are not casual and unthinking but are deliberate and considered and spring ... from the realization that the UK itself may no longer be powerful enough to be placed securely alongside the US and the USSR in the triumvirate of Great Powers. Therefore, the conception of the single Commonwealth and Empire should be built up. This building up process is encouraged, on occasions, both in Washington and Moscow, by those who for one reason or another prefer to deal with the British Commonwealth as a unit, and who seem unaware of the fact that the course of historical development cannot be altered in this way ... If we are not careful our international position as an independent nation within the British Commonwealth will be weaker at the end of this war than it was at the beginning.[10]

The Canadian Government intended to be careful.

On 1 May 1944, a meeting of the Prime Ministers of the Commonwealth, long postponed in deference to Mackenzie King's reluctance to leave his country in wartime for any extended period, held its first session in London. 'The Post-War Commonwealth' was not an item on its agenda. 'Defence Co-operation within the Commonwealth' was. But, whatever the agenda, it was evident to the participants that the meeting would very quickly have to come to grips with the conflicting conceptions of the Commonwealth presented by Smuts and Halifax, on the one hand, and by Mackenzie King, on the other. So it proved.

Mackenzie King first placed his views before the Conference on 4 May, following a review of British foreign policy by Anthony Eden. Curtin of Australia and Fraser of New Zealand had each stated at the conclusion of Eden's remarks that (as Mackenzie King recorded) 'British foreign policy had been sound. I felt,' his account continues,

> it would be a mistake to let the meeting break up without a word or two. I said that I was glad to hear Fraser speak as he did of the soundness of the British policy and also Curtin ... and wanted to associate myself with both Curtin and Fraser ... I had in mind that this foreign policy had been reached as a result of consultation with ourselves and the other Dominions and that it made clear a common policy could be reached without any centralization here in London.

Curtin asked Mackenzie King what he thought of the idea 'of having someone put in the Foreign Office here from each of the Dominions to get more information.' The Canadian Prime Minister replied that he did not think much of that idea. 'I told him,' he wrote,

> that everything over here was on the ratio of 8 to 1. He would see that from the table we were sitting at. I later said to him I thought he would get more information by appointing his own Ministers to the different capitals, where they could gather their own opinions.

It was his impression, Mackenzie King recorded, that the Australian and New Zealand Prime Ministers were at long last beginning to see as he had seen 'the dangers of having matters settled in London.'[11]

For Mackenzie King, the most trying, and the most important, day of the Conference came on 15 May, the day before adjournment, the day for consideration of the draft communiqué. He had lived through such a day before – indeed, thrice before: in November 1923, in November 1926, in June 1937; each was at an Imperial Conference; in each Mackenzie King prevailed. He did not intend to give way now.

The draft communiqué was largely the handiwork of the Secretary to the British Cabinet, Sir Edward Bridges (succeeding Hankey in his famous role), who had shown it to Norman Robertson two days earlier; Robertson had spoken about the draft to Mackenzie King who 'at once asked if a single policy had been set out ... Robertson replied that was the one point he, himself, had caught.' Robertson had asked Bridges to change 'policy' to 'policies.' This had been duly done, with the result that when the draft was placed before the Prime Ministers on 15 May, it recited that they had 'examined together the principles which determine our foreign policies, and their application to current problems.' The British Foreign Secretary did not much care for this formulation, and held out for the original 'policy.' Eden was supported by Curtin and Fraser. Clement Attlee, presiding in Churchill's absence, then declared: 'We are all agreed.' Mackenzie King immediately said: 'No.' He went on to tell them why:

> This is rushing the pace a little too rapidly. I would not agree to the use of the words "one policy." In our discussions, it was settled that our policies would converge. There was no agreement about there being one foreign policy. I took exception to that, saying that it was not true. We were not agreed on all aspects...

Mackenzie King recorded that he had spoken 'pretty emphatically and made it clear I was holding my ground. The matter was not pressed further ... It was well,' he reflected, 'I was present and spoke out ... Every effort was made, despite all that has been said thus far, and the Canadian attitude made so plain. Had I not spoken as I did, we would have been completely crowded out of our true position.'[12]

Immediately following this engagement, the Prime Ministers turned their attention to Commonwealth defence. Once again it was an old story for Mackenzie King. The Secretary of State for Dominion Affairs, Lord Cranborne, read to the meeting what Mackenzie King described as

> a long paper putting forth different suggestions as to policies and so forth, piling up one on top of the other, and among other things, asking for ... an Imperial Joint Board for Defence. Everything that they had been trying for years was jammed into this statement. When Cranborne had completed, Attlee asked me what I had to say. I replied that that statement would be an interesting one for the Cabinets of the different Governments to consider. That I would be pleased to see that the different suggestions made were considered. Frankly I would not undertake to express opinion on any one or give any undertaking respecting it. I went on to say that I thought we had better wait until the present war was over and we saw how it resulted before we started to discuss new methods of organization. I ended up by saying that I did not think we should have been expected to discuss this matter at this time. It was plain from my attitude, and what I said, that [I thought] it was a bit of underhand work. It really amounted to high pressure of the worst kind in trying to shove this kind of thing through, at the last moment ... after we had come to an agreement on a statement which covered the whole proceedings...[13]

The result of this intervention was that the communiqué contained no reference whatsoever to the problem of Commonwealth defence. Once again Mackenzie King had got his way with everything. That evening he recorded in his diary the events of the long day, congratulating himself on his performance. 'It makes me tremble,' he wrote, 'to think of what Canada might be let in for if a different type of person were in office.'[14]

That a different type of person was not in office was in part because of the voters' appreciation of the zeal displayed by their Prime Minister for the care and nurture of Canada's autonomy. Most of them approved wholeheartedly of the way Mackenzie King, in a series of constitutional and political episodes some of which had been provoked by him, others merely exploited by him, had slackened the ties of empire. Mackenzie King was well aware that most Canadians wanted the slackening of those ties. 'You know,' he had confided to Churchill during one of their wartime meetings, 'the minute I cross to England, immediately there is a cry raised that I have gone into the imperialist camp, and a nationalist sentiment begins to develop at home: not in the province of Quebec only, but in the West and in other parts of Canada. What people are really afraid of is the imperialist idea as against the complete independence of the parts.'[15]

But that did not mean – and Mackenzie King was no less aware of this – the Liberal way with the Commonwealth met with the approval of all Canadians. An influential minority clung to the concept of a centralized British Empire, speaking with one voice on foreign and most other affairs. Its members, found almost always within the Conservative Party, were prone to judge the foreign policy of a Canadian government by the extent to which it conformed to and supported the policies of the United Kingdom. By that test it was occasionally found wanting; and on such occasions the voice of the Canadian imperialist resonated through the land – the voice of an Arthur Meighen, or a Tommy Church, or a Howard Green.

By their utterances Mackenzie King professed to be more elated than disturbed: he was usually able to turn them to his political advantage. But he was nonetheless disturbed. Not far beneath their reasoning – reasoning borrowed from Smuts, and from Curtin, and from other overseas philosophers – lay a crude emotional appeal, manipulating the images of empire. King and Queen, Royal Family, Union Jack, Mother Country, Land of Hope and Glory – were not these potent symbols on the hustings still? Who was to say that Canadians, regardless of party, might not be swayed by their skilful exploitation, by charges that the Prime Minister himself was lukewarm in his loyalty? In private negotiation, where reason might prevail, Mackenzie King was sure of his case and of its outcome; in public controversy, where his opponents would deploy irrational forces in their cause, he was not so sure. His wartime diary shows how uneasy their charges made him feel:

*26 May 1940*: The Tories would be the first to shout about it from the housetops that I was ready to sacrifice the British Isles for a new orientation of world power...

*24 June 1941*: No doubt the Tory Press will begin their attacks on me for not going to London and put it down to some difference re war effort, etc. It might come to result in a pretty serious cleavage...

*31 December 1941*: I told Churchill ... they [Conservatives] had tried to pin the badge of isolationism on me. He could not find in Canada a man who had been stronger for British connection than myself, and for Empire unity ... For a long while their chief cry was that I was pro-American. It was true I had been at Harvard and with the Rockefeller Foundation, and had many friends there. I had always felt that would be helpful and ... it had proved to be helpful. That when they saw they could no longer take advantage of that attack they were now coming back to this isolationist talk...

*4 August 1944*: ... [The Opposition] reverted back to an Imperial Council for war; centralized Secretariat and one voice for the Empire. Effort also to make it appear that I was not loyal. I did not use enough expressions of loyalty...

*5 December 1944*: I suppose the Tory Party and others will be saying that I am doing my best to break up the British connection, etc. Unless one were very objective in one's attitude ... one might think one was in a mad-house...[16]

Mackenzie King was not himself very objective in his attitude towards the imperialist minority in Canada. He grossly exaggerated its influence. The moulders of opinion were nearly all on his side of the issue. When, in December 1943, the Montebello Conference* took up the questions 'Is the maintenance of Great Britain as one of the three or four great powers of the world an important Canadian interest? To what extent should Canada contribute to this end? E.g., diminution of autonomy? centralized policies? etc.,' the bloc-unit conception of Empire received scant support. Most of the conferees accepted that the Commonwealth, as one of those present from the Department of External Affairs put it, might best be regarded as 'a tough and enduring alliance,' 'an *entente cordiale* between a group of states which did not bind them to common action, but by practice, tradition and usage to be frank with one another and to attempt to reach common agreement, without insistence upon reaching such common agreement or a joint voice.'†

In the United Kingdom, a very different sort of opinion prevailed in comparable quarters. The Royal Institute of International Affairs had drawn up late in 1943 in preparation for the Third British Commonwealth Relations Conference‡ a draft agenda which was sent to the participating

* See above, 171–3.

† 'The Round Table Reports of the Rapporteurs at the Montebello Conference on "Canada and the Building of the Peace".' Canadian Institute of International Affairs, February 1944 (mimeographed). On 4 August 1944, in the House of Commons, the Prime Minister offered a close approximation of this description, remarking 'that in the British Commonwealth there has been evolved a unique alliance of a peculiarly tough and enduring kind whose members act together not because they are under any strict obligation to do so but because they have the will to act together.' Canada, *H.C. Debates*, 1944, v, 5918.

‡ The British Commonwealth Relations Conferences were unofficial meetings of students of Commonwealth affairs chosen from public and private life by the Institutes of International Affairs in the United Kingdom, Canada, Australia, New Zealand, South Africa, and India. Discussion lasted about a fortnight, and was meant to be strictly confidential. The first Conference had met in Toronto in September 1933, the second at Lapstone, Australia, in September 1938; the

Institutes in the Dominions and India for their comments and suggestions. Officials at the Canadian Institute of International Affairs found the draft profoundly unsatisfactory. 'My first reaction,' wrote E.J. Tarr, the member of the Institute responsible for arrangements for the Conference,

> is definitely unfavourable ... There seems to be an underlying assumption that where the member nations have common interests there should be Commonwealth machinery for furthering those interests. This seems to me to skate over the most important immediate question of all, and practically assumes the desirability of a British bloc, and even, perhaps, the desirability of speaking with one voice.[17]

Nor did further reflection change their mind. The British draft, Tarr wrote a month later to Norman Robertson, 'is apparently based on the assumption that everything that is possible in the way of centralizing machinery is desirable. In other words, it makes a basic assumption which in the opinion of most of us in this country is a false one.'[18]

The Canadian Institute accordingly informed its sister Institute in London that its draft agenda was unacceptable to it. Chatham House responded by arranging a meeting, to be held in New York City early in 1944, at which its representatives and officials of the Canadian Institute might work out a mutually satisfactory programme for the Conference. 'If we get a decent agenda lined up,' E.J. Tarr wrote beforehand, 'I think I can probably get it across.' But if he failed to persuade his British colleagues to agree to a less slanted approach, he thought 'it would be better not to hold a conference. For the British nations to get together now with a view to planning how they will act if a world system doesn't develop would have very bad reactions outside the Commonwealth and would tend to develop a defeatist attitude within the Commonwealth.'[19] There was at least one important member of the Canadian Institute who thought it would be best in any event not to go through with the Conference as planned. This was Brooke Claxton, whose nationalism was then flaming like an oil well as a result of his exchange in the House of Commons with the Conservative advocates of a united-front Commonwealth. 'Instead of having a British Commonwealth conference,' Claxton had written, 'we should have a conference of the countries which are likely to think alike.' However, he conceded that he was 'not too sure that we could go so far as to stand out of it and ... the possible benefit (I think the only benefit)

third met in London between 17 February and 3 March 1945. Lacking any official standing, the Conferences played an important part in shaping Commonwealth attitudes and, occasionally, Commonwealth policies. The London Conference, the first such meeting to be held since the outbreak of war, was exceptionally important: the Canadian participants were right to take it as seriously as they did.

will be to show the Commonwealth nations that their interests are general and not particular.'[20]

The draft counter-agenda which the two members of the Canadian Institute of International Affairs took with them to New York was as carefully drawn as any document destined for a Prime Ministers' Meeting. In addition to such Institute stalwarts as E.J. Tarr, Edgar McInnis, Frank Scott, J.B. Coyne, and George Ferguson, a number of officials of the Department of External Affairs (among them Norman Robertson, Hume Wrong, and A.D.P. Heeney) had offered comments and suggestions. The burden of the Canadian Institute's draft was that the Conference should be encouraged to turn its attention away from the concept of the Commonwealth as a closed and exclusive system, and examine instead the ways in which the member states might best contribute 'to the creation of an effective world system.'

At the meeting in New York City, the Canadians got their way. 'The Chatham House agenda was scrapped,' E.J. Tarr reported, 'and our agenda, with modifications, was the one adopted.' He admitted that 'some of the modifications tended to blur a little the ideas which we had in mind,' adding that it would be 'for those who go to the Conference to see that in the discussions themselves the proper emphasis is placed.'[21]

The Conference had originally been planned for the spring of 1944, but did not get under way until 17 February 1945, delayed by the approaching climax of the war and by difficulties in finding transportation for the delegates. The Canadian Institute assembled a strong team. Its delegation consisted of E.J. Tarr, the chairman, F.A. Brewin, W.A. Irwin, D.R. Michener, Lionel Roy, B.K. Sandwell, Victor Sifton, R.G. Trotter, and L.B. Unwin; two young Service officers, James George and Gerald Graham, then stationed in London, acted as secretaries. Tarr described the group as 'really representative of all shades of opinion here [in Canada] other than the two lunatic fringes'[22] – a fair enough description if the Conservative Opposition Party was to be relegated to the lunatic fringe. The group set sail from Halifax late in January. 'I confess to you,' Tarr wrote to Norman Robertson on the eve of its departure,

> that I am going to this Conference with reluctance ... The splendid qualities of the British which made possible the Battle of Britain are the qualities which are now blinding their eyes to realities, and ... without knowing it they are instinctively trying to turn the clock back and get the Dominions into a power bloc ... The Canadians at the London Conference will constantly have to be saying what will deeply hurt our British friends. Personally I don't relish the job, because in a sense it is a case of kicking a man when he is down.[23]

Blunt speaking began even before the Conference began. Its organizers had arranged for some of the participants to place their views about the Commonwealth before the wider audience of the BBC Home Service. The first in the series of talks was given by F.B. Malim of the British delegation. Malim expounded, with perfect fidelity to the assumptions of the scrapped Chatham House agenda, the doctrine of a united Commonwealth moving as one on the issues of foreign policy and defence policy in the post-war world. This opening statement afforded the Canadian who spoke next a perfect opportunity for rebuttal.

He did not pass it up. George Ferguson – disciple, protégé, and successor of J.W. Dafoe of the Winnipeg *Free Press* – while not a member of the Canadian delegation to the Conference, was a leading spirit at the Canadian Institute; he had played a part in the earlier battle of the agenda, and was fully aware of the significance of the confrontation looming at the London Conference. His broadcast minced no words. 'If I am asked,' Ferguson told his listeners,

> how best the nations of the Commonwealth can organise to maintain the peace, I reply that the best way for this particular group of nations to organise is not to organise at all ... I do not mean there should be no organisation in the world for peace. There must be. But I do mean that it is both artificial and dangerous for the nations of the Commonwealth to attempt to do it on their own. I believe not only that the attempt would break down but I believe too that, as it failed, the major cause of world peace would suffer greatly, and that we should, by making the try, damage the very thing we most want...
>
> It seems to me, and to very many other Canadians as well, that every attempt by Commonwealth countries to form a united front, depends absolutely upon the creation of a far wider common front. It should include not only Britain and the handful of small countries known as the Dominions. It should embrace other powers as well; and inside that larger framework, every member should agree to the greatest possible surrender of national sovereignty for the benefit of all of us. Above all, the larger organization must include the Great Powers – all three of them...
>
> Canadians do of course want the foreign policies of the Commonwealth to march together. But they must be policies, in the plural, and not a policy in the singular, as the statement at the meeting of Prime Ministers last May made very clear. The Commonwealth group is too narrow to meet our minimum needs. We want, we must have, a wider basis for our security.[24]

All this could not have been put more plainly. Ferguson's broadcast, especially when juxtaposed against that which had preceded it, sharpened the positions on both sides. It made their confrontation direct, and inescapable.

On 17 February, the first day of the Third British Commonwealth Relations Conference, that confrontation took place. Discussion commenced immediately on the general question of international security in the post-war world. Lord Hailey, of the British group, introduced this topic. His statement embraced the ideas of Smuts and Halifax. He spoke at some length of the need of the United Kingdom for the unity and support of the members of the British Commonwealth if she were to be able to play an effective part for peace in a world dominated by Russia and America. At the conclusion of his statement, Lord Hailey was asked by a member of the Canadian group whether he 'had in mind a single policy shared by a number of governments; or a community of policies expressed in the world organization by the voices of the several nations which had discussed their policies together.' Hailey's reply was as disconcerting to the Canadians as it was clear to them. He was, he told them, in favour of the single policy, the unified Commonwealth. 'If each [Commonwealth country] came in as an independent sovereign people, the whole effect would be destroyed. What mattered was that other members of the world organization should recognize that in some way [the countries of the Commonwealth] did form an entity and exercised a common policy with the resources of the Commonwealth behind it; that there was known to be some form of machinery for combined action.'[25]

When the Conference resumed the discussion two days later, E.J. Tarr was next to speak. He outlined what he considered to be the 'four fallacious assumptions' contained in Lord Hailey's statement.

The first was the very dangerous and unreal assumption that if the security organization was to be lasting and permanently successful, each of the Big Three must speak for approximately the same quantum of power. Such an organization would have within itself the seeds of its own early destruction. The world was not static and the relative position of countries was bound to change from year to year. There must therefore be a system sufficiently elastic to deal with or disregard shifts in power.

The British conception seemed to be straining after the form, while losing sight of the substance, of Britain's position within the organization. If she took a certain line, the other two parties would surely be aware if she were expressing the common point of view of the Commonwealth nations, and the countries of Western Europe. Her influence would be measured in the light of that knowledge.

The second fallacious assumption was that the influence of the British nations would be greater if they spoke with one voice. On the contrary, it would be greater if they acted as separate entities.

The third assumption was that the Commonwealth was at present, or would become, a functioning political entity. It was a *group* of functioning entities, and being democratic, they could not speak with one voice, unless they formed a federation. And that was not considered practical politics at present, however desirable some may think it to be.

The fourth assumption was that in some way the Commonwealth and Empire formed a desirable regional system for defence. But it was not a defensible unit and a more effective development would be for Australia and New Zealand to try to extend the idea of the Canberra Pact so as to bring in American seapower and for Canada to try to broaden the United States-Canada Pact [of August 1940]...[26]

And that, too, was laying it on the line.

The two competing conceptions of Commonwealth were now very clearly drawn. Between them the Conference continued to wrangle for a fortnight. It was not, in Tarr's view, at all evenly divided. 'We were a solid phalanx against any centralizing development,' he wrote afterwards, 'and in this respect we really didn't differ from Australia or South Africa, and very, very slightly from New Zealand.' But the British stood their ground.

It was in these circumstances that, on 2 March, the day before the Conference adjourned, a venerable figure rose in the room to request permission to make a personal statement. He was Lionel Curtis, the disappointed but not dishonoured prophet of imperial federation. Almost forty years earlier, Curtis had stumped the youthful Dominion of Canada in an unavailing effort to persuade her leaders to join his crusade for a united Commonwealth of Nations.* No one with a sense of history could have listened unaffected by what he now said.

Lionel Curtis began by reminding his audience that his credentials for prophecy had not been entirely shredded by events. He had warned of civil strife in South Africa if Britain went to war with Germany; the Beyers rebellion had followed. He had warned (in 1916) of a second war with Germany if the United States retreated into isolationism leaving Britain alone in Europe; the Americans had retreated, and the war was not yet won. He had worked for Ireland's sovereignty, and Ireland was now sovereign. He had worked for India's freedom, and freedom was on its way. When, therefore, he declared, he saw 'old and dear friends like Lord Cecil, Lord Samuel, Edgar Tarr and George Ferguson again drugging the public mind into thinking that world war can now be prevented by means which have obviously failed since 1919,' he felt he had some excuse for using 'such terrible words' of his friends as he was now obliged to utter. 'You, Mr Tarr' – levelling (so an eye-witness recalls) an accusatory finger at the elderly, grey-haired, and entirely benign figure who had astonishingly become the villain of the drama –

You, Mr Tarr, have told us that "the Commonwealth is not a functioning political entity." Then in plain words it is in your view "a political non-entity." From the chair yesterday you called on us to discuss "Commonwealth

* See James Eayrs, 'The Round Table Movement in Canada 1909–1920,' xxxviii, 1, March 1957, 1–2.

co-operative institutions" and then implored us to soft-pedal the word "institutions." You seem to have forgotten that on a previous day you attached the greatest importance to the Joint Defence Board of Canada and the USA becoming a permanent institution. In your view the mutual relations of Canada and the USA ought to be implemented by institutions. But in your view the mutual relations of states Members of the Commonwealth should not be implemented by institutions.

Then, Curtis went on, there was the question of the relationship of the Commonwealth to a more general international organization. The history of the pre-war years offered an irrefutable answer to that question. The League of Nations had failed to keep the peace; the Commonwealth of Nations, which some sceptics had wanted to 'be liquidated into the League,' had saved the world from infamy and destruction. 'In the face of these facts' – again the accusing finger – 'you, Mr Tarr, are now asking for the liquidation of the British Commonwealth into Dumbarton Oaks.' Curtis referred to the chapter in Grant Dexter's *Canada and the Building of Peace**

in which he recounts the manner in which my old friend Senator Dandurand, acting at Geneva as the agent of Mr Mackenzie King's Government, led the movement for emasculating the League of Nations in the interests of nationalism and national sovereignty. I can picture the sceptical smile which would have spread over the faces of Mr Mackenzie King, of Senator Dandurand, and I must add on your face, Mr Tarr, and on that of George Ferguson, had anyone then ventured to prophecy that the movement which the Government of Canada led at Geneva was forging a vital link in a chain of causes which would lead on to the brutal butchery of a Winnipeg battalion by Japanese bayonets in Hong Kong, and to covering France, Belgium and Holland with Canadian graves.

Senator Dandurand has not lived to see the results of the movement he voiced. But Mr Mackenzie King has lived to see them, and so have you, Mr Tarr, and George Ferguson, who are now voicing his views. Like the nobles of the *ancien régime*, who returned to re-establish the monarchy in France, you have learned nothing and forgotten nothing, although the tragic fruits of your policy are staring you in the face. Once more you are luring public opinion down the primrose path which leads to another wholesale butchery, to a third holocaust...

At an earlier meeting I told you that Mr Bevin has said to us that after this war the British Government will not be able to train mechanized forces on land or in the air in these islands. They will have to train them in the Dominions and especially in Canada. On this Mr Brewin observed that the USA might not

* Written originally as a background paper for the Montebello Conference of December 1943, this book was published in 1944 under the auspices of the Canadian Institute of International Affairs; the published version was submitted by the Canadian Institute as a background paper for the British Commonwealth Relations Conference. Curtis was referring to Section XI, 'Collective Security,' 137–43.

approve of Canada allowing the training of Commonwealth forces on Canadian soil. I am rich in friends and almost think I have more Canadian than English friends. Years of intercourse with them have not disposed me to accept the statements of Mr Tarr and Mr Brewin as expressions of general Canadian opinion. In those statements I recognize the policies of the Liberal Party machine and the CCF Party machine ... I do not believe that Canadians would make any measure required to strengthen the Commonwealth and its defence subject to American approval...

The immediate policy I am here to advocate is simple. I urge that we who boast that we speak the tongue that Shakespeare spoke, the faith and morals that Milton held, should now at last have the candour and courage to recognize that the undertaking we gave in 1926 to keep the routes which unite all parts of the British Commonwealth immune from attack is utterly beyond our resources, as shown by the outbreak of this war and also of the last. We should call on our Government to say this frankly to Dominion Governments, and ask them to discuss how to devise an authority equipped with adequate resources to render the Commonwealth immune from attack...

I have to thank you, Mr Tarr, for giving me time for stating my case, a case which you knew was poignantly levelled against your own.[27]

When Lionel Curtis finished speaking, all eyes rested on the person of E.J. Tarr. As the chairman of the meeting, his was the next word and, as it turned out, the last. 'My head is bloody,' Tarr said unsmilingly, 'but unbowed.' He then adjourned the meeting. Perhaps he was incapable of reply. Perhaps there could be no reply. The poignancy of their confrontation, to which Lionel Curtis had alluded in his closing remark, is in no way lessened by the reflection that, a quarter century later, it is still too soon to say which man made the better prophet. Or if the prophecy of either was any good at all.

## LIBERALS AND LABOUR

'I don't think I am ... enthusiastic about the Conference,' E.J. Tarr had written soon after his return to Canada from London. 'I had a feeling that at the end of two weeks we were just about at the point where a group which really understood what the Commonwealth is should have begun its discussion. I hope the UK group was not a really representative one, but I'm afraid that it probably was.'[28]

The staff of the Canadian High Commission in London had been troubled by a different fear. They were afraid that the Canadians present at the British Commonwealth Relations Conference would form the impression that the views expressed by the United Kingdom participants reflected the views of British policy-makers actual and potential. 'In an attempt to correct this misconception,' Vincent Massey has since recalled, 'I arranged a private dinner for the Canadian delegates, to which I invited five members of the British Cabinet (Attlee, Cranborne, Swinton, Morrison, and Richard Law), as well as the editors of *The Times* and *The Economist*. I had done a little advance planning to bring about a frank conversation.'[29] The conversation was certainly frank. The Canadian delegates told the British Ministers that they 'were worried over the preoccupation of the United Kingdom delegates [at the Conference] with the desirability of integrating the Commonwealth by the establishment of more formal machinery. This attitude was not only contrary to the trend of opinion in Canada but was considered by Canadians to be contrary to the best interests of the Commonwealth and of the world at large. Although the Canadian view was accepted by the United Kingdom delegates it was accepted with regret. The Canadians, on the other hand, did not understand the reasons for regret as they did not consider their views of Commonwealth relations to be second-best.'[30] The British Ministers did all they could to reassure. Lord Cranborne, the Secretary of State for Dominion Affairs, told the Canadian delegates that they should not take Lionel Curtis seriously. His views were logical, Cranborne allowed, in some respects attractive; but they were not then, nor would they become, practical politics. Clement Attlee, then Deputy Prime Minister and a former Dominions Secretary, agreed. He told the Canadians present, in what one of them described as 'a concise and forceful statement,' that he wholly endorsed the present informal arrangements for Commonwealth consultation. 'He deplored the approach to Commonwealth relations of those who wished to devise new paper constitutions.'[31]

Five months later, Clement Attlee had become the head of the new Labour Government of the United Kingdom. He was now in a position to practise what he had preached. Ottawa was not entirely certain that he would. Attlee's own conception of Commonwealth relations it conceded to be sound – that is, to coincide with the conception of the Canadian Government. On the other hand, Attlee was judged to have been less than a complete success during his short stint (February 1942 to September 1943) as Secretary of State for Dominion Affairs: the reticence and taciturnity for which he was already known were qualities not well suited to the task of placating Dominion governments avid for information and for a place in the scheme of things. Moreover, some of the new Prime Minister's Cabinet colleagues were unknown quantities whose inexperience of recent Commonwealth practices, combined with their predeliction for central planning, might make their policies indistinguishable from those of Cecil Rhodes, however different their intentions. Might not the logical mind of Sir Stafford Cripps – an asset, certainly, at the Treasury – prove disastrous at the Dominions Office?* And there was something else to be reckoned with. Labour was in power not in London only, but in Canberra and Wellington as well. The majority of the Commonwealth had gone socialist. Might not this make awkward the position of the non-socialist minority? 'We may become the reactionary Power in the Commonwealth,' a member of the Department of External Affairs had ruminated in a paper written soon after the Labour victory, 'and be denounced as a satellite of the "capitalist," "imperialist" United States.'

All this was speculation of the professional diplomatists. The reaction of the Prime Minister of Canada was far less sophisticated. Mackenzie King reacted to the news with unalloyed satisfaction. 'Looking into the future,' he wrote on 26 July 1945,

> I am not sure Labour winning as strongly as it has may not help the peace of the world. It is only as human brotherhood is established that peace will come. The Conservatives do not rely on international friendships. They rely on force and power. Force and power bring force and power to oppose them. Under a Tory regime for the next few years it is difficult to say how far antagonism might not develop between Britain and Russia and also through Europe. Labour in all the countries will be quicker to recognize common rights and to come to share them in a way which will not place burdens on the people themselves to say nothing of costing their lives...
>
> To me it is a relief also in that at Imperial Conferences and Peace Conferences I know I will not have to be bucking centralized Imperialism again. My sympathies were much stronger with Labour and its point of view than with the Conservatives...[32]

Less than three months after Labour's triumph, Mackenzie King visited the United Kingdom, mainly in order to meet with the members of the new Government and gain some impressions of their personalities and outlook. He was greatly taken by Clement Attlee 'of whom,' he recorded, 'I think more and more as I listen to him in conversation. He is very humble minded; very clear minded ... Is always so gentle and kind. A very true soul.' Souls were one thing; policies something else again. Mackenzie King soon discovered that the new day in Commonwealth relations for which he had hoped when British government changed hands was not yet dawning.

On 2 November 1945, Mackenzie King had his first discussions with members of the new Labour Government on problems of Commonwealth

* This appraisal appears to discount the value of the contribution Cripps made to the Commonwealth of Nations during his trip to India in March 1942; at any rate, official Ottawa experienced more relief than disappointment on learning that a less highly powered politician – Lord Addison – was to take over the Dominions Office on 3 August 1945. (Cripps went to the Board of Trade.)

policy. 'Shown into the Cabinet Council at Downing Street,' he wrote of the occasion,

and had a quiet talk with Mr Attlee, who was seated alone in front of the fire. He later was joined by Lord Addison. The subject they had wished to discuss was the question of strengthening up the more effective co-ordination of the defence of the Empire. Reference was made to the Imperial Council of Defence.

Mackenzie King had been forewarned by Norman Robertson that the British leaders were likely to bring this subject up. He was well prepared to defend himself. He responded, he recorded, immediately:

said ... that at all the Conferences I had attended in 1923 and since, this question of Imperial Defence came up. That I had always to take exception to Canada being represented on that body [the Committee of Imperial Defence]. That I thought I should make very clear that the word "Imperial" was a word to which the members of our Party and the CCF and other parties in Canada denoted centralization in matters of defence, being drawn into all kinds of conflicts in all quarters of the world, etc. That, as a matter of fact, we had not been represented on the Imperial Council at any time, nor was it of the slightest use during the war. That I might say at once our Government would not be favourable to Canada taking a different course at this time in regard to an Imperial Council of Defence than that taken on any previous occasion.[33]

Attlee and Addison appeared to Mackenzie King to be 'quite receptive' and 'prepared to accept what I said'; certainly they had no excuse for being surprised.

An early casualty of the post-war Commonwealth was the old-style Imperial Conference. Once again, it had been Labour which wanted to revive it, Liberals which cut it down. The British Foreign Secretary raised the matter with Mackenzie King in London on 10 October 1945. 'Bevin ... said that he thought ... the best thing to do was to have an Imperial Conference fairly soon and bring the Dominions together. I said to him at once,' Mackenzie King recorded, 'that that did not seem to me to be the step most necessary. That this Russian situation' – a reference to the discovery a fortnight earlier of a Soviet espionage ring in Ottawa – 'could not be met by Britain and the Dominions. It could only be met by closer relations and understanding of the United States and the British Commonwealth.'[34] This view prevailed. Within six weeks, the Prime Minister of the United Kingdom, the Prime Minister of Canada, and the President of the United States were conferring together in Washington.*

Failure to reconvene the Imperial Conference did not go unnoticed nor uncriticized in the United Kingdom, where the critics freely identified the Government of Canada as the culprit responsible for its demise. 'It was

* See below, 279–81.

surely not on the initiative of the United Kingdom Government,' a speaker told a meeting of the Royal Empire Society early in 1946, 'that the Imperial Conference was quietly smothered in its bed ... – put down, like an old dog which has become feeble and smelly, and which must now not be mentioned before children, lest they embarrass by asking what became of him. We can have a shrewd guess who was the principal accessory before that guilty fact. Surely, from all the evidence, it was the representatives of Canada.'[35]

It required no particularly penetrating intelligence to see that this was so. Naturally the representatives of Canada took strong exception to this interpretation of their motive. They had not, to be sure, wished to revive the Imperial Conference in its pre-war form. That stemmed not from their dislike of the Commonwealth but from their attachment to the Commonwealth. It reflected a simple concern for the principles of scientific management. The old-style Imperial Conference, a member of the Department of External Affairs wrote at the time, had been 'superseded by the almost continuous series of functional conferences which accomplish the work with less fuss but with better timing ... The more emphasis there is on doing a job and the less on pure display the better for the health of the Commonwealth.' The Royal Empire Society had always been able to find a role for 'pure display.'

Canada's opposition to the old-style Imperial Conference did not extend to the new-style Prime Ministers' meeting of the kind which had been held in London during May 1944. Its regimen of mostly work and only a little display appealed to Ottawa's pragmatic approach; and when, early in 1946, a Prime Ministers' meeting was proposed by the United Kingdom Government, the Canadian Government accepted the proposal.

It was accepted with some reluctance. 'If I had consulted my own feelings at this time,' Mackenzie King frankly informed the House of Commons on the eve of his departure, 'I would have remained here.'[36] But it was not the notion of the meeting that caused the Prime Minister displeasure. It was its timing. His agenda was already crowded: a Dominion-Provincial Conference was in the offing, the loan to Britain had to be guided through Parliament, the Budget drawn up, his External Affairs estimates worked over. And its tone.

The wording of the British Government's invitation was unfortunate: it certainly angered its recipient. 'I felt quite annoyed,' Mackenzie King wrote on 22 April 1946, 'when I read in it reference to public opinion in Britain being disappointed if I were not present. The public opinion I have to consider is that of Canada. It annoys me beyond words ... to have pressure put on from a Government in Britain as though our Government were in some way subordinate to it.'[37] His annoyance mounted when, about a fortnight later, he received a batch of official papers relating to the forthcoming meeting from the Dominions Office, 'all in form and substance akin to a full fledged Imperial Conference. I felt the time had come when I should speak out.'[38] That evening, he drafted an indignant message of protest to Attlee. On reading it over the following morning, it seemed to him 'in some ways a little more emphatic' in its wording than was proper to send 'to one who I know is having his problems and is a true friend. At the same time,' he reflected, 'I know it is not Attlee who writes the letters or who is controlling the situation. I certainly am not going to have Canada made a puppet of any official in the Dominions or any other official of the British Government.'[39] The letter went off to London substantially as Mackenzie King had first drafted it. Later in the day, Mackenzie King referred to the Prime Ministers' meeting in the House of Commons. 'I wish to make it perfectly clear,' he told the House, 'that I am not going to attempt ... to say what this Government's opinion is with regard to questions of defence, questions of trade, preference and the like ... I shall be careful to refrain from committing anyone.'[40] That assurance, a Commonwealth historian has commented chidingly, 'might perhaps by then have been thought superfluous.'[41]

It was not until 20 May that the Prime Minister of Canada, who had been detained in his capital by the pressure of other business, was able to join his colleagues in London. The Prime Ministers' meeting had turned out, after all, to be less of a Prime Ministers' meeting than a series of bilateral conversations between United Kingdom Ministers and such representatives of the Dominion governments as could find time to attend. By 20 May fourteen sessions had been held. Mackenzie King was present for the last five sessions, which took place between 20 May and 23 May. He was in a crotchety mood. His few interventions in the discussion set new standards of non-commital – his existing standards being already very high. We have already noted his contribution to two of the three important items on the agenda – the draft peace treaties with Italy and the Balkans, and policy towards Germany.* The third item was Commonwealth defence.

On 23 May, Lord Addison read to the delegates a paper on this subject. It had been prepared by the Committee of Imperial Defence. It stressed the heavy financial and manpower burdens that post-war defence requirements were imposing upon the United Kingdom. It implied how much improved the situation would be if the Dominions helped to relieve those

* See above, 177, 194–5.

burdens. The British Foreign Secretary spoke next. He made explicit what Addison had left implicit. It would be extremely welcome, Bevin said, if the Governments of the several Dominions could formally assume responsibility for the defence of their respective regions of the Commonwealth. Both Bevin and Addison then looked expectantly at Mackenzie King. If they really expected a constructive response from the Canadian Prime Minister they were sadly disappointed. Mackenzie King replied briefly and bluntly that he was unable to promise anything of the kind. He did not wish to discuss the subject further.

That being so, the British hopefully turned to another. It concerned military liaison. On 27 May, Lord Addison spoke privately about this matter to Mackenzie King. 'He wanted to know,' the latter recorded,

> whether I would object to having one of the Canadian military authorities at HQ Staff [in London] present [at meetings of the Chiefs of Staff of the United Kingdom] to listen to the discussion for the sake of getting information. Canada being informed of the situation. I said I might as well be blunt and tell him how we viewed these matters. I said Canada was not in favour of a Commonwealth policy. In other words, a single foreign policy for the Empire. That we felt Australia might have one foreign policy; SA another; and ours would necessarily be based on our immediate neighbours, the Americans, for questions of defence, and the like ... Addison said he understood this thoroughly. He then used the words: Would we agree to someone coming in as an observer – give no expression of opinion – but simply to report the situation to the government. I said that I thought as long as it was understood it was simply for the sake of information and that no commitments were to arise nor were we to be regarded thereby as being consulted as distinguished from being informed, I would be agreeable to someone being present...[42]

Here, at least, was something. But it was far from being any thin edge of a wedge, as Attlee and Addison discovered some ten days later when they attempted to press Mackenzie King further on the subject of military liaison. This time their proposal concerned the appointment of military attachés. 'They wanted to know,' the Prime Minister of Canada recorded on 7 June, 'if I would agree to our having representatives of our defence staffs here in a purely liaison capacity to be present at meetings of the General Staff and to listen to discussions to keep us informed and to give information to them.' Mackenzie King had little liking for this project on two counts. In the first place, he distrusted military attachés in general. 'I had a strong feeling,' he had written as recently as 20 May, 'that the military, air and navy attaché business ought to be done away with altogether, and Embassies should be left free to discharge what are obviously their right duties ... The present arrangement seems to recognize war as an institution and to make it a business of all governments to have to do with it.'[43] And in the second place, he distrusted imperial military attachés in particular.* He told Attlee and Addison 'that I would not give any final reply myself at the moment. I would wish to discuss the matter not only with Ministers of Defence but my colleagues in the Cabinet as well.'[44]

The matter was duly brought before the Cabinet, but not until November 1946. By that date Mackenzie King had become even less favourably disposed towards projects of Commonwealth defence than he had been at London during May and June. On 10 November, he recorded his 'concern with the efforts being made to hold the Dominions liable for security of Commonwealth as a whole and to centralize the direction and administration of affairs in London.'[45] On 11 November his concern turned to anger. 'I was quite incensed,' he wrote in his diary that evening,

> when I received a despatch from Attlee, written by the War Office, in a tone which would indicate that Canada had to give an accounting to the United Kingdom as to what she was going to do in the Commonwealth policy – a complete reversal of the order of things which has been the kind of relationship toward different governments in Canada over the last forty years. The worst feature of it all is that after all Canada has done, and before we have been able to begin to meet the obligations arising out of the gifts of money, and the sacrifices of men and materials we have made, that there should come a demand on this country as if it were some Colonial possession of inferior races. I have not been far wrong in sensing the kind of situation which is developing under those at present in control of war policy in London...[46]

He wrote as well that evening to a correspondent in Britain of 'the mischievousness of the emphasis being placed on the "machinery" of Commonwealth defence, and the attempt to bring something of the kind into being.'[47]

The following day, the Prime Minister decided to share his anger and misgivings with his Governor-General who, as it happened, was a Field Marshal of the British Army. Mackenzie King told Viscount Alexander of Tunis

> quite plainly that I thought the [British] Prime Minister's military advisers, whoever they were, were making a mistake. That I had been amazed at what had taken place at the meeting of Prime Ministers, where Ministers had frankly said that they had taken the position that Britain was no longer responsible for her own defence, but that there must be Commonwealth defence, in which each would take a share. No recognition of what had been done or of the success which had attended the flexible method of organization, but an endeavour to get back to centralized control in London. Mentioned the telegram I had received from Attlee speaking of Britain having adopted compulsory training in time of peace and virtually asking us to assume part of the

* See James Eayrs, *In Defence of Canada*, II, 82–5.

cost of what was involved thereby and in tone taking the position that we were expected to give some accounting to the British Government as to how we proposed to meet our obligations to her ... I said I felt entitled to speak in the light of my actions over the years that I have been in office and what I had done to keep Canada united and the Commonwealth united and the relations with the UK friendly.

I found H.E. very responsive. He spoke very nicely of Attlee's government. He said he thought Attlee had done a darn good job; that he had a difficult position. No doubt these communications were put in his hand and he just sent them on. I said I knew all this and knew how these matters were done. I said that somebody had to be told that that was not the way our defence relations between the different nations were carried out. I told him I was simply discussing the matter with him in a very friendly way, not with a view to making representations. He said to me he understood that, but he had his relations with The King and others. Thought he could be helpful in these matters; as G.G. it was part of his duty to help in any way he could. I said I was glad to have him to talk to as I could not talk to some of my colleagues on these matters...[48]

This discussion provides a rare example of the way the efficient and dignified portions of the constitution may interact to its advantage. It shows, too, how far off the mark is the widely-read dictum that Mackenzie King 'did not make a practice of consulting the famous soldier, presumably because he was confident that Alexander's advice on Canadian politics would be quite worthless.'[49] On the contrary, Mackenzie King found Alexander's advice to be invaluable – though not exactly his advice on Canadian politics. 'It was altogether a most helpful conversation,' the Prime Minister wrote of their discussion on 12 November. 'I found him so fair and reasonable in his attitude.'[50] Nor was it by any means the only conversation of importance they had together.

It was against this background that, on 13 November, the Cabinet, in the presence of the Canadian Chiefs of Staff, took up for consideration what Mackenzie King described as 'many of the questions that are likely to come up in seeking to reach a decision on policy as to what it might be most advisable to do in our relations with Britain and the United States.' Prominent among these questions was that of Commonwealth defence. Mackenzie King addressed himself to it in a mood made sour by his recent experience. His mood was not improved when he discovered that his Cabinet colleagues were less eager than himself to make an issue out of it. 'I was surprised to find,' he wrote after the meeting, 'that St Laurent, who was very strong this morning in stating that Smuts was all for centralization and for each of us taking a share in certain proportion of Commonwealth defence, suddenly this afternoon excusing the whole British attitude by saying he thought it was just perhaps a method of finding it the most natural way to deal with the problem of Commonwealth defence. I was quite outspoken in saying I felt it was a reversion to the old order of things which sought centralization and control, in London ... I found it pretty difficult to get our Ministers to speak out.'[51] Their anxiety to avoid a fight was as natural as Mackenzie King's desire to pick one. None saw any political advantage to be gained from battling the dragon of Downing Street once more; whereas for Mackenzie King the episode recalled past triumphs and held out the prospect of yet one more victory on the familiar terrain. 'I can see a battle ahead,' he had written not long before, 'and I may have to speak out pretty plainly. This perhaps will help me to recover some confidence in myself which I have been losing rapidly of late.'[52]

On 15 November, the Cabinet considered the proposal to provide military liaison officers for the High Commission in the United Kingdom. It was no routine proposal and was treated in no routine manner. 'Discussed at length the subject of organization for defence in London,' Mackenzie King wrote after the meeting. 'Arguments pro and con of centralization versus co-ordination.' It need hardly be added that the co-ordinators won the day. To replace the wartime Canadian Joint Staff Mission, constituted by the War Committee of the Cabinet on 8 January 1945, it was agreed to appoint one liaison officer from each of the three Armed Services and from the Defence Research Board. These four officials, practically if not nominally Service attachés, were to be members of the staff of the High Commission in London. They would receive their instructions from the Canadian High Commissioner, and report back to him. Their functions were to be confined to liaison work strictly defined, and they should on no account take part in planning activities of any kind in conjunction with British or other Commonwealth officers. Finally, the decision was taken on the express understanding that whatever subordinate staff might be required by these liaison officials would be kept to the minimum essential number. There was no intention of allowing the Commission to become 'a sort of Coffee House where the dispatches are read and criticized like newspapers' – as Lord William Russell asserted of his embassy a century before.

With that much of a contribution from Canada to Commonwealth defence co-operation, the British Government had perforce to be content. It is not likely that it really expected much more. Attlee, at any rate, knew his man for what he was. 'Mackenzie King' the British Prime Minister of that day wrote retrospectively,

> in contrast to Smuts ... had for the greater part of his career been apprehensive of being dominated by the Government of the United Kingdom and had been almost morbidly so lest Canada should be drawn into European entanglements

without her consent. Undoubtedly, the war years had effected a considerable change in his outlook ... He was, however, still apt to be rather non-commital and to be unwilling to make pronouncements when away from his Cabinet.[53]

## BETWEEN LONDON AND DELHI

The post-war Commonwealth's most important issue had little to do with co-operation for defence among Britain and the old Dominions. It was the issue of India's future. Would the peoples of the sub-continent, after its partition in August 1947, remain within the Commonwealth? Or would they seek their destinies outside, as foreigners in foreign states? In the process by which the outcome was decided, the Government of Canada played a part.

Relations between Canada and the sub-continent had not always been expressive of that spirit of 'entente' discerned by an Indian scholar in 1962, nor of that spirit of 'co-operation' discerned by a Canadian scholar in 1968.* Canada's interest in India was first aroused by the desire to keep Indians out of Canada. 'The Hindoo and all people coming from India,' wrote Sir Wilfrid Laurier in 1909, 'seem to be less adaptable to our ways and manners than all the other Oriental races that come to us.'[54] Had the Prime Minister of Canada consulted only the report on Indian immigration to his country prepared by his Deputy Minister of Labour such was the conclusion at which he was bound to arrive. 'The native of India,' Mackenzie King had written the year before in that report, 'is not a person suited to this country ... accustomed as many of them are to the conditions of a tropical climate ...'[55] Not since Queen Victoria commanded that her Fleet bombard Bolivia had policy reflected so profound a geographical misconception – if misconception it was. The device was too dissembling to endure. 'We have used the climate of Canada,' the Governor-General observed to the Secretary of State for India, 'as a reason for prohibiting Hindu emigration to BC on humanitarian grounds. That consideration will not apply to the Sikhs, who have slept in the snows of the Himalayas.'[56] Policy came accordingly to be based more bluntly on the national interest – or at least upon the notion of national interest held by the Trades and Labour Council which resolved it to require

> the exclusion of certain nationalities and classes of people who, either by temperament, non-assimilative qualifications, habits, customs or want of any permanent good which their coming brings to us, are not a desirable acquisi-

* M.S. Rajan, 'The Indo-Canadian *Entente*,' *International Journal*, XVII, 4, Autumn 1962, 358–84; Dale C. Thomson, 'India and Canada: A Decade of Co-operation, 1947–1957,' *International Studies* (New Delhi), IX, 4, April 1968, 404–30.

tion to our citizenship ... The vast majority of the Hindus now arriving in Canada are by reason of venereal and other diseases absolutely unfitted to be allowed into this country ... They should be altogether excluded from Canada.[57]

And they were. Not by law, but by an ingenious administrative arrangement depending for its effectiveness upon the compliance of the government of the land they wished to leave.

Towards the end of the Great War that government grew restive in its compliance. It was not that the Imperial authorities felt more keenly than the Canadian the injustice and indignity of racist immigration policy. It was that they were more urgently aware of the adverse effect of such a policy upon the war effort of the people of India at a juncture when the war was going none too well for the Allies. Strong pressure was brought to bear upon Sir Robert Borden from the Imperial War Cabinet to make his policy more liberal: 'It is folly,' a British official told one of Borden's colleagues in London, 'to throw life away so prodigally in fighting the ill-will of Germany and at the same time deliberately provoke the ill-will of a nation of three or four times the population of Germany.'[58] Pressure no less strong was brought to bear upon him from his own Cabinet to keep the policy as it was: 'Think it unwise,' the acting Prime Minister cabled from Ottawa, 'to concur in any resolution which changes in any particular the existing situation.'[59] Caught in the cross-fire, Borden sought, and believed he had obtained, a compromise. The resolution adopted by the Imperial War Conference on 24 July 1918 provided that a Canadian citizen of Indian origin could secure the admission of wife (or husband) and unmarried children under 21 years of age. 'Prime importance of this agreement,' Borden telegraphed to his Cabinet after its passage,

is that we have secured formal and public acquiescence by British Government and Government of India in our view that we have absolute control of composition of our population and their assent to such resolutions on immigration as we deem desirable ... Also very important that ... this long outstanding question is now settled on a permanent basis satisfactory to us without wounding self-esteem of India...[60]

But the 'self-esteem of India' was less easily ascertained than Sir Robert Borden supposed. Certainly no viceroy, no secretary of state for India, might claim convincingly to be its custodian; nor could the Sinhas, the Singhs, the Saprus, and the Aga Khans – those appointees of the *raj* to India's delegations at imperial conferences, sitting as silent witnesses from some other planet while the delegates from Britain and the White Dominions talked on, and on. It suited Canada to believe that all was well; that did not mean that all was well.*

* See below, 241–2.

The principal architect – or, at any rate, head draughtsman – of Canada's immigration policies visited India in 1909 (the year of the Morley-Minto reforms). From this early impression, and from the contacts to which his visit led, Mackenzie King formed those ideas which were to govern, forty years later, his response to the project of extending the Commonwealth of Nations into Asia.

Like most other Westerners making their passage to India for the first time, Mackenzie King was overcome by the grim spectacle of the subcontinent's masses and miseries. 'Such darkness I have never seen,' he wrote to his parents from Calcutta, 'such need for enlightenment I have never known.'[61] His belief in the wisdom and justice of the policy of total exclusion was confirmed. 'What I have seen of this country and of the people,' he wrote to Sir Wilfrid Laurier from Colombo, 'convinces me more strongly than ever that they are entirely unsuited for the Dominion; that it is not a kindness to allow them to come, and that it is in every way desirable that Canada should be kept for the white races and India for the black, as Nature appears to have decreed.'[62] He did not, however, share the opinion, then prevailing among British statesmen,* that Nature decreed that the white races should rule the black in perpetuity. 'I believe self-government will come in time,' he wrote again to his parents, 'but my present opinion is that it will require some time.'[63] That was expressed with characteristic precision.†

* For example Lord Kimberley, who was to resume the Secretaryship of State for India convinced that 'the notion of parliamentary representation of so vast a country ... containing so large a number of different races, is one of the wildest imaginations that ever entered the minds of men.' Quoted in R. Coupland, *The Indian Problem: Report on the Constitutional Problem in India* (New York 1944), 26.

† Of the prospects for self-government for those Indians resident in British Columbia, still deprived of the franchise when Mackenzie King became Prime Minister, he remained less sanguine, for reasons which he explained at the Imperial Conference of 1923:

> When we came into office, I had a majority of one behind me in the House of Commons. I think we have a majority of three at the present time. Many of the constituencies were very close. It is conceivable that in British Columbia the difference in the result might be material by increasing a certain vote in some of the constituencies. In other words, were the subject to become one of political discussion, I think it would be possible for a political orator to make it quite apparent to the people of British Columbia that the fate of the Federal Government might depend upon the vote cast by the Indians resident in that Province.

Sensing, perhaps that his audience was not exactly swept along by the force of this argument – 'it may seem,' he conceded, 'that I am straining a little in emphasizing the possible political consequences of giving the franchise to resident Indians in British Columbia' – he added: 'It would not be an exaggeration, it would not be a figure of speech; it is a literal and absolute truth.' Imperial

To 'the Indian problem' in an imperial context, Mackenzie King paid comparatively little attention until the Second World War. He was on this subject a consumer rather than a producer of ideas. At the Imperial Conference of 1926, he recorded without comment Lord Birkenhead's prophecy 'that a representative of India would be speaking with the same authority as prime ministers of self-governing dominions.'[64] At the Imperial Conference of 1937, he recorded as 'rather curious' Lord Zetland's prophecy 'that India could be relied upon to supply regiments for defence purposes,' considering that Zetland had just told the Conference that if the British Empire found itself at war with Germany, 'Nehru ... would avail himself of that moment to bring a rising in India against Britain.'[65] Apart from the discussions at imperial conferences, Mackenzie King's main sources of information about Indian affairs were those among his correspondents who were responsible for the government of the subcontinent. What he learned, for example, from Lord Willingdon (who, like Dufferin and Minto before him, became Viceroy of India immediately after having been Governor-General of Canada) could hardly have conveyed a more dispiriting impression about the prospects for Indian democracy. Willingdon's letters painted a picture of unrelieved gloom:

I am not happy about the prospects. Irwin may have secured a truce, but to me it is a very serious thing for the head of the Govt. to have been negotiating with the head of a political party wh. has been giving us much trouble in past years, to have been treating with this individual as a plenipotentiary arranging terms of peace! The Govt. seem to have abdicated their authority by this action & it will be difficult to restore the situation. [Lord Willingdon to Mackenzie King, 15 March 1931]

I have really had a desperately hard 1st 6 months of my life here, harder than any ViceRoy has ever had I'm sure ... Gandhi that weird little man ... has gone to London wch. will be good for him for he will be up agst. practical difficulties wch. he always tries to avoid. It is an extraordinary thing to me that this individual whom I can't help looking upon as largely a humbug has created for himself in the eyes of the world the characteristics of a saint... [Willingdon to King, 9 October 1931]

The Indian is I fear a person who likes leaning on & at the same time criticizing his British colleague out here, & when he gets responsibility he'll make an awful mess of it unless we are nearby... [Willingdon to King, 5 September 1932]

There is no homogeneity here but a mass of different communities, Princes, Hindus, Mahomedans [*sic*], Depressed Classes among others all out for their own interests & none of them looking on to secure the good of the country as a whole ... I feel certain that the Indian when he's got to do the job will appeal to us British to stay here for long years to relieve him of the responsibility and

Conference, 1923, Stenographic notes of Meetings, E (1923) Series. Thirteenth Meeting, October 29th, 11 A.M., p17. King Papers.

do the main work of administration as before... [Willingdon to King, 21 March 1933][66]

Another informant on India was L.S. Amery, after he had become Secretary of State for India in Churchill's government. Amery was more sanguine than Willingdon had been about the future, but his letters, too, stressed how bleak to him appeared the prospects for Indian self-government:

The real difficulty is that the Hindu majority represented in Congress want to see that achieved at once under the forms of parliamentary majority rule. The 90 millions of Muslims, with a few exceptions, are absolutely determined to reject such a solution and are already drifting into the position of calling themselves a separate nation and demanding the right to be a separate Dominion. How this deadlock is to be solved looks at present like squaring the circle. [L.S. Amery to Mackenzie King, 27 May 1940]

There is such a thing as India apart from Congress agitators declaiming, with a complete misrepresentation of facts, against the iniquities of a tyrannous British government. The real trouble ... in India is not our reluctance to devolve authority but the present incapacity of Indians to agree to any form of India Government under which they are prepared to live together without us. [Amery to King, 16 December 1940]

Giving way to Congress, which is the most vocal element, and the only element which has done any effective propaganda outside of India, means chaos and probably civil war in India. Even a partial surrender to Congress at this moment would seriously upset the war effort, in view of the fact that a full half of the army are Moslems. [Amery to King, 27 December 1941][67]

These appraisals, coming as they did from a Viceroy and a Secretary of State for India, could hardly be taken as a detached assessment, and it is not to be thought that Mackenzie King accepted them as such. Yet when, in early 1943, he finally received a report from one of his own representatives, it was if anything even more pessimistic in tone. It came from Major-General Victor Odlum, who had stopped off in India en route to his new posting as Canada's first ambassador to China. 'In Calcutta,' Odlum wrote,

I saw the other India, the ignorant, dirty, diseased, unsmiling India. It shocked me, in spite of my wide knowledge of the world. This India is *not* fit to accept the responsibilities of government. It is not fit to vote. It is ignorant beyond belief. And, in numbers, it is very great...[68]

By the spring of 1942 the question of whether India was ready for self-government had been displaced by the question of whether India would much longer remain secure under the *raj*. Singapore had fallen on 15 February; and with its fall the Bay of Bengal lay open to the Japanese advance. Rangoon fell three weeks later; and with its fall Bengal and Madras were threatened. 'All down that long flat eastern coast Indians were faced with a similar prospect to that which had faced Englishmen in 1940.'[69] With one important difference. The British people confronted the threat of Nazi invasion united as never before in their history. The Indian people confronted the threat of Japanese invasion divided as never before in their history. They were as yet unsure – not even their leaders were sure – whether the Japanese at their gates were enslavers or liberators. 'Indian reaction was a mixture of vicarious pleasure, surprise, suppressed fear and inertia.'[70] It was a poor recipe for survival, let alone for victory. Much of the blame for it must be borne by the British, whose maladroitness in political warfare reached a nadir in Churchill's statement that the Atlantic Charter applied mainly to Europe. Word that its 'four freedoms' were not for the likes of Asians reached Jawaharlal Nehru in Gorakhpur prison, during the first weeks of what was to have been a four-year sentence. 'So it was that as Calcutta prepared to resist, or to share, the fate of Moulmein, Singapore, and Rangoon, Indian suspicions of British intentions were deepest and the prestige of the British *raj* at its lowest ebb.'[71]

It was in these circumstances that the Canadian Government ventured for the first time into the vexed question of 'the Indian problem,' its misgivings over the wisdom of such intervention from afar doubtless allayed by the reflection that whatever its outcome things could hardly be made much worse than they had become. The occasion for the venture was provided by the arrival in Ottawa of the terms of a draft declaration of British policy with regard to India, which the British Government proposed to make public and to form the basis of discussion between Sir Stafford Cripps and Indian leaders in Delhi. The draft recited the object of British policy as being 'the creation of a new Indian Union which shall constitute a Dominion, associated with the United Kingdom and the other Dominions by a common allegiance to the Crown, but equal to them in every respect, in no way subordinate in any aspect of its domestic or external affairs.'[72] This was both more positive and more precise than the lacklustre and elliptical offer of Dominion status to India after the war broadcast by the Viceroy on 8 August 1940 and which had provoked Nehru's pithy response that Dominion status was 'as dead as a doornail.'[73] But in August 1940 India had seemed secure (even if Britain had seemed otherwise). In March 1942 a promise of Dominion status after the war might not be sufficient to rally the Congress Party behind the war – certainly not a Congress Party demanding immediate independence as the price of its co-operation.

With this thought in his mind, Mackenzie King set about composing a reply to Churchill's despatch in which the terms of the draft declaration had been outlined. More, perhaps, than any other allied statesman he understood the delicacy of the operation. Churchill's confidence in the expediency of his policy for India – which, despite the misgivings of his colleagues in the War Cabinet, 'continued to rest in strong government and the proven valour of India's martial peoples'[74] – was matched only by his resentment of those who dared to challenge his judgment; and if the challenger chanced to be American, his resentment turned to rage. (The only part of Roosevelt's reply to a similar message in which Churchill concurred, according to an adviser of the President, was that admitting it to be 'none of my business.'[75]) Mackenzie King knew the symptoms well: he was determined that his response should not prove counter-productive, and drafted it with even more than his customary care. It read as follows:

> The Canadian Government heartily welcomes the statement of policy laying down the steps it is proposed to take for the earliest possible realization of complete self-government in India. We attach the highest importance to its early issue and believe it is in the interest of all the United Nations that the utmost expedition should be exercised in promulgating the new programme. We believe that a fully self-governing India has a great part to play in free and equal association with the other nations of the British Commonwealth and that a free India, fighting alongside the other free peoples of the world, will strengthen immeasurably the common cause...[76]

This message challenged Churchill's policy: far from wanting 'a free India, fighting alongside the other free peoples of the world,' the British leader adamantly refused to contemplate any major constitutional change in India's status so long as the war remained to be won. Even so, he might have read it in relative calm had it not been for the simultaneous arrival of a second despatch from the Prime Minister of Canada, recounting what the Chinese foreign minister, T.V. Soong, had told Mackenzie King during a recent visit to Ottawa. It was to the effect that Chiang Kai-shek was of the opinion that only the immediate grant of independence to India would save the highly precarious military situation; and that he, Chiang, believed that 'the alleged difficulties which might arise between Mohammedans and Hindus had been greatly exaggerated.' This information, Mackenzie King observed, was doubtless already at Churchill's disposal but he had passed it along in any event: 'I have felt,' he concluded, 'that you might like to know that I felt much impressed by what Soong said to me and that all my colleagues in the government are very strongly of view that no time should be lost in accepting and making known the proposals set forth in your telegram.'[77] Churchill wanted to know nothing of the kind. His reply was brusque to the point of rudeness, and did not conceal, and may not have been intended to conceal, his irritation. 'Matter is far more complicated than it appears,' he cabled to Mackenzie King on 8 March. 'Chiang ... blissfully ignorant about Indian affairs ... In my opinion proposals will certainly be rejected by Congress and become the starting point for new demands.'[78]

Thus rebuffed, Mackenzie King might well have concluded that his usefulness as a mediator between London and Delhi was at an end. But it was no time for false pride or for standing on ceremony. Churchill's reply arrived with the news of the fall of Rangoon. On 15 March the Prime Minister of Canada tried again. 'I have been giving much thought to the situation in India,' his message to Churchill began.

It occurs to me that it might be of assistance to the Government of the United Kingdom and to the success of Cripps' mission were Cripps to be fortified by an expression from each of the self-governing Dominions of their readiness to co-operate with all who may be concerned in peace negotiations in insuring immediate recognition of India's status as one of equality with the other Dominions of the British Commonwealth of Nations ... Having regard to the evolution of self-government in Canada and the position taken by Canada in peace negotiations after the last war, and at subsequent Imperial Conferences with respect to equality of status of all self-governing parts of the British Commonwealth, it might well be that strong assurance to India on the part of Canada as to the helpful role we would be prepared to take on her behalf, might not be without some real effect that this time ... I should like you to know that my colleagues and I would be ready to lend any good offices that may be within our power.[79]

To this second overture Churchill's response was hardly more mollifying than his response to the first. He did set out in more detail the reasons for his disagreement with the approach suggested by the Prime Minister of Canada. 'Question which has to be solved,' Churchill cabled to Mackenzie King on 18 March,

is not one between British Government and India, but between different sects or nations in India itself. We have resigned ourselves to fighting our utmost to defend India in order if successful to be turned out. Congress have hitherto definitely refused Dominion status. Moslems, a hundred millions, declare they will insist upon Pakistan, i.e., a sort of Ulster in the North. We have our Treaties which must be respected with Princes in India, over ninety million. There are forty million Hindu untouchables to whom we have obligations. These are the grim issues which Cripps is valiantly trying to settle. There can be no question of our handing over control during the war. This would break up the Indian Army, eighty-five per cent of which cares nothing for Congress and is loyal only to the King-Emperor. It would render the defence of India impossible. I should strongly recommend your awaiting developments until we see how the Cripps Mission goes.[80]

As Churchill had made plain all along, he did not expect, and perhaps did not hope, it would go well.

By Churchill's reply to Mackenzie King, which read as if the former believed the latter incapable of locating India on a map, L.S. Amery was justifiably disturbed. It could easily have widened the gap between the two governments on what was to be done. Amery wrote at once to Mackenzie King to praise his 'most generous and helpful telegram about India.' He promised to take up with the Viceroy his proposal for an exchange of High Commissioners between Canada and India. And he expressed the hope that it might become possible 'for India to be represented at the Peace Conference by men representative, not merely of the official Government of India, but of the main elements in her political life.'[81] That did not go very far, certainly not as far as the Canadian Government would have liked. But it was as far as Amery could go. It was not his Government and, as he wrote to Mackenzie King after the war, not really his policy either: 'It would be very difficult ... to give [in my memoirs] any intelligible account of my Indian Administration without revealing the fact that Winston and I held diametrically opposite views as to the course to be pursued.'[82] Meanwhile, he soldiered on.

The sharp rebuff from Churchill, even when blunted by Amery, ended for the duration Mackenzie King's desire to take any further initiatives over India. These thus remained confined to one. But even this solitary foray, unsuccessful as it proved, is so much out of character as to call for explanation. Mackenzie King did not normally involve himself or his Government in the affairs of some distant country. 'My whole point of view,' he had himself remarked to the British High Commissioner soon afterwards, 'was that of allowing sleeping dogs lie.' Why did he risk an awakening?

One may guess at four main reasons. There was first the urgency of events. If his intervention was unusual, so were the circumstances which brought it about.

Domestic politics also played a part. The CCF, as its leader, M.J. Coldwell, wrote to the Prime Minister, had 'for some time ... been giving consideration to the situation in India,' and believed 'that every effort should be made by Canada, both as a self-governing Dominion associated with India in the British Commonwealth of Nations and as one of the United Nations, to find a satisfactory solution to a problem which gravely endangers our common cause.'[83] To have remained aloof in the face of this pressure to intervene would have opened his Government to criticism from Coldwell's party which, as Mackenzie King noted, was only too 'ready to make an issue of the Indian situation.' He thought it best to try to head off its criticism by taking its advice.

A third reason was reconciliation – of British and American policies which, on Indian independence, had begun drastically and dangerously to diverge. Roosevelt questioned Churchill's motives, Churchill questioned Roosevelt's competence. The Prime Minister of Canada believed himself to possess a special talent and a unique responsibility for keeping the titans in tandem; and acted accordingly.

Finally, he was moved by the tribulations of the Congress leaders in their struggle for freedom. The periodic imprisonments of Gandhi and Nehru struck a responsive chord in his own past; he sent a message to Nehru in March 1942 telling him of 'the part Mackenzie had taken in the struggle for Responsible Government in Canada, and of my readiness, as his grandson, to do all in my power, and have Canada do all in her power, towards seeing that any undertaking given by Britain to India would be fully implemented.'[84]

But by 1947 Mackenzie King was no longer stirred on India's behalf by the memories of 1837. So far from interesting himself in the rush of negotiations preceding independence and partition, he remained aloof and even reproving. A telegram from Attlee in February, advising the Canadian government that the Labour Cabinet had decided to fix a definite date for India's independence, made him feel 'sad at heart. It left open the way for India to run completely outside of the Commonwealth which she probably will do. Should it unite with other countries of Asia in common attack upon some other parts of the world, this old globe may come to witness the most appalling of disasters with which it has yet been faced.'*

In this deeply pessimistic mood, the Prime Minister of Canada met with his Cabinet on 28 May to consider what should be said in response to the British decision. Within the Department of External Affairs had been prepared, at St Laurent's direction, a draft reply warmly endorsing the admission of India and Pakistan as full members of the Commonwealth. This statement St Laurent read to the Cabinet, expecting its routine approval. He was astonished, as were all present, when the Prime Minister 'snatched it out of [his] hands, pointed out that the original communication must have been addressed to him as head of the government, and commented acidly that he was still Prime Minister and entitled to answer his own correspondence.'[85] Nor did the outburst end there. Mackenzie King, his anger rising as he proceeded, declared that his own answer to

* Quoted in *Record IV*, 34. Mackenzie King was not the only prime minister in the British Commonwealth of Nations to experience misgivings at the prospect of India's independence. Smuts wrote of the Mountbatten mission that it would 'open the way for the new All-Asia anti-European policies which will sow the seeds of the future world conflicts'; and of the independence of Ceylon: 'Am I mad or is the world mad?' Quoted in W.K. Hancock, *Smuts*, II, *The Fields of Force* (Cambridge 1968), 447.

Attlee's message would be very different to that which St Laurent was now suggesting.

> [I] said quite openly that there was not a single member of the Cabinet who was in a position to advise in regard to India, who understood the situation there or realized what implications there might be in tendering advice in a matter of this kind. St Laurent admitted it would mean an obligation of mutual assistance. I said yes, and if Canada's decision pleases one part of India and displeases another, we may find that the other may join in with Russia to form a common cause with her and that, in addition, we would be pulled into some of the civil war that may result from an action which may be taken at this time by Britain. I pointed out that India was a dependency of Britain. She should deal with the matter herself. That this was part of an effort on Britain's part to get rid of her burdens and throw them on to the Dominions. I thought we ought to help bear burdens that were legitimate, but should not go out of our way to load Canada with obligations that we could not see the beginning or the end of.[86]

Two days later Mackenzie King scrutinized another despatch from Attlee on Indian independence. 'I did not think Canada should commit itself one way or the other to anything arising in the present situation beyond indicating that our attitude would be, as far as possible, helpful. We were not consulted about India's independence. We had nothing to do with negotiations, nor do any members of the Government or the people of Canada know anything about India.'[87]

In this far from expansive spirit the Prime Minister revised the text of a statement which Pearson had prepared in anticipation of the British government's announcement that India and Pakistan would become independent on 15 August. His changes, which he described as 'in the nature of abbreviations and avoidance of raising any question about independence within the Commonwealth, vs Dominion status, etc., at this time,' resulted in the cryptic communiqué given to the press on 3 June which, while assuring 'the peoples of India ... of the sympathetic understanding and good will of the government and people of Canada in their efforts to achieve self-government,' merely noted that the results of those efforts 'may be to enlarge the number of states within the British Commonwealth.'[88] It was left to M.J. Coldwell, leader of the CCF opposition, to express the feelings of his countrymen: 'Canada would be pleased to do everything she can to welcome into the family of the Commonwealth the nation which we hope will now emerge in India.'[89]

The Government of the new Dominion of India which became a member of the Commonwealth on 15 August 1947 wished India to remain a member of the Commonwealth. More than that, it wished it to become a republic. Other members of the Commonwealth were thus faced with a problem they had never solved before. Could Commonwealth membership be reconciled with republican status? If so, how?

These questions were canvassed by the Commonwealth Relations Office (as the Dominions Office was re-named in 1947) and the Foreign Office on the eve of the Prime Ministers' Conference held in October 1948, to which the three new Asian Dominions would be sending representatives for the first time.

The British government desired to make every effort to maintain and expand the existing membership of the Commonwealth, even though some of its countries – India, Pakistan, Eire, possibly South Africa, and other Asian and African nations on attaining independence – might be unwilling to accept the precise form of constitutional relationship preferred by the other members. The concept of associate membership for such countries was rejected. It was not desirable, the British felt, that members of the Commonwealth should be divided into two or more classes according to the extent to which they accepted allegiance to the Crown. At the same time, there was no reason why the degree of that acceptance should be identical in every case. New Zealand's might well be different from India's. There was room, there was need, for diversity according to taste and tradition. But there had to be some lowest common denominator of commitment, some minimum constitutional link, some irreducible quota of allegiance below which no member might fall without depriving itself of membership.

This basic bond the British located in acceptance of the jurisdiction of the Crown in the external relations of Commonwealth members. Such an acceptance, they affirmed, need not be inconsistent even with a republican form of constitution provided that the country in question accepted that its 'President' (however elected or appointed) acted, at least for purposes of external relations, as the representative of the Crown. This was the utmost dilution that could be contemplated or tolerated. A country which felt unable to profess so spare and partial an allegiance could no longer be regarded as a member of the Commonwealth. Thus, if Eire were to repeal her Executive Authority (External Relations) Act of 1936, or India declare her unwillingness to recognize the King's jurisdiction for any purpose, they would become foreign states.

These perceptions were relayed to the Canadian government by Sir Norman Brook, Secretary to the British Cabinet, who visited Ottawa in August 1948 on the first stop of his emissary tour of Commonwealth capitals. He met with Mackenzie King on 13 August.

> In conversation, Sir Norman said that the British Government felt that India might wish to become a republic. Give up association with the Crown. The question would come up whether India could be kept in the Commonwealth

of Nations and how. The British Government thought every effort should be made toward that end. The first step would be to seek to have the Government of India appoint its own Governor-General by whatever name they pleased. Same for all the Dominions. Could be called King's Representative or by whatever name they wished. The main thing would be to allow same thing as in Ireland, of maintaining the King's authority in external relations. A third thought was to have the Prime Minister of India made a Privy Councillor. What would be done being something still to be explored...[90]

Following consultations with other Commonwealth governments, Brook returned to Ottawa in September. He now had a more specific proposal, the terms of which have not been disclosed. 'It met with Canadian approval,' writes St Laurent's biographer, 'and was eventually adopted.'[91] That is a considerable over-simplification. The parties concerned were groping towards, rather than negotiating, a solution. That was fine by Mackenzie King. 'I think here,' he wrote of the problem of Crown and Commonwealth, 'Lord Morley's maxim of events helping to determine evolutionary trends is a wise one.'[92]

Events soon unfolded in London, where the Prime Ministers of the Commonwealth convened in October. The question of the compatibility of Commonwealth membership with republican status had not been placed on their agenda. Its omission was deliberate. It was thought best to allow 'the Prime Ministers of the Asian dominions to judge the value of Commonwealth consultation in the light of their personal experience before recommending any final decision about their countries' membership, for it was felt that only by participation in the councils of the Commonwealth at the highest level might misapprehensions be dispelled and understanding of its working be acquired.'[93] But though it was not on their agenda it was much on their minds.

Mackenzie King, no longer leader of his Party but Prime Minister still, had gone to London on what was to be the last of a lifetime's ventures in diplomacy which had begun with his mission to India fifty years before. He fell ill and was unable to attend the meetings; he was able to receive a steady stream of visitors. It is an exaggeration to imply that, as its senior statesman, he dominated the conference from his suite at the Dorchester Hotel. But these bed-side conversations were not without influence on the outcome. 'I must thank you for allowing us to come and see you,' Lord Jowitt, the Lord Chancellor, wrote afterwards.

I do so agree with you that whatever legal difficulties we may have we should be very foolish to take any step which might be construed as throwing anybody out of the "Club" ... I like your suggestion of describing the "Club" as "the Commonwealth of Free Nations." I put this to the Indians and they were obviously attracted by the phrase...[94]

An early visitor to the sick-room was Pandit Nehru. This meeting, writes one authority, 'has been invested with dramatic significance by some commentators. They would seem to have allowed their imaginations to outrun the facts.'[95] But not if the facts are that Mackenzie King made the concept of the Commonwealth more attractive in the mind of the Indian leader than it had been before and disposed him to be conciliatory. 'Your Prime Minister,' Nehru later told a Canadian interviewer, 'showed me and my sister such real friendship, even affection. It helped a lot.'[96] Mackenzie King recorded that he

enjoyed Nehru's visit very much. He reminded me a little of Sir Wilfrid Laurier in his fine, sensitive way of speaking, using his hands, etc. He gave me his views about India. Thought it was best to have the Constitution passed without raising any question of relations within the Empire. Once the Constitution was established, they could then, he thought, work out the relationship of India to the rest of the Commonwealth on the basis of the Citizenship Act. Lord Jowitt had been talking with him along that line, maintaining an independent citizenship in each country, Canada, etc., but acknowledging a Commonwealth citizenship which brought with it certain obligations of co-operation, etc. I gave him my views on the emphasis being placed on Community of Free Nations, rather than having emphasis upon the Crown which would almost certainly be drawn into controversy if it were made the main issue. He saw the point at once and said he regarded it as quite important. I also outlined to him what I had thought of as regards member nations of the Commonwealth qualifying under the Statute of Westminster, etc. This, he also said, was worth carefully looking into...

The talk I had with Nehru made a most favourable impression on me, having regard to his own imprisonment, etc. I gave him a little account of my grandfather's life and the times in Canada in 1837/38, and later.[97]

Before leaving London for New Delhi, Pandit Nehru, in consultation with Sir Stafford Cripps, prepared a memorandum setting forth the terms and modalities which he thought would allow India to remain within the Commonwealth as a republic. India, as specified in the draft constitution awaiting the scrutiny of the forthcoming Congress Party conference at Jaipur, was to be declared 'a sovereign, democratic republic' whose sovereignty would reside in and be exercised by the people of India and their representatives. India would recognize the King as 'the first citizen of the Commonwealth' and, as such, its 'fountain of honour.' For the purpose of fulfilling the obligations of the Crown towards Commonwealth citizens other than Indian nationals, the President, at the request of the Crown, was to act on behalf of the King within the territories of India; a similar arrangement was to apply reciprocally on behalf of Indian nationals in the rest of the countries of the Commonwealth. The new constitution (or a separate statute passed at the same time) would make Indian nationals

Commonwealth citizens, and provide that the nationals of any Commonwealth country would be given the status of Commonwealth citizens while resident in India. Finally, in any new legislation or treaties, Commonwealth countries were not to be foreign states, nor their citizens considered as foreigners. These proposals, Nehru's memorandum stated of them, 'represent a sincere desire to continue the Commonwealth association and what is practicable and adequate at present.'

But for the Law Officers of the Crown sincerity was not enough. Apart from their reservations about finer and more technical points – they had little enthusiasm for Nehru's proposed designation of the King as the Commonwealth's 'first citizen' – the Law Officers considered that Nehru's memorandum provided too tenuous a connection for India to be recognized as a full and equal member of the Commonwealth either in world opinion or in a court of law. The British Cabinet concurred, the Indian Government so informed. Its reply was tart and to the point. 'I am to say in reply to your communication of views of lawyers,' C.R. Attlee was told by Krishna Menon's aide mémoire of 11 December 1948, 'while [Prime Minister Nehru] is grateful to be put in posession of this expression of opinion, neither he nor his colleagues consider that the problem is one of legal formalities and arguments. It is essentially a political problem and is based upon our mutual desires and interests. On our side therefore we do not think it necessary or appropriate to pursue the legal arguments or to find answers to them.'

All this was being closely watched by a Canadian government whose leadership had changed as it went on. (L.B. Pearson became Secretary of State for External Affairs on 10 September, L.S. St Laurent had become Prime Minister on 15 November.) Pearson had discussed Nehru's proposals in Paris with a top official of the India foreign ministry, by whom he was informed that some members of Nehru's cabinet were opposed to retaining any links, however tenuous, with a British crown. If that were indeed so, Nehru's offer was a non-starter not only in London, Canberra, and Wellington – Evatt and Fraser too thought the Indian basis far too frail – but in New Delhi also. There would be nothing for it but 'to fall back on the kind of relationship which is being worked out with Ireland.'[98]

It is interesting – it may be significant as well – that Canada's Prime Minister, Secretary of State for External Affairs, and High Commissioner in India were of Irish descent: that may have disposed them all the more resolutely to find some way to accommodate India's aspirations within the Commonwealth, for 'the kind of relationship which is being worked out with Ireland' evaded rather than solved the problem of reconciling republicanism with Commonwealth membership. Certainly John D. Kearney, reporting reaction from New Delhi, was in sympathy with the spirit of Nehru's proposals, if not with their details.* 'Though individually the elements are weak,' he wrote to Ottawa about them, 'I think the idea of combining a declaration of intention to remain in the Commonwealth, Commonwealth citizenship and an arrangement whereby The King, although empowered to designate and appoint Ambassadors, etc., would delegate these prerogative functions to the President of the Indian Republic, is as strong a link as can be hoped for under the circumstances.' He added that when talking with Nehru a fortnight previously, 'I casually suggested to him that if it were found that Commonwealth citizenship was not a sufficiently satisfactory link, he might bear in mind the idea of The King delegating to the President of India the prerogative functions above mentioned...'[99]

At the year's end, Kearney again reported to Ottawa, this time on how things stood in Delhi after the Congress Party had passed at Jaipur a resolution welcoming India's 'free association with independent nations of the Commonwealth for their common welfare and the promotion of world peace.' He had had a lengthy conversation with Sir Girja Bajpai, the permanent under-secretary of the Indian Department of External Affairs.

Sir Girja thinks well of the suggestion of the proposed link with the Commonwealth through the Crown ... He informed me that in the cabinet a good deal of jockeying for position was going on and that Mr Nehru himself was still between two minds on the subject. Sir Girja asked me my views and I said they were only personal, but I thought it was in the interests of the Commonwealth countries that the Commonwealth link should be sufficiently strong to stand the test of a court decision, and that the mutual benefits derived from the Commonwealth association which have heretofore existed were worthy of being preserved, as far as circumstances permit ... Personally, I doubt the wisdom of placing too much emphasis on the link with the Crown, and I have some misgivings that the United Kingdom High Commissioner may have put it up as sine qua non to India remaining in the Commonwealth ... Tactically such an approach appears to me undesirable because it savours of pressure, and the Indians, like the Irish, easily get their backs up if they imagine the shadow of the big stick is to fall across them...[100]

Meanwhile a shadow of a different sort threatened to darken the outlook for a disinterested and sympathetic Canadian position on the issue of a republican India Commonwealth membership. It was the shadow of migration.

At the British Commonwealth Relations Conference held in London in 1945,† the Indians present revealed to their Canadian colleagues with a

* Kearney before his posting to India had served as High Commissioner in Eire from 1941 to 1945.

† See above, 209–16.

candour rarely up to then in evidence the extent of their resentment of the Dominion's restrictions upon their people's emigration. 'It wasn't part of the Conference,' the chairman of the Canadian delegation reported to their Under Secretary of State for External Affairs,

> but it came out at the Conference that the Indians felt very keenly the stamp of inferiority which we placed upon them by reason of our discrimination ... They all assured us that it would be tremendously appreciated if a treaty could be entered into which would incorporate the principle of mutuality, on the clear understanding that it really wouldn't extend at all present restriction or prohibition of immigration by indirect means ... We promised to bring this matter to the attention of your Department...[101]

The Department of External Affairs duly took the matter under advisement. Nothing was done about it for some time. In May 1948 Kearney brought it up again. 'It seems to me,' he wrote from New Delhi, 'that in view of the large scale program existing for immigration into Canada from Great Britain and Europe, to admit one hundred Indian nationals per annum would constitute by comparison a drop in the bucket.' There were, moreover, a number of compensating political advantages since India had gained independence, of which foremost on his list was that 'the chances of India remaining in the Commonwealth would be improved.' He proposed that the Government pass an order-in-council to allow a hundred Indians to emigrate each year. He had been assured 'that if a courtesy number of Indians were admitted to Canada, the Indian Government would see to it that they were hand-picked and would be people of education and means, and constitute a valuable though unofficial group of ambassadors for India in Canada.'[102]

To a quota for India immigrants the Canadian government eventually agreed, in 1951 – too late to have any salutary effect upon Indian feeling for the Commonwealth.* On the eve of the great decision an awkward situation threatened to develop. The Government of India, averse to the link with the Crown, seemed intent upon making Commonwealth citizenship the symbol of the Commonwealth association. What did Commonwealth citizenship mean in practice? If little more – or even less – than the prerogatives of certain foreigners, then opponents of membership within the Nehru Cabinet might argue persuasively that the Common-

* The arrangement – by treaty rather than by order-in-council – provided for the admission annually of 150 Indian immigrants. The Department of Citizenship and Immigration opened an agency in India to process applications. 'An Opposition member of Parliament asked the Minister in the House why twelve people are needed to select one hundred and fifty immigrants a year. The answer was that when the office opened there were twenty thousand applications.' David C. Corbett, *Canada's Immigration Policy: A Critique* (Toronto 1957), 181.

'His audience ... listened to his remarks in "astonishing silence"...' (p. 180).
Mackenzie King addressing the Paris Peace Conference, 2 August 1946

'..."always wanted to go a little too fast" ' (p. 34n).
Lester Bowles Pearson, January 1950 (PAC)

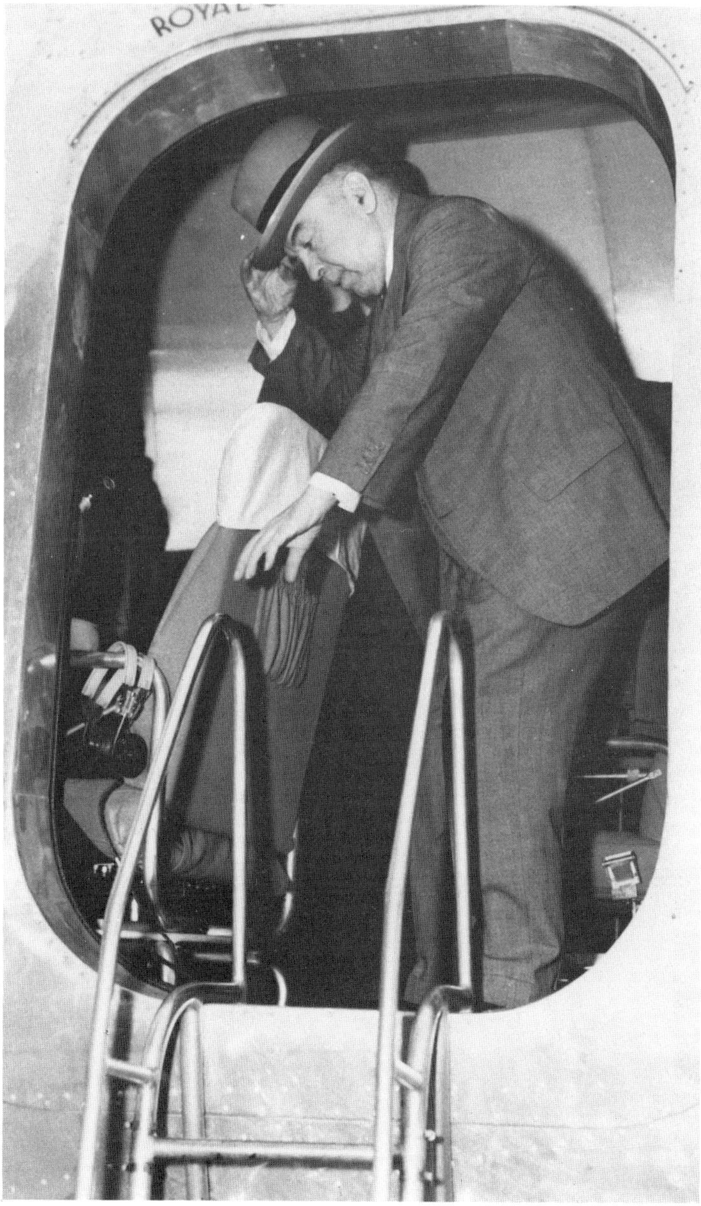

'The descent at first was slow ...' (p. 5).
Mackenzie King arriving at the San Francisco Conference, 1945 (PAC)

'... not just the ideal man, he was the only man' (p. 17).
Andrew George Latta McNaughton (PAC)

'... suffered these indignities with patrician stoicism' (p. 29).
Vincent Massey with Mackenzie King (PAC)

'... he basked in *darshan* ...' (p. 44).
A.D.P. Heeney with Mackenzie King (PAC)

'... clearing ... with Jack ...' (p. 46).
J.W. Pickersgill with Louis St Laurent (PAC)

' "I do not know the personages ..." ' (p. 5).
Mackenzie King at the Paris Peace Conference (Norman Robertson and Brooke Claxton on his right and left)

'... "What sense do they make of ... folly and horror?" ...' (p. 173).
Delegates at the Montebello Conference, December 1943 (CIIA)

wealth was a gigantic farce. So it must mean much more – as much as it meant in the United Kingdom, where Commonwealth citizenship then conferred the right to enter and remain. But if that was what Commonwealth citizenship was to mean in the White Dominion of Canada, not many Canadian citizens and no Canadian government would want India in the Commonwealth.

It fell to Pearson to elucidate the Commonwealth reality as distinct from the Commonwealth ideal for the guidance of the High Commissioner. 'We have some misgivings,' Pearson cabled Kearney on 5 January 1949, 'about having the Commonwealth link with India based primarily on the common status of Commonwealth citizens on a reciprocal basis in view of our immigration policy.'[103] A departmental memorandum elaborated on the sources of this misgiving:

> There are certain clear difficulties, particularly for the white dominions, in any scheme whereby the principal element in the Commonwealth connection would be the "common status." The term "Commonwealth citizen," no doubt, refers to a general principle or concept with no defined content, but at the same time it implies that Commonwealth citizens will be in a special position in some way different from that of aliens. It must be borne in mind that at present Indians, though British subjects in our law, are excluded as immigrants to Canada, in exactly the same way as other persons of Asiatic race, such as the Chinese, while United States citizens and French citizens are placed in a preferred category with white British subjects. Rights and privileges are thus accorded to some aliens which are denied to some Commonwealth citizens. It would seem inevitable that we should find ourselves eventually in an embarrassing position regarding our immigration policy if we agreed to a scheme under which the essential feature of the Commonwealth connection would be the common status of Commonwealth citizenship. This would be a device without any real substance, a mere form which would not give any material concrete benefits to citizens from all parts of the Commonwealth. In fact a very obvious discrimination would continue to be enforced against Commonwealth citizens of Asiatic race. Even though the Indian authorities might be prepared to declare now that they were only interested in the form of common citizenship, it could be expected that before long and in view of the feeling in India regarding racial discrimination they would quite logically demand that some real meaning and significance be given to the outward form.[104]

In 1949 a multiracial Commonwealth had little appeal in Canada, even as an ideal.

To play down citizenship meant playing up the Crown. Yet, as Kearney's despatches reported again and again, the Crown was an unpopular symbol in India. 'An essential feature of republicanism as the Indians understand it is that the individual is subject to no person. To ask Indians to accept allegiance to any man is bad enough, and it becomes far worse when that man happens also to be the King of Great Britain.'[105]

A further difficulty now developed. One of the more promising proposals, emanating from the Indians, had been that a link might be preserved if the King were to delegate part of his prerogative to a future President of India. But the Canadian High Commissioner reported from London that 'the reason why the suggestion ... has been allowed to recede into the background of current thinking about possible forms and symbols of Commonwealth association is that the King himself was not at all receptive to the idea...'[106] That was the end of that.

So soundings taken between the Prime Ministers' Conference of October 1948 and a proposed Prime Ministers' Conference of April 1949 produced not consensus in the Commonwealth but something close to stalemate. India desired Commonwealth membership as a republic, with Commonwealth citizenship as the symbol of association. The White Dominions, wary of Commonwealth citizenship for fear their restrictive immigration policies could be called into question, looked for a solution to allegiance to the Crown. The United Kingdom wavered uncertainly between the belief that allegiance was all or it was nothing.

On the eve of the Prime Ministers' Conference, the British Government was veering to the view that allegiance was nothing. 'I fear the United Kingdom attitude with regard to India and the Commonwealth is becoming far too legalistic and too little realistic,' Kearney had commented from New Delhi in January, and his fears then were well founded. Two months later the lawyers were in retreat, the realists were in charge. When stock was taken once again it was not in an atmosphere of legal quibbling but in a mood of fear. The United States was about to enter its first peacetime alliance with Europe since the eighteenth century, as a makeweight to Soviet power. But where was the makeweight to the power of China, as Mao's Long March neared its triumphant conclusion?

No question loomed more insistently in Foreign Office minds as these considered for a final time the advantages and disadvantages for the United Kingdom and the Commonwealth of India's relations with the Commonwealth. Three possible outcomes were carefully weighed. First, that India remained a member of the Commonwealth, though owing no allegiance to the Crown; second, that India became a foreign state, but in especially close relationship, probably signified by treaty, with the United Kingdom and other Commonwealth countries; third, that India became a foreign state with no close relationship, by treaty or otherwise, with the Commonwealth it left behind.

The advantages of the first hypothesis were discerned to be the following. The retention of India as a member of the Commonwealth would mean that, in the eyes of the world, and in particular of potential aggressors, the size and power of the Commonwealth would remain undiminished. This was of great importance at a time when much of South-east Asia and the Far East was disturbed by civil war and the encroachments of communism in China. The Commonwealth itself would profit by a demonstration of the statesmanship and flexibility of its member governments which enabled the whole of the Indian subcontinent, after being freed from British rule, to choose freely to remain within the Commonwealth. Conversely, confidence in the future of the Commonwealth would be gravely shaken if India followed Burma and Eire, the more especially if it appeared that her sole reason for doing so was the incapacity of the rest of the Commonwealth to accede to her desire to remain on account of legalistic and constitutional forms. The satisfaction of India's express desire to retain membership while repudiating allegiance to the Crown would provide the best possible conditions for establishing confidence and friendship between India and the United Kingdom and other Commonwealth countries, and would enable her fellow Commonwealth members to influence the young Indian state during its years of adolescence – which could be expected to be stormy.

Disadvantages were discerned as well. Allowing India to remain a member of the Commonwealth while owing no allegiance to the Crown might encourage the belief that Commonwealth countries were so anxious to retain India's goodwill as to sacrifice the traditional basis on which Commonwealth membership had always rested. The result would be to make foreign states contemptuous of the Commonwealth and so impair its capacity to deter aggression and anarchy.* Again, having once succeeded in imposing its will upon the Commonwealth, India might try to blackmail Commonwealth governments into accepting or tolerating practices inconsistent with Commonwealth ideals and interests by threatening secession if they did not do so. Conversely, India might place a higher value upon the Commonwealth connection if it were made plain at the outset that membership was difficult to come by, not handed out indiscriminately to all comers. Finally, it was by no means certain that a Com-

* No such contempt had been displayed by the Commander-in-Chief of the German Navy in reporting to the Fuhrer, on 6 September 1940, that 'the British Empire is not expected to collapse owing to the peculiar innate force of the political objectives embodied in the conception of the Commonwealth of Nations.' (Quoted in Mansergh, *Survey ...*, *Problems of Wartime Co-operation ...*, 1.) It is possible that this fact was recalled by those opposed to abandoning allegiance to the Crown as the basis of Commonwealth membership.

monwealth so loosely articulated as to permit membership of a state paying no allegiance to the Crown was preferable to a smaller but more cohesive Commonwealth.

To the hypothesis of an India foreign to the Commonwealth yet retaining with its members, especially with the United Kingdom, a special relationship which might be signified by treaty, officials in Whitehall were not entirely averse. Should such a special relationship form the terms of a treaty, the negotiations might themselves afford an opportunity to achieve a more solid foundation for constructive ties than would mere continuation of the Commonwealth bond. That lack of precision and definition of the Commonwealth relationship so often extolled by spokesmen for the old Dominions did not necessarily augur well, or as well, for the new. India's membership of the Commonwealth imposed upon the United Kingdom some sort of moral obligation to come to India's aid should India be attacked; a treaty or special relationship with a foreign India would no longer impose unilaterally upon one partner so onerous an obligation. And once outside the Commonwealth, India could no longer exert leverage upon the members by threatening to secede. These would be able to deal with India's policies strictly upon their merits, or upon their lack thereof. It might even prove that under the stress of events India would find her loss of Commonwealth membership detrimental to her external safety and internal stability, and so be induced to pursue towards the United Kingdom and other Commonwealth countries more co-operative policies than might otherwise be the case.

It is evident, however, that the British policy planners, seeking possible advantages in the wake of an Indian departure, were straining further than reality. They saw the consequences that loomed ahead, and liked not what they saw. An Indian secession, even on the friendliest of terms, would have world-wide repercussions most of which would be adverse. Not for nothing had the Soviet Union voted for the admission to the United Nations of Burma, which had left the Commonwealth, while vetoing that of Ceylon, which had remained; the Russians would take every advantage of India's new-found isolation, and India might not rebuff Russia's advances. Nor those of the Chinese Communists, then consolidating themselves on the mainland. Finally, an India outside the Commonwealth, with Pakistan within, would not be conducive either to the stability of the subcontinent nor to the tranquillity of the Commonwealth. 'The political dangers of that situation,' the policy planners noted, 'are obvious.'

But in all probability an Indian secession would not be on the friendliest of terms. This was the third hypothesis, and not even the most fanciful scenario could find it advantageous. The dangers, by contrast, were only too obvious, and the planners did not mince their words. An India uncooperative after secession, an India bitter after secession, an India hostile after secession, would be a calamity for British, Commonwealth, and Western policy alike. It would be difficult for the United Kingdom government, or for any Commonwealth government, to exercise any effective influence over the course of Indian affairs. India might well embark upon a frankly anti-Western course. She would turn to Russia, and to China, for support and assistance. These could cause her to fall under communist domination. A communist India joined to a communist China could easily result in the extinction of all western influence in Asia.

Such were the considerations causing the United Kingdom Cabinet to brush aside the misgivings of its legal advisers and of some of its members,* and to make every effort to devise some modality which would allow a republican India to remain within the Commonwealth. 'I may be wrong,' the Canadian High Commissioner reported from New Delhi on 18 March 1949, 'but I think I see in the attitude of the United Kingdom government a disposition to admit India to the Commonwealth without necessarily having any real link with the Crown...'[107] Kearney was not wrong.

The Canadian Government came to the same conclusion as the British. 'There is obvious value in India's continued membership in the Commonwealth, from a political and strategic point of view, particularly in view of the present international situation.' So the Department of External Affairs summed up in a memorandum prepared in mid-March 1949 for its Minister's exposition to the Cabinet. 'This is of importance not only in terms of the Soviet menace but also as providing an important link between the peoples of Asia and the Western countries.'[108]

Britain being bound on keeping India in, there was no need for a major Canadian initiative. St Laurent decided that his presence at the Prime

* Notably the Foreign Secretary. A meeting of the Commonwealth Affairs Committee of the Cabinet on 7 January 1949 began inauspiciously 'with Bevin saying in effect that the Commonwealth ought to be dissolved,' it was not worth the trouble. Patrick Gordon Walker, then Parliamentary Under-Secretary of State in the Commonwealth Relations Office, spoke strongly in favour of fitting 'in India as a republic, based on the reality of a common act of will ... Shawcross attacked this on the ground that unless we had the common crown or common nationality it would not stand up under international law. Cripps and the Prime Minister in effect said that law must be made for people and international law must adjust itself.' A month later Bevin was still arguing 'the Foreign Office line – that it was not worth keeping India in the Commonwealth: it was not going to be morally committed to us, but we to it. To keep India in would lead to the breakdown of the old Commonwealth.' But as the discussion proceeded, 'Bevin warmed up and made some positive suggestions.' Patrick Gordon Walker, *The Cabinet* (London 1970), 135–7.

Ministers' Conference was not essential, choosing to campaign instead in Western Canada. In a message to Nehru explaining this decision, the Canadian Prime Minister stressed his country's attachment to the Crown.

So far as the Canadian Government is concerned, we are satisfied with the present basis of association between the members of the Commonwealth and we do not wish to alter Canada's traditional relationship with the Crown. The Crown is an essential element of our constitution and of our whole parliamentary system of government. We think that the Canadian public would have misgivings in accepting any fundamental change in the present form of Commonwealth association which would appear to weaken the position of the Crown.

The above considerations prompt me to express the sincere hope that you may see your way clear to retaining some link between the sovereign republic of India and the Crown. It seems to me that any alternative presents not only constitutional but also real practical difficulties, for example, we might be hard put to defend against foreign objections the continued exchange of trade preferences.[109]

The real practical difficulty of being hard put to defend against Indian objections the continued restrictions on immigration if Commonwealth citizenship rather than some form of association with the Crown were to become the bond of Commonwealth it was thought prudent not to mention. 'In any event,' St Laurent's despatch concluded, 'you and your colleagues may be assured that the Government and people of Canada earnestly desire that a way may be found through which India can remain a full member of the Commonwealth. Please be assured also of our sincere good will and of our understanding of India's special situation in regard to this matter. I wanted you to know this before you left for London, as well as something of the problems involved from the Canadian point of view in regard to any action which might seem to require a fundamental change in the basis of the Commonwealth relationship.'

Canada was represented at the Prime Ministers' Conference by the Secretary of State for External Affairs; he was the only non-Prime Minister to lead a delegation. Joining Pearson for the occasion was the High Commissioner in India. Max Wershof was flown in from Geneva for his expertise on nationality and citizenship problems. R.A. MacKay and Hume Wright* of the Department of External Affairs completed the Canadian team.

A busy couple of days of consultation preceded the opening meeting of the Conference on 22 April. On 20 April Pearson met privately with Attlee, who impressed him with the 'strong disposition on the part of the

* The Department of External Affairs was able at this time to accommodate both Wright and Wrong.

Government here to do everything possible to keep India in the Commonwealth. Mr Attlee has no illusions about the difficulties in persuading the Indians to accept the King in any other form than that of a symbol of the Commonwealth association,' Pearson reported to Ottawa, 'but he thinks that this might suffice, through a declaration and a consequential alteration in the King's title to include some such phrase as "Head of the Commonwealth".' The next day he talked with the Prime Minister of India.

> Nehru was quite firm that there could be no membership for India in the Commonwealth except on the basis of her Republican constitution but if that basis were accepted then India desired to continue the present association. I pointed out to him that we in our turn did not desire in Canada to alter in any way our present connection with the Crown which met our needs and our wishes, but that we recognized that India's position in this regard was different. Nehru said that there was a good deal of opposition in India to any form of Commonwealth association but that he appreciated its advantages and he also appreciated the position of the Crown as a symbol of such association.[110]

Nehru had brought with him to London a written statement of the Indian position, which Pearson, along with Attlee, was the only delegate to see in advance. Pearson thought the paper 'establishes a satisfactory basis for discussion and possible agreement.' Closer scrutiny the following day by R.A. MacKay disclosed a number of difficulties from the Canadian standpoint. The Indian paper proposed a re-statement of the basis of the Commonwealth association, which the Canadians desired to avoid; there was the troublesome emphasis upon Commonwealth citizenship as an essential element of the Commonwealth association; there was a suggestion that the Commonwealth be given a new title, 'Commonwealth of Free Nations,' about which MacKay commented: 'Obviously to change the title expressly would raise political difficulties in Canada. It would be much better to have any change in title come by usage rather than by public declaration.' He noted that the Indian paper proposed the acceptance of the King as a symbol of free association between Commonwealth countries, and that St Laurent's message to Nehru had expressed the hope that India could retain some link with the Crown, adding: 'The Indian proposals would permit a link with the King in person, though hardly with the Crown, but this is probably as far as they can be expected to go.'[111] So it proved.

The first meeting of the Prime Ministers and Pearson, and their advisers – Pearson brought Kearney and MacKay – was held on the morning of April 23. It lasted two hours. Attlee presided. He told those present that he wanted the discussions to be wholly informal, and that there would be no formal record of them. Their purpose was to determine whether and on what basis India, committed to a republican form of government, could remain a member of the Commonwealth. He then called on Nehru to speak first. The Prime Minister of India elaborated on the proposals of the paper that Attlee and Pearson had already seen. Attlee then called on Pearson to speak but, as the only non-Prime Minister delegate at the meeting, Pearson said that he preferred to wait until the Prime Ministers present had spoken first.

Attlee turned then to J.B. Chifley of Australia, whose main concern was that his country's link of allegiance with the Crown be in no way weakened or disturbed. Fraser of New Zealand echoed this sentiment at length, and suggested that the King should be recognized not only as the symbol of the Commonwealth association but as Head of the Commonwealth also.

The statement by the Prime Minister of South Africa which followed provided the sensation of the meeting. Dr D.F. Malan, who alone at the meeting read from notes prepared beforehand, backed more strongly than any other delegate the continuation of India's connection with the Commonwealth, notwithstanding its proposed republican constitution. He also stated strongly South Africa's intention to adhere to the Commonwealth, even though the link of allegiance to the King was not considered as important as it was to other Dominions. The people of South Africa were conscious of dangers ahead, and did not wish to stand isolated and alone in a world of turmoil. They would need the Commonwealth to see them through.

Liaquat Ali Khan spoke next for Pakistan. Of all Commonwealth countries his would be most immediately affected by the outcome of the meeting. Pakistan, like South Africa, valued the Commonwealth not so much for sentiment's sake as for security's sake. The members of the Commonwealth should declare their readiness to come to the aid of any of their number threatened by aggression. Liaquat Ali Khan thought the meeting should discuss the position of other Commonwealth countries which, like India, wanted Commonwealth membership and republican status simultaneously. He could not pass judgment on Nehru's proposals, he declared, until he had studied them in writing.

For Ceylon, D.S. Senanayake stressed the importance of allegiance to the Crown. He feared that a republican India, if allowed to remain a full member of the Commonwealth, would weaken the association. A decision on Indian membership ought to be deferred. Time would iron out the difficulties, or at least clarify the issues.

Finally it was Pearson's turn. 'After expressing our regrets at the inability of our Prime Minister to attend the Conference,' he reported to Ottawa on his intervention,

I pointed out that in the past the Commonwealth had proved its adaptability in meeting changing situations as they arose, and that I hoped it would be able to do so again. I observed that the Commonwealth was founded on freedom and equality. The question now before us was, did the freedom enjoyed by each member include its right to declare itself a Republic and remain within the family. I added that the nations of the Commonwealth also enjoyed a full equality of status which meant that there should be no inner or outer circle of membership. Canada, I said, was satisfied with the Crown and wished to maintain it, and it was important for us that no one should gain the impression from this conference that Canada's link with the Crown was being weakened or changed. This link reflected the history, sentiments and feelings of the member states and therefore it may vary in strength in the different countries. Heretofore it had been not only the source of common allegiance but also a symbol of the association of the nations which composed the Commonwealth. India although not wishing to be bound by allegiance, nevertheless desired to continue its close and friendly association with the rest of us and agreed to retain the Crown as the symbol of this association. The Canadian Government would welcome Mr Nehru's statement to this effect because it hoped that India could remain in the Commonwealth. In the course of my remarks, I incidentally mentioned that I did not think that the question raised by Mr Liaquat Ali Khan of if how Republics not now connected with the Commonwealth might be admitted to it, was of sufficient immediate importance to be dealt with at this conference. Quite a few at the conference table nodded their assent. I concluded by saying that I was confident that this conference would be capable of finding a solution which would permit India to remain as a Commonwealth member.[112]

Reviewing this initial round of presentations, Pearson was struck by the curious alignment that they revealed. The younger Dominions – Pakistan and Ceylon – had given Nehru the least support; South Africa, though at loggerheads with India, the strongest. 'From my private talks with Mr Attlee,' Pearson's despatch concluded, 'I know that the United Kingdom Government is pleased with Mr Nehru's attitude, and I believe that subject perhaps to some slight modification, the Prime Ministers of the older Commonwealth countries are prepared to agree to India remaining in the Commonwealth on the basis of Mr Nehru's proposals.'

After the opening meeting on 22 April, the British Prime Minister undertook to prepare a draft memorandum for consideration by the delegates at their second meeting on 25 April. Attlee's proposals provided for two declarations: one by the Indian Government affirming India's continuing membership of the Commonwealth after India became a republic and its 'acceptance of the King, Head of the Commonwealth, as the symbol of the free association'; a second by all the other Commonwealth Governments affirming their continued membership of the Commonwealth 'wherein they are bound in unity by their common allegiance to the King, who is also the symbol of their free association,' and recognizing India's continuing membership in accordance with the Indian declaration. Attlee's paper proposed as well that the participants should place on record their agreement that Commonwealth countries were to be distinguished from foreign countries. This would be done by legislation adopting the scheme of Commonwealth citizenship embodied in the British Nationality Act of 1948, and by provisions in treaties and legislation making it clear that other countries of the Commonwealth would not be treated as foreign countries or their citizens as foreigners.

These proposals were scrutinized by the Canadian delegation and found wanting in several respects. Attlee's draft, Pearson and his officials agreed, was too formal in its tone. Much better to work out a clear and simple statement which could be made public at once, presumably in the form of a press release. The device of two declarations, one by India and one by all the rest, was divisive rather than unifying in its impact. It placed India in one category, all the rest in another, and would convey the impression of two-tier membership and two-class status. Reporting to Ottawa on the reception of Attlee's draft – Liaquat Ali Khan had disapproved, Nehru was not completely satisfied – Pearson suggested that the two declarations be re-drafted as one to which all present would signify assent, so stressing their solidarity. St Laurent was much impressed by this idea, and Pearson was accordingly instructed 'to propose or give full support to a single statement to be agreed to by all governments.'

The Canadian delegation had doubts about the phrase 'Head of the Commonwealth'; while useful, it could give rise to misunderstanding if not employed precisely and identically in all parts of the Commonwealth. And Attlee's reference to Commonwealth citizenship would have to be given a restricted meaning, perhaps in a statement reaffirming the right of each Commonwealth country to decide on the content of that term and to have exclusive control over its own immigration policy.

On the basis of these reactions, and those of other delegations, Attlee revised his draft, presenting the revision for discussion at the second meeting of the Conference on the morning of 25 April. There was now a single declaration only, as Pearson had suggested.

> The Government of India have informed the other Governments of the British Commonwealth of Nations that India will shortly become a sovereign independent Republic under the new Constitution to be adopted by the Indian People. At the same time they have declared and affirmed India's desire to continue her membership of the Commonwealth and her recognition of the King, Head of the Commonwealth, as the symbol of the free association of the independent member nations within the Commonwealth.
>
> The other members of the Commonwealth, while making no change in the existing basis of their relations with one another and with the Crown, accept

the declaration of the Government of India as the basis of India's continuing membership of the Commonwealth.

All but the Prime Minister of New Zealand considered this revision an improvement; Fraser felt that Attlee's original draft was preferable for its emphasis on allegiance to the King as the basis of the Commonwealth association for all members except India. There was considerable discussion about the phrase 'Head of the Commonwealth.' Malan did not like it. The Statute of Westminster, he pointed out, made no reference to it, and to adopt the phrase there and then would imply that a fundamental change was being made in the structure of the Commonwealth. Pearson also expressed his doubt. Attlee replied that the term was not intended to suggest the existence of a super-state, and that the phrase that followed it in his draft – 'free association of the independent member nations of the Commonwealth' – surely made that clear. That term, or some other like it, was essential to create a link between India and the Commonwealth when India ceased to pay allegiance to the Crown. Different delegations then produced different drafts – 'The King who symbolizes, as Head of the Commonwealth, the free association...,' 'The King as the symbol of the free association ... and thus the Head of the Commonwealth...,' 'The King, the symbolic Head of the free association of the independent nations within the Commonwealth...' – which it was agreed would be considered later on.

The other aspect of Attlee's revision discussed at length at the second meeting was the phrase 'The other members of the Commonwealth, while making no change in the existing basis of their relations with one another and with the Crown...' That formulation, Chifley and Fraser asserted, did not stress forcefully and positively enough the strength of their countries' feelings of allegiance to the Crown. Liaquat Ali Khan pointed out that if the declaration went too far in that direction, other members might find it difficult to follow India's example if they wished to do so; the wording ought not to preclude other prospective republics from remaining in the Commonwealth. Attlee, Sir Stafford Cripps, and Pearson agreed to try again.

A third meeting convened on 26 April. Malan still bridled at 'Head of the Commonwealth,' and the term was put to one side for the moment. The expression 'British Commonwealth of Nations' caused comment. Fraser and Chifley wanted it used throughout the declaration. Nehru was content that it be used in its first paragraph, but pointed out that the term 'British' implied a political and cultural unity which no longer corresponded to reality; for that reason he did not think it right to use it throughout. Attlee and Cripps thought it best to drop 'British' entirely unless it was used throughout, since its appearance in one paragraph and not in another might be questioned by the press. Pearson did not think this an undue hazard, and sided with Nehru's suggested compromise. That view prevailed.

The drafting team of Attlee, Cripps, and Pearson, helped by Sir Percivale Liesching and Sir Norman Brook, meanwhile had altered 'The other members of the Commonwealth, while making no change in the existing basis of their relations with one another and with the Crown...' to 'The other members, the basis of whose membership of the Commonwealth remains unchanged...' This formulation was opposed by the Prime Ministers of Pakistan and Ceylon, who argued that it implied that other members would be prevented from changing their constitution as India had done. Pearson then proposed that 'remains unchanged' be revised to 'is not hereby changed.' That phrase, too, made its way into the final Declaration – though only after the Conference adopted, at Liaquat Ali Khan's insistence, a minute recording its opinion that 'it could be logically assumed that a future Meeting would accord the same treatment to any other member as had been accorded to India by this Meeting.'

To Attlee's revised draft there had been added, as agreed at the second meeting, a paragraph about the purpose of the Commonwealth. This the third meeting now had before it. 'They remain united,' the draft read, 'as free and equal members of the Commonwealth of Nations which has proved its value as an instrument for free co-operation in the pursuit of peace, security and progress.' Liaquat Ali Khan thought this version inadequate. He thought the members of the Commonwealth should commit themselves to 'mutual assistance' – at which point the Prime Minister of New Zealand interposed to say he would hold up not one of his hands in favour but two. Sir Stafford Cripps, doubtless recalling his interrogation in New Delhi seven years previously, quickly pointed out that the notion of 'mutual assistance' had an unfortunate historical connotation in the Commonwealth and that it was best to leave it out.

But not quickly enough. For the first time in the proceedings Pandit Nehru showed signs of impatience, perhaps of anger. Membership in the Commonwealth, he stated, entailed no such obligation as 'mutual assistance.' Even the word 'security,' which already figured in the draft, was much too strong a term since it implied an obligation to preserve the status quo. It should be struck out, in favour of the word 'liberty.' A Pakistani delegate asked with some asperity whether India was not prepared to preserve the status quo. Nehru replied that India was not prepared to underwrite without question the policies of other member governments. Clearly nettled by now, Nehru took exception to yet another phrase. He did not think it proper to recite that the Commonwealth of Nations 'has proved its value as an instrument.' That implied to him that Commonwealth members had always been right. He could not say in honesty that he thought British policy in India right. The phrase should look to the future, not to the past. He proposed the following alternative: 'Accordingly the United Kingdom, Canada, Australia, New Zealand, South Africa, India, Pakistan and Ceylon hereby declare that they remain united and free as equal and independent members of the Commonwealth of Nations, freely co-operating in the pursuit of peace, liberty and progress.' With only 'as' and 'and' transposed, this version formed part of the final text.

There remained for consideration at a fourth meeting on the morning of 27 April only 'Head of the Commonwealth.' Malan once again expressed his misgiving but, as in the case of Liaquat Ali Khan's objection, the device of a recorded minute, indicating that the use of the term did not imply any change in the constitutional relations existing between members or that the King had any constitutional functions by virtue of that Headship, overcame it. The meeting agreed that the formulation first proposed by Pearson should stand: 'The King, as the symbol of the free association of the independent member nations, and thus the Head of the Commonwealth...' One final touch of drafting was then added: 'thus' was altered to 'as such.'*

By noon the work was done, the Declaration of London complete. Just before lunch the members of the Conference adjourned and repaired to Buckingham Palace to present their handiwork to the King. That afternoon, the Declaration of London was released for publication.

The Governments of the United Kingdom, Canada, Australia, New Zealand, South Africa, India, Pakistan and Ceylon, whose countries are united as Members of the British Commonwealth of Nations and owe a common allegiance to the Crown, which is also the symbol of their free association, have considered the impending constitutional changes in India.

The Government of India has informed the other Governments of the Commonwealth of the intention of the Indian people that under the new constitution which is about to be adopted India shall become a sovereign independent republic. The Government of India has however declared and affirmed India's desire to continue her full membership of the Commonwealth

* 'This "as such",' said V.K. Krishna Menon, claiming credit for it, 'came after half an hour of going backwards and forwards ... The King ... said to me in jest, "What am I now – 'As Such?' " ' Quoted in Michael Brecher, *India and World Politics: Krishna Menon's View of the World* (London 1968), 24.

of Nations and her acceptance of The King as the symbol of the free association of its independent member nations and as such the Head of the Commonwealth.

The Governments of the other countries of the Commonwealth, the basis of whose membership of the Commonwealth is not hereby changed, accept and recognize India's continuing membership in accordance with the terms of this declaration.

Accordingly the United Kingdom, Canada, Australia, New Zealand, South Africa, India, Pakistan and Ceylon hereby declare that they remain united as free and equal members of the Commonwealth of Nations, freely co-operating in the pursuit of peace, liberty and progress.[113]

Later in the day, Pearson broadcast to the people of Canada an account of the work of the week just past and of its significance. 'The report,' he said, 'is short and without frills; just as our meeting was short and without frills.' The problem before the meeting of Prime Ministers and himself had been an easy one to state but far from easy to solve.

In a word it was this. Was our Commonwealth of Nations adaptable and elastic enough to include one nation, India, which was anxious to retain its full partnership in our group? Our report shows this can be done without altering the connection with the Crown as the source of our allegiance which the rest of us cherish and which has not been changed by anything that we have done in London. To Canada the Crown means no impairment of our freedom, but on the contrary symbolizes the continuity of our historical development and the depth and strength of our democratic roots. The King, however, stands for something more than this. He is the symbol of the free association of the members of this Commonwealth of Nations. India joins with the rest of us in accepting The King as such a symbol and as the Head of our Commonwealth.

Thus we will all remain together at a time when, as never before, it is good for us and for the world that this should be so...

Pearson's gifts as a conciliator had been deployed again to good effect. But looking back across the decades the hero of the hour is clearly Pandit Nehru. Had he lost patience in the search for an acceptable formula, had he lost sight of the larger goal beneath the arid constitutional wrangling and legal quibbling, the London Conference might have ended in disaster instead of triumph. Instead he persisted and prevailed. 'It was an act of high statesmanship,' his biographer judges justly, the more so since it was by no means universally acclaimed by all his fellow-Indians. 'Some critics termed it a "betrayal" of Nehru's pledge of "complete independence." To others it was anathema because of racial discrimination in various parts of the Commonwealth, notably in South Africa. To others still it implied an abandonment of non-alignment.'[114] Nehru himself took the criticism in his stride. He admitted that in London he had not held out for the perfect formula, the last comma in the communiqué issued on 27 April 1949. 'It was possible that if I had tried my hardest I might have got a word here and there changed in this declaration.' But he had thought it best not to try, partly because 'I am not used to the ways of the market place,' partly 'because there was nothing more for us to get out of that declaration,' mainly because he thought it was a good thing to 'have begun this new type of association with a touch of healing ... good for us, good for them, and ... good for the world.'[115]

It was not only in India that the opinion was expressed that Nehru had been if anything too generous at the London Conference. 'I have some misgiving,' E.J. Tarr wrote afterwards to L.B. Pearson, 'in that Nehru may have conceded too much in acknowledging the King as the titular head of the Commonwealth, even though it is a purely honorary title so far as India is concerned. I am afraid that before long this may be used in India for political purposes, with motives not soundly national but purely destructive.' Pearson did not think this likely. 'It was not a case of forcing Nehru to make concessions in regard to the recognition of the King as the symbol of the Commonwealth association,' he replied, 'because he seemed to accept that solution of our problem without any difficulty. In the circumstances, it would not have been either easy or appropriate for the rest of us to have been less royalist than Mr Nehru! ... Personally, I would have preferred to leave the expression "Head of the Commonwealth" out, but in its context I do not think it can do any harm. It will, on the other hand, ensure support from quarters which otherwise would have criticized and perhaps refused to accept the declaration.'[116] Later, in Parliament, Pearson spoke of the new Commonwealth made possible by India's membership as 'a bridge between the east and the west.'[117] It was a bridge all the more valuable for having been constructed in a world where almost all the bridges were being blown.

# 5

# Controlling the Atom

Some natural tears they drop'd but wip'd them soon.

*John Milton*

## NORTH ATLANTIC TANGLES I

On 15 June 1942 the Prime Minister of Canada received in his study at Laurier House a small and secret delegation. Accompanying the British High Commissioner, Malcolm MacDonald, were Professor G.P. Thomson, the British scientific liaison officer in Ottawa, and M.W. Perrin, deputy director of what to a very few was known as 'Tube Alloys' – the British project to develop atomic bombs.

For the first time Mackenzie King learned of the impending race with Nazi Germany to invent and produce a weapon of enormous destructive power. But it was not owing to the convention of Commonwealth consultation that he was being let in on this deadliest of wartime secrets. An atomic explosion required splitting the particles of the element uranium, of which only two sources were known to exist. One was in the Belgian Congo, beyond reach of the allies at that stage of the war. The other was on the shore of Great Bear Lake in the Northwest Territories of Canada.

The purpose of the British delegation was now clear – to persuade the Canadian Government to acquire control of the Eldorado Gold Mines Company which owned the pitchblende deposits at Great Bear Lake, and so assure to the Allies a supply of what had suddenly become the most crucial component of the entire war effort. 'The whole business was very secret,' Mackenzie King recorded after his visitors had left, 'but it was represented that it was quite possible that it might, within a very short time, lead to a development that whichever country possessed this mineral would unquestionably win the war...'[1]

The Prime Minister referred MacDonald, Thomson, and Perrin to his Minister of Munitions and Supply, C.D. Howe, and to the President of the National Research Council, C.J. Mackenzie. The five men met in Howe's office that afternoon at 4 PM and talked for about two hours. After the visitors outlined their proposal, Howe at once offered his co-operation. He agreed that government control of the mine was essential. The Canadian Government could not, however, expropriate the Eldorado Gold Mines Company without exciting unwelcome attention. He intended to proceed quietly by buying a controlling interest on the open market on behalf of the Canadian Government. He did not expect any problems; the president of the Company, Gilbert LaBine, was his personal friend. Once the purchases had been made and control secured, the United Kingdom, the United States and, if need be, Canada, could negotiate an agreement on the division of the ore.[2]

The British delegation professed to be delighted at this arrangement, and that evening they met for the second time with the Prime Minister. 'They told me,' Mackenzie King wrote afterwards,

> there had been complete agreement among them as to desirability of Government not only controlling, but owning, the particular mineral deposit in question, and I was asked if I would authorize the Government getting the majority of shares from the owner ... I agreed to this step being taken at once so long as Americans were advised in advance of the intention...[3]

C.J. Mackenzie set out at once for Washington, and on 19 June met with Vannevar Bush, director of the Office of Scientific Research and Development and the key figure in the United States atomic energy project. 'Bush thinks that we should proceed with the acquisitioning of the property,' Mackenzie wrote of their interview, 'and appreciated very much Mr Howe's offer. He thinks there should be an international arrangement as between the United States, the United Kingdom and Canada for post-war control.'[4]

The stage was thus set for C.D. Howe to commence his clandestine takeover. He asked Gilbert LaBine to come to Ottawa and told him what was up. LaBine being willing, they went immediately to prices. 'I am prepared to deliver to you,' LaBine wrote to Howe after their meeting on 7 July, '1,000,303 shares of the stock of Eldorado Gold Mines Limited at a price of $1.25 per share. I shall endeavour to purchase all further shares that I may be able to do privately, and I further agree to deliver 40,000 other shares which I am personally interested in, which is at the moment tied up in a separate account as collateral.' Howe replied: 'Representing His Majesty the King in the Right of the Dominion of Canada I accept your offer ... It is understood,' he added, 'that the details of this transaction will be kept entirely private until an announcement is made officially by the Canadian Government.'[5] A few days later Howe wrote to Malcolm MacDonald to apprise him of these developments. 'Am now taking steps to quietly purchase another million shares from banks and trust companies. Gilbert LaBine is being most co-operative.' He told MacDonald that substantial orders for the 'product' were being received from the authorities at the atomic energy project in the United States, and that he felt this demand might be met by enlarging operations at the mine. 'I am satisfied that the situation is well in hand.' It was not to be so simple.

No principle of Mackenzie King's foreign policy had become more firmly established than the prime necessity of keeping the United Kingdom and the United States agreed upon essentials. Their divergence was considered contrary to Canada's interests and to be avoided at almost any cost. Thrust by possession of uranium ore into the endeavour to create atomic bombs, those few members of the Canadian Government privy to the secret soon found that the traditional role as conciliator of Anglo-American misunderstandings was neither easy nor automatic. For a time Canada created more Anglo-American misunderstanding than she was able to conciliate.

The first misunderstanding arose over the division of the Eldorado output.

Precision in the arrangements by which the United Kingdom was to take delivery of uranium ore had been sacrificed to secrecy. Extreme informality, based on trust and friendship of the few individuals concerned, characterized the early negotiations. Trust and friendship are not invariably the firmest foundations on which to build international relationships fraught with possible conflicts of interest. Or so the Canadians now discovered.

Barely a week after Howe's deal with LaBine, the British submitted, through Malcolm MacDonald, their first order – '20 tons of the purest oxide at present being manufactured at Port Hope refinery.' The British Government, MacDonald reported, were particularly concerned that the oxide be promptly shipped because of the substantial orders which Howe had said were being placed by the United States authorities. Howe told MacDonald that he hoped the British would not need their tonnage right away, at the same time advising LaBine to fill the American orders first. The British did not like this priority at all. 'Our people regard it as essential,' MacDonald informed Howe on 22 July, 'that their order should be delivered to them by the end of September at the latest. They assume that this date will certainly mean interference with the United States deliveries and the matter is being taken up in Washington through our representatives there who will explain the position to the United States authorities with a view to securing their agreement.'[6] It was only then that Howe learned from LaBine the size of the American requirement. The British had ordered 20 tons. The Americans wanted 350.

Sensing trouble, the British attempted at this juncture to negotiate a formal division of control at the source. They proposed a three-fold split – themselves, the Americans, and the Canadians – of the shares of the Eldorado mine. Howe demurred. He had yet to acquire a controlling interest in the Company, he told them, and did not want to proceed to a formal division until he was in full control. 'Some time must elapse before this can be acquired.'[7]

There thus devolved on Gilbert LaBine the awesome responsibility of allocating uranium ore between the two Allies which, nominally partners in the project, were already showing signs of rivalry. He had not sought it in the least. Now that, through no fault of his own, it had become his he did not shrink from it. Years of prospecting in the Canadian north, more years of roughing it on Bay Street, enabled him to take the strain. But the pressure had become intense. On 15 September he wrote to Howe for guidance.

> At the present time we are producing just enough of this material to meet the requirements of the US Office of Scientific Research and Development. About October 15th we will complete the expansion of our production facilities to a point where we can start to fill the twenty ton order for the United Kingdom without interfering with the deliveries to the Office of Scientific Research and Development.
>
> If the order for the United Kingdom cannot wait until that time we would appreciate very much your discussing this problem with the Office of Scientific Research and Development as regards the priority of these orders. We are anxious to supply both Governments but we believe it will be advisable for them to decide between themselves and advise us which order should be filled first...[8]

If the British could wait another month all would be well. The American order would be filled and increased production would henceforth assure supplies to both countries. On 24 September came word from London that delivery might be postponed. Sir John Anderson, Lord President of the Council, who handled British atomic affairs as Howe handled the Canadian, would be satisfied if five tons of the twenty on order reached the United Kingdom not later than 20 November, the rest to follow not later than 31 December. The heat was off.

As the December deadline loomed, the heat came on again. The British were agitated to learn that the Americans were after their 15 remaining tons. A deal was worked out whereby the 15 tons would be sent to the Malinckrodt Chemical Company in St Louis for purification, 5 tons of the purified product to be sent from there to the United Kingdom. But when the time for delivery came, the Americans failed to release the 5 tons. Repeated letters from LaBine and C.J. Mackenzie to their contacts in Washington failed to secure their release.

That no graver crisis arose from this contretemps is explained by the preoccupation of the British authorities with the removal of their atomic energy project to Canada.* By April 1943 the Montreal Laboratory was ready to go to work. It needed uranium oxide to go to work with. On 7 April Malcolm MacDonald asked Howe to supply the Montreal team with 20 tons of oxide. Howe duly relayed the order to LaBine. LaBine now more than justified the British authorities' most dire misgivings. He would be unable, they learned, to fill this order or any other they might place. He had contracted to sell the entire output of the Eldorado mine for the foreseeable future. His customer was the United States Army.

Howe had known nothing of any of this. On 26 May, when word first reached him of what had happened, he wrote to LaBine for an explanation. 'I have no knowledge of any such sale,' he told his friend, 'and I feel sure that you would not dispose of your product in a way that would interfere with filling urgent requisitions from the United Kingdom. In any event, I would be opposed to selling our full output of uranium for a long period in advance under present day circumstances.' LaBine may pardonably have felt that such a guideline was long overdue. What slight glimmering he had received of Howe's general policy in the matter of selling uranium ore had led him to think that it was a policy of America First. Moreover, as he wrote to Howe on 28 May, 'I was of the opinion that it was good policy to accept all contracts that came our way for the refining of ore, in order to give our industry revenue and at the same time protect our company against other interests which were anxious to take on job refining for the US Government.' He added: 'It is true that at the moment we are shipping our entire output of Uranium across the line to our American friends, but we have been definitely led to believe by verbal understanding that they know this is a Canadian company and that the requirements of the governments of both Canada and the United Kingdom should be taken care of.'

This explanation may have reassured Howe. It did nothing to reassure the British authorities. They were coming to have less and less reason for

* See below, 266–74.

relying on verbal understandings with the Americans on atomic energy matters. When word of what had happened reached the highest British authority his reaction was sharp and explosive. Canada's Minister of Munitions and Supply, Winston Churchill growled, had ' "sold the British Empire down the river".'[9] The slight was duly relayed to its subject. Howe was not a preternaturally sensitive soul. But as a Canadian born in the United States he keenly resented any suggestion that his loyalty to Canada – the 'British Empire' was another matter – should be called into question by Churchill or by anyone else. He was upset and fed up. One more remark like Churchill's from a British source could have brought Anglo-Canadian co-operation to an end, or even Howe's cabinet career.

Meanwhile there was a mess, and it needed cleaning up. LaBine was summoned to Ottawa to give an accounting of his contracts. These were distressingly confused. C.J. Mackenzie recorded the unavailing attempts at unravelling:

*14 June.* Meeting in Mr Howe's office with Mr LaBine of Eldorado and Colonel Nichols and Lt-Col. Crenshaw of US Engineers ... Discussion was in connection with the proposed contract for uranium and refining of oxide ... It is a very sticky subject and I was not fully informed as to past contracts which LaBine has with the US Army and how the thing will work out...

*15 June* ... The supply of uranium is in a very confused position and we are not at all sure what contracts LaBine has, how much the Americans have tied up, and whether or not there will be any available to us if we go on our own...

*21 June* ... MacDonald, Mr [W.A.] Akers [director of the British atomic energy project Tube Alloys] and myself went to see Mr Howe about ... the uranium contracts. We all feel that we must get the correct information and it has become apparent that no one of us knows the complete story...

*30 June* ... MacDonald ... very much upset by the lack of exact information on the LaBine-US Army contracts. There does seem to be some confusion and we may have trouble yet as Mr Howe is very fed up with the suggestion that he is selling the British Empire down the river, etc., etc., which of course is all nonsense but it does seem very difficult to get the exact information.[10]

The British found it no less difficult to get at the facts. A senior official who had come to Canada for that purpose reported to London that he had been unable to discover just where LaBine's transactions left Britain's prospective sources of supply. 'You may well wonder how this can be,' he wrote to Anderson, 'after I have had a fortnight here with this as one of my principal preoccupations; but the entire lack of any accurate knowledge of the position is quite staggering.' It did not help matters to learn that Howe seemed unaware of whether such figures as he was able to quote from the contracts referred to ores, concentrates, or oxide; that made quite a difference.[11]

C.D. Howe had not sold the British Empire down the river in any treasonable sense. But he had been more than a trifle careless with its assets. Overburdened and overworked, he had simply been unable to follow with sufficient care the details of what LaBine was doing on the Government's behalf. Unlike his junior colleague Brooke Claxton (who wrote of himself, accurately enough, that his main problem as an administrator was a temperamental inability to delegate authority), Howe picked his right-hand men with care and serenely left them to their own devices. Here is the authentic hallmark of administrative genius, and it is hard to know how Howe could have borne his crushing responsibilities without it. Yet the method is not without its hazards, as Howe now learned to his cost. The strain of the hassle worked havoc with his nerves and health. 'He almost collapsed on the eleventh hole,' Mackenzie, who played golf with him on 10 July, wrote in his diary on that date, 'but got a drink of water and carried on. He is very much in need of a holiday.'

In the event, it was C.J. Mackenzie – a right-hand man if there ever was one – who got Howe, and the country, out of their predicament. On 6 July he went to New York City to see the chief of the American atomic bomb project, General Leslie R. Groves. Mackenzie laid his cards on the table.

> Told Groves that we were in a jam, that the British were accusing Mr Howe of having sold the British Empire down the river by letting the Americans contract for Eldorado oxide, and that as he knew we had become involved when co-operation was assured and that now the co-operation was broken down we were in a mess and wanted their help.
>
> I told him I realized the legal contract with Eldorado was firm but that he also must realize such contracts with private firms in Canada could be easily broken ... He said their program was very tight and to let us have the amount of oxide we needed might embarrass their program, which I said we did not want to do. On the other hand the small amount of oxide which our group needed to get on with its work in Montreal was only a few per cent of their total stocks and we thought something might be done ... I left the meeting very well satisfied that they would do anything they could to help us out...[12]

Mackenzie's confidence was not misplaced. Enough uranium oxide was released by the Americans to allow the team in Montreal to get on with the job for the time being. It did not solve the long-term problem of British supply. However, that was not Canada's look-out. 'I have always felt,' Mackenzie reflected some weeks later, 'that the United States effort is one hundred times greater than any possible United Kingdom effort, that the Americans can get along if necessary without the UK, while the UK can do nothing without the US, and that our best policy is to make sure we get collaboration and also that we will have to change our plans to suit the American situation.'[13]

Mackenzie also cleared the air with the British. On 13 July he had a very frank talk with their High Commissioner in Ottawa.

MacDonald said they were frightened LaBine would be making more contracts with the Americans ... I told him there was not a chance in a million of that happening ... He was all for telephoning Mr Howe to send a wire to LaBine to refrain from entering into more contracts. I told him that in my opinion if he phoned Mr Howe ... on a matter which he, Howe, was getting very fed up with, Mr. Howe would tell him to go to hell and take his whole crowd back to England, and I am quite sure he would have done it ... I said that we all knew that ... he was carrying a terrific load, that he had got the facts mixed (which is not unnatural at all), and that there was no point in making him admit an error just for the sake of it. I told him that in my opinion if it came to a showdown Mr Howe's contributions to the war were so great that no one would bother about a point, which after all was a minor one ... and that if they persisted in bothering Mr Howe about this unimportant matter there would be a real blow-up...[14]

It remained to insure that the fiasco would not be repeated. A first step was to relieve LaBine of his discretionary responsibility in the allocation of contracts. On 28 July, Howe instructed LaBine that henceforth the Government of Canada would be taking delivery of all uranium ore produced in Canada. Releases from what would in effect be the Government's stockpile should be made only on orders from C.J. Mackenzie, who would be acting as the Government's agent. The system was soon put to the test. Eldorado received an order for 7½ tons of uranium nitrate and uranium oxide from the Soviet Union. The Company was duly instructed to inform the prospective Russian purchasers that their order could not be filled.

On 27 January 1944, the Government expropriated the shares of the Eldorado Mining and Refining Company, which thus became a Crown company with its existing officers continuing their jobs as public servants. In announcing this step in the House of Commons, Howe pleaded that no one question the Government's action 'in the interests of military secrecy'; despite his plea, groups of discontented shareholders both in Canada and in the United States, feeling themselves short-changed by the purchase price of $1.35 a share, insisted upon an official investigation of the transaction. This got them nowhere, but widespread publicity about 'Canada's secret mine' was the outcome. The nature of the secret remained undisclosed, at least in 'investment circles,' but in London Sir John Anderson became agitated by the loose talk which he feared would cost lives. 'I understand the reasons for which he was obliged to make the statement on the subject in the Canadian House of Commons,' Anderson wrote to Malcolm MacDonald. 'I hope that he will be successful in his efforts to avoid any further publicity or discussion...' He was particularly concerned that the American authorities, 'who are very security minded on this subject, may feel apprehensive,' and suggested that Howe would be well advised to explain and defend his action before the Combined Policy Committee created by the Quebec Agreement on 19 August 1943.* MacDonald forwarded this somewhat querulous communication to Howe without comment. 'We are doing everything possible to restrict discussion,' Howe replied on 8 February 1944, 'and considering the rather drastic action taken, I think that we are meeting with some success.' He would be glad to report on the matter to the Combined Policy Committee. 'Unfortunately, the time and place of meetings of the Combined Policy Committee are so secret that I have never been able to attend a formal meeting.'[15]

A second cause of North Atlantic tangle was the team of British, European, and Canadian scientists assembled in a makeshift laboratory at the University of Montreal.

The Montreal Laboratory originated in the desire of the British atomic energy authorities to locate their experiments in North America where they would be immune to enemy attack and, no less important, closer to the vital secrets being uncovered almost daily by their American counterparts. As between moving to the United States or to Canada, the British preferred Canada 'for a number of reasons,' as Sir John Anderson explained, 'of which the most important is our fear that owing to the concentration of the Americans on the graphite system [we] might not receive a fair share of facilities and encouragement.'[16] Better, therefore, to set up duplicate and, to some extent, rival facilities than to become understudies in an American establishment. Another reason was that the American authorities doubted the political trustworthiness of the British team, many members of which were scientists of European nationalities who had not acquired British citizenship. From every point of view Canada was thought to provide a more hospitable environment in which to work.

On 17 August 1942, the British Government formally proposed to the Canadian that there be created in Canada an Anglo-Canadian joint nuclear research team, with the British scientists hitherto engaged on slow-neutron research with heavy water at Cambridge University coming out *en bloc* to get it going. The Canadians to whom this proposal was put were most receptive. 'I was very keen on the project,' C.J. Mackenzie wrote at the time, 'and thought there could be no objection to it ... Mr Howe thought the same thing.'[17] In retrospect Mackenzie recalled his reaction to have

* See below, 271–2.

been closer to elation than to mere satisfaction: 'I remember how the whole aspect of this particular phase of nuclear research interested and excited me. There's no doubt that much of my enthusiasm for the plan was influenced by the thought that by co-operating with British science, Canada would be getting in on the ground floor of a great technological process for the first time in her history.' A month later H. von Halban, director of the Department of Scientific and Industrial Research, together with a colleague, came to Ottawa to discuss the project with C.D. Howe. 'I remember he [Howe] sat there and listened to the whole thing,' Mackenzie said many years later, 'then he turned to me and asked: "What do you think?" I told him it was a sound idea, then he nodded a couple of times and said: "Okay, let's go." I suppose that was the moment Canada really grew up, scientifically.'[18]

The scheme for organizing and controlling the joint project, for which there existed no recollected precedent, closely followed Mackenzie's conception, which he described in his diary on 25 September 1942:

> The team should work within the National Research Council structure. At the top would be Mr Howe and Mr Malcolm MacDonald representing the Canadian and United Kingdom governments, with responsibilities for decisions on broad policy. The team would work as a separate unit under the President of the NRC, I to have a small group of internal advisers ... I stressed very strongly that we could only have one single authority in matters of policy...[19]

No less crucial was assurance of United States support. Without interchange of scientific intelligence between the Anglo-Canadian and American projects the whole point of the move to Canada would be lost. On 29 September Mackenzie wrote to Vannevar Bush to tell him so. 'It is the opinion of Messrs Howe, MacDonald and myself that it is essential for us, if the project goes through, to have most intimate and sympathetic co-ordination as between your groups and mine.' Bush replied that there was no need to worry on that score. He and his colleagues also believed that 'adequate and frequent interchange would ... be highly desirable,' and looked forward 'to close consultation with you as the matter proceeds.'[20] In the light of what was to come this assurance seems less than ironclad: the history of diplomacy is littered with negotiations wrecked by failure to arrive at a precise understanding of the meaning of 'adequate.' But at the time Bush's promise seemed satisfactory. There was no point in looking for trouble. The parties concerned were friends as well as neighbours. And, after all, there was a war on.

It transpired soon enough that what the Americans, on the one hand, and the British and Canadians, on the other, meant by 'adequate' were two very different things. The principal civilians, Bush and James Conant, had spoken in good faith but security policy was no longer in their hands. The US Army had taken over. It proceeded to apply standards that were stringent and even harsh. On 28 November Conant told Mackenzie that he thought 'the clamping down of the Army on the interchange of information ... in its present form may be a bit extreme,' and proposed an exchange of letters among W.A. Akers of the United Kingdom, Mackenzie, and himself 'setting forth that in our opinion the fundamental principles have been worked over by so many people that it is not correct to suggest that any one group or any one country has any special right on the information to date.[21] That cut little ice with General Groves, whose fetish for security was such as to cause him to withhold information not just from foreign scientists but from his own.* The result was that the first few months of the Montreal Laboratory was what Mackenzie later described as 'a strange period of frustration and uncertainty ... We found it was well nigh impossible to discover exactly what the Americans were planning to do. US security was so tight, we learned even the smallest fact only through some strange process of scientific-circle osmosis.'[22] It was scant consolation to know that American scientists were similarly handicapped.

On 2 December 1942 came the momentous news – restricted, of course, to a very few – that the reactor at Chicago had gone critical. This gave the *coup de grâce* to adequate interchange of information among the three nominally co-operating countries. The Americans were already genuinely apprehensive about the reliability of the British as custodians of top secrets: they were not reassured by the conclusion of an agreement between the United Kingdom and the Soviet Union of September 1942 concerning an exchange of information on weapons research, word of which reached Washington only in December. They were more and more suspicious that Britain's interest in atomic energy derived less from its military than from its civilian application and that her leaders were looking beyond the bomb to post-war industrial use. The success of the Chicago experiment now convinced them that they could, after all, go it alone. On 28 December, President Roosevelt informed Bush that he was about to approve recommendations put to him by his military and scientific advisers drastically curtailing the type and quantity of information to be communicated to Montreal. On 2 January 1943, Conant wrote to Mackenzie to break the bad news, having previously telephoned to say that the letter then on its way 'might sound more harsh than was really intended.'[23]

* 'Immediately upon taking charge, he had ordered each of the many specialized crews in each of the laboratories to keep their colleagues ignorant of their work.' Nuel Pharr Davis, *Lawrence and Oppenheimer* (New York 1968), 144.

To the British the new American restrictions on scientific intelligence came as both a blow and a betrayal. They wanted to protest in the strongest possible terms, and sought to enlist their Canadian colleagues in order to strengthen their case. They were more infuriated than dismayed to discover that the Canadian reaction was markedly different from their own. 'I am not at all sure that their views are right,' Mackenzie wrote on 7 January, following a meeting at which the British authorities had vainly attempted to persuade him to sign a letter to Conant bitterly critical of the new restrictions, 'and I am quite sure that there are other factors in the picture which have not been disclosed. I can't help feeling that the United Kingdom group emphasizes the importance of their contribution as compared with the Americans and this attitude has been one of the real shortcomings of British diplomacy all through the war.'[24] A week later Mackenzie discussed the situation with Howe before leaving for Washington where he was to meet with Conant and Bush. They agreed 'that we should not get into any embarrassing position due to any high power disagreement as between the UK and the US.[25]

Mackenzie's session with the Americans on 18 January confirmed his feeling that their case was better than the British allowed. 'The restrictions which they were putting on the Anglo-Canadian group were no greater,' Bush and Conant assured him,

> than the restrictions they were putting on their own groups. The Army and the higher military [are] quite convinced that secrecy is of extreme importance and unless they take the precautions stated there will be serious probability of leakage ... I gathered the impression that they were particularly apprehensive of discussing all the details and "know-how" with the Montreal group, and that they felt there was no guarantee that the various nationals – French, Australian, Russian, Czechoslovakian, German, Italian, etc. – could be guaranteed for any length of time. I think there is a great deal to be said for their point of view...[26]

Indeed there was. The scientists at the Montreal Laboratory included Alan Nunn May and Bruno Pontecorvo.

Though Mackenzie sided with the Americans, he was determined 'not to become involved' (as he wrote on 20 January) 'in any unpleasant controversy.' That proved to be more easily resolved than realized. Bridges, as Mackenzie now discovered, are made to be walked over. Malcolm MacDonald understood his partiality for the American position and did not blame him for it. But in London, as the British official historian records, it 'smacked of treachery since it seemed desirable to maintain an unbroken Anglo-Canadian front in the face of American intransigence.'[27] Mackenzie, who had in the British view broken it, now became the object of their ill feeling. A further trip to Washington convinced him more than ever that the British were making the worst of a bad case. 'Conant and Bush ... very much annoyed at the suggestion from England that there was unfair play in the American attitude,' Mackenzie wrote after meeting with them on 24 April. 'They are looking upon the thing as a war project which will be utilized in this present conflct and for that reason they are not opposing the restrictions laid down. They told me there was not the slightest chance of Churchill being able to have Roosevelt move in the case, which of course has been my opinion all along...'[28]

It was not merely in a policy sense that Mackenzie was closer to Washington than to London. His proximity to the American capital enabled him to get the American view at first hand, whereas London's was relayed to him by messengers. In May, however, Mackenzie was able to learn the London line directly. On 11 May he was ushered into the office of Sir John Anderson. 'Rather elderly, well-preserved pompous John Bull,' was Mackenzie's unflattering impression of his antagonist.

> He started off telling me what an awful deal they had from the US. I told him he did not understand the US position or feeling – that they were as sure of the justice of their cause as he was. He would not believe me when I assured him the US were going very fast and we were in danger of being left out in the cold. We talked very frankly and he said that if we could not get an agreement with the US we would have to discuss what could be done in Canada. I told him I could give him that answer in a few words. If they broke off with the US we would have to close down as we could get no priorities or any material and our Government would certainly not support a team in Canada to compete with the US.[29]

This confrontation sharpened the issue but failed to clear the air. In the words of the British official historian, 'it simply left a residue of bad feeling and the memory of it rankled on both sides.'[30]

What was happening was a Canadian foreign minister's nightmare – one wherein hinges stick, linchpins snap, and bridges fall into the sea. But Mackenzie King's rest was undisturbed. He knew nothing of these goings-on. 'I never once had an official conference with the Prime Minister,' C.J. Mackenzie recalled afterwards. 'All of my dealings were through C.D.'[31] But Howe, suspect in London as having sold out to the Americans, was at this stage worse than useless as a peacemaker. It was only when Mackenzie King, at Churchill's suggestion, met with Lord Cherwell in Washington that he learned of the breakdown of Anglo-American interchange, and then in a general way and from the British point of view. 'Both the British and Americans have been experimenting on similar lines,' was how he described the situation in his diary on 19 May. 'The latter have made contracts with Canada for some of the raw material and power needed, and are now unwilling to let the British know what they have done. This is because the [US] Army has got hold of the matter. It has been removed from the realm of the scientists into the hands of the Army. They are as difficult about it in their relation with Britain as Stalin has been in telling of what was being done in Russia.'[32] That interpretation was far removed from how it looked to Canadians closer to the trouble.

Stubborn efforts at the summit, where Churchill and Roosevelt played major roles and Mackenzie King none at all, finally brought the quarrelling partners to a better understanding of each other's difficulties. On 8 August 1943 Sir John Anderson informed Mackenzie King that 'he had reached an agreement which he thought the President and Churchill would both sign. It made,' the Prime Minister noted, 'Canada also a party to the development. Much of the *U.* and *H.W.* are in our country.'[33]

The agreement to which Sir John Anderson referred, since known as the Quebec Agreement, was signed in Quebec City on 19 August.* Four of its five provisions recited obligations of the United States and the United Kingdom in regard to 'Tube Alloys' – never to use 'this agency,' i.e., the atomic weapon, against each other, never to use it against third parties without the other's consent, never to communicate information about it to third parties without the other's consent, and to reserve post-war industrial and commercial applications for future negotiation. The fifth provision created a Combined Policy Committee on which the United States was to be represented by its Secretary of War together with Vannevar Bush and James B. Conant, the United Kingdom by Sir John Dill and J.J. Llewellin, and Canada by C.D. Howe. The Combined Policy Committee was designated as the forum through which information and ideas were to be exchanged. So far as 'scientific research and development' was concerned, such exchange was to be 'full and effective.' But information and ideas relating to 'the field of design, construction and operation of large-scale plants' were to be exchanged in accordance with 'such ad hoc arrangements as may, in each section of the field, appear to be necessary or desirable if the project is brought to fruition at the earliest moment.' It remained to be seen how these principles would work out in practice.

The Combined Policy Committee met for the first time on 8 September 1943. The notice was short and the attendance spotty. No one in Washington had alerted Howe, so no Canadian was present. (The Secretary of War himself had had only a few hours' warning.) The haste with which

* The terms of the Agreement remained secret until 1954, when they were disclosed by consent of the two Governments. Its full text is in the *New York Times*, 6 April 1954.

the meeting was set up reflected the impatience of the British scientists anxious to press on with their research. Thus the key to the success of the work of the Committee was the degree to which it got the flow of information and ideas relating to scientific research and development circulating once more. A committee struck at so senior a level was obviously incapable of attending to the work in necessary detail, and the first act of the Combined Policy Committee was to create a subcommittee on interchange. This was a three-man subcommittee on which Richard C. Tolman represented the United States, Sir John Chadwick the United Kingdom, and C.J. Mackenzie Canada. When all three were in agreement they were empowered to act without consulting the CPC.[34]

The subcommittee met for the first time at the Pentagon on 10 September. Mackenzie was present at this meeting, and at a further meeting on 13 September. He took little part in the proceedings as these quickly became an Anglo-American confrontation over whether what the Americans now proposed to release was sufficiently adequate and generous. Mackenzie wanted no part in that argument: he had already had too much. In any case, as the American official historians observe, 'committees were not the answer. The British members could indicate what they were able to bring to the joint effort. They could make tentative arrangements. But they could not speak with finality, for every decision, every assignment of a scientist, had a long-run impact on the British program.'[35]

Mackenzie's concern was the Montreal Laboratory, whose work was being frustrated by the breakdown of interchange between itself and the American programme at the University of Chicago. Neither Groves nor Conant seemed willing to allow the pooling of resources which logic might suggest – Groves out of his fears for security, Conant out of doubt that the heavy-water process was the quickest way to the bomb. 'They might have let the matter drift indefinitely,' write the American official historians, 'had not Chadwick raised it at a Combined Policy Committee meeting on February 17 1944.' 'The English physicist urged the advisability of building a large heavywater pile in Canada to produce plutonium. He recommended that Great Britain and the United States finance it jointly, use the heavy water produced in the United States, and admit Canada to control.'[36] From this proposal eventually emerged Chalk River.

The meeting of the CPC was attended by Mackenzie on behalf of Howe, who was unable to be present. It was Mackenzie's first appearance at the top. 'Stimson is very kindly,' he noted of the chairman, 'gets up and passes cigarettes and is well disposed, but not terribly knowledgeable as to what the show is all about; that is not unnatural,' Mackenzie added charitably, 'as it is quite involved.' He recorded his impressions as follows:

Bush and Conant were against the decision to go on with the full scale. I do not know what is behind it but I can understand that they would not wish to be in the position of providing all of the material, heavy water, etc. and having our group at a small fraction of the cost of any of the American projects produce in quicker time than they results which they had got at such greater effort. I thought Chadwick's handling was not diplomatic in the sense that he was too honest and pointed out that the method proposed in Montreal could not have been done by the Americans until they got heavy water but that now it was the best and the cheapest method and that we could do it in quicker time, all of which if true would put the US crowd in a dangerous position.[37]

With Bush and Conant refusing to accept Chadwick's proposal to proceed immediately with the joint construction of a heavywater plant, the CPC appointed a subcommittee, consisting of Conant, Chadwick and Mackenzie, to consult with specialists in Montreal and Chicago and report back with recommendations. This took seven weeks to accomplish. On 13 April 1944 the subcommittee's analysis came before the CPC. The heavywater process, so the specialists had argued, was not vital to bomb-production: enough plutonium would be made available by the graphite piles at Hanford. On the other hand, the heavywater method held out the prospect of economical production of fissionable materials of great potential significance for post-war industrial application, and should not be neglected altogether. The thing to do, the subcommittee recommended, was to proceed with the construction of a heavywater plant on an experimental basis, reserving the decision as to whether or not to go 'full-scale' until the results of its experiments were known. All this the CPC accepted. 'The meeting was a very good one,' Mackenzie wrote afterwards, 'and apparently everyone is in agreement on the fundamental principles. The presence of Mr Howe added very greatly to the effectiveness and a decision was taken to proceed immediately.'[38]

For the scientists at the Montreal Laboratory it came, in the words of the British official historian, 'in the nick of time. The demoralisation of the Montreal team, which had grown apace before the Quebec Agreement, had in these winter months of 1943–4 become almost complete. The scientists and engineers had been sent to Canada on the understanding that they were to take part in war work of the highest importance but instead their existence appeared merely futile. The team was in abysmally low spirits and had lost any sense of direction.'[39] There was still disappointment among the group that only a pilot pile was to be built at first, but as work on it went forward the initial enthusiasm was rekindled. The arrival in Montreal at the end of April 1944 of J.D. Cockcroft to take charge of the project gave the team the leadership it had lacked. By mid-July the Chalk River site, about 130 miles west of Ottawa, had been selected, and by autumn the pilot pile, known as NRX, designed. It was hoped that the pile would be in operation by the end of the year. It did not go critical until July 1947. By then, of course, the Second World War was over. But there was a Cold War on.

## 'FIRST AND LAST THINGS'

Nothing in the Quebec Agreement, or anywhere else, obliged Canada's allies to inform her leaders in advance that, with the collapse of Nazi Germany, the atomic bomb would be dropped upon Japan. Nonetheless, in recognition of Canada's past contribution to the building of the bomb, and even more in deference to her coming importance as supplier of uranium, Mackenzie King, C.D. Howe, and C.J. Mackenzie were the only persons outside similar inner circles in the United States and the United Kingdom who knew beforehand when and where the bombs would fall.*

The Prime Minister first learned of the possibility of using the bomb against Japan on 3 February 1945; the deadly secret was conveyed to him in Ottawa by the British High Commissioner. On 9 March, visiting the White House, he was told by President Roosevelt that August was the likely date.

The decision to use the bomb against Japan – though whether as demonstration shot or destroyer of cities was not disclosed – was communicated to a full meeting of the Combined Policy Committee at the Pentagon on 4 July. C.D. Howe, who was present, learned of the decision in this way. The next day, back in Ottawa, he told C.J. Mackenzie that 'the main event will take place in the immediate future.' It was natural and proper that Howe should have relayed this deadliest of all secrets to his trusted deputy and friend, but there was as well a special reason why Mackenzie should be informed. There was public relations work to be done, and Mackenzie was the man to do it. 'The Americans have all their press releases ready,' Howe had told him on 5 July, 'and it is going to be a most dramatic disclosure. They are going to tell a great deal about the project in general terms, all the money spent, where they are working, etc. Mr Howe said we must get busy immediately and get our press releases ready as it is the biggest opportunity Canada has ever had to make an important scientific announcement.'[40] The task took most of the month to complete. 'There is a great deal of work to be done,' Mackenzie wrote on 30 July, 'in getting all the three releases – US, UK and Canada – harmonized. We

* Not even General Smuts, who had learned of Tube Alloys in July 1943, had any advance knowledge of its use against Japan. See W.K. Hancock, *Smuts*, II: *The Fields of Force, 1919–1950* (Cambridge 1968), 437.

will probably have three releases, one brief one to be given by Mr Howe, the second one more detailed and probably a third to go into extensive scientific detail.'

Thus preoccupied, Howe and Mackenzie seem to have been spared any painful scruple as the time for the obliteration of Hiroshima and Nagasaki drew inexorably closer. The Prime Minister was less serene. 'It appalls me to think of what may be involved in even attempting its use,' he wrote in his diary on 4 August. 'It makes one very sad at heart to think of the loss of life that it will occasion among innocent people as well as those that are guilty. It can only be justified through the knowledge that for one life destroyed, it may save hundreds of thousands and bring this terrible war quickly to a close.'*

On the morning of Monday, 6 August, shortly after 11, a note from the British High Commission was delivered to C.D. Howe at his office. Written in Malcolm MacDonald's hand was a terse message: 'The thing has gone off.' Howe at once dictated a few words to the Prime Minister, then presiding at the opening session of a Dominion-Provincial Conference. His thoughts far removed from the cataclysmic event which had just taken place, Mackenzie King momentarily construed its reference to a 'bomb' as having to do with a manoeuvre he had performed a few minutes earlier at the expense of the Premier of Ontario; this grotesquely parochial interpretation vanished in seconds as 'I suddenly realized it was the atomic bomb in Japan.'

Anxious not to repeat the gaffe of a few weeks before (when he had inadvertently broadcast a premature announcement of victory in Europe), the Prime Minister sent word out to Howe to check on the authenticity of the news and received in reply the text of the statement which Mackenzie had previously prepared for the occasion. But it was not until he read the ticker-tape report of President Truman's statement that Mackenzie King told the Conference what had happened.

> I told those present that I had a world-shaking announcement to make. I then mentioned in a word the dropping of the atomic bomb. Read Howe's statement and later the paragraph from the ticker ... [I] was listened to in dead silence...[41]

The statement given to the press by C.D. Howe at noon and read to the Conference by the Prime Minister about an hour later disclosed Canada's part in the scientific research and development which had led to the

* Quoted in *Record II*, 448. Mackenzie King's estimate of the ratio of destruction was drastically at variance with that of the planners who were working in the expectation of an exchange of one life for ten, rather than for 'hundreds of thousands.'

dropping of the bomb – the expropriation of Eldorado to secure the supply of uranium ore, the work at the Montreal Laboratory, the pilot plant at Chalk River. Upon the actual detonation it did not dwell. 'An almost incredible feat of destruction' had been performed, but its true significance lay in its evidence, 'which all can appreciate, that the basic problems of the release of energy by atomic fission have been solved, and that the unbelievable large amounts of energy which scientists have long believed to be associated with matter can now be made available for practical use.' Not all its uses are destructive, the statement noted, 'and we may justifiably expect notable achievements along the paths of peace.' Finally, 'it is obvious that until some appropriate methods are devised to control this new source of energy that has been developed it will not be possible to divulge the technical processes of production or of military application.'[42]

At the end of the day Mackenzie King brooded on its momentous event. 'Naturally it created mixed feelings in my mind and heart. We were now within sight of the end of the war with Japan ... We now see what might have come to the British people had German scientists won the race. It is fortunate,' he added, 'that the use of the bomb should have been upon the Japanese rather than upon the white races of Europe.'* Building the bomb had been 'referred to as the greatest achievement in science. I think it was an equally great achievement in secrecy – a tremendous secret to have kept over four years.' (He did not yet know that this self-congratulation was premature.) He confessed to feeling 'a little concerned about how Russia may feel, not having been told anything of this invention or of what the British and the US were doing in the way of exploring and perfecting the process.'[43]

Years later, C.J. Mackenzie was asked if he had not experienced some emotion – a twinge of guilt, perhaps – on learning that the apparatus which he had helped create had done its job of killing and maiming a quarter of a million people. 'I don't remember feeling anything special,' was his frank reply. 'It's difficult to be philosophical when you're in action. And you must remember we were all out for blood at that particular time. I didn't have to ponder the rights or wrongs of the bomb. It wasn't our baby in Canada.'[44]

No Canadian had given much, or any, thought to the problems the atomic bomb would create for the security and stability of the post-war world.

* The reader of *Record II* will find this reflection rendered on p. 451 by a row of four small dots. The significance of the omission is discussed in James Eayrs, *Greenpeace and Her Enemies* (Toronto 1972), 'Clio and Jack.'

By 1944, Roosevelt, Churchill, and Smuts were giving them anxious thought.* But Mackenzie King was otherwise preoccupied, principally over conscription. C.D. Howe and C.J. Mackenzie, to the extent that they reflected on the future of atomic energy, were concerned to imagine its effects upon industrial development rather than upon international politics. No Canadian counterpart of the Danish physicist Niels Bohr spent his time 'haunting the offices and anterooms of those who had political power or access to it' in the attempt to inspire a vision 'of the change in international relations ... which the atomic bomb must bring.'[45] Nor did the Post-Hostilities Planning Committee consider the political consequences of atomic energy; all its members worked in ignorance of Tube Alloys, and their memoranda necessarily took no account of how the international system for which they planned would be changed on 6 August 1945. C.D. Howe's statement of that date that the Canadian Government had 'studies under way ... as to how future control of production and use of atomic bombs may be achieved' was incorrect. All such studies followed Hiroshima. They did, however, follow quickly.

The first step in working out a policy for controlling the atom was to ascertain from knowledgeable scientists the relevant technical information, of which the diplomatic community as yet knew nothing, upon which any soundly conceived proposals would have to be based. Was the secret of the bomb likely to be preserved for any length of time? Or would other countries, friendly and otherwise, soon find it out? Assuming the secret lost, was the process of converting theoretical knowledge into actual manufacture such as to make it likely that only a very few countries could make atomic bombs even if they knew how? Was uranium the sole form of fissionable material? Where was it to be found?

Questions such as these were put to C.J. Mackenzie in September 1945, with instructions to furnish the Government as quickly as possible with their best available answers, along with answers to any others the scientists might wish to raise. Drawing on the accumulated expertise of wartime, Mackenzie soon had the work in hand. By October the Department of External Affairs, despite a belated beginning, had formulated proposals for the international control of atomic energy which, for technical sophistication no less than imaginative sweep and grasp, bear comparison with those of any government. 'How strange it is,' Mackenzie King mused on

* Roosevelt more than Churchill, and Smuts more than either. At the moment of the Allied invasion of Western Europe, Smuts had written to Churchill urging him to give highest priority to the problem of post-war atomic energy control; Churchill, grimly following the progress of the Allied armies after D-Day, had a somewhat different timetable. See Margaret Gowing, *Britain and Atomic Energy, 1939–1945* (London 1964), 355–6.

11 October after perusing some of the papers, 'that I should find myself at the very centre of this problem, through Canada possessing uranium, having contributed to the production of the bomb, being recognized as one of the three countries to hold most of the secrets and ... having more in my possession of [knowledge] of the Russian system of espionage ... than anyone living excepting the men whose duty it is to keep me informed...'[46]

Canada's policy was outlined for the Prime Minister in a memorandum prepared as background material for his forthcoming discussions with Attlee and Truman by L.B. Pearson. This document set out the five major assumptions underlying the Government's approach to atomic energy control.

The first was that the atomic bomb should be considered not as the latest weapon in the development of military technology since men began to fight with clubs, but rather as what Pearson called 'something revolutionary and unprecedented; a new departure in destruction.' The second was that the bombs dropped on Japan would appear, in the absence of effective international control, not as the ultimate weapon but only as its forerunner. 'Even more devastating bombs are being or could be developed,' Pearson noted, 'which will be to the present bomb as a machine-gun to a breech-loader.' The third assumption was that the secret of the bomb could not and would not be kept for long; within five years the Russians would know all about it. The fourth was that any major industrial power with access to nuclear technology could manufacture nuclear weapons. Finally, any country in the world would one day be brought within range of atomic attack by nuclear-armed rockets travelling immense distances with startling accuracy. No one would be immune.

From these assumptions – read in retrospect they seem remarkably far-sighted – Canada's policy followed. It opted decisively for international, indeed for supranational, control. A 'national solution' was a contradiction in terms. Leaving atomic technology to the traditional rivalries of nation-states would result in 'the most bitter and disastrous armament race ever run. Like every other armament race in history, it would follow the same course, of fear, suspicion, rivalry, desperation and war; only in this case the war would probably mean national suicide.'

This did not mean that the three states temporarily privy to the secrets of the atom should unconditionally surrender them to any interested party. Rather it meant that they should exploit their momentary monopoly so as to bring the terrible new weapon securely under control – so securely that never again could it be used unilaterally in the interests of a single country. The knowledge now possessed by the United States, the United

Kingdom, and Canada could be traded advantageously for a system of international control under the United Nations. Such an offer, put forward in good faith, could be rejected only by those governments whose motives were malign. No harm could come from such an offer being made. If accepted, well and good; if rejected, the world would at least be alerted to the presence of a hostile power.

From this general argument were derived certain key principles which, in Pearson's view, should be embodied in any effective international agreement. National manufacture and use of atomic weapons should be banned. All existing atomic weapons ought to be destroyed, or transferred to the United Nations as trustee. All basic scientific knowledge about nuclear energy should be pooled as required. An international commission of scientists of world stature and repute should be charged by the United Nations to make periodic inspection of all national laboratories, industries, raw materials, and every form of technical development in nuclear physics, and to report their findings annually to the General Assembly.[47]

Pearson's memorandum on atomic energy control deserves a place among the great diplomatic state papers; in its qualities of analysis and prescience* it ranks with Sir Eyre Crowe's of 1 January 1907, George Kennan's of 22 February 1946. Pearson's bore the date 8 November 1945, and had been hastily prepared in response to Truman's decision, totally unheralded in Ottawa, to meet a few days hence in Washington with the Prime Ministers of the United Kingdom and Canada. Mackenzie King had indeed learned of this development while shipboard bound for Europe – the news was brought to him by an itinerant don† – and cut his visit short so as to hasten back to North America, arriving at the venue of the meeting on 10 November. Other Canadians present were Pearson, Norman Robertson, Hume Wrong, C.J. Mackenzie, and C.D. Howe.

Of this entourage, only Pearson (as ambassador) accompanied Mackenzie King when the presidential yacht *Sequoia* bore the three heads

* Pearson had been even more prescient eleven years earlier: 'Consider the release of atomic energy as a destructive agency. We are told that a drop of water contains sufficient of such energy to run a motor car continuously for twenty years. If that energy is ever released (and scientists are hopeful that it will be in the near future) and applied to destructive purposes, we would doubtless have world peace, because the world would be blown to bits.' 'To a Church Group in Ottawa,' 11 April 1934, quoted in Lester B. Pearson, *Words and Occasions* (Toronto 1970), 14.

† D.W. Brogan. 'I well remember one day when the loudspeaker went on and President Truman announced that he, the Prime Minister of Great Britain (Mr Attlee) and the Prime Minister of Canada had called a conference on the problem of the atomic bomb. When I gave this news to Mackenzie King he exploded. "This is the first I have heard of it".' Sir Denis Brogan, 'A Balliol Man,' *The Spectator*, 2 August 1968.

of government down the Potomac River for their first face-to-face talk on atomic energy. It was the morning of Sunday, 11 November – Armistice Day. Pearson recalls that the party went below and sat around the large circular table, covered with green baize, at which President Truman on less weighty occasions played poker with his friends.

I sat beside Mr King. Lord Halifax sat beside Mr Attlee. Mr Truman had with him his Secretary of State, Mr Byrnes, and Admiral Leahy. At one point Mr Truman said, "Now, we will go around the table, and I'll ask everybody's opinion as to what we should do about the bomb." This was the first time I had ever been asked by a head of state to express my views, and in the presence of my Prime Minister, on such a vital subject. I was a little diffident about saying anything. But not much was needed. All I had to say was, "There's only one thing to be done, and that's to get in touch with other powers, especially the USSR, which will become a nuclear power shortly, and draft an agreement for international control of this new destructive force. If the United States is willing to give up national control of the nuclear weapon, when they alone have it, their good faith should be beyond doubt." That was the general feeling of the group...[48]

Following two more days of talk the principals agreed that they should draft, sign, and make public a joint Declaration on Atomic Energy. Each with his advisers was to try his hand at a version and out of these efforts a final product, acceptable to all, would be prepared. The Canadians decided not to complicate this process by a comprehensive statement of their own; they would concentrate instead on those points to which they might make the most useful contribution. The British (in the words of the American official historians) 'covered the entire subject. Their version was more eloquent than the Americans in depicting the dilemma that confronted mankind, but in content it was substantially the same.'[49] On 14 November – the fourth day of discussion – Mackenzie looked over the United States draft. 'Lots of good ideas,' he commented, 'but ... a badly drafted document lacking coherence, etc. I am quite sure that the ideas came largely from Bush. During the morning Pearson, Robertson, Hume Wrong and the PM all were busy working over the draft and the house was saturated with the atmosphere of business as there is a final meeting of the Big Three this afternoon for a final draft.'[50] But there were too many cooks and they were spoiling the broth. That afternoon the conference designated Bush, Anderson, and Pearson as a drafting committee. 'Taking parts of each of the three texts, adding some language here and there, they had a composite draft ready' by 6 o'clock that evening. The plan had been for the three leaders to consider this version the following morning but at the last moment they decided to finish up that night. 'There was nothing to do but take the one copy and join their chiefs and the foreign secretaries in the President's study. It was ten-thirty. For an hour and a half the discussion proceeded. Bush acted as secretary, pencilling the changes in his barely legible scribble. Finally, he read the draft aloud, making a few final corrections as he went. Now there was complete agreement ... [It was] well past midnight...'[51]

The next day, the agreed Declaration was signed by the two Prime Ministers and the President at the White House, shortly after 11 AM. The President read it out to the press while (according to one observer) 'Attlee and King sat slumped in their chairs, looking up only occasionally and blinking eyes that struck reporters as bloodshot.'[52] It was not that they had dined well, it was that they had worked hard.

The Declaration made three main points. It proclaimed its signatories' 'willingness, as a first contribution, to proceed with the exchange of fundamental scientific information and the interchange of scientists and scientific literature' in atomic energy research 'for peaceful ends with any nation that will fully reciprocate.' It announced that they would not share with other nations 'the specialized information regarding the practical application of atomic energy' until such time as 'effective enforceable safeguards against its use for destructive purposes can be devised.' It called for the creation 'at the earliest practicable date' of 'a Commission ... under the United Nations Organization' to formulate proposals for international control.

Canada made two contributions to this statement.* One was to place the proposal to create a commission after the proposals of the principals, so as to avoid any impression that they might be passing the buck to the United Nations. The other was to attach the reference to their decision not to share the secrets of atomic weapons production to their promise to share them when international control was assured, so as to avoid any impression that the conferees conceived their responsibilities exclusively in negative terms. These contributions are not major but they are not unimportant.

On 17 November, C.J. Mackenzie was asked 'to attend a full meeting of the Cabinet where the PM reported on the Washington trip on the atomic bomb proceedings. He handles these things very astutely and used this simple agreement ... as a vehicle for exposing the whole project with its twenty million dollar cost to the Cabinet.'[53] The project in question was

* 'Mackenzie King's diaries for the period from November 10 to December 31, 1945, could not be found after his death, despite repeated searches through all his papers.' (*Record III*, 96.) Until this missing evidence – misplaced, stolen, or destroyed: the hypothesis that Mackenzie King wearied of his daily chore of diary-keeping may safely be dismissed – is restored, no definitive account of Canada's contribution is possible.

the NRX reactor, still slowly and painfully taking shape at Chalk River.

One month later the Prime Minister presented the Declaration on Atomic Energy to Parliament, so providing the House of Commons with its first opportunity to debate atomic energy policy. Mackenzie King's speech was worthy of the occasion. Major portions of it had been prepared from notes drafted by Norman Robertson. Robertson normally detested any form of rhetoric or hyperbole, but confessed to his chief that he had found it 'difficult to avoid the use of apocalyptic language, for we are concerned with the first and last things.'

The Prime Minister began by recounting to the House the events by which Canada had been drawn into the development of atomic energy and recounted Canada's role in its development. He recited the assumptions underlying the Government's approach to its international control: the monopoly of raw materials and expertise necessary to produce atomic weapons was a temporary monopoly; 'even with international measures of supervision and control, it will be but a matter of time before all processes are known to practically all nations.' He recounted his discussions in Washington with Attlee and Truman and set out the terms of their joint Declaration. He then divulged his (and Robertson's) reflections on the nature of the problem posed by nuclear weapons and on the direction in which a solution should be sought. The problem was political. Its solution was some form of world government.[54] Seldom did Mackenzie King miss an opportunity to recite from *Industry and Humanity* where it suited his argument (and sometimes when it did not); but he missed it now. A passage from that early work, written in 1918, prefigured precisely the human condition in the atomic age:

> Who can say the extent to which the application of scientific knowledge and the inventions of science have been devoted to augmenting and perfecting means of human slaughter, on land, and sea and in the air? ... Surely, Industry is something other than was intended by those who contributed to its creation, when it can be transformed into a monster so demoniacal as to breed a terror unparalleled in human thought, and bring desolation to the very heart of the human race.[55]

The scene now shifts from Washington to Moscow. Byrnes and Bevin, somewhat to their surprise, succeeded in obtaining the Soviet Government's ready assent to the United Nations atomic energy commission proposed in the Truman-Attlee-Mackenzie King statement of 15 November 1945. On 27 December the three foreign ministers issued a communiqué which announced their intention to invite the two other Permanent Members of the Security Council, together with Canada, to sponsor a resolution to create the commission at the first session of the General

Assembly. Pearson, who read the communiqué in Washington, considered it 'a very considerable achievement, even though it does not commit the USSR to anything except the establishment of the Commission with agreed terms of reference.' He was worried lest Canada's role as sponsor would inhibit any vigorous Canadian effort to shape the proposed commission to her liking. 'Some of the radio commentators,' he reported to Ottawa, 'speak as if international control of atomic energy is already established. That battle remains to be fought, but nevertheless a good beginning has been made.'[56]

On any fair application of functionalism* Canada was entitled to membership on the proposed commission. Sponsorship would be an aid to membership but did not guarantee it. 'It is essential,' Mackenzie King stressed in a note to Malcolm MacDonald, 'that Canada as one of the sponsors for the establishment of the Commission should be assured of representation on it, whether or not Canada is elected to one of the non-permanent seats on the Security Council.' The work of the Commission was likely to continue for quite some time and it was therefore undesirable for the roster to be changed periodically as new members were elected to the Security Council. Membership of the commission should therefore not be identical to membership of the Council. The Prime Minister proposed that Canada and the Five Permanent Members, together with 'at least one Latin American country and at least one European country,' should be the members of the Commission.[57] The Commission created by the General Assembly on 24 January 1946 consisted of the members of the Security Council, and Canada.

Deriving from stature as a potential nuclear power rather than from status on the Security Council (Canada's bid for Council membership had failed a few days earlier†), this position was unique and, in one respect, anomalous. What was to happen if atomic energy came before the Council? The Department of External Affairs considered that a claim should at once be staked to the right to participate in any Security Council discussion of atomic energy, under Article 31 of the Charter. C.D. Howe disagreed. 'I see no purpose,' he wrote to Norman Robertson on 9 February, 'in making such a demand at this time.' It was highly unlikely, he argued, that the Security Council would fail to follow the recommendations of the Atomic Energy Commission, its membership being identical except for Canada, but if it did Canada could then invoke Article 31. In any event, 'our policies will be ably stated to the Security Council through our partners, both of whom are members.'[58] This advice was not accepted. Instead, the Government sought out, and obtained, British and American assent to the right of Canada's representative to join the Security Council

* See above, 161–2.

† See above, 166–7.

for any discussions of atomic energy. It was the first time since 1942 that Howe's views on any aspect of nuclear policy were overruled, and marked – as he noted wryly on another occasion – 'the entry of diplomacy into atomic bomb discussions.'[59]

One hurdle remained. The British and Americans had agreed: would the Russians? No serious difficulty was anticipated. The Soviet Union had accepted without cavil Canada's membership on the Commission; there seemed no good reason why it should object to Canada's presence at the Council to discuss, but not to vote on, atomic energy matters. When, however, the Canadian representative on the Commission formally applied to the President of the Security Council for permission to participate, the Soviet delegate on the Council sought to employ his veto and would have done so but for an adroit procedural manoeuvre on the part of Evatt of Australia. The episode was not without value, the Canadian representative reported, trying to put the best face on it, for 'Gromyko's effort to exercise the veto against us has undoubtedly served to stimulate those who would question the irresponsible use of the veto by the Russians.'[60]

Having become a member of the Commission Canada had next to nominate her delegate. It would not do to wait much longer, the Government had been warned on 20 March: the United States had appointed Bernard Baruch a couple of days before and already he had assembled a 'substantial number of "alternates and co-workers".'[61] Most of the other members had also nominated, some choosing diplomats, others politicians, others still scientists. Mackenzie King minuted: 'McNaughton – all 3.'

On 7 June, a week before the Commission's first meeting, General McNaughton received his provisional instructions. 'The United States,' he was reminded, 'will call the tune in the Atomic Energy Commission. As the only possessor of atomic weapons, as the leader in the construction of production plants, and as the most powerful industrial nation in the world it is the policy pursued by the United States which will in the end be decisive.' That did not mean that Canada would 'slavishly follow' the American line. But it did mean that her government 'did not wish to go further than the United States and United Kingdom Governments are preparing to go in advocating international control.' The General was warned 'not to take any step to commit the Canadian Government on any issue of importance without further reference to the Government.'[62] The 'Riddell incident' still cast its long shadow over the conduct of Canadian diplomacy.*

* Walter Riddell, as Canadian Advisory Officer at the League of Nations, had on his own initiative recommended the imposition of sanctions against Mussolini's Italy in 1935, only to be publicly repudiated by his Government. See James Eayrs, *In Defence of Canada*, II, *Appeasement and Rearmament* (Toronto 1965), 16–27.

On 13 June 1946, General McNaughton received a telephone call from Bernard Baruch. 'He said,' McNaughton reported to Ottawa after their conversation,

that he had been wanting to get in touch with Cadogan and myself to tell us, in advance, personally, the plan which he had formed for control of atomic energy ... Unfortunately this had not been possible ... However, he said he had gathered ... that I was in close agreement with what he had in mind, namely, the creation of an International Development Authority to be endowed with every power, which would own atomic energy material from the mine to the ultimate product (in his own words, from birth to death) ... The conversation concluded on a very friendly note, Mr Baruch expressing pleasure at our prospective association and his confidence in the outcome, which I reciprocated.[63]

The next morning, at the first meeting of the United Nations Atomic Energy Commission, Baruch presented, in a highly dramatic speech, the carefully formulated American proposals for the international control of atomic energy.

The Canadian Government, like other governments, had not been informed in advance of the Baruch Plan. It had been studying carefully the quasi-official proposals embodied in the outline for international control prepared by David E. Lilienthal and Dean Acheson, some features of which were incorporated in the Baruch Plan announced on 14 June. Parts of Baruch's speech, therefore, came to the Canadian Government as a surprise. The most important of these were (a) the provision that the Permanent Members of the Security Council waive their right of veto in disputes involving atomic energy matters, and (b) the provision that sanctions be applied against any state which refused to abide by the rulings of the proposed international atomic energy authority. Two days after Baruch made public the American plan, McNaughton invited some members of the British delegation to dinner to get their reaction to it. 'They expressed the view frankly,' he wrote afterwards, 'that Baruch had made acceptance of international control so clearly contingent upon prior safeguards and commitments, including acceptance of sanctions on the part of other nations, that they were at a loss to know what first step the Commission should take.' The Australian delegation, he noted, was also baffled.[64]

On 19 June, General McNaughton stated the Canadian position. He was the first delegate to speak since Baruch had spoken. He described the Baruch proposals as 'constructive and imaginative,' and announced that he had been authorized by his Government to say that it supported 'the principles on which these proposals have been based. We feel,' he continued, that in his statement Mr Baruch, on behalf of his Government, has given a lead worthy of a great nation, which recognizes its obligations to humanity. We are well aware that proposals so novel and far-reaching will encounter many difficulties...

The plan which Mr Baruch has suggested will need the most careful study. If accepted as a basis of discussion in this Commission, as I hope it will be, we shall have to examine fully its implications with a view to drawing up concrete and detailed recommendations.

The most obvious of the difficulties to which McNaughton referred was the issue of the veto, of which he then spoke frankly:

The Canadian attitude toward the veto power of the five permanent members in the Security Council is that we have never liked it. We accepted it at San Francisco because it seemed the only basis on which the Great Powers could come together to set up the United Nations.

I suggest, however, that at this stage we should not concern ourselves unduly over the procedure whereby the present decisions of the proposed International Atomic Energy Authority should be taken. Rather, I suggest that we should concentrate on the many other aspects of the proposals put forward by the United States representative on which we must reach agreement before the Authority can be brought into being. If we succeed in achieving a meeting of minds on these aspects, we may find that we have established a degree of confidence which will make it much easier than at present to solve this difficult problem. The question of establishing confidence is certainly a vital aspect of our work at this time. The Canadian delegation believes that this can best be promoted by developing specific proposals on the first matter listed in our terms of reference, namely, "for extending between all nations the exchange of basic scientific information for peaceful purposes."[65]

In this way was 'the functional idea'* enlisted in the fight to control the atom.

After McNaughton finished speaking, five other delegates made statements – those of the United Kingdom, China, Brazil, Mexico, and the Soviet Union. Upon what Andrei Gromyko would have to say everything depended. Unlike Baruch, Gromyko eschewed all rhetoric in his statement. There should be signed at once an international convention prohibiting the production and use of atomic weapons, and pledging their owners – that is, the United States – to destroy all existing bombs within three months of the day the convention went into effect. Thus far his speech had not referred to the Baruch Plan. But then, when he had almost finished, he stated flatly that his government rejected any tampering with the veto. In two meetings, the Atomic Energy Commission appeared to have produced one result – that of instant deadlock.

On 26 June, L.B. Pearson met in New York with General McNaughton

* See above, 161–2.

and George Ignatieff, McNaughton's External Affairs adviser, 'regarding the impasse,' as Pearson reported afterwards to the Prime Minister,

> which seems to be developing in the Atomic Energy Commission, as the United States and USSR confront each other with their own plans and procedures, which they show no disposition to alter or compromise. It appears that Baruch is almost as inflexible as Gromyko himself, and there is not any evidence that the State Department has much influence over him and his associates.

There was one way, he thought, by which the log-jam might be broken. A convention along the lines of the Soviet proposal outlawing the use of atomic energy for destructive purpose – a sort of nuclear Kellogg-Briand Pact – could be signed at once. This would, in Pearson's view, 'meet the Russians up to a point and certainly could do no harm, though, of course, without further measures outlawry would be of no value.' The immediate destruction of all atomic weapons could not be accepted. However, since 'the Russians themselves do not include international sanctions in their own plan, but seem to rely on good faith and national punishment, they could not logically argue that the proposal for prohibition without immediate destruction of bombs was valueless.' McNaughton had seemed interested in this approach, 'and may attempt to develop it further.'[66] The stumbling block was not the Soviet Union but the United States. On 5 July Gromyko asked Ferdinand Eberstadt of the American delegation why it was unwilling to sign a convention outlawing atomic weapons. 'Eberstadt explained ... that such a convention would not fulfill the mandate of the General Assembly. It would accentuate international suspicion. The Kellogg Pact had demonstrated the ineffectiveness of such treaties.'[67]

The rival plans were now on the table. The Atomic Energy Commission was working through three committees: a Control Committee, dealing with general questions of policy; a Legal Committee, concerned with the preparation of drafts; and a Scientific and Technical Committee. It was McNaughton's view 'that we should now try to seek an area of agreement by discussion in committees of detailed aspects of plan and not to continue emphasizing differences in prepared statements which separate the United States and Soviet positions.'[68] This tactic, however commendable in spirit, only concealed the depths of division. The Committees 'are all moving very slowly,' Hume Wrong reported on 1 August,

> and unless some change in the Soviet attitude takes place, it seems inevitable that a deadlock will be reached before very long. The central problem of course arises from Gromyko's insistence that the manufacture, use and possession of nuclear weapons should be banned, coupled with his refusal as yet to admit the need for any special system of international control. His position

seems to be that while admitting the need for certain safeguards, he wants the Security Council to be responsible for dealing with enforcement – a position which of course would preserve intact the Soviet veto in the Security Council.

The scientists have run into difficulties of a different nature in considering the application of atomic energy for peaceful purposes, and technical aspects of control. A number of them are forming the opinion that these matters cannot be usefully discussed without the revelation of important information which is still secret, and the result is that they have not made any real progress...

The general tactics which our representatives are pursuing – and I gather that both the Americans and the British agree with this line – are to seek to avoid a showdown with the Russians for the present, partly in the hope that Gromyko may become able to do something more than repeating his instructions over and over again, and partly because, if it does come to a showdown and the presentation of majority and minority reports, it would be better politically that this should occur after the Paris Conference and not at any rate until shortly before the General Assembly meets on September 23.[69]

Under the Commission's rules of procedure its chairmanship was due to pass to the representative of Canada during the period 14 August to 14 September. On his first day as chairman, General McNaughton met in Ottawa with the members of the Canadian Government's Advisory Panel on Atomic Energy which had been created by a Cabinet decision of 27 March 1946. In addition to McNaughton and Ignatieff, the meeting was attended by Hume Wrong, C.J. Mackenzie, George C. Lawrence (the senior Canadian physicist at Chalk River), and one or two others. McNaughton outlined to the members of the Panel the events leading to the impasse between the American and Soviet delegates, and sought their guidance on what line to follow as Chairman of the Commission during the forthcoming month. Two suggestions emerged from the ensuing discussion. One was that the Canadian delegation should stress whenever possible its view that atomic energy was not a weapon like any other and therefore justified special treatment and procedures even beyond those of the Security Council. The other was to pursue wherever possible a functional rather than a political approach. The second of these suggestions was agreed to, and it was in keeping with it that on relinquishing his chairmanship General McNaughton proposed that the next step the Commission should take was to investigate, through its Scientific and Technical Committee, 'the safeguards required at each stage in the production and use of atomic energy for peaceful purposes.'[70]

These tactics, designed not so much to secure an agreement as to postpone a breakdown, worked only so long as American patience held out. On 29 August, Baruch told McNaughton and Ignatieff 'how anxious he was not to force the pace. He did not want to drive Gromyko into a corner. He was convinced that a slower, educative technique was best; the present emphasis on the work of the Scientific and Technical Committee manifested this conviction concretely.'[71] For the Canadians such an attitude was splendid so long as it lasted. But it could not, and did not, last forever. In fact it did not last a fortnight. By 10 September Baruch met with his advisers to consider whether the time had not now arrived for a showdown. He did not want people to think that the Commission was responsible for inaction. 'If a temporizing procedure was in order, it might better be carried out by the bureaucrats.' To go on as the delegation had been doing in the absence of further contingency planning left the American position vulnerable to Soviet attacks upon it. These could come at any time, initiative would be lost, the results could be damaging. A letter embodying all this, and more, was prepared and sent by Baruch to President Truman on 17 September. There was no response from the White House. On 29 October occurred what Baruch had feared. The Soviet foreign minister addressed the General Assembly and attacked both Baruch and his plan which, he charged, 'proceeds from the desire to secure for the United States of America the monopolistic possession of the atomic bomb.' To these negative remarks Molotov had shrewdly joined a positive proposal. He called for the general reduction of all armaments, nuclear and conventional. When Molotov sat down, the leader of Canada's delegation, L.S. St Laurent, went to his side, shook his hand, 'and assured him that there was no reason why Canada could not live on as amicable terms with her neighbour across the Arctic as with her neighbour to the south.'[72]

Baruch had foreseen, and tried to forestall, this diversion. He had warned against allowing the Soviet Union to seize the initiative in disarmament from the United States. He had recommended combining the problems of atomic energy control with those of conventional disarmament, as Molotov was now proposing. All to no avail. The man already known as adviser to presidents did not care to have advice rejected, especially when rejection made him look like a fool. He was furious. Gone beyond recall was his patience of the autumn weeks. He determined to press for a showdown.

The White House gave its assent on 5 November, and the machinery for showdown was quickly set in motion. The Atomic Energy Commission met in plenary session on 13 November – the first such meeting since July – and adopted (Poland and the Soviet Union abstaining) Baruch's motion requiring its Scientific and Technical Committee to complete its report by 20 December, so that the Commission could submit recommendations to the Security Council by the end of the year. At its next meeting, on 5 December, Baruch placed before its members the draft of what, in the view of his delegation, the report of the Scientific and Technical Committee should say. 'The outline here presented,' Baruch declared, 'is the bone and sinew of any effective international control that may be, that shall be, that must be established if the civilized world is not to be ended.' The United States delegation, 'in the long and protracted series of some seventy meetings of this Commission and its various committees, studying all phases of the subject, [had] found inherent and inevitable in any treaty that is to be written covering this subject three major elements: (1) the erection of an international authority which shall effectively prevent the manufacture and use of atomic bombs for war purposes, and which shall develop the use of atomic energy for social gain; (2) the right of free and full international inspection in support of these purposes; (3) the definite agreement that once a treaty becomes effective, providing for deterrents against offences and punishments for offenders, there can be no "veto" to protect wilful violators or to hamper the operations of the international authority.' He did not ask the Commission to discuss or vote on his proposals at that time. But he did ask that a meeting be called so that 'the position each nation takes on them may be recorded in this Commission's report, which must be drafted by 20 December and presented to the Security Council by 31 December.'[73]

The Canadians were now in a quandary. Statesmanship is the constructive acceptance of the inevitable. But was showdown inevitable? If it was, a case could be made for doing all that could be done to isolate the Soviet Union and expose its obstructionist tactics to the court of world opinion. If it was not, there was still scope for mediation. The Government decided it was not.

Its delegates at the General Assembly were accordingly instructed to speak in a spirit of conciliation.* On 4 December, St Laurent drew a distinction between the use of the veto in the Security Council to block any plan for controlling atomic energy, and its use in the control machinery once a plan had been approved. The former was obviously legitimate, the latter just as obviously illegitimate. It seemed to him, St Laurent stated, more out of hope perhaps than conviction, that Molotov agreed with this. 'As I understood the honourable delegate of the Soviet Union, he envisages

* They did so in the Political Committee on 28 November, 30 November, and 4 December. The texts of these statements are reprinted in *Canada. The United Nations, 1946: Report on the Second Part of the First Session of the General Assembly of the United Nations held in New York, October 23–December 15, 1946*, Department of External Affairs, Ottawa, Conference Series No. 3, 1946, 183–92.

that this international commission will be clothed with powers, which they will exercise autonomously and which will enable them to take the proper measures to make us feel that the international obligations are being respected everywhere.'[74] Molotov, as it turned out, envisaged nothing of the kind. But if mediation was to triumph so terribly close to midnight it was necessary to proceed as if he did, and to display in the cause of nuclear control what St Laurent called 'a holy obstinacy.'[75]

In the chairman of the Canadian delegation to the United Nations Atomic Energy Commission the quality of holy obstinacy ran very deep. It served its purpose now. At the Commission's next meeting, on 17 December, McNaughton again counselled against rushing ahead. 'No final conclusions can reasonably be drawn on matters of such importance ... without the most thorough consideration and discussion.' He spoke as well of 'the need for precision in the use of words ... Unless we weigh our words carefully we run the risk of committing ourselves to statements capable of being misconstrued.' He welcomed the proposals placed before the Commission by Baruch on 5 December as being based on principles which 'accord with the views of the Canadian delegation.' But in his recitation of those principles he pointedly omitted the third of Baruch's 'three major elements' – that which insisted on the waiving of the veto.[76]

For the American delegation McNaughton was now clearly a trouble-maker. On the evening before the showdown meeting of 20 December, Baruch's deputy, Ferdinand Eberstadt, conferred with McNaughton and Ignatieff to try to preserve a united front. Their meeting lasted until 3 AM. The Americans were eager for a showdown with the Russians but not with the Canadians. They accepted McNaughton's plan to propose, when the Commission met in a few hours' time, an amendment to Baruch's resolution of 5 December.

McNaughton's amendment was a bid for time. It required the Commission to express its approval of the principles on which Baruch's resolution had been based, rather than to accept its findings in all their detail. 'When I got to the meeting,' McNaughton recalled years afterwards, 'Gromyko, shrewd as a pet fox, read it in my face that I was going for Baruch. He could see that my papers were not ready, and so he took the floor and talked nonsense, really nonsense, until he saw that I had sorted the notes. Then he said: "I now yield the floor to the representative of Canada," and sat down.'[77] The vote on McNaughton's amendment was 10 to nil in favour, Poland and the Soviet Union abstaining. 'I want to make it quite clear,' Oscar Lange, the Polish delegate, explained, 'that the reason for my abstention is that I want to show the same conciliatory spirit to the representative of Canada as he showed to the representative of Poland.'[78] Gromyko had as much reason to be gracious and more to be grateful, but graciousness and gratitude were not his strong points. 'I said I did not wish to take part in the vote,' was his gruff explanation. Gromyko never had McNaughton figured out.*

The Canadian delegation had thus bought time – though not much time – to make one last drive to common ground. A secret session of the Working Committee had been called for 27 December. That left five days, not counting Christmas Day, to get Baruch to change his mind. They had for this purpose their powers of friendly persuasion, together with a carefully reasoned memorandum showing that waiving the veto was unnecessary. The memorandum had been drafted by Escott Reid,[79] and was circulated among the members of the Commission at its meeting on 20 December. These are its key paragraphs:

47 Article 51 of the Charter of the United Nations states that "nothing in the present Charter shall impair the inherent right of individual or collective self-defence if an armed attack occurs against a Member of the United Nations, until the Security Council has taken the measures necessary to maintain international peace and security." This means that a permanent member of the Security Council cannot protect himself from the consequences of certain types of wrong doing by the exercise of his veto in the Security Council. All he can protect himself against by his veto is the application of sanctions *by the Security Council.* His veto does not protect him, and could not possibly protect him, from condign punishment inflicted on him by his fellow Members of the United Nations.

48 Article 51 would appear therefore to cover the situation which would arise if a permanent member of the Security Council made an armed attack against another Member of the United Nations. However, the Article, by itself, does not cover acts of aggression or threats of aggression which do not constitute armed attack. One such act might be the illicit manufacture of atomic bombs in violation of the international treaties or conventions on the control of atomic energy.

49 However, paragraph 4 of Article 2 of the Charter reads as follows: –

> All Members shall refrain in their international relations from the threat or use of force against the territorial integrity or political independence of any state, or in any other manner inconsistent with the purposes of the United Nations.

* Soviet ideology required Russian diplomats to regard their Canadian colleagues merely as marionettes whose strings were pulled in Washington. Sometimes McNaughton's diplomacy might be so interpreted, but sometimes it ought not to be. A member of the American delegation to the Commission recalls that 'once when McNaughton and Baruch were engaged in quite a violent argument over some point in the plan, I [glanced] at Gromyko and [saw] an extraordinary expression of bewilderment on his face, as though he were trying to figure out whether or not the whole thing was being staged for his benefit.' Frederick Osborn, 'The USSR and the Atom,' *International Organization*, v, 1951, 485.

50 The undertaking in paragraph 4 of Article 2 of the Charter is an undertaking by all the Members of the United Nations – by the permanent members of the Security Council as well as by the other fifty Members of the United Nations.

51 If a permanent member of the Security Council violates its solemn undertaking under paragraph 4 of Article 2, it has violated the most important provision of the Charter of the United Nations. Any such violation would be likely to make other Members of the United Nations feel that *they* are released from *their* obligation under the Charter not to threaten or use force against that delinquent state.

52 The mere existence of the "veto" in the Security Council would make no practical difference. If there came about a situation where it was generally felt that it was necessary to take armed measures against a great power which was threatening the peace of the world, those armed measures would be taken – veto or no veto...

53 Thus, under present circumstances, little would be gained by trying to persuade each of the permanent members of the Security Council to give up its veto over the imposition of military sanctions against a state found to be committing serious violations of the convention or conventions on atomic energy.[80]

*Quod erat demonstrandum*. But not to the satisfaction of the American delegation. 'Baruch quite adamant,' notes one of McNaughton's scribbled memoranda of his urgent consultations with the United States representatives. And another: 'We were not intending to be pushed around.' And still another: 'Eberstadt indicated friendship. No personal feelings had been hurt.' There had evidently been quite a brawl.*

Progress was now harassed from another quarter. Inquiring reporters were on the scent. On 25 December, Thomas J. Hamilton filed a story in the *New York Times* and the Toronto *Globe and Mail* quoting 'sources close to Mr Baruch' as having challenged 'the Canadian view that the abolition of the veto on punishments would make little difference.' An article by Warren Baldwin in the *Globe and Mail* of the same date reported that the 31 December deadline had been agreed to largely in deference to 'the wish of Baruch' and that the Canadian Government was taking the position 'that a matter as critical as the basis for world action on atomic energy is sufficiently important to outweigh all personal feelings.' It also reported a split within the American delegation between those who wanted to press to a showdown and those who felt the Canadians were right to ask for more time. These leaks agitated the principals. 'Hume

* McNaughton Papers. These notes are regrettably too fragmentary to permit reconstruction of the conversations to which they refer. 'Such notes by McNaughton,' his biographer observes, 'were rarely in chronological sequence.' John Swettenham, *McNaughton*, III, *1944–1966* (Toronto 1969), 39.

[Wrong] advises leaving alone,' McNaughton noted after reading Hamilton's despatch. 'Escott [Reid] said things which were not correct. Asked H. to treat as background information.' And on 26 December: 'Press battle continues. Hamilton and Baldwin not liked by the US.'

It was not only by the American delegation that they were not liked. On the morning of 26 December McNaughton was called to the telephone by the Prime Minister of Canada. McNaughton's notes of their conversation are brief but revealing:

> King was worried about newspaper stories of controversy. Does not want impression that Canada against UK and US. Do not defend veto as such. Pearson will come down if needed.[81]

On 27 December the Working Committee met in secret session. McNaughton placed before it a revised version of Baruch's 'findings and recommendations' which were still being carried forward from the Commission's meeting on 5 December. Here was the product of the intensive search for a compromise in which the Canadian and American delegations had been engaged during the past five days. 'The American delegation,' write the official historians of the US Atomic Energy Commission, 'had made some concessions. Eberstadt had worked over the revision with George Ignatieff ... and agreed on a number of textual changes.' But on the issue of the veto the Americans remained firm. The best the Canadians could do was to secure their agreement to a formulation 'less heavily freighted with moral indignation'[82] than Baruch's 'a violator of the treaty should not be protected from the consequences of his wrongdoing by the exercise of any power of veto.' This was now rendered: 'There shall be no legal right, by veto or otherwise, whereby a wilful violator of the terms of the treaty or convention shall be protected from the consequences of violation of its terms.'

The question now was whether to accept or reject the key phrase: 'by veto or otherwise.' Not only the Russians objected to it. Both the British and the French delegates expressed the view that there really was no need to insist upon a specific reference to the veto: the reference to 'legal right' covered the point sufficiently. But Baruch would not hear of this. 'Gentlemen,' he said impressively, 'it is either – or. Either you agree that a criminal should have this right by voting against our position (or you fail to take a stand on the question by refraining from voting), or you vote for this sound and basic principle of enduring justice and plain common sense.' The Working Committee adjourned to mull, during the weekend, what was in effect an American ultimatum.[83]

Left to his own devices it is just possible that General McNaughton would have been tempted to call what he was inclined to regard as an American bluff. But he was not left to his own devices. On the morning of 28 December, the Prime Minister discussed what stand Canada should take with his Secretary of State for External Affairs. 'Both St Laurent and I were wholly at one,' Mackenzie King recorded,

in feeling that Canada should support the American position and that it would be well for Pearson to go to New York to be with McNaughton and the others on Monday. He was to let them know that both St Laurent and myself wished to have the American position supported. As I said to St Laurent, Canada of all countries concerned had the strongest reason for not allowing information concerning the bomb to be disclosed to Russia, unless she would agree not to apply the veto in the case of herself or some friend of Russia's being responsible for starting a conflict against other countries which might lead to a third world war. I pointed out to St Laurent that I thought there should be no misunderstanding as to what Russia's position should be. Much better to have no agreement at all than one which would admit of subterfuges and interpretations that would fail to effect the real purpose of achieving peace. It would be like building a structural piece on quicksand. What was needed was the solid rock of complete truth and understanding.[84]

These instructions were duly conveyed to McNaughton by L.B. Pearson. On 30 December 1946, Canada cast its vote in the Commission in favour of the Baruch Plan and in effect for deadlock.

Deadlock persisted throughout much of 1947, before giving way to discard. In public, at least, General McNaughton remained optimistic, even buoyant. 'There remains,' he conceded in a speech of 30 October 1947, 'a very wide gap between the views of the USSR supported by Poland and those of the rest of the Commission, but I do not think that we should be unduly cast down on that account, and we should certainly not underestimate the value and the significance of the progress which has been made.' He even ventured the hope that 'eventually a way will be found to traverse the opposition of those who presently control the policy of the Soviet.'[85] But on 28 November the Under Secretary of State for External Affairs, L.B. Pearson, reported to the Advisory Panel on Atomic Energy 'that because of the attitude of the USSR, there is no prospect of achieving the effective international control of atomic energy.'[86]

Years later, when the 'solid rock of complete truth and understanding' had still to be located, the atom had still to be controlled, General McNaughton expressed an opinion very different to that of those whose instructions he had been obliged to carry out. The Baruch Plan, he told an interviewer in 1965, was 'insincerity from beginning to end.'[87]

## NORTH ATLANTIC TANGLES II

If atomic energy was not easily brought under international control, it was with no less difficulty shared between the two countries which had collaborated during wartime in its development. To post-war Washington sharing should be done sparingly, if at all. To post-war London sharing was a moral, even a legal, obligation. Here was fertile ground for recrimination. The Canadian Government was anxious to keep clear of it. C.D. Howe especially having been burned once was twice shy. But keeping clear was not going to be easy or even, in some ways, desirable. 'We are the third member of the Combined Policy Committee,' A.D.P. Heeney reminded the Prime Minister on 20 April 1946, 'and a party to the Washington document of November 16th, and it is clearly in our general interest that the difference between the United Kingdom and the United States should be resolved satisfactorily to all concerned.'[88]

It was not only on the Combined Policy Committee* (CPC) that Canada was thrust into the midst of post-war Anglo-American nuclear disputation. She was also involved, however anomalously, in the work of the Combined Development Trust (CDT). This institution came into being on 13 June 1944 with the signing by Churchill and Roosevelt of a 'Declaration of Trust.' Six individuals, appointed and subject to removal by the CPC, were charged with the job of augmenting supplies of the raw materials of atomic energy. These C.D. Howe had sought to confine to uranium – 'I hold the view strongly,' he had written on 17 February 1945, 'that while the Development Trust should attempt to control all Uranium deposits, the Trust should not attempt to control Thorium deposits. The latter material may have doubtful value, and is widely scattered over the earth's surface'[89] – but without success. Canada's membership created, according to the British official historian, 'some uncertainty. In the end Canada willingly agreed that she should not [sign] since the Declaration was governed by the Quebec Agreement which was an Anglo-American document; it was intended, however, that one of the six Trustees should be Canadian.'[90] The Canadian trustee was George C. Bateman.† On 3 June 1944 Howe had written to Bateman as follows:

You are no doubt aware of very secret work being done in the field of radio active materials.

Recently I have been asked to appoint a Canadian Member to a Committee of Six, three to be appointed by the United States, two by Britain, and one by

* See above, 271.

† Mining engineer and friend of C.D. Howe, who had left private enterprise for Ottawa in 1940 to become Metal Controller for Canada.

Canada. The British members of the Committee are Sir Charles Hambro and Mr F.G. Lee. I have nominated yourself as the Canadian member of this Committee ...

I will be greatly obliged if you will accept appointment to this Committee. Canada is not a party to the agreements to be entered into by the Committee but Canada has an interest through being an important source of supply of the material.[91]

On 4 October 1944, Bateman was notified by the American and British co-secretaries 'that the Combined Policy Committee at its meeting on 19th September 1944 formally confirmed your appointment as a Canadian representative among the six members of the Combined Development Trust with effect from the 6th day of July, 1944.'[92]

The future of Policy Committee and Trust came under scrutiny at Washington in mid-November 1945. What was at stake was nothing less than Anglo-American co-operation itself. In the discussions leading to the preparation of the necessary documents the Canadians, who were present for the talks on international control, took little or no part. Anglo-American co-operation was best left to Englishmen and Americans. But in nuclear matters their co-operation necessarily involved Canadian interests, not always to the advantage thereof.

The British and United States delegations drew up between them two documents. One, to be signed by the Prime Ministers and the President, was a brief directive to the Combined Policy Committee, affirming their desire for effective co-operation, agreeing that the CPC and the CDT should continue in 'a suitable form,' and requesting that the CPC recommend appropriate arrangements.[93] This document created no problem for Canada and was duly signed by her Prime Minister.

But there was trouble with its companion. Sir John Anderson, General Groves and their respective assistants had drafted a 'Memorandum of Intention' addressed to the Combined Policy Committee. C.J. Mackenzie read this document on 15 November and did not like what he read.

After dinner I went to the Embassy and saw the draft that had been drawn up by the British and Americans. I observed that as far as Canada was concerned, it was a one-sided bargain that gave all our uranium away and did not provide much assurance of co-operation for our laboratories. It seemed to me that the only thing the British gave was what belonged to Canada and I said I doubted very much that the Minister would approve.[94]

The Minister did not approve. Howe instructed Mackenzie not to sign the Anderson-Groves memorandum.

Its offending paragraphs related to Canada's future relationship with the CDT. They sought to make the Canadian Government a partner within the Trust, with all the commitments and responsibilities, including financial commitments and responsibilities, which partnership implied. They failed to recognize Canada's unique position as supplier of the raw materials of atomic energy and the contribution she had made to its development. 'Canada was the first to acquire all uranium deposits within its borders,' C.D. Howe pointed out for the benefit of L.B. Pearson (who was taking his place at the next meeting of the CPC), 'and perhaps for that reason those forming the Trust were content to proceed with the Trust without asking commitments from Canada. I see no reason why any change in the situation is desirable at this time.' He asked Pearson to press for the re-drafting of the Anderson-Groves memorandum so as to exempt Canadian uranium and thorium from CDT operations, and proposed that Canada's undertaking *vis-à-vis* the CDT be specified as follows:

> Canada will take measures so far as practicable to secure control and possession, by purchase or otherwise, of all deposits of uranium and thorium situated within its area. Canada will develop its deposits and use the product, in the common interest, for scientific research, and military and humanitarian purposes.[95]

To the Canadian representative on the CDT, it was not at all clear that the protection of his country's interests required at this juncture some sort of metallurgical Statute of Westminster. Moreover, it seemed to George Bateman that his chief's understanding of the existing relationship between Canada and the Trust was hazy in the extreme. Howe had referred to Bateman as 'one of the Directors of the Trust, representing the United Kingdom.' But Howe's own letter to Bateman of 3 June 1944 had referred to him as 'the Canadian member,' as did the formal letter of 4 October 1944 from the Trust's co-secretaries confirming his appointment. Nor did Howe seem to grasp the nature of the changes proposed for the CDT in the Anderson-Groves memorandum. As tactfully as he could Bateman tried to explain matters as he saw them. The paragraphs dealing with the CDT, he conceded, had been badly drafted, and on that account 'might convey the impression that the Trust is to be given more authority than is either intended or desirable.' All that was intended was that the Trust might now be empowered to purchase supplies from its member Governments as well as from territories outside their jurisdiction. From Canada's point of view that might be desirable, since 'under the present authority of the Trust, if the US were to stop buying from Canada, we would have no place to sell our concentrates.' It was not proposed that the Trust should have any authority over Canadian mining operations. It might, to be sure, recommend a campaign of exploration and development, but would be in no position to compel it. Allocation of supply remained the responsibility of the CPC. 'It is my understanding,' Bateman concluded, that you approve the principle of having *all* supplies subject to allocation by the CPC. Having regard to this, and on the assumption that Canada is in fact a member of the CDT and the further assumption that the proposed enlarged authority of the CDT is to be exercised as I have set out above, I think it would be difficult to write ourselves into the CPC and out of the CDT.

He proposed that before any final decision, the Government should wait until the drafting subcommittee had revised and clarified the Anderson-Groves memorandum, which would be submitted to Howe in due course.[96]

On 5 December, before C.D. Howe had had an opportunity to respond to these observations, the CPC held a meeting at which Pearson, together with Bateman, was present. 'The Anderson-Groves memorandum was read,' Bateman reported to Howe, 'but there was no discussion.' 'There was, therefore, no necessity, and in fact no occasion, for mentioning the amendments to the Anderson-Groves memorandum contained in your letter to Pearson. As there appeared to be some confusion on certain points, no mention has been made to the Americans of the possibility of our position being altered.'[97] Two days later, with still no guidance from Howe, followed a meeting of the CDT. There the British put forward what was for Bateman an awkward proposal. Under the new terms of procedure, each country, rather than the Trust, should assume financial responsibility for stockpiling production. Bateman had already told Howe that the Trust would bear that responsibility. He now had to tell Howe that it was otherwise. He reported that following the British statement he had informed the meeting, as 'a personal opinion which might be subject to correction when I heard from you,' that 'if the CPC was to have the right of allocation, and that if at the same time the CDT was not prepared to find a market for any material which might not be allocated, we might have to reconsider our position with both CPC and CDT.'[98]

A sixth sense had saved Howe from selling his uranium empire down the river. 'I am sure you appreciate more than before,' he wrote to Bateman in an eagerly awaited letter of 11 December, 'my reluctance in signing the Anderson-Groves memorandum without a great deal more clarification.' He would have no objection to permitting the Trust to allocate all Canadian production not required in Canada, providing the Trust would in turn pay for unallocated material rather than leaving this as a charge upon the producing country. In another letter of the same date he set out his general ideas:

I feel that Canada should not at this time undertake responsibility for financing the Trust. We have spent some $6,000,000 in purchasing Eldorado and are spending $1,000,000 each year in development work which is bringing excellent results in the way of locating new uranium deposits. It seems to me that if we look after the Canadian source of supply at our own expense, that should be our full share.

I have no particular objection to permitting the Trust to allocate our uranium, particularly should the Trust be willing to undertake to purchase any uranium that we do not sell direct to the United States or the United Kingdom. If the Trust will not give such an undertaking, it seems to me that we should be left free to make our own arrangements. We can never hope to do better than break even with Eldorado and we will be fortunate to do that if the market for radium goes to pieces as now seems likely.

I think that Canada should remain a member of CPC, but I am not so concerned about our membership in CDT. Should it be decided that the UK and US desire to operate the Trust without Canada, I will have no objection...

I do not wish to take too narrow a view of Canada's relations to the Trust and and therefore I think we should reserve our position until the results of the Drafting Committee are known. The above thoughts are for your guidance as a member of the Drafting Committee. The Prime Minister feels that we should try to be as independent as possible in all these matters, and while I have not discussed details of the Trust with him, I think I am interpreting his feelings correctly. When the work of the Drafting Committee comes to hand, I will take up the matter with him and with my colleagues in the Cabinet...[99]

The Drafting Committee of the CPC consisted of General Groves, Roger Makins, and L.B. Pearson (who was assisted by George Bateman). Its job was to recast the Anderson-Groves memorandum of 15 November 1945 in a form acceptable to the three Governments. What was required was a post-war version of the Quebec Agreement. By January 1946 a draft Memorandum of Agreement had been prepared. It specified the following.

Subject to any wider agreements for the control of atomic energy, the President and the Prime Ministers would agree not to use nuclear weapons against other parties without prior consultation. Nor would they disclose information or enter into negotiations concerning atomic energy except in accord with agreed common policy or after discussion. Each government would take measures to control and possess all deposits of uranium and thorium within its borders and to acquire desirable deposits elsewhere. The Combined Policy Committee would allocate all raw materials. A reconstituted Combined Development Trust would serve as the agent of the CPC in raw-material matters. In regard to information, there was sweeping provision for full and effective exchange to meet the requirements of the respective national programs. The Combined Policy Committee would be responsible for taking the measures necessary to put this pledge into effect.[100]

After the penultimate meeting of the Drafting Committee, where all this had been agreed to, Pearson reported on its progress to Norman Robertson. 'We will have one further meeting next week,' he wrote on 18 January 1946,

and then turn our drafts over to Secretary of State Byrnes, who will no doubt call a meeting of the Combined Policy Committee ... This gives the Government a couple of extra weeks in which to make up its mind on the fundamental question of participation in these Agreements and in the machinery which they set up ... I discussed this matter with the Prime Minister ... and he was inclined to think that it would be difficult for us to withdraw now. Notwithstanding earlier doubts on the subject, I am inclined to agree with him. In any event, I think that it will be impossible for us to accept the draft Memorandum of Agreement without accepting the Draft Declaration of Trust...[101]

By the end of the war the British Government had decided to develop as rapidly as possible facilities in the United Kingdom for producing atomic power. As between its civilian and military applications – electricity or bombs – priorities had not yet been laid down, but the Experimental Establishment for which planning had begun would obviously require men and materials whatever shape the British nuclear programme might eventually assume. Both men and materials were in short supply and, as it happened, what supply of each there was could only be found in Canada.

During the war, raw materials had been the cause of Anglo-Canadian misunderstanding; now, during these first few months of peace, it was to be manpower which led to strained relations and ill feelings. To this episode the British official history alludes in guarded language. 'It would be difficult to provide enough men for the Experimental Establishment and for Canada; but with careful management and flexible arrangements it could be done and in time Canada would have trained sufficient staff of her own. Meanwhile Chadwick was anxious that the Canadians should not be pressed by the British to go too far too fast; he wanted Britain to play as large a part as possible in Canada but did not wish to prejudice developments at home. The ideal arrangement was that the projects in Britain and in Canada should be complementary, and everyone agreed that there should be the closest co-operation and good interchange of staff between the two projects.'[102]

This was not at all the perspective in which the problem appeared from Ottawa. Even with the best of help from all hands – British and Canadian – the pile at Chalk River was painfully slow in approaching completion. 'Delays familiar to all engineers in all projects were compounded by the need to pioneer many new devices. Faulty castings turned up during radiography. Some stainless steel parts were not up to specifications.'[103] Just when a supreme effort was required to pull everything together the British were preparing to pull out. The first to leave was the director of the Chalk River Project, J.D. Cockcroft, who returned to the United Kingdom in the summer of 1946 to take charge of the British Experimental Establishment. Other key British personnel followed. Not until a year later would the NRX reactor go critical. Howe had hoped for the end of 1945.

The news that British scientists would be withdrawn from Canada to work on atomic energy in the United Kingdom reached the Minister of Reconstruction and Supply (as C.D. Howe had become on 1 January 1946) on the eve of the meeting of the Combined Policy Committee scheduled for 15 February. Irritated by the slow progress at Chalk River, still aggrieved by his abrasive dispute with the British over the wartime allocation of ores and concentrates, Howe was very angry at this turn of events. He prepared a statement for L.B. Pearson to deliver to the CPC. 'He has bluntly said,' C.J. Mackenzie, whom he consulted, recorded after reading his message, 'that the partnership arrangement between UK and Canada will come to an end when Cockcroft returns to UK as withdrawal of the British group is, in essence, changing the original partnership.'[104]

The British could ill afford such a shift in the arms of the North Atlantic triangle as was now taking place. As early as August 1945, George Bateman had reported after a talk in Washington with General Groves that 'Groves considers that the US and Canadian partnership is much more important to the US than the US-UK partnership,' an opinion which Howe was glad to receive and which he professed to share.[105] But the British were in graver difficulty than perhaps they knew. The Memorandum of Agreement was still in draft form. Groves had been one of its drafters but he had no sympathy for one of its provisions. He warned Byrnes that, on the strength of its assurance of full and effective exchange to meet the requirements of the respective national programmes, the British intended to ask the United States for information that would help the United Kingdom develop a large-scale plant for producing fissionable materials. There were two reasons why Washington would be unwise to accede to such a request. One, which Groves stressed in his discussion with the Secretary of State, was that publication of the Memorandum of Agreement (as required by Article 102 of the UN Charter) would adversely reflect upon the sincerity of the attempt of the three governments to work out with the Soviet Union a system of international control of atomic energy.[106] The other – his real concern – was the security risk. Groves was obsessed by security, but it would not be long before many Americans shared his obsession. On 15 February, as the CPC met in Washington, the Prime Minister of Canada issued a statement to the press. It declared that 'information of undoubted authenticity has reached the Canadian Government which establishes that there have been disclosures of secret and confidential information to unauthorized persons, including some members of the staff of a foreign mission in Ottawa.'

Mackenzie King had told President Truman about Gouzenko's revelations soon after the Soviet cypher clerk defected to the Canadian Government in September 1945,* but counter-espionage required that this intelligence be kept a closely-guarded secret. As a result, all but a handful in the American policy community remained in ignorance of the Soviet wartime spy ring in Ottawa until the disclosure of 15 February. In the absence of names and detail – the press statement did not specify the embassy concerned – the Washington rumour mills worked overtime. For once their wildest speculations proved only too well founded.

These circumstances created a most unhappy atmosphere for the British representatives at the CPC meeting that day. The meeting, L.B. Pearson reported, with considerable understatement, 'was an unsatisfactory one.' He told Ottawa how things had gone when Sir James Chadwick had indicated that the British Government would be requesting considerable assistance from the United States to get its own atomic energy project started; they had not gone well. Chadwick's statement 'brought out certain differences of interpretation between the United States and United Kingdom authorities on what was meant by co-operation. General Groves demurred at sending detailed engineering and other information to the United Kingdom authorities to enable them to complete their plans until they were satisfied here that security arrangements were adequate to prevent this information falling into unauthorized hands.' But it was not just the prospect of information falling into unauthorized hands that alarmed Byrnes, Secretary of War Patterson, Acheson, and Groves – the Americans present at the meeting. They were worried lest nuclear weapons stored in the British Isles offer an irresistible temptation to a smash-and-grab raider. If the British had to make atom bombs of their own, better that they should make them in Canada. On this Pearson expressed no opinion.

He did, however, venture his, or rather Howe's, views about the impending evacuation of British scientists from Chalk River. Pearson's intervention took the form of 'a very short but general comment expressing the interest of the Canadian authorities in the United Kingdom developments, and our regret if those developments should in any way prejudice our own Chalk River project in Canada.' Howe, had he been present, would doubtless have employed blunter language. Pearson was more accustomed to the circumlocutions of diplomatic discourse, but he was further constrained in what he said and in his manner of saying it by what he had learned in an informal talk with the British representatives before the meeting began.

* See below, 319–20.

Found Chadwick and Makins anxious and, in the case of Chadwick, inclined to be irritated at the implications [of C.D. Howe's message]. Neither of them understood what we meant by stating that partnership arrangements between the United Kingdom and Canada would be ended by the withdrawal of United Kingdom scientists at Chalk River ... Sir James Chadwick also does not agree that United Kingdom authorities had taken, or intended to take, any steps which would prevent the development of Chalk River. He said that they had let the Canadian authorities know some time ago that their own people would be removed only gradually from Chalk River and in such a way that operations there would not be prejudiced. He asked me whether the statement ... from Mr Howe was to be construed as an official statement from the Canadian Government. If so, they might have to reply by an official statement from their own Government in order to make their own position clear. I ventured to doubt the necessity for any such official governmental exchanges...[107]

There the matter rested. The British scientists were duly withdrawn. Their defection to their own project may not have done the Canadian project great harm but it certainly did it no good. The last move was Canada's. 'The UK have requested Canada to furnish complete plans and specifications of the Chalk River development,' Howe told Bateman on 18 April 1946, 'which we have declined to do when we found that we were bound to secrecy on the design and that we cannot guarantee our US friends secrecy if the plans are sent to the UK.[108]

Whether the British believed that was the real explanation cannot be ascertained. They were not mollified by it. Now it was Chadwick's turn to be angry. 'I am sorry that Chadwick feels that Canada-UK relations in the atomic field have deteriorated,' Howe wrote to Bateman on 13 May.

Personally, I feel that the UK have let us down by pressing us to become the centre of atomic energy work for the Empire, and then, without prior notice, announcing plans for the development in the UK which involve withdrawal of our top personnel. Having spent some thirty million dollars of the taxpayers' money in atomic energy work, my greatest desire is to put our project in such position that it cannot further be interfered with from outside this country. I have told Sir James that we would be glad to extend to the UK every courtesy at Chalk River that the UK is willing to extend to Canada, in connection with UK projects. This should prove to be a satisfactory working arrangement.

I hope you will not let us be put in the position of having created ill feeling in this connection. We are in the happy position of having carried out all our agreements with the UK. I cannot feel that the UK are in the same happy position.[109]

Some months later, Howe disclosed to Pearson a further cause of his aggravation – his 'feeling that the United Kingdom had been using experimental work in Canada not as a basis for Canadian development but in reality for a United Kingdom pile on which a large part of the design work was carried out at Chalk River.'[110]

Meanwhile the Combined Policy Committee was due on 15 April to take up once again the intractable task of devising a mutually satisfactory instrument of post-war atomic energy co-operation.

By the delay – it was five months since Truman, Attlee, and Mackenzie King had reached their agreement in principle – the Canadian government was not unduly disturbed. 'From the Canadian point of view,' A.D.P. Heeney commented on March 20, 'while the present situation is in some ways unsatisfactory, it is questionable whether more precise definition along the lines of the new Trust Agreement would not create more problems than it would solve ... Unless there are any pressing difficulties in the present Canadian situation as a supplier of raw material, or otherwise in our relationship to the Trust, it does not seem to be in our interest to urge any immediate conclusion of the proposed revised agreements.'[111] One such difficulty emerged just before the CPC meeting. 'Our UK friends,' Howe informed Bateman on 14 April, 'seem to be moving towards obtaining control both of the operation of the Eldorado mine and the output therefrom. Canada cannot agree to this and if there is no other alternative we would do well to refrain from holding a membership in the Trust.' Bateman and Pearson were to make sure that under whatever form of Trust the CPC might agree to, 'Canada must be free to operate the mine in such manner as Canada will decide ... While we would like to have the Trust buy our surplus material, the price for an agreement to do so is too high if to obtain it we must surrender all Canadian control of the output.'[112]

The meeting of the CPC on 15 April 1946 marked the nadir of post-war Anglo-American relations in the field of atomic energy. It served only to register that a complete deadlock had arisen between the two governments. 'The Americans are obviously reluctant,' Pearson reported afterwards, 'to give the British the industrial information necessary for the construction of the plants in the United Kingdom. They are in fact, I think, doubtful about the desirability of constructing those plants at all. The British, on the other hand, feel that co-operation, without this complete exchange of information, does not mean anything, and if the Americans insist on this attitude, the Policy Committee and the Trust might as well be abandoned.'[113] Bateman added further details in his account to C.D. Howe:

The real pressure behind the British desire to have a firm agreement and a definition of 'full and effective co-operation' lies in the fact that they are designing a plant and need a good deal of information from the US on engineering design, construction and operation. They state that since V-J Day there has been practically no interchange of information of any value and in the meantime they cannot proceed with the work they have undertaken.

There seems to be a great deal of uncertainty as to what the President and Prime Ministers meant by 'full and effective co-operation.' The British interpret it as meaning that they should receive the information they want from the US while the US claim that President Truman did not have in mind the construction of another plant by the UK. It would appear that the only way in which the matter could be settled would be by an interchange of letters between the President and Prime Ministers stating just what they had in mind and defining what is meant by 'full and effective co-operation.' It is quite obvious that the US does not want to give the UK the information desired and I would consider it doubtful if any solution satisfactory to the UK will be found.[114]

The leader of the British delegation at the meeting was Lord Halifax. He at once reported what had transpired to his Prime Minister. Attlee responded by despatching a sharply worded telegram of protest to President Truman. He sent as well a message to the Prime Minister of Canada, repeating his telegram to Truman and entreating Canada's support for the British case.[115]

This request was received in Ottawa with mixed feelings. It was hard not to experience at least a twinge of sympathy for the British in this latest manifestation of their post-war slide to second-powerdom. Mackenzie King did feel sympathetic. 'The United States are refusing to give the British the information they have about the manufacturing end of the bomb,' he wrote in his diary on 27 April. 'I do not like this at all. It is not square-dealing. If they had a thought of the kind in mind they should have brought it to the surface when we were being asked to sign an agreement on co-operation.'[116] Those closer to the negotiations tempered their sympathy with the reflection that in atomic energy matters the Americans had no monopoly on the double-cross. C.D. Howe in particular bore up cheerfully under the news that the CPC had reached a deadlock. 'It would look as though the last agreement on this subject has been signed,' he wrote to Bateman on 18 April, 'and that the UK will get very little further information with which to design their proposed pile ... I am inclined to think that the Trust agreement will lapse, and if so, no harm will be done as far as we are concerned. I feel that we will always find a market for our uranium regardless of the Trust.'[117] Apart from the future of the Trust there was no reason why Canada should take sides. 'The United Kingdom undoubtedly have as much information as we have,' Howe told Pearson some months later, 'which should be sufficient to enable them to get on with their project, although the time element would be assisted by receipt of more complete information. It seems to me that Canada should not be involved in this argument.'[118] There were additional reasons for not being involved. One was that in the light of the recent revelation of Soviet espionage in Ottawa, Canada's supuport for the British case could have done it more harm than good in Washington. Another was the need to work closely with the United States in the all-important negotiations on international control soon to begin in New York. Finally there was the view of the British representatives in Washington, privately conveyed to Pearson, that 'nothing is likely to result from [Attlee's] intervention, and that, indeed, they would have advised against it.'[119] All factors seemed to counsel lying low.

There was still the problem of how to respond to the request, conveyed to the Prime Minister by the CPC meeting of 15 April, for his understanding of the phrase 'full and effective co-operation' to which, along with Attlee and Truman, he had pledged his government on 16 November 1945. After some thought it was decided to inform the CPC that what Canada understood by 'full and effective co-operation' could be deduced from the fact that a United States official was stationed at Chalk River where he was privileged to know everything that was going on. This response pleased the British and gave no offence to the Americans. Acheson told Pearson that he had received it with interest and had indeed 'expressed some admiration for the ingenuity with which we handled this matter.'[120]

President Truman's interpretation of 'full and effective co-operation' was bluntly conveyed to Attlee on 20 April. He would not have signed the Washington Declaration on 16 November, the President told the Prime Minister, had he known that the British wanted information to help them build atomic plants and atomic bombs in the United Kingdom. They would get no information for these purposes.[121] Thereafter the trickle of intelligence dried up completely. On 1 August 1946, President Truman signed an Atomic Energy Act which made it illegal to turn it back on.

The British were left to proceed on their own as best they could. This turned out to be better than they had allowed the Americans and Canadians to believe. 'The men who had worked in America and in the Tube Alloys project in the United Kingdom,' states the British official history, 'knew a good deal about the processes between which they would have to choose, and the variables which would govern their choice.'[122] Indeed they did. 'In the matter of bombs,' writes an American authority, 'we had no secrets from the British. No one, for example, knew more about fission bombs than James Tuck, then at Oxford. Every significant advance made before 1951 toward the super, fusion or thermonuclear bomb was summed up in a top-secret "Disclosure of Invention".'[123] The co-holder (with John von Neumann) of this patent was a member of the Harwell Atomic Energy Research Establishment, one Klaus Fuchs.

For the remainder of 1946, and throughout 1947, the CPC no longer exercised its intended function as regulator of the flow of information. It still functioned, however, as allocator of raw material. The meeting of 15 April 1946 had attempted to work out an agreement on how to divide uranium oxide between the United States and the United Kingdom. The Canadian supply was not at issue, the total output of Eldorado (at that time less than 300 tons per annum) having previously been sold to the United States Army in a contract due to expire at the end of the year, at which time the Canadian Government would be free to make other arrangements. What was at issue was the production from the Belgian Congo. The British proposed that it should be divided fifty-fifty. The Americans demanded a firm monthly allocation of 250 tons which, the total output being about 330 tons a month, meant a division more like three to one than one to one. The CPC could no more solve the dispute over raw materials than it had been able to solve the dispute over information. It appointed a subcommittee to try to work it out. 'Canada was asked to appoint a representative,' Bateman reported afterwards, 'but as the question involves one of having to do with the purchase of materials with Trust funds to which we are not a contributor, we took the position that we should not appear in the matter officially. I was, however, asked to attend the meetings unofficially, and this I agreed to do. I think there is a fairly strong possibility that if a solution is not found which is satisfactory to the British, they my withdraw from the Trust.'[124]

Two meetings of the subcommittee were held during the next few days. They were inconclusive. The British representatives, Bateman reported, appeared to be greatly concerned. They had reason to be. They had estimated that their nuclear establishment would require 5700 tons of uranium oxide for its next three years' operation. Reports from the Belgian Congo indicated that the mine there was giving out. Their project to go nuclear was thus threatened by the developing shortage of raw materials. Even if the entire Canadian output was switched to them after the expiry of Eldorado's contract with the US Army – and it was yet far from certain that this could be done – it would not be nearly enough to meet their needs. A total of 6000 tons remained in the CPC stockpile. The British had somehow to lay claim to as much of it as possible – not to the lion's share, that was obviously out of the question, but at least to half.

The Americans were very far from being ready to allow them that half, or anything like half. 'Chadwick states that the US wants practically the entire available supply,' Bateman told Howe on 6 May. That was far more than Chadwick thought the Americans needed, and he was right. Their real anxiety, as L.B. Pearson learned when he discussed the raw materials problem with Dean Acheson on 3 May, was not for their own requirements – they thought, as it proved incorrectly, that Colorado would take care of those – but over shipping the uranium oxide 'to such an exposed position as the United Kingdom when it would not, in any event, be required for some time.' There was, of course, an obvious solution to such a difficulty, and Acheson had hinted at it – storing the United Kingdom share in Canada. 'This would certainly turn out to be the best course,' Acheson had remarked, 'if the United Kingdom could be persuaded to return to the wartime arrangements by which Canada was the centre of British Commonwealth atomic energy development schemes.'[125] There was little chance of that, as Acheson probably knew.

Informed of these developments, C.D. Howe was concerned only to protect such Canadian interests as might be affected by them. He was not at all keen at the suggestion that Canada should be the custodian of British supplies or uranium. 'I see no purpose in stockpiling ore, and do not think that we can consider doing so, particularly as we have no adequate security arrangements at the mine.' He was 'quite willing to permit the Committee to allocate our production as between the US and the UK, and have no great preference as to which market we supply.'[126] One lesson had emerged: 'I would like to be self-contained as far as atomic energy is concerned, particularly in view of the tension over supplies...'[127]

In the event the British were able to prise out of the CPC sufficient quantities of uranium oxide to tide them over. With supply solved and information shelved, the Combined Policy people enjoyed an unaccustomedly tranquil twelve months.

Towards the end of 1947, the Canadian Government was astonished to learn that the American authorities wanted to re-examine all aspects of atomic energy co-operation among the United States, the United Kingdom and Canada with a view to reaching a new working agreement to replace that signed at Quebec in August 1943.

For this change of heart and mind a number of factors were responsible, not least the new personnel on the American side. As of 1 January 1947, control of atomic energy policy passed from the hands of General Leslie R. Groves and the US Army into those of the newly created civilian agency, the Atomic Energy Commission. The chairman of the new Commission was David E. Lilienthal, a distinguished public servant and New Deal Democrat who had made his mark as the guiding spirit of the Tennessee Valley Authority. Lilienthal was liberalism personified compared with his predecessor and, while no Anglophile,* infinitely better disposed than Groves towards co-operation with the British in atomic energy matters. So were the new faces in the State Department, where influence had shifted to the sensitive and imaginative group gathered around George Kennan, back in Washington after Moscow to take charge of the Policy Planning Staff just then being formed. 'The bitterest problem after I came in,' is how Kennan has described the condition of Anglo-American relations over nuclear policy following the disarray in which these had been left early in 1946, and he devoted much of his time and energy to its solution.†

Personalities apart, other circumstances made a change in policy imperative. It would no longer be possible to proceed, as before, in utter secrecy. The US Atomic Energy Commission had concluded that, to maintain control of raw materials, it would have to participate in the Combined Development Trust. That meant revealing to Congress, and to the public, the existence of the CDT and its parent body, the Combined Policy Committee, and of the wartime agreements by which these institutions had been created. Of their existence all but the participants themselves had known nothing. It still remained top secret, even to top Congressmen. 'The Commission,' write its official historians, 'thought the Administration would do well to dissolve CPC as quickly as possible, since its continued operation appeared to be illegal under the Atomic Energy Act. If the State Department could assure that the CPC would be disbanded and that Congress would be informed of the wartime arrangement, the Commission was willing to accept membership on the CDT and possibly on the CPC for a temporary period.'[128] For this reason, if no other, the status of these institutions and the authority by which they existed were bound sooner or later to be scrutinized and probably altered. But the State Department would not come clean with Congress for almost a year after the Atomic Energy Commission took charge.

Secrets can never be kept long in Washington. The first inkling of

* 'The State Department staff people ... keep pressing for a broad approach – something that smacks of an alliance. I shall do everything I can to discourage and prevent this ...' Diary entry for 22 November 1947, quoted in *The Journals of David E. Lilienthal*, II, *The Atomic Energy Years, 1945–1950* (New York, Evanston, and London 1964), 259.

† Quoted in Nuel Pharr Davis, *Lawrence and Oppenheimer* (New York 1968), 281. Kennan's own memoirs tell nothing of this story.

the wartime atomic energy agreements reached members of the Congress from the chairman of the Atomic Energy Commission, in the course of a confidential briefing of the Joint Congressional Committee on Atomic Energy on 5 May 1947. Lilienthal recorded that in talking about the raw materials problem he had disclosed that half the output of the Belgian Congo uranium was going to the United Kingdom. 'There was some alarm expressed [at this],' Lilienthal noted,

> and some surprise at learning that Great Britain and Canada actually had had men participating with all four feet in the development of the bomb itself, during the war.[*] Senator Connally said that then you mean that England knows how to make the bomb. The answer is certainly "Yes." I explained that we had been concerned that the Joint Committee and the Foreign Affairs Committee had not previously been informed of our agreements with England and recommended that they learn of these basic agreements directly from the Secretary of State and the Under Secretary. This apparently they will do.[129]

As a result of this exchange, Dean Acheson appeared before the Joint Congressional Committee on Atomic Energy. He told it enough to make Senators Bourke B. Hickenlooper and Arthur H. Vandenberg go in protest to the President. They were particularly concerned at the revelation that Roosevelt had agreed that the United States would not use the atomic bomb against any other country without the consent of the British, and scarcely less concerned at having learned that uranium concentrates were being stockpiled in the United Kingdom 'where it might fall into Russian hands in event of an outbreak of war in Europe and at a time when it was required for the US atomic program.'[130]

Only then was an arrangement made to take the Senators (and indeed the Secretary of Defense, for Forrestal had first heard of the Quebec Agreement not from Truman or Marshall but from Hickenlooper†)

* This surprise reflects Congressional ignorance, not governmental secrecy. The wartime collaboration of British and Canadian scientists in the Manhattan Project had been publicly stated in the communiqués released in Ottawa and Washington immediately after the bombing of Hiroshima. (See above, 275–6.) A more subtle interpretation is that the ignorance was studied. 'Happy men, says Chekhov, are those who keep their eyes shut, and this is what Congress was doing.' Davis, *Lawrence and Oppenheimer*, 282.

† Walter Millis (ed.), *The Forrestal Diaries* (New York 1951), 338. The Quebec Agreement was not the only important atomic energy document to get lost in the shuffle. 'None of the atomic energy people in Washington, from Mr Stimson the Secretary of War downwards, were aware of the existence of the Hyde Park Agreement until April 1945, after Mr Roosevelt died. They had to ask the British Government to tell them what was in the Agreement and to supply a copy. The president's copy was found some years later in the files of his naval aide: someone had seen the heading "Tube Alloys" and had concluded it dealt with naval supplies.' Margaret Gowing, *Britain and Atomic Energy 1939–1945*

into the State Department's confidence. On 16 November, the three men met at the Pentagon with the Under Secretary of State, Robert A. Lovett. They may not have learned everything from him but they learned much they had not known. They were profoundly disturbed. 'Vandenberg declared that he thought the Hyde Park and Quebec Agreements were "astounding" and "unthinkable," and that he felt a tremendous responsibility as Chairman of the Senate Foreign Relations Committee ... He said that failure to revamp the agreements would have a disastrous effect on Congressional consideration of the Marshall Plan...'[131]

There was one further reason for the new approach. The fuel was running low. Colorado was not living up to expectations. Canadian sources were far from enough. The Congo mine was giving out. Already the CPC was looking covetously at South Africa. On 28 June 1947, Lilienthal remarked to Dean Acheson 'that antagonizing the British might make our chance of getting South African materials ... more difficult, and that was very important to this country.'[132]

Not all of this background was known to the Canadian authorities at the time. About the middle of November 1947 they had begun to detect a marked change in the demeanour of American officials concerned with atomic energy matters. At a meeting in Washington on 14 November dealing with declassification of wartime secrets, C.J. Mackenzie was struck by the unaccustomed responsiveness of his United States counterparts. 'Carried on throughout the entire 3 days in the same spirit,' he wrote in his diary. 'It was obvious that all the Commission from Lilienthal down were most anxious to co-operate in every way, and there was no lining up of delegations. Understanding was reached on all matters almost with unanimity.'[133] That in itself was a new departure. But a more momentous novelty was in the making. 'At Blair House with Vandenberg ... and Hickenlooper,' Lilienthal recorded on 26 November, 'while Lovett and I ... presented a proposal that, if it results in agreement, will present a new course of basic policy in the world. It has been months

(London 1964), 341–2. On 14 July 1949, at a meeting at Blair House, Senator Bourke Hickenlooper referred to the wayward Hyde Park Agreement:

> 'One of these wartime agreements is so extra-or-rdinary that the US hasn't even a copy; I had to see it in photostat.' Truman, looking like a tired owl ... suddenly woke up ... He stuck his finger, arm outstretched, at H. and said, 'I've got that document; got it locked up in my safe in the White House and that's where it stays.' H. said, nonplussed, 'I don't refer to the Quebec agreement; I have another one in mind.' The Pres. didn't bat an eye: 'I know the one you mean, and don't you worry about that; I've got it.'

*The Journals of David E. Lilienthal*, 547. Not only the battlefronts were covered by the fog of war.

and months in coming. To my great surprise it was received almost without question, in every essential. The thing we thought would cause the most trouble didn't raise a ripple hardly – the matter of "information".'[134] Within a week Hume Wrong was able to report from Washington what was up. 'It seems obvious from what we have learned so far that the Americans have in mind a complete revision of the existing CPC and Trust Agreements.'[135] On 5 December George Kennan told him the details.

> The first purpose of the talks would be to find a realistic basis of co-operation between the three countries in present conditions. They wished to continue the operations of CDT under a different working name and to substitute for the Quebec Agreement a new working arrangement. This would not be a binding international instrument requiring Senate approval and registration with the United Nations...
>
> The question of the supply of raw materials would be the second major subject of discussion. In this connection the only point which [Kennan] stressed was their desire that a large stockpile should not be accumulated in the United Kingdom ... They wished on strategic grounds that everything above what was needed for [current operations] should be stored at a safer distance from the Continent of Europe. I asked him whether they would raise the allocation as well as the location of raw materials. He said that he expected that they would do so, but did not emphasize the point...
>
> The third major subject would be the exchange of information. He told me that they had succeeded in securing a liberal construction of the McMahon Act, under which they thought that they could exchange information deemed to be "in the national interest." He said that the United Kingdom and Canada would certainly not be the sole beneficiaries ... I told him ... that we were givers rather than receivers of information, and that we would welcome closer co-operation in the areas of direct interest to our own operations...[136]

A meeting of the Combined Policy Committee had been scheduled for 10 December 1947. It would afford the first occasion for the Americans to display their new policy. 'Apparently it is an extraordinarily important meeting,' C.J. Mackenzie, who had been instructed to attend on C.D. Howe's behalf, noted on 4 December, 'and is causing quite a flurry in External Affairs.' And on 6 December: 'Down to Mr Howe's office ... to discuss my proposed visit to Washington. We both agreed that there were no instructions he could give and that we would have to "play it by ear".'[137] Towards its representative the Department of External Affairs was less permissive. Hume Wrong was instructed not to get carried away. Signs of a new liberality within the US Administration were welcomed for what they might prove to be worth. But the Canadian Government did not want to rush into a new agreement on atomic energy co-operation merely for the sake of easing the strain between the State

Department and the Congress. Existing arrangements worked well enough for Canada. Moreover, there was the need to take care that any new announcement of tripartite co-operation did not ruin what slight hope might still remain of ending the deadlock within the United Nations Atomic Energy Commission. Those were the general considerations to be kept in mind. In addition, there were specifically Canadian interests to be safeguarded.

> The Canadian attitude remains unchanged insofar as the CDT is concerned. You will be aware that our position has always been that, while (at the request of the United States and the United Kingdom) a Canadian representative attends meetings of the Trust, Canada is not a member of this body in the sense that we assume obligations thereunder with the other partner nations. This has been clearly understood throughout.
>
> In this same connection, Dr Mackenzie and Mr Bateman will have in mind our relatively minor role as a source of supply and the fact that Mr Howe has always insisted that Canadian production should remain under the sole control of the Government.
>
> The US authorities seem preoccupied with the distribution of stockpiles and military facilities. It has been suggested that they may seek to bargain the exchange of information against an agreement by the United Kingdom to transfer stockpiles and facilities to less exposed territories. In this connection we understand Canada has been mentioned. Unless this country is suggested for such a purpose, we consider that this matter of location is primarily one for discussion between the United Kingdom and the United States. It certainly cannot be assumed that we would be prepared to accede to any such proposal involving Canada.
>
> In our view, the real Canadian interest in these discussions lies in the possibility that they may result in really useful information being made available to us and to the United Kingdom.[138]

More people than usual were in attendance when the CPC meeting got under way at 4 PM on 10 December. The Canadians present included Hume Wrong and Tommy Stone from the Embassy staff in Washington, Mackenzie, Bateman, and George Ignatieff. The chairman of the meeting was the US Under Secretary of State, Robert A. Lovett. 'Witty, clever, kindly and very shrewd,' was how Lovett impressed C.J. Mackenzie. 'He certainly created a marvellous atmosphere and, when the meeting got under way, he proposed that we clarify all of the old issues and disagreements which had become acrimonious at times and that we should try to get a minute to which we could all agree ... I think they really do want our co-operation and are not letting UK in because they just want something.'[139]

The meeting agreed to create two working parties, one (on which Canada was represented by Ignatieff and Mackenzie) dealing with the exchange of information, the other (on which Canada was represented by Bateman and Stone) with raw materials. The information group met for the first time on 11 December, under what Mackenzie described as 'the most auspicious circumstances.' The mood of the Americans seemed to have change completely. The American scientific representative, James B. Fisk of the Bell Telephone Company, a new face at the CPC, 'carried on as he would have in a pure science meeting in 1938. Most of the suggestions for co-operation were his, and it was almost impossible to believe that we were dealing with the same sort of thing we used to ... We are to get all the co-operation we could possibly expect, and the whole thing was eminently satisfactory.'[140]

The new materials group had before it a more intractable problem. 'There is a disturbing difference,' Hume Wrong reported on 12 December, 'between the estimated total production over the five year period in review and the minimum essential requirements of the United States alone. This probably means that the United States will, at the next meeting of the group, request not only the diversion of all world production to this country during the period, but also deliveries from the United Kingdom stockpile to the amount of approximately one-half of supplies now in the United Kingdom.'[141] On 17 December, Bateman added some more details in his report to C.D. Howe: 'Our committee did no more than prepare the detailed statement of supply and requirement figures which showed that the best estimate we could make at this time of supplies over the five years, 1948 to 1952 inclusive, would fall short by some 1600 tons of what the US considered to be their minimum essential program. We did not deal with the question of allocation and it was quite obvious that the US, and I believe also the UK, prefer to have the question of allocation dealt with by a small committee on the political and strategic level.'[142] To C.D. Howe it was quite obvious that Canada should not take sides in the impending tug-of-war. 'This is a problem,' he wrote to Mackenzie King of allocation, 'which involves primarily the United Kingdom and the United States. The comparatively small requirements of the Canadian programme are not in question. Our interest is in the achievement of mutually satisfactory arrangements between the two larger countries.'[143]

Elusive as they had been, such arrangements now miraculously came into view. The British, long accustomed to American intransigence, entered the December 1947 CPC meetings with an intransigence of their own. Their delegation was bound by rigid instructions not on any account to barter away the United Kingdom raw materials position. The conciliatory approach of their American colleagues took the British unawares. Roger Makins returned to London over Christmas to report the possibility that a new day might be dawning; he urged that he be given authority to trade supply for intelligence. Impressed by this, more impressed by the latest figures from the Belgian Congo indicating that the ore was holding out better than anticipated, the British Government authorized Makins to deal on this basis.

A deal was struck. In exchange for information in specified areas, Britain would release all Congo production for 1948 and 1949 to the United States, and would yield ore from her own stockpile if the American programme required it. For Canada the deal was ideal. NRX was to be fuelled from American supply; meanwhile her scientists would gain on the information front. 'I am, of course, delighted with the outcome,' C.D. Howe wrote on 13 January 1948, 'which is all that we could desire.'[144]

There was also a new deal on the political side. The Quebec and Hyde Park Agreements were to be replaced by a new understanding among the three countries concerned. This provided for the continuation of the CPC as the appropriate medium of co-operation in atomic energy matters; for the continuation of the Combined Development Trust under the new name of Combined Development Agency, with Canada a full member; for future allocation of raw materials by the CPC; and for exchange of information and experience. These arranagements were to stay in force until the end of 1949. At that time they might be renewed, or enlarged, as the principals might wish. It was not foreseen that they would lapse.

So that they would not, like their predecessors, sink without trace in the recesses of some forgotten file, the arrangements were incorporated in the minutes of the CPC meeting of 7 January 1948. This was something of an occasion. There was a scurry to find some green baize cloth, for previous meetings had not had much need for this essential prop of diplomatic agreement. Lovett, Inverchapel, and Hume Wrong signed the documents for their respective governments. The meeting, Bateman reported, 'developed into a regular love feast ... They served sandwiches and drinks. I do not think I need say any more than this to indicate the favourable change that has taken place.'[145]

The question had arisen as to what to call the new agreement. One of the Americans suggested *modus vivendi.* 'His British and Canadian colleagues demurred,' the historians of the US Atomic Energy Commission record, 'for the term was most often used to describe the relations between adversaries driven by circumstances to get along together.'[146] But the term stuck, and *modus vivendi* it was. Even in its usual usage it was not inappropriate.

The basis for co-operation had thus been laid. What co-operation there would be now depended on the US Atomic Energy Commission. On

3 May 1948, C.J. Mackenzie had a long talk with its Chairman. 'I gathered,' Mackenzie wrote afterwards, 'although nothing was said, that things have bogged down a bit somewhere in the Commission ... since the last meeting of the CPC and they are having difficulty fulfilling their obligations. They want to get it cleared again on a high level but do not like to take it up until all the current issues – Atlantic Pact, Berlin situation, etc., are out of the way.'[147] There was a reason why things had bogged down a bit. The Commission had learned that Harwell was heading for bomb production.

To Lilienthal that made no difference to the *modus vivendi*. 'We had made a promise,' he wrote on 5 July, 'and we must keep that promise.' But another member of the Commission, Lewis L. Strauss, who had given assent to exchange of information only with reluctance, felt that what had since become known of the progress of the British nuclear weapons effort – it involved a new gas-cooled reactor of impressive design – required that the deal be re-examined in the best interests of the United States. Where would the United States be, he asked rhetorically, if the British nuclear arsenal, now a real possibility, were to be captured by a hostile power?[148] That was the way the President looked at it too. On 9 February 1949 Lilienthal met with Truman, who called his

> attention to a copy of a Modus Vivendi and said that it was necessary to get rid of certain agreements, but that those agreements had been entered into during the war by Roosevelt and others because it was not felt that Britain was a safe place for atomic energy weapon production. He then went on to say that we have got to protect our information and we certainly must try to see that the British do not have information with which to build those atomic weapons in England because they might be captured.[149]

A new North Atlantic tangle, knottier than any of the others, was in the making. The Canadian Government was distressed to see it so but, its own atomic programme unaffected, decided this time to take no active part in the unravelling. One proposal being canvassed in Washington was that the British manufacture and stockpile their nuclear weapons in Canada. When sounded out on this idea, a British spokesman 'retorted that much of British military opinion held Canada as vulnerable as Britain.'[150] (Vulnerable to what or whom the spokesman did not specify.) No one sounded out the Canadians. Miffed a bit at this neglect, C.D. Howe momentarily put his country in the spotlight. Canada had acquired the capacity to build atomic weapons on her own, he announced in a press release of 21 July, but had chosen to explore only the peaceful applications of nuclear power.

In the autumn of 1949, with the *modus vivendi* working poorly on its information side and due in any case to expire at the end of the year, negotiations were resumed, within the CPC and at high bilateral levels, to see if tripartite co-operation on atomic energy might be salvaged after all. From an unexpected quarter these talks were given powerful impetus. 'Heard about Vermont from C.D.,' Mackenzie noted tersely on 20 September. 'Vermont' – otherwise known as 'Operation Joe' – was the codename for the first atomic detonation by the Soviet Union.

The shock-waves from Novo-Ivankovo battered the American bargaining position, and a new one was swiftly devised. 'Nuclear components for British weapons were to be made in the United States. Only a limited number of weapons were to be stored in the United Kingdom, and these were for use only in accordance with common war plans.'[151] To be short of ore and at odds with a nuclear Russia was more than the Congressmen could bear; they panicked.

In such a climate negotiations between Washington and London, with Ottawa intervening only intermittently, continued into 1950. Something much more momentous than a *modus vivendi* might have emerged, maybe an atomic energy treaty. But all hope of that was dashed on 2 February. On that day Klaus Fuchs was arrested in Britain, and later confessed to spying for the Russians.

'The idea we and UK are just trading a hunk of uranium for a hunk of "secrets" – all wet.'[152] So Lilienthal had jotted in his diary on 18 August 1949. He had been right all along, but the Fuchs case shocked Congress beyond reason. Co-operation was the casualty. In 1951, the United Kingdom government asked the Americans to test a British-made atomic bomb on its behalf; the Congress insisted on so many restrictions 'on the access of British scientists to the information to be gotten from the tests and on the mode of procedure' that the British decided to test it themselves. This they succeeded in doing on 3 October 1952; a thermonuclear detonation followed on 15 May 1957. By then there was no longer 'a hunk of "secrets",' only a few crumbs. Nor could these be traded for 'a hunk of uranium,' for there was more than enough to go round. A deal, when it came, swapped not technique for raw materials but equipment – Polaris for Skybolt, both made in USA.

6

# Defending the Continent

Yet living here,
As one between two massing powers I live,
Where neutrality cannot save
Nor occupation cheer.

*C. Day Lewis*

## 'ROLL UP THAT MAP...'

A few minutes before 11 AM on 6 September 1945, the Prime Minister of Canada arrived at the House of Commons for the first peacetime meeting of Parliament in six years. The peace did not begin auspiciously.

Mackenzie King was met at his office by the Under Secretary of State for External Affairs in a state of intense agitation. Norman Robertson told him 'that a most terrible thing had happened.' Half-an-hour earlier, there had shown up at the office of the Minister of Justice a man and wife. The man claimed to be from the embassy of the USSR. He declared that he had in his possession documents which he had procured from the Soviet files there – documents which, he had insisted, would disclose the existence of a massive espionage operation penetrating into the most secret recesses of the government of Canada. As Robertson told his tale, the division bells were summoning Members of Parliament to their places in the Senate Chamber; the Prime Minister barely had time to receive the news before he took his place among them.

Mackenzie King's first reaction to the sensational revelation by Igor Gouzenko was to discount its importance. 'My own feeling,' he wrote later that day, 'is that the individual has incurred the displeasure of the embassy and is really seeking to shield himself. I do not believe his story about their having avowed treachery. There is no doubt that most countries have their secret spies, but that is another matter.'[1]

Such a reassuring interpretation was not permitted to last long. By the following day the Canadian authorities had examined the documents which Gouzenko had turned over to them, and divulged their contents to the Prime Minister. Mackenzie King was horrified. 'Everything was much worse than we would have believed,' he recorded. 'They went right into our Department of External Affairs ... In the cypher room there was an agent of the Russians who had seen and knew all our cyphers and had known what they contained. The same was true at Earnscliffe...[*] In our Research Laboratories here at Ottawa, where we had been working on the atomic bomb, there is a scientist who is a Russian agent. In the Research Laboratory in Montreal where most of the work is done there is an English scientist who is pro-Russian and acting as a Russian agent ...'[2]

The full impact of the disclosure of a Soviet spy ring dawned on the Prime Minister a few days later. 'If there is another war,' Mackenzie King wrote on 11 September 1945, 'it will come against America by way of Canada from Russia.'[3]

That another war would come against America by way of Canada from Russia was a hypothesis which had been considered by post-war policy planners in Ottawa many months before. Nor had they rejected it. 'Assuming that, in the post-war period, Japan and Germany are effectively disarmed,' one such planner had posited as long before as 6 January 1944, 'the most probable threat ... would come from Russia.'[4]

What Canada's location athwart the bomber route between the Soviet Union and North America might mean for post-war policies was deeply pondered by civilian and military planners in Ottawa during the last eighteen months of the war. A meeting of their minds was not easily arrived at.

An early and important contribution to the debate was made by Maurice Pope who, as Chairman of the Canadian Joint Staff Mission in Washington and Army member of the Canadian section of the Permanent Joint Board on Defence, was in a good position to assess what the United States was likely to ask of Canada in the way of post-war defence co-operation. He set down his thoughts in April 1944.

> I believe that on the conclusion of this war it will be held desirable, certainly by the present United States government, and very probably by ours, that the present intimate defence relationship be continued. At the moment we have Defence Plan ABC-22. This Plan was drawn up before the United States came into the war as a belligerent. It was put into effect on the 8th of December, 1941, and will lapse on the cessation of hostilities. As we approach that time I feel sure that the United States will ask us to revise it so as to have it ready to put it into effect when the next war comes ... I do not think it will be possible

* The residence and office of the British High Commissioner.

for Canada not to accede to this request, nor do I think it will lie within Government policy to refuse to do so.

The revised Plan ... will require a statement of the objects or tasks to be achieved and a statement of the forces that will be made available to achieve those objects ... We need think only of a recrudescence of strength of Germany and Japan. This seems rather far-fetched at the present, and I hope will remain so for a long time to come. Public opinion, however, has a short memory, and we may again find ourselves thinking in terms of peace while our present enemies will be actuated by entirely different thoughts and motives. They may again attack us or oblige us in self-defence to make war on them...

There is one exception to this, and that is the possibility that sometime in the future the United States, from their idealistic dislike of Russia, may find their relations with that country somewhat strained ... In such circumstances our position would be a difficult one. To the Americans the defence of the United States is continental defence, which includes us, and nothing that I can think of will ever drive that idea out of their heads. Should, then, the United States go to war with Russia they would look to us to make common cause with them and, as I judge their public opinion, they would brook no delay...

So, therefore, my view is that the defence relationship between the United States and Canada in the post-war period should just be that intimate technical relationship that we enjoy at present. We should renew ABC-22, and take good care that in our defence establishments we should provide adequate forces, not so much as to defend ourselves against possible raids from the enemy (though this would be necessary), but more to ensure that there was no apprehension as to our security in the American public mind. As I used to hold ten years ago when I was in Operations, what we have to fear is more a lack of confidence in the United States as to our security, rather than enemy action. I can put this in another way. If we do enough to assure the United States we shall have done a good deal more than a cold assessment of the risk would indicate to be necessary.[5]

Pope's assessment, set down in a letter to one of his successors at the Military Operations Directorate of National Defence Headquarters, Colonel J.H. Jenkins, was passed around among members of the Working Committee on Post-Hostilities Problems and favourably impressed Norman Robertson, who sent it to the Prime Minister with the notation 'Interesting and I think a correct appreciation.' Mackenzie King read it aloud in the presence of one of his secretaries, who informed Robertson of his reaction. The Prime Minister did not share Pope's fear of a resurgent Germany and Japan.

But Mr King clearly thinks that the Canadian position, as lying between the USSR on the one side and the USA on the other, may have to be worked out with very special care.

We will also have to think in terms of a rising unity of *colour* policy in the Far East generally which, from the point of view of world strategy, might have to regard the Far East as a solid block opposed to the so-called white races generally.

There is the possibility that oil developments in northwest Canada will reach such a scale as to make this area a much more vulnerable one in terms of offensive plans of any possible future enemy. The fact that it lies near the international air routes perhaps emphasizes the strategic aspect of which account would have to be taken.[6]

In May 1944, the Working Committee on Post-Hostilities Problems set itself the task of preparing a paper on post-war defence arrangements with the United States. It took its members the remainder of the year to draft a document on which all could more or less agree.

The Working Committee commenced its labours by scrutinizing on 18 May a paper prepared for its consideration by its Army member, Colonel J.H. Jenkins. Jenkins' memorandum began with the assumption 'that amicable relations between Canada and the United States will continue,'* but on a basis unlike any that had hitherto existed.

In the past the security of the North American hemisphere seemed self-evident in view of the two oceans protecting it. The war has changed this traditional way of thinking in terms of "Mercator's Projection" to that of "Polar Projection" ... Canada is the air highway and the land route (if such is to be possible) for attack on the United States from either the east or west ... No longer is the northern boundary of the United States inviolate to attack. As aviation develops, so will these northern routes increasingly become a world commercial highway and, as such, normal routes for any hostile power with designs against the United States.

All this being so, Canada would become crucially important to American defence plans and planners. It would be difficult in any event to resist United States demands for defence co-operation, but if isolationism were to return 'as a militant form of continental defence mindedness,' then 'the pressure on Canada to maintain commensurate defences might be very strong' – financially embarrassing to meet, politically embarrassing to refuse. For that reason, if for no other, it would be prudent to maintain membership in, and to prepare planning through, the Permanent Joint Board on Defence, 'where the tradition of equality is established and where the Canadian case may be frankly stated.' Statesmanship being the constructive acceptance of the inevitable, Canada ought to accept as a fact of its national life its post-war involvement in United States continental defence arrangements, and to consider as soon as possible the nature of her contribution. Nine areas invited some degree of Canadian co-operation.

* A contrary assumption had dominated defence planning after the first World War; see James Eayrs, *In Defence of Canada*, I, *From the Great War to the Great Depression* (Toronto 1964), 70–8.

First, the defence of Newfoundland, including Labrador. The United States had already acquired 99-year leases for bases at Goose Bay, Gander, and Tor Bay. Their security during the post-war period would be a primary American strategic interest. Canada had accepted the major role for the defence of the area in the Second World War, and would not be able to pull out without the Americans moving in.

Second, the Alaska Highway. While Canada had given no precise undertaking to maintain the route when it was to revert to her control six months after the termination of hostilities, the United States would expect Canada to keep it in good repair for military traffic.

Third, the airfields along the air-routes of northwest Canada. These guarded the approaches to the United States, and the Americans would want them kept both serviceable and secure.

Fourth, radar warning. 'Since questions of attack, or raids, against the United States will be chiefly predicated on air attack from the north, it follows that an adequate warning system – linked up with the airfields chain – will be an important defence provision.'

Fifth, coastal defences. Naval strategy would continue to require the maintenance of strongly defended bases, with heavy anti-aircraft artillery and air striking power for protection. Canada would be expected to provide adequate coastal defence protection of Halifax, Esquimalt, and other areas after the war, as during it.

Sixth, Iceland and Greenland. These areas formed the outer defence perimeter of Canada and the United States in the east, and while not possessing sovereignty, the two countries, together with the United Kingdom, had a vital interest in their protection. It was unlikely, however, in view of the vast expanse of land and ocean for which Canada would also be responsible, that she would be expected to accept any major commitment to their defence.

Seventh, the use of Canadian facilities by the armed forces of the United States. The Alaska Highway, airfields, and seaports were among the facilities that the United States might wish to gain access to as part of its post-war continental defence arrangements.

Eighth, exchange of technical information. 'Any arrangement to extend this into the future is obviously to be encouraged.'

Finally, defence of the sea approaches. For the defence of her own Canada would be primarily responsible, and would be expected to maintain 'first class defended convoy assembly ports and task groups on both coasts.'

'Emphasis in this paper,' its author concluded,

has been given to the desirability and probably the inevitability, of a continuance of the present defensive coordination with the United States. It should be stressed that this coordination is not regarded in any sense as a development of Canadian-United States isolationism, either from world or Commonwealth affairs. Rather it is felt that by taking the obvious steps to make Canada defensively secure, Canada's function as a member of the Commonwealth and of any world security system that may evolve will be considerably enhanced ... Canadian relations with the United States ... should be as a member of the Commonwealth and of a world security organization, and any attempt to form a North American bloc should be resisted in the interests of world peace.[7]

The Working Committee on Post-Hostilities Problems found no serious flaw in this analysis when it met on 18 May to discuss it. It was felt, however, that a revised version of the paper might change the emphasis of the argument here and there. In particular – so the minutes of the meeting record – more should be made of Canadian relations with the Soviet Union, 'and especially defence problems arising out of the possibility of tension between the USA and the USSR, in which Canada, being sandwiched between the two, would inevitably be involved.' Some of the installations manned by and located in Canada for the defence of Alaska, for example, could be turned by the United States into bases for offensive operations against the Soviet Union; 'it was essential that the granting of facilities under the special circumstances of this war should not be used as a precedent for future action in time of peace, if Canadian neutrality were not to be prejudiced.' The Working Committee recommended that the revised paper examine more critically the role of the Permanent Joint Board on Defence, 'as the very fact of its existence might give rise to mistrust on the part of third powers who might not appreciate its defensive character...'[8]

The second draft of the document, dated 26 May, embodied these suggestions and clearly reflects the qualifications of the External Affairs members of the Working Committee of which it had now become an official paper, though far from in its final form. The assumption of the post-war Canadian-American relationship was now more cautiously worded – not 'amicable,' as in Jenkins' first version, but 'close and, unless disturbed by factors which have not hitherto arisen ... characterized by a mutual willingness and ability to reach agreement on all questions of importance.'

The paper next set forth assumptions about the post-war world scene. Germany and Japan, utterly defeated and disarmed, would not constitute a threat 'for a number of years at least.' Europe likewise, with the exception of the United Kingdom and the Soviet Union, would be too weak to threaten any non-European nation, as would China. 'It follows that the USSR is the only nation which would be capable of offering a threat to North America.'

The greatest difficulty in maintaining good relations with the United States would arise if, in the event of tension between the United States and the Soviet Union, the Americans were to demand Canada's support to an extent the Canadian government considered unwarranted. The choices would be unenviable:

(a) Respond to United States pressure for large scale defences in the north (which the USSR might regard as offensive measures) and incur the risk of Soviet hostility, or

(b) Refuse to incur that risk and be faced with the demand that if we will not take the necessary steps ourselves we must give United States forces a free hand.

The paper however discerned an escape from this dilemma in 'the establishment of a world security organization in which the member states had sufficient confidence that they would not embark on individual policies leading to strained relations.' Such an organization, in which Canada, the United States, and the Soviet Union would be represented, 'would alleviate suspicions between the nations ... and ... give Canada an opportunity to try to use her influence for what it was worth to try to prevent the growth of any misunderstanding or tension between the United States and the USSR. Indeed, it may be that we will have to attempt the role of interpreter or intermediary between these countries.'

If the post-war world developed in such a direction, Canada should continue to co-operate closely with the United States through the Permanent Joint Board on Defence, as well as participate in a global security organization. The two should not be mutually exclusive. The Board 'might conceivably be extended to take in other countries such as the USSR.'

If, on the other hand, post-war rivalries and tensions were such as to preclude the development or lead to a breakdown of a world security organization, 'the retention up to a point of the Permanent Joint Board on Defence or some similar body offers the best possibilities. It provides an opportunity to discuss difficult problems frankly and openly in an arena where a tradition of equality has been established ... The Permanent Joint Board on Defence is a practical working model of a regional defence system where weight of counsel is dependent on function rather than on net power.'

In its scrutiny of what a later generation of strategists would call 'alternative futures,' the paper did not overlook the possibility of a situation of tension between the United States and the Soviet Union in which Canadian sympathies were ranged on the Soviet side. Here again, the planners concluded, membership on the Permanent Joint Board on Defence would prove advantageous to Canada. It would permit Canada openly to dissociate herself, for a short term or a long, from joint military planning with the United States. 'Our ability to use our influence towards relieving the tension might be greatly increased by our visibly adopting a position of greater freedom of action.'

These speculations done with, the paper arrived at its conclusions, set out as follows:

(a) That the static or territorial defences of Canada should be closely coordinated with those of the United States in the post-war period.

(b) That this coordination should be carried out through the medium of the Permanent Joint Board on Defence or some similar body.

(c) That the only apparent source of friction which might arise between Canada and the United States would grow out of differing views towards events outside this continent.

(d) In this connection relations between the United States and the USSR are of special concern to Canada and any military co-operation between Canada and the United States should be conducted in such a way as to avoid giving the USSR any cause for mistrust of our intentions.

(e) In joint defence planning with the United States, Canada must accept full responsibility for defence measures within Canadian territory (and if possible in Newfoundland and Labrador). Excessive though these may seem, the new vulnerability of the North American continent requires the acceptance of increased defence responsibilities on the part of Canada.[9]

On 16 June, the Working Committee reported to its parent Advisory Committee that it had prepared a draft paper on post-war defence arrangements with the United States, but that before submitting a final version the Working Committee desired to find out whether certain assumptions on which the paper had been based were generally acceptable. One of these assumptions was the following.

Provided that complete victory is won, and that it is followed by thorough disarmament of Germany and Japan, it may safely be assumed that there is no danger of attack on North America during the ten years after the war. Even if tension were to become acute between the USSR and the US, the problems of recovery and development in the USSR are so great that the possibility of warfare between these two Great Powers during the next decade is extremely remote.[10]

Reaction to this assumption proved mixed on two accounts. It seemed to some members of the policy community that the draft paper placed too much emphasis on the Soviet threat as the *raison d'être* for United States defence planning. North America was not the only, nor even the most likely, locale of conflict. 'If war were to come between the United States and the Soviet Union,' the Working Committee agreed at its meeting of 3 July, 'it would probably come as part of a world conflict, and the fighting would take place in Asia or in Europe.' The paper should be reworded so as to make this clear.[11]

In the second place, there was disagreement as to the likelihood of war. To Maurice Pope, the paper's discounting the probability of Soviet-American conflict within ten years of the end of the war appeared highly realistic. 'I find myself very much in agreement,' Pope wrote to Jenkins from Washington.

> You will find yourselves opposing the American technique of assessing enemy capabilities as against our view of what the enemy will *probably* do. You will find people saying that the enemy is quite capable of despatching a hundred, or a thousand, planes against Gander or White Horse. That is true, but my counter to that is "Will he?", i.e., are there reasonable grounds for assuming that he will? If one guards himself against enemy capabilities everywhere you will soon exhaust your resources...
>
> During the past three years we have done a great deal for the United States without subjecting their proposals to really critical examination. There being a war on, as good neighbours and as little fellows, we were practically obliged to meet their requests and that speedily. As a result we and they have done a number of foolish things which are now a burden on our tax-payers. I think in future if cases of this kind again arise, we would be wise not to accept immediately but to observe that, in our view, in which we have a certain measure of confidence, the proposal or request seems to be exaggerated and to resist their pressure and to suggest to them that they lower their sights.[12]

Pope's views were reflected in the discussion at the meeting of the Advisory Committee on 4 July, the minutes of which record that some members expressed objections to the Working Committee's susceptibility to 'a Russian bogey,' as well as to its implication 'that Canada would have little part in making decisions as to her own policy.'[13]

At the same meeting, however, the Chief of Naval Staff, Rear Admiral G.C. Jones, questioned the validity of the Working Committee's assumption that the possibility of Soviet-American conflict within ten years was extremely remote. 'He thought that this ten year concept had been a fallacy of pre-war planning which persisted until 1939. He questioned also the advisability of including ... political judgments such as ... that the USSR could not be in a position to take part in a war during the next decade.' As a result of 'Jetty' Jones' intervention, the Advisory Committee agreed to regard the ten-year period as a flexible estimate which should be reviewed each year, and on no account as 'a time during which defences could be relaxed or forgotten because at the end of it they would have to be prepared for possible attack.' The Cabinet War Committee, to which the Advisory Committee reported two days later, was similarly briefed:

> Although on present prospects Canadian planning for the ten years after the

war need not take account of the possibility of attack on North America or of the outbreak of war between the US and USSR, there will be considerable military needs to be met by the United Nations during all or part of that period...[14]

On 19 July, the Advisory Committee's memorandum was discussed by the War Committee. Its members decided to strike out a paragraph asserting that 'Canada will not be willing to permit the United States to provide and maintain defence installations in Canadian territory.' On the urging of the Minister of National Defence, J.L. Ralston, it agreed to ascertain the views of the US Chiefs of Staff before giving its approval to the assumption about ten years of peace between the Soviet Union and the United States.

Soundings were duly taken in Washington by General Pope. A US member of the Permanent Joint Board on Defence considered the Canadian assessment overly optimistic. A member of the US Strategic Survey Committee believed that while the United States and the Soviet Union would not come to blows on their own there was a distinct possibility that the United States would be drawn into an armed conflict with the Soviet Union in support of the United Kingdom. But the clinching evidence of disapproval came from a deputy Chief of Staff. 'His reaction was immediate and categorical,' Pope reported.

He thought it extremely unlikely that the US Joint CO's would be disposed officially to state their agreement with the tentative assumption. The United States Services both were hoping and planning to make compulsory military service a feature of the post-war period. They certainly proposed to retain a powerful navy. As for their land and air forces they proposed to remain in a position which would enable them rapidly and at any time to mobilize an army and air force of four and one-half million men. To achieve this policy they would be dependent on Congress. This being so it would be most unwise on their part officially to subscribe themselves to the proposition that the possibility of a major war during the first decade of the post-war period was extremely remote. For if word of this ever reached the ears of Congress the hopes they now cherished and planned to achieve would be dashed against the rocks...[15]

Somewhat chastened by this intelligence, the Ottawa planners went back to their drafting-board.

A meeting of the Working Committee on 25 August considered the text of a third draft. 'It is unwise to ignore the possibility of attack from the Soviet Union,' its minutes record its conclusion. 'At least until the world security organization has proved itself capable of functioning successfully it seems inevitable that every nation will require forces for the dual purpose of defending its own territory from attack and of striking at enemies or potential enemies beyond its territory.'[16]

After further weeks of tinkering, a fourth draft was prepared, and then a fifth. The working assumptions had now been reduced to three succinct statements:

i That international problems arising from purely Canadian-United States relations will cause no irreconcilable conflict of policies and, therefore, any dangerous conflict of policies could only be occasioned by differing attitudes towards events outside this continent.

ii That for several years at least there will be no direct military threat to North America.

iii That the victor nations, including the United States, will maintain larger armed forces than before the war to enforce peace.

The issue of the threat was elaborated in these terms:

The defence problems of Canada and the United States must now be considered as inter-dependent. While it may be held that the east and west coastal areas are still relatively immune from major attack (as long as the British and United States Navies are in being, which will continue to be a basic assumption), the development of air power has diminished the physical isolation of the North American continent by opening up the northern approaches. Defence planning must be re-oriented to take this into account.[17]

Across the top of the document, bearing the title 'Revised Final' and the date 24 October 1944, one of the planners had printed: 'All final drafts are final, but some are more final than others.'

Even so, the finality of the fifth version was for a few days in doubt. 'There may be a hitch with regard to the paper on "Defence Relationship with the United States",' the secretary of the Working Committee informed Hume Wrong a few days after it had given its approval to that document. He had been telephoned by an aide to the Chief of the Air Staff and told that 'Air Marshal Leckie took strong exception to certain parts of the paper on Canada-United States relations and had instructed his deputy at the meeting to report his views. Air Marshal Sully, however, did not arrive at the meeting and the objections were not expressed. I have sent the Secretary a note on the changes made in the Paper at the meeting but I doubt if these will meet the CAS's views ... I should not be surprised ... if we hear from him shortly.'[18]

Leckie's last-minute objections to a document so long in the making were not well received by the top officials of the Department of External Affairs. 'I am inclined to advise that the CAS should be told politely that he ought to have made his points somewhat sooner,' was Hume Wrong's reaction.

I understand that what he objects to is ... the statement that there will be no immediate threat of attack to North America after the war ... Col. Ralston questioned this and the War Committee agreed to check in Washington ... No objection in any case was made to the point by the RCAF when the earlier paper was under consideration ... I am inclined to think the paper should go forward to the War Committee and Leckie should be so informed.[19]

Norman Robertson agreed: 'Leckie could be told that the paper will be considered at next meeting of War Committee when perhaps his Minister could develop the CAS's reservations.' But Leckie's soldierly nature* shrank from pursuing the issue at the political level. 'The CAS to whom your suggestion was transmitted,' Hume Wrong informed Robertson on 18 November, 'has reluctantly withdrawn his objections...'

That was not yet the end of the affair. Loath to carry the argument to the War Committee, Leckie was ready to rally the Chiefs of Staff Committee. He and his fellow Chiefs met on 29 December to discuss 'Whether or not there was good reason for the assumption "That for several years at least there will be no direct military threat to North America".' 'I think their views can best be summed up,' Maurice Pope informed Hume Wrong afterwards, 'by quoting the remarks of Air Marshal Leckie.' Leckie had told the Chiefs:

I still feel that there is grave danger in accepting as an assumption for Post-War Planning any statement which suggests that there will not, or might not be, any military threat to North America over a period of time at the close of hostilities. However, as there appear to be strong opinions to the contrary, and as the changes suggested by Mr Wrong constitute a compromise, I am prepared to accept these changes to the recommendations made by the Chiefs of Staff Committee.[20]

The compromise proposed by Hume Wrong consisted of attaching to the statement that there would be no immediate threat of attack to North America after the war the following qualification: 'It is necessary, however, that the means to meet any such threat should be available during this period.' With that qualification duly inserted, the document came before the War Committee of the Cabinet on 8 January 1945.

There it met with criticism by which the planners could not brush. 'The Prime Minister was of the opinion,' the War Committee minutes record, 'that insufficient emphasis had been given in the report to the importance of Canada's positive contribution to peace in fostering good international relations. This was a central principle of our external policy, as we were too small and vulnerable to rely solely on defence relationships.' It was back to the drafting-board once more.

The Advisory Committee met on 12 January to discuss what to do next. It was told by Arnold Heeney, factotum to the War Committee, that there was no need to start again from scratch.

* See above, 58–9.

Mr Heeney explained that there had been no disposition on the part of the War Committee to disagree with the main contents of the Report. There was some doubt, however, as to the purpose of this paper. It was not clear whether it was intended to recommend certain commitments to be accepted by the Government, or to be a general statement of policy. The Prime Minister, moreover, had expressed the view that Canada could not depend on defence arrangements for its security, but must primarily rely on the establishment of an international system of security. Emphasis, therefore, should be placed on the Canadian contribution to the peaceful settlement of international problems.

Norman Robertson attempted to clarify the purpose of the paper. It was intended 'to recommend a general line of policy and not to furnish a basis for specific commitments. The appropriate Departments would have to work out recommendations with respect to the application of proposals covered in a general manner in the paper.' It might be necessary, Robertson thought, 'to prepare a covering paper containing a projection of the long-range political considerations governing Canadian external policy, and that the specific studies on defence relationship with the United States, the Commonwealth, etc., would have to be related to this paper.' That prospect appeared to dismay Hume Wrong, who had invested so much time and effort in the preparation of a position paper which had still to be approved by the government. Wrong proposed instead that the report, revised to take into account the suggestions of the Prime Minister, go forward to the War Committee at once rather than held back to await the completion of yet another document which might take even longer to run the gauntlet of interdepartmental criticism. The Advisory Committee allowed it to proceed.

So by 23 January 1945, the final version – 'Post-War Canadian Defence Relationships with the United States: General Considerations' – was finished. [It is reproduced below, as Document 1.] It was the product of nearly a year's deliberation and debate within the policy community. It was discussed by the War Committee of the Cabinet on 28 February, and finally approved by the War Committee on 19 July 1945 – though not before the Under Secretary of State for External Affairs assured its members that 'the acceptance of the report by the War Committee would not imply specific commitments on the part of the Government.'

The disclosure of Soviet espionage in Canada caused the Prime Minister to become extremely apprehensive about the vulnerability of North America to attack by Russia. 'This revelation,' Mackenzie King wrote on 11 September 1945, 'gives one a new and more appalling outlook on the world than one has ever had before...'[21] His entries in his diary during the next few weeks reveal the depth of his concern.

*23 September*: I personally feel a great alarm at the encroachment which Russia is making in different parts of the world. So far as this continent is concerned, their possession now of part of the Kuriles, etc., makes clear their arm reaches right over our continent ... I have no doubt that Russia intends to develop the atomic bomb and to go to all lengths in doing this. It looks to me as though she was already very far along the road. To try to fight a war with atomic bombs is just too appalling a thought for words. We are at the edge of a situation of the kind at this very hour...[22]

*1 October*: ... What I feel is that neither the UK, the US or Canada would ever use the atomic bomb as a surprise weapon. I do not feel the same way about a country that uses espionage on a national scale as it is being used against Canada today...[23]

*21 October*: ... deeply concerned about Canada's position in the event of any trouble arising between Russia and other countries ... It would be the battleground ... they were near neighbours of ours and to reach America, would come across Canadian territory.[24]

Mackenzie King was angry as well as apprehensive. 'To think,' he wrote, 'of the Russian Embassy being only a few doors away and of there being there a centre of intrigue. During this period of war, while Canada has been helping Russia and doing all we can to foment [*sic*] Canada-Russian friendship, there has been one branch of the Russian service that has been spying on all matters relating to location of American troops, atomic bombs, processes, etc ... All this helps to explain,' he added, 'the Russian attitude at the Council of Foreign Ministers. Something very sinister there.'[25]

Yet apprehension and anger made poor foundations on which to build Canada's post-war policy towards the Soviet Union. Despite what the Prime Minister regarded, not without reason, as the betrayal of a trust, he was determined to preserve what remained of co-operation between the two countries. On 8 November 1945, the Minister of National Defence spoke on his behalf – he was then en route from London to Washington – to a meeting of the Canadian-Soviet Friendship Rally convened in Ottawa to commemorate the anniversary of the founding of the Soviet state. 'Mr King,' Douglas Abbott told his audience, 'would have been delighted to be here tonight.' That was sheer hyperbole. The rest of his message, presumably prepared in consultation with the Department of External Affairs, brimmed with cordial goodwill:

The friendship that has grown up between Canada and the Union of Soviet States, the two great Northern Neighbours, is one which must be maintained and strengthened. Only the top of the world separates us, and that means we're next-door neighbours in this modern flying age.

But our respect and admiration are founded on something more than just geographical neighbourliness. There is similarity in the vastness of our two countries ... Our two frontiers meet at the North Pole. We have the same climate and the same resources, and we have the same problems in transportation and development. We have populations of mixed racial origins living in harmony together, and on all levels we can do much to learn from each other and to assist each other ... In friendship, and in understanding ... lie all our hopes for the bright world of the future ... That is why the Council for Canadian-Soviet Friendship has the warm support of the Government of Canada today...[26]

That was laying it on with a trowel. By March 1946, when Soviet wartime espionage had become public knowledge and the time had arrived to make a full disclosure to the people of Canada, it was no longer possible to speak in such lavish terms of Canadian-Soviet co-operation. Nevertheless the Prime Minister still hoped, in spite of everything, to keep alive the spirit of entente.

On 18 March – the first meeting of Parliament since the statement of 15 February in which the Prime Minister made public the news that 'Information of undoubted authenticity has reached the Canadian Government which establishes that there have been disclosures of secret and confidential information to unauthorized persons, including some members of the staff of a foreign mission in Ottawa' – Mackenzie King reviewed in detail the events that began on that morning of 6 September 1945, when 'Hon. members may have noticed that at that time the House was kept waiting for a few minutes at least, before I found it possible to come in.' Towards the close of his narrative he turned his attention to 'some of the international aspects of this matter.' He told the House that he had deliberately refrained, in the statement of 15 February, from mentioning the name of the foreign power concerned. 'But before giving out this statement,' he added, 'I did ask the chargé d'affaires of the Russian embassy to come to my office: I read to him the statement, and I told him that the country to which reference was made was the USSR.' Suggestions had been made that the Canadian Government ought to break diplomatic relations with the Soviet Union and require the Soviet Embassy to withdraw. 'I hope,' Mackenzie King commented, 'that no view of that kind will be expressed by anyone in a responsible position.' He went on:

We in Canada want only the best of relations with the USSR, as we do with every other country, and we must not be too ready to judge until we know all the circumstances connected with the particular situation. I believe it is true that there are agencies working, may I put it, at the side of the Russian Embassy which are doing things that possibly are unknown to the ambassador himself and members of his immediate staff. That may be so and it may not be so. At any rate I am not going to be the one to judge as to who has knowledge of this and who has knowledge of that. The time will come when all this can be worked out and, I hope and pray, will be worked out in a manner which

> will let us get rid of whatever there may be of wrong and evil in the whole business and establish the friendliest of relations on a true and sound basis, one which will be above suspicion in every way.

Mackenzie King even went so far as to attempt to exonerate the highest levels of the Soviet government from responsibility for what had happened. 'What I know, or have learned, of Mr Stalin from those who have been closely associated with him in the war, causes me to believe that he would not countenance action of this kind on the part of officials of his country. I believe,' he declared, 'that when these facts are known to him and to others in positions of full responsibility, we shall find that a change will come that will make a vast difference indeed.'[27]

This answer could hardly have been softer; and its author confidently expected it to turn away wrath. 'I tried to prepare the ground for the future,' Mackenzie King wrote in his diary after delivering the speech,

> by separating any knowledge of this business from Stalin, and expressing a certain confidence in him. Also every confidence in the Russian people and my own determination not to allow what had been disclosed to affect the relations of the two countries, but rather be made the instrument for drawing us closer together. That course alone will save the world. An opposite course, one of antagonism and fight, would very soon provoke an appalling situation. If war ever comes between Russian and any part of the British Commonwealth and the United States this country would be the battlefield and everything we value here would be obliterated...[28]

As with Hitler, so with Stalin: Mackenzie King was still prepared to give to tyrants the benefit of doubt. He could not believe that the apparatus of the modern state could fall into the hands of gunmen or lunatics. In 1946, as in 1937, Mackenzie King found it hard to believe 'that our civilization is dominated by carnivorous animals.'[29]

Soviet experts within the Department of External Affairs, while less sanguine than their Prime Minister that Stalin still possessed a store of goodwill for his wartime allies, were not of the opinion that he was girding his country for war. 'Our information indicates ... that the Soviet Union will not be in any position to wage another major war in the near future.' one of their memoranda asserted, 'and that it will take considerably more than three to five years for the Soviet Union to complete her economic and industrial recovery so as to be in a position to wage another long drawn out war.'[30] Nor would the Kremlin choose to fight, even if it could.

> The foreign policy of the Soviet Union, while pursued by different methods and sponsored by a government which is foreign in its political institutions and social structure, is nevertheless the normal expression of the interests of that country. There have been no indications of undue Soviet interest in North America and politically, therefore, it may be judged that there is an absence

of evidence to show the development of any aggressive designs on the part of the Soviet Union against this continent.[31]

Soviet policy is defensive. While there is a resemblance in technique between the diplomatic practices of the Kremlin and those used by Hitler, it would be most misleading to push the comparison far. For instance, the Soviet Government completely controls one seventh of the earth's surface and already possesses, unlike Nazi Germany, a vast field for internal development. The Russian peoples also do not share the German illusion that they are a master race...[32]

We are likely to see, for some time to come, a continuation of the "Cold War," the purpose of which will be to divide and weaken the Western powers ... Probes will be made here and there to see whether further territory can be acquired without running the risk of a major war, but care will also be taken to prevent the "Cold War" from turning into a "hot war"...[33]

These assessments did not differ in their conclusion from the sombre depiction of the sources of Soviet conduct then purveyed to Washington by the US *chargé d'affairs* in Moscow, who likewise argued that the Kremlin's methods, while unscrupulous, were not Hitlerian, so that 'if the situations are properly handled, there need be no prestige-engaging showdown.'* But whereas the Canadian policy community remained calm, the American policy community was galvanized into something close to panic. Kennan's despatch became 'required reading for hundreds, if not thousands, of higher officers in the armed services,' for whom it was heady stuff. Those 'questions so intricate, so delicate, so strange to our form of thought' – questions Kennan had intended not so much to answer as to raise – were banished from military minds. In their place a crude appreciation prevailed. The Soviet Union was the enemy, war a possibility, bombers were the threat, the polar corridor the route.

The US Navy planners were ready converts to this concept, for it enabled the fleet to play a key role in continental defence. 'Operation Frostbite' – an exercise carried out during March 1946 by the new heavy aircraft carrier *Midway*, three destroyers and a tanker – demonstrated to the US Navy's satisfaction that 'carrier-air operations can effectively extend to sub-arctic regions in defiance of ice, snow and frigid winds.'[34]

Still more strident alarmists were to be found among American airmen, for the more drastically they portrayed the threat of Soviet attack the stronger became their case for a mighty national commitment to military aviation. Bombers would be needed to deter the Russian air force. Fighters would be needed to repel the Russian air force. The ambitions of these apostles of air power knew few if any limits. 'Airpower would defend

* See George F. Kennan, *Memoirs: 1925–1950* (Boston & Toronto 1967), 292–5, 547–59.

this nation; airpower would guarantee the success of a new international security organization; airpower would punish aggression wherever it might manifest itself; airpower would save the world. Salvation had come; all America and the world needed to do was to maintain and support a strong United States Air Force – a simple, reliable formula. The airplane was not considered just another weapon; it was the ultimate weapon for universal peacekeeping.'[35] Such was the USAF ideology in 1946. The Americans sat down in briefing rooms and conference rooms with their Canadian counterparts in a frame of mind at once messianic and demanding. The combination augured ill for easy collaboration.

The wartime military partnership between Canada and the United States had been governed by a document drawn up under the aegis of the Permanent Joint Board on Defence during the summer of 1941 and came into formal effect with the United States declaration of war. This document, officially known as Joint Basic Defence Plan No. 2, more familiarly as ABC-22, was, in the words of the official US military history, 'not directed toward hemispheric defense as an end in itself. It was intended instead to supplement the agreements reached in the United States-British staff conversations, the aim of which was to bring to bear against Germany the combined might of the United States and the British Commonwealth when the United States entered the war.'[36] It was thus in no way suited to the situation of the two countries at the end of the war, and the question arose at once of what plans, if any, should be made to take its place.

The Permanent Joint Board on Defence held its first meeting in peacetime in New York City on 7 and 8 November 1945, when the senior US Army and Navy members reported that they had been instructed to 'initiate conversations to provide, in the light of changed world conditions, a continuing basis for joint action of the military forces of Canada and the United States in order to ensure the security of Alaska, Canada, Labrador, Newfoundland, and the northern portion of the United States.' The Canadian members of the Board undertook to seek the views of their government on this proposal.[37]

The Cabinet Defence Committee met to consider it on 4 December, agreeing to recommend to the full Cabinet 'that the United States' proposal for continued collaboration in defence planning be accepted, and that the Chiefs of Staff Committee, with the addition of appropriate civilian officials, be given the responsibility for co-ordinating Canadian participation in the preparation of joint plans...'[38] This recommendation was accepted by the Cabinet on 19 December, 'on the understanding that any new plans for joint defence would be submitted to the Government for decision.'[39]

The joint planning staff assembled for this purpose was first known as the Canada-United States Planning Committee, later as the Military Co-operation Committee. It was composed of Canadian and United States military officers in equal numbers and corresponding ranks, who were also members of the Permanent Joint Board on Defence. Its Canadian members were Commodore H.G. de Wolf, Major General D.C. Spry, Air Vice Marshal W.A. Curtis, Colonel J.H. Jenkins, and Group Captain W.W. Bean. By June 1946 the joint planners had held two meetings. 'At the first of these,' Hume Wrong reported, 'they tentatively agreed on an appreciation which is said to have received the blessings of the US Chiefs of Staff in an earlier version which has not been changed substantially. They are now working on a new basic defence plan which will replace ABC 22.'[40]

Their appreciation argued along the following lines. Geography no longer conferred upon North America the luxury of immunity from major attack by a hostile power. The continent's protective *glacis* of ocean and ice would soon be vulnerable to bombers, guided missiles, submarines. These formidable weapons carriers would bear no less formidable weapons – rockets, bacteria, atomic bombs, the last of which would be available to the enemy (unnamed, but unmistakably the Soviet Union) in three to five years' time.

By 1950, then – or thereabouts – the enemy would be capable of inflicting an all-out attack on North America, using short-range guided missiles, aircraft, and rockets launched both from submarines and from Arctic bases seized for the purpose. It could also engage in long-range bombing with atomic weapons. The targets would be the nerve centres of government, industrial concentrations, and densely populated areas. The attack would follow the shortest route between the Eurasian land mass and the Western hemisphere – across the polar cap and north-east Canada into the industrial heartlands of North America.

Such was the grim contingency discerned by the planners only a few years hence. It was none too soon to make defensive preparations. They recommended accordingly the joint construction by Canada and the United States of an effective air defence system – early warning, meteorological, and communications facilities; a network of air bases deployed as far to the north of potential targets as feasible; fighter-interceptor aircraft; and anti-aircraft defences.

In addition to the air defence system, the planners proposed that a programme of air mapping and photography begin at once. Air and surface surveillance should be undertaken to give warning of enemy infiltration. Anti-submarine and naval patrol of the sea approaches should be instituted, and garrison and mobile forces created to guard against lodgments in the north. Finally, a command structure suited to the needs of joint Canada-United States defence should be contrived and put into effect. All these measures the planners considered urgent. But most urgent was the air defence system.

A Basic Security Plan, dated 5 June 1946, accompanied this appreciation and echoed its forecasts and recommendations, suggesting in some detail a division of labour between Canadian and American forces. [It is printed below as Document 2.]

First in the Department of External Affairs to read these documents was Hume Wrong. 'My feeling is that the appreciation while sound in its general analysis is defective in its estimate of the possible time factors involved,' Wrong wrote after perusing them, 'and also overemphasizes some of the potential dangers. It seems to me to assume a greater capacity in the USSR for waging an offensive war than seems likely to exist now or even within the next decade.'[41]

Next in line was Arnold Heeney who, sensing trouble, immediately briefed the Prime Minister (then returning from Britain an the *Queen Mary*).

> The conclusions of the draft appreciation are grave. They may be modified somewhat by the Canadian Chiefs but they are unlikely to undergo any material alteration before being submitted to the government...
>
> There is no doubt that, from several points of view, these developments will constitute one of the most difficult and serious problems with which the government will have to deal within the next few years. The initiative has been wholly that of the United States but our own military advisers will certainly, on purely defence grounds, reach similar conclusions. They may feel, however, that on all the evidence we have more time than US authorities have estimated...
>
> In these circumstances, the government will probably have to accept the US thesis in general terms, though we may be able to moderate the pace at which plans are to be implemented and to some extent the nature of the projects which are to be undertaken...[42]

In a note accompanying his memorandum, Heeney urged Mackenzie King to give the issues his earliest attention. 'Our own defence and military people will have to receive Cabinet guidance before long. The issues are such that there will be strong opinions held and expressed ... The exposition of the military position as given by the intelligence and planning officers ... is one which I think you should hear, yourself, as soon as there is time...[43]

This proved to be 9 July 1946. At a meeting of the Cabinet Defence Committee the Prime Minister presided. The military planners gave their presentation. Their advocacy failed to produce the effect desired. 'It became perfectly apparent, I think, to all as we listened,' Mackenzie King recorded afterwards, 'that Canada simply could not do what was necessary to protect itself. Our country would be a mere pawn in the world conflict.' So far from giving the green light to the Basic Plan, the Prime Minister flashed the red. 'The great thing,' he told the crestfallen officers, 'was for Canada to be the link that would keep the other two great powers united.' How their plan would accomplish their unity he was unable to understand. 'I drew out how the whole business had been worked out between the planning committee here and opposite numbers in Washington. That up to the present the British had not been brought into the matter ... I said there must be the fullest exchange of views with the British on the whole question of defence.' The plan he had been shown was altogether too bilateral. The military, as usual, wanted to go too far too fast.[44]

Yet though Mackenzie King had no use for the planners' political judgment, he was favourably taken by their technical competence. 'I thought the whole business was well done. The subject was presented on the basis of the polar map, instead of using Mercator's projection. By the polar map, a clear picture was given of how this continent could be attacked from the North.'[45] Henceforth Mackenzie King would have no more use for Mercator's projection than Pitt, on the eve of Austerlitz, professed to have for the map of Europe. But the map of Europe was rolled up only for ten years. Mercator's would not be needed again.*

The Americans were now in something of a quandary. All their assessments stressed the need for urgency. In Ottawa the mood was calm. Yet without the northern neighbour nothing could be done. Was there a way by which the mood might be changed?

Towards the end of August 1946, the US ambassador to Canada ad-

* 'As a map to illustrate the intercontinental relations of the Soviet Union and the United States, in an age of jet planes and ballistic missiles, the conventional Mercator map has serious manifest defects. This map does not portray the clustering of Canada and the Soviet Union around the Arctic Ocean. Viewed from this map, the elaborate system of American air defences in northern Canada makes no sense whatever. Likewise, the conventional Mercator map exaggerates the width of the northern reaches of the Atlantic and Pacific oceans, thereby contributing to the historic American illusion of political and military isolation from the Old World.' Harold and Margaret Sprout, *The Ecological Perspective on Human Affairs. With Special Reference to International Politics* (Princeton, NJ 1965), 126.

dressed himself to this question, in a despatch which rendered the attitudes of the Prime Minister and those around him with admirable sensitivity.

> ...We are convinced beyond question that the Prime Minister realizes the necessity of joint planning and eventual standardization of training and equipment, but that he is using his traditional caution in approaching the subject. That the bulk of his Cabinet and all of the Service Chiefs of Staff go along with him seems from our conversations to be also beyond question. Some want to move faster than others, but all seek the same end, that is, the security of Canada under the United Nations in co-operation with the United States without detriment, if possible, to Canada's position as a member of the British Commonwealth ... There remain some members of the Cabinet ... who are still sceptical of the intentions of the United States. The convictions of these men are so patently honest that the Prime Minister seems unwilling to ride rough shod over their objections. It seems to me that if some way can be found to allay the suspicions of this element and to assure Canada that joint defense with the United States will not lead to withdrawal from the Commonwealth our path would be much easier. This must be done, however, I believe, at the very highest level.[46]

The invitation from the White House duly followed.

Prime Minister and President met in Washington on 28 October 1946. 'Quite early in our conversation,' Mackenzie King wrote afterwards, President Truman

> brought up the question of our common interests in defence. He said he thought it was quite apparent about the US and Canada that each depended in part on the other. There was need for co-ordinating our methods ... The President said that anything in the nature of war between us was inconceivable and that war with any one of the three might certainly bring in the others...
>
> I said I thought what had to be most considered was the way in which the public became informed on these matters. The whole publicity should be agreed to in advance, steps to be taken very slowly and surely. Care would have to be taken not to give the Russians a chance to say we were trying to fight them. The President said there was no aggression in our mind at all. All that we were doing would be to make aggression impossible anywhere.
>
> I spoke of the enormous expenditures the armed forces had made. I said I thought it would be well in regard to any statement we were making of our conversation to make clear that while we had touched on defence it had been with a view to discussing means of effecting economies and effective co-operation between the forces. The President said he thought my judgment was right in referring to the matter in this way. I said one could not take exception in seeking to effect economies in joint defence. The President mentioned that in working out plans he thought further steps should be taken up through Ministers and on a diplomatic level, rather than by the Services. With this I agreed...[47]

It was clear, Mackenzie King reflected at the conclusion of his visit, 'that the purpose of the meeting was to give official sanction in both countries to go ahead and work toward an agreement as a result of which plans for defence would be co-ordinated and developed.' But Mackenzie King had given Truman no such assurance. It was first necessary for him to consult with his colleagues in the Government, and to ascertain their views.

These consultations took place during a series of meetings of the Cabinet Defence Committee and the Cabinet proper during the middle of November 1946. The first meeting of the Cabinet Defence Committee was held on 13 November. The Prime Minister presided. Ministers present included St Laurent, Abbott, Gibson, Claxton, and McCann. The Chiefs of Staff were there, as were the Director General of Defence Research and a sprinkling of senior civil servants. The Chief of the Air Staff, Air Marshal R. Leckie, told the assembled politicians that the Royal Canadian Air Force disagreed with American proposals for the air defence of North America. Speaking for his Service, the Air Marshal related that he was dissatisfied both with the financial implications and with the strategic assumptions of current American thinking on this subject. He noted that the intelligence upon which the joint appreciation was based had been supplied largely from American sources, allowing the implication to stand that the intelligence was on this account not altogether reliable. The view in Washington was that, in any future war, an aggressor would attempt to destroy the war potential of the North American continent before embarking upon expansion elsewhere. He did not himself share that view. His own notion was that any attack upon North America would likely be a feint, no more, not warranting the establishment of an elaborate defence scheme such as the Americans were proposing, with all its inroads upon Canadian territory and possibly upon Canadian resources. He thought it better to press for much more modest proposals.

These remarks by the Government's principal professional adviser on air defence matters made a profound impression upon his audience. No one present was more profoundly impressed than Brooke Claxton who, a month later, was to become Minister of National Defence. Claxton immediately prepared a statement of his own reaction, which he read to the meeting of the full Cabinet which met on the following day. 'Yesterday afternoon,' Claxton told his colleagues,

> the Chief of the Air Staff told us that the United States took the view that the main attack would be launched against them, with the objective of crippling the productive power of the United States.
>
> He went on to say that this was not the view either of the UK or of the Canadian General Staffs, who felt that any attack on this continent would be diversionary, that is, intended to prevent our assisting in the defence against the main attack. Only when the latter was pushed home, would the full resources of the rest of the world be turned against this continent.
>
> My present purpose is not to indicate a preference between the two views, but

to point out, indeed to emphasize in the strongest terms, the fact that there is a fundamental difference in the concepts of the American and Canadian staffs.

This would vitally affect the whole scale of the defence measures which should be established.

Further, this fundamental difference of view arises out of a joint appreciation. On the basis of that appreciation, the Americans say that they are to be the object of the main attack, and we say that at the outset we would be the object of a diversionary attack.

On the basis of this appreciation, the Military Co-operation Committee of Canada and the United States (generally called "The Joint Planners") have been drawing up a plan for submission to the General Staffs of the two countries. In anticipation of this, so that we might better appreciate the situation, Air Marshal Leckie has described to us this plan, and it appears to be based on the American concept. He has added that, having regard to the defence needs of Canada and the resources of Canada, he would not be likely to recommend the adoption of this plan when it comes before him.

I mention this as the background against which we should now consider the President's request that we should endorse the joint planning and that this endorsation should take the form of approval of the appreciation.

That is, we are asked to approve an appreciation when it is a fair assumption that the Americans draw a conclusion from it totally different from that which our expert advisers are likely to draw.

Secondly, we are asked to approve the continuation of joint planning which we now know is going forward on the basis of the American interpretation of the appreciation and which is designed to attain an object which our advisers will probably say is entirely beyond our capacity, even if it is desirable, namely the achievement of a Maginot Line across the north of Canada.

It seems to me that in these circumstances and against this background, our approval of the appreciation and endorsement of the joint planning that is now going on could not but mislead our American partners into the belief that we were going along with them in their concept.

It seems to me that each day that we allow them to continue along the present course will commit us further to acceptance of that course.

It seems to me that as this proceeds we will find that in their view at least we will have acquiesced in the action they have been taking, so that all that remains will be to settle the details and allocate the cost.

Moreover, if it comes down to this, we will be in a weak bargaining position, at least in a much weaker bargaining position than if we were to say to them now, "We simply don't agree with your concept. We can't afford to allocate any considerable proportion of the defence appropriations we can make in support of it. If you insist that this is necessary for your defence, then we would expect that you would contribute a large proportion of the cost."

Wouldn't it be better now, rather than to approve the appreciation and endorse the planning, to enter into the discussion with the Americans at the top political level and clarify the ground there before committing ourselves by allowing a chain of events to appear in the minds of the Americans to commit us?

Shouldn't our reply to the President therefore be that while we agree emphatically that there should be joint planning on the basis of an appreciation to be agreed to by the political representatives of the two countries, we feel that the best way to proceed would be to have the discussion at the political level at once and then to give instructions to the Chiefs of Staff and the Joint Planners?

By following that course, Claxton concluded, 'we would not enter upon the most important action in the peacetime history of this country on the basis of a possible misunderstanding.'[48]

On the following day – the third day of Cabinet discussion of the subject – both the Prime Minister and the Secretary of State for External Affairs spoke along the lines of Claxton's statement. The Cabinet agreed that, while general endorsation could be given to the principle of joint defence planning with the United States, the Government would neither concur in the joint appreciation nor conduct further joint planning until there had been additional discussions between the two countries at a senior diplomatic level.

These discussions took place in Ottawa on 16 and 17 December 1946, in conditions of the utmost secrecy. The meeting was held in a suite of the Chateau Laurier so as to throw the press off the scent (a private home in Rockcliffe had been considered as a possible venue), and the military members of the US team came in civilian dress. The Americans did most of the talking. George Kennan held forth on the nature of the Soviet threat, using language much less alarmist than that of the joint appreciation. 'It was virtually certain,' Kennan told the meeting, 'that the Russians were not planning a direct attack but there was always a danger of a Russian misunderstanding or miscalculation of the situation which might lead to an outbreak of hostilities which did not form part of any long range plan ... Our best policy was to "contain" Russian expansionism for so long a time that it would have to modify itself. This would require the utmost firmness and patience.'[49]

A policy of firmness and patience – especially of patience, for that implied avoiding provocative and hasty preparations of the kind the joint planners were recommending – suited the Canadian planners perfectly. They were delighted by both the tenor and the outcome of the talks. 'The United States delegation made a very good impression,' L.B. Pearson reported to the Prime Minister afterwards. 'There was no attempt ... to present demands or to insist on certain things being done ... They recognized that because we are a much smaller country than the United States and because most of whatever is done will take place on our own territory, it is harder for Canada to reach decisions in these matters than for the United States.'[50] Gone now was any insistence on US fighter bases in the Canadian Far North. The emphasis had switched to mapping and meteorology.

The Canadian government was greatly relieved. 'The suggestions raised by the United States officials,' the Minister of National Defence wrote to the Prime Minister on 8 January 1947, 'do not go nearly as far as those anticipated in the reports previously made to the Cabinet. These suggestions would add little to defence expenditure. Further, they would fit in with any plans ultimately adopted and would assist in the development of the north for civilian as well as for military purposes.'[51] Mackenzie King was pleased too. He had expected the Americans to exert far greater pressure and had steeled himself to resist it. Instead, they had come round to his own way of thinking – that (as he had expressed it earlier) 'our best defence in the Arctic was the Arctic itself. We had better be careful about constructing bases, which ... may become bases from which the enemy himself may operate, but would not operate were they not there.'[52] There would be no Maginot Line up north.

## STRATEGY AND SOVEREIGNTY

The United States throughout 1946 wanted more from Canada than agreement upon an appreciation of the Soviet threat to North America and what should be done to counter it. Agreement was sought as well on certain general principles of defence co-operation, and certain particular proposals for defence co-operation of which the most unsettling was the request to base offensive bombers at Goose Bay. By these demands sovereignty became for Canada as much an issue as did strategy.

Some general principles of defence co-operation had been developed by the Permanent Joint Board on Defence during its meetings on 7 and 8 November 1945. Both in form and content they struck Canadian officials as most unsatisfactory. 'I am struck by the formality of the document,' L.B. Pearson commented from Washington.

> It is almost in treaty form, whereas one might have thought that at this stage something more in the nature of a statement of general principles would have been sufficient ... More important, I think, is the omission of any reference to the United Nations Organization, its provisions, and the machinery set up by them for the security of its members. Surely we cannot work out separate defence arrangements without relating them somehow to general international security arrangements...[53]

Arnold Heeney was still more emphatic in his disapproval. 'The Board's proposals go far beyond a working paper for the instruction of joint planners. They take the form of a basic security pact and contain a number of fundamental military obligations. We had expected something quite different ...'[54] Even the secretary of the Board's Canadian Section, R.M. Macdonnell, conceded that 'the memorandum ... requires amendment both in form and content before it would be acceptable to the Canadian government as an agreement...'[55]

At its next meeting on 21 March 1946, the Board toned down its original version. What emerged was a draft of what would eventually become its 35th Recommendation. The wording was deliberately low key: 'In order to make more effective provision for the security of the northern part of the western hemisphere, the Governments of Canada and the United States should provide for close co-operation between their armed forces in all matters relating thereto ...' Several recommendations followed: interchange of military personnel, standardization of equipment and methods of training, joint manoeuvres and tests, reciprocal availability of military facilities, national mapping and surveying (with an exchange of the results), and 'free and comprehensive exchange of military information.' In this form the draft recommendation was approved by the Chiefs of Staff Committee.

The Cabinet would be a greater hurdle. On 2 May, Hume Wrong briefed the Prime Minister for its meeting one week hence. The draft recommendation, Wrong warned, could be a source of trouble.

> We must face the prospect that in some quarters both at home and abroad there will be a tendency to interpret this Recommendation as equivalent to the conclusion of a defensive alliance between the United States and Canada directed against the possibility of attack by Russia. Such an interpretation may well be placed upon it by the USSR, while in the United Kingdom, and to some extent elsewhere in the British Commonwealth, it may be regarded by some people as impeding co-operation with other Commonwealth countries...[56]

That was enough for Mackenzie King. 'I declined to let Council accept recommendations of the Joint Board,' he recorded on 9 May 1946, 'until after I had a chance to discuss aspects of them with the British.'[57]

Keeping in step with both the United States and the United Kingdom had always been a fundamental principle of Liberal foreign policy, and it was not now to be abandoned. The Prime Minister no more wanted an exclusively Canadian-American agreement on defence co-operation than he had wanted an exclusively Canadian-British agreement, which was not at all. 'This Russian situation,' Mackenzie King had told Ernest Bevin the previous October, 'could not be met by Britain and the Dominions. It could only be met by closer relations and understanding of the United States and the British Commonwealth.'[58]

The United States, however, was as strongly attached to the bilateral approach as was Canada to the multilateral. 'To American defense planners,' write the authors of the official history of the framework of hemisphere defence, 'the success of the wartime alliance with Canada seemed to vindicate the old suspicions of multilateral action and to confirm the preference for bilateral arrangements. While other wartime associations were breaking up with the end of hostilities, the United States and Canada were an example to the rest of the world. Their relationship was indisputable evidence that two partners could work together amicably in time of peace as well as war, and that two nations could each relinquish a measure of independence of action without losing self-respect or national dignity.'[59] That was a natural way for Washington to regard the relationship. It overlooked that the measures of independence of action to be relinquished by each party were not proportionately equal – save in the proportions favoured by the hotel chef, 'who made a hare-pie from hare's meat and horse meat according to the 50–50 recipe, that is to say, one hare and one horse.'*

This, however, was a retrospective verdict, delivered when the passing of time had obscured the issues and softened their angularities. In 1946 the Americans took a more realistic view. They had to, for, had they not, there could have been no satisfactory outcome. As it was, the outcome was satisfactory. It took the form of a compromise. The Canadian government compromised by allowing a bilateral defence agreement with the United States to go forward when it much preferred some form of tripartite arrangement. The United States government compromised by accepting modifications in the 35th Recommendation of the Permanent Joint Board on Defence the purpose of which was to safeguard Canada's sovereignty.

These modifications were accepted by the Joint Board at its meeting on 19 September 1946. '[They] go a long way to meet the objections raised in Cabinet to the original draft,' Hume Wrong informed the Prime Minister afterwards. But the Cabinet had yet to accept the Recommendation. Meanwhile, Mackenzie King was due to meet with President Truman. If Truman inquired about the Recommendation, Hume Wrong advised, 'the line to take is that the question of the wording, timeliness, and possible publication is now under consideration in Ottawa.'[60]

Truman made no inquiry. However, a so-called 'oral message' left with the Prime Minister after his visit to the White House requested that the

* The remark is attributed to General J.B.M. Hertzog of South Africa, who made it *à propos* British influence in his country. See Nicholas Mansergh, *Survey of British Commonwealth Affairs: Problems of External Policy*, 1931–9 (London 1952), 213.

Canadian Government give official approval to Recommendation 35. Mackenzie King put it to his colleagues on 14 November. 'I presented to the Cabinet Recommendation 35 of the Joint Defence Board,' he recorded,

> which sets forth the principles in accordance with which representatives of the two countries can be expected to carry on joint planning. Its various clauses were approved by the Cabinet in the presence of the Chiefs of Staff. It was interesting to observe how completely surprised some Members of the Government were at what was disclosed; equally amazing in some particulars how little some of the Members appreciated the military situation today and what it involves in the way of a complete change in the way in which from now on some old-time conceptions will have to be viewed. It is the greatest problem with which the Canadian Government has been faced since the war.[61]

The following day, possibly for the benefit of his backward colleagues, the Prime Minister secured 'renewed approval by the Cabinet of the 35th Recommendation ... Cabinet put much of today on discussion of its various clauses – a very profitable discussion I thought. I felt much relieved to have Cabinet's view carefully recorded on different paragraphs.'[62] It was decided as well to let the British know all about it. Mackenzie King did not propose to allow them any excuse for petulance or reproach of the kind Churchill had displayed towards him for entering the Ogdensburg Agreement in August 1940.*

The 35th Recommendation had now been approved. Ought it to be published? Hume Wrong for one felt strongly not. 'More than ever an announcement of this sort would look to the Soviet Union, and indeed to nearly everyone, as the conclusion of an intimate military alliance between Canada and the United States – and that, in fact, is what it would amount to. I feel that relations with the USSR should, at any rate, either get better or worse than they are at present before publication takes place.'[63]

That condition, at least, was speedily fulfilled. Relations with the USSR got worse. The Canadian ambassador was recalled from Moscow in January 1947. On 7 February 1947 *Izvestia* informed its readers that Ottawa, overcoming early misgivings, had joined with United States 'ruling circles' to aid their 'imperialist designs' upon the Far North. Molotov threatened Soviet retaliation.

These exaggerations of Soviet propaganda were not the only argument in favour of disclosing the real state of affairs. Reports hardly less lurid were appearing in the press of North America. On 29 June 1946, the *Financial Post* under a series of flamboyant headings – 'Canada "Another

* See James Eayrs, *In Defence of Canada*, II, *Appeasement and Rearmament* (Toronto 1965), 209–10.

Belgium" in US Air Bases Proposal'; 'Hear Washington Insists Dominion's Northern Frontier be Fortified'; ' "Atomic Age Maginot Line" is Feared' – carried a report that while the United States wanted far northern bases, Canada did not. More in this vein appeared later in the year.* L.B. Pearson himself had admitted in an article in a leading American journal that his government was concerned at 'an increasing, and in some of its manifestations, an unhealthy preoccupation with the strategic aspects of the north: the staking of claims, the establishment of bases, the calculation of risks and all the rest.'[64]

By the end of the year, Ottawa felt the time had come to clear the air. This required American approval. Discussions with their US colleagues revealed to the Canadians that

> the State Department was obviously inclined to the view that any public reference to the Recommendation ... was unnecessary and undesirable ... The Canadian representatives succeeded in convincing the United States representatives that because of the interest that had been displayed by the public in northern defence problems, it would be impossible to avoid some sort of statement at the forthcoming session of Parliament. This being so, it seemed desirable to make public the substance of the Recommendation since, if this were not done, there would be no satisfactory answer to the inevitable question – "What arrangements have been entered into with the United States?"[66]

On the understanding that the public statement would 'avoid sensationalism or anything savouring of the provocative and ... be as matter-of-fact as possible,' this procedure was agreed upon by the two governments.

The Prime Minister delivered his statement to the House of Commons on 12 February 1947. Its wording resembled closely that of the 35th Recommendation.† It recited the principles upon which a 'limited' Canadian-American collaboration for joint security would follow – interchange, standardization, shared testing and manoeuvres, reciprocal availability of military facilities. It stressed that 'as an underlying principle all co-operative arrangements will be without impairment of the control of either country over all activities in its territory.' It emphasized that 'no treaty, executive agreement or contractual obligation has been entered into.' Either country could discontinue collaboration at any time. Finally, it pledged that 'neither country will take any action inconsistent with the Charter of the United Nations. The Charter remains the cornerstone of the foreign policy of each.'[66]

* For example, Blair Fraser, 'The Watch on the Arctic,' *Maclean's Magazine*, 1 December 1946; Leslie Roberts, 'Canada Fears US Militarism More than Soviet Expansionism,' *PM* (New York City), 22 December 1946.

† The text of Recommendation 35 has been published in US State Department, *Foreign Relations of the United States, 1946*, V (Washington, DC 1970), 65–7.

That certainly avoided sensationalism or anything savouring of the provocative. It was a far cry from the defence pact recommended by the Joint Board more than a year before. 'An important document, and a far-reaching sequel to the meetings with Roosevelt, at Ivy Lea and later at Ogdensburg,' was how it seemed to a satisfied Mackenzie King. '...Canada itself is getting to be not merely the interpreter between the United States and Britain but the pivot – the pivotal point of union between these two great countries.'[67] A correspondent of *Red Star* employed a different metaphor. 'The greatest British dominion is being made the orbit of polar strategy for American militarism,' wrote V. Fyodorov on 23 February, noting that its prime minister had tried 'in a very peculiar manner to justify the transformation of his country into a *place d'armes* for the armed forces of another country.' It is hard to please all of the people all of the time.

The United States government did not wait until an agreement had been reached with Canada on general principles of post-war defence co-operation before putting to its neighbour practical proposals to protect the security of the continent. Not all of them were easy for Canada to accept. At a time when the United States wished to augment its military presence in the Far North, the Canadian government was anxious to reduce it.

That anxiety was a legacy from the Second World War, when the American presence had grown to what Canadians came to refer to – neither jocularly nor without justification – as a United States occupation. To the Yukon and North West Territories, and the northern prairie provinces, had come American military and civilian personnel to build and man the land and air routes, and the supporting supply facilities, between the United States and Alaska. Principal projects included the Alaska Highway (built by the United States during 1942–3 at a cost of approximately $130 millions); the airfields along the Northwest Staging Route, the Northeast Ferrying (or Crimson) Route, and the Mackenzie Valley; about 60 weather stations; and the Canol Project (an oil distribution system between Norman Wells on the Mackenzie River and Whitehorse, constructed by the United States between 1942 and 1944 at a cost of approximately $140 millions). By the end of 1942 more than 15,000 US servicemen were stationed in Northwest Canada to build, man, and guard these facilities; by 1943, when many of them had been replaced by civilian workers, the number of US civilians alone exceeded that figure. As of 1 June 1943, the 33,000 Americans in the area far outnumbered its Canadian population.

It was not the number of the invaders but their demeanour that caused

Canadians to resent their presence. 'The Americans ... have apparently walked in and taken possession as if Canada were unclaimed territory inhabited by a docile race of aborigines,' the High Commissioner in London wrote following a conversation with an indignant official of the Hudson's Bay Company. 'Large numbers of men have been discovered well established in certain parts of the North without Ottawa knowing anything about the matter at all or any permission having been asked or given.'[68]

There was the additional concern that the Americans might outstay their welcome. When the war which was the reason for their presence came to an end, would they return to whence they came, leaving their plant behind them? That they might be tempted to remain had occurred to the Prime Minister as early as 30 December 1942 when, at a meeting of the War Committee of the Cabinet, Mackenzie King took strong exception to a proposed Canadian-American joint study of the territory being opened up by the Alaska Highway. 'Efforts would be made by the Americans to control developments in our country after the war,' he predicted, 'and to bring Canada out of the orbit of the British Commonwealth of Nations into their own orbit. I am strongly opposed to anything of the kind.'[69] On 17 February 1944, when the War Committee considered the future of the Canol Project, Mackenzie King 'held strongly with one or two others to the view that we ought to get the Americans out of the further development there, and keep complete control in our own hands ... With the United States so powerful and her investments becoming greater in Canada we will have a great difficulty to hold our own against pressure from the United States.'[70] Later that day he spoke 'apprehensively' to Vincent Massey

> of the process of disentanglement which must follow the war when the Americans must withdraw and leave us in full control of our own bases and their wartime installations. The PM showed he had grave doubts as to whether international agreements on this which Canada had secured from the United States provided any practical guarantee against the United States' claims and pretensions. When I suggested that the Americans did not take us seriously enough as a nation, King said that Canadians were looked upon by Americans as a lot of Eskimos...

That was a striking observation, Vincent Massey reflected, 'by a man who has so often been accused of being subservient to American policy.'[71]

The Prime Minister's concern to protect Canada's sovereignty and territory against encroachments by the United States was heightened by his realization, during the first few months of peace, that a new justification for a protracted American presence in the Far North might be provided by the threat of an attack by the Soviet Union. 'If the Americans felt security required it,' Mackenzie King wrote gloomily on 11 October 1945, they 'would take peaceful possession of part of Canada with a welcome of the people of BC, Alta., and Saskatchewan...'[72] And on 21 October: 'I felt perfectly sure that once the Western provinces become alarmed in the matter of their security, they would look to the United States for protection, not to Canada or the Commonwealth. This was something to keep in mind.'[73]

Such fears at first proved without foundation. The process of what Fiorello La Guardia, chairman of the US Section of the Permanent Joint Board on Defence, referred to as 'unscrambling the eggs' went on unmarred by any attempt by the Americans to avoid dislodgment. Canada assumed responsibility for the Alaska Highway on 1 April 1946. Canol had been closed down before the end of the war. Only the future of the air bases (and their supporting weather stations) remained in doubt. But there was no doubt in the minds of US airmen. They not only wanted the bases kept open, they wanted at least one of them reinforced.

On 29 April 1946, the Permanent Joint Board on Defence met to discuss what ought to be done.

The Board were agreed that final decisions could not be reached until the joint Canada-United States planning groups had submitted their recommendations. It was felt, however, that the contemplated studies would reveal the need for a number of air bases in the North and that considerations of prudence and economy indicated the desirability of maintaining these [existing] bases since to close them down and later to bring them back into operation would involve considerable additional expense ... The Board agreed to the following conclusions:

(a) The Northwest Staging Route, including the airways system, is vital to the defence of Canada and the United States. The operation of this route should not be reduced below a level which will provide at all times for the safe transit of large numbers of military aircraft of all types...

(b) The facilities of the Mackenzie River Air Route should be retained pending reassessment...

(c) The aerodromes of the Crimson Route ... are considered to possess great strategic importance ... These facilities should be retained...

(d) Goose Bay is considered vital to the defence of the United States and Canada and should be maintained as a military base on such a scale as to provide for the stationing of operational squadrons as required.[74]

The Cabinet discussed these proposals on 9 May. Mackenzie King recorded that he spoke 'very plainly' at the meeting.

I said I believed the long range policy of the Americans was to absorb Canada. They would seek to get this hemisphere as completely one as possible. They are already in one way or another building up military strength in the North of Canada. It was inevitable that for their own protection, they would have to do that. We should not shut our eyes to the fact that this was going on consciously as part of the American policy. It might be inevitable for us to have to submit to it...[75]

It was in no spirit of rejoicing that the Cabinet gave its qualified approval to the Joint Board's proposals.

It was not just through the Joint Board that the Americans put their requests to carry out various kinds of military operations on Canadian territory. They arrived through the US Embassy, they arrived through Service channels, and by the summer of 1946 they were arriving thick and fast. 'We have had a series of requests this year,' Hume Wrong informed the Prime Minister, 'relating to such matters as the opening of new weather stations in the Arctic islands, the continued operation by the US of existing weather stations in Northeastern Canada, the maintenance in a serviceable condition of far northern air fields, the operation of the Northwest Staging Route, and the provision of facilities for various exercises and training programmes in Canadian territory.'[76] Among the latter was a US Navy request to cruise in northern Canadian waters. 'In Washington they insist on calling this by the dramatic name of "Operation Nanook." We have tried to get them to drop this but they say they have gone too far to change the title. Canadian observers will be with the party and they want to land a few marines for a short period near an RCMP post in the eastern Arctic.'[77]

The ambassador pleaded with his American colleagues to make haste slowly. 'I expressed the hope,' L.B. Pearson reported, 'that the War Department would not press us too hard with urgent requests for quick action in the field of defence in the North. I said that, while developments in the north were perhaps relatively small items in the defence plans in this country, they were for us matters of great importance, strategically and politically.'[78] The Americans reacted sympathetically but firmly. 'Our requests will not be granted until we have justified them,' Pearson's counterpart in Ottawa counselled his government, 'nor will they be granted with the rapidity that was evident under the stresses of war, but they will be given unprejudiced consideration, and where we can offer convincing evidence of the necessity of a project, I believe we may count upon the full support and co-operation of the Canadian Government and the people.'[79] That assessment proved correct.

Of the score or more specific requests made of the Canadian government by the United States for access to facilities in the Far North for continental defence purposes during 1946, two were especially vexatious. One was its request to reinforce the base at Goose Bay, Labrador. The other was its request to maintain a garrison at Fort Churchill.

The air base at Goose Bay had by 1946 become of prime importance to US air force planners. From nowhere else in North America might heavy bombers reach Soviet targets with any prospect of safe return. Its three concrete runways, 200 feet wide by about 6000 feet long, had been constructed in 1942–3 for the North Atlantic Ferry Route. A ninety-nine year lease agreement signed at St John's on 10 October 1944 between the governments of Canada and Newfoundland (then still a 'Dominion in suspense') provided that the facilities at Goose Bay would be available for use by United States and United Kingdom aircraft 'for the duration of the war and for such time thereafter as the Governments agree to be necessary or advisable in the interests of common defence.'[80] Few could have forecast their role as a potential pivot of deterrence.

The Permanent Joint Board on Defence had agreed at its meeting on 29 April 1946 that 'Goose Bay is considered vital to the defence of the United States and Canada and should be maintained as a military base on such a scale as to provide for the stationing of operational squadrons as required.'[81] However, the Cabinet considered this recommendation too permissive. On 9 May, it decided to allow the United States to use the base for military aviation 'on the understanding that Air Force operation ... would be continued without increase in presently authorized establishments.'[82]

This concession did not give the Americans what they were after. A few weeks later, the High Commissioner for Canada in St John's reported to the Department of External Affairs on his conversation with the base US commander and some of his senior officers.

> The talk turned to questions of aviation and I think I should pass on to you that the United States Field Commanders ... appear to be really in earnest in their desire to see the United States established in Goose Bay. They even talked of the necessity of extending the runways to 10,000 feet and of building up a giant base. In their view the North country is taking on great strategic importance and they regard the Goose Bay air base as the natural entrance to this area. They tell me that they wish to keep open not only the existing bases in the far North but to establish more...

The High Commissioner, J.S. Macdonald, added as his personal opinion that 'it would be quite fatal to the development of Canada, as a nation, to have the United States take over the defence of the North Country or to have them muscle in and assume control of even a part of the defences. Not only would it infringe Canadian sovereignty, but it would involve us, sooner or later, in complications and perhaps hostilities with the USSR.'[83]

An informal diplomatic overture was made towards the end of September by the first secretary at the US Embassy in Ottawa, J. Graham Parsons, who approached R.M. Macdonnell 'about the urgent desire of the United States to establish at Goose Bay, on an indeterminate basis and in addition to their present establishment there, a very long range bomber group and a fighter group. No estimate of personnel involved was given but I gather that it would be likely to amount to something in the neighbourhood of 10,000 all told. Parsons wanted to know what would be the best way to bring this to the notice of the Canadian government. My own view,' Hume Wrong added, 'is that it ... should be the subject of a high level approach, not routed through service channels of the PJBD.'[84]

The approach, when made, could hardly have been at a higher level, for President Truman himself broached the problem of Goose Bay when the Prime Minister visited him at the White House on 28 October. 'When he spoke of Goose Bay,' Mackenzie King recorded,

> I mentioned that one consideration was that it belonged to the Labrador section which belonged to Newfoundland. We would have to work in full harmony with them which meant also working with full knowledge so far as the United Kingdom was concerned ... I said I hoped for agreement also and believe it should be possible to reach an agreement. We were a small country in population and wealth compared to the United States. They might wish to put in large numbers of men. I understood they were thinking of some 10,000 in Goose Bay. The President said he did not know the numbers or any details, that would have to be worked out with care and with agreement. He believed it could. I said we had to watch particularly the question of our sovereignty. Not that we entertained any fears on that score, but having regard to the years as they went by and to the view the people would take, large numbers of troops from other countries being stationed out of their own country, or would have to be arranged on the basis of agreement to protect national rights...[85]

This meeting of President and Prime Minister did not produce a meeting of their minds about Goose Bay. On 12 November, Mackenzie King told the Governor General, Viscount Alexander of Tunis, 'what the Americans were contemplating at Goose Bay. He told me he did not think that was necessary at all. Indeed, on these things, he has a most sensible and realistic attitude.'[86]

The Goose Bay problem was high on the agenda of the top-secret meeting of Canadian and US diplomatists and senior service officers held in Ottawa on 16 and 17 December 1946. The Americans minced no words. 'The most probable route of approach to North America,' a US Army Air Force spokesman told the meeting, 'included Iceland, Greenland and the line Newfoundland–Labrador–Eastern Canada, the latter portion of which was only about 1200 miles from the main continental industrial centers.

Goose Bay was considered to be the only suitable base for very heavy bombardment groups and in fact could be said to be the most important all-round strategic air base in the western hemisphere.'[87]

Clearly it would be hard, it might even be impossible, for the Canadians to reject a request put so tenaciously by an American colonel, an American president, and American officialdom in between. Sensing an impending capitulation, L.B. Pearson and A.D.P. Heeney cast about for some protective colouration. Might it be possible, they inquired, to emphasize, for political reasons, the training side of the Goose Bay project? The United States representatives responded by reminding the Canadians of the facts of life. 'Mr Parsons pointed out that Goose Bay was intended for offensive purposes. He added that it was "a facility in being" and there were evident advantages to be derived from this fact.'[88] An enemy was not deterred by concealment of the mechanism of massive retaliation. Here was the Canadians' first lesson in the school for strategy. It was not to be their last.

By the end of 1947, US B-47 bombers were parked at the end of the Goose Bay runways.

On 18 February 1947, *Izvestia* referred disparagingly to the 'construction of barracks in northern ports.' The facility coming closest to this description was the joint Canada-US experimental station at Fort Churchill, Manitoba. If it be granted that the barracks were ramshackle, the 'ports' but one, the Soviets' description is accurate. The Canadian Navy since 1943 had used the site for a radio station. The Army employed it as a base of operations to test snowmobiles during March and April 1945, and again early in 1946 as a base from which to mount 'Operation Musk-Ox' – a military foray into the Arctic. In October 1946, a Joint Services Experimental Station was established. Some 450 Canadian servicemen were billeted at this post, together with about 100 United States servicemen. Their mission was to train military personnel and test military equipment under conditions of extreme cold.[89]

Soon after the Joint Services Experimental Station had been established, the Canadian government received from the United States government a request to station 500 US Army personnel at Fort Churchill for cold weather training during the following winter. The request was refused.[90] The Canadian government did not wish to be outnumbered by Americans on the base. To have reinforced it to maintain numerical superiority would give the Soviet Union grounds for propaganda, if not for complaint.

The Canadian government reasoned that it had nothing to lose and something to gain – namely, whatever confidence the Soviet leaders might be able to vouchsafe at that stage of their history – by letting the Russians see for themselves that this small-scale military establishment created no very grave threat to the security of the Soviet Union. Accordingly, in the spring of 1947, it invited the military attachés of the embassies in Ottawa to visit Fort Churchill at their pleasure. The Russian embassy took up the offer, and the Soviet military attaché duly made the rounds. He was a young major who had fought at Stalingrad and knew an offensive force when he saw one; what he reported to his government is of course not known. At any rate, the Russians did not desist with propaganda.

## POLITICS AND ELECTRONICS

In the Joint Canadian-United States Basic Security Plan drafted by the military planners of both countries in May and June of 1946, protection of the vital areas of Canada and the United States from air attack was considered to be the most important of the several tasks to be undertaken by their respective military establishments. The Plan had assigned each of the armed services of each country a particular mission in the defence partnership. The mission assigned to the Royal Canadian Air Force was to co-operate in an air warning system, together with the necessary complementary communications, navigation, and meteorological systems.

By the end of 1946, the Canadian Government had authorized the planners to proceed with detailed studies of the feasibility of installing 'long range air raid warning equipment so as to protect from surprise attack the main industrial regions of the continent,' such installations 'to be situated in Canadian territory somewhere between the national transcontinental railway and the Arctic Ocean.'[91] By the end of 1947 the planners had completed their studies. They came to the conclusion that the warning game wasn't worth the candle. Several years later, the Minister of National Defence disclosed to the House of Commons the reasoning which led to their unfavourable appraisal. 'A radar chain across the Far North,' Brooke Claxton declared on 26 November 1953,

> might give us early warning of an approaching attack, [but] between this Arctic radar chain and the main radar control system far to the south lay a vast and isolated area in which it was simply not practical to build the complete gridwork of overlapping radar coverage which is necessary to keep attacking planes under continuous observation. Thus by the time any attackers had travelled the hundreds of miles between the first alarm and the nearest desirable target they would be completely lost to our defending control system.

> Therefore such an isolated Arctic radar chain might provide an alarm which might not lead to effective action, while it might nevertheless be likely to immobilize all activities in all target areas. Moreover, it would be very easy to

create this result by "spoofing" raids. That is, an enemy aircraft of any size would come in, being very careful indeed to get picked up on a radarscope. The alarm would go out 2000 or 3000 miles to the south. Activity would stop. The aircraft would either go back home or go in somewhere else...

For these reasons, the Canadian planners had turned in an adverse recommendation. The proposed Arctic radar chain, Brooke Claxton told Parliament, 'never reached the stage of discussion between governments.'[92]

Notwithstanding this adverse recommendation, the Canadian Government continued to be fascinated by the technique of early warning by radar. Governments as well as scientists are prone to yield to what Robert Oppenheimer has termed the temptations of technical sweetness.* 'The miracle of radar,' Brooke Claxton remarked, 'enabled skilled and courageous airmen to win the battle of Britain.'[93] Might it not yet be adapted to help skilled and courageous airmen to win a battle of North America, should it ever come to that? The Canadian Government was reluctant to put the possibility completely out of mind. Nor did it do so. When the American Secretary of Defense met with the Cabinet Defence Committee during the summer of 1948, he found its members much under the spell of what Winston Churchill had aptly called 'the wizard war.' 'They are giving a good deal of thought to a radar screen,' James Forrestal noted in his diary on 16 August, 'although the very great costs involved make it a problem difficult of solution.'[94]

By the end of 1949, the Canadian Government had decided to replace the Arctic radar project by a more modest proposal. 'The territory of Canada is so vast,' declared the White Paper on Defence issued by the Minister of National Defence in that year, 'that it is obviously impracticable to construct a chain or grid of radar warning stations similar in density and consequent effectiveness to the installations during the last war in the smaller areas of Britain or Germany; nevertheless, an early warning system to cover certain vital approaches and areas is being developed.'[95] On 8 June 1950, Brooke Claxton guardedly gave a few more details of the project to Parliament. 'We have a plan,' he stated, 'under which we will do a certain amount of construction of radar sites and equipment each year. We have on order, in the way of equipment ... the latest and most powerful sets, equipment to the value of approximately $25 million...'[96] On 26 November 1953, Claxton disclosed further that 'something more than two years ago, the two governments [of Canada and the United

* '...It is my judgement in these things that when you see something that is technically sweet, you go ahead and do it, and you argue about it only after you have had your technical success.' (*In the Matter of J. Robert Oppenheimer*; *Transcript of Hearing before the Personnel Security Board, Washington, D.C., April 12, 1954 through May 6, 1954*. (Washington, DC 1954), 251.

States] agreed to proceed at once to build up a system working upward and outward from the principal target areas which would give protection to the most vulnerable areas against the most likely forms of attack.'[97] This system, known as the Pinetree Line, was completed in 1954. It consisted of more than thirty radar stations following a route running northeast from Vancouver Island into the Peace River district of Alberta, down through the northern states of the American prairie, up again into Ontario and Quebec, and ending at the Atlantic Coast of Newfoundland. Each station was equipped not only with radar to detect approaching aircraft but with electronic apparatus to direct fighter planes in an ensuing air battle. It was paid for and manned jointly by the United States and Canada, the Americans providing roughly two-thirds of the $450 millions it was said eventually to have cost, and a similar proportion of its personnel.

Modest in cost and conception by comparison with the Arctic warning systems subsequently to be constructed, the Pinetree Line would not have been undertaken but for two external and related developments upon the international scene. One was the enormous increase in North American defence budgets following the outbreak of the Korean War in June 1950. The other was the no less enormous increase in the severity of the Soviet threat to North America.

In 1946, the official United States appreciation of that threat considered that the Soviet Union would acquire the capability to mount a very long range aerial bombardment, possibly with atomic weapons, beginning by about 1950. The Canadian Government, on the advice of its Chiefs of Staff, refused to subscribe to this appreciation, which it regarded as overly alarmist and as tending to distract attention from the central theatre of conflict, namely, Europe.* It continued to abide by a more conservative appraisal at least until 1948. Early in that year, the Chief of the General Staff had given his senior officers his personal appraisal of the Soviet threat to North America. General Charles Foulkes considered that while 'there is no doubt that the Russians are capable at the present time of over-running the whole of the Continent of Europe ... I don't think we have yet reached the stage where a complete air invasion [of North America] is on.' The main Soviet deficiency, General Foulkes believed, 'is that of a strategical air force.' However he noted that the Russians 'are developing a strategical air force. It was very astonishing that in the May Day demonstration last year the Russians produced in the air four-engine jet bombers and two-engine jet fighters and the air experts had no idea they had any such weapons.' In any event the Russians would wait until

* See above, 341–3.

they possessed nuclear weapons before mounting an all-out attack upon North America. That would be anywhere from between three years to fifteen years from then. 'A conservative estimate,' General Foulkes concluded, 'is about ten years, that is, about 1957. However, if Russian scientists find some more expeditious method of extracting sufficient fission material from uranium and can devise some new simpler device for exploding the bomb, the time limit may be cut down to a matter of five years.'[98] The Canada-United States joint appreciation in effect immediately prior to the Soviet Union's detonation of a nuclear device in September 1949 – two years in advance of the most pessimistic Western forecast* – considered that not until 1957 would the Soviet Union possess a stockpile of nuclear weapons large enough to be able to inflict a devastating blow against North America – a stockpile slightly in excess of 50 bombs, delivered by long-range aircraft and merchant shipping deployed in harbours.

The immediate impact of the Soviet nuclear detonation upon Western strategy was a radical revision of the assumptions of United States military planners concerning the date and scale of a surprise nuclear attack upon North America. In December 1949, the Canadian planners were informed by their American colleagues in Washington that the Pentagon was now working on the assumption that the Soviet Union would by July 1954 possess a nuclear arsenal of at least 150 atomic bombs capable of delivery on targets in North America not only by long-range aircraft and merchant shipping but by missiles launched from submarines with a range of between 400 and 600 miles. 'The U.S. Planners now state,' one of the Canadian officers present at the meeting reported to the Chief of the General Staff on 15 December 1949, 'that whilst the previous estimate of over 50 was serious enough, they now considered that the figure of 150 might well prove critical and if delivered without warning on this continent might so injure our capabilities that the war would be lost in the initial few days of the Soviet offensive.' It was to offset this dire possibility that work on the Pinetree Line was begun almost at once.

If the Pinetree Line was the product of increases in the overall costs of

* Even the most pessimistic Western forecaster did not then know that work on the Soviet atomic bomb had begun in Moscow as early as June 1942, with the decisive breakthrough – that of a self-sustaining chain reaction – being achieved on 24 December 1946. These events were disclosed only in August 1966, by the biographer of Professor Igor V. Kurchatov, the Director of the Soviet 'Moscow Project.' See *The Times* (London), 19 August 1966; *The New York Times*, 19 August 1966.

defence and in the severity of the Soviet threat to North America, the Distant Early Warning and Mid-Canada Lines were the product of advances in weapons technology and strategic sophistication.

Early in 1951, the United States Air Force entered into a contract with a number of scientists on the faculty of the Massachusetts Institute of Technology, under which the scientists were to engage in an intensive study of the best means of solving the outstanding problems of continental defence. Project Charles (for the Charles River on the banks of which MIT is situated), in which Canadian scientists from the Defence Research Board were unofficial participants, 'did not recommend construction of the Arctic warning systems but it did call attention to the very great value of additional warning.'[99] It also recommended that a permanent laboratory be created for exclusive and continuing study of continental defence problems. This recommendation was implemented in September 1951 with the creation, again as the result of a contract between the USAF and MIT, of the Lincoln Laboratory; it was intended to become, in the words of the US Secretary of the Air Force, 'the Manhattan Project of Air Defense.'[100]

Throughout the winter and spring of 1951–2, the Lincoln scientists worked on the problems of detecting and intercepting enemy air attack on North America. During the summer of 1952, a group of scientists, including Canadian scientists, assembled at the Laboratory to survey the work already done and to recommend future policy. In due course the Lincoln Summer Study Group produced a report. The report was nominally top secret but, as its sponsors wished to bring pressure upon the Administration for its implementation, its contents were in due course leaked to confidants in the American press; in their column for 16 March 1953 the Alsop brothers published a full account of the report's findings and recommendations. The Lincoln Group had

> 1) estimated that in two or three years the Soviet Union would have sufficient planes and atomic weapons to cripple the United States in a surprise attack; 2) declared that existing and planned American defenses were inadequate and improperly integrated and that under optimal conditions would achieve only a 20 percent kill-rate; and 3) argued that new and probable technological break-throughs made it feasible to develop an air defense system which could hope to achieve a kill-rate of 60 to 70 percent. Specifically, the report recommended the construction of a distant early warning radar line across northern Canada to give three to six hours warning of approaching enemy bombers, an integrated and fully automatic communications system for air defense forces, and improved fighter planes and homing missiles for interception. Finally, the report urged that the distant early warning system be given top priority...[101]

The recommendations of the Lincoln Group met with vigorous and varied opposition from within the American policy community, and were accepted only after prolonged argument and much delay. The USAF, sponsors of the project, did not at first support its findings. While the Air Force bore primary responsibility for continental defence, it was at this time preoccupied with the wholly different and indeed competing tasks of forging the Strategic Air Command, conducting tactical air operations in Korea, and creating air forces for the defence of Western Europe. Strongly imbued with the spirit of the offensive – 'the bomber will always get through' – many of its senior officers were reluctant to take on continental defence as a prime mission. 'The attitude of the Air Force was ambivalent. Continental defense was motivated in part with its support and in part over its opposition.'[102]

As for the Administration, its response reflected the inter-service and intra-service feuding so characteristic of major weapons procurement programmes and policy innovations during the years before Robert McNamara brought a kind of order to the chaos. Its response was to procrastinate. Its response resembled, in the words of the Alsop brothers, 'that of a man who hopefully consults other doctors, seeking a pleasanter verdict, when his own physician orders him to a painful and dangerous operation.'[103] It procrastinated so long that no decision had been reached by November 1952, when the Administration was defeated. The incoming Eisenhower team, confronting a major policy dilemma the moment it took office, was no more able than its predecessor to reach a prompt decision. The new President's counsellors were divided. Vice-President Nixon, Secretary of State Dulles, and Under Secretary of State Bedell Smith wanted to implement at once the Lincoln Group's recommendation to build the distant early warning system. Secretary of the Treasury Humphrey, Budget Director Dodge and – unexpectedly – Secretary of Defense Wilson just as strongly opposed early implementation of the plan, noting that the Lincoln Group, while unable to give any precise figure as to its cost, had agreed it would amount in the end to 'billions of dollars.' 'Caught between the conflicting demands of defense and economy, the President reportedly told senators and congressmen that "his dilemma was giving him sleepless nights".'[104]

It was in this atmosphere of indecision and doubt that the Minister of National Defence visited Washington for the purpose of ascertaining the views of the Eisenhower Administration on a variety of military and strategic matters, and, in general, to size up the character and outlook of the individuals upon whose judgment and decisions the safety and welfare of Canada would, in the last analysis, depend. On 27 February 1953, Brooke Claxton met with the service Secretaries, their deputies, and with the US Chiefs of Staff. He was on the whole favourably impressed and reassured by what he saw and heard.* Naturally the question of the Arctic radar screen came up for discussion.

In January 1953, the new Administration had urgently requested the Canadian Government to grant permission to build at once two experimental radar stations on territory near Herschell Island in the Canadian Arctic, for the purpose of demonstrating the feasibility (or otherwise) of an early warning system of the kind recommended by the Lincoln Group. (Soon afterwards, the Americans altered their request: only one such station would have to be built, but it would have to be built at once.) To this project, code-named Project Counterchange, a name for some reason later changed to Project Corrode, the Canadian Government gave its assent. The Americans could build the station at their own expense, but on one condition. There should be created at once by the two governments a Joint Military Study Group, whose job it would be to study those aspects of the North American air defence system in general, and of its early warning component in particular, which were of mutual concern to the two governments. The Canadian Government hoped by this device to escape a situation wherein it would be presented with plans for radar construction which its own expert advisers had had no opportunity to scrutinize and study. That had happened, to Canada's disadvantage, more than once in the past: the Government was determined that it should not happen again. To emphasize its concern, it stressed in its message authorizing the construction of the experimental radar station that it would not consider any proposals for an Arctic radar chain unless and until it had received a report on the project from the Joint Military Study Group.

This message had reached the State Department on the day that the Minister of National Defence was paying his visit to Washington. Brooke

* 'Mr Wilson and his associates,' Brooke Claxton reported to the Prime Minister after his meeting with them,

> showed the same friendly attitude towards Canada as was shown by their predecessors. It happens that most of them have had extensive business interests as well as social associations with Canada. They were full of praise for the economic position and general development of the country. It seemed to me that these were men of unusual business experience and capacity but that they had had little or no working experience of government or politics. The immensity of the scale of the defence operation in the United States should not of itself be staggering to men having the experience and capacity of this team. More difficulties will result from the extraordinary variety and complexity of problems arising out of defence organization and planning today and perhaps above everything else, the difficulties of maintaining consistently good relations with Congress, the press and the people.

Brooke Claxton to L.S. St Laurent, 10 March 1953, Claxton Papers. This assessment proved to be both shrewd and accurate.

Claxton reported that he had found 'Mr Wilson and his colleagues [to be] all aware of this project and ... acting on the assumption that it was urgent and important.' They readily agreed to accept the Canadian condition. A Military Study Group was accordingly created. It comprised a Canadian and an American section, and was advised by a combined Canadian-American scientific team. The head of the Canadian section was Air Vice Marshal Frank Miller, then Vice-Chief of the Air Staff. The Military Study Group began its appraisal of the early warning radar system in the spring of 1953.

Brooke Claxton took advantage of his meeting with the American defence leaders to weigh in heavily on the side of the anti-early warning group. 'I told Mr Wilson, Mr Anderson and a number of others,' he reported to the Prime Minister afterwards, 'that we were by no means persuaded that the proposed additional screen would add sufficiently to our defence to justify the expenditure of money and manpower.' He adverted to the argument which (as he was later to tell Parliament) had caused the Canadian planners to report adversely on an Arctic early warning system in 1947: 'I pointed out that the appearance of a single identified enemy aircraft might result in our alerting all of North America. This idea had not been suggested to them before.' He could not form any clear impression as to whether the Americans were moving towards or away from the recommendations of the Lincoln Group. 'I gathered that Mr Wilson and his assistants were not familiar with the background and in any event had had no opportunity to give any serious consideration to this matter.'[105]

The Eisenhower Administration did not long soldier on in ignorance. By the summer of 1953 no fewer than three separate reports on continental defence lay upon its desks. There was the report of the Lincoln Summer Study Group. There was the report of the Kelly Committee (a group of civilian experts under the chairmanship of Marvin J. Kelly, president of the Bell Telephone Laboratories, appointed by Defense Secretary Lovett). There was the report of the Bull Committee (a group of government officials under the chairmanship of Major General Harold Bull, a long-time associate of President Eisenhower, appointed by Secretary of Defense Wilson). These reports, so far from catalyzing decision, served the divided factions of the Eisenhower team as a pretext for further delay. July 1953 found the National Security Council still deadlocked over the competing considerations of improving defence and curtailing expense.[106]

The deadlock was abruptly broken on 12 August 1953. On that date the Soviet Union exploded a hydrogen bomb. On 6 October, the National

Security Council gave its approval to NSC 162, a paper which 'identified the Soviet threat as "total," declared that the Soviets had the ability to launch a nuclear attack against the United States, argued that national defense had to have clear priority over other goals, and recommended that a much greater effort be made to improve continental defenses.'[107] The Lincoln Summer Students had at last prevailed. Their programme for continental defence had been adopted almost intact. It would cost roughly $20 billion over a five-year period. Most of the expense would be for Arctic early warning.

On 6 October 1953 – the day the National Security Council endorsed NSC 162 – the Minister of Trade and Commerce happened to be in Washington on official business. C.D. Howe found his friend Charles Wilson, and other Pentagon personnel, in an exceptionally uncommunicative frame of mind. 'No one would say a word,' he reported to Brooke Claxton. 'The President had instructed all concerned not to discuss either the Russian hydrogen bomb or continental air defence ... I was asked by reporters to discuss continental air defence. My reply was that I could not discuss it since it was top secret for all except readers of *Colliers' Magazine*.'[108]

*Colliers'* had just caused Brooke Claxton, and some of his Cabinet colleagues, intense annoyance and concern by publishing, in its issue for 16 October, an article by William A. Ulman under the title 'Russian Planes are Raiding Canada's Skies.' As the lurid title implies, the article charged that owing to the failure of the United States and Canadian Governments to provide North America with an adequate air defence system, Russian bombers and reconnaissance aircraft had been able to violate northern air space with impunity. Nor was that all. 'Apart from the statement which gave rise to the highly exciting title to the effect that Russian planes are thick overhead,' Brooke Claxton wrote agitatedly to C.D. Howe after reading the offending exposé, 'the article ... contains a remarkably full, detailed and accurate account not only of everything having to do with air defence, but everything that is being considered in connection with it. Had this appeared in a report given by some clerk in the Pentagon to a communist informer,' Claxton added, 'there can be no doubt but that the poor clerk could have been tried for treason and executed. Unquestionably it is the most sweeping breach of security ever to take place. Moreover, it is just the kind of thing the Russians would want to get...'[109]

What further incensed the Minister of National Defence was that the *Colliers'* article was by no means the only leak of its kind. There had appeared in the *Saturday Evening Post* for 22 August and 29 August two articles by General Omar N. Bradley, who until that month had been chairman of the Joint Chiefs of Staff; under the title 'A Soldier's Farewell,' General Bradley had dealt in what to the security-obsessed Claxton seemed like harrowing detail with the condition of the continent's radar defences, which he pronounced imperfect. In the November issue of *Fortune* (published in early October), Charles J.V. Murphy's 'The US as a Bombing Target,' disclosed what was virtually the Pentagon's estimate of Soviet targeting policy, citing 163 possible targets in the United States and Canada for attacking Soviet bombers. Worst of all was a series of articles published in the *Washington Post* by Marquis Childs, on 11 September, 12 September, and 13 September. The article of 12 September bore an Ottawa dateline, and had been written following the correspondent's visit to the Canadian capital. It contained the following passage:

> In the midst of the argument over the Lincoln Line, Canada came up with a new idea for an intermediary line based on more advanced technology. This was the brainchild of a group of brilliant scientists at McGill University in Montreal, among them those who contributed the pioneering development of radar and the proximity fuse at the beginning of World War II. The McGill Fence, as it is now known, could be far less costly and could be built much more quickly. But even more important, the skilled manpower required to operate it would be a fraction of that required for the Lincoln Line. What is more, the radar network now being completed to protect a part of Canada and the United States would serve as a backstop.

Childs' despatch, Brooke Claxton noted grimly, was 'the first public reference ever made to [the McGill Fence] so far as I know.'[110] He may well have been right.

Exercised by what he regarded to be damaging breaches in security in these various accounts, the Minister of National Defence was even more distressed by the thought that they were not so much evidence of the vigour and enterprise of American journalism as they were evidence of a conspiracy to which Washington itself was a party. 'Obviously, this all forms a pattern,' Brooke Claxton had written to the Prime Minister on 23 September, 'the design of which must be inspired by the Administration. It is not too much to suggest that the reason for this flood of propaganda is not so much the increased fear of attack by Russia as growing fear of the hostility of the electors when it becomes apparent that the Republican Party's promises to balance the budget and cut taxes while strengthening their defences has not got the slightest chance in the world of being carried out ... Apparently the Administration had it in mind that the anger of the electorate may be flooded out in a wave of fear of atomic attack.'

Brooke Claxton was himself an intensely political animal with a sophisticated understanding of the processes of American policy-making: he was the last person to be either surprised or dismayed by what he well knew to be Washington's standard operating procedure in situations of this kind. He was also an intensely nationalistic animal, with the Canadian nationalist's resentment of his country's destiny daily determined by developments in the United States over which its government was unable to exercise control. It had been precisely to prevent such a slippage of sovereignty that the Cabinet, when granting permission earlier in the year for the Americans to build their experimental radar station in the Canadian Arctic, refused to consider any proposal to proceed with a Far Northern early warning system that had not been previously studied and approved by its own experts. Now, it appeared to Claxton, the US Administration was attempting to force the hand of the Canadian Government by creating among the North American public – for as many Canadians, proportionately, as Americans read *Colliers'* and the *Saturday Evening Post* – a demand for defence so insistent and widespread that Ottawa would be forced to go along with any United States plan, however misguided Canadian planners might consider it to be. 'It may not be too much to say,' Claxton wrote to St Laurent,

> that the line of action that may be taken may prove to constitute the most serious setback to [the] work [of Canada and the United States] together for joint security since the end of the Second World War, and bring about a situation which might, to some extent at least, endanger the extraordinarily harmonious relations which have existed between Canada and the United States. If there appears to be any serious justification for this extreme view, then it would appear to be desirable that we should take steps at once to make our apprehensions known to the Administration at Washington.
>
> One approach to this might be that just as the United States Administration would readily recognize that no steps could be taken to carry out a programme of additional continental defence without the co-operation of Canada, so it would be advisable to discuss the matter fully with Canada before starting currents of opinion in the United States which would virtually force our taking additional steps.[111]

This was plain talk – but only in private. Washington, meanwhile, was planning some plain talk – in public. On 17 September, Brooke Claxton was aghast to learn, from the syndicated column of that date published by the Alsop brothers, that

> President Eisenhower has now approved plans for one of the most remarkable experiments in government ever undertaken in this country. These plans call for seven reports to the American people, all related to one aspect or another of the threat to national survival inherent in the growing Soviet air-atomic

capability. The series of reports is tentatively scheduled to start Sunday evening, Oct. 4, and to continue every Sunday evening until Nov. 15. This project – known as "Operation Candor" in the inner circles of the Government – will start, as presently planned, with a vitally important speech by the President. In this speech President Eisenhower expects to tell the people in broad strokes, but frankly and factually, the hard truth about the national situation. This Presidential report to the people is to be followed by six further nation-wide radio and television reports by Administration leaders, all dealing with the problem of national survival in the nuclear age...

This program, of course, is subject to change. The President might even conceivably change his mind, and cancel the whole project. Short of this, it might in the end be so watered down as to serve no useful purpose, or even turned into a political stunt ... Yet as of now, this program for trusting the American people with the truth looks like a remarkably courageous and wholly admirable experiment in government.[112]

The Canadian political climate had never been propitious for the flowering of 'Operations Candor,' or even of 'Operations Candour.' It was not propitious now. Brooke Claxton had many qualities of the statesman just as he had many qualities of the politician. But candour was not among them.* 'Anything like "Operation Candor",' he wrote at once to the Prime Minister after reading the Alsops' account, 'would almost certainly have serious consequences.' An extraordinary number of these crowded his mind.

Emphasis on home defence would lead to a disproportionate amount being put into purely defensive measures.

It would be accompanied or followed by releases or leaks on the location and effectiveness of existing defence works giving Russia the information it most keenly desires.

Since attack can only come over Canadian territory, it would place responsibility for the alleged defencelessness of New York and Chicago on our failure to make adequate provision.

It would increase enormously the pressure on us to add to our own defence measures, which we could only do by increasing the defence appropriation or reducing our contribution to NATO.

What has just been said would be equally true in the United States, so that greater insistence on local defence would further reduce US participation in NATO abroad and mutual aid.

Any reduction in the US contribution would be used by the European countries

* 'It is difficult for any member of a government,' Brooke Claxton had remarked in the House of Commons in the course of one of his earliest statements as Minister of National Defence, 'and particularly the Minister of National Defence, to put before either Parliament or the people all the considerations which enter into the making of a defence policy.' Canada, *H.C. Debates*, 1947, I, 413.

as an excuse for their further letting up in their efforts, defeating the purpose of NATO and adding to liability to attack.

An operation of this kind would lead to a spate of speculative articles, breaches of security and the like, which would upset public opinion and further reduce the power of the administrations in the States and here and abroad to plan effectively so as to make the most economic and efficient use of their combined resources to build up collective security through joint action.

Finally, the whole operation would greatly bolster up the strength and morale of the forces behind the Iron Curtain, just at a time when the continued steady development of our strength can probably be combined with a willingness to sit around a table and discuss measures that may be taken to eliminate the threat and danger of war.[113]

It is hard to say which aspect of Operation Candor caused Claxton the most concern. Was it the policy of stepped-up continental defence to the propagation of which it was to be devoted? Or was it the tactics of propagation proposed? If the latter, Claxton's anxieties were soon dispelled. The US Administration, as the Alsops had foreseen, declined to mount Operation Candor on anything like an all-out scale. On 8 October, President Eisenhower declared that 'the Soviets had the capability of atomic attack on us, and such capability would increase with the passage of time.' But the President also stated that he had no intention of disclosing details either of Soviet offensive power (insofar as the Administration could pretend to be privy to them), or the details of American retaliatory capability. The President's statement was correctly interpreted as 'something of a victory for those members of his Cabinet who have argued against dramatic disclosures in the field of atomic energy.'[114] Operation Candor had not exactly become Operation Duplicity: but it was far from being the frank and fearless confrontation of the public with all the known facts that the Alsops had hoped for and that Claxton had deplored.

There remained the policy of improved continental defence, as distinct from the methods of putting it across. Brooke Claxton's opposition to the policy diminished considerably when, in the middle of October, he received from the Joint Military Study Group a report recommending the immediate creation of an additional radar early warning chain. The route proposed was roughly along the 55th parallel of latitude – some several hundreds of miles to the north of the Pinetree system, following an arc along the points Prince Rupert-Flin Flon-Upper James Bay-Northern Labrador, but even more hundreds of miles south of the far northerly warning system recommended by the Lincoln Group. This recommendation, coming as it did from his own military advisers, suggested to Brooke Claxton a new approach, which could be crudely stated as 'If you can't beat 'em, join 'em,' or, perhaps more accurately, 'When rape is inevitable, relax and enjoy it,' or, certainly more elegantly, 'Statesmanship is the constructive acceptance of the inevitable.' Even before the adoption of NSC 162, Claxton had faced up to the fact that should the United States decide to improve its defences by means of additional radar warning facilities on Canadian territory, it would be exceedingly awkward and perhaps impossible for the Canadian Government to refuse to offer the necessary co-operation. The real issue would be the terms on which its co-operation would be forthcoming. 'If United States government policy develops as forecast,' he wrote in a memorandum of 3 October,

it will, of course, create many serious problems for Canada. The Canadian Government may or may not be convinced, when United States projects are proposed, that they are reasonably necessary when weighed against global strategic factors and political obligations overseas; as well as against the possibility of air attack taking new forms in the next decade. However, it may be very difficult indeed for the Canadian Government to reject any major defence proposal which the United States Government presents with conviction as essential for the security of North America.

If new United States defence projects in Canada, and in particular new radar defences, should become inevitable, the Canadian Government will be faced by the question whether Canada should share in the cost and operation of the new projects or whether the United States should be allowed to develop and operate them exclusively with United States money and men. If Canada is to share in these projects, how will that affect the level of future defence expenditures and, in particular, Canada's continuing share of NATO defences in Europe?

By mid-October, following receipt of the recommendations of the Military Study Group for the construction of what was eventually to be known as the Mid-Canada Line, at least a partial answer to these questions had begun to take shape in Brooke Claxton's mind. Canada should, on its own initiative and at its own expense, proceed with the construction of the radar chain along the 55th parallel.

An all-Canadian contribution to continental defence, Claxton reasoned, was desirable on several counts. First of all, it was feasible. One of the by-products of the adverse appraisal of an Arctic radar system made by the Canadian planners in 1947 had been the institution of work, under the auspices of the newly-created Defence Research Board, on 'certain development projects which produced the equipment ultimately employed in the Mid-Canada Line.'[115] Canada possessed not only the geography in which to go it alone: she possessed, as well, the technology. (That was, for her, an unusual combination.) Nor was this the sole aspect of feasibility. An all-Canadian effort, due mainly to the technology embodied in the radar apparatus contrived by the McGill scientists, would be relatively modest in cost. Keeping the project under Canadian control would enable the Government to avoid the inflated and excessive expenses which, as the wartime experience of the Alaska Highway and the Northwest Staging Route had shown, was the inescapable consequence of joint participation with the United States: 'Our paying for it all,' Claxton argued, 'would not involve us in a greater outlay than whatever might be considered as a proper share of a joint operation.' There was yet another financial inducement, urged upon Claxton by the Minister of Trade and Commerce. An all-Canadian venture would ensure that Canadian manufacturers of equipment, particularly of electronic equipment, would receive their fair share, perhaps more than their fair share, of the valuable contracts that construction of the system would be sure to call into being. 'The strategic importance of industrial production,' C.D. Howe reminded Brooke Claxton at this time, 'cannot be overlooked in defence planning nor the need to develop alternative sources of supply in this country. If the Canadian electronic industry is to play an effective part in the joint defence of the North American continent, it must be given an opportunity to participate in the actual production of electronic equipment, particularly in the field of radar.'[116]

Important as were these technological and financial considerations, the clinching argument, in Brooke Claxton's view, was political. 'Making this suggestion now,' he wrote to the Prime Minister on 21 October,

> would moreover give us the initiative and enable us to tell our own people and the Americans that we were quite prepared to do anything we thought necessary in continental defence.
>
> I feel quite certain that the Americans will not remain content with a line along the 55th parallel but will ultimately want to go for something like the Lincoln Project or even more.
>
> Our taking the initiative with regard to the McGill Fence would put us in a better position to say, "Well, we think we have done what we thought was necessary for continental defence. If you want to go on and do more, we are not going to stand in the way," and keep our self-respect without having to put out too great an expenditure of materials, man-power and money.[117]

These arguments carried the day, although not immediately. The first decisions of the Canadian Government, taken in November 1953, were to conduct further feasibility studies of the Mid-Canada Line. These were completed by June 1954. On 23 June, Brooke Claxton wrote: 'We are putting to the Cabinet Defence Committee tomorrow the proposal that we should proceed alone with the McGill Fence.'[118] The proposal was endorsed without opposition.

As Brooke Claxton had predicted, the United States was not content to repose its confidence solely in the Mid-Canada and Pinetree Lines. The immediate prospect, following completion of the Mid-Canada Line, was that enemy attackers would attempt to outflank it.* This consideration led to the project to extend the radar coverage along the 55th parallel 'by a set of "seawings" – airborne and shipborne radars extending from Alaska to Midway in the Pacific and from Labrador to the United Kingdom in the Atlantic.'[119] The cost of the extension turned out to be as great, or greater, than the cost of the Mid-Canada Line itself – a factor of which the Canadian Government was not unmindful in taking the decision to proceed on its own with the McGill Fence. 'Obviously they are beginning to get really bothered about the seaward wings,' Brooke Claxton had written following a visit to Ottawa by the Secretary of the Air Force and some of his colleagues in June 1954. 'The cost in men and money of doing something effective over both oceans is something to worry about ... Our thought about this is that if we [build the Mid-Canada Line] on our own we should leave the seaward wings largely to the Americans.'[120] In the event, the seaward wings were left entirely to the Americans.

In addition, the Canadian decision to proceed independently with the Mid-Canada Line strengthened the case for constructing the Distant Early Warning (DEW) Line along the 70th parallel. The two systems (as the Lincoln Group had pointed out) were complementary, not competing. With the Mid-Canada Line as a backstop, the DEW Line would be less vulnerable to countermeasures and deception, particularly as each system employed essentially different types of electronic apparatus. In June 1954, the Joint Military Study Group recommended acceptance of the DEW Line project to the two governments, and in an announcement issued on 27 September 1954 by the Defence Departments of the two countries it was stated that they 'had agreed in principle that there was a need for a distant early warning line across the far northern part of North America and had directed that detailed planning for such a line should be initiated at once.' On 19 November, it was announced that 'the two Governments

* 'I think it is the view of most of our people,' Brooke Claxton wrote in June 1954,

> that the United States today is far more exposed to attack over sea than over the North and with the McGill Fence and further developments that we are certainly going to make, the relative position will likely continue the same trend. As I see it, the Russians today only have aircraft for a one-way flight. On a one-way flight, those aircraft could reach anywhere in the United States and they might get to Mexico. These aircraft have a limited ceiling and a relatively slow speed. They would be sitting ducks for fighters if they were picked up at all. On these assumptions, the right course would be to go over the sea at night and in bad weather and strike at the targets without warning, crossing as little land as possible...

Brooke Claxton to A.D.P. Heeney, 23 June 1954, Claxton Papers.

have now decided to proceed with the construction of the Distant Early Warning Line.' Finally, on 20 May 1955, there was tabled in the House of Commons the text of the Agreement of 5 May which set out 'Conditions to Govern the Establishment of a Distant Early Warning System in Canadian Territory.'*

It is the way with weapons systems to become obsolete on becoming operational. In this respect the DEW Line ran true to form. No sooner had the system detected its first intruder – no doubt a civil airliner on a Great Circle Route – than the Soviet Union issued its historic communiqué of 26 August 1957. 'A super long distance intercontinental ballistic rocket has been released,' it proclaimed, which flew 'at a very high unprecedented altitude,' covered 'a huge distance in a brief time,' and 'landed in the set area.' It did not take long for the message of this delphic communication to be interpreted. Henceforth the missile was the message.

* For details of this document, and an analysis of the difficulties with which it was designed to deal, see James Eayrs, *Canada in World Affairs: October 1955 to June 1957* (Toronto 1959; 1965), 148–52.

*End of Vol. III*

DOCUMENTS

CHRONOLOGY OF EVENTS

NOTE ON THE SOURCES

REFERENCES

# DOCUMENT 1

REPORT OF THE ADVISORY COMMITTEE ON POST-HOSTILITIES PROBLEMS, 'POST-WAR CANADIAN DEFENCE RELATIONSHIP WITH THE UNITED STATES: GENERAL CONSIDERATIONS,' 23 JANUARY 1945 (DEPARTMENT OF EXTERNAL AFFAIRS FILES)


*Summary*

1 The paper is based upon the following assumptions:

a It may be assumed that international problems arising from purely Canadian-United States relations are unlikely to bring about a conflict of policies serious enough to prejudice general friendly relations and that, therefore, any threatening difference of view would only be occasioned through differing attitudes towards events in other parts of the world. The possibility, however, of the United States being moved to exert undue pressure on Canada, particularly as respects matters of defence, should not be overlooked.

b That for several years at least a direct military threat to North America is unlikely, although the means to meet such a threat should be available during this period.

c That the victor nations, including the United States, will maintain larger armed forces than before the war to enforce peace.

2 The present war has brought about the following developments:

a Opinion in both countries has gone far towards recognizing that the two oceans no longer provide full protection for North America and that the ultimate security of the continent depends on the maintenance of peace in Europe and Asia.

b Adequate protection against air-borne attacks, especially from the North, Northeast and Northwest, has become an essential part of North American defences.

c The defence of Canada, Newfoundland, Alaska, Greenland, Iceland, Bermuda and the West Indies is recognized as vital to the defence of the United States.

d Neither Canada nor the United States is likely to reduce its defences to the pre-war level.

3 It is concluded:

a that the defences of Canada should be closely co-ordinated with those of the United States after the war;

b that the Permanent Joint Board on Defence will continue to be a valuable means of facilitating this co-ordination;

c that relations between the United States and the USSR are of special concern to Canada;

d that in joint planning with the United States, Canada should accept full responsibility for all such defence measures within Canadian territory as the moderate risk to which we are exposed may indicate to be necessary;
e that Canada should continue to accept responsibility for the local defence of Newfoundland and Labrador, and that the part of the United States in the defence of these territories should be limited to the operation of their leased bases in Newfoundland;
f that the new vulnerability of this Continent necessitates the maintenance of larger Canadian armed forces than before the war;
g that the exchange of technical information on military research and development between Canada and the United States should continue and that Canada should maintain the means of making an effective contribution to such exchange.

*Introduction*

1 In view of the disparity between Canada's military strength and that of the Great Powers, the governing principle of Canadian policy should be to continue to foster and maintain good international relations, generally between all nations, particularly with the United States. Any policy which would create unfriendliness between the United States and Canada would, in the long run, be inimical to Canadian interests.

2 Although it is not possible at this stage to foretell the exact conditions under which Canadian-United States defence relations will operate in the post-war period, enough data are available to indicate the broad outline of the problems which Canada will be required to face.

3 It may be assumed that international problems arising from purely Canadian-United States relations are unlikely to bring about a conflict of policies serious enough to prejudice general friendly relations, and that, therefore, any threatening difference of view would only be occasioned through differing attitudes towards events in other parts of the world. The possibility, however, of the United States being moved to exert undue pressure on Canada, particularly as respects matters of defence, should not be overlooked.

4 It is probable that after the war, a world security organization will be set up. Whether or not this is so for several years any direct military threat to the North American continent is unlikely in view of the exhaustion and war weariness of the nations of the world. It is necessary, however, that the means to meet such a threat should be available during this period.

5 Nevertheless the victor nations will have to retain considerably larger armed forces than before the war to police Germany and Japan, and to provide a reserve capable of maintaining peace, by force if necessary. The policy of any future world organization for the preservation of peace is certain to be based on military action as a last resort, but to be effective this instrument must be ready for instant use when required. There appears to be general agreement that the maintenance of adequate forces by the victor nations must be an essential element in the world security system.

6 It may be assumed, therefore, that, although there will be virtually no risk of general war for some years, military preparation within the United Nations will not be allowed to fall into neglect, and that the United States will not again allow its military power to become so far out of step with its world interests as before this present war.

*Current Situation*

7 In the past, Canadian 'defence' planning has been based on a strong British Navy, and on the premise that the United States would be a benevolent neutral if not an ally in the event of Canada being at war. Developments of this war have not changed these two fundamentals, but other factors have come into being necessitating a review of certain aspects of Canada's defence planning particularly vis-à-vis the United States.

8 Because of the belief in the immunity of attack to the North American continent provided by the Atlantic and Pacific Oceans, and the control exercised by the British and United States Navies, planning for defence against attack on the United States or Canada was considered of minor importance. Both countries could count on adequate time to prepare for war after the actual outbreak of hostilities. While these conditions held, there was no liaison between Canada and the United States for mutual defence planning – there was no apparent need for it.

9 The present war has changed these conditions, and the defence problems of Canada and the United States must now be considered as inter-dependent. While it may be held that the East and West coastal areas are still relatively immune from major attack (as long as the British and United States Navies are in being, which will continue to be a basic assumption), the development of air power has diminished the physical isolation of the North American continent by opening up the northern approaches. Defence planning must be re-oriented to take this into account.

10 Canada, lying across the shortest air routes from either Europe or Asia, has now become of more direct strategic importance to the United States. Consciousness of the need for close co-ordination in defence began to grow even before the war, but it was the fall of France that forcibly brought to the fore the need for practical action. Thus, at a time when the defeat of Britain seemed possible, and with Canada at war but the United States at peace, the Canada-United States Permanent Joint Board on Defence was established.

11 The essential importance of Newfoundland and the Maritimes to the security of both Canada and the United States was fully recognized in the earliest meetings of the Board. At the first meeting, as a direct result of its recommendations, Canada agreed to despatch further forces to Newfoundland and to undertake further defence measures there. One of the main topics of the second meeting of the Board was the defence of the Maritime Provinces. Eventually, following the recommendation of the Board, a joint defence plan was evolved by the Service members and accepted by the Governments of both countries.

12 Nearly all the tasks set out in this plan involved measures to be implemented in Canada, Newfoundland and Alaska. It is possible that if Canada had not been able to carry out the defence measures required on Canadian territory the United States would have done so, even though the United States was not then at war.

13 This attitude of the United States became more apparent after the entry of that country into the war. If Canada had refused or failed to undertake projects which formed part of United States plans (such as the Crimson Air Staging Route), or measures in Canadian territory for the special protection of the United States (e.g. the Radar Chain across Northern Ontario to protect industrial installations in the mid-continent), the United States was willing and even anxious to proceed alone. As time went on, it became increasingly apparent that the existence of major military installations in Canada built, paid for and operated by the United States might impair Canada's freedom of action. That difficulty has been mitigated, if not eliminated, by the Canadian Government's decision, agreed to by the United States, to reimburse the United States for construction costs of all airfields and certain other facilities of continuing value erected in Canada by the United States.

14 Thus, developments in the present war have brought about a new set of defence relationships between Canada and the United States of which the following are the most significant:

a Opinion in both countries has gone far towards recognizing that the two oceans do not provide full protection for North America from attack, and further that the ultimate security of the continent depends on the maintenance of peace in Europe and Asia.

b Both the United States and Canada have accepted the fact that in addition to protection against seaborne attack they must have adequate protection against airborne attack, especially from the North, Northeast and Northwest.

c Canada along with Newfoundland, Alaska, Greenland, Iceland, Bermuda and the West Indies will continue to be vital to the defence of the United States. As aviation develops the northern routes will increasingly become world commercial highways. By the same token they will become potential routes for hostile powers with designs against the United States, and could conceivably be used by the United States for offensive purposes.

d Although no immediate threat of attack may be discerned, neither country is likely again to reduce its defences to the pre-war level.

### *Canadian Defence Policy in the Post-War Period*

15 In the circumstances, the United States may be expected to take an active interest in Canadian defence preparations in the future. Moreover, that interest may be expressed with an absence of the tact and restraint customarily employed by the United Kingdom in putting forward defence proposals. Pressure along these lines will doubtless develop in accordance with the trend of United States post-war foreign policy. It is unlikely that isolationism in the United States will return to its traditional form, but it is quite possible that it may develop as a militant form of continental defence-mindedness. If such is the case, the pressure on Canada to maintain defences at a higher level than

would seem necessary from the point of view of purely Canadian interests might be very strong.

16 Since Canada lies astride the overland route between the United States and the USSR, any serious deterioration in their relations would be embarrassing to Canada. The best hope of Canada being able to avoid such embarrassments lies in the establishment of an effective world security organization in which the leading military powers actively co-operate to secure jointly the settlement of international disputes.

17 Whether there is a security organization or not, it is clear that defence planning for Canada and the United States should be co-ordinated. This co-ordination, which would in fact constitute a regional defence system, would not conflict with the purposes of the world security organization, but would take its place as part of a plan of universal security. In this way one part of the world might be better provided against outside attack, and would be available as a safe base from which punitive operations might be launched against a country attempting to break the peace.

18 To facilitate this co-ordination the Permanent Joint Board on Defence is an appropriate piece of machinery. Through the Board, representatives of two countries (the one great and the other relatively weak) meet together on an equal footing. It is quite conceivable that in the post-war period there may not be a great deal for the Board to do. Nevertheless, its mere existence is a useful public symbol of the mutual confidence which exists between Canada and the United States. Moreover, there is a great advantage in having available a body that can consider potentially controversial questions of defence before government policy in either country has become fixed. The Board will continue to be available to recommend joint defence plans, and as an agency to facilitate discussion and exchange of information.

*Implications of the Policy*

19 While the actual defence measures that will be required cannot be discussed at this point, there can be no doubt that, with or without world security obligations, Canada will be required to carry a greater peacetime defence commitment than ever before. It seems clear that in future it should be part of our policy to accept full responsibility for such measures of local Canadian defence as the moderate nature of the risk to which we are exposed may indicate to be necessary. Furthermore, the general responsibility of Canada for the local defence of Newfoundland and Labrador has been recognized and accepted by the Canadian Government during the war as an inevitable consequence of their geographical proximity. It is desirable that the role of the United States in these territories should be limited to the security of their leased bases, particularly at Argentia and Stephenville, from the first named of which the more extended defence of the North-West Atlantic would be carried out.

20 This closer tie-up with the United States need not conflict with the Canadian tradition of basing military policy and training upon British practice. However, if Canada and the United States are to be efficient in the defence of North America, common experience between the national forces will be

desirable in time of peace (e.g. the pooling of information and possibly the carrying out of occasional joint exercises).

21 Since the basis for exchange of technical information must be mutual, it is necessary that adequate technical establishments staffed by well-trained scientists and research personnel be maintained in Canada, capable of undertaking independent research and development of a high quality, the results of which would be available as a basis for the exchange of such information.

22 This closer liaison with the United States is in no sense an isolationist policy. If any single lesson has emerged from the present conflict, it is that no nation can ensure immunity from attack merely by erecting a defensive barrier around its frontiers. Canada's first lines of defence at the present time extend far out into the Pacific in the West and to Europe in the East. With the growth of air power, frontier defences have become less significant. It is not intended that Canada should base its defensive policy exclusively on collaboration with the United States. On the contrary it is considered that Canada should accept a fair share of responsibility in an international security organization along with the other Nations both inside and outside the Commonwealth.

*Conclusions*

23 It is concluded, therefore:

a that the defences of Canada should be closely co-ordinated with those of the United States in the post-war period.
b that the Permanent Joint Board on Defence will continue to be a valuable means of facilitating this co-ordination and also as a medium for the informal discussion of mutual defence problems.
c that the source of major friction between Canada and the United States is more likely to grow out of differing views towards events outside this Continent. Particularly in view of Canada's geographic position astride the overland route between the USA and the USSR, Canadian defence arrangements with the United States will be greatly influenced by the general character of the relations between the US and the USSR.
d that in joint defence planning with the United States, Canada should accept full responsibility for all such defence measures within Canadian territory as the moderate risk to which we are exposed may indicate to be necessary.
e that Canada should continue to accept responsibility for the local defence of Newfoundland and Labrador, and that the part of the United States in the defence of these territories should be limited to the operation of their leased bases in Newfoundland.
f that because of the new vulnerability of the North American continent, quite apart from any obligations under a world security organization, Canada must accept increased defence responsibilities and maintain larger armed forces than before the war.
g that the exchange of technical information on military research and development between Canada and the United States should continue, and that Canada should maintain the means of making an effective contribution to such exchange.

# DOCUMENT 2

## JOINT CANADIAN-UNITED STATES BASIC SECURITY PLAN, 5 JUNE 1946 (KING PAPERS)

### SECTION I INTENTION

1 This Plan is intended to provide for the co-ordinated or joint action of Canadian and United States armed forces in the defence of the territory of Canada, Newfoundland and the United States, including Alaska, and the protection of the vital sea and air communications associated therewith, in order to ensure the ultimate security of Canada and the United States.

### SECTION II CONCEPT

2 In the past North America has been comparatively immune from heavy attack by a hostile power, due to the geographical barriers created by the Atlantic and Pacific Oceans and the frozen wastes of the Arctic. Technical developments in the art of warfare occasioned by scientific progress have lessened this immunity and portend that it will diminish progressively. Hence the necessity of modifying the concept of defence for the United States and Canada. The principal advancements in the science of war responsible for this change are:

a The increased range of application of destructive power and armed force resulting from the development of modern aircraft, amphibious technique, guided missiles, and advancement in the technique of submarine warfare.
b The increased destructive capacity of weapons such as the atomic bomb, rockets, and instruments of biological warfare.

3 To counter these changes in forms and scales of attack possible against North America, co-operative action of Canadian and United States armed forces will be required for purposes connected with:

a The protection of vital areas of Canada and the United States against air attack.
b The defence of Alaska, Canada, Newfoundland (which includes Labrador) and the United States.
c The protection of essential shipping within the northern portions of the Western Atlantic and Pacific Oceans.
d The protection of land, sea and air lines of communication in Canada and the United States.

### SECTION III JOINT MISSION OF THE UNITED STATES AND CANADA

4 To defend the territory of Canada, Newfoundland and the United States, including Alaska, and to protect the vital sea and air communications associ-

ated therewith, in order to ensure the ultimate security of Canada and the United States.

SECTION IV JOINT TASKS

5 To accomplish the joint mission, the tasks set forth in this section are those which will be undertaken jointly by the armed forces of Canada and the United States.

*Joint task one*: Protect vital areas of Canada and the United States from air attack.
*Joint task two*: Defend the northern area of Canada and Labrador and protect the land, sea and air communications associated therewith.
*Joint task three*: Defend Alaska and protect the land, sea and air communications associated therewith.
*Joint task four*: Defend Newfoundland (excluding Labrador) and protect the land, sea and air communications associated therewith.
*Joint task five*: Defend eastern Canada and the northeastern portion of the United States and protect the land, sea and air communications associated therewith.
*Joint task six*: Defend western Canada and the northwestern portion of the United States and protect the land, sea and air communications associated therewith.
*Joint task seven*: Protect overseas shipping in the northwestern Atlantic.
*Joint task eight*: Protect overseas shipping in the northern Pacific.

SECTION V DIVISION OF TASKS

6 Joint Task One. PROTECT VITAL AREAS OF CANADA AND THE UNITED STATES FROM AIR ATTACK

*Canadian Tasks*

| | |
|---|---|
| Air Force | Co-operate in the establishment and operation of an air warning system and those communication, navigation and meteorological services necessary for an effective common air defence.<br>Provide necessary facilities and forces for interceptor defences for the common protection of vital areas. |
| Army | Establish and operate anti-aircraft defences in Canada and outlying bases under Canadian jurisdiction. |
| Navy | Support Air Force and Army. |

*United States Tasks*

| | |
|---|---|
| Army and Army Air | Co-operate in the establishment and operation of an air warning system and those communication, navigation and meteorological services necessary for an effective common air defence.<br>Provide the necessary facilities and forces for inter- |

| | |
|---|---|
| | ceptor and anti-aircraft defences for the common protection of vital areas.<br>Establish and operate anti-aircraft defences in the United States and at outlying bases under United States jurisdiction. |
| Navy | Support Army and Army Air in the air defence of vital areas. |

7 Joint Task Two. DEFEND THE NORTHERN AREA OF CANADA AND LABRADOR AND PROTECT THE LAND, SEA AND AIR COMMUNICATIONS ASSOCIATED THEREWITH

*Canadian Tasks*

| | |
|---|---|
| All Services | Deny the use by the enemy of the northern areas of Canada and Labrador between Alaska and the Straits of Belle Isle.<br>Provide elements of mobile forces.<br>Specific tasks shall include: |
| Air Force | Conduct air operations required to defend the area.<br>Co-operate with the Navy in the protection of sea communications in the coastal zone. |
| Navy | Protect sea communications in the coastal zone. |
| Army | Conduct ground operations required to defend the area. |

*United States Tasks*

| | |
|---|---|
| All Services | Assist Canadian Services in the defence of northern Canada and Labrador. |

8 Joint Task Three. DEFEND ALASKA AND PROTECT THE LAND, SEA AND AIR COMMUNICATIONS ASSOCIATED THEREWITH

*Canadian Tasks*

| | |
|---|---|
| Army<br>Air Force | Protect the Canadian portion of the Northwest Staging Route, including the air fields, communications system, highway, and ancillary defence installations. |
| All Services | Assist the United States Services in the defence of Alaska. |

*United States Tasks*

| | |
|---|---|
| All Services | Deny use by the enemy of Alaska and the Aleutians.<br>Specific tasks shall include: |
| Army and Army Air | Defend Alaska and the Aleutians including associated land and air communications.<br>Conduct air operations required to defend the area.<br>Support Naval Operations. |

| | |
|---|---|
| Navy | Protect sea communications in the coastal zone.<br>Support the defence of Alaska. |

9 Joint Task Four. DEFEND NEWFOUNDLAND (EXCLUDING LABRADOR) AND PROTECT THE LAND, SEA AND AIR COMMUICATIONS ASSOCIATED THEREWITH

*Canadian Tasks*

| | |
|---|---|
| All Services | Defend Newfoundland in co-operation with the United States Services.<br>Specific tasks shall include: |
| Army | Conduct ground operations required to defend the area.<br>Provide anti-aircraft ground defences.<br>Provide coast artillery defences for Canadian Naval bases. |
| Air Force | Conduct air operations required to defend the area.<br>Co-operate with the Navy in the protection of sea communications in the coastal zone. |
| Navy | Protect sea communications in the coastal zone.<br>Provide and operate the necessary Naval bases, including Naval seaward defences therefor. |

*United States Tasks*

| | |
|---|---|
| Army and Army Air | Defend United States bases.<br>Co-operate with Canadian Services in the defence of Newfoundland. |
| Navy | Support the defence of United States bases.<br>Assist Canadian Services in the defence of Newfoundland. |

10 Joint Task Five. DEFEND EASTERN CANADA AND THE NORTHEASTERN PORTION OF THE UNITED STATES AND PROTECT THE LAND, SEA AND AIR COMMUNICATIONS ASSOCIATED THEREWITH

*Canadian Tasks*

| | |
|---|---|
| All Services | Defend Eastern Canada.<br>Assist the United States Services in the defence of Northeastern United States.<br>Specific tasks shall include: |
| Army | Conduct ground operations required to defend the area.<br>Provide anti-aircraft ground defences.<br>Provide coast artillery defences for Naval bases. |
| Air Force | Conduct air operations required to defend the area.<br>Co-operate with the Navy in the protection of sea communications in the Canadian coastal zone. |

| | |
|---|---|
| Navy | Provide and operate necessary Naval bases, including naval seaward defences therefor. |

*United States Tasks*

| | |
|---|---|
| Army and Army Air | Defend the Northeastern portion of the United States, including land and air communications. Conduct air operations required to defend the area.<br>Support Naval operations. |
| Navy | Protect sea communications in the United States coastal zone.<br>Support the defence of the Northeastern portion of the United States. |
| All Services | Assist the Canadian Services in the defence of Eastern Canada. |

11 Joint Task Six. DEFEND WESTERN CANADA AND THE NORTHWESTERN PORTION OF THE UNITED STATES AND PROTECT THE LAND, SEA AND AIR COMMUNICATIONS ASSOCIATED THEREWITH

*Canadian Tasks*

| | |
|---|---|
| All Services | Defend Western Canada.<br>Co-operate with the United States Services in the defence of the Strait of Juan de Fuca-Puget Sound area.<br>Assist the United States Services in the defence of Northwestern United States.<br>Specific tasks shall include: |
| Army | Conduct ground operations required to defend the area.<br>Provide anti-aircraft ground defences.<br>Provide coast artillery defences for Naval bases. |
| Air Force | Conduct air operations required to defend the area.<br>Co-operate with the Navy in the protection of sea communications in the Canadian coastal zone. |
| Navy | Protect sea communications in the Canadian coastal zone.<br>Provide and operate necessary Naval bases, including Naval seaward defences therefor. |

*United States Tasks*

| | |
|---|---|
| Army and Army Air | Defend the Northwestern portion of the United States, including land and air communications.<br>Conduct air operations required to defend the area.<br>Support Naval operations. |
| Navy | Protect sea communications in the United States coastal zone. |

| | |
|---|---|
| | Support the defence of the Northwestern portion of the United States. |
| All Services | Co-operate with Canadian Services in the defence of the Strait of Juan de Fuca-Puget Sound area. Assist Canadian Services in the defence of Western Canada. |

12 Joint Task Seven. PROTECT OVERSEAS SHIPPING IN THE NORTHWESTERN ATLANTIC

*Canadian Tasks*

| | |
|---|---|
| Navy | Co-operate with the United States Navy in the protection of overseas shipping. |
| Air Force | Support Naval operations. |

*United States Tasks*

| | |
|---|---|
| Army and Army Air | Support Naval operations. |
| Navy | With the co-operation of the Royal Canadian Navy, protect overseas shipping. |

13 Joint Task Eight. PROTECT OVERSEAS SHIPPING IN THE NORTHERN PACIFIC

*Canadian Tasks*

| | |
|---|---|
| Navy | Co-operate with the United States Navy in the protection of overseas shipping. |
| Air Force | Support Naval operations. |

*United States Tasks*

| | |
|---|---|
| Army and Army Air | Support Naval operations. |
| Navy | With the co-operation of the Royal Canadian Navy, protect overseas shipping. |

SECTION VI IMPLEMENTATION

14 This Plan will be placed in effect by the Chiefs of Staff of Canada and the United States when so directed by the Governments of Canada and the United States.

SECTION VII PREPARATORY MEASURES

15 Certain measures will require implementation immediately in order to ensure the proper functioning of the Plan in the event of emergency. Therefore, the implementation of preparatory measures will be effected by specific agreements which will be embodied in annexes to this Plan when approved by appropriate authorities. Preparatory measures of particular urgency include:

a Investigation and establishment of the essential elements of a common system of air defence.
b Program of air photography, mapping and charting.
c Conduct of tests of equipment, clothing and supplies under Arctic conditions and collection of scientific data in Arctic region.
d Familiarization of appropriate personnel of the armed forces of both countries in military operations under Arctic conditions.
e Collection of strategic information necessary for military operations in Canada, Newfoundland and Alaska.

SECTION VIII CO-ORDINATION

16 Co-ordination of the military efforts of the United States and Canada shall be effected by mutual co-operation except where unified command is determined to be appropriate. The forces of each nation shall be assigned tasks for whose execution such forces shall be primarily responsible. These tasks may be as assigned in this Plan or by agreement between the Chiefs of Staff concerned.

17 When operating on a basis of mutual co-operation, the forces of each nation shall aid and support to their utmost capacity the appropriate forces of the other nation. During such operations, the Chiefs of Staff of each nation will retain the strategic direction and command of their own forces.

18 Unified command may be established over any United States and Canadian forces operating in any area or areas, or for a particular operation:

a When agreed upon by the Chiefs of Staff concerned; or
b When the Commanders of the Canadian and United States forces concerned agree that the situation requires the exercise of unified command, and further agree as to the service that should exercise such command. All such mutual agreements shall be subject to confirmation by the Chiefs of Staff concerned, but this provision shall not prevent the immediate establishment of unified command by local commanders in cases of emergency.

19 Unified command, when established, shall vest in one commander the responsibility and authority to co-ordinate the operations of the participating forces of both nations by the setting up of task forces, the assignment of tasks, the designation of objectives, and the exercise of such co-ordinating control as the commander deems necessary to ensure the success of the operations. Unified command shall authorize the commander concerned complete freedom of movement of all forces of either nation or any service under his command to any area within his jurisdiction. Unified command, however, shall not authorize a commander exercising it to control the administration and discipline of the forces of the nation of which he is not an officer, nor to issue any instructions to such forces beyond those necessary for effective co-operation.

20 The assignment of an area of responsibility to one nation shall not be construed as restricting the forces of the other nation from temporarily extend-

ing appropriate operations into that area, as may be mutually agreed between commanders concerned.

SECTION IX CO-OPERATION AND LIAISON

21 For all matters requiring common action, each nation shall require its commanders to establish liaison with and co-operate with appropriate commanders of the other nation.

22 Each nation will seek to provide the forces and within its own territory the military installations necessary for the implementation of this Plan. So far as is practicable, each nation will make available its bases, harbours, and repair facilities for use by the forces of the other.

23 Arrangements for mutual use of areas and facilities during peace for training, tests, manoeuvres or exercises will be made by special agreement. Similar arrangements will be made by special agreement for stationing of combat forces during peace in the territory of the other nation.

24 To facilitate common decision and action, Canada and the United States will establish when necessary in Washington and Ottawa, respectively, officers of all Services who will be charged with the duty of representing their military Services, vis-à-vis the appropriate military service of the other nation. They will also arrange to assign liaison officers where needed for effecting direct co-operation between commanders of forces in the field.

SECTION X REVISION

25 This Plan will be subject to review and any necessary revision annually, or at lesser intervals, if required. It will be the responsibility of the Canada-United States Permanent Joint Board on Defence to initiate this review not later than July 1st of each year. This review will include the preparation of a joint appreciation.

SECTION XI ANNEXES TO THE PLAN

26 Preparatory measures, military forces and facilities to be provided, organization and command responsibilities, and communication principles are set forth in annexes to the Plan. These annexes will be revised from time to time as necessary. (Annexes are under preparation and when approved by appropriate Canadian and United States authorities will be included in the Plan.)

# DOCUMENT 3

EXTRACTS FROM AN ADDRESS BY THE CHIEF OF THE GENERAL STAFF, LT-GENERAL CHARLES FOULKES, TO OFFICERS OF ARMY HEADQUARTERS, 28 JANUARY 1948 (FOULKES PAPERS*)

I want to talk to you today about the present strategic situation and also about the year's work...

...We have only one enemy and that is Russia. I think it is quite obvious to you all that the world is slowly dividing itself into two armed camps. Those of the democracies under the leadership of United States; those of the communist regime under the leadership of Russia. Some people believe that these two opposing ideologies must some day meet in open conflict. Some people believe it is inevitable that Russia and United States will go to war. Some other people think that all the Russian is doing is establishing this 'Cordon Sanitaire' from the Baltic and down to the Mediterranean and is now trying to round it off in Greece. It will be very interesting to watch whether Russia stays behind this 'Cordon Sanitaire' or whether she expands further into Europe. If this happens, we will be able to decide very conclusively on which theory the Russian is working. Whether she is seeking security or whether she has an idea of world domination.

During the last year there have been many significant events. First of all there was the Russian refusal to participate in the Marshall Plan and further to disallow the Satellites to take any part in the restoration of Europe under the leadership of the United States. Then you will recall this was followed up very quickly by the Truman Doctrine in which the president of the United States established a stop line in Greece and is determined to make Russia stay behind the borders of the satellite countries. Perhaps you may have noticed the repeated announcements in the press about the Russian possession of the Atomic Bomb secret and it is significant that the Russians refused to agree to the Baruch plan for control of Atomic energy. As you know, in the Baruch plan the US are prepared to give to Russia the Atomic Bomb secret providing the Russians agreed to inspection. However, I feel that no matter what assurances the Russians give in regard to inspection they will never allow inspection to be carried out. It is also very clear through the vitriolic attacks on the United States and on UK that chances of reaching solutions to any of the problems are extremely difficult. Some observers believe that Russia will eventually leave the UN and that there will be formed in the UN a defensive alliance against Russia. Those of you who read Mr Pearson's speech of two days ago will

* 'I have gone through my papers and I can find little dealing with the early period after the war. All that has turned up is a verbatim report of an address I made in Jan. 1948, which is unedited and quite rough, but it may give you some clues to our thinking in those days.' General Foulkes to the author, 8 July 1967.

observe the indications that this is the way in which Mr Pearson believes will be the final outcome. The final stroke last year was the failure of the Conferences of Foreign Ministers in London to agree on the unification of Germany. It is quite obvious that Russia would like to have Germany unified provided it could be unified on the Soviet scheme. But Russia has no intention of allowing Germany to be unified so that it will be a buffer between the allies and the Soviet Union. So that I think we can say that this year has brought a considerable deterioration in the International situation. We are much worse off this December than we were when we started last January. Now the thought which must come up in all our minds is, what are the chances of war?

Because war is our business, I feel that in this question of the chances of war we must carefully weigh the capabilities of our potential enemy and the probabilities of war. An examination of the Russian capabilities show that there is no doubt that the Russians are capable at the present time of overrunning the whole of the continent of Europe. All that is really required is the order to start the quick march. There are in Russia at the present time about three million men under arms. So that task would be accomplished fairly easily. Their main deficiency is that of a strategical air force. Although we are finding, to the surprise of most of the air experts of the world, that the Russians are developing a strategical air force. It was very astonishing that in the May Day demonstrations last year the Russians produced in the air four-engine jet bombers and two-engine jet fighters and the air experts had no idea they had any such weapons. So I think we ought to bear in mind that the Russian is making very good use of the scientists and the aircraft craftsmen which she took out of Germany at the end of the war. I consider that Russia is capable of opening a new war on conventional lines at any time, although such a war would be restricted to the land mass of Europe, Asia and North Africa because the state of shipping in the Soviet Union would not permit an overseas campaign and I don't think we have yet reached the stage where a complete air invasion is on.

Now let us look at the probabilities. I do not consider that any nation will start a planned war without the belief in an early victory. I do not think any dictator will sit down to plan a war which is going to last 6 or 7 years. It is an early victory that every aggressor looks for. An early victory requires surprise. The Germans in the last war thought they could gain surprise by using the blitzkrieg and they did. They overran Europe in a very short order. In future the surprise will most likely be some form of the 'Super Blitzkrieg' based on extravagant use of atomic energy and a sudden, tremendous, unexpected, powerful blow designed to break the will of the people to resist and may be accompanied also by a combination of BW or CW and all other kinds of frightfulness. This leads me to the conclusion that no nation will attempt a planned war until it possesses sufficient atomic weapons for this 'Super Blitzkrieg.' This applies equally to Russia as to the United States.

Well, the question in your minds must be, 'When will Russia be ready? When can Russia have sufficient atomic bombs to start a war?' Well, to use a slang phrase – that's perhaps the $64 question. The guesses are all from three to fifteen years. It's not so much the atomic bomb secret but it's the tremendous engineering plant which is required to produce sufficient fission material and the extensive intricate mechanism for exploding the bomb. A conservative estimate is about ten years, that is about 1957. However, if Russian scientists find some more expeditious method of extracting sufficient fission material from uranium and can devise some new simpler device for exploding the bomb, this time limit may be cut down to a matter of five years.

We have, in our planning, always considered the Russian as the aggressor, the one to start the war. We have based our plans upon the estimates of when we expect Russia will be ready to go to war. I think it is very important to consider now whether Russia will ever start a war. You may wonder which kind of communism the Russian will practice. Will it be the militant type that strives for conquest of the whole world as is happening at the present time. I suggest to you that the spread of communism is increasing every day and is becoming extremely alarming. Some of you must have listened to the Prime Minister make his charge against Communism about two weeks ago and I think will all agree that the Prime Minister is not an alarmist. You must have noticed Mr Bevin's plan for uniting the Western Democracies against Russia. I think many of you must be wondering how the penetration of communism in all parts of the world can be stopped especially in those depressed countries. It is quite easy to imagine, if the Marshall Plan fails, a Communist Italy, Greece and even a Communist France. We can also see the difficulties if the rest of Germany becomes Communist. What will happen if the Russians gain control of the Ruhr, if they peacefully penetrate into the Middle East, if they get control of the Persian oil, make a foothold into India which is in just the right mood for accepting communism, and all of this can be done under the guise of self-determination of the people. How we are going to stop this infiltration and this expansion into the land mass of Europe and Asia is very difficult to predict...

Now I want to talk about the effect of war on Canada. What will happen? Will we be invaded, will we be bombed, or will we just be frightened to death? Well, I believe that the day of complete air invasion has not yet arrived. I also mentioned earlier that invasion by sea was not on with the present facilities. I am quite sure we are going to be bombed, it is rather likely we are going to be frightened to death – we all were in the last war. But the attack upon Canada will be designed to tie down troops and to upset the morale. I think we have got to look at this question a little deeper. Perhaps it is better if we look at it in two different periods of time. The first one, let us look at Canada in the conventional or accidental war, that may happen between 1950–52 and then look at Canada's role in the, what you might call, 'Super-Blitz' war, one which may happen in 1952–57.

In the conventional war, I see it being fought as roughly like this. Russian strategy will be to take the easiest thing first. We usually all do this. The Russian is not a bit different to the rest of us. What we expect will happen is that there will be just a quick march by the Russians and I think it will be quite simple for them to take over the rest of Europe. There will be penetrations into the Middle East, inroads into India, certainly penetrations up into Scandinavia and Korea. An attempt to seize the Middle East to prevent the Western Powers from establishing bases, and an attempt to put the UK out of the war completely.

The Allied strategy should be to hold the bases in the Middle East and in Central Africa so that we will have a base from which we can attack the Russian lines of communication from the start. That is why we are vitally interested in this part of the world. It is necessary for us to support the survival of the UK not by stuffing it full of troops as we did the last time but we will have to be able to put in the supplies to keep the Island going. The early intervention of UK, Canada, and all the other Western Allies to win the war in the first stage when it is in Europe and prevent it spreading to North America. We hope we will be able to deliver atomic bomb attacks on Russian cities and quickly show the Russians what this war is going to be like.

The roles of the Canadian Army in this kind of a war are very simple. Our first role is the territorial defence of North America. The second is to provide the maximum force within the minimum time to take part in a UK-US effort outside of Canada.

I want to say a word about the territorial defence of Canada. The territorial defence has been planned for some time as a joint US-Canada project under the Canada-US Basic Security Plan. This plan has been revised and is being put into effect at the present time. The Plan calls for the security of North America as a base for operations against an enemy elsewhere. The Plan has been designed and is being implemented on the basis that the full Plan will be capable of operation within 12 months of 1952, or within one month of 1957. This Plan provides for an air interceptor and air warning system across Northern Canada which is now being undertaken; protection of the coast and the shipping lanes and a certain amount of anti-aircraft defence.

The commitment so far as the Canadian Army is concerned is as follows. First of all the provision of the minimum forces required for defence. I want to emphasize it is the minimum we require for defence. Secondly, the provision of a Force immediately available under the Security Council of the United Nations. As you perhaps have noticed, there has been a great deal in the press about a defensive alliance of countries against Russia. If that defensive alliance is to materialize to prevent aggression, then Canada will have to be ready to make her contribution. The last role is the preparation of the maximum forces in the shortest possible time for employment outside of Canada. For the actual territorial defence they do not look to attacks on this country to be of a serious nature. As I mentioned earlier we expect spasmodic raids designed to tie down as many troops in this country as possible and to upset morale. We can expect landing parties, up to a battalion, to be landed in the Canadian North, either by air or by ice-breaker. The main thing is we must be prepared to see off any landings in the Canadian Arctic.

To meet these requirements what we need first of all is a sound command system to provide for the territorial and local defence of Canada without interfering with the main task of mobilizing the striking force, to proceed elsewhere. For that purpose we have arranged the Command system so that Eastern and Western Commands will become operational Commands and take over the territorial defence of Canada. Quebec, Central and Prairie Commands will be organized as training Commands except for matters of purely local defence. So that this means the defence of Canada will be the responsibility of Western and Eastern Commands.

It is my intention to start training the Commands as divisional staffs so they can take over the first divisions which we will require. The mobile reserve which will be required to deal with any limited invasion of this country will be the Active Force Brigade Group, which as you know is now in the process of completing its individual training. It will be trained and equipped as an air transportable brigade. It will be centrally located, very flexible, and be capable of dealing with any limited invasion which may be attempted.

I want to say a word about Coast Defence. In co-operation with the Royal Canadian Navy and the Royal Canadian Air Force, the Army is responsible for the continuation of the functioning of the vital ports against bombardment and sabotage. As you know, our coast defence equipment is obsolescent and the development of new aerial weapons minimizes the role of coast defence. Similarly in anti-aircraft defence most of our equipment is out of date but we are now working on the development of new equipment and the maintenance of operational techniques. We have under consideration at the present time the formation of Joint Coast Defence and Anti-Aircraft Schools, one on the East and one on the West coast, where we hope that we will be able to carry out a certain amount of dual purpose training.

The mobilization of the Reserve Army will provide a broad coverage across the whole country which will meet in the initial stages the question of protecting the vulnerable points. These can be relieved later by Veterans Guard and police organizations as and when they can be formed. The striking force which is our main force is the Reserve Force. It is being organized on the basis of two Corps and we expect to mobilize it a corps at a time.

I think this would be a good time to say a word about new developments and how they may affect the operation of the Army in a war during the next few years. Most of these new developments are weapons of mass destruction, much more suitable to be used against towns and cities than on the tactical battlefield, where well trained soldiers do not provide suitable targets for atom bombs. The soldier soon learns that there are only two types in modern battle, 'the quick' and 'the dead.' We should examine our tactical doctrine to ascertain the effect of these new developments on the tactical battlefield.

There is no doubt that we must learn to avoid concentration of troops, stores and materials. Never again will we be permitted to repeat the dense concentrations which occurred in Southampton, Plymouth, Bristol, during the invasion of France. Nor will we be able to stuff as many troops in the Beachhead as we did in Normandy. Wide dispersion is the order of the day from now on.

This wide dispersion for protection requires greater mobility so that we can concentrate quickly to fight and then disperse for protection. We require more secure, more adequate, more efficient communications. I am quite sure that we must develop a type of wireless set which the stupidest man in the Army can use, and that's going to be quite a job. What we need is a push-button set with three or four buttons on it, one will say battalion, the other brigade, the other division, and the other corps, and that is what we need. There is no doubt that more efficient communications are going to be required if a more flexible force is to be achieved.

It is also going to require a much higher standard of training and leadership of the junior leaders. We are going to be forced to work in smaller groups. No longer will the divisional commanders and the corps commanders be able to keep their thumb on the battle the way they tried to in the last war. We are going to have to depend upon small groups, more mobile and operating at greater distances from their base. It looks as if our present organization would serve to start; but I am quite sure that what we have got to do, and do very quickly, is to streamline our organization and equipment. If we are going to depend on airlifts, if we are going to rely on available shipping, we are not going to be able to cart around the numbers of people and the numbers of vehicles we did in the past. I do not think we will go to war with two ADCs and a batman any more, nor will we have a caravan. We will quite likely have a sleeping bag and a jeep. I'm quite sure that all the frills that we were so used to towards the end of the war are gone, gone forever. We are studying how we can streamline our organization to just keep in the bare essentials to fight and win the battle. I'm quite sure we must lighten our equipment because if we fight in the Arctic where our loads have to be carried in a snowmobile or where they have to be transported by air the one thing that is perfectly obvious is that it must be much lighter than it is at the present time. So it is obvious we must do a great deal more thinking about our organization for war to eliminate every frill and streamline our organization, equipment and our demands on transport...

Now let us look at the next war which you might call the 'Super Blitz' or the 1957 variety. I emphasized earlier that this type of war, which is a planned war, will be based on gaining surprise and I'm quite sure that the tremendous value of a surprise attack will not be missed by our opponent. It will include the novel use of new weapons in an attempt to overcome the will of the people to resist in the early stages. I'm quite sure that we must consider the psychological effect of this type of attack on the people of this country and the people to the south of us. There is a great deal of defeatist talk both in this country and the United States. And it is of a most dangerous variety. Some of the scientists are saying that there is no defence against the atomic bomb. It is either a case of self destruction or appeasing the enemy. I am afraid there has been too much talk about no defence against the atomic bomb. This defeatist talk was the cause of the collapse of France in the first war. Whereas in Great Britain where it looked at a time that survival was in doubt, the heavier the bombs came the more determined was the will to resist. I believe that the Canadians and the Americans will measure up in the same manner as the people in the UK. I'm quite sure we will stand up to the atomic bombing just as well and perhaps a lot better than the Russians.

What is the pattern of new war? What I suggest to you is that it is going to be a combination of several things; but the main conflict will be between the United States and Russia. With the emphasis on a sudden terrific devastating surprise attack. Everything is thrown in for one big bid for world domination. I am quite sure that after the first attack by Soviet Russia, the United States will commence retaliation attacks. We will see a terrific bombardment one way and then another until all of the atomic bombs are finished. It is possible that the main attack may take place on the United States war industry in an effort to knock it out. I suggest that after the atomic warfare, or perhaps at the same time, it will be accompanied by CW or BW attacks or both. You all realize that atomic weapons do destroy property as well as lives. Those that are not killed are left out in the open or are evacuated to some other place. People in the open, people crowded into towns without adequate public services, lacking organization and control and in low morale are most vulnerable to CW and BW attacks and I am quite sure our enemy will appreciate this point.

I want to say a word about CW because we relapsed, as you all know, during the last war into a position of false security. I think we all tossed away our gas capes and respirators in the early stages of the war. You must be aware that the Germans had a type of gas which was odourless and could not be detected. This gas was very lethal. We also suspect that the Russians were able to secure these types of gases when they overran Germany. So that we may expect to meet in the next unpleasantness, types of Chemical Warfare which are tasteless, odourless and we have no method yet of detecting them. So that Chemical Warfare is still a problem to be dealt with in modern war.

A word about the Bacteriological Warfare. I feel this is over-emphasized at the present time. It is really not a weapon yet. No opportunity has been given for us to try it out on human beings. The Russians may have tried it out by now; we don't know. However, it is not quite as powerful as Brook Chisholm would have you believe but it has a great potential. It is easy and cheap to manufacture. It does not destroy property but it is a bit difficult to control especially if we contemplate occupation of the country later. There are grave risks also of starting world epidemics. It is more effective against people and cattle in the open and against people of a low standard of hygiene and sanitation. Looks to me to be a good weapon for use against the Russians. Some of the types which you may be familiar with are the bubonic plague, anthrax, undulant fever ... There are many ways of distributing this business; either from the air by spraying or from bombing, air bursting or it can even be spread by infected vermin or infected insects, although this method is a bit uncertain. However, there are some brighter points, that is, our experts tell us that protective devices are in the offing, and perhaps in the not too distant future they will have perfected serums and vaccines and treatments for all these various types of diseases. So that before we go to the next war they may be able to pump us full of the vaccines against all these various plagues. I do want you to bear in mind that it is a potential weapon but it is not a proved weapon yet.

I believe that this super blitz will be accompanied or in combination with attacks of BW and CW but sooner or later it will be necessary to capture and occupy the enemy territory and impose our will on our opponents. I am afraid I cannot subscribe to the very popular theory that we can win the next war by dropping bombs. If we have learned anything from the last war, I think you will all agree that although we bombed hell out of the Germans, and certainly shelled hell out of them, we did not really get any satisfaction until we really got in there with a bayonet and got him by the scruff of the neck and sat on him for a bit, which I am sure we will have to do with the Russians.

After we do frighten them to death with atomic bombs it will still be necessary for us to get down to conventional warfare, and seize parts of his country, and bring him to his heels. In this case I think we may start out with limited air invasion. Instead of forming beachheads, we will have to form air-heads and advance from these air-heads to vulnerable points in which we can exert our will on the opponent. We will have to follow up the air invasion very quickly by a seaborne invasion. On the other hand we might have to repel a similar invasion on this continent. Therefore there is every indication that normal fighting will still be one of the jobs to be done. I want you to bear in mind that I have given you one version of this 'Super Blitzkreig' war. It may start with an atomic attack on the United States and at the same time commence a massed land force attack on Europe, a bombing attack on UK and France, Middle East, India, Korea.

I would like you to examine with me Canada's position in such a war. It is likely that we will be very much like the infantry soldier in the next war. We will get the shorts, some bombs aimed at the United States will drop on Canada. I am quite sure we must expect that we will get some of the atomic bombs on this country either by accident or on purpose. There will be an air defence system across the Northern part of this country and the object of this air defence scheme will be to bring down the airplane carrying atomic bombs before it reaches Chicago. This might mean that Canada will be on the receiving end. The one thing that we can be sure about is that there will be destruction, chaos, casualties in the thousands, cities laid waste, essential services destroyed, complete and utter confusion, panic and distress in certain areas in Canada at the beginning of the war. There will be sabotage and subversive activities on a scale that we have never known before. So I consider that the main task of the Canadian Army in the first few months of the 'Super Blitz' war will be to restore and maintain the high morale of the Canadian people, to render aid and succour to the distressed, to assist in the maintenance of law and order, in bomb clearance, rescue work, emergency treatment and the restoration of essential services.

I suggest to you that if the Reserve Force is well up to strength before the war begins we should be able to mobilize it immediately. This force will provide a well disciplined, completely reliable and self-contained force, complete with its equipment so that it can operate anywhere in Canada. This force will ensure the maintenance of a sound morale across the whole country. It is probable that we will have a civil defence scheme organized but those civil defence schemes are apt to be on a local basis and I think, if we are realistic, we will appreciate that the local defence outfit will perhaps go up in smoke with the rest of the city which is attacked; therefore, the aid must come from outside. I feel that the Reserve Force, if it is fully equipped, fully mobile, and the GOC has complete control, he will be capable of moving it in and providing the essential services, restoring order and providing immediate aid. In short carrying out the same role in the beginning of the war that we finished the last war where we moved into liberated countries assisting in the restoration of normal essential services and running the country until such time as the civil services could take over.

This is going to mean that army control must be flexible. It requires that our Command system must really work and that by that time we have decentralized control to commands. If we extend the Ranger system into the northern part of Canada to augment the Reserve Force, we shall be in a good position to deal with this phase of the war. After the super blitz part is over, then I think we must be ready to either resist invasion or be ready to start invasion on conventional lines...

Now, I have talked a little longer than I intended but I did want to put you completely in the picture as to what may happen in the future ... I would like to say that I was extremely pleased with the progress which we have made over the past three years. When you realize that we have demobilized an Army of about half a million, without serious trouble, we have set up another Army which, I hope, will be up to strength by this time next year. The Reserve Force is well organized with an Officer Corps which I think is going to serve us well in the next year. This has not been accomplished by the efforts of one or two people, it has been done by the combined efforts of all and a large part of it by the people at Army Headquarters. I am extremely pleased with the progress we have made, it has been steady, in some places perhaps a bit slow, but in every case according to an agreed plan. I do want to impress upon you the necessity to continue this process of decentralization. It is essential for our future, especially if we get into a war. What we want at Army Headquarters is a small thinking Headquarters devoid of detail administration. I still feel that too much detailed administration is being done here, which keeps the strength in Ottawa far too high. This matter requires constant review.

We have accomplished a lot in the past year but there are still many problems to be solved in the year we are approaching.

# DOCUMENT 4

EXTRACTS FROM AN ADDRESS BY THE CHIEF OF NAVAL STAFF, VICE ADMIRAL H.T.W. GRANT, TO THE MONTREAL UNITED SERVICE INSTITUTION, 16 FEBRUARY 1948 (DIRECTORATE OF HISTORY, DEPARTMENT OF NATIONAL DEFENCE)

*'The Navy's Role in Events of Today and Tomorrow'*

...The Fleet consists of one aircraft carrier, one cruiser, and six destroyers in commission, with the odd frigate and minesweeper to assist in training and for extraneous commitments, such as weather ships.

In reserve is a second cruiser, five destroyers, a dozen mine-sweepers and two or three frigates.

This reserve of ships is very small and bears absolutely no relation to our requirements in the event of war. At the end of the recent conflict, we had 348 anti-submarine escort vessels and never had sufficient for the work in hand.

However, it is financially out of the question with our present estimates to lay up in reserve large numbers of ships which sooner or later will be obsolete, which deteriorate very rapidly (particularly in the East), and which cost no less than $100,000 each per year for the minimum of caretaking.

The composition of the post-war fleet differs from its 1939 version in that we have graduated to aircraft carriers and cruisers. There are those who argue that two or three additional destroyers could be manned and operated for the price of one cruiser and that the latter's value against submarines would be much greater.

This is partially true, but at this stage the value of larger ships must be assessed in other ways. For one thing they afford essential training for officers and men in equipment not installed in the smaller ships and provide seagoing experience to the more senior officers of every branch. Further, cruisers are eminently suitable for the elementary sea training of young officers and men, whilst destroyers, with their limited space, are not...

With regard to the other type of big ship, i.e., carriers, perhaps it is unnecessary to point out that in the course of the late war, seaborne air power proved itself a vital factor, not only in defence against submarines, but in the operation of the Fleet.

The advent of air power at sea has brought about a highly significant change in strategy and tactics. Its proper use, however, is that of another weapon and I suggest that it only serves to enhance the importance of sea power. The fact that both our maritime strategy and our battle tactics must be made to conform to this new and powerful weapon makes it imperative that officers and men of the Fleet should thoroughly appreciate the change. For this reason, the Royal Canadian Navy has integrated Naval Aviation into its organization.

The cost is high both in manpower and dollars, but a nucleus for the inevitable expansion is worth the price.

At this stage it is pertinent to examine broadly the effect of the atomic bomb in Navies and on Naval Strategy.

There is, of course, no lack of statements to the effect that Navies, as we have known them, are on their way out, and, indeed, that the conventional defence of the past, a strong Navy, Army and Air Force, is obsolete.

These writers contend that the war will be won by atomic bombs planted by agents or submarines or sent in by rockets and that the victory will go to the country which lands the most, soonest. This last statement presupposes that we have actually achieved the push-button stage and that atomic bombs can be directed at will against an enemy.

It seems at this time wholly reasonable and a safe assumption that rockets with atomic warheads, capable of thousands of miles of range, are not to be expected for at least another 25 years, nor can a large sub-sonic bombing aircraft, operating at extreme range and without heavy fighter escort, be considered a sufficiently reliable means of delivering precious atomic bombs against a strong and well-alerted enemy.

While the effects of the new weapon may well alter the strategic conception of Naval Warfare, such as relegating the Straits of Gibraltar, the Panama Canal or the Suez Canal to a position of lower priority, it cannot be said that these waterways will altogether lose their strategic importance.

It seems absurd to suppose that any weapon can sweep away every other weapon, for there is no implement of war, even the atomic bomb, which can be used effectively without the support of other weapons.

...Precedent would indicate that any defeated country must be invaded and occupied before its defeat is consummated. Destruction by bombs is not enough. This occupation force must be transported overseas and kept supplied by sea – hence a continuing role for the Navy to protect this shipping.

It may be that the advance of science and engineering will eventually make it possible to produce atomic bombs cheaply and rapidly. If this happens, they would probably be used for attacking ships at sea, but, whereas one bomb can produce devastation over one square mile of city, that area at sea does not necessarily contain any large number of ships.

Also important is the fact that a Fleet at sea is not easily located nor easily destroyed for it embraces the two principles of mobility and dispersion. I would say that the ability to retaliate, if attacked, is certainly enhanced by having a bomb launching base which cannot be plotted on a map. A Fleet armed with atomic bombs and practically self-supporting with its Train, which has disappeared into the vastness of the sea during a crisis, would surely be an additional element to give pause to an aggressor.

Turning now to the Navy's role in peace, it is worthwhile pointing out that the duty of training a Reserve is only one of its functions. It is essential to maintain the Fleet itself at the highest possible state of efficiency, for it will be at action stations the day war breaks out, and it follows that the proportion of Active Service personnel to Reserves must be relatively higher in the Navy than in the land forces.

...Whilst long-range aircraft would appear to be ideal for world policing, it must be remembered that their stay above the troubled area in peace is transitory. They cannot land without infringing sovereignty, nor support themselves without a friendly base reasonably close at hand. I suggest that for a Naval task force moving on the free sea the problem is far less complicated. The danger of precipitating violent incidents is reduced, and the power that can be brought to bear is both greater and far more prolonged.

Certainly, the sea highways are open to ships to move wherever they will without affecting sovereignty. Within the hulls of cruisers and above is carried the necessary concentration of armament and magazines, whilst the aircraft carrier has its own reconaissance planes on board.

You are, of course, aware of the importance which all the Services attach to scientific research. By far the most pressing problem from the Naval angle is the improved detection of the fast submarine.

Here is a weapon of great offensive power which loses nothing and possibly gains in importance in future warfare. Defence against the submarine has always called for an effort out of all proportion to the strength of the sporadic attack...

At the moment it is unfortunately true that the submarine has the upper hand in the see-saw struggle with anti-submarine forces ... With the advent of the atomic bomb, the submarine future has brightened, for if it remains difficult to detect, it will be difficult to attack. Further, it has a very reasonable degree of protection against gamma rays...

Submarines are readily adaptable for the release of controlled missiles, but I do not agree with the school of thought which suggests that warships of the future should all be submersible.

Whilst the size of the Royal Canadian Navy has precluded the operation of every type of vessel, submarines amongst them, we nevertheless are actively engaged with the problems of anti-submarine warfare. Our A/S forces exercise continuously with both British and American submarines, and our procedures are being standardized.

In conclusion, I would say that certainly the greatest impact of the changing scene of modern warfare pertains to the time scale of preparation.

It is now more important than ever before that we have the best possible force afloat at the outbreak of hostilities, for it is probable that such action as the enemy can take will be directed against the centres of industry and our commercial ports, in order to gain the initiative before industry and ship-building can swing into war production.

For our generation at least, sea power is not outmoded and as far as power is concerned, it is certainly one of the immediate answers to peace.

# DOCUMENT 5

EXTRACTS FROM AN ADDRESS BY THE MINISTER OF NATIONAL DEFENCE, THE HON. BROOKE CLAXTON, TO THE ADVISORY COUNCIL MEETING, NATIONAL LIBERAL FEDERATION, 26 FEBRUARY 1951 (CLAXTON PAPERS)

...May I say at once that every cent spent on the defence of Canada assists in the defence of the United States. I repeat: Every single cent we spend defending Canada helps to defend the United States, for this reason. There is only one enemy and that is Russia, and there are only two avenues of attack: one is from Siberia in the northwest down south of the Aleutians or across east of the Rockies; the other is from northern Russia across Spitzbergen and Iceland, the southern tip of Greenland and down Labrador to the industrial centres of the United States.

These are the only two avenues of attack and both go through Canada, so that every cent spent on the defence of Canada is directly to the advantage of the United States. Let us have no false pride about taking help from the United States. We must build our defence resources to make the best use we can of them.

Of these two avenues of attack, this on the east is considerably the shorter if the object is to get at the industrial targets of Canada and the United States. I think it is even shorter than the avenue on the west coast, and this was always considered as being the most likely avenue of attack to be followed by the Russians. That may surprise you, but the view now is that this is at least as likely, and the reason for that is that the prevailing wind from west to east, adding 25 miles an hour to the speed of aircraft, would add about 10 per cent to the effective range; so that aircraft coming from Siberia might be able, with the same expenditure of gasoline, to reach somewhere in the vicinity of the objective attained by aircraft coming from the east.

We know that the Russians have a number of heavy bombers of the B29 type which were made in the United States and used from 1942 on. The Russians got some by accident and copied them. We do not know how good their copies are, but we do not think they are a great deal better than the original aircraft.

These aircraft have a range of about four thousand miles one way, so that they can reach virtually any part of North America, travelling one way, and they are capable of dropping the atomic bomb, one per aircraft. But they are not capable of doing that and returning except for limited areas unless they have the good fortune to be able to refuel. They cannot carry both bombs and men. They are fitted to carry one or the other; and our information is that as these aircraft are limited in number – probably they have not more than 400 – the military advantages of their carrying bombs would be much greater than the military advantages of carrying men, because each aircraft will carry only forty men. It is therefore very unlikely that any part of North America will be exposed to attack by men except for the purpose of creating panic and diversion. Consequently neither the United States nor we think that it is necessary for us to have any considerable force in Canada for the defence of Canada.

We have a specially raised, trained and equipped airborne brigade group for the purpose of defending Canada in Canada, and the United States has a specially raised, trained and equipped airborne division for the purpose of defending the United States in the United States, and both will be used together.

It is noticeable, after all this hullabaloo about not sending an airborne brigade to Korea, that the United States did not send a corresponding Division 82 airborne division to Korea either, the reason being that it was specially trained for the defence of North America by the use of paratroopers and the like.

These two formations are considered quite enough for the job, and they would not do the job by keeping the enemy out. They could not. But once a few Russians got in they could be cleaned up wherever they were as fast as we could do it. That is the theory. I do not know whether the Russians have heard about the theory, and I do not know whether the theories stick or will be changed. But that is the best military view of the United States and Canada working together, and it is completely agreed to by the North Atlantic Treaty nations.

As part of our defence we shall be working in co-operation with the United States on the screening of radar stations of the latest type and great range of power to protect this approach, and it will be for the Americans to do the same job ... On this side we shall have them so arranged as to constitute defence in depth. There will be a ring of vessels equipped with radar off both coasts, and we shall not provide any vessel for that ring; the United States will do it. The radar in connection with each of the stations costs some $6,000,000 and is of the latest type. It will not become obsolete. According to the mathematics of the subject it will not leave room for improvement but will be as nearly perfect as we shall ever get it. One quarter of the combined network of the United States and Canada will be in Canada, and the Americans will contribute one-third of the cost of the equipment in Canada, which we think is a fair basis, since a good deal of the equipment is being installed exclusively for the purpose of defending the United States and not to defend Canada at all.

It is impossible for the United States and Canada, using all the resources of money, men and communications industry, to completely cover a continent of seven million square miles. In England there is a greater density of population and they could keep out only ten per cent of the aircraft that attacked. It is impossible to make North America impregnable or impenetrable, and the question arises: How much of our resources can we usefully put into static defence of North America? The answer is, just as little as we can get away with, because that is not the place to defeat the enemy. The place to defeat the enemy is in Russia, not Canada; and that is fundamental to the whole thinking.

We shall be equipped with the very latest aircraft, F-86E and CF-100. These are the best of their type. They are not produced in quantity yet because it was not possible to produce them. The first F-86E to be produced was produced exactly two weeks after the first plane was produced in the United States, and that despite the fact that we had to wait on the United States for many parts and modifications. It was a magnificent feat of production.

One factor limiting the number of aircraft we shall produce in Canada will be not money or men but the number of jet engines we can get. There is a world shortage and the first of ours will be produced only towards the end of this year.

We have persuaded the Americans to treat us as Americans in the allocation of jet engines so that we shall get enough jet engines to keep Canadair going to equip one squadron after another until we have forty squadrons of air force equipped. England's job is to look after seaward defences of harbours, and escort across the North Atlantic. We must specialize on things that particularly relate to our own defence, which we can do better than others. The basic defence, apart from our own local defence of our own coast, defence against the enemy abroad will be the responsibility of the United States. It is beyond our resources to get into that game. We shall be fully occupied with our coastal defence on both coasts and escort across the North Atlantic.

In addition to the jobs we shall have to do for the Army and Air Force in Canada, we have also to discharge our undertakings under the United Nations charter and the North Atlantic treaty. In connection with the United Nations charter, we have had three destroyers at Korea, with a considerable proportion of naval forces there. We had heavy transport squadrons working from the start with 12 North Star aircraft. Now the Princess Patricias are engaged and will be followed in a matter of weeks by the balance of the brigade group going there.

We will not be pushed into any situation where we are biting off more than we can chew, because this effort of Canada is not an effort of which any country in the world need be ashamed. It is an all-out effort. Don't let Howard Green of Vancouver say that it is something to be ashamed of. It is something which the world at large, as well as Canadians, will recognize we have reason to be proud of. Indeed, it may become difficult to justify it on the ground that it is higher than other countries.

In addition to a brigade group, we have agreed to build up a force of eleven squadrons of aircraft on the other side. That is an enormous undertaking. It will require nearly 800 aircraft of the latest type at a cost of half a million each, and that will take some time.

*Vis-à-vis* the United States, they said they would have six divisions in Europe. If we have a brigade group, which is a third of a division, that is not a bad proportion, even from the manpower point of view, with what the United States is doing.

All this adds up to an immense bill. The defence appropriation this year will be $1,600,000,000, and that will be the first installment in a three year programme. This will be more, proportionately, either on a per capita basis, or as a percentage of national income, than any country in the North Atlantic

Treaty Organization except the United States. From the financial point of view, on any basis of comparison, we shall be doing more than The Netherlands, Italy, Belgium, Denmark, Norway, Portugal, France and the United Kingdom; and our defence bill this year is ten times what it is in Australia – and they have not got conscription there yet either!

These comparisons that appear in the newspapers are dreadfully misleading. We do not like making comparisons because you cannot make a fair one. But if people go on making comparisons that misrepresent the position of Canada, I will make them so as to represent Canada's position in the most favourable light. And if we make such comparisons you will see the same newspapers which are now saying we are not doing enough changing their tune and say, 'Others ought to be doing more; why should Canada do everything?'

All this is a gigantic programme and I can assure you it is being approached by the Government with a great sense of responsibility. I do not know how many of you appreciate quite fully the efficiency at his job of leadership of Mr. St. Laurent, our Prime Minister. I do not believe he ever had anything to do with defence matters in his life until he entered the Cabinet in 1941, but he shows the most complete and sympathetic understanding, and if he can do anything for our armed forces he does it. To a greater degree than any Prime Minister he is supported in every way, and in consequence of his leadership what do we see? We see my own province of Quebec and other French-speaking parts of Canada contributing to the armed forces of the country men in proportion to population. And magnificent troops they are too...

That is the picture, and it seems to me it is very desirable indeed that we should know what it is and back it up, because we are fighting for our existence. We are fighting for our existence against forces that none of us who might survive could live with.

The effort that we are called upon to make is the kind of effort that the Canadian people want; it is the effort that we must make if our democracy is to survive. It is not a war effort but an effort for peace – an effort to ensure peace by being willing to pay the increased premiums that we think are necessary. In this I am sure we have the support of the people of Canada and, I am sure, the support of the Liberal party as a whole. Thank you very much.

# CHRONOLOGY OF EVENTS, 1943–9

1943

| | |
|---|---|
| 22 July | First meeting on post-hostilities problems |
| 19 August | Quebec Agreement |
| 8 September | Italy surrenders |
| | First meeting Combined Policy Committee |
| 1 November | Four Power Declaration on Post-War International Organization, Moscow |
| 9 November | UNRRA |
| 11 November | Legation at Washington becomes embassy |
| 4–12 December | Montebello Conference |
| 10 December | Legations at Moscow, Chungking, Rio de Janiero become embassies |

1944

| | |
|---|---|
| 1 January | Leckie CAS |
| 2 January | Vanier arrives Algiers |
| 14 January | Nelles resigns |
| 15 January | Jones CNS |
| 24 January | Halifax's Toronto speech |
| 28 January | Eldorado Mines expropriated |
| 1–16 May | Prime Ministers' Conference, London |
| 3 May | Murchie CGS |
| 6 June | Allies invade Normandy |
| 9 October | Dumbarton Oaks Proposals |
| 13 October | Howe Minister of Reconstruction |
| 1 November | Ralston resigns |
| 2 November | McNaughton Minister of National Defence |
| 27 November | Power resigns |

1945

| | |
|---|---|
| 4–11 February | Yalta Conference |
| 17 February–3 March | Third British Commonwealth Relations Conference, London |
| 8 March | Gibson Minister of National Defence for Air |
| 12 April | Roosevelt dies |
| 8 May | Germany surrenders |
| 25 June | UN Charter |
| 16 July | Atom bomb test, Trinity |
| 17 July | Potsdam Conference |
| 26 July | Labour Government in UK |
| 6 August | Hiroshima |
| 9 August | Nagasaki |

| | |
|---|---|
| 15 August | Japan surrenders |
| 20 August | McNaughton resigns |
| 21 August | Abbott Minister of National Defence |
| | Foulkes CGS |
| 6 September | Gouzenko defects |
| 30 September | Mackenzie King talks with Truman, Washington |
| 15 November | US-UK-Canada Declaration on Atomic Energy |

1946

| | |
|---|---|
| 1 January | Howe Minister of Reconstruction and Supply |
| 9 February | Reid CNS |
| 5 March | Churchill's Fulton speech |
| 2 April–23 May | Prime Ministers' Conference, London |
| 16 June | Baruch Plan |
| 29 July–15 October | Paris Peace Conference |
| 3 September | Mackenzie King resigns from Secretary of State for External Affairs |
| 4 September | St Laurent Secretary of State for External Affairs |
| | Robertson High Commissioner in UK |
| | Pearson Under Secretary of State for External Affairs |
| | Wrong ambassador to US |
| 28 October | Mackenzie King talks with Truman, Washington |
| 12 December | Claxton Minister of National Defence |

1947

| | |
|---|---|
| 10 March | Foreign Ministers' Meeting, Moscow |
| 12 March | Truman Doctrine |
| 7 April | Defence Research Board |
| 5 June | Marshall Plan |
| 15 August | India and Pakistan independent |
| 1 September | Curtis CAS |
| | Grant CNS |
| 20 October | Kashmir invaded |

1948

| | |
|---|---|
| 5 January | National Defence College |
| 19 January | Howe Minister of Trade and Commerce |
| 25 February | Prague *coup d'état* |
| 17 March | Brussels Pact |
| 17 May | State of Israel proclaimed |
| 20 June | Berlin blockade |
| 10 September | Pearson Secretary of State for External Affairs |
| | St Laurent Minister of Justice |
| 15 November | Mackenzie King resigns; St Laurent Prime Minister |

1949

| | |
|---|---|
| 1 March | Heeney Under Secretary of State for External Affairs |
| 31 March | Newfoundland enters Confederation |
| 4 April | Atlantic Pact |
| 22–29 April | Prime Ministers' Conference, London |
| 29 April | Declaration of London on republican status for India |
| 11 May | Berlin blockade lifted |
| 29 August | Soviet nuclear test |

# NOTE ON THE SOURCES

The major published sources, apart from the books and articles cited in the references, are: the Debates of the House of Commons of the Parliament of Canada; the annual reports of the Department of External Affairs and the Department of National Defence; and *The Mackenzie King Record*, an edited version of the Prime Minister's diary for the period September 1939 to November 1948.

A complete list of the collections of unpublished documents on which this book is based is cited below (citation does not imply full or unrestricted access in each case); the collection is described by the name under which it appears in the references, followed by the name of its present custodian.

*Prime Ministers*

Borden Papers (Public Archives of Canada)
King Papers (Public Archives of Canada)
Laurier Papers (Public Archives of Canada)

*Cabinet Ministers*

Abbott Papers (The Hon. Mr Justice Douglas Abbott)
Claxton Papers (Public Archives of Canada, Mrs Brooke Claxton)
Howe Papers (Public Archives of Canada)

*Public Servants and Military Officers*

Foulkes Papers (Literary Executors of General Charles Foulkes)
Mackenzie Papers (Dr C.J. Mackenzie)
McNaughton Papers (Public Archives of Canada)
Massey Papers (Massey College Library, University of Toronto)

*Institutional*

Air Force Headquarters files (Directorate of History, Department of National Defence)
Army Headquarters files (Directorate of History, Department of National Defence)
CIIA Papers (Canadian Institute of International Affairs)
Department of External Affairs files (Historical Division, Department of External Affairs)
Naval Headquarters files (Directorate of History, Department of National Defence)

*Other*

Tarr Papers (Canadian Institute of International Affairs)

# REFERENCES

INTRODUCTION: PERSONALITIES AND POLICIES


1 R. MacGregor Dawson, *The Conscription Crisis of 1944* (Toronto 1961), 109–10
2 Frank H. Underhill, *Canadian Forum*, July 1946
3 Quoted in W.K. Hancock, *Smuts*, II, *The Fields of Force, 1919–1950* (Cambridge 1968), 444n
4 Bruce Hutchison, *The Incredible Canadian* (Toronto 1952), 425–6
5 Vincent Massey, *What's Past is Prologue* (Toronto 1963), 448
6 Escott Reid, 'The Birth of the North Atlantic Alliance,' *International Journal*, XXII, 3, Summer 1967, 428
7 L.B. Pearson to Vincent Massey, 1 April 1942, Massey Papers
8 Quoted in J.W. Pickersgill and Donald Forster, *The Mackenzie King Record*, IV, *1947–1948* (Toronto 1970), 139–40. [hereafter cited as *Record IV*]
9 Quoted in J.W. Pickersgill, *The Mackenzie King Record*, I, *1939–1944* (Toronto 1960), 361–2. [hereafter cited as *Record I*]
10 Quoted in Norman Ward (ed.), *A Party Politician: The Memoirs of Chubby Power* (Toronto 1966), 164
11 *Ibid.*, 390–2
12 Quoted in *ibid.*, 255
13 Quoted in *Record IV*, 272
14 Canada, *H.C. Debates*, 1944, VI, 6602
15 Quoted in Dale C. Thomson, *Louis St Laurent: Canadian* (Toronto 1967), 10
16 Quoted in *ibid.*, 18
17 Quoted in *Record I*, 445
18 Thomson, *op. cit.*, 134–6
19 *Ibid.*, 196
20 *Ibid.*, 206–7
21 *Ibid.*, 225
22 Quoted in *Record IV*, 164
23 Thomson, *op. cit.*, 301
24 *Globe and Mail* (Toronto), 18 March 1958
25 L.S. St Laurent to Brooke Claxton, 16 November 1953, Claxton Papers
26 Thomson, *op. cit.*, 141
27 *Ibid.*, 311
28 Dawson, *op. cit.*, 35–6
29 John Swettenham, *McNaughton*, III, *1944–1966* (Toronto 1969), 70
30 Quoted in J.W. Pickersgill and D.F. Forster, *The Mackenzie King Record*, II, *1944–1945* (Toronto 1968), 442. [hereafter cited as *Record II*]
31 Quoted in *ibid.*, 462
32 Hutchison, *op. cit.*, 401
33 Canada, *H.C. Debates*, 1945, 2nd Session, I, 1130
34 Quoted in *Record I*, 479
35 Quoted in *ibid.*, 519
36 Hutchison, *op. cit.*, 326
37 Quoted in J.W. Pickersgill and D.F. Forster, *The Mackenzie King Record*, III, *1945–1946* (Toronto 1970), 296. [hereafter cited as *Record III*]
38 Quoted in *ibid.*, 373
39 Quoted in *ibid.*, 373

40 'Autobiography,' Claxton Papers
41 Quoted in *Record III*, 393–4
42 C.P. Stacey, 'The Life and Hard Times of an Official Historian,' *Canadian Historical Review*, LI, 1, March 1970, 29
43 Quoted in *Record IV*, 140, 154
44 Quoted in *ibid.*, 378
45 'Autobiography,' Claxton Papers
46 Brooke Claxton to T.W.L. MacDermot, 3 October 1951, Claxton Papers
47 'Autobiography,' *ibid.*
48 *Ibid.*
49 *Ibid.*
50 Vincent Massey to Hume Wrong, 7 January 1944; J.L. Ralston to Massey, 27 August 1943, Massey Papers
51 Quoted in *Record II*, 141
52 Quoted in *Record III*, 271
53 Quoted in *ibid.*, 271
54 Hume Wrong to Mrs G.M. Wrong, July 1927, Wrong Papers
55 Massey, *op. cit.*, 139
56 Quoted in *ibid.*, 235
57 L.B. Pearson to Vincent Massey, 9 June 1942, Massey Papers
58 'H. Hume Wrong,' *External Affairs* (Ottawa), VI, 3, March 1954, 76
59 *Ibid.*, 76
60 'Pearson Reminisces,' *The Globe and Mail* (Toronto), 11 November 1968
61 Quoted in John Robinson Beal, *The Pearson Phenomenon* (Toronto 1964), 55
62 Quoted in *Record I*, 216
63 Massey Papers
64 *The New York Times,* 26 October 1946
65 Quoted in Beal, *op. cit.*, 79
66 'Organizing the United Nations for Peace,' address by L.B. Pearson to the Canadian Club, Toronto, 13 March 1944 (mimeographed)
67 Quoted in *Record IV*, 121, 135–6, 140, 146, 161, 161
68 Peter C. Newman, *The Distemper of Our Times* (Toronto 1968), 286–7
69 *Ibid.*, 287
70 E.L. Woodward, 'The British Foreign Service,' in J.E. Mclean (ed.), *The Public Service and University Education* (Princeton, NJ 1949), 175
71 L.B. Pearson to Vincent Massey, 8 July 1942, Massey Papers
72 Escott Reid to author, 29 October 1969
73 Robert Speaight, *Vanier: Soldier, Diplomat and Governor General* (Toronto 1970), 195
74 Quoted in *ibid.*, 227–8
75 Quoted in *ibid.*, 292
76 Quoted in Massey, *op. cit.*, 335
77 *Dana Wilgress Memoirs* (Toronto 1967), 147
78 J.D.B. Miller, in *The Canadian Forum*, August 1959
79 Sir William Hayter, *The Diplomacy of the Great Powers* (London 1960), 65
80 'Memorandum on the Introduction of Certain Features of the British Cabinet Office into Canada,' by the Warden of Hart House (J.B. Bickersteth), August 1927, Massey Papers
81 *Record I*, 'Introduction,' 7
82 Hankey interview with R. MacGregor Dawson
83 P.C. 1121, quoted in R. MacGregor Dawson, *The Government of Canada* (4th ed., revised by Norman Ward, Toronto 1963), 248
84 Diary entry, 9 August 1938, King Papers
85 Peter C. Newman, 'The Ottawa Establishment,' *Maclean's Magazine*, 22 August 1964

86 King Papers
87 *Ibid.*
88 Diary entry, 23 August 1939, *ibid.*
89 *Record I*, 'Introduction,' 6
90 *Record II*, 'Preface,' x
91 Canada, *H.C. Debates*, 1927, II, 2459
92 Thomson, *op. cit.*, 243
93 Newman, *op. cit.*, 235
94 Thomson, *op. cit.*, 263–4
95 *Ibid.*, 324–5
96 'Memorandum on the Introduction...,' *op. cit.*
97 King Papers
98 Quoted in *Record I*, 177
99 Claxton autobiography
100 John Porter, 'Higher Public Servants and the Bureaucratic Elite in Canada,' *Canadian Journal of Economics and Political Science*, XXIV, 4, November 1958, 496
101 King Papers
102 Quoted in *Record II*, 63
103 Maurice A. Pope, *Soldiers and Politicians* (Toronto 1962), 279
104 Quoted in *ibid.*, 283
105 *Ibid.*, 303
106 Morris Janowitz, *The Professional Soldier* (Glencoe, Illinois 1960), 377–8
107 Quoted in James Eayrs, *In Defence of Canada*, I, *From the Great War to the Great Depression* (Toronto 1964), 41
108 Quoted in Janowitz, *op. cit.*, 379
109 *Ibid.*, 379
110 Dawson, *op. cit.*, 27
111 Quoted in *Record I*, 587–8
112 Quoted in *Record II*, 164
113 Diary entry, 20 May 1946, quoted in *Record III*, 223–4
114 Diary entry, 7 June 1946, quoted in *ibid.*, 248
115 Quoted in James Eayrs, *In Defence of Canada*, II, *Appeasement and Rearmament* (Toronto 1965), 82
116 J.G. Hadwen to author, 6 August 1960
117 Pope, *op. cit.*, 177
118 'Reid Warns Our Navy Too Small,' *Ottawa Morning Journal*, 7 November 1946
119 Norman Ward (ed.), *A Party Politician: The Memoirs of Chubby Power* (Toronto 1966), 232
120 Interview with Air Marshal R. Leckie, 15 December 1967
121 Quoted in *Record I*, 691
122 Quoted in *ibid.*, 689
123 Lt-Gen. G.G. Simonds, 'Where We've Gone Wrong on Defence,' *Maclean's Magazine*, 23 June 1956
124 Interview with General Charles Foulkes, 9 November 1967
125 'Autobiography,' Claxton Papers
126 *Ibid.*
127 *Ibid.*
128 *Ibid.*
129 *Ibid.*
130 *Ibid.*
131 *Ibid.*
132 Canada, *H.C. Debates*, 1953–4, VI, 6521
133 *Montreal Gazette*, 17 January 1955
134 Canada, *H.C. Debates*, 1955, V, 4893

135 'Autobiography,' Claxton Papers
136 Canada, *H.C. Debates*, 1950, 2nd Session, 105
137 Lt-Col. Herbert Fairlie Wood, *Strange Battleground: Operations in Korea and their Effects on the Defence Policy of Canada* (Ottawa 1966), 259
138 Quoted in Eayrs, *op. cit.*, 169
139 Colonel C.P. Stacey, *Six Years of War: The Army in Canada, Britain and the Pacific* (Ottawa 1955), 128
140 'Autobiography,' Claxton Papers
141 Quoted in Wood, *op. cit.*, 162–3
142 Canada, *H.C. Debates*, 1952–3, IV, 3808
143 *Report of the Department of National Defence for the Fiscal Year Ending March 31, 1951* (Ottawa 1951), 13
144 James Jackson, 'Military Colleges,' letter in the *Globe and Mail* (Toronto), 8 June 1966
145 'A Report on the Canadian National Defence College,' privately communicated.
146 Quoted in Adrian Preston, 'The National Defence College of Canada, 1948–1968: An Historical Analysis of the First Twenty Years.' (unpublished manuscript)
147 Quoted in *ibid.*
148 Captain D.J. Goodspeed, *A History of the Defence Research Board of Canada* (Ottawa 1958), 58
149 *Ibid.*, 89
150 John W. Holmes, 'The Relationship in Alliance and World Affairs,' in John Sloan Dickey (ed.), *The United States and Canada* (Englewood Cliffs, NJ 1964), 109
151 Quoted in Aron Drutz, 'Interface: Man and Machine,' *Perspectives in Defense Management* (Industrial College of the Armed Forces, Washington, DC), June 1969, 31
152 C.J. Mackenzie to Norman Robertson (no date), quoted in Robertson to Vincent Massey, 18 April 1945, Massey Papers
153 R.J. Sutherland, 'The Strategic Significance of the Canadian Arctic,' in R. St J. Macdonald (ed.), *The Arctic Frontier* (Toronto 1966), 271

CHAPTER ONE: RE-ESTABLISHING THE MILITARY

1 'Notes on Post-War Army Organization,' 4 March 1943, Army Headquarters files
2 'Memorandum on Post-War Problems: Some Army Aspects,' 14 September 1943, Department of External Affairs files
3 Maj.-Gen. K. Stuart, 'Memorandum for the Minister,' 21 October 1943, Army Headquarters files
4 'Canadian Defence Relations with the United States,' 9 August 1944, Department of External Affairs files
5 R.M. Macdonnell to Escott Reid, 26 August 1944, *ibid.*
6 Maurice Pope to Reid, 24 August 1944, *ibid.*
7 'Summary of Army Post-War Plan,' 11 July 1945, *ibid.*
8 'Canadian Participation in the Policing of Europe,' 7 September 1943, *ibid.*
9 Air Commodore K.M. Guthrie, 'Brief on Post-War Planning for the Royal Canadian Air Force,' 14 December 1943, Air Force Headquarters files
10 'Precis on Plans for the RCAF, Post War,' no date, Department of External Affairs files
11 'The Continuing Royal Canadian Navy,' no date, *ibid.*
12 *Ibid.*
13 'Post-War Canadian Navy,' 21 January 1944, Naval Headquarters files
14 Director of Plans to Assistant Chief of Naval Staff, 14 August 1944, *ibid.*

15 'Post-War Canadian Navy,' 21 January 1944, *ibid.*
16 'The Continuing Royal Canadian Navy' (no date), Department of External Affairs files
18 Quoted in *Record II*, 73, 75
19 Quoted in *ibid.*, 115–16
20 Quoted in J.D.F. Kealy and E.C. Russell, *A History of Canadian Naval Aviation 1918–1962* (Ottawa 1965), 39, reference 5
21 *Ibid.*, 36
22 George Ignatieff to Hume Wrong, 28 June 1945, Department of External Affairs files
23 Lt-Col. Herbert Fairlie Wood, *Strange Battleground: The Operations in Korea and their Effects on the Defence Policy of Canada* (Ottwa 1966), 17
24 'Strategic Factors Affecting Canada's Post-War Military Requirements,' 5 July 1945, Department of External Affairs files
25 Minutes of the Ninth Meeting of the Advisory Committee on Post-Hostilities Problems, 31 July 1945, *ibid.*
26 Wood, *op. cit.*, 17
27 Lt-Col. D.J. Goodspeed (ed.), *The Armed Forces of Canada, 1867–1967: A Century of Achievement* (Ottawa 1967), 155
28 Canada, *H.C. Debates*, 2nd Session, 1945, I, 765
29 *Ibid.*, 876
30 *Op. cit.*, II, 1368
31 *Ibid.*, 1712–13
32 *Op. cit.*, I, 1136
33 *Op. cit.*, II, 1365
34 *Op. cit.*, I, 1181, 1185
35 *Op. cit.*, II, 1373–5
36 *Ibid.*, 1378
37 *Montreal Standard*, 16 April 1946
38 'Speech to the Combined Services Club Meeting, Cornwall, Ontario,' 15 April 1946, Abbott Papers
39 Canada, *H.C. Debates*, 1946, V, 5042
40 *Ibid.*, 5059–60
41 *Op. cit.*, 1947, I, 412
42 *Ibid.*, 417
43 Quoted in *Record IV*, 6
44 'Autobiography,' Claxton Papers
45 Quoted in *Record IV*, 10
46 'Autobiography,' Claxton Papers
47 *Ibid.*
48 'Address to Officers of Army Headquarters,' 28 January 1948, Foulkes Papers
49 Canada, *H.C. Debates*, 1947, I, 413
50 *Op. cit.*, VI, 5270
51 *Ibid.*, 5270
52 *Ibid.*, 5298
53 *Ibid.*, 5275
54 Quoted in *Record III*, 394
55 Quoted in *Record IV*, 9
56 Quoted in *ibid.*, 183
57 Canada, *H.C. Debates*, 1947, VI, 5294
58 Goodspeed, *op. cit.*, 230
59 Canada, *H.C. Debates*, 1947, VI, 5294
60 'Autobiography,' Claxton Papers
61 Canada, *H.C. Debates*, 1947, VI, 5327
62 *Op. cit.*, 1948, VI, 5779, 5810

63 *Ibid.*, 5783
64 *Ibid.*, 5785
65 *Ibid.*, 5797
66 *Ibid.*, 5785
67 C.D. Howe to Crawford Gordon, 10 November 1945, Howe Papers
68 Memorandum by Air Marshal W.A. Curtis, 5 April 1948, 'Acceleration of Development Programme at A.V. Roe's – XC 100 Airframe and TR 5 Engine,' *ibid.*
69 C.D. Howe to Brooke Claxton, 12 April 1948, *ibid.*
70 Canada, *H.C. Debates*, 1948, VI, 5804
71 'Address by Lt-Gen. C. Foulkes, CB, CBE, DSO, to Officers of Army Headquarters, 28 January 1948' (privately communicated)
72 Wood, *op. cit.*, 18
73 Canada, *H.C. Debates*, 1948, VI, 5807
74 *Ibid.*, 5803
75 'Autobiography,' Claxton Papers
76 A.D.P. Heeney to Mackenzie King, 20 July 1945, King Papers
77 'Extract from Note of Conclusions Reached by the Cabinet on Friday, 3 August 1945 in respect of the continuing requirements of the Services in Stage II, European occupation forces and the larger question of post-war arrangements,' Army Headquarters files
78 A.D.P. Heeney to Mackenzie King, 9 August 1945, King Papers
79 Quoted in *Record III*, 356
80 Quoted in *ibid.*, 364
81 Quoted in *Record IV*, 9
82 'Autobiography,' Claxton Papers
83 Canada, *H.C. Debates*, 1946, V, 5044
84 Quoted in *Record III*, 364
85 Quoted in *ibid.*, 374
86 Quoted in *ibid.*, 368
87 Diary, entry 12 December 1946, King Papers
88 Canada, *H.C. Debates*, 1946, V, 5034
89 *Ibid.*, 5035
90 'Autobiography,' Claxton Papers
91 *Ibid.*
92 *Ibid.*
93 Canada, *H.C. Debates*, 1947, I, 366
94 *Ibid.*, 368
95 *Ibid.*, 521
96 'Autobiography,' Claxton Papers
97 *Ibid.*
98 Diary, King Papers
99 'Report Upon the Administrative Organization of the Department of National Defence, December 1948,' Claxton Papers
100 H. of C. Special Committee on Defence, *Minutes of Proceedings and Evidence*, no 6, 9 June 1964, 165
101 Lt-Gen. G.G. Simonds, 'Where We've Gone Wrong on Defense,' *Maclean's Magazine*, 23 June 1956
102 H. of C. Special Committee on Defence, *Minutes of Proceedings and Evidence*, no 6, 9 June 1964, 182–3
103 'Autobiography,' Claxton Papers
104 *Ibid.*
105 *Ibid.*
106 Canada, *H.C. Debates*, 1951, III, 2868

107 H. of C. Standing Committee on National Defence, *Minutes of Proceedings and Evidence*, No. 21, 16 and 17 February 1967, 1228
108 Canada, *H.C. Debates*, 1945, II, 1374
109 *Op. cit.*, I, 1135
110 *Op. cit.*, 1947, I, 413–14
111 *Op. cit.*, VI, 5276
112 'Autobiography,' Claxton Papers
113 Canada, *H.C. Debates*, 1948, VI, 5782
114 'Autobiography,' Claxton Papers
115 Canada, *H.C. Debates*, 1948, VI, 5786
116 *Op. cit.*, 1945, 2nd Session, II, 1774
117 *Op. cit.*, 1950, 2nd Session, 105
118 *Ibid.*, 102
119 *Ibid.*, 102
120 *Ibid.*, 102
121 Quoted in Wood, *op. cit.*, 169
122 Canada, *H.C. Debates*, 1945, 2nd Session, II, 1509
123 *Ibid.*, 1512
124 *Ibid.*, 1513
125 *Op. cit.*, 1946, V, 5030–1
126 'Autobiography,' Claxton Papers
127 'Memorandum,' 6 April 1944, Naval Headquarters files
128 Waldo E.L. Smith, *The Navy Chaplain and his Parish* (Ottawa 1967), 210–11
129 *Report on Certain 'Incidents' which Occurred on Board H.M.C. Ships Athabaskan, Crescent and Magnificent, and on other Matters concerning the Royal Canadian Navy* (Ottawa, October 1949), 33
130 John D. Harbron, 'Royal Canadian Navy at Peace 1945–1955: The Uncertain Heritage,' *Queen's Quarterly*, LXXIII, 3, Autumn 1966, 322
131 'Autobiography,' Claxton Papers
132 Frank H. Ellis, *Canada's Flying Heritage* (Toronto 1954), 96
133 H. Forbell and B. Gallant, 'Armed Forces Histories' (a study prepared for the Royal Commission on Bilingualism and Biculturalism) unpublished
134 G.N. Tucker, *The Naval Service of Canada*, I (Ottawa 1952), 154
135 Quoted in *Record I*, 519–20
136 Canada, *H.C. Debates*, 1946, V, 5020
137 Commander Marcel Jetté, *Report on Recruiting of French-speaking Canadians* (Ottawa, 1951 mimeographed), Directorate of History, Armed Forces of Canada
138 Quoted in *What's Past is Prologue: The Memoirs of Vincent Massey* (Toronto 1963), 470
139 Canada, *H.C. Debates*, 1945, 2nd Session, II, 1631
140 *Ibid.*, 1771–2
141 'Autobiography,' Claxton Papers
142 'Address by Lt-Gen. C. Foulkes...,' *op. cit.*

CHAPTER TWO: UNITING THE NATIONS

1 Winston S. Churchill, *The Hinge of Fate* (Boston 1950), 802–4
2 The Rt Hon. The Earl of Avon, *The Eden Memoirs: The Reckoning* (London 1965), 366
3 Quoted in *ibid.*, 443
4 'Memorandum on War Aims,' 2 November 1939, quoted in James Eayrs, *In Defence of Canada*, II, *Appeasement and Rearmament* (Toronto 1965), 234
5 Quoted in *ibid.*, 234–5

6 Quoted in *Record II*, 153
7 Quoted in *Record III*, 31
8 'Post-War International Organization,' 7 August 1943, Department of External Affairs files
9 Quoted in *Record I*, 678–9
10 King Papers
11 Quoted in *Record I*, 679
12 Minutes of the Fourth Meeting of the Working Committee on Post-Hostilities Problems, 12 October 1943, Department of External Affairs files
13 'Canadian Planning for the International Settlement,' 22 February 1944, *ibid.*
14 Charles A.S. Ritchie to Hume Wrong, 23 February 1944, *ibid.*
15 Minutes of the Seventh Meeting of the Advisory Committee on Post-Hostilities Problems, 15 March 1945, *ibid.*
16 Hume Wrong to L.B. Pearson, 11 May 1944, *ibid.*
17 Memorandum by Hume Wrong, 12 June 1944, *ibid.*
18 Minutes of the Seventh Meeting of the Advisory Committee on Post-Hostilities Problems, 15 March 1945, *ibid.*
19 D.K. MacTavish to George Ignatieff, 18 April 1945, *ibid.*
20 Memorandum by Hume Wrong, 'Politico-Strategic Planning,' 25 July 1945, *ibid.*
21 R.M. Macdonnell to Hume Wrong, 15 August 1946, *ibid.*
22 Minute by John Holmes on Memorandum by George Glazebrook (no date), *ibid.*
23 Quoted in B.S. Keirstead, *Canada in World Affairs, September 1951 to October 1953* (Toronto 1956), 37
24 Minutes of the Third Meeting of the Advisory Committee on Post-Hostilities Problems, 28 March 1944, Department of External Affairs files
25 *Ibid.*
26 Hume Wrong to Dana Wilgress, 13 May 1944, *ibid.*
27 *Ibid.*
28 Ambassador to Moscow to Secretary of State for External Affairs, 16 February 1944, *ibid.*
29 Memorandum, 25 March 1944, *ibid.*
30 'Organizing the United Nations for Peace' (mimeographed)
31 23 February 1944, Department of External Affairs files
32 *Ibid.*
33 Hume Wrong to Charles A.S. Ritchie, 1 April 1944, *ibid.*
34 Ruth B. Russell, *A History of the United Nations Charter* (Washington, DC 1958), 473
35 Minutes of the Twenty-ninth meeting of the Working Committee on Post-Hostilities Problems, 25 August 1944, Department of External Affairs files
36 Mackenzie King to Leighton McCarthy, 1 March 1943, King Papers
37 McCarthy to Mackenzie King, 21 April 1943, *ibid.*
38 Quoted in *Record I*, 553
39 L.B. Pearson to Norman Robertson, 18 July 1944, Department of External Affairs files
40 King Papers
41 L.B. Pearson to Norman Robertson, 18 July 1944, Department of External Affairs files
42 King Papers
43 *Ibid.*
44 Minutes of the Twenty-ninth meeting of the Working Committee on Post-Hostilities Problems, 25 August 1944, Department of External Affairs files
45 Department of External Affairs files
46 Hume Wrong to Norman Robertson, 11 September 1944, *ibid.*

47 Memorandum, 14 September 1944, *ibid.*
48 King Papers
49 Escott Reid to Norman Robertson, 23 September 1944, Department of External Affairs files
50 Mackenzie King to Winston Churchill, 28 September 1944 (telegram), *ibid.*
51 Diary entry, 13 March 1947, quoted in *Record IV*, 27
52 Hume Wrong to Mackenzie King, 20 December 1944, Department of External Affairs files
53 Norman Robertson to J.E. Read, 10 June 1945, King Papers
54 Quoted in *Record II*, 385
55 Quoted in *ibid.*, 386–7
56 Diary entry, 14 May 1945, King Papers
57 Canada, *H.C. Debates*, 1944, v, 6064
58 Quoted in Robert Sherwood, *Roosevelt and Hopkins: An Intimate Story* (New York 1948), 707
59 Vincent Massey to Mackenzie King, 20 April 1943, Massey Papers
60 L.B. Pearson to Norman Robertson, 1 February 1944, Department of External Affairs files
61 King Papers
62 Secretary of State for External Affairs, Ottawa, to Secretary of State for Dominion Affairs, London, 2 August 1944 (telegram), *ibid.*
63 *Ibid.*
64 Memorandum of 12 January 1945, communicated to the Governments of the United States, United Kingdom, Soviet Union and China and the Provisional Government of the French Republic, *ibid.*
65 Hume Wrong to T.C. Davis, 20 February 1945, Department of External Affairs files
66 Wrong to L.B. Pearson, 5 March 1945, *ibid.*
67 Wrong to Norman Robertson, 13 January 1946, King Papers
68 L.B. Pearson to Robertson, 23 January 1946, *ibid.*
69 Diary entry, 13 February 1946, quoted in *Record III*, 163

### CHAPTER THREE: SETTLING EUROPE

1 Quoted in F.L.W. Wood, *The New Zealand People at War: Political and External Affairs* (Wellington 1958), 362
2 Lt-Gen. Maurice A. Pope, *Soldiers and Politicians* (Toronto 1962) 279
3 Quoted in *Record II*, 469
4 Quoted in *Record III*, 307
5 G.P. deT. Glazebrook, *Canada at the Paris Peace Conference* (Toronto 1942), 29
6 N.A.M. Mackenzie to W.A. Mackintosh, 22 April 1929, CIIA Papers
7 Mackenzie King to Thomas Vien, 11 April 1936, King Papers
8 Diary entry, *ibid.*
9 Canada, *H.C. Debates*, 1943, II, 1405
10 E.J. Tarr to Vincent Massey, 22 September 1943, CIIA Papers
11 Tarr to B.K. Burge, 27 October 1943, *ibid.*
12 Escott Reid to Norman Robertson, 15 December 1943, *ibid.*
13 The Round Table Reports of the Rapporteurs at the Montebello Conference on 'Canada and the Building of Peace' (mimeographed), *ibid.*
14 Escott Reid to Norman Robertson, 15 December 1943, *ibid.*
15 'A Healthy Spot,' *Collected Shorter Poems, 1930–1944* (London 1950), 145
16 Quoted in *Record III*, 6
17 Quoted in Canada, *H.C. Debates*, 1945, 2nd Session, I, 491
18 *Ibid*, 492

19 Quoted in *Record III*, 183–4
20 Quoted in *ibid.*, 225
21 Quoted in *ibid.*, 227–8
22 Quoted in *ibid.*, 270
23 Quoted in *ibid.*, 290–1
24 Quoted in *ibid.*, 292
25 Quoted in *ibid.*, 292–3
26 Quoted in F.H. Soward, *Canada in World Affairs: From Normandy to Paris, 1944–1946* (Toronto 1950), 207
27 Quoted in *Record II*, 447
28 Pope, *op. cit.*, 320
29 *Ibid.*, 312
30 *Ibid.*, 312
31 Canada, *H.C. Debates*, 1947, v, 4823
32 Brooke Claxton to Mackenzie King, 17 September 1946, King Papers
33 Canada, *H.C. Debates*, 1948, IV, 3634
34 'Memorandum for the Under-Secretary,' 5 July 1943, Department of External Affairs files
35 Secretary of State for External Affairs to Secretary of State for Dominion Affairs (telegram), 5 July 1943, *ibid.*
36 Minutes of a Meeting to Consider Post-Hostilities Problems, 22 July 1943, *ibid.*
37 'Report by the Army Representative of a Meeting of the Working Committee on Post-Hostilities Problems,' 3 August 1943, *ibid.*
38 'Canadian Participation in the Policing of Europe,' 7 September 1943, *ibid.*
39 Norman Robertson to High Commissioner (London), 3 December 1943, *ibid.*
40 Hume Wrong to C.A.S. Ritchie, 22 January 1944, *ibid.*
41 Quoted in *Record I*, 642
42 Quoted in *Record II*, 77
43 C.P. Stacey, *Arms, Men and Governments: The War Policies of Canada, 1939–1945* (Ottawa 1970), 65
44 Quoted in *Record III*, 123
45 Dale C. Thomson, *Louis St Laurent: Canadian* (Toronto 1967), 181
46 Quoted in *Record III*, 126
47 Quoted in *ibid.*, 176
48 Canada, *H.C. Debates*, 1946, v, 5043
49 *Op. cit.*, 1947, I, 954
50 *Ibid.*, 975
51 L.B. Pearson to Norman Robertson, 14 March 1947, Department of External Affairs files
52 *Ibid.*
53 Quoted in *Record IV*, 27
54 'Policy Towards Germany,' 14 September 1943, Department of External Affairs files
55 Pierre Dupuy to Secretary of State for External Affairs, 30 March 1944, *ibid.*
56 'Policy Towards Germany,' 20 August 1943, *ibid.*
57 R.B. Bryce to Hume Wrong, 31 October 1945, *ibid.*
58 Dana Wilgress to Secretary of State for External Affairs, 30 June 1944, *ibid.*
59 Quoted in James Eayrs, *In Defence of Canada*, II, *Appeasement and Rearmament* (Toronto 1965), 236
60 Quoted in *Record I*, 431
61 Quoted in *Record III*, 228
62 Canada, *H.C. Debates*, 1947, I, 6
63 Robert A. Spencer, *Canada in World Affairs: From UN to NATO, 1946–1949* (Toronto 1959), 29

64 Canada, *H.C. Debates*, 1947, I, 7–11
65 Hume Wrong to C.A.S. Ritchie, 22 January 1944, Department of External Affairs files
66 Minutes of the Fifth Meeting of the Advisory Committee on Post-Hostilities Problems, 25 October 1944, *ibid.*
67 *Ibid.*
68 Dana Wilgress to the Secretary of State for External Affairs, 30 June 1944, *ibid.*
69 Quoted in Norman Robertson, 'Memorandum for the Prime Minister,' 8 April 1944, *ibid.*
70 L.B. Pearson to Hume Wrong, 13 October 1944, *ibid.*
71 'Control Machinery for Europe – Canadian Participation,' 19 October 1944, *ibid.*
72 Minutes of the Seventh Meeting of the Advisory Committee on Post-Hostilities Problems, 15 March 1945, *ibid.*
73 Secretary of State for External Affairs to Acting Assistant Under Secretary of State for External Affairs, 14 May 1945, *ibid.*
74 Norman Robertson to General J.C. Murchie, 10 July 1945, *ibid.*
75 Hume Wrong to Maurice Pope, 6 February 1945, *ibid.*
76 Quoted in Pope, *op. cit.*, 277
77 Quoted in *ibid.*, 283
78 *Ibid.*, 324

## CHAPTER FOUR: COMPOSING THE COMMONWEALTH

1 Quoted in *Record I*, 637–8
2 Quoted in Nicholas Mansergh (ed.), *Documents and Speeches on British Commonwealth Affairs, 1931–1952*, I (London 1953), 578–9
3 Quoted in Vincent Massey, *What's Past is Prologue* (Toronto 1963), 393
4 Quoted in *Record I*, 638
5 Quoted in *ibid.*, 638
6 Mansergh, *op. cit.*, 568–75
7 Canada, *House of Commons Debates*, 1944, I, 39–42
8 Quoted in *Record I*, 641
9 L.B. Pearson to Norman Robertson, 1 February 1944, Department of External Affairs files
10 Pearson to Robertson, 17 November 1944, *ibid.*
11 Quoted in *Record I*, 670–1
12 Quoted in *ibid.*, 686
13 Quoted in *ibid.*, 687
14 Quoted in *ibid.*, 687
15 Diary entry, 22 August 1941, King Papers
16 Quoted in *ibid.*, 118, 217, 329–30; quoted in *Record II*, 55, 266
17 E.J. Tarr to J.W. Dafoe (and others), 26 November 1943, Tarr Papers
18 Tarr to Norman Robertson, 20 December 1943, *ibid.*
19 *Ibid.*
20 Brooke Claxton to Clifford Sifton, 10 January 1944, *ibid.*
21 E.J. Tarr to F.R. Scott, 26 February 1944, *ibid.*
22 Tarr to Norman Robertson, 26 March 1945, *ibid.*
23 Tarr to Robertson, 24 January 1945, *ibid.*
24 George Ferguson, 'The Only Way to Peace,' *The Listener*, 25 January 1945
25 British Commonwealth Relations Conference, 1945, v, 'Miscellaneous Memoranda' (unpublished), CIIA Papers
26 *Ibid.*
27 Tarr Papers

28 E.J. Tarr to Norman Robertson, 26 March 1945, *ibid.*
29 Massey, *op. cit.*, 420–1
30 Quoted in *ibid.*, 421
31 Quoted in *ibid.*, 421
32 Quoted in *Record II*, 446
33 Quoted in *Record III*, 92
34 Quoted in *ibid.*, 55–6
35 *United Empire: The Journal of the Royal Empire Society*, XXXVIII, 1947, 167
36 Canada, *H.C. Debates*, 1946, II, 1348
37 Quoted in *Record III*, 202
38 Quoted in *ibid.*, 220–1
39 Quoted in *ibid.*, 221
40 Canada, *H.C. Debates*, 1946, II, 1348
41 Mansergh, *Survey of British Commonwealth Affairs ... 1939–1952*, 324
42 Quoted in *Record III*, 242
43 Quoted in *ibid.*, 223–4
44 Quoted in *ibid.*, 248
45 Quoted in *ibid.*, 364
46 Quoted in *ibid.*, 364
47 Mackenzie King to Sir A. Shuldham Redfern, 11 November 1946, King Papers
48 Quoted in *Record III*, 365–6
49 R. MacGregor Dawson, *The Government of Canada* (Toronto 1970), 161
50 Quoted in *Record III*, 366
51 Quoted in *ibid.*, 366
52 Quoted in *ibid.*, 364–5
53 C.R. Attlee, *As It Happened* (London 1954), 177–8
54 Sir Wilfrid Laurier to Earl Minto, 13 April 1909, Laurier Papers
55 *Report by W.L. Mackenzie King, C.M.G., on Mission to England to Confer with the British Authorities on the Subject of Immigration to Canada from the Orient and Immigration from India in Particular* (Ottawa 1908), 7
56 Earl Grey to Lord Crewe, 8 December 1908, Grey Papers
57 Resolution of Trades and Labor Council, September 1906, Laurier Papers
58 A.P. Ledingham to J.A. Calder, 17 April 1918, Borden Papers
59 Sir Thomas White to Sir Robert Borden, 20 April 1917, *ibid.*
60 Borden to Cabinet, 27 July 1918, *ibid.*
61 Mackenzie King to Father and Mother, 29 January 1909, King Papers
62 Mackenzie King to Sir Wilfrid Laurier, 31 January 1909, Laurier Papers
63 Mackenzie King to Father and Mother, 21 January 1909, King Papers
64 Diary entry, 22 October 1926, *ibid.*
65 Diary entry, 25 May 1937, *ibid.*
66 *Ibid.*
67 *Ibid.*
68 Victor W. Odlum to Mackenzie King, 4 May 1943, *ibid.*
69 R. Coupland, *The Indian Problem: Report on the Constitutional Problem in India* (New York 1944), 263 (part 2)
70 Michael Brecher, *Nehru: A Political Biography* (London 1959), 276
71 Nicholas Mansergh, *Survey of British Commonwealth Affairs: Problems of Wartime Co-operation and Post-War Change, 1939–1952* (London 1958), 144
72 Quoted in Coupland, *op. cit.*, 336 (part 2)
73 Quoted in Brecher, *op. cit.*, 270
74 Mansergh, *op. cit.*, 145
75 R.E. Sherwood (ed.), *The White House Papers of Harry L. Hopkins*, II (London 1949), 516, quoted in Mansergh, *op. cit.*, 146
76 Mackenzie King to Winston Churchill (telegram), 6 March 1942, quoted in Nicholas Mansergh (ed.), *Constitutional Relations Between Britain and India:*

*The Transfer of Power 1942–7*, I, *The Cripps Mission, January–April 1942* (London 1970), 349–50
77 Mackenzie King to Churchill (telegram), 6 March 1942, quoted in *ibid.*, 350
78 Churchill to Mackenzie King (telegram), 8 March 1942, King Papers
79 Mackenzie King to Churchill (telegram), 15 March 1942, quoted in Mansergh, *Constitutional Relations ...* , 427
80 Churchill to Mackenzie King (telegram), 18 March 1942, quoted in *ibid.*, 440–1
81 L.S. Amery to Mackenzie King, 17 March 1942, quoted in *ibid.*, 436
82 Amery to Mackenzie King, 12 February 1948, King Papers
83 M.J. Coldwell to Mackenzie King, 27 October 1942, *ibid.*
84 Quoted in *Record I*, 408
85 Bruce Hutchison, *The Incredible Canadian* (Toronto 1952), 424
86 Quoted in *Record IV*, 42
87 Quoted in *ibid.*, 43
88 Quoted in Canada, *H.C. Debates*, 1947, IV, 3771
89 *Ibid.*, 3771
90 Quoted in *Record IV*, 371
91 Dale C. Thomson, 'India and Canada: A Decade of Co-operation, 1947–1957,' *International Studies* (New Delhi), IX, 4, April 1968, 409
92 Quoted in *Record IV*, 388
93 Mansergh, *Survey ... Problems of Wartime Co-operation ...* , 250
94 Viscount Jowitt to Mackenzie King, 26 October 1948, King Papers
95 Mansergh, *op. cit.*, 250n1
96 Quoted in Thomson, *op. cit.*, 409–10
97 Quoted in *Record IV*, 404–5
98 L.B. Pearson to Escott Reid, 30 November 1948, Department of External Affairs files
99 John D. Kearney to Secretary of State for External Affairs, 25 November 1948, Department of External Affairs files
100 Kearney to Secretary of State for External Affairs, 29 December 1948, *ibid.*
101 E.J. Tarr to Norman Robertson, 26 March 1945, Tarr Papers
102 'Mr Kearney's Proposal for a Quota System of Immigration from India to Canada – Extracts from his despatch No. 168 of May 27, 1948,' Department of External Affairs files
103 L.B. Pearson to John D. Kearney, 5 January 1949 (telegram), *ibid.*
104 'India and the Commonwealth: A Preliminary Survey,' 3 March 1949, *ibid.*
105 John D. Kearney to Secretary of State for External Affairs, 13 January 1949, *ibid.*
106 Norman Robertson to Secretary of State for External Affairs, 26 January 1949, *ibid.*
107 John D. Kearney to Secretary of State for External Affairs, 18 March 1949, *ibid.*
108 'India and the Commonwealth,' 17 March 1949, *ibid.*
109 L.S. St Laurent to Pandit Nehru, 31 March 1949 (telegram), *ibid.*
110 L.B. Pearson to Secretary of State for External Affairs, 21 April 1949 (telegram), *ibid.*
111 'Comment on Indian Proposals,' 22 April 1949, *ibid.*
112 L.B. Pearson to Secretary of State for External Affairs, 23 April 1949 (telegram), *ibid.*
113 Quoted in Nicholas Mansergh (ed.), *Documents and Speeches ...* , II, 846–7
114 Brecher, *Nehru*, 579–80
115 Quoted in Mansergh (ed.), *Documents and Speeches ...* , 854–7
116 L.B. Pearson to E.J. Tarr, 4 May 1949, Tarr Papers
117 Canada, *H.C. Debates*, 1949, 2nd Session, II, 1834

CHAPTER FIVE: CONTROLLING THE ATOM

1 Quoted in *Record I*, 413
2 Margaret Gowing, *Britain and Atomic Energy, 1939–1945* (London 1964), 182–3
3 Quoted in *Record I*, 414
4 Diary entry 19 June 1942, Mackenzie Papers
5 Gilbert LaBine to C.D. Howe, 7 July 1942; Howe to LaBine, 7 July 1942, Howe Papers
6 Malcolm MacDonald to C.D. Howe, 15 July 1942; Howe to MacDonald, 16 July 1942; MacDonald to Howe, 22 July 1942. Howe Papers
7 C.D. Howe to Malcolm MacDonald, 5 August 1942, *ibid.*
8 Gilbert LaBine to C.D. Howe, 15 September 1942, *ibid.*
9 Quoted in Gowing, *op. cit.*, 185
10 Mackenzie Papers
11 Gowing, *op. cit.*, 185
12 Diary entry 6 July 1943, Mackenzie Papers
13 Diary entry 19 September 1943, *ibid.*
14 Diary entry 13 July 1943, *ibid.*
15 Sir John Anderson to Malcolm MacDonald [no date]; C.D. Howe to MacDonald, 8 February 1944. Howe Papers
16 Quoted in Gowing, *op. cit.*, 188
17 Diary entry 17 August 1942, Mackenzie Papers
18 Quoted in 'The Atom Secrets,' *The Globe Magazine* (Toronto), 28 October 1961
19 Mackenzie Papers
20 Quoted in Wilfrid Eggleston, *Canada's Nuclear Story* (Toronto 1965), 56
21 Diary entry 29 November 1942, Mackenzie Papers
22 Quoted in 'The Atom Secrets,' *op. cit.*
23 Diary entry 2 January 1943, Mackenzie Papers
24 Diary entry 7 January 1943, *ibid.*
25 Diary entry, 15 January 1943, *ibid.*
26 Diary entry 18 January 1943, *ibid.*
27 Gowing, *op. cit.*, 197
28 Diary entry 24 April 1943, Mackenzie Papers
29 Diary entry 11 May 1943, *ibid.*
30 Gowing, *op. cit.*, 197
31 Quoted in 'The Atom Secrets,' *op. cit.*
32 Quoted in *Record I*, 503
33 Quoted in *ibid.*, 532
34 Richard G. Hewlett and Oscar E. Anderson, Jr, *A History of the United States Atomic Energy Commission*, I, *The New World, 1939–1946* (University Park, Pennsylvania 1962), 280
35 *Ibid.*, 281
36 *Ibid.*, 282–3
37 Diary entry 17 February 1944, Mackenzie Papers
38 Diary entry 13 April 1944, *ibid.*
39 Gowing, *op. cit.*, 274
40 Diary entry 5 July 1945, Mackenzie Papers
41 Quoted in *Record II*, 451
Howe Papers
42 'Press Release by Honourable C.D. Howe, Minister of Munitions and Supply,'
43 Quoted in *Record II*, 451
44 Quoted in 'The Atom Secrets,' *op. cit.*
45 Gowing, *op. cit.*, 348

46 Quoted in *Record III*, 60
47 L.B. Pearson, 'Canadian Memorandum on Atomic Warfare,' 8 November 1945, King Papers
48 Lester Pearson, *Peace in the Family of Man* (Toronto & New York 1969), 12
49 Hewlett and Anderson, *op. cit.*, 464
50 Diary entry 14 November 1945, Mackenzie Papers
51 Hewlett and Anderson, *op. cit.*, 464
52 *Ibid.*, 465
53 Diary entry 17 November 1945, Mackenzie Papers
54 Canada, *H.C. Debates*, 1945, 2nd Session, III, 3632–52
55 W.L. Mackenzie King, *Industry and Humanity: A Study in the Principles Underlying Industrial Reconstruction* (Toronto & Boston 1918), 3–4
56 L.B. Pearson to Hume Wrong, 28 December 1945, King Papers
57 Mackenzie King to Malcolm MacDonald, 29 November 1945, Howe Papers
58 C.D. Howe to Norman Robertson, 9 February 1946, *ibid.*
59 Howe to George C. Bateman, 12 October 1945, *ibid.*
60 General A.G.L. McNaughton to Hume Wrong, 15 July 1946, McNaughton Papers
61 A.D.P. Heeney to C.D. Howe, 20 March 1946, Howe Papers
62 'Provisional Instructions for the Canadian Representative on the Atomic Energy Commission,' 7 June 1946, McNaughton Papers
63 General A.G.L. McNaughton to Department of External Affairs, 13 June 1946, *ibid.*
64 McNaughton to Department of External Affairs, 16 June 1946, *ibid.*
65 United Nations, Atomic Energy Commission, Official Records, No. 2, Second Meeting, 19 June 1946, 19
66 L.B. Pearson to Mackenzie King, 27 June 1946, King Papers
67 Hewlett and Anderson, *op. cit.*, 587
68 General A.G.L. McNaughton to Department of External Affairs, 25 July 1946, McNaughton Papers
69 Hume Wrong to C.D. Howe, 1 August 1946, Howe Papers
70 'Minutes of the Advisory Panel (Atomic Energy), Seventh Meeting, August 14, 1946,' McNaughton Papers
71 Hewlett and Anderson, *op. cit.*, 595
72 Dale C. Thomson, *Louis St Laurent: Canadian* (Toronto 1967), 197
73 United Nations, Atomic Energy Commission, Official Records, No 7, Seventh Meeting, 5 December 1946, 91–2
74 *Canada. The United Nations, 1946: Report on the Second Part of the First Session of the General Assembly of the United Nations Held in New York, October 23–December 15, 1946*, Department of External Affairs, Ottawa, Conference Series No. 3, 1946, 190
75 *Ibid.*, 195
76 United Nations, Atomic Energy Commission, Official Records, No. 8, Eighth Meeting, 17 December 1946, 103–7
77 Quoted in John Swettenham, *McNaughton*, III, *1944–1966* (Toronto 1969), 119
78 United Nations, Atomic Energy Commission, Official Records, No. 9, Ninth Meeting, 20 December 1946, 141
79 George Ignatieff to author, 7 September 1966
80 'Observations of the Canadian Delegation on the Resolution proposed by the United States (AEC/15 of 14th December, 1946, as revised by the United States Delegation on 17th December, 1946),' quoted in *Canada. The United Nations, 1946...*, 196–7
81 McNaughton Papers
82 Hewlett and Anderson, *op. cit.*, 615

83 *Ibid.*, 616–17
84 Quoted in *Record III*, 405–6
85 'National and International Control of Atomic Energy,' Address to University of Toronto Engineering Society, 30 October 1947, McNaughton Papers
86 L.B. Pearson, 'Memorandum to the Advisory Panel on Atomic Energy,' 28 November 1947, *ibid.*
87 Quoted in Swettenham, *op. cit.*, 124
88 A.D.P. Heeney to Mackenzie King, 20 April 1946, King Papers
89 C.D. Howe to C.J. Mackenzie, 17 February 1945, Howe Papers
90 Gowing, *op. cit.*, 300
91 Howe Papers
92 H.H. Bundy and Wm. L. Webster to George C. Bateman, 4 October 1944, *ibid.*
93 Hewlett and Anderson, *op. cit.*, 467
94 Diary entry 15 November 1946, Mackenzie Papers
95 C.D. Howe to L.B. Pearson, 30 November 1945, Howe Papers
96 George C. Bateman to Howe, 4 December 1945, *ibid.*
97 Bateman to Howe, 5 December 1945, *ibid.*
98 Bateman to Howe, 7 December 1945, *ibid.*
99 Howe to Bateman, 11 December 1945, *ibid.*
100 Hewlett and Anderson, *op. cit.*, 468
101 L.B. Pearson to Norman Robertson, 18 January 1946, Howe Papers
102 Gowing, *op. cit.*, 332
103 Eggleston, *op. cit.*, 182
104 Diary entry 14 February 1946, Mackenzie Papers
105 George C. Bateman to C.D. Howe, 10 August 1945; Howe to Bateman, 17 August 1945. Howe Papers
106 Hewlett and Anderson, *op. cit.*, 478
107 L.B. Pearson to A.D.P. Heeney, 16 February 1946, Howe Papers
108 C.D. Howe to George C. Bateman, 18 April 1946, *ibid.*
109 Howe to Bateman, 13 May 1946, *ibid.*
110 Howe to L.B. Pearson, 9 December 1946, *ibid.*
111 A.D.P. Heeney to Howe, 20 March 1946, *ibid.*
112 Howe to George C. Bateman, 14 April 1946, *ibid.*
113 L.B. Pearson to A.D.P. Heeney, 16 April 1946, King Papers
114 George C. Bateman to C.D. Howe, 15 April 1946, Howe Papers
115 Quoted in Francis Williams, *A Prime Minister Remembers* (London 1962), 110–12
116 Quoted in *Record III*, 218
117 C.D. Howe to George C. Bateman, 18 April 1946, Howe Papers
118 Howe to L.B. Pearson, 9 December 1946, Howe Papers
119 A.D.P. Heeney to Howe, 14 June 1946, *ibid.*
120 L.B. Pearson to Heeney, 3 May 1946, King Papers
121 Hewlett and Anderson, *op. cit.*, 480
122 Gowing, *op. cit.*, 338
123 Nuel Pharr Davis, *Lawrence and Oppenheimer* (New York 1968), 282
124 George C. Bateman to C.D. Howe, 15 April 1946, Howe Papers
125 L.B. Pearson to A.D.P. Heeney, 3 May 1946, King Papers
126 C.D. Howe to George C. Bateman, 23 August 1946, Howe Papers
127 Howe to Bateman, 13 May 1946, *ibid.*
128 Hewlett and Anderson, *op. cit.*, 654
129 *The Journals of David E. Lilienthal*, II, *The Atomic Energy Years, 1945–1950* (New York, Evanston, & London 1964), 175–6
130 Arthur H. Vandenberg, Jr (ed.), *The Private Papers of Senator Vandenberg* (Boston 1952), 360

131 *Ibid.*, 361
132 *The Journals of David E. Lilienthal*, *op. cit.*, 215
133 Diary entry 14 November 1947, Mackenzie Papers
134 *The Journals of David E. Lilienthal*, *op. cit.*, 260
135 Hume Wrong to L.B. Pearson and A.D.P. Heeney, 4 December 1947, Howe Papers
136 Wrong to Department of External Affairs, 5 December 1947, *ibid.*
137 Diary entries 4 December 1947, 6 December 1947, Mackenzie Papers
138 A.D.P. Heeney to Hume Wrong, 9 December 1947, Howe Papers
139 Diary entry 10 December 1947, Mackenzie Papers
140 Diary entry 11 December 1947, *ibid.*
141 Hume Wrong to A.D.P. Heeney, 12 December 1947, Howe Papers
142 George C. Bateman to C.D. Howe, 17 December 1947, *ibid.*
143 Howe to Mackenzie King, 24 December 1947, King Papers
144 Howe to George C. Bateman, 13 January 1948, Howe Papers
145 Bateman to Howe, 9 January 1948, *ibid.*
146 Richard G. Hewlett and Francis Duncan, *A History of the United States Atomic Energy Commission*, II, *Atomic Shield, 1947–1952* (University Park, Pennsylvania, & London 1969), 283.
147 Diary entry, Mackenzie Papers
148 Hewlett and Duncan, *op. cit.*, 287–8
149 *The Journals of David E. Lilienthal*, *op. cit.*, 465
150 Hewlett and Duncan, *op. cit.*, 293
151 *Ibid.*, 308
152 *The Journals of David E. Lilienthal*, *op. cit.*, 565
153 Dean Acheson, *Present at the Creation: My Years in the State Department* (New York 1969), 321

### CHAPTER SIX: DEFENDING THE CONTINENT

1 Quoted in *Record III*, 9–10
2 Quoted in *ibid.*, 11
3 Diary entry, King Papers
4 Lt-Comm. G.F. Todd, 'Post-War Strategic Security of Canada,' Department of External Affairs files
5 Maj.-Gen. Maurice Pope to Col. J.H. Jenkins, 4 April 1944, *ibid.*
6 J.A. Gibson, 'Memorandum for the Under Secretary,' 12 April 1944, *ibid.*
7 'Canadian Defence Relationships with the United States,' 11 May 1944, *ibid.*
8 Minutes of the 21st Meeting of the Working Committee on Post-Hostilities Problems, 18 May 1944, *ibid.*
9 'Canadian Defence Relationships with the United States,' 26 May 1944, *ibid.*
10 'Post-War Defence Arrangements with the United States: Preliminary Paper,' Report to the Advisory Committee from the Working Committee on Post-Hostilities Problems, 16 June 144, *ibid.*
11 Minutes of the 22nd Meeting of the Working Committee on Post-Hostilities Problems, 3 July 1944, *ibid.*
12 Maj.-Gen. Maurice Pope to Col. J.H. Jenkins, 27 June 1944, *ibid.*
13 Minutes of the Fourth Meeting of the Advisory Committee on Post-Hostilities Problems, 4 July 1944, *ibid.*
14 Memorandum to the Cabinet War Committee from the Advisory Committee on Post-Hostilities Problems, 6 July 1944, *ibid.*
15 Canadian Joint Staff, Washington, DC, to Chief of the General Staff (telegram), 5 August 1944, *ibid.*
16 'Revisions to Third Draft, Canadian Defence Relationships with the United States,' 25 August 1944, *ibid.*

17 'Post-War Canadian Defence Relationship with the United States: General Considerations,' 24 October 1944, *ibid.*
18 J.W. Holmes to Hume Wrong, 27 October 1944, *ibid.*
19 Wrong to Norman Robertson, 3 November 1944, *ibid.*
20 Maurice Pope to Wrong, 4 January 1945, *ibid.*
21 Quoted in *Record III*, 19
22 Quoted in *ibid.*, 29
23 Diary entry, King Papers
24 Quoted in *Record III*, 71–2
25 Quoted in *ibid.*, 30–1
26 Abbott Papers
27 Canada, *H.C. Debates*, 1946, I, 52–3
28 Quoted in *Record III*, 155
29 Frank H. Underhill, 'The Close of an Era: Twenty-Five Years of Mr Mackenzie King,' *Canadian Forum*, September 1944
30 C.S.A. Ritchie, 'Memorandum on the Appreciation of the Requirements of Canadian-United States Security,' 14 June 1946, Department of External Affairs files
31 'Memorandum on Soviet Motives in Relation to North America,' no date, *ibid.*
32 Hume Wrong, 'The Possibility of War with the Soviet Union,' 28 June 1946, *ibid.*
33 Dana Wilgress to L.B. Pearson, 25 May 1948, King Papers
34 Quoted in Vincent Davis, *Postwar Defense Policy and the U.S. Navy, 1943–1946* (Chapel Hill, NC 1966), 222
35 Perry McCoy Smith, *The Air Force Plans for Peace, 1943–1945* (Baltimore & London 1970), 18
36 Stetson Conn and Byron Fairchild, *The Framework of Hemisphere Defense* (Washington, DC 1960), 383–4
37 R.M. Macdonnell, 'Memorandum for Cabinet: Postwar Defence Collaboration with the United States,' 12 December 1945, Department of External Affairs files
38 E.W.T. Gill to Macdonnell, 7 December 1945, *ibid.*
39 Memorandum by Norman Robertson, 19 December 1945, *ibid.*
40 Hume Wrong to Robertson, 12 June 1946, *ibid.*
41 Wrong, 'Memorandum,' 11 June 1946, *ibid.*
42 A.D.P. Heeney, 'Memorandum for the Prime Minister,' 12 June 1946, *ibid.*
43 Heeney to Mackenzie King, 12 June 1946, *ibid.*
44 Quoted in *Record III*, 266
45 Quoted in *ibid.*, 266
46 'The Ambassador in Canada (Atherton) to the Secretary of State,' 28 August 1946, quoted in US Department of State, *Foreign Relations of the United States*, 1946, v (Washington, DC 1970), 54
47 Quoted in *Record III*, 362–3
48 Claxton Papers
49 'Memorandum of Canadian-United States Defense Conversations Held in Ottawa in Suite "E" Chateau Laurier Hotel, December 16 and 17, 1946,' quoted in US Department of State, *Foreign Relations of the United States*, *op. cit.*, 70
50 L.B. Pearson to Mackenzie King, 23 December 1946, King Papers
51 Brooke Claxton to Mackenzie King, 8 January 1947, Claxton Papers
52 Quoted in *Record III*, 370
53 L.B. Pearson to Norman Robertson, 29 January 1946 (telegram), Department of External Affairs files
54 A.D.P. Heeney to Robertson, 1 February 1946, *ibid.*
55 R.M. Macdonnell, 'Memorandum,' 8 March 1946, *ibid.*

56 Hume Wrong, 'Memorandum for the Prime Minister,' 2 May 1946, *ibid.*
57 Quoted in *Record III*, 219
58 Quoted in *ibid.*, 55–6
59 Conn and Fairchild, *op. cit.*, 408
60 Hume Wrong, 'Memorandum for the Prime Minister,' 26 October 1946, Department of External Affairs files
61 Quoted in *Record III*, 367
62 Quoted in *ibid.*, 368
63 Hume Wrong to Norman Robertson, 30 September 1946, Department of External Affairs files
64 L.B. Pearson, 'Canada Looks Down North,' *Foreign Affairs*, July 1946, 643–4
65 R.M. Macdonnell, 'Memorandum for the Prime Minister,' 23 December 1946, Department of External Affairs files
66 Canada, *H.C. Debates*, 1947, I, 347–8
67 Quoted in *Record IV*, 24
68 Quoted in Vincent Massey, *What's Past is Prologue* (Toronto 1963), 371
69 Quoted in *Record I*, 436
70 Quoted in *ibid.*, 644
71 Quoted in Massey, *op. cit.*, 396–7
72 Quoted in *Record III*, 60
73 Quoted in *ibid.*, 72
74 Journal of the Permanent Joint Board on Defence, 29 April 1946, Department of External Affairs files
75 Quoted in *Record III*, 219
76 Hume Wrong, 'Memorandum for the Prime Minister,' 26 October 1946, Department of External Affairs files
77 Wrong to Norman Robertson, 12 June 1946, *ibid.*
78 L.B. Pearson to Robertson, 21 June 1946, *ibid.*
79 'The Ambassador in Canada (Atherton) to the Secretary of State,' in US Department of State, *Foreign Relations of the United States, 1946* (Washington, DC 1971), V, 55
80 Stanley W. Dziuban, *Military Relations between the United States and Canada, 1939–1945* (Washington, DC 1959), 188–9
81 Journal of the Permanent Joint Board on Defence, 29 April 1946, Department of External Affairs files
82 Memorandum by Hume Wrong, 10 May 1946, *ibid.*
83 J.S. Macdonald to Wrong, 30 August 1946, *ibid.*
84 Wrong to Norman Robertson, 30 September 1946, *ibid.*
85 Quoted in *Record III*, 362
86 Quoted in *ibid.*, 366
87 'Memorandum of Canadian-United States Defense Conversations Held in Ottawa in Suite "E" Chateau Laurier Hotel, December 16 and 17, 1946,' quoted in US Department of State, *Foreign Relations of the United States, op. cit.*, 73
88 Quoted in *ibid.*, 73
89 Margaret A. Carroll, 'Joint Experimental Station, 1946–1964,' in C.S. Beals and D.A. Shenstone (eds.), *Science, History and Hudson Bay*, II (Ottawa 1968), 907–32
90 Hume Wrong, 'Memorandum for the Prime Minister,' 26 October 1946, Department of External Affairs files
91 Hume Wrong to Mackenzie King, 26 October 1946, King Papers
92 Canada, *H.C. Debates*, 1953–4, I, 362
93 *Ibid.*, 362
94 Quoted in Walter Millis (ed.), *The Forrestal Diaries* (New York 1951), 474
95 *Canada's Defence Programme, 1949–50* (Ottawa 1949), 12–13

96 Canada, *H.C. Debates*, 1950, IV, 3377–8
97 *Op. cit.*, 1953–4, I, 362
98 'Address by Lt-Gen. C. Foulkes, CB, CBE, DSO, to Officers of Army Headquarters, 28 January 1948' (typescript, privately communicated)
99 R.J. Sutherland, 'The Strategic Significance of the Canadian Arctic,' in R. St J. Macdonald (ed.), *The Arctic Frontier* (Toronto 1965), 268
100 Quoted in Samuel P. Huntington, *The Common Defense: Strategic Programs in National Politics* (New York & London 1961), 329
101 *Ibid.*, 329–30
102 *Ibid.*, 328
103 Quoted in *ibid.*, 330
104 *Ibid.*, 332
105 Brooke Claxton to L.S. St Laurent, 10 March 1953, Claxton Papers
106 Huntington, *op. cit.*, 330–3
107 *Ibid.*, 334
108 C.D. Howe to Brooke Claxton, 9 October 1953, Claxton Papers
109 Claxton to Howe, 5 October 1953, *ibid.*
110 Claxton to L.S. St Laurent, 23 September 1953, *ibid.*
111 *Ibid.*
112 'Experiment in Truth,' *New York Herald Tribune*, 17 September 1953
113 Claxton to St Laurent, 23 September 1953, Claxton Papers
114 James Reston in *The New York Times*, 9 October 1953
115 Sutherland, *op. cit.*, 268
116 Howe to Claxton, 13 October 1953, Claxton Papers
117 Claxton to St Laurent, 21 October 1953, *ibid.*
118 Claxton to A.D.P. Heeney, 23 June 1954, *ibid.*
119 Sutherland, *op. cit.*, 269
120 Claxton to Heeney, 23 June 1954, Claxton Papers

# INDEX

*(Officers and titled persons are listed under the highest rank and title attained during 1943–9.)*